The Evolution of American Legislatures

The U.S. Congress and the state legislatures have roots in the representative bodies of the past. Indeed, since the first colonial assembly of 1619, the institutional development of American legislatures has been marked by continuity. Beginning with the ways in which colonial assemblies followed British precedents, Peverill Squire traces their evolution into distinct institutions. He next charts the formation of the first state legislatures and the Constitutional Congress. He then describes the creation of territorial and new state legislatures, and includes a chapter devoted to odd cases, such as Oregon, Kansas, and Hawaii. Finally, he turns to the institutionalization of state legislatures in the nineteenth century and their professionalization since 1900. Squire demonstrates that, although throughout the nation's history dozens of new legislatures have been established, each was based on existing models and driven by the practical need for governance and regularized decision making. In the conclusion, reviewing the historical trajectory of American legislatures, Squire suggests how they might further develop over the coming decades.

Squire's approach will appeal to historians. At the same time, his focus on the evolution of rules, procedures, and standing committee systems, as well as member salaries, legislative sessions, staff, and facilities, will appeal to political scientists and legislative scholars.

Peverill Squire holds the Hicks and Martha Griffiths Chair in American Political Institutions and the Frederick A. Middlebush Chair in Political Science at the University of Missouri.

LEGISLATIVE POLITICS & POLICY MAKING

Series Editors

Janet M. Box-Steffensmeier, Vernal Riffe Professor of Political Science,
The Ohio State University

David Canon, Professor of Political Science, University of Wisconsin, Madison

The Evolution of American Legislatures

Colonies, Territories, and States, 1619–2009

PEVERILL SQUIRE

The University of Michigan Press • Ann Arbor

First paperback edition 2014
Copyright © by the University of Michigan 2012
All rights reserved

Published in the United States of America by
The University of Michigan Press
Manufactured in the United States of America
⊚ Printed on acid-free paper

2017   2016   2015   2014   5   4   3   2

A CIP catalog record for this book is available from the British Library.

Library of Congress Cataloging-in-Publication Data

Squire, Peverill.
    The evolution of American legislatures : colonies, territories, and states, 1619–2009 / Peverill Squire.
        p.   cm. — (Legislative politics & policy making)
    Includes bibliographical references and index.
    ISBN 978-0-472-11831-1 (cloth : alk. paper) — ISBN 978-0-472-02840-5 (e-book)
    1. Legislative bodies—United States—History.   2. Legislative bodies—United States—States—History.   3. United States. Congress—History.   I. Title.

JK1021.S69   2012
328.7309—dc23

                                                        2012011075

ISBN 978-0-472-03583-0 (pbk. : alk. paper)

For my parents, Rusty and Peggy (Vashon Island),
and my children, Russell (Madison) and Emma (St. Peter)

Acknowledgments

I have been fortunate to receive a great deal of assistance in locating the vast materials I draw on in this book. The University of Missouri library staff expeditiously filled my endless requests to retrieve old books from the depository. The interlibrary loan staff successfully located almost all of the obscure materials I requested. I benefited from visiting libraries at the University of Illinois, Springfield, the University of Iowa, and the University of Washington. I made great use of the materials at the State Historical Society of Missouri and the excellent collection of state legislative journals at the library archives of the Wisconsin Historical Society. A visit to the South Carolina Department of Archives and History helped resolve a question about standing committees in the colonial Commons House. I was also able to track down a few bits of useful information by visiting the Idaho Legislative Reference Library.

Through the wonders of e-mail I was able to work with archivists and librarians at the Hawaii State Archives, the State Library of Louisiana, the Maine State Law and Legislative Reference Library, the Historic New Orleans Collection at the Williams Research Center, the Oregon State Archives, and the Research Center of the Utah State Archives and Utah State History. Professor Kevin Leyden and Ashley Harpster at West Virginia University kindly tracked down information I needed from that state's first House journal. I am grateful for all of their assistance.

I am in great debt to my friend Gerhard Loewenberg who read early drafts of every chapter and always gave me the correct blend of encouragement and criticism. The thoughtful comments given by the anonymous reviewers improved the final product. Melody Herr and her colleagues at the University of Michigan Press deserve my thanks for helping fashion a long manuscript into what I hope is a lasting contribution.

Contents

1 ◆ Tracing How American Legislatures Changed Over Time

The 50 state legislatures and U.S. Congress are deeply rooted in the representative bodies that preceded them beginning with the first colonial assembly that met in Virginia in 1619. These roots explain the shape of today's legislatures. Indeed, the evolutionary path of American legislatures evidences remarkable organizational continuity over its almost 400-year time line. The colonial assemblies that were the first American legislatures morphed almost directly into the original state legislatures. In turn, the original state legislatures became the unattributed models for the Congress created by the Constitution. Finally, the original state legislatures, Congress, and existing state legislatures functioned as blueprints for newer state legislatures as each was established.

These evolutionary relationships are important because they help explain why modern American legislatures are organized and structured the way that they are. But there is an unappreciated reason why this evolutionary process matters. Tucked away in *Information and Legislative Organization*, Krehbiel notes in passing, "Legislatures in their primitive states are egalitarian collective choice bodies." He goes on to add, "However, over time (and usually very quickly) abstract egalitarian principles give way to concrete policy-making needs" (1991, 248). In Krehbiel's view these policy-making needs drive the rise of rules, leadership structures, and committee systems. An important observation generated by the story presented here is that, at least in the American context, there have never been any primitive legislatures. Even the first assembly in Virginia—a midsummer meeting of a handful of men stuck in a hot and humid outpost in the New World—was not an egalitarian collective choice body because, as I will show, it operated with a set of procedures and structures inherited from the English House of Commons. Thus, while over the course of American history there have been dozens of newly established legislatures, none of them was ever primitive because each newly established body was modeled on existing legislatures and because they were driven from their outset to meet concrete policy-making needs of those they were charged with governing.

My goal in this book is to reveal the evolutionary line that ties American legislatures across four centuries. Remarkably, although scholars have uncovered important fragments of this evolutionary story, no one has assembled all of the pieces in one place. Consequently, students of legislatures and American political development have largely been unaware of it.[1] That means that the organizational development of American legislatures over their long histories has not been used to inform our understanding of the modern institutions. In the following chapters I document the strong links that run from the initial Virginia assembly to the legislatures that exist today and use those links to offer a better and more complete understanding of why American legislatures have evolved as they have.

Evolution and Legislatures

Evolution is usually conceived as a biological process of change over time in some population, involving, among other things, natural selection, mutation, and hybridization. From a biological perspective, there are two types of evolution. Adaptive evolution suggests that natural selection allows for the transmission of advantageous traits from one generation to the next. Neutral evolution introduces a random element to the process, as genetic flukes result in population changes over time. Does either biological perspective offer insights into the process by which legislatures evolve?

One might argue that there is an element of natural selection in the evolution of legislative institutions because rules and procedures that have worked well in existing legislatures are often adopted by newly established legislatures, while failed features fall by the wayside. In contrast, neutral evolution does not appear to fit the pattern of legislative evolution, because it does not evidence randomness. Legislative evolution involves a series of conscious decisions made by people entrusted to make them. And it is on this score that attempts to impose features of biological evolution on the process of legislative evolution founder.[2] Legislatures are the creations of people making a series of deliberate choices, and not the product of random events.

This reality, then, might lead one to glibly associate legislative evolution with intelligent design. But this notion also does not translate well because there is no single designing intelligence driving the change in legislatures over time. Consequently, in the context of legislative evolution, intelligent design is better thought of as rational design. And to push this line of thought even harder, what is really in evidence is bounded rational design. Those who initially established American legislatures and those who influenced how they changed over time were informed by their understanding of what worked and what did not work among the limited number of legislatures with which they were familiar. They did not have the time, resources, or expertise required to survey all possible, or even very many, options for legislative design. They made decisions using the limited information available to them.

Thus, the notion of evolution I employ in this study is a fairly simple one: legislatures change over time because of a series of purposeful decisions. Importantly, people who controlled decisions about legislative design were influenced by those legislatures with which they were familiar. Features thought functional in existing legislatures were adopted, and those that were thought not to work were discarded. This approach is compatible with organization theory–based perspectives used to explain specific aspects of legislative evolution over briefer time periods (Cooper 1977; Cooper and Brady 1981; Davidson and Oleszek 1976; Moncrief and Jewell 1980).

The theory offered here posits that when fashioning new legislatures, political leaders do not seek to reinvent the wheel; rather they borrow from those legislatures with which they are familiar. If this is true then we ought to be able to find clear and convincing evidence of institutional lineages. Thus, I expect that a legislative offspring will, under most circumstances, look much like its institutional parent. There are several ways legislative DNA might get transferred. Most obviously, it could be passed on through constitutional design. It also might be relayed through the adoption of existing procedural rules and organizational structures. Finally, shared personnel could pass it along.

In the analysis that follows there are two distinct and important observations that emerge from the examination of how American legislatures have evolved since 1619. The first is that newly established legislatures start their organizational existence at the point of development of existing legislatures. This happens because those who design new legislatures model them on existing ones. Consequently, even legislatures created in the most remote and primitive locations are, comparatively speaking, the equivalents of their longer-established brethren in terms of structures and rules. This is important because it identifies the mechanism by which newly established legislatures in frontier locales populated by inexperienced lawmakers overcame their limitations.

Evolution, however, is not just about inception. It also involves change within an organization over time. Thus, the second observation is that as American legislatures age they become more complex organizations. They do so in response to external demands made on them and to meet the needs of members, both as individuals and in groups, factions, or parties. But, while all American legislatures have become more complex over time, they have not done so in exactly the same ways. Thus, at a macrolevel American legislatures have evolved along the same path, but upon closer examination each has blazed a somewhat different trail. How they came to differ is part of the story told here. I examine the organizational evolution of American legislatures to draw attention to the sequence by which these institutions developed over their long histories. I focus on the effect of early contexts on the shape of the organizations, the dependence of later development on the formative paths taken earlier, and on the tendency for innovations to be layered onto earlier features.

Measures of Legislative Evolution

To identify and measure change in the critical attributes of American legislatures, I use the concepts of organizational boundaries and internal complexity, first employed by Polsby (1968) as measures of the institutionalization of the U.S. House during the nineteenth century.[3] These measures have subsequently been used in the study of the evolution of many other legislatures and have proven to be relevant indicators of central characteristics in a variety of settings. Unlike indicators that focus primarily on political parties and partisan calculations (e.g., Binder 1995, 1996; Schickler 2001), Polsby's measures are applicable to legislatures such as the colonial assemblies and early state legislatures that existed before the advent of party organizations. Although they may not explain why or predict when legislatures change, these measures are useful for gauging how legislatures as organizations evolve over an extended period.

I examine the rise of representative assemblies and bicameral legislatures as important aspects of boundedness. But I spend more time detailing the development of rules and standing committee systems as evidence of increasing organizational complexity. Focusing on rules and committee systems is vital because they are essential features that help structure legislative decision making. Configuring decision making is a daunting challenge for legislatures because they are unusual organizations composed of an ever-changing roster of members, each of whom is usually endowed with an equally weighted vote (Loewenberg 2011, 49–50). To succeed legislatures must overcome coordination, collective action, and collective choice problems (Wilson 1999). Leadership is the typical solution to the coordination problem. As will be documented in the following chapters, at a minimum presiding officers were provided for new legislatures at their outset, and over time more complicated leadership structures were usually elaborated. Collective action problems involve workload management, with the division of tasks among committees the most common solution adopted. Again, as will be seen, newly established legislatures adopted the committee structures in vogue at the time. These too typically became more extensive over time.

Collective choice is the most difficult problem for legislatures to solve because of lawmakers' conflicting policy preferences. Rules and procedures are the mechanisms devised to solve the problem of sorting among these preferences. They are critical because they induce stability that legislatures would otherwise lack (Cox 2000). As I will demonstrate, American legislatures started with inherited sets of rules and procedures, which allowed them to sidestep this obstacle. And, once more, rules and procedures became more sophisticated over time.

Examining how early legislatures overcame these various challenges is important because the possibility of organizational dysfunction would appear to be acute. In most cases they were frontier assemblies populated by members unfamiliar with parliamentary practices. Thus how American legislatures came to successfully structure and govern themselves—how they institutionalized—are key questions to explore.

I also spend time uncovering the evolution of member compensation, legislative session length, and staff and facilities. These are central components of legislative professionalization, and they affect the informational capacity of legislatures, thereby influencing the substance of policy decisions (Squire 2007). Institutionalization, professionalization, and their relationship are discussed in chapters 6 and 7. For the moment it suffices to say that they are each part of the evolutionary story.

Using these various measures of legislative evolution, it is possible to examine the development of representative institutions during the colonial and early national eras. Almost every existing study of the evolution of legislatures is limited to tracing developments since the nineteenth century. But to understand the legislative institution as it exists today we must know whether its development is the product of modernity or is independent of modern society (Hibbing 1999, 164). Studying the organizational evolution of early American legislatures is therefore important because it enables us to learn whether the characteristics of contemporary legislatures are the result of increases in complexity, specialization, and differentiation in society at large as a number of scholars allege (Bensel 2000, 354–55; Katz and Sala 1996, 25–26; Silbey 1983, 622) or if they have quite a different functional origin.

In this regard it is critical to keep in mind that the colonial assemblies and early state and territorial legislatures developed in the absence of political parties. And as each of these institutions evolved over time, new or revised rules and structures were usually introduced incrementally rather than in one fell swoop. Taken together, these two facts suggest that early American legislatures were focused more on overcoming coordination, collective action, and collective choice problems—that is, figuring out the decision-making process—than they were on allowing one group or faction to design methods to dictate the content of the decisions they were making. Not being organized by parties or factions that were cohesive and enduring from session to session indicates that rules and structures were devised more for functional than for political purposes. In the examination of legislative evolution that follows I present evidence that partisan explanations for many developments may be less general than explanations focused on changes in the organizational environment, such as workloads.

Diffusion Models and Legislative Evolution

In the following chapters, I demonstrate that newly established American legislatures were modeled on existing legislatures. This would suggest that legislative evolution can be thought of as a case of policy diffusion. But what kind of diffusion model might fit?

Actually, there are several different dimensions to this question as it applies to legislatures. The first is what is being diffused. In Hibbing and Patterson's terms, my focus is on "structural diffusion," such as the number of chambers, and "procedural diffusion," notably parliamentary rules and committee systems. I devote only a little attention to "normative diffusion," or the informal mechanisms governing member behavior, and mention "policy diffusion" only in passing. The second dimension is a distinction between "hegemonic diffusion" and "multifaceted diffusion."

Hegemonic diffusion posits that a single entity dominates the diffusion landscape and functions as the primary model to be emulated. In contrast, multifaceted diffusion suggests a diversity of available models from which to choose (Hibbing and Patterson 2006, 120–21). Initially, one might anticipate the existence of a hegemon in American legislative evolution because of the more or less common social, economic, and cultural context in which the diffusion took place (Power and Rae 2006, 188). We might think that the British Parliament was a hegemon for the colonial legislatures, but as will be detailed in chapter 2, that was not the case, at least not to the extent commonly assumed. The U.S. Constitution might be seen as a hegemon for legislatures established after its creation because it requires the adoption of a republican form of state government. But this requirement makes a very weak case for hegemonic diffusion; indeed it does not rule out the creation of a parliamentary legislative form. More important, as American legislative evolution is viewed in finer and finer detail, the reality of multifaceted diffusion rather than hegemonic diffusion becomes apparent.

If American legislative evolution appears to be a case of multifaceted diffusion, there is still a question about the particular diffusion mechanism in play. Given that legislative evolution involves conscious decisions made by political elites it would seem reasonable to assume that some sort of learning model fits. There are several different diffusion models that emphasize learning. The first is information cascades, where adopters "may have no other information than the knowledge of whether others have adopted the policy." We might imagine that adopters on the frontier operated with such limited information. But as will be seen, backwoods elites were often aware of at least a basic set of options available to them. So, for example, the fact that bicameralism dominated among early state legislatures does not establish that option as the only one available for later adopters to consider because in a number of cases unicameralism was debated. A better fit to the circumstances here is offered by two other learning models. The first is learning and availability, where adopters "tend to base their decisions on only those instances that are available to them. . . . The result is that the choice set of policy makers will be limited to policies of states that are immediately accessible." The other is learning and reference groups, where adopters "prefer policy models from [states] that are similar to theirs" (Elkins and Simmons 2005, 42–45). Aspects of each of these two models comport with the story uncovered in this study. Those creating new legislatures tended to look to legislatures with which they were familiar and imported their structures and rules. This was the simple, easy, and rational way to design a new legislature.

Tracing American Legislative Evolution

How, then, did American legislatures evolve? Colonial assemblies developed over a 157-year period and, as discussed in chapter 2, although they eventually looked superficially like their British parent, in fundamental ways they evolved to become distinctly different institutions. When independence was declared, the colonial lower houses became state lower houses with little more than a name change, as figure 1.1 suggests and chapter 3 documents. Upper houses changed more significantly in most states, becoming elected rather than appointed bodies. Overall, however, there was considerable organizational continuity between the colonial-era legislatures and those institutions that succeeded them after the break with Britain. This evolutionary process, however, was not deterministic. As shown in figure 1.1, there was a second evolutionary line consisting of the Continental and Confederal Congress and the much less well-known provincial congresses. These latter institutions were temporary bodies that bridged the gap between the colonial and statehood eras. The institutional features of this second evolutionary line were discarded in the original state constitutions and the federal constitution.

Perhaps more controversial is the claim in chapter 3 that the original state legislatures were the models for the Congress created by the Constitution. It is true that several of the most influential voices in the writing of the Constitution disparaged the existing state legislatures. Yet, in every elemental characteristic—number and name of houses and the relationship between them, the legislature's ability to name its own leaders and adopt its own rules, and the power of the executive veto—the Congress under the Constitution closely resembled the original state legislatures. It bore no relationship at all to the Congress that existed under the Articles of Confederation, which was a unicameral chamber that fused legislative, executive, and judicial powers, and granted each state, not each legislator, a vote. Indeed, as figure 1.1 suggests, the evolutionary line from the Continental Congress and provincial congresses to the Congress of the Confederation ceased with the creation of the Congress created by the Constitution.

Legislatures created after the establishment of the Constitutional Congress bear some resemblance both to it and to state legislatures that existed at the time they were started. The impact of the Constitutional Congress on state legislatures was, in fact, immediate, as both Georgia and Pennsylvania switched to bicameral legislatures shortly after the Constitution was adopted, in part to conform to the new national structure. But the evolutionary line for state legislatures established after the original 13 is varied,

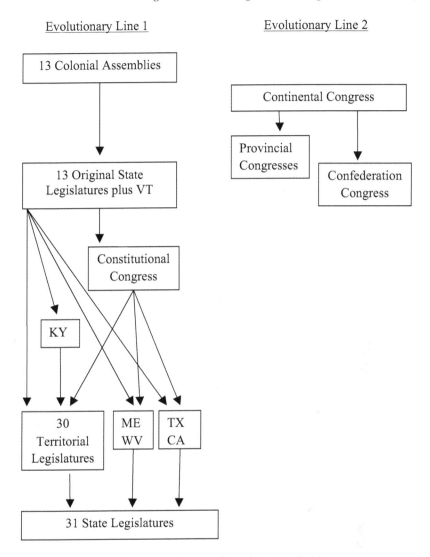

Fig. 1.1. The main evolutionary lines of American legislatures

and not every state went through the same developmental phases, as figure 1.1 suggests. A total of 31 states were admitted to the Union only after first being territories.[4] They all had territorial legislatures that preceded the creation of their state legislatures, and these bodies are the focus of chapter 4. Several states, however, bypassed being territories, and their evolutionary stories are necessarily different. Although it was not admitted to the Union until 1791, Vermont wrote its first constitution and created its legislature at the same time as the original 13 states. Kentucky was admitted as a state a year after Vermont, again without having been a formal territory. Legislatures in both Maine, which was carved out of Massachusetts in 1820, and West Virginia, which separated from Virginia during the Civil War, were related to their parent state legislatures in differing degrees. Finally, California and Texas became states without passing through a territorial stage; the former having no predecessor legislature, the latter having been an independent republic with a bicameral national assembly. The evolutionary stories in Hawaii, Kansas, Oregon, Tennessee, and Utah, all of which experienced legislatures that preceded, or in the case of Kansas competed with, their territorial legislatures, also merit examination, as do, for reasons that will be explained, the Legislative Assembly of San Francisco and the General Assembly of the Indian Stream Republic. These odd cases and their implications for understanding legislative evolution are detailed in chapter 5.

After legislatures are established, the evolutionary focus shifts to how they change over time. Chapter 6 examines this question by documenting the institutionalization of state legislatures during the nineteenth century. Over this time, state legislatures greatly expanded parliamentary rules and procedures. Similarly, standing committee systems became a standard feature, although with some distinctive nuances across the states. Legislatures also came to acquire dedicated facilities and rudimentary staffs. Chapter 7 examines the professionalization of state legislatures across the twentieth century and into the twenty-first century. During this time, many, but not all, state legislatures professionalized, with increased member pay, more frequent legislative sessions, and greatly improved staff resources and facilities. Again, although state legislatures continued to evolve in the same direction, they did so at very different paces and with very different results.

The final chapter explores where legislative evolution is apt to go from here. One possibility that has been floated is that state legislatures are in the process of deinstitutionalizing. A second possibility is that they are deprofessionalizing. They could, of course, be experiencing both or neither process. These possibilities are examined. The answers to these questions matter because where American legislatures were in the past and how they got to their current point tells us a great deal about where they are apt to go in the future.

2 ◆ The Colonial Assemblies and the Beginnings of American Legislatures

Representative assemblies emerged in each of the American colonies within a decade or two of their coming under English control, despite the fact that the colonies were settled by different people at different points in time for different reasons.[1] By *American colonies* I mean those that were eventually incorporated into the original 13 states. Assemblies were, of course, established in other British colonies in North America. Indeed, the second colonial assembly established, just a year after Virginia's first met, was in Bermuda. The influence of the assemblies in colonies that were not incorporated into the United States on those that were should not be minimized. For instance, South Carolina's assembly was greatly influenced by its counterpart in Barbados (Kammen 1969, 54). Indeed, Barbados was an important referent for many colonies. When the Maryland House claimed the power to pass an elections bill, the governor responded by noting that not only was that assertion of legislative power new to the colony, it was "not practiced in Virginia, Barbadoes, or any other of his majesties plantations,' &c." (Ridgely 1841, 84). But the focus of this chapter will be on the assemblies that later became American state legislatures.

It is important to emphasize that assemblies arose for different reasons in different colonies. In Virginia, an assembly first met in 1619 because the failing colony's commercial directors hoped it would promote much needed economic stability (Billings 2004, 5–7; Bosher 1907, 734–35; Kammen 1969, 13–15; Kukla 1985, 284). Assemblies in Maryland, Massachusetts, and Connecticut were rooted in their early charters, but colonists pushed for their establishment. After the 1650s, external proprietary boards determined that assemblies were essential structures for the development of successful societies (Kammen 1969, 19, 32).

A chronology of the emergence of representative assemblies in the American colonies is provided in table 2.1. It is critical to appreciate that the assemblies were not, in any simple sense, clones of the English parliamentary system. Even the official who created the first Virginia Assembly molded it "to fit the design of the company's corporate culture, not to resemble Parliament" (Billings 2004, 6). Moreover, it is important to keep in mind that the assemblies were established throughout the seventeenth century and into the eighteenth century, a period during which Parliament itself was undergoing dramatic changes (Norton 1989). Most significant, a parliamentary system developed in Britain, something that never took root in the American colonies. Consequently, the legislatures that developed in the colonial era arguably had more in common with Parliament of the Tudor period than with Parliament following the Glorious Revolution (Huntington 1968, 109–21).

Yet, despite that fact that the assemblies emerged at different times and for different reasons and the reality that their distant parent government was not a static model to emulate, the colonial bodies quickly came to resemble one another (Andrews 1944, 40; Greene 1961, 453–54; Kammen 1969, 58, 69). This convergence might be considered surprising because "each colony constituted an almost wholly separate political environment" with "virtually no common political life" (Greene 1975, 27–28). Moreover, the colonies "lacked a common political culture" (Beeman 1992, 412), in part because British colonists hailed from various regions of that country, and each group brought a somewhat different political culture with it (Fisher 1989). But in their struggles to assert power the assemblies came to assume virtually the same set of responsibilities across the colonies.

Perhaps the most elemental power of a legislature is lawmaking. Some of the colonial assemblies exercised the right to initiate legislation from their inception, while others only gained that power over time (Kammen 1969, 64). But they all came to be lawmaking bodies. The range of issues on which the assemblies legislated is demonstrated by the collection of laws passed by the Pennsylvania Assembly between 1715 and 1718, listed in table 2.2. During this four-year period the Assembly adopted measures dealing with government revenue ("an Act for Raising a Supply of one *Penny per Pound* and four *shillings* a head"), law enforcement and justice ("For the Advancement of Justice"), public welfare ("For Supplying some defects in the Law for the Releif of the Poor"), elections ("For the better

TABLE 2.1. The American Colonial Assemblies

Colony	Year Assembly Established	Initial Assembly Membership Size	Assembly Membership Size, 1770	Year Assembly Became Chamber in Bicameral Legislature	How Upper House Filled
Virginia	1619	22	118	1642–80[a]	Appointed
Massachusetts	1634	24	125	1644	Elected by lower house[b]
Connecticut	1637	12	138	1698	Elected
Maryland	1637–38[c]	24	58	1650	Appointed
New Haven[d]	1639	4	—	Unicameral	
Plymouth[e]	1639	17	—	Unicameral	
Rhode Island	1647	24	65	1696	Elected
North Carolina	1665	12	81	1691	Appointed
South Carolina	1671	20	51	1691	Appointed
New (East) Jersey	1668	10	24	1668	Appointed
West Jersey[f]	1681	34	—	1696	Appointed
New Hampshire	1680	11	34	1692	Appointed
Pennsylvania[g]	1682	42	36	Unicameral	
New York	1683	18	27	1691	Appointed
Delaware	1704	18	18	Unicameral	
Georgia	1755	18	25	1755	Appointed

Source: For Delaware, Bushman, Hancock, and Homsey 1986; Conrad 1908, 78–79; and Munroe 1979, 72; for Georgia, Jones 1883, 463–65; and Gosnell and Anderson 1956, 14; for New Jersey, Moran 1895, 33–34; in general see Kammen 1969, 11–12; Frothingham 1886, 18–21; Greene 1981, 461; and Moran 1895.

Note: — = not applicable.

[a]Kukla (1981, 10; 1985, 289; 1989, 110–12) holds that bicameralism appeared in 1643; Walthoe (1910, 1) places it a bit earlier; Bailey (1979, 28) puts it in the 1650s; Kammen (1969, 12) before 1660; and Billings (1974, 234), Frothingham (1886, 19), and Miller (1907) not until the 1680s. More recently, Billings (2004, xx, 27) revised his view, dating the rise of bicameralism in Virginia to around 1642 or 1643.

[b]After 1691, members of the upper house were elected by the lower house.

[c]The year depends on the calendar used. Maryland may have had an assembly as early as 1634–35: the Assembly journal of 1637–38 makes reference to "an Act of Generall Assemblie held at S[t] Maries on the six and twentieth day of Feb[ry] 1634" (Browne 1883, 23). The earlier assembly was deemed illegal, and no official records of it were kept (Riley 1905, 1).

[d]Connecticut absorbed New Haven in 1664.

[e]Massachusetts annexed Plymouth; the final meeting of the Plymouth General Court was in 1692.

[f]New Jersey was separated in 1676 into East Jersey, which continued under the existing government, and West Jersey. East Jersey and West Jersey were reunited in 1702, and the first assembly met in 1703 with 13 councilors and 24 representatives, 12 from each region.

[g]Pennsylvania was bicameral from its first assembly in 1682 until a new charter in 1701 instituted a unicameral system.

Regulating of Elections of Sheriffs, Coroners, and Assessors"), economic regulation ("Impowering the Justices to settle the Prices of Liquors in Publick Houses, and Provender for Horses in Publick Stables"), transportation ("For Establishing a Ferry over *Delaware*, at the Falls"), and even women's rights ("Concerning Feme Sole Traders").[2] While some of these measures were relatively simple, others were complex pieces of legislation; the justice bill, for example, ran to 14 printed pages.

By the early eighteenth century the assemblies were permanent components of colonial government and recognizable legislative organizations (Kammen 1969, 57). Their strong resemblance to each other would seem to document the power of path dependency with initially disparate bodies coming to look alike over time. But, as will be argued below, when examined more closely their evolutionary paths did not always take the same route or arrive at exactly the same destination. Indeed, in an extreme ex-

TABLE 2.2. "Acts and Laws" Passed by the Pennsylvania Assembly, 1715–18

Act	Page Length
To Enlarge the time for putting in Execution An Act, Entitled an Act for Raising a Supply of one penny per pound and four shilling a Head	3
For Reviving of Actions and Processes lately depending in the Courts of the County of *Chester*	2
For Raising a Supply of one *Penny per Pound* and four *shillings* a head	8
For the better Regulating of Elections of Sheriffs, Coroners, and Assessors	2
For laying a Duty upon sundry Liquors retailed in this Province	4
For the more Effectual raising of County Rates and Levies	12
For the Advancement of Justice	14
For Supplying some defects in the Law for the Releif of the Poor	4
To Supply some Ommissions in a Law, entituled, *An Act for Raising a Duty of Tonnage upon Ships and Vessels*	2
For the better Encouraging of Trade the of [*sic*] this Province	3
For laying a Duty on Wine, Rum, Brandy and Spirits, Cyder, Hops and Flax Imported into this Province	6
Concerning Feme Sole Traders	2
For continuing the Duty upon Negroes brought into this Province	4
For Raising a Duty upon Tonnage of Ships and Vessels	2
For Erecting Houses of Correction and Work-Houses in this Province	4
For Erecting a Ferry to the Landing near *Daniel Cooper*, and also to *Glouchester* in the Western Division of *New Jersey*	2
For Establishing a Ferry over *Delaware*, at the Falls	2
For Continuing the Ferry from *Bristol*, in the County of *Bucks*, to *Burlington* in the Western Division of *New-Jersey*	1
Impowering the Justices to settle the Prices of Liquors in Publick Houses, and Provender for Horses in Publick Stables	2

Source: Laws of the Prov. of Pennsylvania 1718.

ample, one sibling legislature—Nova Scotia—evolved completely differently from its American cousins by adopting a parliamentary system (Massicotte 2006). Moreover, the institutional survival of the assemblies was not predestined. Another sibling, a federal assembly established in the Leeward Islands in 1682, failed and disappeared from the political landscape by early in the eighteenth century (Higham 1926).

The Establishment of Institutional Boundaries

As Polsby notes, "the differentiation of an organization from its environment" is a critical step in the evolution of an institution (1968, 145). When first established the early colonial assemblies had to differentiate themselves from their environments in two fundamental ways. First, they had to evolve from being folkmoots inclusive of all a colony's freemen to smaller representative bodies. Second, these emerging representative assemblies had to change from being part of amorphous lawmaking entities with the governor and council to being separate chambers in bicameral legislatures. For later legislatures these fundamental boundaries were delineated by charters and constitutions; the early assemblies had to establish them themselves.

The Rise of Elected Representatives

How did colonial assemblies come to be representative bodies? In Virginia, the issue was settled immediately. While the government had a governor and councilors, they met from the beginning of the General Assembly with two elected representatives from each of the colony's plantations and corporations. But things were different to the north. In simple terms, the original governmental form for the early New England colonies consisted of a governor, a council, and an assembly comprised of the colony's freemen (Morey 1893–94, 204).[3] Each of these governing units—the governor, the councilors, and the assembly—was a distinct entity. But they made most important decisions collectively in what was usually referred to as the General Court.

The assemblies, however, rapidly evolved into representative bodies as it became geographically impracticable for all freemen to participate in their regular (and often frequent) sessions (Haynes 1894, 22–23; Langdon 1966, 85–86; Moran 1895, 43; Morey 1893–94, 206–9; Young 1968, 154). In 1638, for example, the Plymouth General Court, which met three or four times a year, made this decision.

> Wheras Complaint hath bine made that the ffreemen were put to many
> Inconveniencyes and great expences by theire Continewall attendances
> att the Courts It is therefore enacted by the Court and the Authoritie
> thereof for the ease of the seuerall townes of this Gou^rment; that euery
> towne shall make Choise of two of theire freemen and the towne of Ply-
> mouth of foure to bee Comittes or Deputies to joyne with the bench to
> enact and make all such laws and ordinances as shalbee Judged to bee
> good and wholsome. (Pulsifer 1861, 91)[4]

Even after this decision the freemen were still expected to attend the annual General Court election session. In 1649, the General Court eased this
requirement for one community on the colony's periphery: "It is enacted
that the towne of Rehoboth shall haue liberty yearely to make choice of 2
freemen of their inhabitants to be assistant[s]." This privilege was extended
to all Plymouth towns in 1652 (Pulsifer 1861, 55, 59).

Across the early colonies each town or county eventually came to elect
representatives to speak on its behalf (Klain 1955, 1112–13; Shurtleff 1853a,
118; Trumbull 1850, 22). In later colonies such representation was established from the start. In 1668, New Jersey governor Carteret issued a
proclamation for the first meeting of the assembly, requiring the freeholders in each town "To make Choice and appoint Two able men . . . to be your
Burgesses and Representatives for you" (Whitehead 1880, 57). Similarly, a
decade and a half later, instructions given to the New York governor authorized the calling of a general assembly, "of all the Freeholders, by the p^rsons
who they shall choose to rep^rsent [them]" (O'Callaghan 1853, 331).

The Establishment of Boundaries between Legislative Chambers

How did colonial assemblies become distinct legislative chambers? In general, bicameral legislatures emerged from unicameral bodies because of the
distinction between councilors, as appointed agents of the Crown or proprietors, and assembly members, as elected agents of the colonies'
freemen. As separate chambers developed, labels for the members of each
body were devised. Councilors were typically referred to as *magistrates* or
assistants. Assembly members took many names. In Virginia they were
called *burgesses* because they were elected from boroughs. Maryland initially used several titles; a journal entry in 1674–75 stated, "It is this day ordered by the Bu[rgesses], Dep^{tys} or Delegates of this Province . . ." (Browne

1884, 441). Similarly, documents from the first New Jersey Assembly reveal the use of two names for its members, referring to them as *burgesses* and *deputies* (Leaming and Spicer 1758, 77, 90). By 1703, they were called *representatives* (*Jour. and Votes of the H. of Reps. of the Prov. of Nova Cesarea* 1872). Across the assemblies *deputy* was the term most commonly used.

The council and the assembly first became unmistakably separate bodies in Massachusetts (Kammen 1969, 22–23; Morey 1893–94, 212). The exact steps in the development of bicameralism, however, were somewhat unclear. Through the early 1630s, the magistrates and deputies developed divergent interests that led to conflicts between them. The most prominent dispute involved the legal case of a peripatetic pig. A Boston widow claimed that her sow left her yard and wandered over to a sea captain's property, where it was killed. The widow sued for compensation. Legally, the issue involved the interpretation of two laws: one passed in 1631 that said "that all swine that are found in any mans corne shalbe forfeit to the publique" and the other passed in 1633 holding "that it shalbe lawfull for any man to kill any swine that comes into his corne" (Shurtleff 1853a, 86, 106). The magistrates largely sided with the wealthy sea captain, while most of the deputies backed the less well-to-do widow (Hosmer 1908, 64–66). This difference of opinion had two consequences. First, the General Court opted out of swine regulation, decreeing that "All former orders concerning swine are repealed" and delegating power over such ordinances to the towns (Shurtleff 1853a, 119). Second, and more important, it forced an enduring split between the magistrates and deputies.

Accordingly, as John Winthrop wrote in his journal, "there fell out a great business upon a very small occasion" (Hosmer 1908, 64). In 1636 a working arrangement was reached between the council and the assembly. Its language contains the glimmerings of a bicameral legislature and even conference committees.

And whereas it may fall out that in some of theis Ge[ner]all Courts, to be holden by the magistrates & deputies, there may arise some difference of [j]udgm^t in doubtfull cases, it is therefore ordered, that noe lawe, order, or sentence shall passe as an act of the Court, without the consent of the great^r p[art] of the magistrates on the one p[art], & the great^r number of the deputyes on the other p[art]; & for want of such accorde, the cause or order shalbe suspended, & if either p[art]e thinke it soe materiall, there shalbe forthwith a comitte chosen, the one halfe by the magistrates, & the other halfe by the deputyes, & the comittee soe chosen to elect an vmpire, whoe togeather shall have the power to heare & determine the cause in question. (Shurtleff 1853a, 170)

This decision may also reflect a political calculation on council's part, because as new towns were established the number of deputies grew and "the magistrates would, in a few years, have lost all their weight in the legislative part of government" (Hutchinson 1765, 449).

The separation became permanent in 1644 (Hosmer 1908, 164). At that point it was agreed that the deputies and the magistrates would sit apart, bills proposed and passed by one body would be sent to the other body, and both bodies would have to agree to a bill for it to become law.

Forasmuch as, after long experience, wee find divers inconveniences in the mann^r of o^r [pro]ceding in Co^{r}ts by ma^{trats} & deputies siting together . . . It is therefore ordered, first, that the magistrates may sit & act busines by themselues, by drawing up bills & orders wch they shall see good in their wisdome, wch haveing agreed upon, they may p[re]sent them to the deputies to bee considered of, how good & wholesome such orders are for the country, & accordingly to give their assent or dissent, the deputies in like mann^r siting a[part] by themselues, & consulting about such orders & lawes as they in their discretion & exp[er]ience shall find meete for com[m]on good, wch agreed upon by them, they may p[re]sent to the magistrats, who, according to their wisdome, haveing seriously considered of them, may consent unto them or disalow them; & when any orders have passed the ap[pro]bation of both ma^{trats} & deputies, then such orders to bee ingrossed, & in the last day of the Court to bee read deliberately, & full assent to bee given.

Even this accord, however, failed to finally settle the issue. In 1646 the deputies had to vote again, "that the House of Depu^{t}s should continew in the setting aparte & acting a[par]te from the Magis^{ts}." They went on to assert that bicameralism was "the most suitable to their condi[ti]ons" (Shurtleff 1853b, 58–59; 1854, 62).

Although the legislatures in most of the other colonies also became bicameral, they did not follow the same path to that destination as in Massachusetts. In Rhode Island it took almost 50 years of campaigning to force the change. In 1664 the General Assembly's journal noted, "Ther having been a long agetation about the motion whether the magistrates shall sitt by themselves and the deputyes by themselves," it was resolved that the next assembly should address the issue. But several subsequent assemblies failed to resolve the matter. The first real step toward bicameralism was finally taken in 1668, when the General Assembly held, "It is ordered and enacted, that the Deputies have liberty for halfe an howers time to withdraw themselves, and then immediately to returne; and that for the future the like liberty is, and shall be allowed to the Deputies if they or the major part of them shall desire it, and that in the time of their absence, noe act shall pass as a law." Even then, however, efforts were made to keep the deputies and magistrates sitting together. In 1672, a measure passed authorizing, "ffor the keepinge of the Magistrates and Deputies in love together, for the ripeninge of their consultations, and husbandinge of their time, the Generall Treasurer shall give order and pay for a convenient dinner for the Magistrates and Deputies in Generall Assemblies." Although there is evidence that by this time the two chambers considered themselves separate entities, their partition was not formalized until 1696 (Bartlett 1857, 63, 124, 144–45, 151, 223, 445, 472; 1858, 313).

In Connecticut, few conflicts arose between the elected assistants and the deputies. Still, a process of separate consideration of legislation evolved over the last quarter of the seventeenth century (Morey 1893–94, 213–14). A formal split was recognized in 1698: "this Gener¹ Assembly shall consist of two houses; the first shall consist of . . . Assistants, which shall be known by the name of the Upper House; the other shall consist of such deputies as shall be legally returned from the severall towns within this Colonie, . . . which shall be known by the name of the Lower House." Both chambers were to be powerful: "And it is further ordered that no act shall be passed into a law of this Colonie, nor any law already enacted be repealed, nor any other act proper to this Generall Assembly, but by the consent of both houses" (Hoadly 1868, 267).

The course of separation in New Hampshire was fuzzy. The 1679 royal commission that made the colony independent from Massachusetts established a separate council and assembly. During the relatively few times the assembly was called together during the 1680s it appears it sat separately from the council. But on many occasions the council and governor enacted laws without the consent or even the participation of the assembly (Moran 1895, 14–15). It is not until 1692 that clear evidence of separate and powerful bodies appears in the records, with the journals of each chamber making references to actions taken in "the other house" (Bouton 1868, 108; 1869, 3–4).

After only a few years operating in a unicameral legislature, Maryland deputies sensed a critical difference in their perspectives compared with those of the councilors. According to the Assembly journal, in 1642, "Robert Vaughan in the name of the rest desired that the house might be Seperated & the Burgesses to be by themselves and to have a negative but it was not Granted by the Lieu^t General." It took until 1650 for a formal separation of the two bodies to occur. At that point it was decided, "That this p^{r}nt assembly during the continuance thereof bee held by way of Vpper & Lower howse to sitt in two distinct roomes a part, for the more convenient dispatch of the busines therein to bee consulted of." Both chambers had to consent for a bill to become law (Browne 1883, 130, 272). Even after this seemingly unequivocal pronouncement unicameralism returned briefly in the mid-1650s, and only from 1660 on was Maryland's assembly permanently bicameral (Falb 1986, 46–59; Jordan 1987, 26–33).

A weak commitment to bicameralism also surfaced in South Carolina, but with a different twist. The colony initially enjoyed a bicameral legislature (Moran 1895, 49). During the 1670s, however, it appears that lawmaking power was centered in the Council with the Assembly relegated to a minor role. In the 1680s a system was instituted where councilors, noblemen, and representatives sat together, but a majority of each group had to pass a measure for it to become law, effectively creating a tricameral body. It was not until 1691 that a more typical bicameral legislature was fashioned (Kammen 1969, 35).[5] There were, however, unceasing tensions between the houses, as will be discussed below. Indeed, in the mid-1740s—a half century after the advent of bicameralism in the colony—the lower house changed its name to the General Assembly from the Commons House of Assembly and attempted unsuccessfully to deny the upper house any role in the legislative process (Sirmans 1961, 384–85; Weir 1969, 490–91).

In several other colonies it is not clear when bicameralism emerged. The concession that established the right to create a legislature in New Jersey appeared to call for a unicameral body (Kammen 1969, 37; 232; Moran 1895, 28). During the initial session in 1668, however, the deputies' secretary sent a message to the governor and council saying, "We Have read and perused the Contents of several Acts of yours presented" (Leaming and Spicer 1758, 84), phrasing that suggests a separation between the lawmakers. In this case the initiative for sitting apart appears to have come from the seven councilors, who may have calculated that they would be outvoted by the ten deputies if they sat together (Moran 1895, 27–28). It also seems that the two groups sat apart in a second session held later that same year, apparently making the deputies unhappy. At the end of the brief meeting they sent an angry message to the governor and council, complaining, "We finding so many and great Inconveniencies by our not setting together, and your apprehensions so different to ours, and your Expectations that Things must go according to your Opinions" (Leaming and Spicer 1758, 90). Although seven years would pass before another session was held, bicameralism was formally recognized by the Lords Proprietors in 1672, who announced "that in all Generall Assembly's, the Governor and his Council are to set by themselves, and the Deputies or Representatives by themselves" (Whitehead 1880, 100–101). Acrimony, however, continued to be a hallmark of the relationship between the houses for several decades (Moran 1895, 31–33; Whitehead 1880, 354–65). Indeed, in a nasty exchange of letters in 1681, the councilors accused the deputies of suffering "Lucifers Pride" in assuming "to yo^{r}selues the title of the generall assembly, the truth is if you were all persons quallified for Dep^{tis} yett true wisdome would teach you better manners than to stile Yo^{r}selves the Generall Assembly" (Whitehead 1880, 364).

In 1676 New Jersey was split into East Jersey, which continued under the existing government, and West Jersey which had to create a new governmental structure (Moran 1895, 33; Whitehead 1880, 205). The 1677 *Concessions and Agreements* created a unicameral general assembly (Leaming and Spicer 1758, 404–5). The assembly first met in 1681 and continued to assemble regularly for several years. But by the early 1690s it suffered from political instability, and in 1696 bicameralism was introduced to resolve the problem (Kammen 1969, 38). The two Jerseys were reunited in 1702, with a bicameral legislature that met for the first time in 1703. Bicameralism was actually so well established by that point that the speaker's appeal to the governor on behalf of the House included a call for conference committees: "That if any mis-understanding shall happen to arise between the Council and this House, that in such a case a Com^{ee} of the Council may be appointed to Confer with a Com^{ee} of this H^s for the Adjusting and Reconciling such Differences" (*Jour. and Votes of the H. of Reps. of the Prov. of Nova Cesarea* 1872, 4).

When New York was authorized to establish a legislative body in 1683, the Duke of York's instructions appeared to call for a bicameral body. The governor was told, "there shall be a Gen^r Assembly . . . in ord^r to consulting wth yo^{r}selfe and the said Councill what laws are fitt and necessary . . . [the] said Gen^r Assembly shall have free liberty to consult and debate among themselves all matt^{rs} as shall be apprehended proper to be established for laws" (O'Callaghan 1853, 331). That the councilors and the representatives sat apart would appear to be established by two notations added to the end of *The Charter of Libertys and Privileges granted by his Royal Highness to the Inhabitants of New-York and its Dependencies*, a historic measure passed by the assembly. The initial notation says, "The Representatives have assented to this bill, and order it to bee sent up to the Governo'r and Councell for their assent," and it was signed by the speaker. That was followed by a second note saying that the governor and Council gave their assent as well. The *Charter* provided for a bicameral legislature, requiring that "the major part" of the representatives must agree to all bills (Brodhead 1871, 661). But after first consenting to the *Charter*, royal assent was subsequently withdrawn and the General Assembly dissolved. For several years lawmaking was left to the governor and his councilors. The Assembly was only revived in 1691 after Leisler's Rebellion was put down, and from that point forward it operated as a bicameral body. Interestingly, Leisler's insurgent government had featured its own bicameral assembly (Moran 1895, 37–38).

The storyline in North Carolina is muddled. The assembly was established as a unicameral body in 1665, but over time councilors and assembly members began to consider legislation separately, and they were formally recognized as distinct chambers in 1691 (Bassett 1894, 55–58; Moran 1895, 47–48). Perhaps the most puzzling case, however, is Virginia. Kukla (1981, 10; 1985, 289; 1989, 110–12) holds that Virginia became bicameral in 1643, while Walthoe (1910, 1) places the split a bit earlier, Bailey (1979, 28) puts it in the 1650s, Kammen (1969, 12) dates it before 1660, and Beverley ([1722] 1855, 187–88), Billings (1974, 234), Frothingham (1886, 19), and Miller (1907) say it did not happen until the 1680s. More recently, Billings (2004, xx, 27) revised his earlier view and, persuaded by Kukla's analysis, dates the rise of bicameralism in Virginia to around 1642 or 1643.

Even if Virginia became bicameral in 1642–43 as the best evidence indicates, the commitment to it was, at least initially, uncertain. In 1653, a dispute over naming the House speaker hints at the existence of separate chambers but with an unclear division between them. A message from the Council begins with an admission of that body's reluctance to get involved in House decisions: "Not to intrench upon the right of Assemblies in the free choice of a speaker." The message then goes on to suggest the House choose someone other than the burgesses' preference. In response, the House sent a committee to the governor and Council with a charge to "request of them their reasons, wherefore they cannot joyne with vs the

Burgesses in the business of this Assembly, about the election of Lev't Coll *Walter Chiles* for Speaker of this Assembly" (McIlwaine 1915, 86).

Regardless of when bicameralism might have happened in a particular case, it became the established norm in the colonies. Indeed, among the other assemblies formed in the Americas during the seventeenth century, only Bermuda's remained unicameral; Barbados, St. Kitts, Antigua, Montserrat, Nevis, and Jamaica all became bicameral (Kammen 1969, 11–12). Moreover, the final generation of assemblies established—the Bahamas in 1729 (Craton 1962, 112–25); Georgia in 1755, Nova Scotia in 1758 (Beck 1957, 24–25), West Florida in 1766 (Howard 1947, 43–44, 108–17), and Prince Edward Island in 1773 (MacKinnon 1951, 13–16)— were all created as bicameral bodies.[6]

It is important to note that the direction of cameral change was not universal. Pennsylvania took the opposite path, starting with a bicameral legislature in 1682 and switching to a unicameral system with its new charter in 1701. Actually, the Council did not disappear but lost its role in the legislative process (Leonard 1948b, 406–11). The Delaware Assembly, which was spun out from the Pennsylvania Assembly in 1704, was created as a unicameral body like its parent chamber, and it remained so until the Revolution. Both New Haven and Plymouth were unicameral throughout their truncated histories. There was some debate on the matter in Plymouth (Langdon 1966, 94–95). In June 1650 a committee of the General Court held, "And y^t for the futuer as formerly in the making and Repealling of lawes and aiornment of Courts wherein Comitties are Requeset; The Magestraits and Comitties or Deputies bee Concidered together as one body" (Pulsifer 1861, 57, 155). There is no evidence that the New Haven General Court ever strayed from its plan that their magistrates and deputies "shall sitt together" (Hoadly 1857, 115).

There is another aspect of bicameralism as it developed in the colonies that merits comment. Although the lower houses came to enjoy the political upper hand, in each colony both houses exercised influence in the legislative process. Thus, it was possible for one house to impede the wishes of the other house and for tensions between them to fester. Upper-house and lower-house members had different perspectives, as we might expect given that they usually attained office through different mechanisms. For example, in his diary a member of the Virginia House in the 1750s complained, "It is remarkable that some, who were Once Burgesses and hearty for a Removal, as Councillors are against it" (Greene 1965, 99). Such differences in opinion often incited great passions. A witness to a debate in a

Maryland conference committee wrote, "This dispute, though managed with good sense and spirit, breathes an acrimony, virulence, and unmannerly invective not honorary to the parties and inconsistent with the rules and dignity of parliament" (Quincy 1915–16, 469).

Cameral conflict became particularly pronounced in South Carolina, where, as noted earlier, great animosity developed between the two chambers. It was reported that during a 1773 debate in the Commons House a member snarled, "And, Mr. Speaker, if the Governor and Council don't see fit to fall in with us, I say, let the General duty law and all *go to the Devil*, Sir. And we go about our business" (Quincy 1915–16, 452, italics in original). Excerpts from letters written in 1764 by Henry Laurens, a member of the lower house, attest to the fact that clashes between the chambers were a chronic feature of South Carolina legislative life. In one he complained about a measure that had passed in both chambers, "It stuck sometime with the Council . . . & would have remained there I do believe till doomsday if it had not been a necessary instrument to save appearances & take off the imputation of outragiousness in a quarrel that the two Houses are unhappily engaged in." Another involved "A very unhappy difference of opinion between our House of Lords & House of Commons respecting the Salary or gratuity (usually allowed to Governours)" that "brought forth a proroguation, annihilated upwards of Twenty five essential Laws the existence of which depended upon the Session of the House of Assembly" (Rogers 1974, 381–82, 389). The discord between the chambers even prompted remarkably petty behavior; in 1760 the Council president twice refused to receive a message from the House simply because the messenger failed to deliver it at what he considered the proper spot on the floor (Lipscomb 1996, 507).

Finally, it must be emphasized that the advent of bicameralism in the colonies represented an effort by lower-house members to establish institutional boundaries. It was not an attempt by either the colonists or the Crown to simply imitate the British system. While it is true that colonists often cited Parliament's two houses to justify their desire for a similar-looking system (Johnson 1938, 21; Lokken 1959a, 574; Moran 1895, 13, 26), bicameralism in the colonies differed from the British version in two fundamental ways. First, the historical reasons behind the split between the House of Commons and the House of Lords were not the same reasons that drove the colonies to develop separate legislative chambers. Bicameralism emerged in England over representation of different social classes (Taswell-Langmead 1946, 169–71). In contrast, bicameralism in America was triggered by policy disagreements between groups holding office through different means. Thus, for example, in South Carolina, "Everyone recognized that the composition of the upper house did not reflect a separate stratum of society comparable to that of the British Lords" (Weir 1969, 492). Second, the House of Lords was in the main a hereditary body and thus politically independent of both the Crown and the people. In contrast, upper-house members in most of the colonies were appointees of the Crown or the proprietor and thus politically tied to them (Luce 1924, 47–50; Main 1967, 3, 199–200; Pole 1969, 68; Sirmans 1961, 387). By the mid-1750s, the South Carolina Council's lack of political independence from the Crown led to a substantial decline in its political power and public standing. Notable South Carolinians refused to accept appointment to it (Sirmans 1961, 390–91; Weir 1969, 491). The Commons House went so far in 1770 as to ask that the Crown appoint an additional upper house composed of politically independent men (Greene 1963, 406–7). And, as table 2.1 showed, upper-house members in Connecticut and Rhode Island were elected by the freemen of the colony, while in Massachusetts they were elected by members of the lower house.

These distinctions and their significance were well understood at the time. Tracing the history of New Hampshire, one scholar noted, "The institution of an house of peers in Britain was the result of the feudal system. . . . But there was nothing similar to this in New-England. . . . A council, whether appointed by [the king] or chosen by the people could not form a distinct body, because they could not be independent" (Belknap 1784, 173–74). Similar reasoning was offered by South Carolina Commons House Speaker Rawlins Lowndes, who in 1773 argued, "The Lords, are a permanent body; inheriting the right of Legislation, independent of the Crown." In contrast, "The Council, are appointed during the pleasure of the Crown. . . . They hold their offices . . . at will; and, therefore want that most essential requisite of independency" (Drayton 1821a, 121). Such sentiments were long held and deeply felt. During a dispute in 1700, an earlier Commons House speaker contended that the council could not be termed "an upper house, as they differed in the most essential circumstances, from the House of Lords in England." Accordingly, he encouraged his members to refer to the councilors as "the proprietors' deputies" (Ramsay 1858, 28–29). And in 1775, after the governor sent a message addressed to "Mr. Speaker and Gentlemen of the *Lower-House* of Assembly," Speaker Lowndes shot back, "The style of *Lower-House*, is by no means applicable to us; it implies, that there is *another House* in this *Colony*, dignified with the appellation of Upper-House of Assembly; which we absolutely deny" (Drayton 1821b, 12–13, italics in original). An English observer at the time of the Revolution concurred with such assessments, generalizing that across the colonies, "The Council, or (as it is called) Upper House of Assembly, is an humble imitation of the House of Lords" (Stokes 1783, 243).

There never was an American House of Lords, and there is no evidence that the colonists ever intended to create one. Indeed, when such a hereditary body was proposed for Massachusetts in 1635 the Council rejected the idea (Kammen 1969, 23). The reality is that bicameral systems in the colonies developed in response to local conditions and problems. The idea of two chambers was, of course, familiar to the colonists, and outside of Pennsylvania and Delaware they promoted such systems. But the sequence of events that produced bicameralism differed across the colonies and differed from that in England.

The Rise of Boundaries between the Assemblies and Their External Environments

Over time, the colonial assemblies established other boundaries that were later created for Congress and the state and territorial legislatures at their outsets. The assemblies successfully pressed claims of parliamentary privilege for their members, thus establishing a bright line between them and other governmental bodies (Cook 1931, 262; Clarke 1943; Greene 1963, 212–16; Young 1968, 158). In 1661, for example, Virginia enacted a law stating "that none of the burgesses of any assembly nor any of their attendance shalbe arrested from the time of their election, untill tenn days after the desolution of the assembly wherein he serves as a burgesse" (Hening 1823, 107). The assemblies also asserted the right to impeach other government officials, although only Pennsylvania was explicitly granted that power by its charter (Clarke 1943, 39–53; Hoffer and Hull 1978, 1979; Young 1968, 158). Finally, they also successfully asserted the right to establish their own rules and to select their own leaders (Cook 1931, 261; Falb 1986, 120; Greene 1963, 216–19; Wendel 1986, 173), powers that are central but overlooked aspects of institutional boundaries (Rosenthal 1996, 190).

Perhaps the most convincing evidence for increased boundedness in an institution is the rise of leadership ranks that are impermeable to entry by outsiders and the increase in apprenticeships (Hibbing 1999, 159). Over time, colonial speakers came to serve for longer periods within the chamber before achieving the highest post. In 1700, speakers spent a mean of 2.3

years in the assembly before assuming the top position. By 1750 the mean apprenticeship was a more impressive 8.5 years. Speakers also came to serve longer tenures once in the post. In 1700 speakers served for an average of 5.5 years. Fifty years later the average had increased to 11.3 years (Wendel 1986, 175). Clearly, leadership structures in the assemblies evolved in such a way as to make lateral entry from the outside difficult, further confirming their establishment of institutional boundaries. But, again, not every assembly developed in the same manner. In this instance, the Bermuda and Barbados assemblies evolved a very different approach to filling their speakerships. In each, a new speaker was routinely elected at the beginning of every fourth session (Labaree 1930, 200–201). Overall, however, better-prepared and longer-serving speakers proved important because they were sufficiently strong to help their institutions meet the increasing demands placed on them (Olson 1992, 559–60; Wendel 1973).

Legislative Evolution: Increasing Internal Complexity

Increased internal complexity is another characteristic associated with legislative evolution. It is a difficult concept to measure. One suggestion is to examine "the growth in the autonomy and importance of committees, in the growth of specialized agencies of party leadership, and in the general increase in the provision of various emoluments, and auxiliary aids to members in the form of office space, salaries, allowances, staff aid, and committee staffs" (Polsby 1968, 153). On almost all of these dimensions the assemblies evolved to become more complex organizations. The only exception was a failure to develop specialized party leadership because organized parties were not part of colonial politics. But the assemblies became more complex in another significant way: through the adoption of increasingly sophisticated rules and procedures. Arguably, it was the development of these more complex rules and procedures that allowed colonial assemblies to thrive.

Changes in Legislative Service

During the eighteenth century colonial assemblies developed into institutions organized to meet the demands of their constituents (Olson 1992; Longmore 1995; Rainbolt 1970, 422). The ties were so strong that the assemblies occasionally adjourned specifically to allow members to return to their districts to assess the voters' opinions on important proposals (Olson

1992, 554). Still, while colonial lawmakers were clearly concerned with their constituents' views, they were cognizant of what would later come to be called the Burkean dilemma. One burgess noted in his diary that he and his colleagues grappled with the question, "Whether a Representative was obliged to follow the directions of his Constituents against his own Reason and Conscience or to be Governed by his Conscience" (Greene 1965, 116). Other lawmakers ruminated on this quandary. When he accepted the speakership of the House of Burgesses, John Randolph made this speech to his colleagues.

> We must consider ourselves chosen by all the People; sent hither to represent them . . . And surely, a Desire of pleasing some, and the Fear of offending others; Views to little Advantages and Interests; adhering too fondly to ill-grounded Conceits; the Prejudices of Opinions too hastily taken up; and Affectation to Popularity; Private Animosities or Personal Resentments; which have often too much to do in Popular Assemblies, and sometimes put a Bias upon Mens Judgments, can upon no Occasion, turn us aside in the Prosecution of this important Duty, from what shall appear to be the true Interest of the People; Tho' it may be often impossible to conform to their Sentiments, since, when we come to consider and compare them, we shall find them so various and irreconcileable. (McIlwaine 1910, 240)

Much of the assemblies' time was consumed with dealing with petitions, which were the most common vehicle for constituents to call for legislative action on problems of interest (Higginson 1986, 153–55; Olson 1992, 556–58). Lawmakers often responded to these concerns by introducing legislation focused on local issues (Bailey 1979, 59–60; Haight 1984). For example, Richard Bland, a mid-eighteenth-century burgess, introduced "a Bill, To prevent Hogs running at Large in the Town of Port Royal" and "a Bill for destroying Crows and Squirrels in the County of Accomack" to address problems troubling his constituents (Rossiter 1953, 41).

As demands on colonial lawmakers increased, legislative sessions became longer. In Virginia, the first General Assembly in 1619 met for only five days in midsummer, adjourning earlier than anticipated because the lawmakers were too hot and too sick to continue. The Assembly's journal entry on August 4 notes, "This daye (by reason of extream heat both paste and likely to ensue, and by that meanes, of the alteration of the healthes of the diverse of the general Assembly) the Governour, who himself also was not well, resolved should be the laste of this firste Session." Indeed, one Assembly member passed away during the brief session (Van Schreeven and Reese 1969, 35, 53). Over time, the General Assembly came to meet in longer sessions. The burgesses met for an average of 89 days prior to 1728, 157 days from 1728 to 1749, and 176 days during the final period, 1750 to 1776 (Pargellis 1927b, 156). Similar numbers are found in New York, where the Assembly met for an average of 76 days annually from 1691 to 1727 and 108 days from 1728 to 1775.[7]

Longer sessions, of course, asked more of the legislators. The South Carolina Commons House was particularly demanding. It was customary for it to meet for up to eight months a year, and when in session it met six days a week for six hours each day (Sirmans 1966, 241). Such long hours were not unusual. Under the rules adopted by the Maryland assembly in 1642, a member was considered late if he failed to arrive by the third beating of the drum. The first beating was to "be as near as may be to sunrising and half an hours distance between each beating" (Browne 1883, 131). In 1646, the Plymouth General Court agreed to convene at seven in the morning during the "summer tyme" and at eight during the winter. They opted to break for dinner at eleven, and then met again, "vntill a convenient hower in the euening as the Go[ver]nor shall think meete" (Pulsifer 1861, 49). Working into the night was common; on several occasions the New Jersey Assembly "Ordered That Candles be brought in" (*Jour. and Votes of the H. of Reps. of the Prov. of Nova Cesarea* 1872, 11, 220, 223). A member of the Pennsylvania Assembly wrote in his journal that on February 2, 1762, "The House resumed the Consideration of the Road Bill, which took up the whole day." The matter was only settled, "In the Evening after a long & laborious Debate" (Foulke 1884, 413). The same was often true in Massachusetts (Zemsky 1971, 20). Thus, even sessions held over relatively short time periods took a toll on members. In 1757, the Connecticut General Assembly was in session between May 12 and June 8. During that span it met a total of 24 days, usually every Monday through Saturday. By the end, one deputy confided in his journal, "I am heartily weary of ye long Session" (Turner 1975, 56).

Changing Salary Structures

Given the time demands made on lawmakers, the colonies had to address several questions regarding their salaries. The first was whether or not to pay legislators at all. Assembly members in most of the colonies came to be compensated for their services, in large part because there were too few wealthy individuals who could afford to serve without some form of remuneration (Luce 1924, 521). Indeed, concerns were expressed early on about the willingness of potential lawmakers to serve given the financial costs associated with doing so. In 1631 Massachusetts decreed that for "any Deputy for the General Court . . . their necessary expences, shall be defrayed" (Whitmore 1889, 133–34). In 1645, the General Court argued explicitly that financial incentives were required to get people to serve. In justifying legislative pay, the Court noted that it was "sensible" of the many demands made on lawmakers "wch dayly increaseth, & wch necessarily occasioneth much expence of their time, to y^e [prej]udice of [their] families & estates." Consequently, it was reasoned that legislators needed to be compensated so "none be unequally burthened, or discouraged fro^m doing s^{r}vice to ye country" (Shurtleff 1853b, 101).

Pay also was seen as a necessary inducement in Rhode Island. Initially, the colony's lawmakers received no compensation. But attendance proved to be a problem, prompting a decision to pay members to get them to participate. A journal entry in 1672, for example, noted, "ffor the encouragement and ingadging of the Magistrates and Deputies to attend the Generall Assemblyes," the lawmakers voted to give each magistrate a four-shilling per diem and each deputy three shillings. The colony also assessed a financial penalty for failing to show: Not attending without an acceptable excuse cost a member a substantial fine of six shillings (Bartlett 1857, 433–35, 443).

Such a carrot-and-stick approach to legislative service was common. The New Haven General Court fined absent members 20 shillings, "vnless some providence of God hinder, wch the said Court shall judge of" (Hoadly 1857, 115). Pennsylvania imposed a higher fine if an absence deprived the House of a quorum (Leonard 1948a, 224). Tardiness was also punished; in Connecticut the fine for being an hour late was the entire three shilling per diem, and a harsh ten shillings was assessed for missing the whole day (Hoadly 1868, 269). Several other colonies also fined members for tardiness (Cook 1931, 266–67; Clarke 1943, 181–82). In some colonies nonmonetary penalties were exacted. In Georgia, which did not pay a salary, unexcused absences brought a formal rebuke by the speaker in front of the assembly (Corey 1929, 117–18).

Such penalties did not just sit on the books; the assemblies could be tough taskmasters when it came to judging the excuses given by tardy or absent members. For instance, in South Carolina, where poor attendance was occasionally a problem, the House was skeptical of a letter sent by Thomas Wright, claiming that he was "very much indisposed & incapable of attending the Service of the House." The members voted to reject the excuse and decided that Wright would not be allowed to take his seat until "he has made proper Concessions to the Sattisfaction of the House." They further ordered "That Mr. Wright do forthwith attend the Service of this House or send a Certificate from Some Physician that his bad State of health will not admit of his Coming up to Town." The House sent its decision by special messenger to Wright's house—at the lawmaker's expense. When the messenger reported back that he found Wright "Sick in Bed" the House told the messenger to "Either continue there with him, or Carry him to any other convenient Place till he is able to Travell." Eventually Wright recovered his health and returned to the House's good graces (Lipscomb 1996, 181, 189, 191, 198).

Not all assemblies evolved exactly alike on the question of pay. In addition to Georgia, lawmakers in South Carolina also received no compensation (Luce 1924, 525). Indeed, in 1746 by a vote of 11 to 18 the Commons House rejected a measure proposing a per diem (Easterby 1958, 101). Some years later the colony's lieutenant governor wrote that members disdained the idea of taking pay even though their counterparts in Virginia and North Carolina did (Smith 1903, 115). But, while members of the South Carolina House may have held themselves above being paid, they were willing to organize the legislative calendar around the demands of their working lives. In 1758, for example, lawmakers rearranged the dates by which government bureaucrats had to submit their accounts for review, because under the existing schedule, "the Sessions is protracted to an unreasonable Length & Gentlemen from the Country are obliged to attend in Town at a Time when their Presence in the Country is of Utmost Consequence to their Private Affairs" (Lipscomb 1996, 172). Of course, other assemblies also scheduled matters to accommodate the needs of their members. A Pennsylvania lawmaker noted that the Assembly opted to adjourn when it "would be most convenient for them to be at home about their . . . affairs, it being Seed Time" (Foulke 1881, 61).

The next question faced by the colonies that chose to compensate their lawmakers was who should cover the cost. In some colonies the constituency paid, while in others the colony did (Luce 1924, 522). In some cases who paid changed over time. In Connecticut in 1670, the legislative journal reveals, "This [General] Court orders that the Treasurer for the future shall make payment of the sallary formerly granted to the Deputies (by this Court,) out of the Country Rate, in the respective places where they dwell" (Trumbull 1852, 142). Similarly, a report on conditions in New York to the royal commissioners for trade and plantations noted, "the Assembly Men have a Salary assigned them, but that the method of raising it as usual by a County levy was found more inconvenient than by a Public Tax, and that the sum apply'd by the said Assembly to themselves was in lieu of the County Levy to which they had a Right" (O'Callaghan 1855, 559). In Virginia, who was held responsible for paying the burgesses switched back and forth between the colony and the counties or parishes (Miller 1907, 96).

Even when it was settled who should pay, subsidiary issues cropped up. In Massachusetts in 1645 it was decided "that each towne shall beare ye charges of y^{ir} owne deputies at ye Gen^{r}all Co^{r}t." But this approach imposed a considerable financial burden on the smallest communities. Consequently, eight years later the General Court held "that such townes as haue not more then thirty ffreemen shall henceforth be at li[ber]tie for sending, or not sending, deputyes to the Gen^{ll} Court." (Shurtleff 1853b, 140; 1854, 320). Another problem was that towns occasionally did not come up with the money to pay their representatives when they were responsible to do so. Consequently, in 1672 Rhode Island passed a clever law, holding that when a town failed to pay its representative, the "Deputy may or shall discount soe much as his rate or tax shall be untill such said debt be paid" (Bartlett 1857, 474).

The third question faced by the colonies was how much lawmakers should be paid. Again, the answer varied. In the first Virginia General Assembly only the officers were compensated, and it was decided "That every man and manservant of above 16. yeares of age shall pay into the handes and Custody of the Burgesses of every Incorporation and plantation, one pound of the best Tobacco, to be distributed to the Speaker, and likewise to the Clerke & sergeant of the Assembly" (Van Schreeven and Reese 1969, 69).[8] By 1636 all Virginia lawmakers were paid, and each county was charged with covering the expenses incurred by its representatives. But the burgesses were compensated in various fashions. In 1641, for example, "Accomac" county required "every tithable person to perform half a day's labor" in the burgesses' fields, or if they were unable to do so, to pay 10 pounds of tobacco to compensate their representatives for their "paines and cares" (Bruce 1910, 435–37). During the 1660–61 legislative session the burgesses established a standard per diem. They opted for this approach for two reasons. First, the public was unhappy with what they thought were inflated expense claims by the burgesses. Second, the burgesses wanted to confront the willingness on the part of some potential candidates to offer to work for less.

> WHEREAS, the excessive expenses of the Burgesses causing diverse misunderstandings between them and the people occasioned an injunction to make an agreement with them before their election which may probably cause interested persons to purchase votes by offering to undertake the place at low rates and by that meanes make the place both mercenary and contemptible, *Bee itt therefore enacted by this present grand assembly*, that the allowance for their maintenance be ascertained to one hundred and fifty pounds of tobaccoe per day besides their charge in goeing and comeing. (Hening 1823, 23, italics in original)

This reasoning apparently failed to assuage the voters. When the Assembly passed the same legislation again the following year, they prefaced the measure by acknowledging, "WHEREAS the immoderate expences of the burgesses causing diverse heart burnings betweene them and the people . . ." (Hening 1823, 106).

Still, resentment toward the salaries paid lawmakers continued to build, finally reaching such a point that in 1676–77 the House voted to cut their own pay. Admitting that their wages were "complained of as greivous and burthensome to the people" the burgesses reduced their salary to 120 pounds of tobacco and caske per day. They also reined in travel expenses in order "to prevent the greate charge that may accrue by burgesses comeing to assemblies in sloopes and boates." Members coming from Northampton and Accomack counties were allowed "sixty pounds of tobacco per day and noe more," to cover the cost of a sloop and two people to sail it. Other burgesses who had to come by water were limited to 36 pounds of tobacco per day to pay for two people to row them. Those coming by horse were granted 10 pounds of tobacco and caske per day to cover their expenses. Payments for ferry passages also were covered. A few years earlier, the House had begun covering the cost of two horses and a servant for each burgess, both during a session and in traveling to and from the meeting place (Hening 1823, 309–10, 398–99).

By 1720, the burgesses were paid a per diem, "out of the Publick money after the Rate of 10 shill[ings]" (McIlwaine 1912, 264). Payments "in mony" at 10 shillings a day became standard from that point on (e.g., Greene 1965, 101). In 1722 an additional sum of 50 pounds was allocated to the speaker, and 20 pounds was set aside for the chair of the Committee for Propositions and Grievances (McIlwaine 1912, 344), signaling the additional work and importance of both posts.

Concerns about colonial lawmakers' wages also came from London. Among the instructions to North Carolina's governor in 1730 was one that stated, "In case you find the usual Salaries or pay of the Members of the Assembly too high you shall take care that they be reduced to such a moderate proportion as may be no grievance to the country" (Saunders 1886a, 93). Virtually the same language can be found in the instructions issued to New Hampshire governors (Batchellor 1904, 510, 623).

Pay schemes varied across the colonies. Early in its history members of the Maryland House were, like their Virginia counterparts, paid in tobacco. In 1642, the burgesses from St. Mary's were given 40 pounds of tobacco for each day in session. The burgesses from Kent Island were paid an additional travel expense: the hire of a boat and "1 Servant and his diett for 20 days at 30 [pounds per] day" (Browne 1883, 143). Covering lawmakers' travel expenses became common across the colonies. In 1671, Connecticut decreed that each town "shall pay for the hyer of their Deputies' horses, which they ride upon to the seuerall sessions of the Generall Courte" (Trumbull 1852, 154). Eventually, the colony came to cover the cost of travel to and from the assembly for all members. When the assembly met in Hartford in 1698, deputies from Fairfield and New London were allowed three days of travel expenses, deputies from New Haven were allowed two days, and deputies from Hartford one day. When the Assembly met in New Haven in later years, travel reimbursements were recalibrated accordingly (Hoadly 1868, 269, 344).

Other expenses also came to be covered. The Plymouth General Court voted that for its assistants, "the charge of theire Table be defrayed" (Pulsifer 1861, 219). And nonfinancial benefits were occasionally granted to lawmakers. At varying times in the mid-seventeenth century deputies in Connecticut, Massachusetts, and New Haven were freed from obligations to participate in local military training exercises (Hoadly 1857, 374; Trumbull 1850, 62, 350; Whitmore 1889, 227).

Compensation was a recurring issue in most assemblies because it was important to lawmakers. Indeed, among only a handful of measures to pass during the first session of the New York Assembly in 1683 was "AN ACT for the Allowans to Representatives." That bill began by acknowledging, "WHEREAS the severall Representtatives of the Assembly cannot

Officiate thatt honorable and great Trust reposed in them, without being att much Charge" (Lincoln, Johnson, and Northrup 1894, 121; Lincoln 1909, 10). Because pay often failed to cover actual living expenses (e.g., Purvis 1986, 42) legislators grumbled about it. Consequently, it is not surprising that in Connecticut, "Vpon complaint of the Deputies that their sallerie was not sufficient" the General Court voted that their wages should be drawn from the colony's treasury (Hoadly 1868, 181). Similar concerns were registered in New Hampshire: "Whereas the allowance for . . . the Members of the Council and assembly is not sufficient to defray the Charges necessary when they attend." It was decided to pay members of the Council eight shillings a day and members of the Assembly six shillings a day, to be paid out of the "Publick Treasury" (Bouton 1870, 242).

An important fact to note about the development of pay schemes for colonial lawmakers is that they occurred at the same time Parliament was doing away with legislative remuneration. Evidence of payments to members of Parliament can found as early as the thirteenth century. In 1463, the Borough of Weymouth paid its members 500 mackerel for their service (House of Commons Information Office 2009, 5). Members were paid for their attendance, and by 1580 the House of Commons instituted rules fining those who were absent without leave for the session and withholding wages of those who were absent without leave for part of the session (Taylor 1884, 18). But, toward the end of the seventeenth century legislative salaries disappeared. In Samuel Pepys's diary, he records a March 30, 1668, dinner party conversation among important men as lamenting, "But all concluded that the bane of the Parliament hath been the leaving off the old custom of the places allowing wages to those that served them in Parliament" (Pepys 1905, 635). Efforts to resurrect pay began by 1780, but it was not reinstituted until 1911 (House of Commons Information Office 2009, 6). Thus, lawmaker pay is another instance where the assemblies evolved in a different fashion than Parliament.

Changing Staff Resources

Staff assistance for the assemblies developed slowly. As noted in passing above, the first Virginia General Assembly employed a clerk, a position with deep roots in English parliamentary history (Phelps 2004). In 1648, the Massachusetts General Court decided, "It is hearby ordered, that as there is a secretary amongst the magistrates . . . so there shall be a clarke amongst the deputies." They opted to provide the clerk with the necessary resources to do the job: "there be provided, by the auditoʳ, four large paper books, in folio, bound up with velum & pastboard, two whereof to be delivered to the . . . clarke of the House of Deputies, one to be a [j]ournall . . . the other for the faire entry of all laws, acts, & orders . . . that shall passe" (Shurtleff 1853b, 259).

Although they were not direct participants in floor activities—Benjamin Franklin confessed that when he served as the Pennsylvania Assembly's clerk "I grew at length tired with sitting there to hear the debates, in which . . . I could take no part" (Franklin 1921, 120)—clerks became important cogs in the legislative system. Indeed, in 1685 the Virginia House assigned a specific room (the "porch") for their clerk's use, a decision which led to a battle with the governor over control of the space (Yonge 1904b, 120–23). As a result of their increasing centrality, clerks were eventually allowed to hire assistants, a move that contributed to better record keeping (Cook 1931, 264, 283; Falb 1986, 127–30; Leonard 1948a, 235; Olson 1992, 561–62). This was a key development because at the start of the eighteenth century, legislative records were very poorly kept. They were stored in "taverns, homes, and college rooms and in Pennsylvania, in one small trunk that seems to have been carried from place to place" (Olson 1992, 547). When the New Hampshire House voted to appoint a new clerk in 1745, they had to name a committee to "go to Mr. James Jeffry the late clerk of the House of Representatives & demand of him all the Books, Records & files that belong to this House & bring them directly to the House" (Bouton 1871, 263), suggesting that the materials were neither in the custody of the House nor even physically present in or near the chamber.

By the end of the colonial era the situation was much improved. The assemblies were sufficiently staffed so that clerks could notify the public about legislative schedules in advance and keep much more detailed minutes of floor business. Assemblies started publishing their journals—New York was the first in 1695 (*Jour. of the H. of Reps. for his Majestie's Prov. of N.Y.* [1695] 1903)—as well as codifications of the laws they passed (Barker 1940, 167; Cook 1931, 264; Hasse 1903; Leonard 1948b, 394; Olson 1992, 562–64; Surrency 1965). This activity created new financial opportunities. Franklin admitted that "besides the pay for the immediate service of clerk, the place gave me an opportunity of keeping up an interest among the members, which secured to me the business of printing the votes, [and] laws, . . . that, on the whole, were very profitable (Franklin 1921, 99–100).

Changing Facilities

Assemblies also came to acquire buildings dedicated to their use. Initially, they met in makeshift facilities. The journal of the first Virginia General Assembly reveals, "The most convenient place we could finde to sitt in was the Quire of the churche" (Van Schreeven and Reese 1969, 15). Over the next several decades the assembly continued to meet in churches and also in the governor's house (Yonge 1904a, 46). In 1641 the colony occupied the first of several statehouses in Jamestown, this one being a home purchased from a bankrupt former governor and paid for by the imposition of a tax of two pounds of tobacco per household (Hening 1809, 226; Yonge 1904a, 46). It appears that this facility burned to the ground sometime in 1655 or 1656 (Tyler 1900, 111; Yonge 1904a, 47). The second statehouse was fashioned from a building purchased by the colony shortly thereafter, and it was used for three or four years before it too burned (Yonge 1904a, 52). The lack of a building dedicated to their use forced lawmakers to meet in taverns and by 1663 they were campaigning for another statehouse both because of the expense of renting and "the dishonor of our Lawes being made . . . in Ale-houses" (McIlwaine 1914, 27). This time lawmakers opted to raise the funds needed to build a new statehouse through a voluntary subscription rather than a tax. Toward this end the "burgesses of this present grand assembly have voluntarily subscribed severall considerable summes and quantityes of money and tobacco" (Hening 1823, 38). The third statehouse was either purchased or built a few years later, but it was destroyed during Bacon's Rebellion in 1676 (Tyler 1900, 114). The General Assembly took occupancy of the fourth statehouse in 1685, financing it with money collected from a liquor tax (McIlwaine 1914, 235–36; Yonge 1904b, 119). This facility was distinguished by the appearance of a wood bar to separate the burgesses from the spectators (Yonge 1904b, 123). In 1698, it was lost to fire (Tyler 1900, 116; Yonge 1904a, 48). As a result of continually losing statehouses, it is estimated that lawmakers met in taverns for a total of 17 years between 1641 and 1699 (Yonge 1904a, 46).

In 1699, the capital was relocated to Williamsburg to make it more accessible to the colony's growing population. The General Assembly met at the College of William and Mary until it moved into the newly constructed "Capitoll" in early 1705. In the new building, "The west wing was set apart for the use of the general court and the council, the east wing was for the hall of the burgesses and their committee rooms, while the room over the porch was used for conferences between the council and the burgesses"

(Pargellis 1927a, 74–75). Like its Jamestown predecessors, this facility burned to the ground in 1747, forcing the Assembly to again meet at the college until the statehouse was rebuilt in 1755 (Yonge 1904b, 124).

Similar stories, but with fewer fires, unfolded in a number of other colonies. In New York, an act was passed in 1704, "For the appointing fitting up & ffurnishing a Roome for the Sitting of the General Assembly & a Lobby to the Same in the Eastern part of the City Hall of the City of New York" (Lincoln, Johnson, and Northrup 1894, 569). That decision enjoyed the enthusiastic support of the governor, who in a letter to the Lords of Trade confided that the measure was "an Act I readily consented to because till this time the Assembly has always sat in a Tavern, which I thought was a scandalous thing" (O'Callaghan 1854, 1115). The Rhode Island Assembly rotated its sessions among several towns, and for many years lawmakers made use of available facilities, meeting in taverns, private homes, and even barns. The first dedicated statehouse was constructed in Newport in 1690, and in succeeding years other statehouses (which also doubled as county courthouses) were built in Providence, Rochester (Kingston), Bristol, and East Greenwich (Bicknell 1920, 645–47; Taylor 1900, 211–17). The Pennsylvania Assembly moved into a new capitol in the 1730s or 1740s.[9] Previously, the Assembly had met in a variety of places. Among them were a house they rented from a widow, Thomas Makin's schoolhouse, for which they paid Makin, who was also the Assembly clerk, twenty shillings "in Consideration of the Inconviniency this Assembly hath put him to," and the Bank Meeting House (Etting 1891, 5–7; *Votes and Proc. of the H. of Reps. of the Prov. of Pa., vol. the First* 1752, 89; *Votes and Proc. of the H. of Reps. of the Prov. of Pa., vol. the First, Part the Second* 1752, 63). The decision to build the statehouse had been prompted by a feeling that it was "very incommodious as well as dishonourable for the Assembly of this Province to be obliged annually to hire some private House to met and sit in, while imployed in the Service of the Publick" (*Votes of the H. of Reps.* 1734, 46). Maryland completed its first statehouse in 1697 or 1698. In 1699 the building was nearly destroyed by a lightning strike that killed one of the delegates and injured several others. In 1704 the ill-fated facility burned to the ground. The second statehouse served from 1706 to 1769 before falling into disrepair (Riley 1887, 66–67, 80–81). Maryland was in the midst of constructing its third capitol when the Revolution started. Several other colonies also came to build statehouses (Daniel and Daniel 1969; Hitchcock and Seale 1976; Lounsbury 2001).

In general statehouses were designed to be functional. A traveler in

1773 commented that the Virginia capitol "is more commodious inside than ornamental without" and that Pennsylvania's was "rather well calculated for use than elegance or show" (Quincy 1915–16, 465, 476). Another description of the Pennsylvania statehouse around the same time was similar in tone: "The Assembly room is furnished in a neat but not elegant manner" (Jordan 1899, 418). A letter writer in 1769 derided the Maryland statehouse, remarking that "The building has nothing in its appearance expressive of the great purposes to which it is appropriated" (Riley 1887, 81). As noted above, others agreed, and the building was torn down shortly thereafter. But even if these capitols were not aesthetically pleasing, at a minimum they provided lawmakers the space they needed to conduct their business.

Not all assemblies were fortunate enough to get their own facilities. The North Carolina governor built a large government building in the early 1770s, but he used it to house his office and the Council. The Assembly only met there during joint sessions; otherwise they convened in the "roomier courthouse or school" (Cook 1931, 258; Dill 1955, 117; Hitchcock and Seale 1976, 8–9). The Georgia Assembly met in houses, the Assembly downstairs and the Council upstairs (Corey 1929, 111). Other newer colonies also lacked the resources and time to build capitols. Thus the Bahamas House first met at the home of Samuel Lawford (Craton 1962, 115), while the inaugural West Florida Assembly gathered at a house rented by the government (Howard 1947, 44).

Ultimately, however, most legislative business came to be conducted in official settings. Massachusetts House committees initially met over a meal at a tavern on the colony's tab. Such circumstances were not unusual. Committees in South Carolina also met in taverns and private homes during the 1730s (Frakes 1970, 66). In 1741 Massachusetts tightened controls over such arrangements (*Jour. of the Honourable H. of Reps. of His Majesty's Prov. of the Mass., 1741* 1741, 77). By the early 1750s most committees were convening in meeting rooms in the Court House attic (Zemsky 1971, 13). Along the same lines, a wing was later added to the Pennsylvania statehouse to accommodate committee meetings; prior to that they met in courthouses and the Coffee Shop (Leonard 1948b, 386).

There were occasions when assemblies temporarily abandoned their statehouses. According to a letter written by Benjamin Franklin, in 1764 the Pennsylvania Assembly left its regular meeting place because "Our old speaker, Mr. Norris, has been long declining in his Health. During the Winter Session he was unable to come to the Statehouse, and the House met at his Lodging" (Labaree 1967, 218). A smallpox outbreak in Charleston in 1760 forced the South Carolina Commons House to relocate to a safer environ, "at Mr. Legg's House in the Village of Shem-town on Ashley River" (Lipscomb 1996, 754).

The Evolution of Standing Committee Systems

Organizationally, how did the assemblies cope with the demands made of them? Initially, they relied exclusively on ad hoc committees to aid in information gathering and decision making. Indeed, two ad hoc committees were created on the first day of the first Virginia General Assembly in 1619 (Van Schreeven and Reese 1969, 25–27). Their use was imported from England by the speaker, John Pory. The House of Commons had come to employ ad hoc committees during the latter part of the sixteenth century (Dean 1996, 21; Neale 1949, 371–79; Elton 1986, 106), and Pory had served on several of them while he was a member between 1605 and 1611 (Powell 1977, 25, 30). The use of short-term committees as a means for the division of labor can be taken as evidence of increasing internal complexity, but here it highlights another critical point: Even a new legislature created in a wilderness an ocean away from any institution like it may be organizationally sophisticated because it can employ rules and structures developed by existing bodies.

The use of ad hoc committees was universal across the assemblies. In Massachusetts temporary committees were established at almost every point in the legislative process. Thus, "it was not at all unusual for a major bill to be proposed by one committee, drafted by another, revised by a third, revised again by a fourth, and cast into its final form by a fifth." More than 400 committees were appointed, and in excess of 1,600 individual committee assignments were made during the 1756–57 legislative session (Zemsky 1971, 13).

Ultimately, however, standing committees were established in most assemblies to handle recurring matters of importance, as detailed in table 2.3.[10] Assemblies in Pennsylvania, South Carolina, and Virginia even came to employ subcommittees (Frakes 1970, 84, 94; Olson 1992, 560). Standing committees never completely supplanted ad hoc committees in any of the assemblies, marking them as an example of the layering of a new process atop an existing one. During the 1769 to 1771 session of the South Carolina Commons House, for example, 59 ad hoc committees were appointed, even though standing committees exercised considerable power in the chamber.[11]

TABLE 2.3. Standing Committees in Colonial Assemblies, circa 1770

Colonial Assembly	Number of Standing Committees	Standing Committees
Connecticut	0	
Delaware	2	Aggrievances
		Elections and Privileges
Georgia	2	Grievances
		Priveleges and Elections
Maryland	3	Accounts
		Grievances and Courts of Justice
		Elections and Privileges
Massachusetts	1	Petitions as may be brought in, praying for Liberty to make Sale of Lands
New Hampshire	0	
New Jersey	0[a]	
New York	2[a]	Inspect what Laws are expired, or near expiring
		Privileges and Elections
North Carolina	4	Privileges and Elections
		Propositions and Grievances
		Public Accounts
		Public Claims
Pennsylvania	4	Accounts of the General Loan Office, and other Public Accounts
		Aggrievances
		Correspondence
		Minutes of this House
Rhode Island	0	
South Carolina	4	Grievances
		Priveleges and Elections
		Correspondence
		Laws Near Expired or Expiring
Virginia	6	Courts of Justice
		Privileges and Elections
		Propositions and Grievances
		Public Claims
		Religion
		Trade

Source: Candler 1907b, 11–12; Harlow 1917, 259–61; *Jour. of the Honorable H. of Reps. of His Majesty's Prov. of the Mass.* 1770, 98; *Jour. of the H. of Asm.* 1771, 6; *Jour. of the Votes and Proc. of the GA of the Col. of N.Y.* 1771, 5; Kennedy 1906, 190–91; *Votes and Proc. of the GA of the Prov. of N.J.* 1769, 7; *Votes and Proc. of the H. of Reps. of the Gov. of Del.* 1770, 194–95; *Votes and Proc. of the H. of Reps. of the Prov. of Pa.* 1771, 207; *Votes and Proc. of the Lower H. of Asm. of the Prov. of Md.* 1771, 257. The South Carolina committees were taken from a microfilm copy of the unpublished, handwritten journal entry for June 27, 1769. On January 17, 1770, three audit committees (Public Treasury, Powder Receiver, and Commissary General) were appointed. The microfilm is held at the South Carolina Department of Archives and History.

[a]New Jersey operated with a Committee of Grievances. It operated as a committee of the whole house (*Votes and Proc. of the GA of the Prov. of N.J.* 1769, 7). Similarly, New York created a Grand Committee for Grievances, a Grand Committee for Courts of Justice, and a Grand Committee for Trade (*Jour. of the Votes and Proc. of the GA of the Col. of N.Y.* 1771, 4–5). These grand committees were specialized committees of the whole house. The New Jersey Assembly established a standing committee of the more common form in 1772.

Virginia's standing committees evolved to function much like those in modern American legislatures. They first appeared in the House in the mid-1650s. In 1656 a Committee for Review of the Acts was appointed. It produced a revised code of statutes, which was adopted by the Assembly of 1657–58 (Hening 1809, 421; Leake 1917, 14–15). The committee was re-created in 1658 (Hening 1809, 512), and it evolved into the Committee for Propositions and Grievances (Billings 2004, 38–39).[12] Over time, other standing committees were added. All of them, save for Public Claims, had an analogue in the English House of Commons (Harlow 1917, 3–5; Jameson 1894, 263).

Although the Virginia standing committee system had parliamentary roots, it developed differently than its parental counterpart. During the seventeenth and eighteenth centuries standing committees withered away in the House of Commons (Jameson 1894, 259–60; Redlich 1908, 210–11), but in Virginia they became central to the legislative process. As early as 1658 the journal of the House of Burgesses began noting that particular pieces of legislation were "referred" to a specific standing committee (McIlwaine 1915, 106–7). Referrals became more common over time (McIlwaine 1914, 122–24, 198–99). Standing committees also came to acquire other powers. In 1712, the Committee on Propositions and Grievances was allowed to "send for present Records Journals and other Papers they shall from time to time have Occasion of" (McIlwaine 1912, 5). This power was extended to other committees beginning in 1727 (McIlwaine 1910, 6–7).

By the middle of the eighteenth century the development of standing committees in the House of Burgesses was such that they "were vigorous, hard-working groups, actively engaged in legislative work" (Harlow 1917, 14). Committees framed and amended legislation before it was sent to the chamber's floor. Procedures were so well established that petitions presented to the House were quickly referred to the appropriate standing committees (Bailey 1979, 29; Greene 1965, 79; Harlow 1917, 14–17). By 1768, the Committee of Courts of Justice had its own clerk, and the Privileges and Elections and the Propositions and Grievances committees shared another clerk (Kennedy 1906, 174). And the House added standing committees to handle emerging societal problems. The Committee on Religion was created in 1769 in response to heighted religious tensions in the colony (Longmore 1996, 780). The system became so central to the legislative process that when Thomas Jefferson sketched plans for a new capitol building in 1776 he designated separate rooms for each of the six standing committees (Wenger 1993, 82–84).

The committee system in Virginia evolved to become the most sophisticated and complex among the assemblies. But Pennsylvania's standing committees were also well rooted. Indeed, among the first acts taken by the newly formed Assembly in 1682 was the creation of three standing committees: a Committee for Elections and Privileges, a Committee for Justice and Grievances, and a Committee on Foresight for the Preparation of Provincial Bills (*Votes and Proc. of the H. of Reps. of the Prov. of Pa.*, 1682 1752, 1). From that point forward, standing committees were a regular feature.

By 1770 almost every assembly had at least one standing committee. Several were created in the first Georgia House of Assembly: on the second day a Committee of Propositions and Grievances and a Committee of Privileges and Elections were formed (Candler 1907a, 13). And in some assemblies standing committees became central to the legislative process as they were in Virginia; South Carolina's, for example, were powers by the middle of the eighteenth century (Frakes 1970, 84).

As in Virginia, assemblies in other colonies came to give their standing committees the power to send for persons and papers, for example, in Pennsylvania in 1724 and Georgia in 1769 (Candler 1907b, 11–12; *Jour. of the Votes and Proc. of the Reps. of the Prov. of Pa.* 1725, 2–3). Both standing and ad hoc committees came to engage in serious efforts to gather and analyze information, through holding hearings and traveling to conduct investigations (Olson 1992, 562; Miller 1907, 109; Zemsky 1971, 14). In 1762, a member of the Pennsylvania Assembly recorded in his journal, "This day ye Committee heretofore appointed to attend the Indian Treaties brought in a report in writing, giving a pretty full acc't of ye manner in which the Affairs were transacted at Easton." The following day he noted, "The Committee of Accounts reported how far they had been able to Settle them, and the Committee of incidental Charges produced their Settlement" (Foulke 1881, 62–63). Virginia occasionally employed interim committees to help set the agenda for the next legislative session. For instance, in 1660–61 a burgess and the clerk were appointed to a committee to "review all the acts, peruse the records . . . and present a draught of them with such alterations & amendments as they shall find necessary to the next assembly." They were paid fifteen thousand pounds of tobacco for "their paines" (Hening 1823, 34).

All of this suggests that committees were established to provide assemblies with information. The process the assemblies evolved to decide contested elections highlights their informational role. Most were not given explicit formal authority over who sat among them; they had to fight for that power. Seizing on a 1604 precedent from the English House of Commons, the assemblies claimed the right to control their own memberships, in a few instances very quickly—Virginia in its first assembly in 1619 (Van Schreeven and Reese 1969, 17–19) and Massachusetts in 1647 (Shurtleff 1854, 119)—and at a somewhat slower pace in others (Clarke 1943, 132–50; Greene 1963, 189–99). Once attained, the assemblies exercised this power. The House of Burgesses expelled a member because he was "notoriously knowne a scandalous person, and a frequent disturber of the peace of the country, by libell and other illegall practices" (McIlwaine 1915, 84). A former New Jersey speaker was removed for being "in Contempt of his Majesties Authority" and in "Breach of the Trust reposed in him by this house" (*Jour. of the Votes of the H. of Reps. of His Majestys Prov. of N.J.* 1716, 14).

By late in their histories most assemblies had passed laws asserting their powers to settle disputed elections (Clarke 1943, 154–57). Because there were no organized political parties in the colonies, partisanship was not a motivation in deciding disputed elections. But contested elections were reasonably frequent; over the final 50 years of its existence about 8 percent of elections for the Virginia House were appealed to that chamber for resolution (Kolp 1992, 656). Over time, procedures to handle contested elections became systematized in most of the assemblies. Once a dispute was brought to an assembly a committee was assigned to investigate it. Virginia was the first to use a committee for such a purpose in 1663, and most other assemblies followed suit: Maryland in 1678, Pennsylvania in 1682, South Carolina in 1692, New York in 1699, New Jersey in 1710, North Carolina in 1739, and Georgia in 1755 (Clarke 1943, 145–46).[13] Only the New England assemblies failed to employ such committees; instead they devised other mechanisms to investigate election disputes. In Massachusetts, for example, a joint committee of lower- and upper-house members met to make an inquiry (Clarke 1943, 144–45).

The available evidence suggests that the assemblies investigated disputed elections rigorously. In 1727 the Committee on Privileges and Elections in the Virginia House of Burgesses was empowered to "meet as often as they find necessary" and "to send for Persons, Papers, and Records for their information" (McIlwaine 1910, 5–6). By 1770, the elections committees in Georgia, New York, and North Carolina enjoyed similar powers

(Candler 1907b, 11; *Jour. of the H. of Asm.* 1771, 6; *Jour. of the Votes and Proc. of the GA of the Col. of N.Y.* 1771, 5). More generally, facts, not personal preferences, drove verdicts (Clarke 1943, 146–47; Greene 1965, 70–71, 89; Kolp 1992, 656). Thus, these committees appear to have served primarily an informational function.

How the assemblies handled committee assignments changed over time. Initially, an elite group of members dominated committee slots in most assemblies. In Georgia (Corey 1929, 124), Maryland (Jordan 1987, 175), Massachusetts (Zemsky 1969), New Jersey (Batinski 1987, 66; Purvis 1986, 106), Pennsylvania (Tully 1977, 96), and Virginia (Greene 1959), committee assignments were doled out unequally, with just a handful of assembly members getting most of the posts and consequently making most of the important decisions. But, at least in Virginia, which relied heavily on standing committees, power became more decentralized over time. A bias in favor of burgesses from the Tidewater region greatly dissipated between 1730 and 1766 (Detweiler 1972). Perhaps even more important, committee membership sizes grew throughout the eighteenth century, allowing more members to be given positions (Bailey 1979, 33–34; Greene 1959, 486; Pargellis 1927a, 84–85). By 1748, the speaker started giving each burgess at least one standing committee assignment (Greene 1959, 486). In later years the House developed a custom of adding members to standing committees over the course of a session. In 1774, the Committee on Propositions and Grievances started with 37 members but grew to 73 members by the end of the session (Harlow 1917, 13). A similar trend also was evident in Pennsylvania (Ryerson 1986, 116). Expanding committee sizes increased the number of members able to exercise influence. It may also have been an administrative response to recurring problems with absenteeism and a need to achieve committee quorums (Harlow 1917, 13).

It is important to emphasize that in their details committee systems evolved differently across the colonies. For instance, in 1770 both New York and New Jersey employed one or more grand committees (*Jour. of the Votes and Proc. of the GA of the Col. of N.Y.* 1771, 5; *Votes and Proc. of the GA of the Prov. of N.J.* 1769, 7). They were modeled on similar bodies in Parliament and functioned as specialized committees of the whole house (Harlow 1917, 8; McConachie 1898, 8). In New York the grand committees appear to have been for form only; those for Grievances and Courts of Justice seldom met, and the one for Trade never met at all (Harlow 1917, 8). The chamber's two standing committees actually carried the legislative burden. And New Jersey's committee system was in flux. At its session in 1772 the

Assembly established its first standing committee, Publick Accounts (*Votes and Proc. of the GA of the Col. of N.J.* 1772, 11).

The rise of standing committees in the assemblies sheds light on explanations for their subsequent emergence in Congress. Gamm and Shepsle (1989) find that organizational imperatives and the rational actions of individual actors each contribute to the development of standing committees in the House and Senate. Jenkins (1998) argues that Speaker Clay's political calculations and the distribution of party support in the House explain standing committee development in that chamber. The experience across the assemblies, where standing committee systems arose slowly and incompletely over time, would suggest that organizational needs primarily drove this innovation. Partisan scheming, of course, cannot explain what happened. Thus, the assemblies' need to make information-gathering and decision-making processes more efficient is the most plausible explanation for the development of standing committees across the colonies. But legislative leaders making rational calculations in pursuit of their own goals might have played a role in establishing standing committees in at least some chambers, because their development in Pennsylvania and Virginia roughly coincided with the appearance of strong speakers (Lokken 1959b; Olson 1992, 559–60).

Finally, the establishment of standing committee systems in the assemblies is significant for another reason. As noted above, standing committees disappeared in Parliament at the same time their numbers and importance grew in most colonies. This is compelling evidence that colonial legislative systems evolved independently (Harlow 1917, 3; Jameson 1894, 259–61). While the idea for both ad hoc and standing committees were taken from Parliament, many of the assemblies developed committee systems that looked and, more important, functioned very differently.

The Evolution of Parliamentary Rules and Procedures

The rules and procedures initially used by the assemblies were taken from English parliamentary practices (Clarke 1943, 174; Greene 1969, 345–47; Johnson 1987, 350–51; Kukla 1981, 14–16; Pargellis 1927a, 83; 1927b, 1560; Peterson 1983; Plaisted 1976). Although the English House of Commons did not authenticate its Standing Orders until the eighteenth century, several volumes compiling precedents were published before then, among them Hooker's *Order and Usage* in 1571 (Snow 1977, 70–71) and Smith's *De Republica Anglorum* in 1583 (1906). Selected passages from each are presented in box 2.1a and box 2.1b. These excerpts touch on matters of parliamentary protocol, such as admonitions to take one's hat off when speaking and to not disparage one's fellow lawmakers. They also specify legislative procedures, notably the practice of requiring three separate readings of a bill, a routine that had become standard in the House of Commons during the sixteenth century (Dean 1996, 21; Elton 1986, 90; Neale 1949, 369). In the context of this study these passages are noteworthy because they resurface in the rules and procedures promulgated by the early colonial assemblies. This should not be a surprise because the procedures discussed in these two volumes along with those in William Hakewill's *The Manner How Statutes are Enacted in Parliament by Passing of Bills* (1641) were well known to "engaged Stuart Englishmen" (Billings 2004, 235).

Over time there were two important developments in regard to legislative rules and procedures used in the assemblies. First, they became more intricate and sophisticated. Second, they began to respond to issues relevant to local legislative experiences. These changes led legislative rules and procedures to become progressively less like those used in Parliament, even though their original roots always showed.

The first Virginia Assembly in 1619 operated under procedures lifted from those used in the House of Commons. The obvious means of conveyance was Speaker Pory, a former Member of Parliament. Thus, the Assembly used three readings for each bill (Van Schreeven and Reese 1969, 55). Although incomplete in their application (Billings 2004, 8), the employment of parliamentary procedures in the first Assembly greatly facilitated legislative decision making. Indeed, a journal entry on the final day of the session notes, "It is fully agreed at this Generall Assembly, that in regarde of the great paines and labour of the Speaker of this Assembly (who not onely first formed the same Assembly and to their great ease & expedition, reduced all matters to be treatted of into a ready method" (Van Schreeven and Reese 1969, 69).

Rules and procedures were rarely compiled in early assemblies. Among the first sets of rules collected were those adopted by Maryland in 1647–48, presented in box 2.2. By that point, the Assembly had been in existence for just over a decade. In 1637–38 it had employed a shorter list of six unnumbered rules, one of which prohibited "vncivill or contentious termes," another that specified "nor shall any one speake above once to one bill or matter at one reading," as well as one that held "every one that is to speake to any matter, shall stand vp, and be vncovered and direct his speech to the Lieuten^t

Box 2.1a. The English Parliamentary Roots of American Legislative Rules: Excerpts from Hooker's *Order and Usage*, 1571

- Also every one ought to be of a quiet, honest, and gentle, behavior, none taunting, checking or misusing an other in . . . any unseemly woords or deeds, but all affections set a parte to doo and indever in wisdome, sobrietie & knowledge, that which that place requireth.
- And if any one doo offend or misbehave himself: he is to be corrected and punished by the advise and order of the residue of the house.
- Also every person of Parlement ought to keep secret and not to disclose the secrets of things spoken and doon in the Parlement house, to any manner of person unlesse he be one of . . . the same house: upon pain to be sequestred out of the house, or otherwise punished, as by the order of the house shalbe appointed.
- Also none of the Parlement house ought to departe from the Parlement: without speciall leave obteyned of the Speaker of the house, and the same his licence be also recorded.
- Also when any . . . Burgesse dooth enter and come into the lower house . . . every such person ought to be grave, wise and expert: so ought he to show him self in his Apparail, for in times past: none of the councellers of ye Parlement came otherwise then in his gown, and not armed nor girded with weapon, for the Parlement house is a place for wise, grave and good men, to consult, debate, and advise how to make Lawes, and orders for the common welth, and not to be armed as men redy to fight, or to trye matters by the Swoord . . .
- Also every Bil whiche is brought into the house: must bee red three severall times, and upon three severall dayes.
- Also when any Bil upon any reading is altogether by one concent rejected, or by voices after ye third reading everthrown: it ought not to be brought any more to be red during ye Sessions of Parlement.
- Also whensoever any person dooth speak to any Bill: hee ought to stand up, and to be bare headed, and then with all reverence, gravitte, and seemly speech, to declare his minde.

Source: Passages taken from *The Order and Usage how to keep a Parliament in England in these dayes, collected by John Vowel alias Hooker gentleman, one of the Citizens for the Cittie of Exeter at the Parlement holden at Westminster Anno domine Elizabethae Reginae decimo Tertio. 1571*, reprinted in Snow (1977). The passages used here are found on pages 185 to 191.

Box 2.1b. The English Parliamentary Roots of American Legislative Rules: Excerpts from Smith's *De Republica Anglorum,* 1583

- All bils be thrise in three diverse dayes read and disputed upon, before they come to the question.
- He that standeth uppe bareheadded is understanded that he will speake to the bill. If moe stande uppe, who that first is judged to arise, is first harde, though the one doe prayse the law, the other diswade it, yet there is no altercation. For everie man speaketh as to the speaker, not as one to an other, for that is against the order of the house.
- It is also taken against the order, to name him whom ye doe confute, but by circumlocation, as he that speaketh with the bill, or he that spake against the bill, and gave this and this reason.
- He that once hath spoken in a bill though he be confuted straight, that day may not replie, no though he would chaunge his opinion. So that to one bill in one day one may not in that house speake twise, for else one or two with altercation would spende all the time. The next day he may, but then also but once.
- No reviling or nipping wordes must be used. For then all the house will crie, it is against the order . . . So that in such a multitude, and in such diversitie of mindes, and opinions, there is the greatest modestie and temperance of speech that can be used.
- The speaker hath no voice in the house, nor they will not suffer him to speake in any bill to moove or diswade it.
- After the bill hath been twise reade, and then engrossed and eftsoones reade and disputed on ynough as is thought: the speaker asketh if they will goe to the question. And if they agree he holdeth the bill up in his hande and sayeth, as many as will have this bill goe forwarde, which is concerning such a matter, say yea. Then they which allow the bill crie yea, and as many as will not, say no: as the crie of yea or no is bigger, so the bill is allowed or dashed.

Source: Sir Thomas Smith ([1583] 1906, 54–56)

Box 2.2. Early Legislative Rules in the American Colonies: Maryland General
Assembly, 1647–48

1. That noe one of the howse shall use any reuylling speeches or name
   any one by name but by another signification Viz. the Gent. that
   spoke last or the like.
2ly. That noe one shall speake aboue once att one reading to any Bill
   wth out lycence of the Gou^{r}. And if 2 p[er]sons rise up together, the
   Gou^{r} shall Appoynt who shall speake first. And noe one shall interrupt another, or speake till the other hath ended.
3ly. That noe one shall deliuer his opinion or speake to any bill sitting,
   But shall stand up reuerently and bareheaded directing his speech
   to the Gour.
4ly. That euery Bill proposed to the howse shall be read 3 seuerall
   dayes before it shall be uoted to engrosm^{t}. And that betwixt euery
   such reading one day shall be intermitted unlesse with speciall lycence of the Gou^{r}.
5ly. That before the grall day of Sessions for the enacting of all the
   Lawes, notice shall bee gyuen 3 dayes before, att the least to all the
   County of St. Maries to make their personall appearance, if they
   shall like thereof.
6ly. That noe one shall come in the howse of Assembly (whilst the
   howse is sett), wth any weapon uppon perill of such fine or censure
   as the howse shall thinke fit
7ly. Any of the 16 members bownd to attend the Assembly th^{t} shall be
   absent from the howse att the hower & place appointed, shall be
   fyned (after the number of Ten of them shall be p[rese]nt with the
   Gou^{r}. & the Clerk), in the Summe of 50 [lb] Tob. unlesse lawfull
   excuse shall be shewen: to be imployed in defraying the charges of
   this p[rese]nt Assembly.
8ly. All misdemean^{rs} wch shall happen in the howse shall be censured &
   fyned by the howse. To be employed as afore.
9ly. Any one of the sixteen members th^{t} shall not attend the house,
   eyther through sicknes or other urgent occasion, shall have power
   to constitute another Proxie in his roome during such his absence

Source: Browne (1883, 215–16)

[Governor] as President of the Assembly" (Browne 1883, 4–5). Each of these provisions was essentially the same as ones listed by Hooker or Smith.

The 1647–48 rules were slightly more elaborate than the 1637–38 rules, but they were still clearly grounded in accepted parliamentary practices of the time. Again reviling speeches were banned, members were to speak only once on an issue, and they were to stand bareheaded and to direct their speech to the presiding officer. In addition, members were not to enter the chamber "with any weapon." This last rule is like one found in Hooker. By 1650 the Maryland version would evolve to specifically mention guns and by 1666 to prohibit swords (Browne 1883, 273; 1884, 65). The Assembly's rules were changed in another interesting regard in 1650. In 1647–1648, the fine of 50 pounds of tobacco imposed on members who were absent without an acceptable excuse was directed toward "defraying the charges of this [present] Assembly." Two years later the fines were redirected (Browne 1883, 216, 274) "towards the releife of the Poore of the Province." There was an English precedent. The *Journal of the House of Commons* reveals that on January 30, 1563, November 9, 1566, and again on April 2–5, 1571, the House determined that for various violations of parliamentary protocol, the offending member would pay four pence to "the Poor-mens Box."[14]

Colonial assemblies did not all use the same rules, even at their beginning. The Rhode Island General Court was in its infancy when it adopted a set of 10 rules in 1648 (Bartlett 1856, 213–14). Some terminology differed from that used in Parliament or in Maryland. For instance, the presiding officer was referred to as the *moderator*, a term used at the time at the local government level (Brunkow 1980, 244), rather than the speaker.[15] Some rules, however, were clearly grounded in the practices of the House of Commons. Most notably, assembly members were to speak only once to a matter, when they spoke they were to stand up with their head uncovered, and they were to avoid using "nipping terms." All of these rules were found in Hooker or Smith, or both.

Over time, rules in the assemblies evolved to become longer and more detailed. The rules used by the South Carolina Commons House at the end of the seventeenth century are listed in box 2.3. They are longer and more complex than those used in Maryland and Rhode Island 50 years earlier. And, while they still show clear ties to English parliamentary practices—one historian claims, "The procedure and customs of the English House of Commons were imitated by the Assembly as far as possible" (Whitney 1895, 51–52)—they also evidence the development of new and distinctive features.

Box 2.3. More Developed Rules: The South Carolina Commons House of Assembly, 1692, 1696, and 1698

1692:

1. When any man Intends to Speake he is to Stand upp Uncovrd and to Address himselfe to the Speaker, Who: Usually calls such [per]sons by name: that the House may take notice who itt is that Speakes

2. If more than one Stands upp att once the Speaker is to Determine who was first upp & he is to Speake & y^e: Others Sitt downe & Unlesse he Whoe was first upp Sitt downe againe & Give way to y^e: other or thatt Some Memb^{br}: Stand upp & acquaint y^e: House y^t an other was upp before him whome y^e: Speaker calls and the house adjudges itt Soe

3. When a Memb^r is Speakeing none is to Stand upp or interupt him till he has done Speakeing & Sate downe, and then any other may arise and Speake observing y^e: Rules

4. That When M^r: Speaker Desires to Speake he ought to be heard wth:out Interuption if the house be Silent and nott in Dispute/

5. That if any Question be upon a bill y^e: Speaker is to Explain but nott to Sway the house wth—argum^{ts}= or Disputes

6. Thatt If any Memb^r: hisses or Disturbeth any one in his Speach, shall answer itt att the barr—

7. If Any Memb^r: (the house Sitting and in p^{r}sence Use any Reflecting words of or offend y^e: Authority of their Majties y^e: Governo^r. or this house he is to be Called to y^e: barr & there Answer the Same=

8. Any Memb^r: (y^e: house Sitting Departing y^e: house wthout Leave from the Speaker Shall be fined any Sume nott Exceedeing 2^s=6^d= And if they Shall Absent hime or them selves wth=out Leave as aforesaid Shall be fined 5^s: for Each day he so absents him selfe Unless he gives y^e: house Sattisfactory Reasons for his soe absenting

9. When any Memb^r. Speakes to a bill lett him stand upp Uncovered & Direct his speech onely to y^e: Speaker or Chaire & although upon the answer of an other Memb^r. he hath further matter, to alleadge in defence of his first argum^{ts}: ag^t y^e: Answere yett he shall nott make any further discourse on y^e: Same Day to

prevent Expence of time betwixt two Disputtants or talketive
Persons and that if more than one Memb^r: Stand upp att once,
The Speaker shall ord^r. who the [per]son shall be thatt ought to
Speake first

10. In: y^e: Assembly, they are to Vote by yeaes and nays and if itt be
Doubtfull wch of them is the Greater Number then the yeas to
draw forth & y^e: noes are to stand still

11. All Bills are Either Unanimously Rejected att first or Else allowed to be debated

12. After any bill hath been twice Read on two Sevall days then itt is
ingrossed & read y^e: third time & then, y^e: Chaire man is to aske
(if they will have itt putt to y^e: Question whether a Law or nott
Law—

13. If any bill be Rejected y^e: Same shall nott be any Moore
[pro]posed that Session—

14. Any Memb^r: fayling or neglecting to meete att the houre of ad-
journm^t (wth out Shewing a Sattisfactory reason to the house)
Shall be fined in any Sume nott Exceeding Two shillings and Six
pence

15. (**Added by 1696**) While the house is Sitting: noe man ought to
Speake or Whisper to another to the End the house might not
be Interupted, when any are Speakeing, but Every one is to In-
tend the business of the house/

16. (**Added by 1696**) Ord^rd that the Majority of Tenn Members of
this house or any Number above may from time to Time ad-
journe the house [pro]vided the Speaker be one Butt for any
thing Else not Less then Sixteen memb^rs—Shall have power/

17. (**Added by 1696**) That Till the business in agitation be Ended
noe new motion of any new matter Shall be made w^thout Leave
of the house/

18. (**Added by 1698**) Ordered—That no member of The House
Smoak In The House The House Sitting/

Source: Salley (1907, 6–7; 1908, 8–10; 1914, 8–10)

In 1692, the Commons House adopted fourteen rules, which by 1696 were supplemented by three more rules, with another one added by 1698. The first, second, fifth, ninth, and tenth rules were very similar to passages from Smith, while the eighth and tenth rules were tied to excerpts from Hooker. Still, several of the rules demonstrate the evolution of legislative procedures. The eleventh rule held that all bills were either unanimously rejected at the first reading or allowed to be debated. The seventeenth rule prevented motions on new matters from being entertained while another issue was being debated, unless the Assembly voted to allow it. The sixteenth rule instituted a quorum requirement that ten members could adjourn the Assembly if the speaker were among them, but "not Less then Sixteen memb^{rs} Shall have power." And the eighteenth rule prohibited members from smoking while the Assembly was in session.

Once again, rules differed across the colonies. Among the ten rules employed by New Hampshire in 1699, the second, fourth, and ninth were clearly drawn from English precedents. Others, however, reveal some changes. The third rule, for example, allowed members to speak twice to an issue rather than the traditional limit of once. The sixth rule permitted the speaker to vote in the event of a tie rather than always staying above the fray. In *Order and Usage* Hooker says the speaker may vote in the event of a tie, but it is not clear whether this was accepted behavior in Parliament at the time (Snow 1977, 170). The eighth rule provided for a speaker pro tem to preside in the speaker's absence. The tenth rule granted the chamber explicit control over its membership. The fifth rule disallowed members to "smoak tobacco in the house" on penalty of a fine (Bouton 1869, 67–68).

Up to the time of the Revolution, legislative rules in the assemblies continued to evolve. In Maryland, there was "the general development of a more effective internal organization within the lower house" leading to "the slow but sure establishment of influential precedents contributing to achievement of the delegates' objectives" (Jordan 1987, 173). By 1760 the Georgia Commons House, which had only been established five years earlier, was employing a sophisticated set of 29 rules (Candler 1907a, 421–25). But perhaps the most advanced rules devised were those used in Pennsylvania and Virginia.

Pennsylvania's rules adopted in 1767 were numbered and totaled twenty-two (see box 2.4). The rules were still grounded in those first used in Parliament: In this case, the first, tenth, eleventh, twentieth, and twenty-first had parallels in Hooker, the fifth and seventh in Smith. But more recent procedural developments also appeared in the Pennsylvania rules. Lawmakers could speak twice to an issue, as they could earlier in New

Hampshire. There were other advancements specific to Pennsylvania. In the thirteenth rule the speaker was given explicit authority to name members to committees, an important power given their prominence in the Assembly's legislative process. This represented a change; in the original Assembly rules in 1682 standing committees had been elected by the membership (*Votes and Proc. of the H. of Reps. of the Prov. of Pa., 1682 1752*, 1). The fourteenth and fifteenth rules delineated the sequence by which legislation would be considered, starting with allowing any member to introduce a bill, a first reading that would only present the proposal for the lawmakers' consideration, and then a second reading after which amendments could be offered and the bill could be killed. Finally, the seventeenth rule established a cloture procedure by which four members could demand an end to a "tedious" debate and move the previous question. A procedure to cut off debate actually had a long history in Pennsylvania; in 1682 a resolution allowed the speaker on his own initiative to stop "superfluous and tedious" speeches (*Votes and Proc. of the H. of Reps. of the Prov. of Pa., 1682 1752–54*, 2). The use of the "four member rule" language can be traced back to 1703 (McConachie 1898, 24).[16]

Box 2.4. Advanced Rules: Province of Pennsylvania House of Representatives: "Rules for Better Regulating the Conduct and Attendance of the Members," 1767

First, That any Member carrying himself indecently towards the Speaker or any of the Members, by Reflections or otherways, in the House, or shall transgress this or any of the subsequent Rules, shall, for the first Offence, be reproved, for the second, and other Offences, fined, as the House thinks fit, not exceeding Ten Shillings.

Secondly, That all Members offering to speak, stand up and direct his Speech to the Chair, and speak pertinently to the Occasion, and having ended, to sit down. None to speak above twice to one Matter (especially upon Bills) without Leave of the Speaker.

Thirdly, That none presume to interrupt another, nor offer to speak until the first sits down.

Fourthly, That the Members forbear talking to each other, and keep Silence, unless when they have Occasion to speak, in Order as aforesaid.

Fifthly, That no Member endeavour to pervert the Sense of another's Speech.

Sixthly, That the Speaker have Power to stop all unnecessary, tedious and superfluous Discourse, and to command Silence when needful.

Seventhly, That the members avoid naming others, when they have Occasion to observe or take Notice of their Speech; but have Respect to the Time of their speaking, or to the Seat they have, as right or left Hand of the Chair, &c.

Eightly, That no Member presume to go in our out of the House before the Speaker, (he being present) nor depart the House without his Leave.

Ninthly, That upon Debates and passing of Bills, the Majority of Votes shall govern; and when the Votes of the Members are equal in Number, the Speaker may have the casting Vote.

Tenthly, The Speaker may, with the Consent of the House, require any Member offending, to stand at the Bar, and there receive the Censure of the House.

Eleventhly, That no Member presume to divulge the Debates or Secrets of the House.

Twelfthly, That no Member who is against the Body of a Bill, shall be appointed to be of a Committee concerning that Bill.

Thirteenthly, That the Speaker have Power to nominate Persons for Committees, and that none who are nominated refuse the Service; not that any of the Members shall be hereby debarred of their Privilege of nominating Persons, if they think fit, or rejecting such as are nominated by the Speaker; in which Case the Opinion of the House shall govern.

Fourteenthly, That Bills to be passed into Laws, may be brought in by any particular Member, or received by them or the Speaker from others, and presented to the House, who is to order the Clerk loudly to read them, and, after reading to be respectfully delivered to the Speaker, and him to mark or note (by Breviate or otherwise) all Bills, and declare the Nature and Use of the same; which, if not rejected, to cause to be read a second time; and after deliberate Consideration thereon, and Amendment made, if needful, cause it to be read a third time and sent to the Governor, as the House shall think fit, for his Assent; but that no Bill be read twice in one Day, except on extraordinary Occasions.

Fifteenthly, That at the first Reading of Bills, the Members avoid any close Debate, and seriously deliberate on the Contents, in Order to their better Information before the second Reading; and that the said Bills do lie on the Table for the Members to peruse; and that no Member presume to carry a Bill or other Paper out of the House without Leave.

Sixteenthly, That all Questions put by the Speaker, to know the Mind of the House, be answered by the Members in the Affirmative, by standing up, and those in the Negative, by keeping their Seats.

Seventeenthly, That if it shall at any Time happen, that a Debate prove tedious, and any four members shall stand up and request the Speaker to put the Matter in Debate to the Vote, he shall not refuse it.

Eighteenthly, That after the Meeting of any Assembly (the Regularity of Elections being first inspected) Committees shall be appointed on the several Occasions of their Sessions, so far as they have Knowledge thereof, wherein the Commands of their Crown shall be preferred, and next that of the Governor; after which, Inspection shall be made into the Laws for Safety of the Government.

Nineteenthly, That the Door-Keeper always wait on the Speaker for his Orders to ring the Bell.

Twentiethly, That every Member absent from any Meeting of the House, shall be liable to be sent for by the Members present, at the Expense of such absent Member.

Twenty-firstly, That every Member who shall absent himself from the Service of the House, without Leave from the Speaker for so doing, shall be subject to a Fine of Five Shillings for every Day's Absence, unless such Member can assign to the House a satisfactory Reason for the same.

Twenty-secondly, That such Members as do not appear at the Place of Meeting, within half an Hour after the Bell ceases to ring, in the Fore- and Afternoon, shall pay One Shilling; but if a Quorum be not present at the same Time, then each absent Member shall pay Two Shillings; and Eighteen-pence for every Hour's Absence after, unless he can shew Cause, to the Satisfaction of the House, which shall be determined by an immediate Vote.

Source: Votes and Proc. of the H. of Reps. of the Prov. of Pa. (1767, 3–4)

Pennsylvania was not the only assembly with extensive rules. In 1769 Virginia's House of Burgesses compiled 28 rules from an accumulation of chamber precedents. They were gathered by the Committee of Privileges and Elections, which had been specifically charged with the task. The committee packaged what they collected as "the ancient Rules and standing Orders of the House, with others, which they think ought be observed" (Kennedy 1906, 192, 323). These rules represented a dramatic increase from the five rules the chamber had adopted in 1658 (Hening 1809, 507–8). The earlier rules had been centered on English precedents, but with a Virginia twist: all fines were specified in pounds of tobacco. Among the misbehaviors punished was appearing in the House "with overmuch drinke." With each successive offense for being drunk the amount of tobacco a member was fined increased. Three rules were added by 1663, the traditional one limiting members to speaking only once on an issue (with a fine of 20 pounds of tobacco for any violation), a requirement that all fines be paid by each Saturday of the session, and a final one creating a penalty of 20 pounds of tobacco for "every member that shall pipe it after the house is begun to be called over" (Hening 1823, 206–7). In this last matter the House of Burgesses acted well ahead of Parliament; the *Journal of the House of Commons* does not reveal any prohibition on tobacco use until March 23, 1694. There was some tinkering with the language used in the five rules the Burgesses carried over in 1663. The one covering the use of alcohol, for example, was rewritten to say that an offending member was "disguised with drink" (McIlwaine 1914, 25).

The more numerous rules adopted in 1769, of course, still had roots in Parliament's procedures. An admonition to avoid "all indecent and disrespectful Language" and the prohibition "That a Question being once determined . . . cannot again be drawn into Debate, during the same Session" were both found in Hooker. But a number of rules unique to Virginia had been added over time. There were procedural rules requiring that the clerk read the orders of the day before the House proceeded to any other business and that all bills were to be taken up in the order they were introduced, unless the House decided otherwise. Specific quorum rules were set; 15 members with the speaker could adjourn the House, 30 were needed to issue a call, and 50 to proceed to other business. Quorums were also established for the standing committees: 11 members for the Religion, Privileges and Elections, and Propositions and Grievances committees, and 5 members for other committees. Burgesses were prohibited from chewing tobacco while the House was in session. Finally, several rules covered the process by which election contests were to be settled, while another rule explicitly banned the use of "Bribery, and other corrupt Practices" to gain election as a burgess.

The evolution of legislative rules and procedures beyond those used in Parliament occurred across most of the assemblies. Indeed, each assembly developed some distinctive characteristics. Quorum rules were adopted. The first was established by the 1629 Massachusetts Bay Colony Charter, which held that 7 of the 18 assistants along with the governor or deputy governor were sufficient for the "dispatching of all such buysinesses" (Shurtleff 1853a, 10–11). This quorum standard is notable because it was put in place 11 years before the English House of Commons first established one (Redlich 1908, 75–76). But in the colonies they were recalibrated from time to time to meet the needs of particular assemblies and their attendance patterns (Clarke 1943, 174–75; Cook 1931, 259–60; Greene 1963, 216–19; Luce 1922, 24–27). Virginia frequently changed its quorum for conducting business, from 25 of its 56 members (45 percent) in 1720, to 41 out of 84 members in 1748 (49 percent), 25 out of 104 members in 1756 (24 percent), and 50 out of 116 members excluding the speaker (43 percent) in 1766 (Pargellis 1927a, 83; Miller 1907, 111). Some quorum rules were considerably looser than those in Virginia. Maryland approved a remarkably lax standard in 1642: "Any tenn members of the house at any time assembled at the usuall or appointed time (whereof the Leivten[t] Generall & Six Burges's to be Seaven) shall be a house unless sickness do hinder that number In which Case only the members present to make the House" (Browne 1883, 146). The 1663 Rhode Island charter established its quorum as whatever number of deputies attended, a rule that was reaffirmed in subsequent years (Bartlett 1857, 472). The Bahamas assembly reduced its quorum requirement when there was urgent business (Clarke 1943, 175). Some quorum rules were very strict; Pennsylvania required two-thirds (Leonard 1948a, 223).

More important, over time quorum rules became more complex, as in Virginia. Most assemblies devised at least two quorums: a higher standard for transacting business and a lower one for adjournment (Bassett 1894; Clarke 1943, 175). Additional quorum requirements were concocted for specific issues in some colonies. In 1769, New Jersey imposed a higher quorum requirement for decisions regarding government revenues than for other subjects: "but not less than sixteen be a sufficient Number to proceed to any other Business; nor less than eighteen, when any Money is to be raised, or applied." Three years later the numbers were adjusted to 20 and 24 respectively (*Votes and Proc. of the GA of the Prov. of N.J.* 1769, 7; *Votes and Proc. of the GA of the Col. of N.J.* 1772, 6). In 1762, the Bahamas assembly set a quorum requirement that required virtually every member to be present for a measure to pass but allowed a lower quorum for the conduct of other business (Clarke 1943, 175).

It is worth noting that the strategic opportunities offered by quorum rules were well understood by politicians of the time. In 1748, the South Carolina governor grumbled that "A Party of pleasure made by a few of the Members renders it often impossible for the rest to enter upon Business, and sometimes I Have seen a Party made to go out of Town purposely to break the House as they call it (well knowing that nothing could be transacted in their absence)." Their motivation for doing so was "to prevent the Success of what they could not otherwise oppose" (Greene 1963, 217). Such calculated behavior was not isolated to South Carolina. In a 1747 letter to the Board of Trade, the North Carolina governor registered a similar complaint about a group of his lower-house members.

> And being generally united under the conduct of a few designing Men who found their account in Keeping Public Affairs in confusion they have made the Governor and Council, and remaining Members of no weight in the Legislature for they could not so much as meet unless they thought fit to be present and after they were met if they did not like any Bill, they withdrew Privately and then the Majority of Burgesses being absent, no more Business could be done, so that the very being of Assemblies depended upon their whim and Humour, and not on the King's Writ; and Governours Proclamation and Prerogation. This is no Imaginary Consequence, but a real effect which has happened more than once within these four years past. (Saunders 1886b)

The Pennsylvania Assembly also witnessed a number of efforts to exploit quorum rules for political advantage (Leonard 1948a, 224).

Norms and rules governing lawmaker behavior became more stringent over time. Many of the rules focused on parliamentary protocol, and they covered a broad range of activities (Andrews 1926, 227–28). As noted above, the use of tobacco was regulated, but it appears that some accommodations were made. A member of the Connecticut assembly wrote in his journal that after a joint session with the upper house, "we moved to our house & were pretty soon dismissed for a Smoking spell." Such breaks were allowed with some frequency (Turner 1975, 34, 36).

Rules on member behavior were enforced (Andrews 1926, 228). In 1703, Captain Joseph Wadsworth, a Connecticut deputy, was admonished for using "reproachfull words" during a debate. He was forced to pay a fine of 10 pounds to the colony treasury (Hoadly 1868, 453). Wadsworth proved to be a serial offender; in 1708 he was reproached by the Assistants for threatening a sheriff in the gallery ("I will break your head, or knock you down") and again in 1715 for assailing the integrity of legislation that had passed (Hoadly 1870, 492–93). Similar events transpired elsewhere. During a 1736 debate on a measure "to prevent the taking away of Lands against the Will of the Proprietors, for building Water-Mills," Burgess Daniel McCarty accused some of his colleagues of voting "with a View to his own Interest." He was scolded by the speaker "that no such Expressions ought to be used." A motion then passed the House, "That M^r *McCarty* do, in his Place, explain himself." McCarty then "stood up in his Place, and said, He had no Design to reflect upon the House, or any Member in it . . . but if the House thought him in the wrong, he was sorry for it." The House passed a motion accepting the apology (McIlwaine 1910, 298). An incident along these lines occurred in Massachusetts. During House proceedings a deputy got into a heated argument with the speaker over a parliamentary ruling. After the deputy said, among other things, "If the Speaker puts a nonsensical Question, I have a Right to oppose it" and "When I began to speak, I observed the Speaker treated me with an uncommon Degree or Warmth of Temper" the House voted to require him to apologize to the speaker and the full membership. The deputy refused to ask for forgiveness and withdrew from the chamber. Ultimately, his colleagues rejected a motion to expel him (*Jour. of the Honourable H. of Reps. of His Majesty's Prov. of Mass.* 1756, 127–28, 260).

Overall, the assemblies came to control floor behavior to a greater degree than Parliament did at the time (Andrews 1926, 227–28). In a letter to an English friend, Benjamin Franklin, at the moment the speaker of the Pennsylvania Assembly, noted, "The Governor intimates that we are deficient in Good Breeding. I suppose he is in the right, and that Gentlemen on your side the Water will be of the same Opinion; but I hope they will make some allowance for Assemblymen bred in the Woods of America, and not expect the same Politeness in them as in a Governor fresh from Court" (Labaree 1967, 220). To overcome any deficiencies in good breeding and manners, colonial lawmakers imposed on themselves high behavioral standards.

Over time, rules became more elaborate in most of the colonies. Initially, assemblies limited members to speaking once on an issue as Parliament did. But, as mentioned earlier, that constraint came to be loosened. Even as early as 1644, Massachusetts began to provide some leeway: "noe member of this howse shall speake twice to one case att one time beefore e[ver]y one (y^t will) haue spoken." Members had to wait until "after some pawse, to see if any other will speake," at which point they could talk again, but only with permission of the House (Shurtleff 1854, 4). By the 1760s, when members were being allowed to speak twice in New Hampshire, Pennsylvania, and Virginia, Delaware went them one better by allowing its members to speak to "any one Matter or Thing" three times. This was something it could afford to do because it was a very small body of only 18 members (*Votes and Proc. of the H. of Reps. of the Gov. of Del.* 1770, 193). In larger bodies limitations were necessary because debate could consume a great deal of time, particularly on complex legislation. In Pennsylvania, a member wrote in his journal about "Consideration of new ways and Means for raising Money, which held ye House Chiefly Employed for about four weeks, upon which Arose Very Serious & Arduous debates." This particular lawmaker proved a keen judge of his colleagues, noting that during the debates "B. Franklin & John Dickenson Greatly distinguished themselves" (Foulke 1881, 68).

Following established parliamentary precedent most assemblies required multiple readings of a bill. And, generally, bills that failed at any stage of the process could not be reintroduced during the same session (Clarke 1943, 176; Cook 1931, 273). This rule was occasionally contested, with Virginia's burgesses looking to Parliament's procedures for guidance (Greene 1965, 88). But, although there were similarities in legislative procedures across the colonies, there were also notable differences. In Georgia a member requested that the chamber bring a bill on a particular subject. If the chamber agreed, the speaker appointed a committee to draft the measure with the original sponsor named as a member. Once the legislation was written, it was given a perfunctory first reading. After the second reading the measure was referred to the Committee of the Whole where it was debated and amended as needed. If the bill was agreed to following amendment, it was given a third reading, after which it was almost always passed (Corey 1929). The process in Pennsylvania was similar to Georgia's in that the second reading was the crucial phase, and a Committee of the Whole was used to amend a bill. One difference was that, as noted earlier, in Pennsylvania the speaker could bring a bill up for a vote of disfavor prior to the second reading. If the majority voted to kill the measure the clerk took the bill and wrote "Dashed" across its back (Leonard 1948b, 383–84).

The sequence in North Carolina differed from that elsewhere in that a bill received intense scrutiny during each of its three readings (Cook 1931, 271–80).

The typical route that a bill followed was to be considered fully in one house prior to being first considered in the other house. But, as was often the case, some assemblies developed distinctive procedures. The rules in the Plymouth General Court required that a bill be introduced in one session but not be voted on until the next session, thus allowing the deputies time to consult their constituents (Kammen 1969, 24). In both North Carolina and South Carolina, and once in a while in Maryland, a bill would first be read in one house and, if approved, then sent to the other house, which, if it approved, would send it back to the originating house (Cook 1931, 271–72; Clarke 1943, 176; Smith 1903, 105). This iterative procedure was followed through all subsequent required readings. A potential problem was that the final chamber to act could pass a version of the legislation that was unacceptable to the other chamber. South Carolina experienced problems along these lines. In 1748, the Commons House forced a change back to the traditional three readings in one chamber prior to sending a bill to the other chamber, but the process reverted to the iterative process the following year (Smith 1903, 106–7). A completely different process developed in New Hampshire. There each house would debate the general merits of proposed legislation. If the proposal enjoyed support in both houses, a joint committee was appointed to draft a bill (Clarke 1943, 176).

How the assemblies handled the consideration of legislation usually became more complicated over time. The Virginia House followed tradition by requiring all bills to be read three times. The initial reading was essentially preliminary. Serious consideration of the measure followed the second reading: "A bill might then be referred to a committee of the whole house, to a standing committee, to the committee that prepared it, or to a special group varying in size from four to twelve." Subsequently, "Debate and amendment could follow the third reading, and the ample opportunity for thorough understanding of the amendments was ensured by the practise of reading them as many times as the bill itself had been read." Procedures evolved to the point that by 1750 at least four different means existed by which a burgess could strategically delay consideration of a measure: a motion to adjourn during a debate, moving that the orders of the day be read, moving the previous question, and offering amendments (Pargellis 1927b, 148, 152–53). The use of a rule to move the previous question is noteworthy because of the central role that procedure plays in current partisan theories of legislative evolution. Examples of its use can be found in New York (Leder 1963, 679) and, as noted above, in Pennsylvania. The previous question was likely imported from Parliament, where it appears to have been incorporated as early as the 1670s, although often used for different purposes (Grey 1769, 113, 321; Plaisted 1976, 8; Timberland 1742, 210, 217).

Riders also came to be employed in Virginia. One burgess wrote in his journal, "I met with a thing this day called a Rider to a bill." He explained, "When a bill is engrossed and can't be amended Substantially, if 'tis necessary to alter it and yet save it, a clause is proposed to be added which is produced, engrossed and read as the bill, and the question put upon it whether it shall pass as a Rider. If it does, then it passes again in the bill." The member noted that only one rider per measure was permitted (Greene 1965, 99).

Various voting procedures evolved across the assemblies. Some chambers employed yeas and nays (e.g., *Jour. of the Honorable H. of Reps. of His Majesty's Prov. of the Mass.-Bay* 1750, 195–96); others used teller votes and standing votes. A few used written ballots. The Virginia House appears to have made use of both the taking of divisions and the employment of tellers, as described in a burgess's diary entry in 1752.

> When a Division happens, if 'tis relating to things intirely in the house, vizt, about Clerks, etc., Ays on one Side No's on the other. But if 'tis about any matter in the House that Some are against and some for, those against the resolution in the house, such as Reports of any Committee, Go out of the house on the division. Tellers are appointed of each Party. One going out is Stopped and Counteth those within. Another from within counteth those who went out as they come in. (Greene 1965, 69–70)

North Carolina and South Carolina also used teller voting (Cook 1931, 272–73; Easterby 1958, 90, 101, 183, 381). But South Carolina employed other methods as well. In 1773, a visitor recounted that "the members gave their votes by rising from their seats, the dissentients did not rise" (Quincy 1915–16, 452). In some assemblies a member could request that an oral vote be recorded (Olson 1992, 565). Other variations in voting rules appeared. In West Jersey a two-thirds vote of the members was required to enact legislation (Pomfret 1956, 96). In New Hampshire in 1745 abstentions were not allowed; if a member was present for a vote he had to take a position in favor or against, or face the censure of the House (Bouton 1871,

325). In 1738, the New York General Assembly ordered "That upon any Question being put, the Names of such Members in the House as do neither vote for the Affirmative or Nagative shall be put in a Column be themselves, under the Names of Neuters" (*Jour. of the Votes and Proc. of the GA of His Majesty's Col. of N.Y.* 1738, 24).

Not every assembly adopted increasingly sophisticated rules and procedures. The very small body in Delaware approved a simple set of five rules in 1769, which it continued to employ throughout the rest of the colonial era. The five rules actually represented a decline; the chamber had operated with six rules from 1749 to 1769 (Bushman, Hancock, and Homsey 1986, 150; *Votes and Proc. of the H. of Reps. of the Gov. of Del.* 1770, 131, 194–95). And even if adopted, rules could be ignored. A former Massachusetts speaker complained the House was "not strict in conforming to some of the most useful rules of parliament." Specifically, he noted, "a bill, after rejecting upon a second or third reading, is sometimes taken up and passed suddenly the same session." Overall, he lamented that rules were "too frequently by votes . . . dispensed with" (Hutchinson 1768, 438–39). But more generally, stricter adherence to accepted parliamentary practices became the norm across the assemblies (Olson 1992, 559).

Each assembly, however, evolved its own culture and accepted behaviors. Some developed norms that were extraordinarily different from those found elsewhere. Many of the trappings of the English parliamentary system were employed in South Carolina, even on the eve of the Revolution. Thus, a visitor in 1773 recorded, "The *first* thing done at the meeting of the house is to bring the mace (a very superb and elegant one which cost ninety guineas) and lay it on the table before the speaker. This I am told is the way in the Commons of G[reat] B[ritain]." He went on to add, "The Speaker is robed in black and has a very large wig of State, when he goes to attend the Chair (with the Mace borne before him) on delivery of speeches, etc."

After writing admiringly of the pomp surrounding the start of the session, the visitor was aghast at the antics of the members during the rest of the meeting.

> The members of the house all sit with their hats on, and uncover when they rise to speak; they are not confined (at least they did not confine themselves) to any one place to speak in. The members conversed, lolled, and chatted much like a friendly jovial society, when nothing of importance was before the house: nay once or twice while the speaker and clerk were busy in writing the members spoke quite loud across the

room to one another. A very unparliamentary appearance. The speaker
put the questions sitting, and conversed with the House sitting. (Quincy
1915–16, 451–52, italics in the original)

The visitor was told by Charles Cotesworth Pinckney, then a member of
the Commons House, that his colleagues always sat with their hats on as
he claimed members of the British House of Commons did (Quincy
1915–16, 447).

In contrast, in Pennsylvania, where Quakers dominated the Assembly
membership (Ryerson 1986, 112), legislative sessions were strikingly similar to Friends meetings. Thus even as late as the 1750s, "Silences were
common as members waited for inspiration to speak, and when debate was
done the Speaker might simply declare the sense of the House rather than
call for a vote" (Tully 1977, 95). Yet, even in Pennsylvania tempers could
wear thin. In 1762, a member reported, "an obstinate dispute with indecent invectives & bitter altercations" over a highway bill (Foulke 1884,
411).

Perhaps even more important, while the assemblies initially imported
rules and precedents from Britain, over time substantial organizational and
procedural differences developed (Barker 1940, 157–60; Greene 1969,
345–46; Sirmans 1966, 69). The colonies started looking not just to Parliament for guidance on questions about structures and procedures, but to
each other as well. Established assemblies influenced the operations of new
assemblies. Thus, those in Georgia and Nova Scotia looked to South Carolina and Massachusetts for models (Greene 1961, 458). Massachusetts also
helped shaped the assemblies in Connecticut and Plymouth, and indirectly
influenced those in East New Jersey, New Hampshire, New Haven, New
York, and Nova Scotia (Kammen 1969, 54). The Bahamas House "adopted
as a matter of course all procedures and privileges made customary in the
English and colonial parliaments up to that time" (Craton 1962, 125).[17] Indeed, even established bodies began to look to each other for guidance.
When, in 1764, a group of Philadelphia residents petitioned the Pennsylvania Assembly to request that their deliberations be open to the public, a
committee was appointed to "examine the Journals of the House of Commons, and report the Usage and Practice thereof . . . and to enquire likewise
what the Practice is in the other *American* colonies." The committee, which
included Benjamin Franklin among its eight members, subsequently reported, "we have examined the Journals of the House of Commons" and
"With Regard to the Practice in the Colonies, we have not been able to ob-

tain perfect information concerning all of them; but we understand, that in the Provinces of *Maryland* and *Virginia* the Assembly Doors are left open . . . but that in the neighboring Provinces of *New-Jersey* and *New-York* the Practice is, as hitherto it has been in this Province, to keep the Doors shut" (*Votes and Proc. of the H. of Reps. of the Prov. of Pa.* 1764, 54, 57–58, italics in original). By 1773, a visitor to the Pennsylvania Assembly observed, "Their debates are not public, which is said now to be the case of only this house of commons throughout the continent" (Quincy 1915–16, 476).

Thus, over time information on rules, procedures, and organization came to be gathered both from the House of Commons and from the other assemblies. This is important because looking toward each other for direction allowed the assemblies to increase their opportunities to evolve independently from Parliament. But the impact of Parliament's rules on those used in assemblies was sufficiently profound that it was still apparent at the end of the colonial era. Writing just before the start of the Revolution, an English observer said, "The proceedings of the Houses of Assembly in the Colonies are conducted, and their Journals kept, in a manner much conformed to those of the two Houses of Parliament" (Stokes 1783, 243).

Explanations for the Organizational Evolution of the Colonial Assemblies

The evidence presented in this chapter shows that over the seventeenth and eighteenth centuries, the colonial assemblies established clear institutional boundaries and became more complex organizations. Although originally modeled in part on Parliament, they evolved to become very different kinds of legislative bodies. Certainly, the assemblies did not evolve exactly alike. The Virginia House, for example, had a more complex standing committee system than did its counterparts in other colonies.

But the organizational evolution of the assemblies a century before a similar process started in the U.S. House implies that legislative development is less about modernization and more about the adoption of internal structures and procedures that function to make the organizations more efficient and more responsive to the needs of both members and constituents. This view is consistent with the observation that over time legislatures evolve into more complicated organizations (Krehbiel 1991, 248). An important finding of this chapter is that this process is not time bound to the modern era.

Beyond describing familiar evolutionary processes, does the development of the assemblies offer any insights into the forces driving the changes? As mentioned several times in this chapter, partisan machinations cannot explain what happened for the simple reason that organized political parties rarely surfaced during the colonial era. Only occasionally was factional politics in evidence, and when it was, it was always ephemeral. Only Rhode Island developed anything like the modern American party system, with two ongoing factions that "drew up lists of candidates, circulated them, spent large sums of money on campaigns . . . and rewarded the faithful with office." At the other extreme, "Far from producing parties, Virginia scarcely produced factions" and had "no organized parties, factions, clientage system or bureaucracy" (Greene 1979, 40; Main 1973a, 5, 11). If political parties drive legislative evolution, Rhode Island ought to have produced the most developed assembly and Virginia the least developed. If anything, the historical record suggests the opposite relationship.

There are two alternative reasons proposed for the evolutionary process found in the U.S. House, each focused on a changing organizational environment: increased workload and increased membership size (Polsby 1968, 164–65). It might also be hypothesized that a legislature becomes more organizationally developed as its membership becomes more stable.

Increased Workload

It would seem reasonable to conjecture that the assemblies became more complicated organizations in response to the increased demands being made on them. There are two sorts of data available on assembly workloads: the number of petitions from constituents and the number of bills passed. Over the course of the 1700s the number of petitions presented to most assemblies climbed significantly (Bailey 1979, 62; Batinski 1987, 7; Harlow 1917, 19; Leonard 1948b, 376–80; Longmore 1995, 428; Olson 1992, 556–58; Purvis 1986, 179). Between the second and sixth decades of the eighteenth century, the number of petitions grew substantially in seven of the nine assemblies for which data have been collected. Over the next decade the numbers continued to increase in six of them. The importance of petitions in the legislative process increased as well. Approximately half of all laws passed by the assemblies during the eighteenth century originated as petitions (Bailey 1979, 64; Olson 1992, 556; Purvis 1986, 178; Tully 1977, 99). Not surprisingly, as the number of petitions climbed assemblies developed specific rules governing how they could be submitted (Leonard 1948b, 379; Olson 1992, 556).

Another piece of evidence suggesting that assemblies experienced greater workloads over time is the amount of legislation they passed. There was a substantial increase in law production in most colonies between the 1730s and the 1760s. The number of new laws increased substantially in seven of the ten assemblies for which there are data, while they held at virtually the same number in two and dropped in only one. The increase in bill production is tied to a dramatic swelling of the legislative agenda. Problems such as defense, Indian relations, and transportation that had been resolved at the local government level in the early years proved to require colony-wide solutions in later years (Olson 1992, 552, 562–63).

Given the evidence it seems reasonable to claim that the assemblies became more complex organizations at the same time they experienced increasing workloads. These data are, of course, only suggestive. They cannot sort out whether workload drove organization, or organization drove workload. More data might allow us to tease out the correct relationship. But it is possible that they happened together with an increase in one leading to an increase in the other in a series of feedback loops.

Membership Size

Legislative membership size might be related to organizational complexity with larger assemblies requiring more elaborate rules to help manage them. The assemblies began as relatively small bodies, as table 2.1 showed. By the time of the Revolution, most were larger, some considerably so. There were, however, substantial differences in their sizes. Assemblies varied from small chambers of 18 to 36 members in Delaware, Georgia, New Hampshire, New Jersey, New York, and Pennsylvania, to much larger chambers with 118 to 138 members in Connecticut, Massachusetts, and Virginia. Assemblies in Maryland, North Carolina, Rhode Island, and South Carolina were of moderate size, with between 51 and 81 members (Corey 1929, 112; Greene 1981, 461; Harlow 1917, 63; Main 1966; Lutz 1999, 65–66). Because representation was based on geography, membership growth was driven by increases in the numbers of towns and counties. In 1752 the Virginia House had 94 members—2 from each of the 45 counties and 1 from each of the 4 boroughs. By 1774 the number of counties had grown to 61, increasing the House's membership to 126 (Griffith 1970, 18).

Do these data suggest membership size is related to organizational complexity? On the one hand, assemblies increased in membership over time. On the other hand, while probably the most developed assembly, Virginia, was among the largest bodies, so was the less developed assembly in Massachusetts. Delaware, with its simple rules, was very small, but so was Pennsylvania, with its sophisticated rules. So, overall, on this relationship the picture is, at best, mixed.

Membership Stability

In and of itself, increased membership stability may not necessarily produce legislative development. Arguably, however, increasing membership stability rates are apt to be associated with increasing levels of development for several reasons. As members serve longer it seems likely that they will adopt rules that place greater value on serving apprenticeships prior to being awarded leadership positions. Complexity in structure may increase as longer-serving members seek to exploit asymmetries of information and talent (Krehbiel 1991, 248). Longer-serving members also have greater incentive to seek influence in legislative decision making (Squire 1988a, 1988b, 1992a). Thus greater membership stability should increase the probability that legislators will adopt increasingly complex rules and procedures.

Over time, assemblies enjoyed increasingly stable memberships. From 1696 to 1775, turnover dropped in every assembly save New Jersey, and the decline was almost always impressive (Greene 1981). In the most extreme case, turnover in Pennsylvania dropped to a mean of 18 percent in the decade from 1766 to 1775 from a mean of 62 percent in the decade from 1696 to 1705. And well over half of the "new" members in later decades were actually former legislators returning to the institution (Ryerson 1986, 130; Tully 1977, 181–82). Many Pennsylvania members served for more than 15 terms, even though elections were annual events (Leonard 1948a, 238). Such longevity was not unusual. Members of the Connecticut Assembly came to average around 9 terms in office, even with semiannual elections (Daniels 1986, 40). Thus, the evidence shows that assemblies evolved into more complex organizations at the same time their memberships were stabilizing. But, once again, the direction of causation is not clear.

Conclusions

Almost all of the colonial assemblies in America began as seemingly rudimentary entities operating at the periphery of the English world, populated by members who almost never had any parliamentary experience. Although they would seem good candidates to be dysfunctional the assemblies managed to legislate productively and to represent their constituents' interests on a wide range of issues. They were successful because the rules and procedures they inherited from Parliament allowed them to begin operation as something well beyond primitive organizations with inexperienced members. The assemblies did not have to invent decision-making rules; they simply had to learn to apply them.

At a macrolevel, the assemblies appear to have followed very similar evolutionary paths. Almost all of them became bicameral, and they almost all became much more complicated organizations, with standing committees and increasingly sophisticated procedures. In the case of rules and committees, the assemblies were initially modeled on Parliament, and their parliamentary roots continued to show throughout the colonial era. But at a microlevel, noticeable differences emerged across them. Although there were regional similarities—the South Atlantic bodies looked much alike, as did those in New England, and older bodies often influenced younger ones—each assembly evolved its own mix of organizational characteristics over its own time line. By the 1770s, they looked and operated only a little like Parliament; importantly they also were in no way mirror images of each other.

The similarities at the macrolevel and the dissimilarities at the microlevel both hint at the same driving force that explains the change in legislative organizations over time. At the macrolevel they adopted similar forms because they were familiar. But beyond familiarity the rules they imported also had a demonstrated record of organizational success. In that regard, they met the functional needs of the assemblies. At the microlevel, however, differences evolved because each colony faced somewhat different governing tasks and organizational obstacles.

But in all of the colonies, the assemblies became institutions that acquired and analyzed information in response to problems constituents brought to them. In every way they became recognizable yet distinctive legislative organizations. Indeed, the assemblies were sufficiently successful as representative bodies that they were the main political engines pushing the colonies toward political independence. Their success in that endeavor actually created the next evolutionary obstacle for them to overcome: managing the transformation to state legislatures from colonial assemblies.

3 ◆ The Original State Legislatures

The colonial assemblies led to the original state legislatures. But, while the transmission of organizational rules and structures to the new legislatures from the old assemblies appears direct, the transition between them was actually interrupted by a little noticed institutional detour: the provincial congresses. While that deviation offered an alternative evolutionary path, as will be demonstrated it was one not taken.

In examining the development of the original state legislatures, three important facets of American legislative evolution will be emphasized. The first is the observation that over time a legislative institution becomes increasingly complex, as documented in chapter 2 about the evolution of the colonial assemblies. The second is the fact that new legislative institutions begin at the point of development of existing legislatures. That is, each new generation of American legislatures starts further along the evolutionary path than its predecessors, because new legislatures inherit the organizational advancements developed by existing legislatures. Thus, the new state legislatures began their existences as sophisticated organizations. The third is that not every evolutionary development succeeds, and not every path gets followed. In this case I show that the Continental and Confederal Congress and the provincial congresses both fall outside the successful evolutionary line.

The Interregnum and the Rise of the Provincial Congresses

By 1774 the colonial assemblies were legislatures in full. They legislated on a wide range of issues, they operated with reasonably sophisticated rules, and almost all of them had at least a few standing committees. But, as the rift with Great Britain widened, most assemblies found themselves in tenuous positions. Only those in Connecticut, Delaware, and Rhode Island enjoyed sufficient powers that they could not be prorogued or otherwise prevented from meeting by their governors (Nevins 1924, 45). Because the assemblies were in the vanguard of the independence movement, governors were loath to allow them to meet. Consequently, to fill the governing gap created by the largely absent assemblies and the disintegrating royal authority, an improvised institution was quickly devised. The solution was the provincial congress, a stopgap organization that looked and acted more like the Continental Congress than the colonial assemblies.

The provincial congresses were to govern during the interregnum between colonial governments and whatever legal structures would succeed them (Brenaman 1902, 7–38; Cushing 1896; Lincoln 1906, 477; Silver 1895; Walker 1905). In some colonies the rise of the provincial congress overlapped with the demise of the assembly. In North Carolina, the final assembly met from April 4 to April 8, 1775. But the first provincial congress had met several months earlier—August 25 to August 27, 1774. The second provincial congress assembled in direct competition with the final assembly, not only meeting for much the same time (April 3 to April 7) but also in the same town, New Bern, and with similar personnel. Indeed, John Harvey served as both the speaker of the assembly and the moderator of the congress (Connor 1913, 340–42). In New Hampshire three provincial congresses met prior to the final meeting of the assembly. The provincial congress's growing dominance as New Hampshire's governing body is demonstrated by the fact the third provincial congress was attended by 109 delegates representing 71 towns, while only 37 representatives representing 36 towns participated in the final assembly that convened the following month (Andrésen 1976, 158; Walker 1905, 19, 21). Moreover, the final assembly took its policy direction from the provincial congress (Walker 1905, 27). An overlap between the congresses and the assemblies troubled some politicians. A member of both South Carolina bodies wrote to his son, "On Thursday the 1st. June the Provincial Congress, & on the same day the General Assembly are to meet in Charles Town, if the Lt. Governor permits the latter to do business & we are told he will, methinks there will be some hazard of Clashing Jurisdictions." The meetings did overlap, but a clash was avoided when the assembly only passed a previously agreed-upon tax bill and then adjourned (Chesnutt 1985, 158–59). A few colonies were spared collisions. The last meeting of the New York assembly was April 3, 1775; the first meeting of the provincial congress was the following month (Lincoln 1906, 472–77).[1]

Colonial governors clearly saw provincial congresses as subversive organizations. Writing to the governor of South Carolina, Massachusetts governor Thomas Gage complained, "This Province has some time been and now is in the new fangled legislature termed a Provincial Congress, who seem to have taken the Government into their hands" (Cushing 1896, 129). The British government understood the threat. Lord Dartmouth, Secretary of State for the Colonies, wrote Governor Gage "that the first essential step to be taken towards reestablishing government would be to arrest and imprison the principal actors and abettors in the Provincial Congress (whose proceedings appear in every light to be acts of treason and rebellion)" (Sparks 1847, 507). In a broadside, Governor Gage went public with his administration's fears.

> WHEREAS, a Number of Persons unlawfully assembled at *Cambridge*, in the Month of *October* last, calling themselves a *Provincial Congress*, did in the most open and daring Terms, assume to themselves the Powers and Authority of Government, independent of, and repugnant to his Majesty's Government . . . All of which Proceedings have a most dangerous Tendency to ensnare His Majesty's Subjects, the Inhabitants of this Province, and draw them into Perjuries, Riots, Sedition, Treason and Rebellion. (*Proclamation* 1774, italics in original)

The public recognized that the provincial congresses challenged the established political order. In Pennsylvania, those loyal to the Crown and therefore opposed to the calling of a provincial congress published a broadside making their case in verse, which included this snippet of doggerel.

> Faction that Fiend, begot in Hell—
> In *Boston* nurs'd—here brought to dwell
> By *Congress*, who, in airy Freak,
> Conven'd to plan a *Republick*?
>
> (*Address of Liberty, to the Buckskins of Pennsylvania, on hearing of the intended Provincial Congress* 1775, italics in original)

In turn, the provincial congresses came to acknowledge that they were usurping the assemblies. Responding to a letter written by the departing New Jersey governor calling for a meeting of the assembly, the provincial congress pleaded, "That in the opinion of this Congress the Proclamation of William Franklin, Esq. late Governor of New-Jersey . . . appointing a meeting of the General Assembly, to be held on the 20th of this instant, June ought not to be obeyed" (*Letter from His Excellency William Franklin, Esquire; to the Honorable Gentlemen of His Majesty's Council, and the Gentlemen of the House of Representatives of His Majesty's Province of New-Jersey* 1776).

In the end, the provincial congresses supplanted the assemblies in almost all of the colonies. Aside from Connecticut, Delaware, and Rhode Island, where the legislatures enjoyed sufficient independence to render provincial congresses unnecessary, only the Pennsylvania Assembly continued to control its colony's politics up until June 1776. Only at that late point was a provincial conference of committees held to push for the creation of a new governmental structure (Gibson 1934; Kruman 1997, 24–28; Nevins 1924, 101–8). Elsewhere the upstart bodies became dominant. By November 1775, the South Carolina Provincial Congress had literally replaced the assembly by commandeering the statehouse (*Exts. from the Jours. of the Provincial Cong. of S.C.* 1776, 1). Thus, the congresses were, in a very concrete sense, revolutionary bodies. In filling the power vacuum, they, like the Continental Congress, exercised executive and judicial functions in addition to legislative functions. This mix of activities leads some to claim that "the provincial congress bore only faint resemblance to the colonial legislatures" (Kruman 1997, 22). Such assertions overstate the differences between the institutions. While the assemblies had not assumed executive functions, they had exercised judicial powers. And, more important, both assemblies and provincial congresses made laws.

Indeed, the provincial congresses were intended to be lawmaking bodies. The initial Massachusetts announcement stated, "That the exigencies of our public affairs demand that a provincial congress be called, to concert such measures as may be adopted" (*Boston Post Boy* 1774). The Georgia provincial congress spelled out its authority, specifying, "That all legislative powers shall be reserved to the Congress" (Candler 1908a, 277). Much of the provincial congresses' efforts were devoted to getting their provinces (the term they used instead of colonies) on a war footing. This involved not only large matters such as raising and supplying militias, but also lower-profile measures, such as one establishing the status of conscientious objectors (*Min. of the Provincial Cong. and the Coun. of Safety of the St. of N.J.* 1879, 407–10). More mundane war-related legislation also was passed, for instance, bills detailing which sheep could be slaughtered and when (*Proc. of the Convs. of the Prov. of Md.* 1836, 7; *Jour. of the Provincial Cong. of S.C.* 1776, 75). Nonmilitary issues surfaced as well; the New Jersey provincial congress passed legislation to conduct a census for tax purposes

(*Min. of the Provincial Cong. and the Coun. of Safety of the St. of N.J.* 1879, 435). They also tackled economic and legal issues. A letter written by a South Carolina member noted, "We have resolved in a provincial Congress that no Suits for the recovery of debts Shall be instituted, nor Mortgages Levied by any Lawyer or Magistrate" (Chesnutt 1985, 48). The Virginia conventions—the name used there and in Maryland—passed laws encouraging the development of saltworks and outlawing counterfeiting of continental paper currency (Hening 1821, 122–26, 134).

There were several important contrasts between the assemblies and the congresses. Most obviously, the provincial congresses, like the Continental Congress, were unicameral; almost all of the colonial legislatures were bicameral. A proposal to create a second chamber in Massachusetts failed in late 1774, foundering on concerns about representation (Cushing 1896, 165–67). But perhaps the biggest difference between the provincial congresses and the assemblies was membership size. The congresses were much larger bodies. In Massachusetts, the first provincial congress had 293 members, whereas the final General Court had only 140 members. As mentioned above, New Hampshire's third provincial congress was considerably larger than the final assembly that met at roughly the same time. Maryland's Conventions were attended by up to 141 members, roughly twice the size of the assembly (*Proc. of the Convs. of the Prov. of Md.* 1836, 19). The January 1775 South Carolina provincial congress listed 183 members, about three times as many members as the assembly (*Exts. from the Jours. of the Provincial Cong. of S.C.* 1775, 5–8). The August 1775 session of the North Carolina provincial congress had 184 members, more than twice the size of the assembly (*Jour. of the Proc. of the Provincial Cong., of N.C.* 1775, 4–6). The May 1775 meeting of the New Jersey provincial congress had 87 members, again more than twice as many members as the assembly (*Exts. from the Jour. of Proc. of the Provincial Cong. of N.J.* 1775, 3–4). The July 1775 session of the Georgia provincial congress was attended by over 100 delegates, roughly three times the size of the assembly (Candler 1908a, 229–30). In most of the cases the membership increases came from delegates sent from previously underrepresented backcountries (Jackson 1985, 286–89; Patterson 1973, 109–10, 282).

The fact that these bodies were so large did not go unnoticed at the time; indeed their great size was taken as a measure of their representativeness. In August 1775, the Virginia convention passed a declaration observing, "The delegates of the people, then met in full Convention, the most numerous Assembly that had ever been known in this Colony" (Brenaman 1902, 24). Numbers also took on political significance in Georgia. The first meeting of the provincial congress in January 1775 had delegates from only 5 of the 12 parishes; the assembly meeting at the same time had members from all 12 parishes. Consequently, at that point the provincial congress did not assert that it spoke for the entire province (Candler 1908a, 42–43). But, by July 1775, when over 100 delegates drawn from all the parishes met, the congress wrote to a royal official boasting, "In these very critical and alarming times, the good people of this Province . . . have accordingly chosen a large number of persons to meet together at Savannah." They then noted, "These, being accordingly met, (to be distinguished from the usual representation,) have styled themselves a Provincial Congress, and from the number and character of their names . . . your Excellency will be convinced the Province was never more fully represented in any Assembly" (Candler 1908a, 249).

The addition of representatives from the peripheries impacted the operations of the congresses. This was, perhaps, most noticeable in South Carolina, where the assembly had been dominated by wealthy planters (Waterhouse 1986). An assembly visitor had commented that "a great majority of the house are dwellers in Charlestown, where the body of the planters reside during the sickly months" (Quincy 1915–16, 454). A patrician member of both the Commons House and the first provincial congress complained about the new representatives.

> During the deliberation & debates in Congress upon the articles of Nonexportation and Compensation; . . . the Deputies who were Sent to represent the frontier Inhabitants commonly denominated Back Woods-Men, unaccustomed to the formalities of parliament; Moving, Seconding, debating, Committing, Sauntering, Reporting, amending, declaiming, Recommitting &c, murmured against delay & procrastination_ according to their Ideas, every thing might have been completed with extreme facility & no more words than are necessary in the bargain & Sale of a Cow,_ from So much talking, So many "fine Speeches," Jealousies arose or were instilled in their breasts; "the Rich Rice-Planter & the Towns-people had Schemed to weary them out in order to thin the House & transact business their own way." (Chesnutt 1985, 39)

Fortunately for the functioning of the provincial congresses, there was considerable membership continuity between them and the assemblies. In New Hampshire, 13 men were members of both the Fourth provincial congress and the final assembly, which met over the same time period (Walker 1905, 27). A similar situation prevailed in South Carolina; in 1775, the Commons House was largely populated by members of the provincial congress (Chesnutt 1985, 159). In both Massachusetts and Virginia a large percentage of the members of the first provincial congresses had previously served in the assemblies (Nevins 1924, 61). There was great membership stability across the provincial congresses as well. Of the 107 members of the fourth provincial congress in New York, 23 had served in all three previous congresses and only 6 were serving for the first time (Lincoln 1906, 486). Almost half of the members of New Hampshire's fifth provincial congress had served in the fourth congress (Walker 1905, 40). Thus, while the congresses were new, in many cases their members were experienced legislators.

Because the provincial congresses were both concocted quickly—they were "creations of haste and anxiety" (Nevins 1924, 60)—and never conceived by their members to be anything other than temporary bodies, little thought was initially given to their rules and structures. Thus, some important organizational features had to evolve in response to experience. For instance, leadership structures changed even over the brief histories of the provincial congresses. The leader of the initial Virginia convention was referred to as both the moderator and the president; subsequent conventions used only the latter title (Brenaman 1902, 13, 15–16). In North Carolina the first two provincial congresses were led by a moderator, the final three by a president (Connor 1913, 342–43). Both the Maryland conventions and the Massachusetts provisional congress underwent a slightly different transformation, each starting with a chair before transitioning to a president (*Proc. of the Convs. of the Prov. of Md.* 1836, 6, 39; *Jours. of the Provisional Cong. of Mass.* 1838, 15, 84). In New Hampshire, John Wentworth was elected chair of the first provincial congress and president of the second congress. When Wentworth could not attend the third congress because of health problems the body was led instead by a president pro tem (Walker 1905, 11, 14, 19). The New Jersey provincial congress elected a president, and later added a vice president (*Exts. from the Jour. of Proc. of the Provincial Cong. of N.J.* 1775, 5, 8).

Most early provincial congresses formally adopted few parliamentary rules. An exception was the Virginia convention, which at the beginning of its meetings explicitly adopted "the same rules and orders" used in the House of Burgesses (*Proc. of the Conv. of Del. for the Counties and Corporations in the Col. of Va., March 1775* 1775, 5; *Proc. of the Conv. of Del. for the Counties and Corporations in the Col. of Va., July, 1775* 1775, 5; *Proc. of the*

Conv. of Del., May 1776 1776, 9). This allowed for sophisticated parliamentary maneuvers. Reporting on events in a letter to George Washington, George Mason confessed, "During the first part of the Convention, Partys run so high, that we had frequently no other Way of preventing improper Measures but by procrastination, urging the previous Question, & giving Men time to reflect." He went on to detail that "The Convention, not thinking this a time to relye upon Resolves & Recommendations only, and to give obligatory Force to their proceedings, adopted the Style & Form of Legislation, changing the word *enact* into *ordain*." In turn, "their Ordinances were all introduced in the Form of Bills, were regularly referred to a Committee of the whole House, and underwent their Readings before they were passed" (Chase 1987, 164, italics in original). Pennsylvania's conference of committees, which as noted earlier was far slower to be put in motion than its counterparts in the other colonies, adopted 10 rules derived from those used by its assembly (*Min. of the Proc. of the Conv. of the St. of Pa.* 1776, 5–6). Even in the absence of formally adopted rules, however, common parliamentary procedures appear to have infiltrated the workings of most provincial congresses. Notably, they usually made use of a committee of the whole (Candler 1908a, 243; *Jour. of the Proc. of the Provincial Cong., of N.C.* 1775, 20; *Jour. of the Provincial Cong. of S.C.* 1776, 20; *Jours. of the Provisional Cong. of Mass.* 1838, 309; *Min. of the Provincial Cong. and the Coun. of Safety of the St. of N.J.* 1879, 384).

Eventually formal rules were adopted in some of the other colonies, but only after several congresses had met. In South Carolina parliamentary rules were adopted sporadically. Thus, on February 7, 1776, the congress passed two rules: one prohibiting members from speaking more than twice on a question, the other assessing a fine of 20 shillings for failure to attend a session. Additional rules were adopted on February 12 (members absent without leave to be sent for at their own expense) and February 24 (members absent and who live more than 65 miles from "Charles-Town" to be sent for at their own expense) (*Jour. of the Provincial Cong. of S.C.* 1776, 12, 23, 59–60). In April 1776, the North Carolina provincial congress created a committee to "draw up Rules and Decorum to be observed in Congress," but no subsequent list of rules appeared (*Jour. of the Proc. of the Provincial Cong. of N.C.* 1776, 13).

Some provincial congresses adopted a complete slate of rules. In Massachusetts a committee in the second provincial congress drafted a set of ten rules, which were adopted on April 29, 1775 (*Jours. of the Provisional Cong. of Mass.* 1838, 164–65). A few weeks later on May 18, the fourth provincial congress of New Hampshire adopted a set of eight rules (Bouton 1873, 471). Both sets of rules were grounded in accepted parliamentary practices, and they share a striking number of similarities. Given the timing of the adoptions and the proximity of the two provinces, it is likely that New Hampshire adapted its rules from those devised by its neighbor. This supposition is further supported by two circumstantial bits of evidence. First, the New Hampshire provincial congress did not opt to adopt the set of ten rules used by its assembly (cf. Bouton 1873, 373), instead they arrived at a different set of rules. Second, on April 26, 1775, the third New Hampshire provincial congress named Nathaniel Follsom, Josiah Bartlett, and Samuel Hobart to be "immediately sent as a Committee from this Convention to the Provincial Congress of the Massachusetts Bay to deliver to them a letter from us & . . . report the effect of their mission as soon as may be" (Bouton 1873, 461). The journal for the second Massachusetts provincial congress reports that they met the New Hampshire committee the same day that the chamber adopted its set of ten rules (*Jours. of the Provisional Cong. of Mass.* 1838, 164). All three of the New Hampshire committee members served again in the fourth provincial congress, which assembled roughly two weeks later and adopted the set of eight rules. Thus it seems plausible that the New Hampshire committee returned from their trip with a copy of the Massachusetts rules, which were then slightly reworked, omitting only the rules regarding committee appointment procedures.[2]

In contrast to New Hampshire, the Maryland convention, which waited until August 1776—more than two years after its first meeting—to adopt formal rules, chose to hew closely to those long used by its assembly (*Proc. of the Convs. of the Prov. of Md.* 1836, 216–17; *Votes and Proc. of the Lower H. of Asm. of the Prov. of Md.* 1773, 3). The assembly's prohibition against bringing swords or weapons onto the floor was carried over into the convention's rules virtually verbatim. For the majority of rules that were continued, the convention's version made changes in capitalization, and a president was substituted for the speaker. Only two rules were substantially different, those being assembly rules that pertained to the bicameral sequence of the legislative process, which were replaced with rules appropriate for a unicameral body.

It is worth pointing out that the Continental Congress also operated with relatively few rules early in its history. It adopted four rules in September 1774 and then waited until July 1776 before replacing those with a more elaborate set of twelve rules (Jillson and Wilson 1994, 307–8). The rules adopted by the Continental and Confederal Congresses were influenced by the experience of members grounded in their colonial legislative procedures (Wilson 1999). The Confederal Congresses' use of ordinances, for example, was likely taken from South Carolina's use of that form of legislation (McCormick 1997, 416). The rules developed by the provincial congresses, however, were not modeled on the Continental Congress's 1774 rules.

Like the Continental Congress the provincial congresses relied heavily on ad hoc committees. But over time some established standing committees to deal with important issues routinely confronting them. The South Carolina provincial congress used ad hoc committees whose members were elected by ballot, but it also came to employ a standing Committee on Public Accounts. That committee represented a point of continuity with the assembly. In 1776 the congress directed that the current members of the Committee on Public Accounts who had also sat on its Commons House predecessor were to deal with a petition that was left unresolved from the colonial era (*Jour. of the Provincial Cong. of S.C.* 1776, 21, 38. 50).

Other provincial congresses also created standing committees. In its April 1776 session, the North Carolina provincial congress created a Committee on Privileges and Elections and a Committee of Claims (*Jour. of the Proc. of the Provincial Cong. of N.C.* 1776, 6, 14), both of which were deeply rooted in the assembly's history (Cook 1931, 266, 277; Harlow 1917, 259–61). In addition, a Committee of Secrecy, Intelligence, and Observation was established to assist with the war effort. Although these standing committees played a role throughout the congress, it would be a mistake to think they represented well-institutionalized structures; at different points during the session the committees were referred to as the Committee of Claims and military Accounts, and the Committee on Secrecy, War, and Intelligence (*Jour. of the Proc. of the Provincial Cong. of N.C.* 1776, 6, 16). The Georgia provincial congress created a Committee of Intelligence (Candler 1908a, 243). The fourth New Hampshire provincial congress appointed two standing committees, one on safety, the other on supplies (Walker 1905, 29–30, 38), a novel development because their assembly had been notable for not using standing committees (Harlow 1917, 259–61).

Voting rules differed across the provincial congresses. In South Carolina, votes were granted to individual members, and teller votes were recorded (*Jour. of the Provincial Cong. of S.C.* 1776, 1). A different rule, one reminiscent of that used in the Continental Congress, was employed in New Jersey: "*Ordered*, That all votes be taken from the counties respectively, so that the vote of each county be taken as one." This approach was again used the following year (*Exts. from the Jour. of Proc. of the Provincial Cong. of N.J.* 1775, 7; *Min. of the Provincial Cong. and the Coun. of Safety of the St. of N.J.* 1879, 172). The first meeting of the Maryland convention adopted a similar unit rule: "It being moved from the chair to ascertain the manner of dividing upon questions, it was agreed, that on any division each county have one vote, and that all questions be determined by a majority of counties." By 1776, that rule had been dropped and members voted as individuals (*Proc. of the Convs. of the Prov. of Md.* 1836, 5, 310). New York also voted by county, assigning counties no fewer than two votes and no more than four votes (Lincoln 1906, 500; Sparks 1832, 70–71).

Because they were never intended to be permanent structures, the provincial congresses had to plan for their demise. In Massachusetts, the solution adopted was for the government to revert to the charter of 1691, significantly modified by investing executive powers in the Council rather than a governor (Cushing 1896, 17). This system carried through until the state adopted a constitution in 1780. Other states wrote constitutions more quickly. One question they faced was the provincial congress's role in that process. Georgia's provincial congress took no part in writing the state constitution. It dissolved itself, and then elections for delegates to the constitutional convention were held (Candler 1908a, 282). In New York, the provincial congress undertook the task of constitution writing and simply relabeled itself: "Resolved and Ordered, That the style and title of this House be changed from that of 'The Provincial Congress of the Colony of New York,' to that of 'The Convention of the Representatives of the State of New York'" (Lincoln 1906, 487). After writing a constitution the convention disbanded, and elections were held for the new state legislature. New Jersey followed New York's lead a few days later, resolving, "That this house from henceforth, instead of the style and title of the Provincial Congress of *New-Jersey*, do adopt and assume the style and title of the Convention of the State of *New-Jersey*" (*Jour. of the Votes and Proc. of the Conv. of N.J.* 1776, 75). Curiously, New Jersey's constitution had been adopted two weeks earlier before the change in name. Without any name change, the Maryland convention wrote the state constitution while juggling other legislative business (Silver 1895, 52–53). Once finished it too disbanded, and elections were held for the legislature.

Not every provincial congress disappeared with the rise of the new regime. In three states—New Hampshire, South Carolina, and Virginia— the provincial congress transformed itself into the lower house of the new state legislature (Brenaman 1902, 38; Kruman 1997, 22–23). In New

Hampshire, the constitution, which was intended to be temporary but lasted until 1784, was thrown together in one week and put into immediate effect (Noyes 1976, 202). In a broadside the provincial congress announced to the public, "we do Resolve, that this Congress, assume the Name, Power and Authority of a House of Representatives, or Assembly, for the Colony of New-Hampshire. And that said House, then proceed to choose Twelve Persons . . . to be a distinct and separate Branch of the Legislature, by the Name of a Council for this Colony" (*In Congress at Exeter* 1776). Similarly, following the adoption of its constitution the South Carolina provincial congress opted to start calling itself the General Assembly and then elected the upper house from its members. The transition was so seamless that the body continued recording its business in the same journal (*Jour. of the Prov. Cong. of S.C.* 1776, 81–82, 112, 126). As a congress member wrote in a letter, "let me tell you that an Act by the Provincial Congress passed on the 26th by which a form of Government is established, the Congress metamorphosed in the twinkling of an eye into a General Assembly" (Chesnutt 1988, 194).

The State Constitutions and the State Legislatures

Constitutions were written in 11 of the 13 new states—Connecticut and Rhode Island opted to continue under their existing charters, making only slight cosmetic changes to them (Bartlett 1862, 522, 582; Hoadly 1894, 3–4). With the exception of Massachusetts, these constitutions were written with some haste. In Pennsylvania, "The constitution was the hurried and necessarily imperfect work of actual revolution" (Selsam 1936, 183). Typically they were not written by learned scholars enjoying the luxury of time and study. In New York, "Rather, it was a group composed of mostly young men surrounded by the activities of war, in frequent fear of capture, compelled to change their meeting place half a dozen times, who were setting up a government to meet the needs of the immediate situation" (Colvin 1913, 30–31). Similarly, an observer of the events surrounding the writing of the New Hampshire constitution asserted, "The convention was composed chiefly of men who knew nothing of the theory of government, and had never before been concerned in public business" (Belknap 1791, 399).

The outlines of the new legislatures are shown in table 3.1. Save for the fact that for the first time the upper houses became elected in the places where previously they had been appointed, most constitutions produced new legislatures that looked very much like the old legislatures. But which old ones did they mimic? In designing the new state legislatures constitution writers reverted to their colonial models, not to the provincial congresses or Continental Congress. Thus, in New York, "the Assembly was continued substantially as it had existed under the colonial system. . . . The Senate possessed substantially the powers which had been enjoyed by its predecessor, the Colonial Council." In Virginia, "The structure of the new

TABLE 3.1. The Design of the Original 13 State Legislatures

State (date of constitution)	Lower House Name	Approximate Lower House Membership Size[a]	Lower House Term of Office	Upper House Name	Upper House Membership Size[a]	Upper House Term of Office
Connecticut (continued charter)	House of Deputies of Representatives	138	6 months	Council	12	1 year
Rhode Island (continued charter)	House of Deputies	55	6 months	Council or Assistants	12	1 year
New Hampshire (Jan. 5, 1776)	House of Representatives or Assembly	Variable	1 year	Council	12	1 year
South Carolina (March 26, 1776)	General Assembly	199	2 years	Legislative Council	13	2 years
Virginia (June 29, 1776)	House of Delegates	126	1 year	Senate	24	4 years
New Jersey (July 2, 1776)	General Assembly	39	1 year	Legislative Council	13	1 year
Delaware (Sept. 21, 1776)	House of Assembly	21	1 year	The (Legislative) Council	9	3 years
Pennsylvania (Sept. 28, 1776)	House of Representatives	78	1 year	Unicameral		
Maryland (Nov. 8, 1776)	House of Delegates	80	1 year	Senate	15	5 years
North Carolina (Dec. 18, 1776)	House of Commons	70	1 year	Senate	32	1 year
Georgia (Feb. 5, 1777)	House of Assembly	90	1 year	Unicameral		
New York (April 20, 1777)	Assembly	70	1 year	Senate	24	4 years
Massachusetts (June 16, 1780)	House of Representatives	Variable	1 year	Senate	40	1 year

Source: See the initial state constitution for every state (1776 version for South Carolina) but Connecticut and Rhode Island. For Connecticut, see Purcell 1918, 188–89; and *Roll of State Officers and Members of GA of Conn. from 1776 to 1881* 1881, 5–7; for Rhode Island, see Bartlett 1863 and Polishook 1969, 22–23.

[a]Few constitutions provided explicit membership sizes for lower houses. Most have to be calculated using the number of counties in each state (or towns in the case of most New England states) at the time the particular constitution was adopted. The size was variable in several New England state legislatures because towns could opt not to send representatives to a session of the legislature.

House of Delegates differed little from that of the colonial House of Burgesses," while in Maryland, "The House of Delegates was but the continuation of the previous Lower House of Assembly, unchanged" (Beeman 1972, 44; Lincoln 1909, 1; Silver 1895, 52).

There was some debate over alternative forms and structures. In South Carolina, where like New Hampshire the constitution was intended to be temporary, members of the provincial congress argued over the imposition of term limits. A proposal to limit members to two successive terms was ultimately defeated (*Jour. of the Provincial Cong. of S.C.* 1776, 85). Virginia had the advantage of not only a little bit more time to develop its constitution but also a stable of political leaders who were well versed in theories of government. An early proposal by George Mason called for a legislature composed of a "Lower House of Assembly" and an "Upper House of Assembly." He suggested, "Let each House settle its own rules of proceeding" (Rowland 1892, 444–45). Thomas Jefferson elaborated on Mason's draft, calling for a "house of Representatives" and a "house of Senators" (Ford 1893, 13). Jefferson's name for the upper house stuck and became the national standard, but his proposal that its members enjoy nine-year terms was rejected. For the most part it was Mason's design of the legislative branch that was written into Virginia's constitution (Pate 1930, 105–6).

New York debated a number of different legislative schemes. At one point the convention adopted a proposal to give the governor standing as a member of the legislative branch with a right to veto but not originate legislation. The idea appeared to be rooted in New York's early colonial history when the governor sat as a member of the council, voted on bills, and decided ties, all while still retaining a separate veto power as the executive. At the urging of John Jay the convention ultimately reversed its position on this novel structure. The convention did make some stylistic changes to the initial draft, for example, passing an amendment to change the name of the upper house to the senate from the council. For the most part, continuity with the earlier legislative regime prevailed as with the language used in regard to the lower house: "That the General Assembly thus constituted shall chuse their own speaker, be judges of their own members, and proceed in doing business in like manner as the former Assemblies of the Colony of New York did" (Lincoln 1906, 501–5, 515).

Constitutions across the new states made few structural changes to their lower houses, in large part because the assemblies had evolved to be republican institutions (Morey 1893–94, 220). The continuation of bicameralism was generally assumed. Indeed, all five of the governmental plans submitted to the Virginia convention included a bicameral legislature (Pate 1930, 106). In its constitution, which it adopted one week before Pennsylvania adopted its constitution, Delaware shifted to a two-house legislature, thus following the pattern set by those states that had already written constitutions. There is no indication that continuation of a unicameral system was seriously contemplated (*Proc. of the Conv. of the Del. St.* 1776). A single-chamber legislature was adopted only in Pennsylvania, where Benjamin Franklin's arguments in favor of staying with such a system carried the day (Fisher 1897, 80; Selsam 1936, 185–86; Sparks 1844, 408–9; Stourzh 1953, 1108–9), and in Georgia, which used Pennsylvania's constitution as its model (Moran 1895, 53), probably because Buster Gwinnett, who served as a Georgia delegate to the Continental Congress in Philadelphia and was presumably familiar with Pennsylvania's constitution, chaired the committee that wrote it (Cashin 1985, 254–55; Williams 1989, 571). As will be discussed in chapter 5, Pennsylvania's 1776 constitution was the model used in Vermont, which also created a unicameral legislature.

The most noticeable change in the lower houses was a sizable increase in the number of seats compared to their colonial predecessors (Harlow 1917, 63; Main 1966; 1973b, 201–3; Lutz 1999, 65–66). Increased membership size was an effort to make a chamber more representative, and most of the new seats came from previously unrepresented towns and inland areas (Beeman 1985, 231–32; Jackson 1985, 297–98; Main 1966, 404; Zagarii 1987, 42–43). Of course, increases in membership and representativeness had already occurred with the provincial congresses and were simply carried over to the new legislatures.

Other important features of the new state constitutions were grounded in the experience of the colonial assemblies (Squire and Hamm 2005, 29–34). One notable example is the provisions allowing each house to adopt its own rules and to select its own leaders, powers seen today as being of considerable importance in explaining how both Congress and state legislatures have evolved (Stewart 2001, 67–68; Rosenthal 1996, 190). Explicit language allowing the legislature to select its own leaders appeared in nine constitutions, while five specifically authorized the legislature to devise its own rules.

Another significant provision involved the power to originate tax legislation. Over time, assemblies had asserted control over taxation (Greene 1963, 51–71). Most of the new constitutions continued the tradition by granting the lower house exclusive rights to initiate tax bills, with New Hampshire's being the country's first formal statement to that effect. Most states followed New Hampshire's lead. A second question concerned the ability of the upper house to amend tax bills passed by the lower house. A majority of constitutions forbade the upper house from amending tax bills.

Finally, three constitutions gave their governor some form of a veto. The language in Massachusetts's constitution was largely lifted into the U.S. Constitution and gave the executive the power to reject legislation and the legislature the right to override the veto with a supermajority vote of two-thirds. The other two vetoes were very different (Fairlie 1917, 474–75). The South Carolina constitution of 1776 maintained the colonial tradition of an absolute executive veto, one that the legislature could not override. When South Carolina adopted a permanent constitution in 1778, the governor was not granted any veto power. The veto in the New York constitution provided that a council of revision composed of the governor, the chancellor, and the judges on the state supreme court could reject legislation passed by the legislature. In turn, a two-thirds vote of all members in the legislature could override the veto.

Given these continuities, it seems clear that the state legislatures were designed using the assemblies as the model. When these characteristics are stacked up, it also is apparent that the new legislatures were not modeled on the Continental Congress or the provincial congresses. Indeed, as table 3.2 reveals, when examining fundamental legislative rules and structures—number of houses, separation of powers, fundamental voting rules, the power to choose its own leaders and adopt its own rules, control over taxation, and an executive veto—the evolutionary line runs from the colonial assemblies, to the new state legislature, and then to the Congress under the Constitution. The basic characteristics of the Continental and Confederal Congress and the provincial congresses made them very different kinds of legislative bodies. The rules and structures employed by the Confederal Congress led to its failure (Wilson 1999). Those who wrote the U.S. Constitution in 1787 recognized the problems and created a legislature modeled on the more successful state bodies. A decade earlier those who wrote the state constitutions had arrived at similar decisions.

Continuities with the Colonial Assemblies in Rules and Committees

Although the new state legislatures were structurally rooted in their colonial predecessors, they were, in some senses, not fully established governmental bodies. Created in the midst of war, in several cases they existed in

TABLE 3.2. Commonalities in Fundamental Characteristics among the Original American Legislatures

Institution	Separation of Powers	Cameral Status	Fundamental Voting Rule	Explicit Power to Choose Own Leaders and Rules	Origin of Revenue Powers	Executive Veto
State Legislatures	Yes, found in all 13 states	Bicameral in 11 of 13 states	Each member given equal weighted vote	Yes, found in 9 states[a]	Yes, lower house in 7 states[b]	Yes, found in 3 states[c]
Congress under the Constitution	Yes	Bicameral	Each member given equal weighted vote	Yes	Yes, lower house	Yes
Continental Congress and Confederal Congress	No	Unicameral	Each state given equal weighted vote		Fused powers	
Provincial Congresses	No	Unicameral	Varied, in some each county given equal weighted vote or county votes were weighted		Fused powers	

Source: Constitutions in eleven states that wrote them; Squire and Hamm 2005, 31–34.
[a]Language found in DE, GA, MA, MD, NC, NJ, NY, SC (1776 and 1778), and VA.
[b]Language found in DE, MA, MD, NH, NJ, SC (1776 and 1778), and VA.
[c]Language found in MA, NY, and SC (1776).

transitory states for several years. The first meeting of the New York legislature took place in improvised facilities in Kingston; the assembly met in Evert Bogardus's house, while the senate convened in Abraham Van Gaasbeck's home (Lincoln 1906, 573–74). It took nine days for a quorum to be present in the House (*Votes and Proc. of the Asm. of the St. of N.Y.* 1777, 4). A few months later the legislature had to discontinue its session because of the impending arrival of British forces. New York's legislature was not the only one to suffer such indignities. In 1781, British troops forced the Virginia legislature to flee Richmond for Charlottesville and then Charlottesville for Staunton (Dabney 1961). A handful of delegates were captured during the second flight, among them Daniel Boone. Fortunately, Boone and the others were paroled after a day or two on the promise not to take up arms (Wyllie 1960). The South Carolina legislature had to abandon Charleston because of the British, and it was forced to meet under army guard in Jacksonborough, a small town where the Senate assembled in the courthouse and the House in the jail (McCrady 1902, 560–63). In many cases appropriate accommodations were hard to find. Even by 1784, a committee of the Georgia House of Assembly charged with finding the chamber a suitable meeting place reported "That the House at Present in the Temporary Possession of Hezekiah Wade is a fit Place for the Purpose" (Candler 1908b, 422).

Even in turbulent circumstances, however, the continuities with the assemblies were strong. Colonial laws were largely carried forward by the new legislatures (Emery 2006). Customs also carried forward. At the beginning of each legislative session the New York Assembly continued, as it had in colonial times, to inform the governor, "that the House are ready to proceed to business and wait His Excellency's *commands.*" Such deferential form was sustained until 1823 (Lincoln 1906, 576, italics in original). A mace originally purchased in England for the speaker of the Virginia House of Burgesses continued to be used by the speaker of the House of Delegates until 1792. At that point the delegates decided, "It is inconsistant [sic] with the principles of a republican government, that any badge or appendage of Kingly pomp should remain therein," and it was stopped (Bedini 1997, 17). Connecticut continued to use the same opening session rituals it had followed during the colonial era (Swift 1795, 70–71).

From an organizational perspective, evidence for continuity should be located in rules and committees. On the one hand, we might not anticipate continuity because the new governments were revolutionary and might have avoided rules and procedures used by the government against which they were rebelling. In addition, the new state legislatures often met in different locations than the last colonial assemblies had met, creating logistical problems that might have made procedural continuity challenging. For instance, among the first motions passed by the first New Jersey General Assembly was "That the Speaker do employ some Person to bring from *Burlington* the Chest with all the Books and Papers belonging to the Assembly" (*Votes and Proc. of the GA of the St. of N.J.* 1777, 7). On the other hand, it seems reasonable to think that a reliance on existing rules would be expedient.

Certainly, the new state legislatures had very little time to innovate. Thus, on the third day it met, the journal of the new Pennsylvania House of Representatives stated, "The rules of a former house of assembly, respecting the order of the house, being read, were amended, and adopted as amended." These rules were largely the same rules the Pennsylvania House used in 1767 (cf. *Votes and Proc. of the H. of Reps. of the Prov. of Pa.* 1767, 3–4; *Jours. of the H. of Reps. of the Com. of Pa.* 1782, 98–99). The differences in the first 18 rules were largely cosmetic, mostly being changes in grammar and capitalization. An occasional reference to the state was added, and the amount of money a member could be fined was altered. The 1776 rules dropped three from those used in 1767 (the nineteenthly, twentiethly, and twenty-firstly) that dealt with the role of the doorkeeper and with how member absences were to be handled. Overall, few rule changes accompanied the transition to a state legislature from a colonial assembly.

Similarly high levels of continuity were witnessed in Maryland. The first seven rules adopted by the first House of Delegates were the same as the first seven rules adopted by the Maryland Convention, and, therefore, much the same as those used in the Lower House of Assembly in 1773 (*Votes and Proc. of the H. of Dels. of the St. of Md.* 1777, 2). Even the admonition against bringing a sword on the chamber floor was carried over (as it had been since 1666). Only the final two rules differed, the eighth taking account of the return of bicameralism by establishing a procedure where the House would read a bill twice on separate days before sending it to the Senate, and then once again after it returned, and the ninth that required members to take an oath before serving unless prevented from doing so by "religious principles."

Perhaps even more telling was the revival of colonial-era rules in the New Hampshire House. The House pushed aside the rules employed by the provincial congress in favor of returning to the rules used by the assembly. Indeed, the first ten rules were the same in the new state lower house in 1776 as in the colonial lower house in 1775, save for an alteration in the ninth rule to raise the number of members needed for a quorum to 30 from 18, a concession to the increased size of the body's membership (cf. Bouton 1874, 8–9; 1873, 373). The new house added two more rules to the ten it inherited, one saying that a vote would only be valid if passed by a majority of the members present, and the other holding that no new motion could be made until a pending motion was settled.

Arguably, the strongest example of continuity was in Georgia, where the state Commons House of Assembly in 1780 used essentially the same rules as the colonial Commons House of Assembly in 1764. The only change in the first 25 rules was minor; rule V was revised to require ten members for a quorum from the previous eight members. Rule XXVI was new and mandated that members put a motion in writing. All of the other rules used in 1780 that did not appear in the 1764 rules were actually incorporated by assemblies in either 1768 or 1769. Thus, 4 years after statehood, the lower house in Georgia was still operating under rules adopted 12 years before independence (Candler 1907b, 564–66; 1907c, 151–55, 615–16).

Finally, the rules adopted by the new Delaware House of Assembly were largely taken from those used by its colonial predecessor. The assembly had adopted a relatively simple set of five rules in 1769, which it continued to employ through the rest of the colonial era (*Votes and Proc. of the H. of Reps. of the Gov. of Del.* 1770, 193–94; Bushman, Hancock, and Homsey 1986, 150). The state constitutional convention adopted the same set of rules, with one new addition preventing delegates from reading any book or printed papers while the convention was in session. The first meeting of the state House of Assembly then adopted the rules as they had been configured by the constitutional convention (Bushman, Hancock, and Homsey 1986, 206, 234–35). The nine-member upper house, the Council, also quickly adopted a short set of five rules (*Min. of the Coun. of the Del. St.* 1887, 11–12). Given the minuscule size of both chambers it is not surprising that they saw no need for elaborate procedures to guide their actions.

Upper houses were reconfigured, and as elected bodies they had weaker ties to the appointed councils that preceded them in most of the colonies. Not surprisingly, then, they too looked to the assemblies for their rules. In the Virginia Senate, a committee that included George Mason drew in part on rules used by the House of Burgesses. The Senate adopted an elaborate set of 33 rules, the first 18 of which were largely taken from rules compiled by the Burgesses in 1769 (cf. *Jour. of the Sen.* 1776, 8–9; Kennedy 1906, 323–25). The added rules were noteworthy in that they delineated the legislative process in considerable detail, including one rule involving the calling of the previous question. Again, the fact that a rule on calling the previous question immediately appeared in a new legislative chamber in a state that was not riven by faction or party suggests that its existence may well be explained by a need for organizational efficiency rather than by any partisan maneuvering.

What about continuity with standing committees? As discussed in chapter 2, by the time of the revolution, most assemblies had standing committees. Like rules of procedure, standing committees carried over to the new state legislatures from their predecessors. For example, not only did the Georgia state Commons House of Assembly continue the Committee on Privileges and Elections and Committee on Grievances that existed prior to the revolution, they used almost exactly the same language to institute them. Indeed, the changes were limited to grammar and capitalization; there was no substantive change between the language used in 1769 and the language used in 1780 (Candler 1907b, 11–12, 554).

The same was true in Virginia, which had had the most elaborate standing committee system among the assemblies. The House of Delegates in 1777 took the extensive language it used to create six standing committees almost directly from the language the House of Burgesses had used in 1769. The vast majority of alterations were grammatical; a few were made to recognize the change in governmental status, thus the change from "Trade of this Colony" to "trade of this state." The strong ties between the colonial and state houses were, however, initially strained. In 1776 the first House of Delegates chose to create only three of the traditional six standing committees, doing so using only the mellifluous phrase, "Ordered, that a Committee of . . . be revived" (*Jour. of the H. of Dels. of Va.* 1776, 5; *Jour. of the H. of Dels. of Va.* 1777, 4–6; Kennedy 1906, 190–91).

Continuity in committees also was evident in New Jersey. The first sitting of the final session of the assembly established two committees: a Committee of Grievances that met once a week as a special committee of the whole house ("do set every *Wednesday*") and a standing Committee of Publick Accounts (*Votes and Proc. of the GA of the Col. of N.J.*, 1772, 6, 11). Using the virtually the same language, the initial state General Assembly recreated the same two committees (*Votes and Proc. of the GA of the St. of N.J.* 1777, 6–7).

Not every new chamber maintained its existing committee system in all of its parts. In New York, the final assembly had operated with two standing committees—one called Privileges and Elections and the other focused on expiring laws or near-expiring laws—and, as discussed in chapter 2, three grand committees—Grievances, Courts of Justice, and Trade (*Jour. of the Votes and Proc. of the GA of the Col. of N.Y.* 1775, 5). The new state assembly altered its committee structure by dispensing with the grand committees. Both Grievances and Courts of Justice were reconstituted as standing committees with just seven members assigned to each of them. Courts of Justice was granted jurisdiction over expired and near-expiring laws. The standing Committee of Privileges and Elections was continued, but new standing committees were established on revising militia laws and ways and means (*Votes and Proc. of the Asm. of the St. of N.Y.* 1777, 13). In the session held the following year, most of the new structure was maintained, except for the demise of the Committee on Revising Militia Law and the recreation of a separate standing committee devoted to expired and expiring laws (*Votes and Proc. of the Asm. of the St. of N.Y.* 1779, 5).

The evidence here strongly supports a claim that the new state legislatures inherited almost all of their rules and structures directly from their colonial predecessors. In contrast, the provincial congresses were, at best, distant relatives. The next question about the evolutionary process is to assess whether the new legislatures became more complex as they matured.

Legislative Service between 1776 and 1789

Over the course of the sixteenth and seventeenth centuries, legislative turnover declined across most of the assemblies, as noted in chapter 2. As their direct descendants, what was the experience of the new state legislatures? There are good reasons to expect that the attractiveness of legislative service changed, at least initially. After all, the new legislatures were founded during a rebellion, and had the British triumphed, state legislators may well have been tried as traitors. Thus, serving in the new legislatures had a potential downside.

There were other problems that might have made service unattractive. Some legislatures had a permanent meeting location—Maryland always assembled in Annapolis. Others were more nomadic—between 1777 and 1789 North Carolina's legislature met in Fayetteville, Halifax, Hillsboro, New Bern, Smithfield, Tarboro, and Wake Court House (Connor 1913, 453–57). Salaries were not much of an enticement. In 1777, New Hampshire paid its legislators a per diem of six shillings and four pence per mile traveled to the meeting place. They were paid the same sums in 1784, 1785, and 1787 (Bouton 1874, 695; Batchellor 1891, 81, 212, 790).

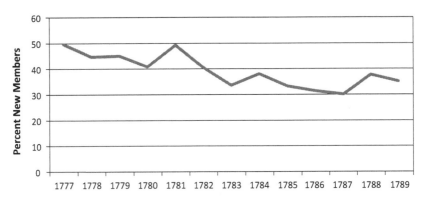

Fig. 3.1. Percentage of new members in the Virginia House, 1777–89

Despite the apparent lack of incentives for service, remarkably, membership turnover was not a significant problem. As figure 3.1 reveals, turnover in the Virginia House of Delegates started at 50 percent in 1777 and then generally declined over the next decade and a half, hitting just 30 percent in 1787.[3] The New York Assembly enjoyed similar stability. During the first decade of its existence only about a third of its members were new each session. Many legislators had considerable experience: about 36 percent served in three or more sessions (Gunn 1980, 278). Such steadiness may have enhanced the prospects for institutional development.

The Continuing Evolution of the New State Legislatures

Between their inception in 1776 and 1777 and the establishment of the Congress under the Constitution in 1789, state legislatures had an unfettered opportunity to develop. They did so largely in response to their own state needs and political contexts. Again, this evolution can be demonstrated through examination of rules and committee structures.

After taking their initial rules from those used by their colonial predecessors, the new state legislatures generally developed increasingly sophisticated and complex rules over the next decade and a half. For example, the comparatively advanced set of 19 rules adopted by the Pennsylvania House in 1776 became an even more developed and complicated set of 25 rules by 1782. Minor changes were made in 1777, 1778, 1780, and 1781, typically grammatical in nature or directed toward altering fine amounts. In 1782, however, substantive changes to the rules were made. Left in were variants of majority voting rules (1782 rule X) and rules governing member behavior (1782 rules XI through XV). Notably, the long-standing cloture rule closing a debate that "proves tedious" also was kept (1782 rule XVI). Weeded out were some of the other rules dealing with decorum (1776 and 1777 rules I, V, VI, and X), several on procedures (1776 and 1777 rules XVI and XVIII), and a few specifying how committees were to be composed (1776 and 1777 rules XII and XIII) (*Jours. of the H. of Reps. of the Com. of Pa.* 1782, 98–99, 160–61, 233, 392, 527–28; *Min. of the First Sess., of the Seventh GA of the Com. of Pa.* 1782, 721–22).

While a few rules added in 1782 restated behavioral expectations (1782 rules I, XVIII, and XIX), the majority more clearly delineated legislative procedure. The order of business was specified (1782 rule II), as was the treatment of petitions, memorials, and reports (1782 rules III and IV). Motions were now required to be "reduced to writing," if requested (1782 rule V). Perhaps most important, rules governing the use of the "previous question" were incorporated (1782 rules VI, VII, and VIII).

As George Mason's letter to George Washington showed, the previous question was familiar to legislators of this era. It was raised in the Pennsylvania conference in 1776 that pushed the colony toward independence: "It was moved, that the previous question be put, viz. Whether this question shall be now put? And it was put accordingly, and carried in the negative" (*Jours. of the H. of Reps. of the Com. of Pa.* 1782, 38). In the Pennsylvania House in 1780 a motion for the previous question was overruled on a bill for the gradual abolition for slavery (*Min. of the First Sess. of the Fourth GA of the Com. of Pa.* 1780, 213). This action might have been the motivation for including an explicit provision covering its use in the rules in 1782.

Committee assignment procedures also changed. Up to 1782, committees were nominated by the speaker (1776 and 1777 rule XII). In 1782, the power to name committees was shifted to the full house (1782 rule XXIV). This change would seem to suggest that power was being decentralized. If so, it was only a short-term trend. Control over committee appointments reverted to the speaker in 1783 using the same language in the 1776 rules, and it remained there in 1784 (*Min. of the First Sess., of the Eighth GA of the Com. of Pa.* 1783, 10; *Min. of the First Sess., of the Ninth GA of the Com. of Pa.* 1784, 27).

The increasingly complex rules developed in Pennsylvania are particularly significant because they, along with those used in Virginia, largely influenced the rules subsequently adopted by the newly created U.S. House and Senate (McConachie 1898, 10). Some minimize the influence of the rules used by the assemblies and state legislatures on the rules used by the Confederal and Constitutional congresses (Jillson and Wilson 1994; Wilson 1999). But it appears that the sophisticated features developed by the national legislature were largely drawn from those first used by the state legislatures.

The rules used in the Maryland House of Delegates also became more complicated over time, although this transformation occurred in fits and starts. As noted earlier, in its first meeting in 1777, the House adopted 9 rules, 7 of which were taken from the rules used by both the colonial assembly and the provincial convention. Those rules were adopted again verbatim in 1778. In 1780, however, the rules were drastically revised. Almost all of the rules used by the earlier houses were dispensed with. The prohibition against bringing a sword on the chamber floor, however, was kept (1780 rule 24). In place of the old rules, the House adopted a set of 32 rules. Among the new rules were two governing the use of the previous question (rules 11 and 13). Others specified the legislative process in considerable detail. Over the next few years, these rules were only tinkered with, just small bits of language added and dropped without changing their substance. The admonition against bringing a sword on the floor was finally omitted in 1785. By 1789 the House was using a set of 30 rules, virtually identical to those first devised in 1780 (*Votes and Proc. of the H. of Dels. of the St. of Md.* 1778, 2; *Votes and Proc. of the H. of Dels. of the St. of Md.* 1781, 3–4; *Votes and Proc. of the H. of Dels. of the St. of Maryland* 1786, 2–3; *Votes and Proc. of the H. of Dels. of the St. of Md.* 1790, 2–3).

Further evidence of increased rules complexity is found in New Hampshire. As noted earlier, the initial New Hampshire House adopted a reasonably simple set of 12 rules in 1776, mostly focused on decorum. By 1784, the House operated under a more detailed set of 19 rules. Some rules carried over, but those added were directed toward resolving questions about the handling of motions and the process by which committees were appointed. A twentieth rule allowing the house to enforce other rules was added in 1786. By 1789 the rules had been whittled to 15, but those pertaining to the handling of motions were made considerably more detailed. Indeed, although the number of rules declined, those that were kept were longer and more involved (Batchellor 1891, 70–73, 619–21; 1892, 591–92).

Not every state legislature came to adopt sophisticated sets of rules during this time period. In 1784, the Delaware House put in place a relatively simple set of six rules mostly focused on protocol. Those rules were readopted in 1785. The next year a seventh rule was added, requiring the reading of the previous day's minutes prior to the start of legislative business each morning. This set of seven rules was then readopted in 1787, 1788, and 1789. Thus the Delaware rules became only trivially more complex (*Votes and Proc. of the H. of Asm. of the Del. St.* 1785, 4; *Votes and Proc. of the H. of Asm. of the Del. St.* 1786, 4; *Votes and Proc. of the H. of Asm. of the Del. St., At a Sess* 1786, 4; *Votes and Proc. of the H. of Asm. of the Del. St.* 1787, 2; *Votes and Proc. of the H. of Asm of the Del. St.* 1788, 4; *Votes and Proc. of the H. of Asm. of the Del. St.* 1789, 4). Similarly, the rules in the North Carolina House of Commons changed remarkably little between 1778 and 1789; in both years a simple set of thirteen rules focused almost exclusively on parliamentary etiquette was employed. The major difference was that in 1789 the use of teller voting was specified (*Jour. of the H. of Commons* 1778, 2; *Jour. of the H. of Commons* 1790, 2).

What drove the increase in the complexity of legislative rules? Examinations of modern American legislatures emphasize partisan motivations, generally finding that majority parties write rules to meet their needs. Did parties drive the increasingly complex rules in this era, particularly in regard to the adoption of previous question rules? It does not appear that they did. In the period after independence political parties in the states were, at best, embryonic (Hall 1972; Risjord and DenBoer 1974). Some voting blocs appeared in state legislatures prior to 1789. Usually, but not always, these were organized along a split between urban and cosmopolitan legislators and their rural and localist colleagues (Main 1973b). Conceivably, these voting blocs could have devised legislative rules to advance their interests. If so, it is not obvious why lawmakers in Pennsylvania and Maryland were more vigorous in pursuing such rules changes than were their counterparts in Delaware and North Carolina.

Alternatively, rules may be becoming increasingly complex because legislatures as organizations require them in order to facilitate decision making. As more decisions are put before them legislatures require rules that assist the members in sorting among possible alternatives. More decisions to be made and more conflict over making those decisions may have driven the early state legislatures to revise their rules accordingly.

Additional evidence of increased complexity is provided by an examination of standing committee systems in the state legislatures. By 1770, standing committees had been established by a majority of the assemblies. But, "This period between 1776 and 1790 rather than before is the time when the standing committees really came into extensive use" (Harlow 1917, 78). By 1789, 10 of the 13 original state legislatures used at least a few standing committees, as shown in table 3.3. A standing committee was usually, but not always, identified by a specific name. More important, a standing committee was instituted for an extended period, as in Delaware where the language stated, "be a Committee of Grievances for the ensuing year" (*Votes and Proc. of the H. of Asm. of the Del. St.* 1788, 4). Finally, a standing committee was typically assigned bills at multiple points in time or designated to be the recipient of all legislation on a particular topic.

The greatest increase in standing committees was in Massachusetts, which had eight in 1789 compared with only two in 1775. Consequently, the new statehouse that opened in 1798 had "twenty smaller [rooms], plainly finished for the use of committees" (*Newburyport Herald* 1798). Virginia, which had six standing committees in 1777, used only five in 1789. The colonial-era Committee on Trade was dropped in 1783 and replaced with a Committee of Commerce. Eventually, that committee also disappeared (Harlow 1917, 76). The other state legislatures with standing committees generally had three or four of them, typically committees on accounts, elections and privileges, grievances, and courts of justice (with Maryland combining the last two into a single committee). Many of these committees had colonial-era predecessors. Several of the committees in 1789, however, were novel, suggesting that state legislatures were responding to different policy demands being made on them. Examples along these lines were committees dealing with agriculture and manufactures in Massachusetts, Indian affairs in North Carolina, and public roads, bridges, causeways, and ferries in South Carolina.

Perhaps the most important development was the role standing committees took in the legislative process. By 1789, standing committees in Massachusetts, New York, North Carolina, Pennsylvania, South Carolina, and Virginia were drafting and amending legislation (Harlow 1917, 77). Thus, they had evolved to play a central role in lawmaking. During the colonial era only standing committees in Virginia and to a lesser extent in Pennsylvania and South Carolina had exercised similar powers.

Only three state legislatures were without standing committees in 1789—Connecticut, New Hampshire, and Rhode Island—each of which continued to rely exclusively on ad hoc committees. New Hampshire, however, had at least dabbled with standing committees. In 1785, the House had created one standing committee "to consider all Petitions from sick and wounded officers & soldiers and report thereon" and another "to

TABLE 3.3. Standing Committees in the Original State Legislatures, 1789

State	Standing Committees
Connecticut	None
Delaware	Elections and Privileges
	Grievances
Georgia[a]	Priviledges and Elections
	Standing Committee of Accounts
	Standing Committee on Petitions
Maryland	Elections
	Grievances and Courts of Justice
Massachusetts	Accounts
	Applications for the Incorporation of Towns
	Applications for New Trials
	Finance
	Petitions for the Abatement of Taxes
	Petitions for the Encouragement of Agriculture and Manufactures
	Petitions for Naturalization
	Petitions for the Sale of Real Estate
New Hampshire	None
New Jersey	Accounts of the Treasurer
	Public Accounts
New York[b]	Courts of Justice
	Grievances
	Privileges and Elections
	Ways and Means
North Carolina	Claims
	Indian Affairs
	Propositions and Grievances
	Public Revenue
Pennsylvania	Accounts
	Claims
	Ways and Means
Rhode Island	None
South Carolina[c]	Accounts
	Courts of Justice
	Privileges and Elections
	Public Roads, Bridges, Causeways, and Ferries
	Religion
	Ways and Means
Virginia	Claims
	Courts of Justice
	Privileges and Elections
	Propositions and Grievances
	Religion

Source: Candler 1908b, 421; Harlow 1917, 78; *Jour. of the Asm. of the St. of N.Y.* 1789, 7; *Jour. of the H. of Commons* 1790, 2, 6; *Jour. of the H. of Dels. of the Com. of Va.* 1789, 3–4; *Min. of the First Sess. of the Fourteenth GA of the Com. of Pa.* 1789, 8–9; *Votes and Proc. of the Fourteenth GA of the St. of N.J.* 1789, 6–7; *Votes and Proc. of the H. of Asm. of the Del. St.* 1789, 4; *Votes and Proc. of the H. of Dels. of the St. of Md.* 1790, 2.

[a]The committees for Georgia are from 1784.

[b]A committee to examine expired or soon to expire laws also was appointed.

[c]The committees for South Carolina are for 1791 and taken from Harlow 1917.

consider of the Petition of the Selectmen of Cornish and all similar matters and report thereon." In 1789 the House voted down a proposal to create a committee "to whom shall be referred every Petition addressed to the Legislature of a private nature" (Batchellor 1891, 344–46; 1892, 672). It appears that the organizational advantages of standing committees were becoming widely recognized if not universally instituted.

Finally, how did the young state legislatures actually operate? They maintained schedules similar to those used during the colonial era. For instance, by law the Connecticut House had to meet at eight in the morning during the May session in Hartford and at nine during the October session in New Haven (*Acts and Laws of the St. of Conn.* 1784, 28). Floor behavior also was familiar. A German visitor to the Pennsylvania Assembly in the mid-1780s provides information on how that chamber functioned. Noting one change, that "The doors are open to everybody," the visitor reported that the speaker sat in the front of the chamber, "at a table, in a rather high chair." The speaker controlled the agenda, and members had to direct their comments to him. Legislators' behavior generated more comment: "The members sit in chairs at both sides of the [speaker's] table . . . but seldom quietly, and in all manner of postures; some are going, some standing, and the more part seem pretty indifferent as to what is being said." When the speaker called for a vote, "those in the affirmative rise, and those in the negative remain sitting." Finally, the visitor noticed that "the members of German descent (if as is sometimes the case, from a lack of thorough readiness in the English language they . . . do not properly grasp the matter under discussion . . .) are excused for sitting doubtful until they see whether the greater number sits or stands." At that point, the ethnic German members "do the same so as always to keep with the largest side" (Schoepf 1911, 382–83).

There were problems integrating "backwoodsmen" into the new legislatures. When Daniel Boone was elected to represent the far west Fayette County (now in Kentucky) in the Virginia House in 1781, he was named to the Propositions and Grievances Committee and several ad hoc committees. But shortly thereafter he was among several Delegates who failed to show, and the "serjeant at arms" was ordered to take him into custody (*Jour. of the H. of Dels. of the Com. of Va.* 1828, 7, 20, 28, 40, 46, 61).[4] Boone's biographers speculate that he was absent because he preferred hunting to legislating (Faragher 1992, 213–14; Morgan 2007, 304). But eventually frontier representatives acclimated. Indeed, Boone appeared to enjoy legislative life during his final term in 1791 (Morgan 2007, 377).

Conclusions

By 1789 state legislatures were reasonably well-developed institutions, ones that are, perhaps, surprisingly similar to their current counterparts. The first state legislatures took little, if anything, from the Continental Congress or the provincial congresses. Instead, they emerged from their colonial predecessors, lifting their initial rules and structures almost directly from them. Relatively quickly, they adopted longer and more sophisticated rules and created more standing committees to deal with a wider range of routine policy matters before them.

The different political context in which the state legislatures operated compared to their colonial predecessors prompted some noticeable changes. Prevailing notions about parliamentary privilege, for example, evolved in response to changing circumstances. Because state legislators were not wielding privilege as a shield against the Crown, by 1789 the reach of such claims was greatly constrained (Stevens 1989). More generally, during the 13 years after independence, state legislatures changed as organizations in response to a new set of demands being made on them.

4 · The Missing Link: Territorial Legislatures

There is a gap in our understanding of American legislative evolution. As noted in chapter 1, most, but not all, state legislatures after the original 13 were preceded by territorial legislatures. In this chapter I point to these bodies as a missing link in the storyline of American legislative evolution. In terms of organization, the territorial legislatures led directly to their successor state legislatures. This is an important observation because the territorial legislatures existed in frontier contexts that were different from the ones in which the original state legislatures had developed.

The Development of Territorial Legislatures

The Confederal Congress enjoyed one (and only one) domestic policy success: it developed and passed the Northwest Ordinance of 1787, which created a process for bringing new states into the Union. That procedure was essentially enshrined in law by Congress in 1789 and employed in the development of most of the states that were subsequently added to the original 13. As the process was originally conceived, new territories would go through several governing stages before they were admitted as states. The initial or district stage placed power in the hands of a governor and three judges, all appointed by the U.S. president and confirmed by the U.S. Senate. Collectively, the governor and judges exercised legislative power, although they were limited to adopting laws used in the original states. At first there were questions about whether territories had to use the exact laws in place in one or more of the states, or if they could take existing laws and mold them to meet local circumstances. It also was unclear if original states meant only the first 13 or any existing state. Finally, there was uncertainty over whether the governor was part of the legislative process along with the judges or was supposed only to react to what they proposed, and whether a majority of judges could constitute a quorum sufficient to pass a law in the absence of the governor. These procedural kinks were worked out relatively quickly. The governor sat with the judges as a legislature, and they took laws from the existing states and fit them to territorial circumstances (Eblen 1968, 88–93). The legislative process developed in the seven territories where district stage governments existed (Northwest, Southwest, Mississippi, Indiana, Michigan, Missouri, and Illinois) so that the governor and judges met annually for a few days or a few weeks to adopt laws (Eblen 1968, 88–89; Philbrick 1930, cccc–cccclvi). Although the governors and judges were active lawmakers (Galbreath 1921; Jenks 1918; Pease 1925; Philbrick 1930), it is worth noting that elected territorial legislatures established in the second governing stage rewrote most of the laws adopted during the district stage (Eblen 1968, 108–9).

Second-Stage Legislatures

Although the process Congress created set specific population thresholds before a district-stage government could be replaced by a second-stage government, it never held territories to those standards. Territories with first-stage governments gained the right to move to the second stage when sufficient political pressure in favor of doing so was brought to bear on Congress (Eblen 1968, 53). With the second stage, legislative power was taken from the governor and judges and vested in a separate and distinct legislature. All seven of the territories created with first-stage governments eventually moved on to second-stage governments. Beginning in 1838 with the creation of the Wisconsin Territory Congress ceased to establish first-stage governments in new territories, and second-stage governments became the starting point.

The legislatures created under second-stage territorial governments changed in two significant ways over time, as table 4.1 demonstrates. In six early territories (Northwest, Southwest, Mississippi, Indiana, Missouri, and Alabama) bicameral legislatures were created by Congress, but only the lower house—called the House of Representatives in every territory—was elected. The upper house—always called the Council or Legislative Council except in Florida, Hawaii, and Alaska where it was the Senate—was, in these early territories, appointed by the U.S. president from a list of candidates nominated by the territorial lower house or, in the case of Michigan, by the voters. In practice, the president often informally dele-

TABLE 4.1. Territorial Legislatures in the United States

Territory (subsequent state name if different)	Years: Territory Established	Years: Territorial Legislature Met	Upper House Size[a]	How Composed	First Territorial Legislature: Lower House Size	How Composed	Initial Meeting Place
Northwest[b] (Ohio)	1788	1799–1801	5	APNH	22	E	Cincinnati, a house
Southwest[b] (Tennessee)	1790	1794–95	5	APNH	11	E	Knoxville, courthouse
Mississippi[b]	1798	1800–1817	5	APNH	9	E	Natchez, Government House
Indiana[b]	1800	1805–16	5	APNH until 1809, then E	7	E	Vincennes, two-room house of Antoine Marchal
Orleans (Louisiana)	1804	1804–05	13	APNH	Unicameral in 1805	E	New Orleans, Principal[c]
		1805–11	5	APNH	25 E from 1806 to 1811		New Orleans, hotel de ville[c]
Michigan[b]	1805	1824–35	9	APNV until 1826, then 13 E	Unicameral		Detroit, Council House
Missouri[b]	1812	1812–20	9	APNH until 1816, then E	13	E	St. Louis, large stone house of Joseph Robidoux[d]
Illinois[b]	1809	1812–18	5	E	7	E	Kaskaskia, two-story building
Alabama	1817	1818	6	APNH	12	E	St. Stephens, Douglass Hotel
Arkansas	1819	1820–35	5	E	9	E	Post of Arkansas, R. Crittenden's house
Florida	1822	1822–45	13	APNH until 1826, then E	Unicameral until 1838; then House 16 E		Pensacola, three-story home of Juan de la Rua
Wisconsin	1836	1836–48	13	E	26	E	Belmont, two-story wood frame building
Iowa	1838	1838–46	13	E	26	E	Burlington, Zion Church
Oregon	1848	1849–59	9	E	18	E	Oregon City, First Methodist Church
Minnesota	1849	1849–57	9	E	18	E	St. Paul, Central House Hotel
New Mexico	1850	1851–1909	13	E	26	E	Santa Fe, Palace of the Governors
Utah	1850	1851–95	13	E	26	E	Great Salt Lake City, Council House

Washington	1853	1854–88	9	E	20	E	Olympia, second floor of a dry goods store
Nebraska	1854	1855–67	13	E	26	E	Omaha, two-story brick building
Kansas	1854	1855–61	13	E	26	E	Pawnee, two-story stone building
Colorado	1861	1861–76	9	E	13	E	Denver, House in rented small frame building, Council in separate building
Nevada	1861	1861–64	9	E	15	E	Carson City, Abraham Curry's Warm Springs Hotel
Dakota (South Dakota; North Dakota)	1861	1862–89	9	E	13	E	Yankton, private residence
Arizona	1863	1864–1909	9	E	18	E	Prescott, two-room log building
Idaho	1863	1863–89	7	E	11	E	Lewiston, Little Log School house
Montana	1864	1864–89	7	E	13	E	Bannack, House in two-story log structure, Council in one-story residence
Wyoming	1868	1869–90	9	E	13	E	Cheyenne, House and Council met in separate buildings a block apart
Oklahoma	1890	1890–1905	13	E	26	E	Guthrie, rented building
Hawaii	1898	1901–59	15	E	30	E	Honolulu, Iolani Palace
Alaska	1912	1913–58	8	E	16	E	Juneau, two floors of Elks Building

Source: Generally, the Organic Acts creating the various territories (U.S. Senate 1900) and Clarence Edwin Carter, ed., *The Territorial Papers of the United States* (Washington, DC: U.S. Government Printing Office, 1934–): See Carter 1936, 309; 1937, 96, 643; 1938, 421; 1949, 554–55; 1950, 252–53, 644; 1952, 305, 486; 1956, 391; 1958, 619. Additional sources include *Acts Passed at the First Sess. of the Leg. Coun. of the Terr. of Orleans* 1805; *Acts, Resolutions, and Memorials, Passed by the First Annual, and Special Sessions, of the LA, of the Terr. of Utah* 1852, 210; Barns 1877, 189; Billon 1888, 44; Blackmar 1904, 2420; Childs 1859, 187; Darcy 2005; Eblen 1968; Fortier 1904, 36; Fowell 1956, 253; Gaston 1912, 426; Graham 1888, 309–10; Hall 1904, 388–89; Hatfield 1976, 136; Hill 1915, 181–82; *History of Tennessee* 1887, 207; Housman 1935, 380; Hudson 1904, 45–46; *Jour. of the First Sess. of the LA of Okla. Terr.* 1890, 3; *Jour. of the H. of Reps. of the Terr. of the US, North-west of the River Ohio at the First sess. of the GA* 1799, 205; *Jour. of the Proc. of the H. of Reps. of the USA, South of the River Ohio* [1794], 1852, 14, 40; Larson 1968; Larson 1978, 72–73; Litter 1929, 95–96; *Off. Directory and Legislative Man. of the St. of Mich.* 1887, 233–35; Martin 1944, 35–36; Morris and Maguire 1978, 31; Rowland 1905, 284–85; Scharf 1883, 558; Shoemaker 1914, 27; Spence 1975, 186–87; Spicer 1927, 74; Thwaites 1906, 257; Tripp and Worst 1904, 226–27; Twain [1872] 1996, 187–88.

Note: APNH = appointed by president of the United States from a list of candidates nominated by voters in territory; E = elected by voters; APNV = appointed by president of the United States from list of candidates nominated by territorial House of Representatives; APNV = appointed by president of the United States from a list of candidates nominated by the Council or Legislative Council acting collectively as the legislature.

[a] The upper house was called the Council or Legislative Council except in Florida (after it became bicameral), Hawaii, and Alaska, where it was called the Senate. In every territory that had one, the lower house was called the House of Representatives.

[b] Territory had initial district stage government, with governor and three judges collectively acting as the legislature.

[c] The Principal and the hotel de ville were the same facility, the city hall (Bradley 2002, 106).

[d] One source (Billon 1888, 44) says the first meeting was held in the home of Pierre Chouteau, Sr.

gated power to choose the Council to the governor, who was, of course, also a presidential appointee. An appointed upper house was not chosen to emulate the American colonial experience under British rule but rather promoted, primarily by James Monroe, as a method to enhance congressional control over the territories (Berkhofer 1972, 256).

Pressure built within the territories, however, for elected representatives. A petition to Congress from residents of Orleans Territory argued, "Your petitioners are fully impressed with the idea that legislative powers are never better, nor more satisfactorily exercised than when committed to those persons who are elected for that purpose by the people themselves, whose conduct must be regulated by those very laws thus made" (*Missouri Gazette* 1808). Similar sentiments also surfaced in Florida, as demonstrated by a call for voters to make good selections in the territory's first election: "Congress . . . to gratify what was then thought to be the general wish of the people of this Territory; and with a view of making an experiment which might determine how far the inhabitants were capable of making a suitable selection of persons to frame laws conducive to the welfare and prosperity of the country, directed that the members of the Legislature should be elected by the people" (*East Florida Herald* 1826). Similar requests were made by other early territories (e.g., Rowland 1905, 185).

These appeals proved powerful, and in Indiana, Missouri, Florida, and Michigan the council eventually became an elective office; the other territories with appointed councils became states (with elected upper houses) before that change could take place. When Illinois was carved out of Indiana, it was immediately given the right to elect its upper house, something Indiana had had to fight to achieve. Every territory created from Wisconsin through Alaska was established with an elected upper house (Eblen 1968, 157–59).

The second significant change involved the number of houses in territorial legislatures. Unicameral legislatures were created in three territories: Orleans, Florida, and Michigan. A 13-member appointed Legislative Council initially constituted the Orleans territorial legislature, but after only a single year public pressure on Congress and a modification in President Jefferson's ideas on institutional design produced a change to a bicameral system with a 5-member appointed upper house and a 25-member popularly elected lower house. Both Florida and Michigan had unicameral territorial legislatures for much longer periods. Congress opted for a single chamber for these territories because both were poor, and it was thought that their residents would be unable to finance two houses. Over time public pressure for a bicameral system mounted in Florida, something that was achieved after 16 years (Morris and Maguire 1980). Although Michigan also had the option to pursue a change to a bicameral legislature, the issue was broached only once and unsuccessfully, probably because voters were content with the performance of the Council and because they did not wish to pay the taxes necessary to support an additional house (Eblen 1968, 160; Sherer 1979, 177). Concerns over the costs of territorial legislatures were not confined to Florida and Michigan. A Wisconsin newspaper wondered, "The appropriation to defray the expense of the next session of the Territorial Legislature is $17,250. Will the next session of the Legislature do Wisconsin as much good as the above amount would do, if expended in improving roads?" (*Milwaukee Sentinel* 1844).

By the time Wisconsin Territory was created, Congress had greatly standardized the structure of territorial governments. From that point on the legislatures were all created as bicameral bodies, although there was some discussion about making Utah's territorial legislature an appointed unicameral body as a way of preventing polygamous forces from taking political control of the territory (Eblen 1968, 160). Thought was also given to making Alaska's territorial legislature unicameral; indeed the U.S. Senate passed legislation to do so, but the House refused to go along with the plan (Harrison 1992, 36–37; Spicer 1927, 75).

One thing that did not change over time was that in the overall governing scheme, territorial legislatures were subordinate to Congress. Congress retained the right to overturn any decision made by a territorial legislature, power occasionally exercised through the territorial era (e.g., *NYT* 1878b), even to the point of declaring all the laws passed by the second and third Montana territorial legislatures to be null and void (Jackson 1943). One contentious issue between the early territories and the federal government concerned the financing of territorial government. Starting with Florida Territory, Congress covered the costs of paying territorial lawmakers' per diems. Over time this decision had consequences for territorial legislatures because Congress subsequently passed measures that required biennial sessions rather than annual sessions and limited membership sizes, sometimes to the consternation of territorial residents who clamored for greater representation (Spence 1975, 186–87). Biennial sessions and fewer legislators saved the federal treasury money.

Congress gained further control over territorial legislatures when it passed the Harrison Act in 1886. The measure was written largely in response to abuses by the Arizona territorial legislature (Lyon 1984). Arizona's thirteenth territorial legislature, referred to at the time as the "thieving, bloody, fighting Thirteenth," became notorious for, among other flaws, a spending binge (Rice 1928, 80). It increased the territory's bonded debt to $622,944 from $350,000, approved $19,967 for printing when Congress had set the maximum at $4,000, and reimbursed members $1,141 above the established federal limits. In addition, the 36 legislators hired 51 clerks, 4 pages, and 2 janitors (Lyon 1984, 212), a large number of employees at a time when Congress itself had very little in the way of support staff. Arizona's need for that level of assistance was doubtful. At one point during the session several committee clerks were "directed to report to the Territorial Librarian, for the purpose of assisting in arranging the books in the library" (*Jours. of the Thirteenth LA of the Terr. of Ariz.* 1885, 289). And to make matters worse, many of the hires were suspect. A councilor appointed his wife to be the clerk of the committee he chaired. Reportedly, she got paid $360 for 60 days work and "never wrote a line during the session" (*Arizona Champion* 1885b). Another reporter noted that "a few members were shameful in the appointment of unsavory females, who performed no duties other than to cater to their owners and sign the vouchers" (Rice 1928, 82). Other territories took notice of Arizona's unrestrained behavior. Wyoming's governor sent his territory's lawmakers a U.S. Interior Department report listing the excesses, leading that legislature to publicly tout the fact that it "has no committee clerks and no unnecessary officials" (*Daily Tombstone Epitaph* 1886).

Congress responded by limiting the sorts of decisions territorial legislatures could make (Lyon 1984, 215–16). It prohibited them from laying out roads or highways, locating county seats, licensing toll bridges or ferries, or authorizing private railroads. Congress also decided that territorial government debts could not exceed 1 percent of a territory's taxable assets. This standard, which at the time Arizona clearly exceeded as did Dakota and New Mexico, greatly constrained territorial legislatures. Indeed, it is argued that the burden it placed on territorial finances delayed Arizona statehood by a number of years (Lyon 1984).

The Frontier Context of the Territorial Legislatures

Given that territorial legislatures were governmental institutions established in almost every case at the edge of the frontier, there are several obvious questions about the legislators who served in them. First; what sort of people were territorial lawmakers? Second, how long did they serve? Finally, what did they do in office? Answers to these questions require an examination of travel, facilities, pay, and legislative life.

Who Served in Territorial Legislatures?

Obviously, territorial legislatures were populated for the most part by pioneers. Consequently, it is not surprising that during their early sessions most legislatures were populated by young men. The average age in the first Washington territorial legislature was only 28 years old (Brazier 2000, 3); in the first Arizona territorial legislature the figure was 37 years old.[1] A majority of the members of the initial Iowa territorial legislature were under 28 years old (Parvin 1900, 22). One member of the first Florida Council, a nephew of President Madison, was only 19 when he was appointed (Morris and Maguire 1978, 26). Even legislative leaders could be young: the speaker of the initial Wisconsin territorial House was 24 years old (*Sheboygan Press* 1936).

There were age qualifications enforced in the territories; even if not expressly stated, implicitly they were set at 21, the age at which the franchise was granted. Not every potential lawmaker was old enough. In 1853 it was reported that the New Mexico territorial legislature refused to seat a member because he was too young. Unfortunately, his age was not given (*NYDT* 1853). An 18-year-old was nominated for the Kansas Council but had to decline because he was not yet of legal age (Ballard 1908, 241). A 20-year-old, Lafe Nuckolls, served in the initial Nebraska Council, but only because, as another member recalled, "Some one, pending the arrival of Judge F. to swear us in, asked him his age. Lafe answered at once: 'Ask my constituents, as Henry Clay once said'" (Bennet 1898, 90).[2]

A young membership impacted legislative behavior. Only 2 of the 13 members of the first Dakota House were over 35 years old; indeed, the second member to serve as speaker during the session was only 22 years old. Perhaps not surprisingly, "the [Dakota] sessions often resembled a college fraternity meeting." For instance, the bachelor-dominated House jokingly referred a divorce petition to the Committee on Internal Improvements (Lamar 1956, 78–79, 93). Similar behavior surfaced in other chambers dominated by the young. In the waning hours of the first Washington territorial legislature, lawmakers spent their time passing fanciful bills for fun, among them one to regulate poker games (Meany 1909, 163). The initial Montana Council passed an unsolicited measure giving a local rancher the right to use "No. 84" as his brand because he was a native of England and pronounced the number as "*highty-four*," which the lawmakers found amusing. The recipient of the new brand was present when the measure passed, and delighted by it, he jumped to his feet and said, "Come boys, adjourn! Come let's liquor." Accordingly, "The motion was put and declared carried, the whole crowd voting, 'Aye'" (Thompson 2004, 208–9). After the Wisconsin territorial House in a fit of pique passed a memorial to Congress complaining that the local federal marshal had failed to disburse "one solitary cent," Council members tweaked their lower-house colleagues by amending the measure to say "one solitary red cent." Neither the House nor the Council would relent on the wording, and the memorial never got sent (Strong 1870, 32). Fortunately, as territorial legislatures matured, so did their members; 23 years after the first Washington territorial legislature lawmakers averaged 43 years of age (Brazier 2000, 26), and for the most part the adolescent high jinks disappeared.

Member occupations were largely dictated by a territory's economic basis. Thus, about two-thirds of the members of the first Iowa territorial legislature were farmers (Parvin 1900, 20); while in Arizona the modal category was miner (Wagoner 1970, 43). Some territorial legislatures had unusual occupations represented in them. In the first New Mexico territorial legislature seven members were Catholic priests, one of whom was elected president of the Council (Twitchell 1912, 291). At least a few lawyers, however, appeared in every territorial legislature, and their training often proved useful in establishing legislative procedures. In the initial Northwest territorial legislature, five members were attorneys, one of whom, a graduate of Princeton, was primarily responsible for compiling the rules under which the Council operated (Burnet 1847, 290–97, 311; Graham 1888, 312). Indeed, although typically few in number lawyers were often given leadership positions. The first president of the Washington Council (Warren 1988) and the presiding officers of both chambers of the initial Wisconsin Territorial Legislature (*Sheboygan Press* 1936) were lawyers.

Newly settled territories were, save for New Mexico and Hawaii, served by lawmakers who had been born outside the territory. None of the 27 members of the first territorial legislature in Minnesota had been born there. The states of New York, Pennsylvania, and Vermont each contributed three members, but five Canadian natives constituted the plurality (Flandrau 1900, 58–59). Of the 39 members of the first Kansas territorial legislature, only one had been born in the territory; Kentucky natives constituted the plurality. The median time having lived in the territory for the members of the first Kansas House was only a single year.[3] The vast majority of lawmakers had migrated to the territory after living in Missouri, a fact that, as discussed in chapter 5, had implications for territorial politics on the critical issue of slavery. The dearth of native-born members barely changed if at all as territories grew older. In 1879—25 years after its first meeting—no Washington lawmakers had been born in the territory. Instead, they hailed from 14 different states, Maine being the leader with five members, and from Denmark, Germany, Ireland, and Scotland (Brazier 2000, 28). Legislators at this point in time were, however, longtime territory residents, having lived in Washington for a median of 18 years.[4]

A number of the territories were acquired by the U.S. government from other countries, which created citizenship issues that had to be resolved. Many territorial inhabitants only acquired American citizenship when the territory was integrated into the United States. Given their numbers, it is not surprising that some of these new Americans participated in territorial politics. The heavy French presence in Orleans Territory led President Jefferson to appoint men with bilingual language skills to the initial Council. The president's decision the following year to push for second-stage government with an elected assembly was motivated in part by his desire to reduce French influence (Peterson 1965, 48–50). Still, the official volumes containing the laws passed by the Orleans legislature alternated pages in English with pages in French (*Acts Passed at the First Sess. of the First Leg. of the Terr. of Orleans* 1807; *Acts Passed at the Second Sess. of the First Leg of the Terr. of Orleans* 1807; *Acts Passed at the First Sess. of the Second Leg. of the Terr. of Orleans* 1808; *Acts Passed at the Second Sess. of the Second Leg. of the Terr. of Orleans* 1809; *Acts Passed at the First Sess. of the Third Leg. of the Terr. of Orleans* 1810; *Acts Passed at the Second Sess. of the Third Leg. of the Terr. of Orleans* 1811). The use of French in Louisiana legislative life actually continued well into the nineteenth century. Article 104 of the 1845 constitution stated that "members may address either house in the French or English language" and required the Senate secretary and the House clerk to be conversant in both. The same requirements appeared in Article 101 of the state's 1852 constitution.

The Orleans experience was not unusual. One member elected to the first Mississippi territorial legislature had to relinquish a pension he received from the British government before he could assume his seat (Rowland 1905, 308). Several former Spaniards served in the early Florida Council, including one who had recently been a colonel in the Spanish Army (Martin 1944, 35; Morris and Maguire 1978). These members were appointed because they were "looked up to by the Spanish population as their first men" (Morris and Maguire 1978, 29). The New Mexico territorial legislature was so dominated by naturalized Mexicans that for many years it conducted legislative business in Spanish and provided interpreters for the minority of its members who spoke only English (Davis 1857, 254–55; *NYT* 1873a).[5] The cost of interpreters was not covered by the federal government, so the territory had to pay (*Acts of the LA of the Terr. of N.M.* 1874, 126). In 1878 the territorial governor complained about the expenditure. In his legislative address he argued, "Interpreting for the Legislature is a useless and disgusting expense, and a disgrace to the Territory. After thirty years occupation of the country, there is no man in it of sufficient intelligence to be elected to the Legislature who does not understand both languages" (*Denver Daily Tribune* 1878). Yet, both chambers were still appointing interpreters as late as 1899 (*H. Jour.* 1899, 4). One of the first acts of the new Colorado territorial House was to appoint a Spanish interpreter and to request 12 copies of the rules "be printed in the Castillian language, for the use of the members from New Mexico" (*Daily Colorado Republican* 1861c). Again, the legislature continued this approach in subsequent sessions even though "The [federal Treasury] Department have declined paying an interpreter for our Mexican members, and if one be employed it must be at the expense of the Territory" (*H. Jour. of the LA of the Terr. of Colo.* 1864, 26). According to a news report, the Senate of the first Hawaii territorial legislature was "made up of an exceedingly cosmopolitan membership. There are native Hawaiians without the slightest admixture in the blood, Americans, Englishmen, a Russian, and representatives of mixed races where the Oriental and South Sea blood is joined with the Caucasian" (*Independent* 1901a). The session was dominated by home rule supporters who insisted on conducting legislative business in Hawaiian despite the fact that Congress had mandated the use of English; consequently translators were employed, and bills and speeches were given in both languages (*NYT* 1901). Indeed, House rule number 14 specified: "The Interpreter and Translator shall faithfully and truly interpret the discussions, motions, resolutions and other matter before the House from English to Hawaiian, or *vice versa*" (*Jour. of the H. of Reps.* 1901, 60).

Territorial legislatures were more diverse than might be expected in another regard. In 1879, William Jefferson Hardin, an African American, was elected to the Wyoming territorial House. Hardin, a barber in Cheyenne, proved an active legislator and on occasion presided over the House. He was the only representative to serve in both the sixth and seventh legislatures, but then he chose not to run for a third term and moved out of

Wyoming (Hardaway 1991). African Americans also served in the Oklahoma territorial House in 1890 and 1893.[6]

No women served in territorial legislatures during the nineteenth century. They were first elected in Hawaii in 1925 and Alaska in 1937 (Cox 1996, 330–31). Some territorial legislatures, however, were in the vanguard of the women's suffrage movement. The Wyoming territorial legislature granted women full voting rights in 1869, becoming the first government in the United States to do so. Lawmakers may have been motivated by more than a sense of social justice. There are indications that they thought the measure would generate needed attention for the territory, perhaps increasing its appeal to potential settlers. Democrats also calculated that passing women's suffrage would win them the newly enfranchised voters' support, securing the party control of the territory. A few years later when women voters appeared to lean in the Republicans' favor, Democrats contemplated repealing the measure. Wyoming's Republican governor resisted the move, stating in his opening legislative address, "Two years more of observation of the practical working of the system have only served to deepen my conviction that . . . our system of impartial suffrage is an unqualified success" (*NYT* 1873b). A few territorial legislatures followed Wyoming's lead. The Utah territorial legislature gave women the right to vote in 1870, but Congress rescinded the legislation in 1887. Washington territorial lawmakers passed women's suffrage bills in 1883 and 1888, but both times the territorial Supreme Court declared the measures unconstitutional. The first legislation adopted by the initial Alaska territorial legislature was a bill giving women the right to vote.

Membership Turnover

Few lawmakers served for long in territorial legislatures, and turnover was high. In the second Northwest territorial legislature in 1801, 64 percent of the members had not participated in the first legislature in 1799. In the second session of the Alabama territorial legislature, which met in November 1818, 56 percent of the members were new to the body, even though the first session had only adjourned in February earlier that year.[7] In territorial legislatures that met over longer periods, turnover typically increased over time. As can be seen in table 4.2, turnover rates averaged well over 80 percent in many territorial lower houses and over 90 percent in a few, meaning that with each new session almost all of the members had not served in the previous session. The lack of experienced lawmakers in most

TABLE 4.2. Membership Stability in Territorial Lower Houses

Territory (total number of sessions)	Territorial House of Representatives		
	Highest Session Percentage New Members (not including first session)	Lowest Session Percentage New Members (not including first session)	Mean Percentage New Members over All Sessions (not including first session)
Arizona (25)	100	83	92
Idaho (15)	100	79	92
New Mexico (38)	100	64	91
Dakota (18)	100	64	88
Oklahoma (9)	100	73	88
Mississippi (8)	100	76	88
Nebraska (12)[a]	97	70	88
Washington (25)	100	74	88
Wisconsin (5)	94	83	88
Minnesota (8)	95	72	87
Montana (17)[a]	100	3[b]	83
Oregon (9)	96	68	82
Nevada (3)	85	75	80
Indiana (5)	81	67	75
Arkansas (10)	91	38	74
Iowa (8)	92	39	71
Ohio (2)	—	—	64
Alabama (2)	—	—	56
Utah (31)	92	19	50
Michigan (5)[c]	77	30	48

Source: Calculated by author from membership rosters in Brantley 1947, 228–29; Darcy 2005; Davis 1912; Gilkey 1901, 131–43; Hailey 1910, 77–280; *Iowa Off. Register* 1907, 107–8; *Legislative Man. Containing the Cons. of N.D.* 1903, 117–25; *Legislative Man. of the St. of Minn.* 1889, 155–61; *Legislative Man. of the St. of Wis.* 1872, 185–96; Neb. Blue Book 1922, 36–42; *Report of the Secretary of the Terr., 1909–1910 and Legislative Man., 1911* 1911, 183–217; Rolfe 1904, vol. III, 277–95; Rowland 1925, 476–80; Thornbrough and Riker 1950, 953–57; Wagoner 1970, 505–29; http://arcweb.sos.state.or.us/pages/records/legislative/recordsguides/histleg/territorial/index.html; http://www.legislature.mi.gov/%28S%28wdadce550e4irr45mvv11we1%29%29/mileg.aspx?page=MM2003-2004&chapter=3; http://www.archives.state.ut.us/research/guides/legislative-assembly-rosters.pdf; http://www.leg.wa.gov/History/Territorial/Documents/territorial_assembly_members.pdf; http://montanahistorywiki.pbworks.com/w/page/21639731/Montana's-Elected-Officials.

Note: — = not applicable.

[a]The Nebraska sessions tabulated here include the 1858 special session. The Montana sessions include several extraordinary sessions.

[b]The eighth regular session followed the eighth extraordinary session by eight months and had all but one member return. The next lowest turnover rate among Montana sessions was 73 percent.

[c]Michigan had a unicameral Legislative Council. The members of the first council (1824–25) were appointed. Members of the second through sixth councils were elected. The data for Michigan are for the elected councils only.

chambers was striking. Over the 25 sessions of the Washington territorial legislature, a total of 573 individuals served in the two houses; 70 percent of them held office for only a single term and another 18 percent for only two terms (Brazier 2000, 35). Similar figures are found in other territorial legislatures. In Nebraska, 79 percent of House members served only one term; in Iowa 64 percent did. Indeed, during some sessions it was hard to keep track of the members. In Wisconsin, the 26 seats in the House during the four sittings of the Fourth Legislative Assembly were held by 69 different lawmakers.[8]

High turnover impacted legislative operations because of organizational memory loss and policy discontinuity. It also meant that leadership often fell to members with no experience. In accepting his election as the speaker of the first Missouri territorial House, William C. Carr conceded, "Unaccustomed to parliamentary proceedings, I feel much diffidence in my abilities to discharge the duties of the trust in such manner as may be most conducive to the dignity of the house and the proper dispatch of business." He went on to add, "Perhaps this diffidence ought to be the more seriously felt, when I recollect that the great majority of the members may be equally with myself, unaccustomed to deliberative bodies of this kind" (*Missouri Gazette* 1812). Other leaders made similar confessions. At the beginning of the fourth session of the Washington territorial House the newly elected speaker admitted in his acceptance speech, "I bring to the task no great amount of experience in parliamentary proceedings. . . . As I was never before present at the organization of a deliberative body, it may be that my remarks have been rather more extended than was proper, and they may be of a different character from what is customary on such occasions" (*Pioneer and Democrat* 1856). Such inexperience brought consequences. The speaker of the first Hawaiian territorial House had to rescind his initial set of committee assignments when it was pointed out to him that he had only put three members on each committee rather than the five members required by the rules (*Jour. of the H. of Reps.* 1901, 45).[9] And that was not his only mistake. A few days later a local newspaper had to admonish, "When there are three 'motions' before the House, we humbly suggest to the Speaker to call the motion which is to be voted on, and not as this morning simply blurt out 'who are in favor of the motion before the House,' and then have the vote recorded of members who really didn't know what motion they were called upon to deal with" (*Independent* 1901b). On occasion, even the use of proper parliamentary language proved challenging. A presiding officer in the first Oklahoma House had to be told to stop saying on voice votes, "The cheer thinks the ayes has it" (Peery 1929b, 439). Given the complexities of legislative procedures, it is not surprising that freshly minted lawmakers tossed into leadership positions made errors.

There are several plausible reasons why turnover was so high. First, territories were usually unsettled areas sprawled across large geographic expanses. Although the Northwest Territory was centered on what is today Ohio, it encompassed an area that now includes several other states, and some of the territorial representatives came from what is today Michigan. Similarly, a few of the lawmakers in Indiana Territory came from what is now Illinois, in Mississippi from Alabama, in Missouri from Arkansas, in Michigan from Wisconsin, in Wisconsin from Iowa (including the first two speakers of the Wisconsin territorial House), in New Mexico from Arizona, in Oregon from Washington, and in Idaho from Montana. Consequently, many legislators had to travel long distances to the legislative meeting place, and these trips were almost always arduous and dangerous. Second, until territories were well established the communities in which legislatures met were rustic at best and the meeting places usually rudimentary facilities. Finally, pay was low and did not compensate for either the difficulty in traveling to the legislature or the time taken away from family and work. Consequently, little about participating in a territorial legislature would entice a member to continue to serve. Moreover, even if a member wished to continue, life on the frontier was treacherous, and fate might not allow it to happen.

Travel to and from the Legislative Meeting Site

Territorial legislatures usually met when there was time available for members to leave their homes and jobs and spend several weeks traveling and in session. Thus they tended to be scheduled during the winter months. A journalist's account of his 70-mile trip to Bannack for the first meeting of the Montana territorial legislature documents the unpleasantness of long treks at that time of year through largely unsettled areas in northern parts of the country: "Two days' travel, overturned and broken-down coaches, . . . frozen drivers and passengers, wearied and worn-out mules and cayuses, hungry and thirsty travelers, grumbling at everything . . . these make up the experience in these days of a journey hither from Virginia [City]" (*MP* 1864).[10] In a letter to his father a member of the initial Wisconsin Council complained about his trip to Belmont: "I arrived here on Sunday afternoon after a tedious ride of six days. The weather was cold and disagreeable, with much snow and rain." Writing to his wife a few days earlier, the lawmaker had put a slightly more positive spin on the trip. After grumbling about the snow, he said, "We had however a very agreeable journey otherwise."[11] Travel was trying in all territories. At the most extreme, the Alaska territorial governor estimated that the members of the first territorial legislature had an average round-trip of over 2,500 miles to get to Juneau. Their journeys were by foot, steamship, horse-drawn sleigh, and dog team.[12] According to a member of the first Washington territorial House, "Nearly the entire legislature journeyed to and from the capital in boats, and it took two good hard days' tugging at the oars to get there from Seattle" (Barton 1891, 280). Several members of Wisconsin territorial legislature canoed down the Mississippi River for the session held in Burlington (now in Iowa) (Fisher 1918, 279). Idaho territorial lawmakers "Mounted on saddle horses or mules" and had "days of toilsome travel over rugged mountain trails such as had formerly been traversed only by Indians" (McConnell 1913, 115). Montanans were motivated to seek a separation from Idaho because "In many instances legislators were compelled to traverse hundreds of miles and to undergo severest hardships in order to attend the first session of the Idaho legislature" (Sanders 1910, 53). An Arizona reporter recalled "seeing one of the prominent statesmen of old Pima County, emulating the Man of Sorrow, by journeying into Prescott on the back of a jackass" (Rice 1928, 80). Even the advent of railroads did not necessarily make travel in the territories easy. In Arizona, to go by train from Phoenix to the territorial capital of Prescott required going through Los Angeles, over 320 miles to the west (Lyon 1984, 220).

The vast areas governed by territorial legislatures and the difficulties of travel and communication made being a lawmaker challenging. This problem was particularly acute in geographic areas that did not feel tied to a territory's core. In 1829, Henry Dodge, a prominent citizen in Dodgeville, Michigan Territory (now in Wisconsin), wrote to the territorial delegate to Congress complaining (with perhaps only slight geographic exaggeration), "At present, we have but two representatives for five counties; there are thirteen in the territory, and the seat of our territorial legislature is from 800 to 1000 miles from us." He went on to argue, "It is not to be expected that so small a representation can effect any important measure for this remote section of the territory, when the legislature is permitted to sit but sixty days; it is, in fact, but a nominal representation" (Smith 1854, 431). A similar complaint was registered by a newspaper in Olympia (now Washington) while that community was situated in Oregon Territory.

> The Legislative Assembly of Oregon has now been in session *five weeks*, and more than *two-thirds* of the allotted term of the session will have expired before we will be able to lay before our readers any of the proceedings of that body. That our representative . . . will use his utmost endeavors to have the rights of his district respected, and the interests of his constituents properly regarded, the people of northern Oregon have every confidence; and it is to be hoped that the day is not far distant when he will be called upon to legislate for his fellow-citizens in a territory of *their own*, instead of being compelled to undergo the fatigue, and incur the expense of a journey of near three hundred miles, to advocate the cause of his constituents in an assembly of *strangers* to our people and to the wants of their territory. (*Columbian* 1853, italics in original)

Problems with getting members to the meeting place also created organizational challenges. The start of the first Florida Council was delayed for 42 days while waiting for a sufficient number of members to make up a quorum to arrive (Morris and Maguire 1978, 30–31). Sometimes a quorum was never achieved. Only one of the six members of the initial Alabama Council ever appeared in St. Stephens. The lonely councilor assumed the presidency, appointed a secretary and a clerk, processed legislation, and finally, adjourned the Council *sine die* (*Jour. of the LC of the Ala. Terr. at the First Sess.* 1818). He was able to sidestep the obvious lack of a quorum because he was the only person in a position to formally raise a parliamentary objection.

But more than just being long and physically demanding, travel to various meeting places could be dangerous. The first president of the Washington Council drowned on his trip back home to Seattle from Olympia when his canoe capsized in a storm off Vashon Island (Brazier 2000, 5; Warren 1988). A member-elect of the initial Florida Council perished at sea on his trip to Pensacola, and four of his colleagues barely survived another shipwreck on their way to the meeting (Morris and Maguire 1978, 31). Even the legislative session itself could prove dangerous. During Florida's first session yellow fever swept through Pensacola; the Council president died from the disease, and several other lawmakers fell ill. The legislature was forced to retreat to the presumed safety of a farm located on the outskirts of the city (Martin 1944, 35–36; Morris and Maguire 1978, 35). Local populations occasionally posed a threat. A crowd of Chillicothe citizens, angered by a lawmaker's efforts to shift the Northwest territorial legislature's meeting place back to Cincinnati, mobbed his residence and broke through the front door. According to a witness, the legislator "met them in the passage with a brace of loaded pistols, and drove them back into the streets" (Burnet 1847, 333–34).[13] A rump caucus of the Nebraska territorial legislature sent a resolution to the governor from their meeting place in Florence claiming they had been "forced to adjourn to . . . the nearest, place of safety, by the disorganizing and turbulent acts of a minority of their own body, aided by the violence of an unrestrained mob at Omaha, causing a well-grounded apprehension as to the personal safety of the majority" (Woolworth 1904, 223). In 1813 the Indiana territorial legislature shifted its meeting place to Corydon from Vincennes because of the "hostile disposition of the Indians" in the latter (Ewbank and Riker 1934, 26).

Legislative Facilities

Generally, legislatures in newly established territories used whatever facilities were available. The New Mexico territorial legislature was fortunate to have for its use the Palace of the Governors, a public building first constructed in the early seventeenth century. The Council room was described as a "comfortable one, with a good hard floor" with "pine desks . . . ranged round the wall facing inward." There was one problem: "Figured calico is tacked to the walls to prevent the members carrying away the whitewash on their coats." The House met in a slightly larger room notable for having a "small gallery separated from the body of the room by an adobe wall breast high" (Davis 1857, 170).

Most other territorial legislatures did not fare as well. In *Roughing It*, Mark Twain, a journalist at the time, commented on the first Nevada territorial legislature's facilities: "[A local businessman] offered his large stone building just outside the capital limits. . . . He also furnished pine benches and chairs for the legislature, and covered the floors with clean saw-dust by way of carpet and spittoon combined. . . . A canvas partition to separate the Senate from the House of Representatives was put up by the Secretary" (Twain [1872] 1996, 187–88). Such primitive accommodations were common. Arizona's initial territorial lawmakers used a crude and cold two-room log cabin with a dirt floor (Waggoner 1970, 40). The members apparently took solace from the claim that their facility, even if unimpressive, was still thought superior to the one used by Colorado's territorial legislature (Pedersen 1966, 49). The Illinois territorial legislature first met in a "rough building . . . of uncut lime-stone. . . . The lower floor, a large and cheerless room, was fitted up for the House, whilst the Council sat in a small chamber above; around a circular table" ("Illinois' First State House" 1938, 100).

The initial session of the Alabama territorial legislature paid $8 a day to use two rooms in the Douglass Hotel, a sum that also covered the cost of furniture and fuel (*Jour. of the H. of Reps., of the Ala. Terr. at the First Sess.* 1818, 17–18). In the second session the legislature rented two rooms in Mr. Alston's house for $12 a day, which again also covered furniture and fuel (*Jour. of the H. of Reps., of the Ala. Terr. at the Second Sess.* 1818, 7). Iowa's first territorial legislature met in Burlington's Old Zion Methodist Church; the House used the first floor, the Council the basement. During the second session the House stayed put—a member recalled "the pulpit of the church answering for the Speaker's chair"—but the Council found the basement too damp and moved their sessions to a small Catholic church nearby (Lathrop 1888, 99; Pioneer Law-Makers' Association of Iowa 1894, 55). The inaugural Minnesota territorial legislature assembled in a hotel; the House convened in the dining room while the Council used the ladies parlor upstairs. Because the dining room continued to be used by the hotel, the House started its daily sessions only after the breakfast dishes were cleared. At 11:30 when dinner was served, "the members would then pick up their desks and pile them in what was known as the office; their papers they generally put in their pockets." The afternoon session ended when supper was ready (Murray 1908, 110). The first Wyoming Council and House met in separate buildings a block apart, an inconvenience salvaged by the fact that both meeting places were close to a wholesale liquor house that had a sample room that lawmakers frequented (Larson 1978, 73–74). The first Montana House rented a room over a store. A councilor bought an unfinished log building in Virginia City and had it disassembled and moved to Bannack where it was reassembled for use as the Council chamber (Thompson 2004, 208). One of the Council's first votes was in favor of a proposal to buy a curtain for the front window (Spence 1975, 25–26).

When a territorial legislature relocated to a new community it often had to scramble to find facilities. Montana's territorial legislature moved to Virginia City in 1866. Initially, the Council met "in the room over John S. Rockfellow's [grocery] store" while the House assembled in "the building formerly called the People's Theater" (*MP* 1866b). Within a short time a door was installed between the Council chamber and the El Sol Billiard Hall next door, allowing lawmakers easy access to that establishment's "First Class Billiards Tables, Prime Liquors, and No. 1 Cigars" (*MP* 1866c). The following year the representatives moved to Con Orem's Melodeon Saloon-House (Spence 1975, 190). A visitor described the makeshift hall this way.

> A cheap double ingrain carpet is spread over half the room where the members sit, and one of Con.'s private poker rooms has been metamorphosed into a platform for the Speaker of the House. A rudely-carved and daubed eagle, with wide-spread pinions, is suspended back of the Speaker's chair; and, in order that irreverent strangers may know the solemn presence they attain when they jostle in by mistake to imbibe one of Con.'s "smashes," the eagle supports a painted placard declaring the sacred purpose to which the rooms has been dedicated. (McClure 1869, 385)

The council remained in their store loft just down the street.

Occasionally a territorial legislature operated in a facility constructed specifically for it. When the Wisconsin territorial legislature met in Burlington, it assembled in a building built for just that purpose, with the House meeting on one floor and the Council on the other. Both rooms had a railing across them to separate the chamber from the lobby. The rooms were larger than those lawmakers had used the year before in Belmont, and according to the local paper, "Instead of being crowded around a small table, as heretofore, each member is provided with a desk—a very real improvement, all will agree." But before the session was completed the building burned down along with much of the town—lawmakers joined the town folk in a futile fight against the blaze. In a subsequent committee report, the legislature absolved its members of any responsibility for starting the fire (*Wiscousin Territorial Gazett* 1837a, 1837b, 1837c). The House had to finish the session in a room over Weber & Remey's store, while the Council used the west room of McCarver's building (Lathrop 1888, 98; "The Beginnings of Burlington" 1921, 359–60). A different misfortune befell the Arkansas territorial legislature. It met from 1821 to 1831 in the "State House," a dedicated (and rent-free) capitol that was nothing more than a small frame building. Eventually it became too dilapidated to use, and the legislature spent its final session in makeshift facilities, the House using the Presbyterian meetinghouse and the Council the Baptist meeting-house a block away (Ross 1971; White 1964, 158, 176).

Even the best-laid plans could go astray. In 1851 the Utah territorial legislature decided to found a new town in the center of the territory—Fillmore (in Millard County)—to become the capital. By 1855, one wing of the planned state house was finished. Acknowledging that it was "a large new building," two visitors concluded, "Though very remarkable for the country, it would be thought insignificant elsewhere." Perhaps more important, they found the new city to be "a dirty place" with houses that had "the same poor look" (Remy and Brenchley 1861, 344). Lawmakers apparently agreed with the negative assessments; they spent only the 1855–56 session in Fillmore. Unhappy with the living accommodations and the considerable distance from the territory's population centers to the north, during the next few years legislators held only a few perfunctory and poorly attended sessions there and then would adjourn to Salt Lake City (DN 1856c, 1856d, 1858b). By 1860 the legislature was permanently resettled in their original capital and debating how to dispose of the Fillmore State House (DN 1860b).

When the legislature returned to Salt Lake City it met initially in the Social Hall and then moved to rooms in the Court House that the city made available (DN 1860b). A reporter who ventured into that facility on the final evening of the 1863 session found it spare.

> We first went into the Council Chamber, which certainly did not present a very gorgeous appearance. The desks and chairs occupied by the Councilors were of the most plain, primitive order imaginable. No upholsterer had been employed to make them showy, easy, and comfortable. The tables of the President and secretaries were not costly nor elegant. . . . The walls of the Hall were bare and unadorned, with the exception of a national banner, "the old flag," which was spread out and nailed to the wall behind the President's chair. There were only five candles burning, three of them on the secretaries' table, to which the President had to repair whenever he read or signed a document. The fire in the stoves had nearly ceased to burn for the want of fuel.

The House's situation was the same: "On retiring from the Council Chamber we went into the Representatives Hall, where there was more artificial light, as there were more candles burning, but otherwise there was a great similarity in the general appearance of things as compared with what had been witnessed in the 'Upper House'" (*DN* 1863a). Even a quarter century later many in the territory were reticent to invest in better facilities. Given congressional limitations on how often the legislature could meet and on the number of lawmakers, it was thought it would be "a decidedly unwise piece of public financiering to erect and furnish elegant halls and committee rooms solely for the accommodation of thirty-six men for six weeks every other year" (*Salt Lake Herald* 1888).

Beyond suffering poor facilities, territorial legislators often had to provide their own supplies. The first session of the Iowa territorial legislature was disrupted by what became known as the "pen-knife and tin-pan controversy" when lawmakers had to cajole the territorial secretary to provide them the basic materials they needed to do their job (Parvin 1865; *Wisconsin Territorial Gazett* 1838). The reluctance of the Kansas Territorial Secretary to supply desks, stationery, and copies of the laws led legislators to seek his arrest (*Freedom's Champion* 1859). Prior to a meeting of the Utah territorial legislature, the local paper complained that "the members will have to furnish their own seats, fuel, stationery, and whatever else may be necessary for their use and comfort." The story noted that members of the previous legislature had been provided no candlesticks, very few inkstands, no penknives, and only one cent's worth of paper per day. They compared the situation to that found "in some of the primitive school houses in new settlements on the confines of civilization" (*DN* 1859).

As might be expected, living accommodations tended to be austere. The dining room used as the legislative chamber by the initial Minnesota territorial House also functioned as a boarding room at night: "The desks and chairs were piled up at one side of the room, and the vacant part of the floor was covered with straw ticks and Indian blankets, upon which some of the members would sleep" (Murray 1908, 110). Such lodgings were common. A visitor to Kaskaskia during the first meeting of the Illinois territorial legislature reported that the 12 lawmakers and the doorkeeper "all boarded at the same public house, and lodged in the same room" (Reynolds 1855, 165). A member of the first Wisconsin Council recalled that the only boardinghouse in Belmont accommodated "The whole of the [five-member] Brown [County] delegation . . . in one room, about fifteen by twenty feet, and our lobby friends roomed with us. Our beds were all full, and the floor well-spread with blankets and over-coats for lodging purposes" (Childs 1859, 187–88). In a letter to his wife another councilor characterized the accommodations more positively: "We have a very comfortable framed house for a boarding or eating house; and the members from our county have a good room in another comfortable building as lodging apartments."[14]

An unanticipated by-product of living in crowded boardinghouses was socialization in the byzantine ways of a legislature. One of the youngest members of the second Northwest territorial House wrote, "My inexperience led me to tremble at the responsibilities of the position, but the benefit of associating with, and enjoying the confidence of, such men as Governor St. Clair, [council members] Burnet and Sibley, and others with whom we boarded at Gregg's, and who were all exceedingly friendly, was very great." As result of these interactions, "I was encouraged to take an active part in business, and of necessity became accustomed to debate the measures I wished to have adopted" (Cutler 1890, 56).

The lack of adequate accommodations worked against a community's long-term prospects to retain the capital. After the Arkansas territorial government relocated to Little Rock a resident fretted in a letter to the local newspaper that legislators were unhappy because the town only had one tavern, a single boardinghouse, and a family that took boarders. Lawmakers, the writer reported, wanted at least two taverns and more boardinghouses (Cash 1942, 234). Similar complaints were registered about Madison once it became Wisconsin's territorial capital. According to a legislative investigation its three hotels assured that they would "be fully prepared to accommodate the members of the Legislative Assembly with board, rooms, &c., comfortably." A skeptical committee, however, was concerned that there would not be "sufficient rooms for the transaction of business." Lawmakers contemplated moving to another town but ultimately decided that no better option existed in the territory (*Jour. of the Coun., First Sess. of the Second LA of Wis.* 1838, 16).

Pay as an Inducement to Serve

The first territories had difficulties generating enough revenue to cover the costs of their governments. Starting with Florida, Congress appropriated funds to pay for territorial legislatures. They set legislative pay, usually at $3.00 a day during the session, plus a reimbursement for each 20 miles traveled to the meeting place (Eblen 1968, 155–56). Most territorial legislators considered the wage to be too low. A Montana lawmaker complained, "Wood sawyers or choppers can make more than the government allows legislators" (Spence 1975, 188). Other observers agreed. A Utah paper editorialized, "However much honor may accrue through being a member of our Legislature, there is assuredly no pecuniary advantage. There is not a man in it but could make more means by remaining at his ordinary business" (*DN* 1869). During the first session of the Washington territorial legislature, a local newspaper commented, "Seriously, $3.00 per day is just exactly no compensation at all. . . . [A] person, however meritorious and able, but *poor*, cannot afford to become a representative." It went on to advocate that "the members of the legislature should receive a compensation conformable to the price of labor, the expense of living, and the high price of everything required, necessary for an existence in the territory" (*Pioneer and Democrat* 1854b, italics in original). There also were complaints that the federal scrip and greenbacks issued to pay territorial lawmakers traded for less than face value, compounding the problem (McConnell 1913, 116–17; Spence 1975, 188; *Wisconsin Enquirer* 1841). Low salaries even caused a Utah paper to joke, "One of the members of the House exhibits quite a taste for mathematics—a very necessary qualification for legislators to possess . . . and without which, with the mere nominal pay they receive in this Territory, they would be liable to have the cash in pocket at the close of the Session representing thus, $0.00" (*DN* 1856b). Even with federal support, territorial budgets were never flush, and although lawmakers tried different ways to increase their wages they were generally unsuccessful. Indeed, territorial governments occasionally did not have sufficient financial resources to pay legislators their meager wages; in 1863, Washington Territory had to take out a $2,000 loan to give lawmakers enough money to get back home after the end of the session (Brazier 2000, 13). Similarly, on several occasions Iowa had to borrow money to pay its legislators (Briggs 1916, 19).

The compensation may have been considered inadequate but it still mattered to territorial lawmakers. Before the first meeting of the Montana territorial legislature in 1864, many Democratic members were reluctant to swear the "iron clad oath" of office. The pledge had been passed by the Republican-controlled Congress in 1862 and required all government officeholders other than the president and vice president to swear that they had "never voluntarily borne arms against the United States" and "voluntarily given no aid, countenance, counsel or encouragement to persons engaged in armed hostilities thereto." Thus those involved with the Confederacy or sympathetic to it were unable to make such declarations (Hyman 1954, 22–23, 158–59). In Montana, the GOP-appointed governor said that lawmakers could not be paid until they took the oath. The threat made lawmakers back down. According to a journalist, "This touched the Madison County delegation in a tender place, and with such wry faces as a patient makes who takes distasteful purgatives, and such contortions as one would make after over-eating turkey buzzards, they swallowed the 'iron clad' 'without mental reservation or evasion'" (*MP* 1864). A battle over wages and the "iron clad" also took place in Idaho. Unpaid because they refused to take the oath, angry lawmakers broke into and vandalized the legislative chambers. Not trusting the word of the territorial secretary—their suspicions deepened because his predecessor had absconded to Hong Kong with the contents of the territorial treasury—legislators confronted him and shouted threats such as "skin him" and "shake it out of him." They then physically attacked the secretary in an effort to get their pay. After order was restored two territorial judges decided that a substitute oath was acceptable, and the members were given the money due them (Jackson 1945, 316–18; Wells 1976).

Regardless of a territory's fiscal circumstances lawmakers demanded their pay. Even though Utah lawmakers from northern communities had not bothered to attend the token sessions held in Fillmore, they still pressed to be compensated for them (*NYT* 1859). A Salt Lake City paper seemed almost amused by this sort of behavior: "The forty days having expired on Friday evening last, or more properly speaking on Saturday morning, as it was long after midnight, the Legislative Assembly adjourned *sine die*, and soon thereafter the members were seen leaving the city for their respective homes, but not till they had received their per diem and mileage, and that too in CASH" (*DN* 1860a).

The Challenges of Daily Life

Even if a lawmaker wanted to continue to serve, the vagaries of frontier life might conspire against such hopes. Some died while engaged in routine activities. A member of the first Wisconsin territorial House perished when, as one of his colleagues eulogized, "In returning to his home from the town of Dubuque, after night, in the month of February last, his horse fell, threw him, and put a period to his existence" (*Jour. of the H. of Reps. of the LA of Wis.* 1837, 6). Other deaths were more unusual: upon their return home from the inaugural Arizona territorial legislature two members were killed by Apaches (Pedersen 1966, 51). Pacific County in Washington had extraordinary trouble getting a representative safely to the first meeting of the territorial House. Their initial choice died unexpectedly before the election. His successor passed away en route to the session. The third man elected got to Olympia and was sworn in, but after joining his new colleagues for drinks at a bar that night he collapsed and died. Finally, a lobbyist was elected to the seat and managed to survive the rest of the session (Brazier 2000, 4; *Pioneer and Democrat* 1854b).

Legislative Life

There was little to do in many of the places where the territorial legislatures met, especially early in a territory's existence. A correspondent covering the Wyoming territorial legislature noted that in Cheyenne, "the chief day diversion seems to be the assembling at the station at noon-time to see the overland express trains which pass each other here, it being exactly half way between the terminal stations of the Union Pacific Railroad" (*NYT* 1873b). In Montana, the Virginia City paper touted the entertainment value of the legislature itself: "Many spectators who witness the proceedings of the law making wiseacres that will dwell in our midst next month, may prefer the discussions to the acting of the Irwins, Belle Douglass, Hosmer and others" (*MP* 1866b). If the legislature proved insufficiently amusing, the city's residents also organized a mock "Third House" that met regularly to lampoon the territorial body's actions (McClure 1869, 410–11; Miller 1960, 97–98). But even if entertainment of sorts was offered in some early capitals (and, to be fair, there was in Cheyenne, Virginia City, and elsewhere), other aspects of normal community life might still be absent. Decrying the fact that Omaha had become the temporary capital of Nebraska, one resident lamented that the influx of visitors meant "Clean sheets and good victuals are a luxury" (*NYDT* 1856a). The Iowa territorial governor's private secretary complained that during the first territorial legislature, "there were seventy-five young men, all of us eligible to matrimony, but not a young woman in all the city of Burlington. There was one maiden lady, older than my mother" (Parvin 1900, 22). A former resident of St. Stephens, Alabama, recalled that in the town of her youth, "A theater flourished, balls were frequent, and there was a prevailing indifference to anything that savored of religion. . . . There never was a church building, nor even a church organization, in the town nor for miles around it" (Welsh 1888–89, 210).

Still, the lack of services associated with urban life may have produced some unanticipated benefits. The sergeant at arms for the Iowa territorial House in Burlington commented, "A new code of laws had to be formed, and there were few amusements and no dining out to divert members"

(Taylor 1890, 519). Similarly, when Utah territorial lawmakers met in Fillmore, one of the newly built community's virtues was "The members of the Assembly are . . . undisturbed by the sights, sounds, amusements, customs and practices common to most large cities, hence their deliberations are calm and mature" (*DN* 1856a).

Given the lack of amenities, it is not surprising that alcohol played a large role in legislative life, as it did in most aspects of frontier society (Winkler 1968). A doorkeeper in the Washington territorial legislature kept a supply of whiskey just outside the chamber, and members were said to partake of it prior to starting the legislative day (Brazier 2000, 4). A teetotaling member of the first House recalled a celebration after adjournment.

> I had made arrangements for a large canoe and crew of Indians to take me home on the morning after adjournment, and was hurrying to the boat, when a "committee from headquarters" gave chase. Headquarters was the place where the "boys" were having a high old time. I was captured and taken back to headquarters. I was offered a glass of whisky, and upon declining, the crowd yelled . . . "Make him drink! Make him drink." They grabbed me by the collar, and I settled back for what I supposed was going to be a nasty fight, when [Council clerk] Elwood Evans spoke up as follows . . . "No, boys, don't make him drink. I propose that we drink to the health of the only member of the Legislature who consistently lives up to the principles of the Maine liquor [prohibition] law." This seemed to satisfy the crowd. They drank most heartily to my health and I made my escape to the waiting canoe. (Meany 1909, 163)

Remarkably, a similar tale was related by an abstentious member of the initial Montana Council. According to the lawmaker's memoir following the final Council meeting, "it seemed that nine-tenths of the men in Bannack were drunk," and some of them hauled him to a saloon to be forced to drink beer. The councilor managed to wiggle free, knocking open a tap on a barrel of beer in the process. He escaped when everyone turned their attention to the open spigot (Thompson 2004, 210–11).

Most territorial legislatures reported problems because of alcohol. The first president of the Iowa Council missed a week of the session because of a bender (Parvin 1900, 23). A reporter covering the initial Nebraska territorial legislature noted that toward the end of each daily session some member "speaks half an hour on nothing, and some hungry or thirsty member moves an adjournment, and a few minutes after the drinking saloons are well patronized" (*NYDT* 1856b). According to a Montana newspaper, "Whisky is the propelling power of the Legislature. . . . Follow a member from the Legislative Hall, and he will lead you into the adjoining saloon" (*MP* 1868b). A local resident agreed, saying "Whisky will suffer when these fellows gets here. . . . about all they do is drink whiskey and play Billiards" (Spence 1975, 191). Even before Arizona's thirteenth legislature earned its label as the "thieving, bloody, fighting Thirteenth," a reporter had noted, "The present session can get away with as much Arizona bug juice as any of its predecessors" (*Arizona Silver Belt* 1885a).[15] Some important policy decisions were influenced by drink. On the question of where to locate the Iowa territorial capital, an observer recalled that during a tie vote one member "was drunk and he didn't know the difference between Iowa City . . . and Mt. Pleasant, so that the members favorable to each of the two places would try to get on either side of him and control him, but the friends of Iowa City outdid the Mt. Pleasant boys and they got his vote" (Parvin 1900, 24). Over time territorial legislators cleaned up their act, at least a bit. Montana lawmakers reportedly drank much less by the end of the territorial era, and the legislature had taken the lead in proposing laws to tamp down various forms of vice (Petrik 1985, 4; Spence 1975, 191). By its final session the Dakota House had a Committee on Temperance (*Jour. of the H. of the Seventeenth Sess. of the LA* 1886, 50).

Legislative Behavior

A frontier legislature fueled by whiskey was apt to be wild and woolly and the territorial bodies certainly fit that description. Conflict and contention flourished, as reported by a correspondent who characterized a debate in the first Nebraska territorial legislature this way.

> Hon. Mr. A. gives Mr. B., "the gentleman from ___ county," a severe lecturing before the . . . House for not voting on his side of the question—says he agreed to, and if he don't behave himself he'll go and tell his constituency how badly he behaves, [etc.]. Mr. B. comes the indignant—says Mr. A. lies if he makes such and such assertions, and Mr. A. is not better than he should be, and reckons he ain't much afraid of him. (*NYDT* 1856b)

Intemperate language often led to physical altercations (e.g., Brazier 2000, 10, 17; Rice 1928, 83–85). In Kansas, "A fight occurred in the Council Chamber this morning, before that honorable body met. Dr. Brooks of Westport, struck Councilor McDonald between the eyes. The difficulty originated about a preemption claim" (*NYDT* 1855a). In Arizona, the "bloody, fighting" in the "thieving, bloody, fighting Thirteenth," came from the fact that "no other legislative body that ever assembled in Arizona, have indulged in so many fisticuff discussions. Scarcely a day passes without a scrap" (*Arizona Silver Belt* 1885b). The territory's lawmakers became accustomed to violent episodes. A few years later another paper reported on a fight between two "very gentlemanly" lawmakers over the handling of a bill. Noting that "all men make mistakes, and loose [*sic*] their temper at times," the story went on to say, "The contest was quickly over, both men apologized to the house, and all was serene in short order" (*Arizona Daily Citizen* 1901). Along the same lines, a Minnesota lawmaker recalled that when "William R. Marshall was addressing the House, a member in a seat in from of him called him a liar. Marshall, with the agility of a cat, jumped over his seat and before anyone realized what was going on knocked the member out of his seat to the floor; returning to his seat, he apologized to the House and proceeded with his remarks." Accordingly, "The matter was dropped there and was never heard of again" because "This was pioneer ethics" (Murray 1908, 112).

Occasionally the mayhem escalated, as described in this account of a meeting of the Oklahoma Council.

> During the argument against a certain point of order raised, Brown of Oklahoma, who has made himself generally obnoxious during the session, personally insulted Brown of Logan. The latter retaliated in a severe manner, when Bixler of Cleveland, who was in the chair . . . peremptorily ordered the Sergeant at Arms to seat Brown. The Sergeant at Arms at once advanced toward Brown, at the same time calling for the Assistant Sergeant. The two took Brown by the throat, when a hundred lobbyists rushed in and interfered. The Chair left his post and all was confusion. Brown of Oklahoma personally attacked Brown of Logan, and the two scuffled backward and forward. Editor Grier of the *State Capital* sat at the press table, and being a very warm friend of Brown of Logan, and a bitter enemy of Brown of Oklahoma, rushed upon the two and drew a slung-shot, prepared, if necessary, to defend the Logan delegate. Howls and a

general fusillade of epithets rent the air. . . . For an hour the Chair had no control over the members.[16]

It comes as no surprise that "Little business was transacted during the remainder of the day and the Council finally adjourned" (*NYT* 1890b).

Violence was often resorted to as a way of solving parliamentary problems in territorial legislatures. When a disgruntled group of Dakota House members was unsuccessful in getting the two-thirds vote needed to replace the speaker, they hatched a plan to forcibly unseat him, toss him out a window, and install a new speaker to serve while the old one recovered from his injuries. After the speaker learned of the plot he requested protection from the governor. The governor initially provided guards but later had them removed and called the speaker a coward. Humiliated, the speaker resigned. That did not, however, spare him from violence. The now ex-speaker was later thrown through a saloon window by his legislative opponents, and in another ugly episode, he jumped through a window to escape attackers (Lamar 1956, 85; Tripp and Worst 1904, 228–29).

Even more extreme violent behavior occasionally occurred in territorial legislatures. There were duels involving lawmakers (Quaife 1922, 280; Sherwood 1947, 188–89). But most fighting was not choreographed by rules; rather, tempers overheated and fists or worse starting flying. Following an angry exchange on the Arizona Council floor one of the councilors involved spied his tormentor walking down the street and, according to a witness, he "secured possession of a wrench used in a city hydrant, and rushing up behind . . . attempted to brain him with the three-foot bar." Only another lawmaker's intervention prevented the assault (Rice 1928, 83). Such attacks were not isolated events. A member of the Nevada territorial House beat the president of the Council with a piece of wood, rendering him senseless (*DN* 1861a). After the New Mexico Council failed in an effort to remove the territory's chief justice, angry words were exchanged between the judge and a councilor when they ran into each other at a billiard hall. Each drew his gun and the councilor shot the chief justice to death (*MP* 1868a; *National Republican* 1867; *NYT* 1867).

But the most notorious incident occurred in Wisconsin, where a lawmaker was murdered on the Council floor. A heated conversation between two councilors over a gubernatorial nomination escalated into a physical altercation. After battling for a few minutes one of the lawmakers drew his gun and shot the other, who died a few minutes later. Rather than accept the assailant's resignation the members of the Council voted to expel him (Quaife 1922; Strong 1870, 26–28).[17] The episode cost the legislature public support. In its aftermath, a paper reported, "There is a petition afloat to do away for the present with the Territorial Legislature. From what we have seen, we believe the people generally to be in favor of the project. About $250,000 have been expended to defray the expenses of our Legislature, and the best man in the body last year was shot in the Council Chamber. Can the present Legislature do any good?" (*Milwaukee Sentinel* 1842). The shooting even reverberated internationally: Charles Dickens, who visited the United States in 1842, specifically cited it as evidence of an American propensity for violence (Dickens 1898, 282–83).

Basic parliamentary civilities were often lacking among territorial lawmakers, as in this reporter's description of the inaugural Nebraska territorial legislature.

> You see a motley group inside of a railing in a small room, crowded indeed to an overflowing, some behind their little schoolboy desks, some seated on top of the desks, some with their feet perched on the top of their neighbor's chair or desk, some whittling—half a dozen walking about in what little space there is left. . . . The clerk, if he chooses, jumps up to explain the hows and whys of his journal. A lobby member stalks inside the bar, and from one to the other he goes about talking of the advantages of his bill. A row starts up in the Secretary's room or somewhere about the building and away goes the honorable body to see the fun. (*NYDT* 1856)

Such ill-mannered behavior was common. New Mexico's lawmakers were said to "sit in their seats and puff away at their cigarritos while the House is in session" (Davis 1857, 255). Dakota representatives "brandished pistols to get recognition from the speaker and had drinks sent in from a nearby saloon" (Lamar 1956, 79). The tables were turned in the Idaho territorial House. According to a news account, "some smart young member undertook to disparage a decision, when the speaker laid his revolver on the desk. . . . The young man at once found that he had intended no disrespect" (*St. Paul Daily Globe* 1889). Councilors acted no better. An observer of the Montana Council was taken aback when he saw that "the members sit around the stove, smoking, whittling, and cracking jokes, while the ordinary routine of legislative business is going on" (McClure 1869, 385). Visitors in public galleries also behaved badly. A reporter observed of a crowd watching a contentious debate in the Nebraska territorial House, "They cheer their champions and hiss their opponents—they talk loud and strong" (*NYDT* 1857).

Makeshift legislative facilities occasionally contributed to the parliamentary chaos. When the Wisconsin territorial legislature moved into its first permanent capitol in Madison in 1838, the building was unfinished. The flooring was incomplete, and the basement was still open, which allowed hogs to take up residence. A legislator boasted that during the sessions in this facility, "We had a great many smart members in the House, and sometimes they spoke for Buncombe.[18] When members of this ilk would become too tedious, I would take a long pole, go at the hogs, and stir them up; when they would raise a young pandemonium for noise and confusion." The result was "The speaker's voice would become completely drowned, and he would be compelled to stop, not, however, without giving his squealing disturbers a sample of his swearing ability" (Childs 1859, 191).

Parliamentary procedures were abused as well. Territorial lawmakers were not above shenanigans to produce their preferred outcome. When the Minnesota territorial House passed a bill to move the capital to St. Peter from St. Paul, supporters of the latter city focused their energies on preventing the measure from making it out of the Council. During the final days of the legislative session the bill's supporters made a push to pass it, and it looked like they were going to be successful. But unfortunately for those backing St. Peter, the only properly enrolled and correctly engrossed version of the bill went missing, and the chair of the Committee on Enrolled Bills went missing as well. The Council met for 123 straight hours—cots and meals were brought into the chamber to accommodate the members—without being able to overcome the procedural problems caused by the absence of the only copy of the bill on which the body could take action. When the session reached its legal end, St. Peter's chance to become the capital disappeared. It was later learned that during his absence the chair of the Committee on Enrolled Bills was happily ensconced in a nice hotel in St. Paul, where, as one account delicately noted, "It is not believed that he lacked any of the comforts of life, nor that he pined in absolute solitude" (Folwell 1956, 385). Indeed, the sergeant at arms was "spending his nights in [the absent lawmaker's] room playing cards with him, reporting each morning that [he] could not find him" (Hall 1904, 31). Some lawmakers also visited their absent colleague. At the same time the properly enrolled and correctly engrossed version of the bill was allegedly locked away in a St. Paul bank safe (Dean 1908, 9–15; Eustis 1904, 52–53; Fowell 1956, 383–85; Hall 1904, 26–34; Thompson 1973, 240–43).

Amazingly, that was not the only instance of a pilfered bill derailing the legislative process in a territorial body. When a member of the Arizona territorial House failed to prevent the passage of a railroad bond measure his constituents adamantly opposed, he asked the speaker to allow him to review the official copy of the bill because he claimed it might contain a technical error. Once the representative had the bill in his possession, he strolled out of the chamber with it and hid in the attic of a nearby building. Futile efforts were made to locate the missing lawmaker and bill, with officials canvassing all of the places he was known to frequent, even his sleeping wife's bedroom. Because the representative's actions occurred on the final day of the legislative session, his swiping of the measure killed it. The thief's colleagues were so enraged that they voted unanimously to expel him from the body and to prevent him from ever holding office again. Upon reflection, however, they decided that such punishment was too severe, and they voted instead to simply censure him (*Arizona Silver Belt* 1885c; Rice 1928, 89–90). And after the Oklahoma territorial House had adopted a motion to reconsider a measure to relocate the territorial capital, several lawmakers filched the copy of the bill that the speaker had signed. Their effort was foiled by a mob of irate colleagues and spectators who captured the thieving lawmakers and the stolen bill after a four-block chase (*NYT* 1890a).

Although part of the problem in territorial legislatures may have been a lack of legislative experience, clearly they also suffered from the unwillingness on the part of many members to play by parliamentary rules. George Curry was a newly elected Democratic member of the New Mexico Council and unfamiliar with legislative procedure when he became the body's president in 1894. Despite his inexperience, things went relatively smoothly until the end of the session, when several controversial gubernatorial nominations came before the Council. In order to secure the nominations, Curry waited until the Republican councilors left the chamber to caucus. He then had one of his own absent members arrested by the sergeant at arms and brought back to the Council, thereby making the required quorum. At that point Curry had the chamber doors locked, and he pushed through the nominations without giving the Republicans any opportunity to block them. In the meantime, the Republicans had figured out the president's ploy, and they tried to break down the doors using long poles. But before they could make their way into the chamber, the nominations had been passed, and the Council had adjourned. Afterward, a Republican leader gave the Democratic president a grudging compliment, saying, "Curry, I don't think you need any instruction in *unparliamentary* procedure" (Hening 1958, 88–89, italics in original).

Given the lack of appreciation for the rules, it is not surprising that corruption was an issue in territorial legislatures. Some thought that low legislative pay contributed to the problem, because of "roguishly inclined officials, who will help themselves to make up the deficiency in their salaries" (*MP* 1866a). Any such inclination was exacerbated by the fact that private interests were always part of the territorial legislative scene. At the start of one new session, an Idaho newspaper observed, "Lobbyists are quite as numerous [as] members" (*Idaho Tri-Weekly Statesman* 1866). In Arizona, it was claimed that "Lobbyists with corruption funds were present during the entire session" (*Mohave County Miner* 1887). A Wyoming reporter expanded on the theme, finding, "The lobby is no new thing in the Territories. There are as keen and persistent hangers-on as can be found at Albany or Harrisburg. . . . The Assembly rooms swarm with men who want to lobby this friend into office or that enemy out, or want a favorite measure to go through, or a swindling law to be protected" (*NYT* 1873b). With large sums of money at stake persuasion efforts that crossed ethical lines were to be expected. Indeed, as will be pointed out in chapter 6, established state legislatures suffered from similar problems during the nineteenth century.

Some bribery efforts were relatively subtle. A member of the first Wisconsin territorial legislature reported being offered stock to vote to locate the capital in Madison (Childs 1859, 188). One of his colleagues corroborated the charge, recalling, "Before another debate . . . it was discovered that Madison was fast coming into favor . . . and stories were put into circulation of a certain stock company, owners of the city of Madison, with thirty-six shares in all—just the number of the two houses of the Legislative Council; and that most of the members . . . were stockholders" (Draper 1872, 390). These allegations were well known at the time (Rodolf 1900, 368). Similar stock schemes were suspected elsewhere. Referencing a measure to relocate the Nebraska capital to a proposed new community, a territorial legislator wrote to a friend, "I am on the committee and will report its immediate passage. . . . I have some shares as you may know" (Potts 1988, 176). In Kansas it was alleged, "Several members took the position that the Legislature was bribed by a direct interest in some paper town, for the purpose of securing the capital nearby" (*NYT* 1858a; *Freedom's Cham-*

pion 1867). An observer of the ill-fated effort to move the Minnesota capital to St. Peter recalled, "it was stated at the time, and undisputed by the persons accused, that every member of either branch of the legislature voting for the capital removal had deeds for town lots in St. Peter already in his pocket" (Hall 1904, 27–28). Some reports had it that the governor and the secretary of the territory were in on the St. Peter stock venture (Thompson 1973, 241).

Other bribery efforts were more blatant. Backers of a successful effort to move the Arizona territorial capital to Phoenix reportedly had a $10,000 "boodle" at their disposal to help persuade legislators (Ehrlich 1981, 240). And not every effort to illegally influence the legislature involved the location of the capital. A slush fund of some $125,000 was reportedly assembled to influence voting on a New Mexico measure to have the territory cover the cost of dubious militia warrants (Hening 1958, 85). When a banking bill lost by a single vote in the Kansas Council, a newspaper said, "It is rumored also that one councilor had been *bought*" (*NYDT* 1855a). Many observers who followed territorial politics considered corruption to be endemic to the legislative enterprise. A correspondent covering the first Montana territorial legislature complained, "there are in this assembly, some of the most venal, corrupt, and shameless legislators in the world." He went on to object that "Men openly in the streets propose to sell votes for a given price, and in any legislative body that ever before congregated, would be kicked out incontinently" (*MP* 1865b). Along the same lines, a reporter characterized a number of Arizona lawmakers in the "thieving, bloody, fighting Thirteenth" legislature as "traitors, bribe givers and takers" (Rice 1928, 81). Another paper concurred with that assessment, commenting, "There are but few who can go back to their constituency with clean hands. It has been percentage and divy all the way through" (*Arizona Champion* 1885a, 28). The notion that the legislature was corrupt was so widely held that a few weeks after it adjourned a location notice for a new mine in the territory was formally registered under the name, "Thieving Thirteenth" (*Arizona Champion* 1885c).

Not every legislature was thought to be riddled with corruption, but those that were not were seen as exceptions to the general rule. At the end of one legislative session a Colorado paper commented, "Probably no body of men sitting as a territorial legislature were ever more free from all taint of corruption or dishonesty—a record honorable in the extreme when we consider the gross and open manner in which bribery runs riot in similar bodies in other states and territories" (*Rocky Mountain News* 1874). Similar accolades were awarded in Utah. Following the adjournment of the legislature, a newspaper extolled, "If the world in their blindness could but discern truth, light and life, they would most heartily commend and strive to imitate the worthy example set by Utah's Legislators, for the jealousies, animosities, pipe-layings, wire-workings, lobbying, quarreling and other kindred deviltry springing from unchecked selfishness find no place in our Legislative Halls" (*DN* 1858a).[19]

Some attempts were made to deal with the problem. The Wisconsin territorial House charged a member with accepting a $300 bribe to push for a ferry grant and the body conducted a detailed investigation of the matter (*Jour. of the H. of Reps. of the LA of Wis.* 1837, 249–54; Appendices 7 and 9). Ultimately, the member resigned his seat, while his former colleagues passed a resolution declaring he was "unworthy of confidence" (*Legislative Man. of the St. of Wis.* 1872, 186). It is not clear, however, how seriously concerns about corruption were taken. Commenting on the Wisconsin case a New Orleans paper asserted, "If all legislators who receive bribes were expelled, there might be a considerable thinning among our wise men throughout the country" (*Daily Picayune* 1838). Referring to a measure "which makes it a criminal offense for any person to attempt to influence legislation" a Wyoming reporter struck a similarly cynical note: "Should such a bill pass it will probably rid the Legislature of a great annoyance and send the members home with light hearts as well as light pockets at the end of their term" (*NYT* 1873b).

Given such cynicism, it was to be expected that territorial legislators would become the subjects of jokes. One apocryphal story that circulated centered on constituents alarmed by a lawmaker's fine clothes upon his return home. When asked about where he had gotten the money, the legislator said, "members don't have anything to do evenings, and instead of reading novels or attending the wicked theater they gather in little crowds around the table." There, "the one who has four of a kind of something or other rakes in something or other they call a pot." The punch line was "somehow or other our esteemed Representative always has more of a kind than any one else" (*Puget Sound Argus* 1881).

It is worth pointing out that territorial legislators did not always exploit their position, and some lamented the patent corruption. Rafael Chacón (1986, 312), who served as both a member of the New Mexico Council and as that body's principal secretary, wrote of his time in the legislature, "I was able to note, to my great disillusionment, the political manipulations in which honor and dignity were sold and respectability forgotten." At times lawmakers behaved quite honorably. During a tense series of tie votes to determine the president of the Arizona Council, in the excitement of the moment one of the councilors forgot to register his preference, giving the other side the victory. But the winning candidate refused to accept the post given the flawed nature of the tally, and the voting continued until a compromise candidate was agreed upon (Rice 1928, 81). In New Mexico, Council president George Curry refused to go along with an effort to seat a fellow Democrat in a contested election, instead giving his pivotal vote to the Republican candidate he thought was the legitimate winner (Hening 1958, 81–82). Over time it appears that procedures and rules in territorial legislatures became more ingrained and more widely followed. By the final years of New Mexico's territorial period adherence to accepted parliamentary practices had become the norm, if only to help convince Congress that the territory was ready to be admitted as a state (Hening 1958, 233). For the most part, however, territorial legislatures were never tame institutions.

Policy Making

Territorial legislatures legislated across a wide range of policy areas. As an example, the 47 laws and 2 resolutions passed by the second session of the Alabama Territorial Legislature in 1818 are given in box 4.1. The list provides insight into the variety of issues tackled by territorial lawmakers. Much time was spent locating the territorial capital (law no. 30), but also to establishing city and county boundaries (nos. 2, 4, 9, 16, 17, 37, 43, 45) and to creating structures for local governance (nos. 13, 39). The legislature granted divorces (nos. 6, 7, 14, 19, 22) and dealt with common law marriages (no. 11) and estate matters (nos. 10, 15). Considerable legislative energy was devoted to developing election laws (nos. 1, 31, 38) and to the mechanics of the judicial system (nos. 5, 8, 24, 29, 33, 34, 35, 41, 44). Economic development commanded extensive attention (nos. 3, 12, 18, 23, 25, 27, 32). And, of course, laws were passed both to generate revenue for the territorial government and to spend it (nos. 20, 26, 36, 42, 47, 48, 49). Finally, miscellaneous measures were adopted (nos. 40, 46), including two dealing with slavery (nos. 21, 28). Many of the bills were relatively simple, having just one or two sections. But several were quite complex, notably one with 22 sections creating a governing authority for the port of Mobile, and another to charter a bank that had 12 sections, one of which had 13 subsections. Thus the evidence supports a claim that territorial legislatures were serious lawmaking bodies. Indeed, during its first session, the Alabama territorial legislature passed a law repealing usury restrictions, claiming, "We believe ours is the first legislature in the Union which has made all obligations recoverable let the rate of interest be what it may" (*Mercantile Advertiser* 1818).

Particularly during their first few sessions, territorial legislatures fixated on pork barrel issues, notably where to locate the capital, the penitentiary, and the university (Brazier 2000, 6; Ehrlich 1981; Folwell 1956, 260–62;

Box 4.1. Titles of Acts and Resolutions Passed by the Second Session of the First Alabama Territorial Legislature, 1818, in Chronological Order

An Act:
1. to apportion the representatives among the several counties in this Territory, according to the returns of the late Census, and for other purposes (3)[a]
2. to extend the corporate limits of Huntsville (2)
3. for the government of Ginholders and for other purposes (5)[b]
4. to incorporate the town of Mooresville and for other purposes (4)
5. providing for the establishment of seats of justice in the several counties therein named (5)
6. to divorce Mary P. Moore from her husband Gabriel Moore, and to change her name from Mary P. Moore to Mary P. Caller (1)
7. to divorce Maria Fuller from her husband William Fuller (1)
8. authorizing county courts to grant private ways, in certain cases (2)
9. to incorporate the town of Athens in Limestone county (4)
10. for the relief of Ann Hughes, guardian of the infant heirs of Raleigh Hughes, deceased (2)
11. to make lawful and obligatory certain marriages therein named (2)
12. to restrain the issuing of small notes, commonly called change bills (1)
13. to enable house-holders in the several counties in this Territory, wherein the Public Lands have not been offered for sale, to perform all the duties which by existing laws are required of free-holders (2)
14. to divorce certain persons therein named (4)
15. to authorize the administratrix and administrator of Henry Cannon deceased, to sell certain real estate (2)
16. to alter & ascertain more particularly the boundaries of the county of Shelby, & to lay off a new county in the north east part thereof, to be called and known by the name of St. Clair county (8)

17. to alter and establish the boundaries of Cahawba county (1)
18. to establish a Bank in the town of Mobile (12 sections, one with 13 subsections)
19. to divorce Gray Syms from his wife Catharine Syms (1)
20. to increase the compensation of the Public Printer (3)
21. to authorise David Norris to manumit his negro woman slave, Nancy (1)
22. to divorce John Barron from his wife Clarissa Barron (1)
23. to regulate Sales at auction (7)
24. to alter the times of holding the Superior courts in the counties of Limestone, Cotaco, Lawrence, Franklin, and Lauderdale (3)
25. to change the mode of increasing the capital stock in the Planters and Merchant Bank of Huntsville, and the Tombeckbe Bank, & for other purposes (5)
26. to authorise the appointment of a keeper and translator of the Spanish records and papers, in the Alabama Territory (2)
27. to authorise the leasing of lands named therein named (3)
28. to provide for the disposition of slaves imported into the Territory contrary to the laws of the United States (2)
29. to authorise the Governor of the territory to offer rewards for the apprehension of criminals (2)
30. providing for the temporary and permanent seats of government (11)
31. to establish elections precincts in the county of Monroe (1)
32. concerning Hawkers and Pedlars (5)
33. to authorise deeds of conveyance to be acknowledged and rights of dower to be relinquished before clerks of courts (2)
34. to alter the times of holding courts in the southern district of this Territory (2)
35. to fix the permanent seat of Justice for the county of Mobile, in the town of Mobile, and to authorise the erection of a court house and Jail (3)
36. to alter the mode of assessing and collecting taxes (2)
37. to divide Montgomery county, and to establish the county of Autauga (6)
38. to make election precincts in the counties therein named (8)
39. for the government of the Port and Harbor of Mobile (22)
40. for the relief of William Jordan (2)

41. to appoint Commissioners to fix the place for the permanent site of justice for the county of Clark (4)
42. to amend the laws creating a tax on lands (2)
43. concerning the middle District (1)
44. supplemental to the laws now governing Judicial proceedings (10)
45. to alter and establish the boundary lines between the counties of Autauga & Dallas (1)
46. for the benefit of certain persons therein named, and to provide a contingent fund (3)
47. providing for the compensation of the convention (1)

Resolution:
48. to increase the compensation of the secretary, clerks, and door-keepers
49. for the relief of William D. Gaines

Source: Acts Passed at the Second Sess. of the First GA of the Ala. Terr. (1818)
Note: [a]The number of sections in an act is given in parentheses.
[b]A ginholder is a person who owns a cotton gin.

Lamar 1956, 84–86; Murray 1908, 115–18; Peery 1929a; 1929b; Potts 1988; White 1964, 30–32; Winslow 1908). Given the potential financial windfalls at stake, as well as local pride, these decisions were highly contentious. According to one lawmaker, during a legislative battle over relocating the capital of Dakota Territory, "a little blood was shed, much whisky drank, a few eyes blackened, revolvers drawn, and some running done" (Tripp and Worst 1904, 228). A conflict in the Nebraska territorial legislature over relocating the capital was characterized as "one continued personal and local fight, a constant attempt at bargain, sale, and argument." The House speaker ordered a lawmaker arrested and was in turn threatened by his legislative opponents to the point "that he dared not occupy the chair" (Potts 1988, 175–76). In another scuffle over a different measure to relocate the capital the speaker was roughed up by an enraged visitor who leapt from the gallery, grabbed him by the throat and threw him under a table (Potts 1988, 178; Wakeley 1917, 67–71; Woolworth 1904, 222). An eyewitness reported that the events "almost make one think that hell had given a holiday and turned all the devils loose in the Nebraska Legislature" (*NYT* 1858b).

Passions were aroused because failing to keep the capital could prove devastating to a community—St. Stephens, Alabama's first territorial capital, lost that status in 1819 and not long afterward became a ghost town (St. Stephens Historical Commission, 1–2). Indeed, several of the communities that hosted the first territorial legislatures failed to thrive after the capital moved elsewhere. Illinois relocated its capital to Vandalia in 1820, in part because of the flooding threat posed to Kaskaskia by the Mississippi River. Those fears proved well founded. In 1844, Kaskaskia, which was already in decline after losing the capital, was devastated by a flood. Another flood in 1881 destroyed what little remained of the town. Today, the only remnant left of Kaskaskia is a sliver of farm land on the west side of the current river channel. It is the only part of Illinois on the western bank of the Mississippi. Bannack, the first territorial capital of Montana, is now a state park (Sherfy 1999, 93), as is Arkansas Post, Arkansas's first territorial capital.

Given the stakes, it is not surprising that losing the capital could be harmful to the community's legislators. When Arizona Councilor C. C. Stephens was unsuccessful in landing the state capital or the state insane asylum for his Tucson constituents (instead he got a university), they berated him unmercifully, as recounted in a local newspaper.

> If C. C. Stephens think he can kick Pima County from one end of the Territory to the other, utterly ignore her and the wants of the people as if he were an avowed enemy, instead of a servant pledged to faithfully represent her interests in the Legislature and then after all his contemptible acts seek to smooth things over by the sop of a Territorial University, that nobody asked for and which at best can be realized in a far distant future, he will find that it will not go down.

When the councilor returned to Tucson to defend his actions the audience responded by pelting him with "ripe eggs, rotting vegetables, and supposedly, a dead cat" (Wagoner 1970, 211).

Some policy areas in which territorial legislatures were involved are not associated with legislatures today, most notably the granting of divorces. Even early on many territorial lawmakers had qualms about performing this judicial function (Magruder 1981). One concern was that divorce petitions consumed valuable legislative time (Brazier 2000, 8; Burnet 1847, 325; Ewbank and Riker 1934, 30–31; "Legislative Divorces" 1844; Martin 1944, 41–42; McClure 1869, 372; McConnell 1913, 370–71; Murray 1908,

112, 117–18; Spence 1975, 184; Strong 1870, 23, 37–38; Wagoner 1970, 59–60). Another was that they occasionally generated political scandals, as happened when territorial legislatures in Arizona and Washington granted their governors divorces (Altshuler 1989; Brazier 2000, 9, 17–18). Finally, the mixing of the political and the personal made many lawmakers uncomfortable, because, as one wag observed, "The legislative Council says that as parties go courting to get married, they must go courting to get unmarried" (*Seattle Gazette* 1864). Indeed there were concerns that the process tended to be one-sided. A Montana paper claimed, "In most cases it is the man who applies to the Legislature, and where this is the case, it is fair to presume that he is in the wrong and seeks legislative action to obtain that which a court of Justice on full hearing would never grant" (*MP* 1868b). Eventually, many new state constitutions took away the legislature's power to grant divorces. As a Wisconsin newspaper observed just before statehood, "The favor which this pioneer bill among the divorce applications has met in both branches of the Territorial Legislature, will doubtless ensure that body as much of this sort of business as they have the time and disposition to attend to. Happily, the Constitution forbids any such 'special Legislation' in future" (*Milwaukee Sentinel* 1848). Congress terminated the ability of the remaining territorial legislatures to grant divorces in the Harrison Act of 1886.

In spite of the obstacles they faced, evidence suggests that, at least during their first few years, territorial legislatures were efficient lawmaking organizations. As can be seen in table 4.3, almost all of the measures introduced into the first Illinois territorial legislature ultimately made it into law. A plurality dealt with the court system, but the rest touched on a number of other issues, among them one that repealed gambling laws. Only a bill regulating court procedures was vetoed by the governor (James 1901, 76, 113). One of the few pieces of legislation that failed to make it through the legislature was a measure to "amend the several laws concerning the militia and for the relief of Quakers, Drunkards, etc." which passed the House but was stopped in the Council. These data suggest that the seven-member House saw its role as initiating legislation, while the five-member Council operated in a more reactive manner.

The rhythm of the legislative process in the territories was much the same as in contemporary legislatures (cf. Loomis 1994). Sessions started slowly. A reporter decided that even at its halfway point, "one of the most notable characteristics of the Wyoming Assembly is the entire absence of hurry about anything" (*NYT* 1873b). At a similar point in Hawaii's first session a Honolulu paper carped, "'To do or not to do' seems to be the motto of both branches of the Territorial Legislature, with an awful accent on the 'not to do'" (*Independent* 1901c). The glacial pace of the twelfth Utah territorial legislature was noted by a local paper, which concluded, "During the first week of the session there was but little business done." The paper rendered the same verdict on the second week: "The Legislative Assembly does not seem to have done much business." The final days of the session, however, were characterized differently, "The proceedings of the Legislative Assembly, during the last three days of the session, were very voluminous" (*DN* 1862a, 1862b, 1863b). Actually, the frantic pace of the closing hours had been anticipated by another observer. Early in that session a correspondent had mused, "The duties of the members have not been very onerous, at least very little work has been done. To be sure, toward the close there is a turning up of the sleeves that looks like hard work, and it is probable that at the last hour the law-making business will assume an unwonted briskness" (*NYT* 1863). The same pattern was observed in Arizona, where on the fourteenth day of the thirteenth session, a paper complained, "thus far nothing has been accomplished." Several weeks later the complaint was, "As usual, the most important measures have been kept for the close, and the next two weeks will see the passage or defeat, of the leading bills" (*Arizona Silver Belt* 1885a, 1885b). And in Kansas, where few bills passed early, on the final day "In about six hours . . . the House had passed *between eighty and ninety bills*. . . . They just set the mill to grinding, and then kept the hopper full" (NYT 1858a, italics in original).

TABLE 4.3. Bill Introductions and Passage Rates in the 1812 Illinois Territorial Legislature

Chamber	Number of Bills Introduced	Number of Bills That Passed Chamber (percentage of introduced)	Number of Bills That Passed Both Chambers and Were Enrolled (percentage of introduced)	Number of Bills Approved by Governor (percentage of introduced)
Council	7	6 (86)	5 (71)	5 (71)
House	33	29 (88)	25 (76)	24 (73)

Source: Calculated by the author from data in James 1901, 157–70, and Philbrick 1950, 50.

The Organizational Development of Territorial Legislatures

By and large, territorial legislatures were rough-and-tumble organizations run by rough-and-tumble men, almost none of whom had any prior legislative experience. As a member of the Northwest Council wrote of his colleagues, "Many of them, it is true, were unacquainted with the forms and practical duties of legislation" (Burnet 1847, 289). During an early vote in the first New Mexico House, a member heard his name called, and he "approached the speaker's chair and said, '*Que quieres usted de mi, señor?*' (What do you want with me, sir?)" This happened three times before the lawmaker understood what was expected of him (Davis 1857, 171). Consequently, a little knowledge about the legislative process marked a man as a potential leader. A member of the first Nebraska Council recalled, "All the parliamentary law I knew I had gained from study of Jefferson's Manual, which I had borrowed after my election." His admitted "meager knowledge of the subject" did not prevent his colleagues from determining that he was "the most capable and best equipped member to put into the chair as *pro tempo* president of the council" (Bennet 1898, 89).

Being located on the frontier also meant that territorial legislatures confronted unusual institutional challenges. For instance, on August 27, 1794, the Southwest territorial House "ordered, that Mr. Kelly and Mr. Beaird, have leave of absence to go on a scout against the Indians" (*Jour. of the Proc. of the H. of Reps. of the Terr. of the USA, South of the River Ohio* [1794] 1852, 5). Yet, in many ways, territorial legislatures were remarkably successful organizations. In the first session of the Northwest territorial legislature the backwoods lawmakers completely revised the territory's laws, passing legislation dealing with, among other things, debtor relief, Indian relations, legal protection for French residents, the establishment of courts, and contract, divorce, real estate, and criminal laws (Graham 1888, 311). Given the extraordinary challenges territorial legislatures faced, what led to their success?

Their saving grace was the rules and structures they inherited from existing legislatures. Despite the reality that territorial legislatures were located on the frontier, and territorial legislators were anything but genteel in their behavior or schooled in parliamentary procedure, in fundamentally important ways the institutions looked and operated much like their established state counterparts. On the first day of the inaugural regular session of the Northwest territorial legislature in 1799, the frontier lawmakers elected the leadership positions found in established American legislatures of the time: the Council a president, secretary, doorkeeper, and sergeant at arms, the House a speaker, clerk, doorkeeper, and sergeant at arms. They instituted sophisticated rules. Both ad hoc and standing committees were created. Indeed, by the third decade of the nineteenth century newly established territorial legislatures immediately instituted full-blown standing committee systems. Where did territorial legislators get their rules and structures?

Rules and Procedures

The vast majority of early territorial legislators had no previous legislative experience. But fortunately, a few did. The first president of the Washington Council had served in the California state legislature (Warren 1988, 26). Arthur Ingram, who served in both the Wisconsin and Iowa territorial councils, had earlier in his life spent five years as a member of the Virginia House of Delegates (Taylor 1890, 522). Among the initial Alaska territorial lawmakers were men who had been members of the California, Oregon, and Washington state legislatures.[20] Occasionally, a staff member had a legislative background, as was the case with the secretary of the Minnesota Council who had previously worked in the Wisconsin territorial legislature (Folwell 1956, 256).

Otherwise, inexperienced territorial lawmakers made use of whatever informational resources they had available to them. In most cases these were limited. The young assistant to the Iowa territorial secretary who was sent east to secure books for the new territorial library later confessed, "Now, I had never seen a legislative body in session. I had no idea or conception of what the members required for the convenience of their work" (Parvin 1900, 22–23). Consequently, frontier legislators scraped together whatever bits and pieces of existing parliamentary practices they could find. During the first session of the Washington territorial legislature, the territorial library held a smattering of legislative journals, including several from the U.S. House and Senate, as well as a few from state legislatures in Iowa, New Hampshire, New York, and Texas, and territorial legislatures in Minnesota and New Mexico (*Jour. of the H. of Reps. of the Terr. of Wash.* 1855, 154). The first Wyoming territorial legislature had at its disposal legislative journals from Colorado and Nebraska (Larson 1978, 74). According to a member of the initial Alaska territorial legislature, "We had a copy of one of the proceedings of the Oregon legislature and on that we organized and started in."[21]

Working off existing rules and procedures is, of course, a rational act. None of the new territorial legislatures started from scratch, instead their rules and procedures were taken from predecessor legislatures. The Southwest Territory was carved out of North Carolina. Given that the territory had been represented in the North Carolina legislature it is not surprising that the new territorial legislators turned to their parent body for the substance of their parliamentary rules. Table 4.4 maps the rules used by the North Carolina House and Senate onto the rules adopted by the new Southwest territorial House. As can been seen, all the territorial chamber's rules and procedures were taken from its parent bodies. This is likely because John Sevier, a former North Carolina state senator and a member of the Council, consulted on the rules used by the territorial House (Gilmore 1887, 271). The first Alabama territorial House explicitly adopted "the rules which governed the house of Representatives of the Mississippi Territory at their last session" (*Jour. of the H. of Reps., of the Ala. Terr. at the First Sess.* 1818, 7–8). The inaugural Washington territorial House followed the same pattern: "The Oregon rules were read and adopted" (*Jour. of the H. of Reps. of the Terr. of Wash.* 1855, 10). Although it went unattributed, both the initial Wisconsin territorial House (*Jour. of the H. of Reps. of the First Terr. Assembly of Wis.* 1836, 5–9) and Council (*Jour. of the Coun. of the First LA of Wis.* 1836, 5–8) lifted their rules almost completely from those used by their parent legislature, the Michigan Council (cf. *Jour. of the Proc. of the Sixth LC of the Terr. of Mich*, 1834, 8–12).

The rules and procedures adopted by new territorial legislatures could be surprisingly complex. The first Northwest territorial House adopted 55 rules (*Jour. of the H. of Reps. of the Terr. of the US, North-west of the River Ohio at the First sess. of the GA* 1799, 12–16). The first 38 rules fell under the heading of "Touching the Duty of the Speaker" and involved the speaker's powers as well as the details of legislative procedure and member responsibilities and decorum. Some of the procedural rules were sophisticated, including three dealing with moving the previous question. One rule appeared under the heading of the "Duty of the Door-keeper." The final 16 rules, under a section heading "Of Bills," provided guidance on the introduction, reading, enrolling, and engrossing of legislative proposals.

Like other territorial rules, those adopted by the Northwest territorial House were rooted in rules used by existing legislatures. In this case, the vast majority—39 out of 55 rules—were taken virtually word for word from those adopted by the U.S. House in 1795 (cf. *Jour. of the H. of Reps. of the US* 1795, 24–29). Another 11 were very similar to U.S. House rules.

TABLE 4.4. Mapping the Rules of Decorum in the 1789 North Carolina House of Commons and the Rules of Decorum in the 1792 North Carolina Senate onto the Rules of Decorum in the 1794 Southwest Territorial House of Representatives

Rule Number (chamber)	1789 North Carolina House of Commons 1792 North Carolina Senate — Rule	Rule Number	1794 Southwest Territorial House of Representatives — Rule
1 (Senate)	When the Speaker takes the chair each member shall take his seat, and on the appearance of a quorum, the journal of the preceding day shall be read.	1st	When the Speaker is in the chair, every member may sit in his place with his head covered.
IV (House)	That no person shall come into the House, or remove from one place to another with his hat on, except those of the Quaker profession.	2nd	That every member shall come into the house uncovered and shall continue so at all times, but when he sits in his place.
I (House)	No person shall pass between the Speaker and the person speaking.	3rd	No member, in coming into the house, or removing from his place, shall pass between the Speaker and a member speaking, nor shall any member go across the house, or from one part thereof to the other whilst another was speaking.
II (House)	That no member should be allowed to speak but in his place, and after rising and addressing himself to the Speaker; shall not proceed until permitted by the Speaker's calling him by name.	4th	When any member stands to speak, he shall stand in his place uncovered, and address himself to the Speaker, but shall not proceed to speak until permitted so to do by the Speaker, which permission is granted by naming the member.
III (House)	That no person shall stand up or disturb another while he is speaking.	5th	When any member is speaking, no other shall stand or interrupt him; but when he is done speaking, and taken his seat, any other may rise, observing the rules.
VI (House)	The Speaker ought to be heard without interruption, and when he rises the member up shall sit down.	6th	When the Speaker desires to address himself to the house he shall rise, and be heard without interruption; and the member then speaking shall take his seat.
XI (House)	When two or more members are up together, the Speaker shall determine who rose first.	7th	If more than one member attempt to speak at any time, the Speaker shall determine who was up first.

8th	When any motion shall be before the house and not perfectly understood, the Speaker may explain, but shall not attempt to sway the house by argument or debate.	11 (Senate)	When any question shall be before the house that is not perfectly understood, the Speaker may explain, and shall be heard at all times without interruption.
9th	He that digresseth from the subject, to fall on the person of any member, shall be suppressed by the Speaker.	10 (Senate)	No personal reflections to be permitted; and any member reflecting upon another, shall be immediately called to order.
10th	Exceptions, taken to offensive words, to be taken the same day they shall be spoken, and before the member who spoke them shall go out of the house.	VII (House)	That no person shall be called upon for any words of heat, but on the day on which they were spoken. -
11th	Whatever is spoken in the house, may be subject to the censure of the house.	XII (House)	Whoever violates any of the above rules shall receive such censure as the house shall direct.
12th	Whenever any matter is in debate before the house, it shall be determined or postponed before any new business shall be introduced.	13 (Senate)	Whenever any question is in debate before the house, it shall be determined or postponed before any new motion shall be introduced; unless to amend it, to adjourn, or for the previous question.
13th	No member shall speak more than twice without leave, in the same question, unless it be in a committee of the whole house.	V (House)	That no person shall speak more than twice to one question, upon any debate, without leave, except in a committee of the whole House.
14th	No question shall be put on any motion, unless seconded.	X (House)	That the House shall not proceed to debate on any motion unless the same is seconded, and immediately reduced to writing, provided any member requires the same.
15th	Every member making any motion, which is not of course, shall before making such motion, reduce the same to writing.		
16th	If there shall be an equality of votes for and against any question, the Speaker shall declare whether he be a yea or nay; but shall in no other case give his vote.	VIII (House)	Whenever the members are equally divided, the Speaker shall determine the question, but not vote on any other occasion.
17th	No member shall depart the service of the house without leave.	IX (House)	That no member shall depart the service of the house without leave.
18th	Upon adjournment, no member shall presume to move until the Speaker arises and goes before.	22 (Senate)	When the house adjourns, no member shall walk out before the Speaker.

Source: *Jour. of the H. of Commons, St. of N.C. 1790*, 2; *Jour. of the Sen., St. of N.C. 1793*, 3; *Jour. of the Proc. of the H. of Reps. of the Terr. of the USA, South of the River Ohio* [1794] 1852, 3–4.

Only 5 rules used by the Northwest territorial House were not taken from the U.S. House; 2 of these, however, appeared in the rules used by the first Kentucky House in 1792 (*Jour. of the H. of Reps. at the First Sess. of the GA for the Com. of Ky.* 1792, 4–5).[22] Interestingly, both the Kentucky House and the Northwest territorial House numbered their rules, something which the U.S. House at the time did not do.

In turn, the Northwest territorial House rules were imported by legislatures established later. Four of the Northwest territorial House's lineal descendents, the Indiana territorial House, the Illinois territorial House, the Indiana House, and the Illinois House, took their rules almost verbatim from those used by the Northwest territorial House. The rules even migrated to less familial legislatures; the Mississippi Council used a pared-down version—37 of their 39 rules were the same as those used in the Northwest territorial House, including two not found in the U.S. House rules (James 1901, 87; *Jour. of the H. of Reps. of the First Sess. of the First GA of the St. of Ill.* 1818, 15–19; *Jour. of the LC, at the First Sess. of the Fourth GA of the Miss. Terr.* 1807, 12–16; Thornbrough and Riker 1950, 31; Walsh 1987, 92).

The importance of inheriting developed rules and procedures should not be underestimated. New territorial legislatures operated under very trying circumstances with members who had very little exposure to parliamentary practices. Importing rules provided them the structure they required to begin making decisions and allowed the speaker of the first Arizona territorial House to tell his members at the conclusion of the session, "Without Legislative experience when you arrived in this capital, you have conducted your business with the order and system of the sages of a senate" (Farish 1916, 130). It is hard to imagine that any new legislature composed of inexperienced lawmakers could make such a claim if it had had to start from scratch.

Typically, once put in place the rules used in a territorial legislature were adopted without changes in its subsequent sessions. For example: "*Resolved*, That the Standing Rules for the government of the second Legislative Council of the Territory of Michigan be, and they are hereby declared to be the Standing Rules for the government of the present Council" (*Jour. of the LC of the Terr. of Mich.* 1828, 8). Occasionally a chamber opted to tinker. Of the 60 rules adopted by the fourteenth Idaho territorial House, almost all were taken from those used by the thirteenth House; 3 rules were new, and 4 rules were amended in some fashion (*Jour. of the H. of Reps. of the Fourteenth LA of the Terr. of Idaho* 1887, 28–29).

Generally, rules changes accrued slowly and in piecemeal fashion (e.g., Thornbrough and Riker 1950, 159, 161, 269, 371, 599, 696). By the 1830s, however, legislative manuals provided new legislatures authoritative guidance on procedural issues. In the Iowa Council members relied on *Jefferson's Manual* as the source for legislative rules and procedures during their first session, and they formally recognized those rules as governing their procedures in their second session. Later sessions simply revised the rules used in the previous session, often making few or no changes (Briggs 1916, 40–41). A similar pattern unfolded in the Kansas Council with its initial rules relying on *Jefferson's Manual* (*Jour. of the Coun. of the Terr. of Kan.* 1855, 9–11). Subsequent sessions more thoroughly elaborated and codified the rules (*Rules for the Gov. of the LA of the Terr. of Kan.* 1858). Given high levels of membership turnover, rule evolution had to accommodate member inexperience even in established territorial legislatures. In 1888, a Wyoming Council special committee on rules, which had consulted "Jefferson's, Cushing's, Robert's, Manual of Parliamentary Practice; also Smith's Parliamentary Rules, and the Wisconsin 'Blue Book,'" reported, "Several new and important rules have been added, and it is confidently believed by the committee that the new rules in relation to the manner of introducing bills and moving the 'previous question' will be of great service to members who have but little experience in parliamentary practice" (*Coun. Jour. of the Tenth LA of the Terr. of Wyo.* 1888, 13–14). Territorial lawmakers appreciated that only through the use of proper parliamentary procedures could their legislatures function and thrive.

Standing Committees

Over time, standing committees became integral to the functioning of territorial legislatures and a valuable mechanism for enhancing organizational continuity. Initially, early territorial legislatures mimicked the existing state legislatures and Congress by relying on ad hoc committees to address specific issues. Thus, in the first Indiana territorial House the speaker quickly appointed seven ad hoc committees to address specific issues identified by the territorial governor in his address to the body (Thornbrough and Riker 1950, 48–49). Additional ad hoc committees were named throughout the rest of the session. Other early territorial legislatures also employed numerous ad hoc committees. But even in these bodies, standing committees usually appeared. The Southwest territorial House used a large number of ad hoc committees, but it also appointed a standing committee on propositions and grievances (*Jour. of the Proc. of the H. of Reps. of the Terr. of the USA, South of the River Ohio* [1794] 1852, 7–8). The Northwest territorial House similarly relied heavily on ad hoc committees, but it established two standing committees: privileges and elections, and ways and means (*Jour. of the H. of Reps. of the Terr. of the US, North-west of the River Ohio at the First sess. of the GA* 1799, 3). By 1812, ad hoc bodies were being termed *select committees* in the Illinois territorial House, which used a number of them but also had a standing committee on enrollments (James 1901, 95–96). In 1813, the Missouri territorial House operated much like its Illinois counterpart just down the Mississippi River in Kaskaskia, using select committees and a single standing committee on enrollments (*Missouri Gazette* 1814).[23]

Over time, standing committees played a more prominent role in the legislative process. In its second session the Mississippi territorial House employed a number of ad hoc committees to deal with specific proposals; for example it "Ordered that a Committee of three be appointed to revise the Judiciary system and a law establishing fees of certain officers, taking into view particularly the inconvenience under which the County of Washington is placed by its great distance from the actual residence of the Territorial Judges." At the same time, however, the body also appointed three standing committees: "ways and means," "previledges and Elections," and "claims" (McCain 1940, 16–17). By the eighth session the standing rules or orders of the Mississippi House required the establishment of seven standing committees: elections, ways and means, claims, accounts, propositions and grievances, revisal and unfinished business, and enrolled bills (*Jour. of the H. of Reps. of the Miss. Terr.* 1814, 6–8). Not surprisingly, given the transmission of rules and structures the same seven standing committees appeared in almost the same (nonalphabetical) order in the first Alabama territorial House, after that territory was fashioned from the eastern part of the Mississippi Territory (*Jour. of the H. of Reps., of the Ala. Terr. at the First Sess.* 1818, 21).

As standing committees became the institutional norm in state legislatures, they appeared immediately in newly established territorial legislatures. The initial Florida Council established two four-member standing committees—one on judiciary matters, the other on revenue—even though the body only had eight or nine members in attendance (Morris and Maguire 1978, 33). The following year seven standing committees were created as part of the Council's rules (Morris 1982). The Wisconsin territorial House and Council created virtually identical standing committee systems within days of their first meetings. Each chamber created eight standing committees. The differences between the two were minor. The Council, for example, established a Finance Committee, while the House had an Expenses Committee (*Jour. of the H. of Reps. of the First Terr. Asm. of Wis.* 1836, 16; *Jour. of the Coun. of the First LA of Wis.* 1836, 14). The Washington territorial House created 15 standing committees on the second day of its first session; on the third day of its first session the Council established essentially the same set of 15 standing committees (*Pioneer and Democrat* 1854a). In its first session the Kansas Council created 13 standing committees, while 10 standing committees were established in the House (*Jour. of the Coun. of the Terr. of Kan.* 1855, 23; *Jour. of the H. of Reps. of the Terr. of Kan.* 1855, 36–37). Within the first few days of its inaugural session, the Colorado Council created 13 standing committees and the House 16 standing committees (*Daily Colorado Republican* 1861a, 1861b).

Most of the standing committees created across the territories were generic, covering topics such as education, finance, and roads that constitute the basic stuff of American legislative policy making. But a few were tailored to meet the specific needs of particular territories. In the mid-1850s, for example, the Utah territorial House had a Committee on Herding. A decade later, it boasted a Committee on Roads, Bridges, Ferries, and Kanyons (*DN* 1856e, 1857, 1860c, 1861b, 1862a). Given the importance of lead mining in the development of Wisconsin's economy, it is not surprising that the territorial House had a Committee on Mining and Smelting (*Jour. of the H. of Reps., First Annual Sess. of the Fifth LA of the Terr. of Wis.* 1847, 23).

Once established, standing committee systems in territorial legislatures were quite stable. All eight of the standing committees created by the first Wisconsin Council in 1836 were still in existence in 1841. The Claims Committee disappeared after 1841, while an Agriculture and Manufactures Committee appeared in each of the final three meetings. After the 1841 session the Public Expenditures Committee was split into the Territorial Expenditures Committee and the Legislative Expenditures Committee. Otherwise there was impressive continuity (*Jour. of the Coun. of the LA of Wis.* 1841, 23; *Jour. of the Coun. of the Fourth LA of Wis.* 1843, 63; *Jour. of the Coun. of the Third Annual Sess. of the Fourth LA of the Terr. of Wis.* 1845, 19–20; *Jour. of the Coun., First Annual Sess. of the Fifth LA of The Terr. of Wis.* 1847, 21). A similar picture of consistency is found in the Utah territorial House from 1856–57 to 1857–58. Over those two sessions there was only a slight twist in the names of two committees: Herding became Herding and Herd Grounds, and Corporations became Incorporations (*DN* 1856e, 1857). As shown in table 4.5, during the three sessions of the House between 1860 and 1863 there were no changes in the committee structure or names.

There was a surprising degree of committee membership continuity given high levels of membership turnover in the chambers. At the low end, committee member carryover rates in the Wisconsin Council from 1841 to 1847 ranged from 11 percent to just 3 percent. More impressive figures were found in the Utah territorial House, where, as shown in table 4.5, between 26 and 36 percent of committee members carried over from one ses-

TABLE 4.5. Standing Committees and Carryover of Member Assignments in the Utah Territorial House of Representatives, 1860–61 to 1862–63

1860–61 Committees	1861–62 Number of Committee Members	Members Returning from Previous Session	1862–63 Number of Committee Members	Members Returning from Previous Session	Members Serving All Three Sessions
Judiciary	3	2	5	0	0
Claims and Appropriations	3	3	3	3	3
Petitions and Memorials	3	2	3	2	1
Revenue	4	3	4	0	0
Elections	3	1	4	0	0
Counties	3	1	4	1	0
Road, Bridges, Ferries and Kanyons	4	0	4	1	0
Education	3	0	4	0	0
Engrossing	3	1	3	1	1
Printing	3	0	4	2	0
Agriculture, Trade, and Manufactures	4	2	4	1	1
Militia	4	1	4	2	1
Incorporations	3	0	4	0	0
Library	4	1	4	1	1
Public Domains and School Lands	5	1	5	0	0
Penitentiary	3	2	3	2	1
Number of committees: 16	Total committee assignments: 55	Percentage carried over: 36	Total committee assignments: 62	Percentage carried over: 26	Percentage carried over: 15

Source: Assignments reported in *DN* 1860c, 1861b, 1862a.

sion to the next, and 15 percent served on the same committee all three sessions between 1861 and 1863. None of these figures compares favorably to those found in the modern U.S. Congress, but given high chamber turnover levels, they do suggest that there was a reasonable expectation of organizational memory on many standing committees. This is important because it is another mechanism that allowed territorial legislatures to overcome their considerable limitations.

The Role of Political Parties

To this point, political parties in the territorial legislatures have only been mentioned in passing. In large part, this is because their influence on the early territorial bodies was limited. This is understandable because prior to the advent of railroads and the telegraph, territories were distanced from national politics in both time and space. Although territorial governors (and council members initially) were political appointees, lower-house members had, at best, only loose party affiliations. In their memoirs on the Northwest territorial legislature neither Burnet (1847) nor Cutler (1890) indicates that partisanship played any role in legislative organization. A close observer of the first Iowa territorial legislature recalled that in regard to leadership positions, "there were no politics then in these selections." It was only during the second meeting of the legislature that party caucuses formed (Parvin 1900, 21). Partisanship played little role in Minnesota (Van Koughnet 1933, 131). The initial Nebraska territorial legislature organized around a regional split between "North Platte" lawmakers and "South Platte" lawmakers, and not around parties (Bennet 1898, 89).

The combination of the rise of national issues surrounding the Civil War and technological advancements linking the peripheries more closely with the rest of the country brought political parties into greater prominence in the territories. But partisan distinctions were often a bit fuzzy in practice. In Washington national party positions on slavery and states' rights drove local politics in the latter part of the 1850s (Johannsen 1951). But even then, minority party lawmakers were named committee chairs (Bird 1958, 65). In Montana, bills passed in the first legislature by the Confederate-sympathizing Democratic majority were routinely signed into law by the Republican governor, a Lincoln appointee (Housman 1935, 376–82). The existence of viable minor parties in Oklahoma and the election of fusion candidates to the territorial legislature make it difficult to uncover partisan effects on legislative organization in that body (Darcy 2005).

All of this suggests that, at least in most territorial legislatures, partisan calculations are unlikely to explain the initial adoption of rules and legislative structures. Given that rules and structures did not change dramatically from one session to the next, party is not a strong candidate to explain how territorial legislatures evolved. Instead, organizational needs to meet the external policy pressures on them appear to provide a more reasonable explanation.

Conclusions

Although operating under trying circumstances, territorial legislatures represented the strong democratic impulse embodied in the U.S. Constitution (Lawson and Seidman 2004, 124). They labored with members who were "unskilled in parliamentary logic" (Graham 1888, 310). Membership turnover was remarkably high. Facilities were lacking, and staff support was limited. Reflecting on his experience as a member of the first Montana Council, one lawmaker wrote, "Creating a whole code of laws for a new [territory] without the aid of a library . . . was not a task of easy performance, and it has always been a wonder to me that we made as much of a success of our work as we did" (Thompson 2004, 207). Yet these challenged organizations managed in every case to successfully govern their territory to the point of its admission to the Union as a state. I argue that this is the result of legislative structures and procedures given to the territorial legislatures by the existing legislatures of the time, which allowed the new organizations to overcome the handicap of limited legislative experience among their members. In particular, rules of proceeding, which structure decision making and constrain member behavior, allowed territorial legislatures to legislate with few hindrances. Standing committee systems allowed for the development of both organizational continuity and organizational memory. Territorial legislatures passed on many of these structures and rules to their state legislative progeny, allowing those organizations to begin their operations at a point even further along the evolutionary path.

5 · The Odd Evolutionary Cases

The original 13 state legislatures emerged almost directly from their colonial predecessors, as documented in chapter 3. In chapter 4 it was shown that another 31 state legislatures evolved straight out of their territorial legislatures. That leaves the evolutionary stories behind 6 state legislatures unexplained. In addition, earlier legislative bodies preceded territorial legislatures in 4 states. Competing legislatures arose in another territory, only 1 of which left an evolutionary imprint. Each of these evolutionary oddities merits examination. There also are 2 other unusual legislatures created during the nineteenth century that shed light on the evolutionary process.

These cases present intriguing developmental twists. The first 6 are instances where there was no territorial legislature prior to the creation of the state legislature.

- In 2 cases—Vermont and Kentucky—the state was not among the original 13, but its legislature was established prior to the start of the territorial process. Thus, as figure 1.1 suggested, Vermont's state legislature was a direct descendent of the original state legislatures, while Kentucky's had ties to the original 13, plus Vermont and the Congress under the Constitution.
- In 2 cases—Maine and West Virginia—a new state was carved out of an existing state. The relationships between these new states and their parent states were not, however, parallel, with implications for their legislatures.
- In one case—Texas—a national legislature preceded the state legislature. Despite the regime change there was considerable continuity between the 2 legislatures.

- In the final case—California—the state legislature had no predecessor.

In 4 cases a territorial legislature was preceded by one or more other legislative bodies. Some of these had direct ties to their successors, while others had only tangential connections.

- Feeling isolated from and ignored by the governing authorities in North Carolina, a group of western counties in what would become the northeast section of Tennessee established a provisional state government that included a bicameral legislature.
- In Oregon, several iterations of a unicameral provisional legislature were devised to make laws while the United States and Great Britain vied for political control of the area.
- Prior to the creation of Utah Territory, Mormons founded the State of Deseret, complete with a two-chamber general assembly.
- The final case—Hawaii—is similar to Texas in that a national legislature existed before the territory was brought under the control of the United States. Unlike every other legislative body in American history, however, even the councils of the colonial era, one of the Kingdom of Hawaii chambers was reserved for nobles, some of whom were women. But between the legislatures of the Kingdom of Hawaii and the creation of the territorial legislature was sandwiched a bicameral legislature established under the Republic of Hawaii.

Another legislature deserves attention for its unusual evolutionary role.

- In Kansas, the Free State Legislature arose to not only challenge the proslavery territorial legislature but to ultimately supplant it in the state's evolutionary line.

Finally, two other little known legislatures merit consideration. Each had virtually no impact on later legislatures, but they demonstrate the pervasiveness of legislative institutions in American civic life during the nineteenth century.

- In California, three local legislative assemblies were established to partly fill the governing vacuum created by the absence of a territorial legislature. The most important of these was in San Francisco.

- The Indian Stream Republic was founded in a sliver of disputed land between northern New Hampshire and British Canada, and to fill the governing void residents created a General Assembly with distinctive features.

The important question about each of these curiosities is whether its experience confirms or contradicts the evolutionary story developed in the preceding chapters. That is, although each of these situations was unusual, to what extent were there ties between the predecessor and successor legislatures? Did they share constitutional features, procedural rules, committee structures, or legislative personnel? In each case, is the legislative oddity just a historical footnote, or is it an important part of the story about how the state legislature evolved? Even where a predecessor legislature's evolutionary contribution was limited, however, the creation of these bodies across a wide range of conditions and circumstances demonstrates an American propensity to turn to legislative bodies rather than to alternative structures when there is a need to create a government. What is of particular interest is the fact that this proclivity surfaced even in the most remote of places where other sorts of governing structures might have been more easily, more economically, and more efficiently established.

The Vermont Legislature

Even prior to the American Revolution, political control over the geographic area encompassed today by Vermont was contested by both New Hampshire and New York. After 1776, the Congress under the Articles of Confederation failed to resolve the dispute, in large part because its members were unwilling to be seen as agreeing to the dismemberment of either of the competing states. Consequently, Vermont declared its independence, and while it sided with the 13 states in the war with Britain, it existed in something of a political netherworld, not really a state, and not really an independent country (Onuf 1981). This anomalous status continued until Vermont was admitted to the union in 1791.

As a means to pressure Congress to bring it into the new union as a state, Vermont adopted a constitution in 1777. Vermonters did not, however, turn to either New Hampshire or New York for inspiration. Indeed, they explicitly rejected using New York's constitution as a model because it was deemed too conservative (Jones 1939, 382–83). Rather, at the urging of Dr. Thomas Young, a noted revolutionary figure of the time (Maier 1976), they looked to Pennsylvania for guidance. Young wrote, "I have recommended to your committee the Constitution of Pennsylvania, as a model, which, with a very little alteration, will, in my opinion, come as near perfection as any thing yet concocted by mankind" (Chipman 1849, 27). Young's advice was heeded, and Vermont clearly based its 1777 constitution on the one adopted by Pennsylvania the year before. Some scholars even go so far as to claim, "The constitution of Vermont was . . . copied almost word for word from the constitution of Pennsylvania" (Fisher 1900, 86). A close comparison of the two documents, however, reveals a number of important differences between them (*Cons. of the St. of Vt.* 1891, 42–44).

In regard to the creation of the legislature, the drafters of the Vermont constitution relied heavily on the Pennsylvania model. Most obviously, they created a unicameral legislature as in Pennsylvania, using language that simply substituted the word *Vermont* for *Pennsylvania*. The Vermont constitution lifted its quorum rules and the requirement to keep its chamber doors open directly from Pennsylvania's constitution. Only very slight wording changes were made in the requirements to publish votes and proceedings weekly, to allow the governor and public to comment on bills before final passage ("To the end that laws, before they are enacted, may be more maturely considered, and the inconveniency of hasty determination as much as possible prevented"), and in the formal style of legislation.

Still, the writers of the Vermont constitution deviated some from the Pennsylvania legislative model. They did not adopt any term limits, whereas Pennsylvania limited its legislators to serving three years out of six. A more minor difference was that a recorded vote could be demanded by two members in Pennsylvania, but in Vermont such a request required support from one-third of the membership. And, while both constitutions stated that the legislature should be composed of "persons most noted for wisdom and virtue," Vermont imposed only a one-year residency requirement "for foreigners" while Pennsylvania required a two-year residency and cast no aspersions on the recently arrived.

Thus, in most substantive ways, the fundamental structure of the Vermont House of Representatives was based on the Pennsylvania House of Representatives. Yet, in terms of the rules and internal structures adopted by the new Vermont body, it looked and operated much more like its New England contemporaries than it did its Mid-Atlantic parent. In 1779 the Assembly adopted its first set of formal rules (Crockett 1924, 78). Unnumbered, the rule count was between seven and nine depending on how the dense language in one long paragraph is parsed. The rules focused primarily on parliamentary etiquette, with only one speaking to procedural matters. Although not taken directly from the rules used elsewhere, they bear greater resemblance to the 12 rules employed by the New Hampshire House in 1776 than they do to the more elaborate and sophisticated 19 rules adopted by the Pennsylvania Assembly that same year (Bouton 1874, 8–9; *Jours. of the H. of Reps. of the Com. of Pa.* 1782, 98). Moreover, like the New Hampshire House, the Vermont Assembly did not use standing committees. In contrast, the Pennsylvania Assembly employed several of them.

Prior to statehood the Vermont General Assembly was an itinerant body. Between 1778 and 1791 its sessions ricocheted among nine different towns, including one not located within its boundaries (Crockett 1924, 1925, 1928, 1929; *Jour. of the Proc. of the GA of the St. of Vt.* 1791).[1] But some evolution can be discerned in the latter part of the prestate era. Initially the legislature met several times a year. By 1783 it was meeting twice a year, in February and then again in October. By 1788 it was meeting only in October, save for a January session in 1791 just prior to admission as a state. Organizationally, the legislature became slightly more complex. While there is no evidence of standing committees in the first state General Assembly in October 1791, by that time the simple, unnumbered rules adopted in 1779 had expanded to 15 numbered rules. Moreover, the 1791 rules were less centered on member etiquette; instead they devoted considerably more attention to procedural matters (*Jour. of the Proc. of the GA of the St. of Vt.* 1791, 6–7). Thus, consistent with the experience of the colonial assemblies and early state legislatures, over the course of its relatively brief prestatehood period, the Vermont legislature evolved to become a bit more sophisticated organizationally.

The Kentucky General Assembly

Compared with the Vermont legislature, the Kentucky General Assembly was even more of an evolutionary hybrid. In many ways it was a product of the turbulent politics of the 1780s and early 1790s. Although Kentucky broke away politically and geographically from Virginia, its parent legislature was not, for the most part, the model used for the new Kentucky legislature. Rather, the conflicting political forces that played out in the development of Kentucky resulted in a legislature that drew its features from several different sources.

Getting to the Kentucky constitution in 1792 was a drawn-out process that involved both negotiations to be freed from Virginia's government and political battles over the new structure that would replace it. Between 1784 and 1790 there were nine unsuccessful constitutional conventions (Coward 1979, 6). In addition, there were a number of political organizations, notably the Danville Political Club, and newspapers that provided ongoing forums for debating constitutional issues. During these extended discussions one legislative topic emerged on which there was widespread agreement: any Kentucky legislature ought to be apportioned on the basis of population rather than by county as in Virginia. Beyond that matter, there was a considerable gap between what the more conservative landed gentry wanted in the way of a legislature and the sort of body envisioned by the less well-to-do frontiersmen, who were fervent democrats. The conservative elements in Kentucky argued for a bicameral legislature, where something along the lines of an aristocratic upper house would act as brake on the impulses of the more representative lower-house rabble. Less fortunate Kentuckians much preferred a unicameral legislature because they argued it would wipe out the sorts of class distinctions entrenched by upper houses with stringent membership qualifications found among the original states. The frontiersmen also argued that one chamber would be less expensive to fund (Coulter 1924, 667–69, 672).

Despite the fact that it was populated by political neophytes who "shared a remarkable lack of preparation for the task before them," the tenth Kentucky constitutional convention managed to successfully cobble together a document that proved acceptable to both camps (Coward 1979, 21). The delegates may not have been well trained in politics or the law, but they were shrewd enough to look to existing constitutions for guidance. Although some scholars see the Kentucky constitution as being drawn from the federal constitution (Coulter 1924, 677), while others find kinship with Virginia's 1776 constitution (Thorpe 1898, 134), a close examination reveals that it was largely taken from the Pennsylvania constitution of 1790 (Barnhart 1941, 34), with a smattering of provisions lifted from several other state constitutions.

The ties to the 1790 Pennsylvania constitution are particularly pronounced in regard to legislative provisions. The language in the Kentucky constitution creating a bicameral General Assembly was taken word for word from the Pennsylvania constitution, changing only the name of the state. Among other provisions lifted from the Pennsylvania constitution were those allowing each house to choose its speaker and other officers, the requirement that the senate select a speaker pro tem, quorum standards, the right for each house to determine its rules of proceedings, the ability of two members to force a recorded vote, the need to keep a journal, and the obligation to keep the doors of the chamber open unless "the business shall be such as ought to be kept secret." A few provisions were tweaked only slightly. For instance, the age of eligibility for serving in the Kentucky house was set at 24 years rather 21 years as in the Pennsylvania constitution. Similarly, both constitutions stated that members would be paid out of the state treasury, but Kentucky went on to specify the amount at "six shillings a day during their attendance on, going to, and returning from the Legislature." This represented the first time a state had designated a specific legislative salary in its constitution (Luce 1924, 528).[2]

The most significant deviation from the Pennsylvania constitution came in the process by which members of the Kentucky senate were to be elected. In Pennsylvania senators were directly elected to four-year terms by eligible voters. Kentucky's constitution also set the senate term at four years but looked to the Maryland constitution of 1776 for election mechanics. Using very similar language, Kentucky mimicked Maryland's electoral college system of senate election. Thus, voters in each county in Kentucky would choose electors, who in turn would meet to elect the members of the senate. This system was replaced by direct elections in the state's 1799 constitution.

Structurally, then, the Kentucky General Assembly looked much like the Pennsylvania General Assembly, albeit with a senate elected using the Maryland method. But in creating the internal organization of the legislature, the state looked elsewhere for inspiration. The rules adopted by the Kentucky House were taken almost completely from those adopted by the U.S. House in 1789 (cf. *Jour. of the H. of Reps. at the First Sess. of the GA for the Com. of Ky.* 1792, 4–5; *Jour. of the H. of Reps. of the US* 1789, 9–12). Thus, the same four topic sections were employed in the same order: the duty of the Speaker; decorum and debate; bills; and committees of the whole house. Of the 51 rules adopted by the Kentucky House, only 5 were altogether different from those used in the U.S. House.[3] Another 3 rules were only slightly different.[4] The rest were identical, although the Kentucky House omitted some rules used by the U.S. House.

The standing committee system in the Kentucky House was taken from yet a third source. Even before it adopted its rules on the second day of its existence, the House created its standing committees (*Jour. of the H. of Reps. at the First Sess. of the GA for the Com. of Ky.* 1792, 3–4). The configuration they adopted was taken straight from the Virginia House of Delegates. Not only did the Kentucky House establish the same five standing committees as in the Virginia House—Religion, Privileges and Elections, Propositions and Grievances, Courts of Justice, and Claims—but they did so in exactly the same nonalphabetical order (cf. *Jour. of the H. of Dels. of the Com. of Va.* 1791, 3–4). Moreover, the Kentucky House used the same enacting language and much the same wording setting quorums for the conduct of committee business, differing only in the number of members required to be present.

The initial meeting of the Kentucky legislature was held in Lexington in a "rude two-story log building." A month later the legislature reassembled in Frankfort in Andrew Holmes's house (*Off. Man. for the use of the Courts, St., and County Officials and GA of the St. of Ky.* 1900, v). But, although it was established on the frontier's edge and first met in rudimentary facilities, the Kentucky General Assembly was never a primitive organization. Most of its constitutional features were taken from the Pennsylvania constitution of 1790, the most modern document governing one of the original states, newer even than the federal constitution. The Kentucky House's legislative rules were lifted from those used by the U.S. House, the most complex and sophisticated procedures then available. The standing committee system mirrored that in Virginia, which was the most developed of any American legislature. Thus, at its inception, the Kentucky legislature was, even if located in the wilderness and populated by frontiersmen, arguably the most advanced legislature of its time.

The Spin-off Legislatures: Maine and West Virginia

Both Maine and West Virginia were spin-offs from existing states. But Maine's departure from Massachusetts was amicable, while West Virginia's Civil War split from Virginia was acrimonious. Thus, a relevant question for this study is whether the feelings surrounding the two breakups influenced the new state legislatures that were established. Did positive attitudes in Maine lead to its legislature being created in the image of its Massachusetts parent? Did negative views in West Virginia force the new state to distinguish itself from its secessionist progenitor?

Although some convention delegates argued against doing so, Maine largely modeled its constitution on the one in Massachusetts. But this was done primarily for reasons of expediency rather than a sense of familial obligation (Banks 1970, 153). Those who were to draft the Maine document needed a starting point, and the Massachusetts constitution seemed the obvious choice.

Legislatures loomed large in the convention debates. Indeed, the original draft of the constitution included an appeal to the "Great Legislator of the Universe," a phrase that was later replaced by "Sovereign Ruler of the Universe." When discussing specific legislative provisions, convention delegates referred to features in a number of states, but they usually fixed on those in Massachusetts. In several instances they pointed out what they saw as flaws in the Massachusetts system that they wished to avoid in creating the Maine legislature. One delegate made these comments.

> We want a House of Representatives that shall not be too large to transact the public business in a reasonable time; and which shall be large enough to embrace the talents and integrity of the State. Gentlemen seem to me to have erroneous ideas of the objects of a Legislative body. These have originated, no doubt, in some degree from the construction of the Legislature of Massachusetts—a Legislature the worst constructed in the Union—It is a perfect anomaly—there is nothing like it in any other State. Its House of Representatives has at times consisted of nearly seven hundred—sixty of which made a quorum.

Another asserted, "We are never to have a Representative body, I trust, like that of Massachusetts." Indeed, a newspaper correspondent covering the convention reported, "But there was one fact that ought not to be lost sight of, for it seemed to be in the mouth of every member of the Convention; when they first came together, and that was, let there be *a small house of representatives and senate* compared to the legislature of Massachusetts" (Perley 1820, 70, 123–24, 152, italics in original).

Sometimes, however, the Massachusetts experience was seen as a positive point of reference. In regard to the size of the upper house, one delegate noted, "And from thirty-one to thirty-three or four, was the number of members, which for many years, transacted the business in the Senate of Massachusetts. This was considered a suitable number for the whole State; and . . . it may be so considered for this State." Similarly, during a debate over the mechanics of compensating legislators, another delegate observed, "Forty years' experience, in Massachusetts, has proved that there is no risk in trusting the Legislature to establish their own compensation" (Perley 1820, 151, 155).

In the end, the Maine convention fashioned a legislature much like the one in Massachusetts, but with a few notable differences. Perhaps most obviously, Maine chose to call its representative assembly the *legislature* rather than the *general court*, the label used in Massachusetts. More important, the convention ended up establishing a considerably smaller legislature than the notoriously large one in Massachusetts. Otherwise the similarities between the two institutions were pronounced. Most of the provisions structuring the relationship between the two houses and giving each chamber the power to establish its own rules, to select its own leaders, and to judge the qualifications of its members were virtually the same between the two constitutions. All passed the convention with no discussion (Perley 1820, 155, 167–68).

In terms of actual operations, the similarities between the Maine and Massachusetts legislatures were, if anything, even more striking. Not surprisingly, there was some membership overlap; 8 of the original 20 members of the Maine senate had previously served as legislators in Massachusetts (Williamson 1832, 676). The 57 rules adopted by the Maine House were taken almost word for word from the rules used by Massachusetts (cf. *Rules and Orders to be Observed in the H. of Reps. of the St. of Maine* 1820, 3–12; *Rules and Orders to be Observed in the H. of Reps. of the Com. of Mass.* 1818, 3–14). The few differences between the two sets of rules were minor. The Maine House, for example, folded Massachusetts's House Chapter 1 Rule V into its Chapter 1 Rule II. In the Maine House one-fifth of the members could demand a calling of the yeas and nays; in Massachusetts it took one-third of the members. Some changes were positively trivial; in Massachusetts (Chapter II Rule II), "No person shall sit at the table, except the Speaker and Clerk," while Maine (Chapter II Rule II) identified different furniture and took a more flexible stance on seating: "No person shall sit at the Desk of the Speaker or Clerk, except by permission of the Speaker."

The Maine House also adopted virtually the same set of standing committees as used in the Massachusetts House.[5] The rules governing committees were exactly the same. The only differences between the two houses came in the names of two committees. The Committee on Turnpike Roads and Bridges in Massachusetts became the Committee on Canals, Turnpike Roads, and Bridges in Maine. In the other instance Maine understandably turned the Massachusetts Committee on the Subject of Eastern Lands into the Committee on State Lands. In sum, the Massachusetts parentage of the Maine legislature is clear.

In many ways, the development of the West Virginia constitution was similar to the process that had unfolded in Maine. The Virginia constitution of 1850 was clearly an important touchstone during the writing of the

West Virginia constitution. In debates the legislative experience in Virginia was sometimes cited favorably. When discussing the proposed constitution's requirement that all engrossed bills be signed prior to the end of a legislative session, the chair of the committee overseeing the writing of the legislative department noted that he had spent time in Richmond during the final days of a session. He said, "I recollect staying up one night to see it through. Bills after reported on by the committee on engrossment were signed by the speaker before the adjournment. The legislature had to keep in existence until the bills were all regularly signed."[6] Sometimes, the reference was unfavorable. For instance, an opponent of a provision calling for biennial sessions cited the Virginia experience to argue against it: "I believe there session after session has been extended either by the governor or the legislature, or there has been a piece put on the end of the regular session. So from a practical experience the attempt that has been made in Virginia under the clause in the constitution for biennial sessions may be considered a failure."[7]

In the end, some notable differences emerged between the Virginia and West Virginia legislatures as structured by their respective state constitutions (Callahan 1909, 19–20). West Virginia opted to use the collective name *legislature* rather than *general assembly* as in Virginia (but at the same time it kept the name *House of Delegates* for its lower chamber). It also chose to have the legislature meet annually rather than biennially as Virginia did. The Virginia House had 152 members and gave them two-year terms; the West Virginia House initially had 47 members and gave them one-year terms. The Virginia Senate had 50 members and four-year terms; the West Virginia Senate had 18 members and two-year terms. After considerable debate the Virginia prohibition against bank officers and ministers serving in the legislature was dropped in West Virginia. West Virginians included a provision that did not allow anyone who had participated in a duel to serve in the legislature. And they took language from the Indiana constitution that prevented those "who may have collected or been entrusted with public money" from serving in the legislature until the candidate had "duly accounted for and paid over such money according to law."

Many provisions in the two constitutions, however, were virtually identical. Language specifying that bills could originate and be amended by either house, requirements for the keeping and publication of legislative journals, and the recording of votes on the request of one-fifth of a chamber's members were essentially the same. Indeed, during the constitutional convention the chair of the committee that composed the legislative section admitted about one provision, "The last clause of that section is: 'If a senator or delegate remove from the district or county for which he was chosen, his office shall be thereby vacated.' This is copied from the seventh section of the fourth article of the Virginia Constitution."[8]

In terms of its constitutional features, West Virginia's legislature was at least partly modeled on Virginia's. Organizationally, it was a different story. Indeed, it appears that not only did West Virginia ignore the Virginia model, it charted a very different course. The initial West Virginia House adopted a complex set of 94 rules. The first 3 rules were unusual—the third rule stated, "The Speaker shall arrange with the Ministers of the several Religions denominations, at or near the seat of government, to open the sittings daily with prayer"—suggesting that they were developed without the use of any direct model (*Jour. of the H. of Dels. of the St. of W.Va.* 1863, 3–14).

By comparison, the Virginia House in 1861 used only 50 rules, many of which had little in common with the rules adopted in West Virginia (*Jour. of the H. of Dels. of the St. of Va.* 1861, 4–10). The rules used in West Virginia also were unlike the set of 65 rules employed in the Ohio House or the 62 rules used in the Pennsylvania House, both of which are neighboring states and potential models (*Jour. of the H. of Reps. of the St. of Ohio* 1857, 164–69; *Man. of Rules for the Gov. of Both Branches of the Leg. of Pa.* 1863, 56–64).[9]

A comparison of provisions governing the previous question documents the distinctiveness of West Virginia's rules. In the West Virginia House, the rule required that the previous question be demanded by 7 members, gave the principal sponsor of the pending matter the right to make a concluding speech (if he had not already spoken twice on the matter), and allowed pending motions to commit, amend, or postpone to first be resolved. In contrast, Virginia's rule was much briefer, required a demand by 20 members, and did not address the resolution of any pending motions. The provisions in Ohio and Pennsylvania also differed in important respects, including the number of members required to press the demand, and in the handling of various motions (cf. *Jour. of the H. of Dels. of the St. of Va.* 1861, 6; *Jour. of the H. of Dels. of the St. of W.Va.* 1863, 8; *Jour. of the H. of Reps. of the St. of Ohio* 1857, 167; *Man. of Rules for the Gov. of Both Branches of the Leg. of Pa.* 1863, 59).

West Virginia created a distinctive set of standing committees. As can be seen in table 5.1, it only established 13 standing committees, while each of its potential models formed far more. Moreover, the Virginia House relied in part on joint committees, something West Virginia chose not to do. Even the names of the committees in West Virginia almost always differed from those used in the other three chambers.

In creating new legislatures political leaders have the freedom to make choices. Although both Maine and West Virginia were spun out of existing states they pursued different evolutionary paths. Some leaders in both new

TABLE 5.1.   Standing Committees in the Initial West Virginia House of Representatives and in Three Possible Model Institutions

West Virginia (1863)	Committee Analog in Lower House of		
	Ohio (1857)[a]	Pennsylvania (1863)[a]	Virginia (1861)[a]
Elections and Privileges	Privileges and Elections		Privileges and Elections
Taxation and Finance	Finance	Ways and Means	Finance
Military Affairs	Militia	Militia System	Militia Laws
Judiciary	**Judiciary**[b]	Judiciary System (general) Judiciary System (local)	Courts of Justice
Education	Common Schools and School Lands	**Education**	Schools and Colleges
Counties, Townships and Municipal Corporations	New Counties	New Counties and County Seats	County Organization
Private Corporations and Joint Stock Companies	Corporations	Corporations	
Roads and Internal Navigation	Roads and Highways	Roads, Bridges, and Canals	**Roads and Internal Navigation**
Forfeited and Unappropriated Lands			
Claims and Grievances	Claims	Claims	Claims
Humane and Criminal Institutions	Benevolent Institutions Penitentiary		Penitentiary Lunatic Asylums
Printing and Contingent Expenses	Public Printing	Printing	
Executive Offices			Executive Expenditures (Joint)

Source: Jour. of the H. of Dels. of the St. of Va. 1861, 7; Jour. of the H. of Dels. of the St. of W.Va. 1863, 11; Jour. of the H. of Reps. of the St. of Ohio 1857, 164; Man. of Rules for the Gov. of Both Branches of the Leg. of Pa. 1863, 60.
   [a]The Ohio House had 28 standing committees, the Pennsylvania House 24 standing committees, and the Virginia House 18 standing committees and 6 joint committees.
   [b]Names in bold indicate those used by West Virginia House of Representatives.

states were reluctant to model the legislature after their predecessor body, and in notable ways each offspring managed to distinguish itself. But Maine, with its more amicable political split, was far more likely to reuse Massachusetts's rules and standing committees than West Virginia was to recycle Virginia's procedural characteristics following their rancorous separation. This suggests that there are circumstances that curb the willingness of those who create new legislatures to inherit legislative structures and processes.

The Congress of the Texas Republic

After Texas declared its independence from Mexico, some 60 of its citizens gathered to write a constitution to govern the new nation. Most of the delegates had migrated from the United States, and they used that country's governing structures as their model. Although they met under austere conditions and had little reference material available, some of them had previously served in the U.S. Congress, a state legislature, or a state constitutional convention, and consequently they brought considerable experience to their task. In regard to the design of the legislative branch the convention drew heavily on the U.S. Constitution, but it also borrowed provisions from state constitutions. Indeed, one historian concludes, "it may be said that in the matter of choosing legislators, in the structure and composition of the legislature, and in its rules of procedure, the congress of the Republic of Texas was nothing more than a state legislature with its name changed" (Richardson 1928, 192–96, 210).

A number of legislative provisions in the Texas constitution were taken directly from the U.S. Constitution. The Texas language making the vice president of the Republic the president of the Senate and allowing him to vote only in case of a tie was virtually identical to language in the U.S. Constitution. The same was true of the words used to allow the Senate to choose all its other officers including a president pro tem, as well as those specifying the role of each chamber in the impeachment process and the right of each house to set its own rules.

Other sections pertinent to the legislature, however, were taken from state constitutions. Like the U.S. Constitution, the constitution of the Republic of Texas allowed each house to expel a member with the concurrence of two-thirds of the members. But an additional clause stating that a member could not be expelled a second time for the same offense was borrowed from the 1812 Louisiana constitution. A provision allowing each chamber to imprison any person "guilty of any disrespect to the House by any disorderly conduct in their presence" first surfaced in the Massachusetts constitution and then appeared in different versions in the South Carolina constitution of 1790, Georgia constitution of 1798, Indiana constitution of 1816, and Illinois constitution of 1818. The language used in both the 1796 and 1835 Tennessee constitutions was the most similar to that in the Republic of Texas constitution.

Some of the choices the Republic of Texas convention delegates made had far-lasting consequences. The delegates set the quorum to conduct legislative business for each house at two-thirds, an unusually high standard that also appeared in both the 1796 and 1835 Tennessee constitutions, as well as in the 1816 Indiana and 1818 Illinois constitutions. The provision also appeared in the Arkansas constitution adopted, like that of the Republic of Texas, in 1836. This quorum standard potentially allows a small minority to thwart the will of a large majority, something that was tried unsuccessfully during the seventh Texas Congress by a group of dissident representatives pushing to make Austin the capital (Lindley 1942, 62). The two-thirds standard first set in the Republic constitution has carried through each subsequent Texas constitution, laying the foundation for the infamous Democratic flight to break quorum during the 2003 legislative battle over redistricting.[10]

Although it was a national assembly, the Republic of Texas Congress actually looked and operated like an American territorial legislature. The initial Congress met in Columbia on the Brazos in a large dogtrot house—a building with two separate rooms covered by a single roof with a breezeway between the two rooms designed to help keep the building cool during the hot months (Collier 2000, 30). It was described as being "meager in every respect" (Spaw 1990, 3). The building's larger room was used by the House once a partition was removed. The Senate used the smaller room. Committees met in the shed (Lubbock 1900, 36). Given the rustic character of the first capitol it is not surprising that one representative wore a buckskin suit he had appropriated from an Indian. He slept each night on a blanket on the House floor (Lindley 1942, 52). Many others had to sleep under a large live oak tree (Lubbock 1900, 36).

The Congress relocated several times over its nine sessions, moving from Columbia to Houston to Austin, back to Houston, and finally to Washington. The moves were mostly driven by financial considerations. The decision to relocate to Washington was prompted by the expense of facilities in Houston and a promise by Washington to let the Congress use an appropriate building there at no cost (Lubbock 1900, 148). Members were paid a bit more than territorial legislators: the speaker of the House and the president pro tem of the Senate each received a $7 per diem, while other members got a $5 per diem (*Laws of the Republic of Texas* 1838, 69). Perhaps the slightly higher pay accounted for the Congress's comparatively higher membership stability rates. Membership turnover in the Senate ranged from a low of 31 percent to a high of 60 percent, with a median of 44 percent, lower figures than those reported for territorial legislatures in table 4.2.[11] Still, life in the various capitals was not always inviting. During the 1837 session in Houston, poor drinking water made a large number of Congress members sick. When the Congress met in Austin one government employee later recalled, "At nights I felt safer at my quarters than on the streets, and you were pretty sure to find a Congressman at his boarding house after sundown" (Lubbock 1900, 67, 143). As with their territorial counterparts, some Texas lawmakers might have continued to serve if the vagaries of frontier life had not claimed them. One senator became identified as a Regulator in the infamous Regulator and Moderator feud; subsequently a group of Moderators surrounded his house and shot him to death as he tried to escape by jumping into a nearby lake (Lindley 1942, 156). Not surprisingly, violence occasionally spilled over into the Congress. After a senator publicly questioned the performance of the Texas surgeon general the offended physician came to the Senate chamber and beat his accuser with a bullwhip. And the Congress itself occasionally behaved in an amateurish fashion. When a senator about whom legal residency questions had been raised failed to attend the sessions examining his case, his colleagues voted to move their meetings to the absent senator's home, "flushing out the recalcitrant and, possibly, very ill legislator" (Spaw 1990, 37, 69).

As with other frontier legislatures, however, the Congress of the Republic of Texas took on the trappings of the lawmaking bodies of its time. Clerks, assistant clerks, a sergeant at arms, a doorkeeper, and a translator were hired (*Laws of the Republic of Texas* 1838, 70). Actually, a surprising number of Congress members had previous legislative experience. Over the nine sessions it met, a total of 11 members had earlier service in American state or territorial legislatures. Another 3 had been members of Mexican legislatures.[12] Finally, the first vice president of the Republic and president of the Senate, Lorenzo de Zavala, not only had served in both houses of the Mexican Congress but also had been a member of the Spanish Cortes (Lindley 1942, 197). Still, most Texas lawmakers were not conversant with parliamentary procedures. When Senator Robertson was called to order by a colleague during a particularly heated debate, Robertson turned to the presiding officer and said, "Mr. President, I am called to order. I do not know that I am out of order, but this I do know, I will not come to order at the command of the gentleman. But, Mr. President, if you will just knock that little hammer down on me, I will squat like a partridge" (Lubbock 1900, 108).

Where did the Republic Congress get its rules and structures? The first Republic House apparently used the U.S. House rules (*Telegraph and Texas Register* 1836). On the first day of its first session, the Senate adopted the rules used by the Texas Constitutional Convention (Spaw 1990, 5). In turn, the convention had taken its rules from those used by the U.S. House (cf. Gammel 1898, 7–13; *Jour. of the H. of Reps. of the US* 1835, 694–705). There were some necessary substitutions in the language used. For example, "Touching the Duty of the Speaker" was altered to read "Touching the Duty of the President." Later in the first session the Senate adopted *Jefferson's Manual* to supplement its chamber rules. The second Senate revised the rules and again augmented them with *Jefferson's Manual* (Spaw 1990, 7, 33). Early in the fourth Senate a member pointed out that despite having met for a week the chamber had yet to adopt any rules. The president held that the rules of the previous Senate were still in force until such time as new rules were adopted. A few days later a committee appointed to review the rules reported a slightly revised version of them, which was adopted after being amended to include two new rules. The fifth Senate adopted the same rules as the fourth Senate, and the sixth Senate likewise followed suit, although it later slightly revised one rule (Smither 1931, 47, 53; 1940, 3, 84).

Determining that the "assiduous exertions of committees" was the best way to deal with the press of legislative business, the first Republic House immediately established 12 standing committees (*Telegraph and Texas Register* 1836). The Republic Senate also quickly created a standing committee system. In its first session the Senate established 11 standing committees, the same set as in the Republic House save for one on foreign relations. Most of these committees carried through in one form or another to the first Texas state Senate, as shown in table 5.2. A few committees were added over the course of the nine Republic Senate sessions. By and large, however, the committees put in place in the first Republic Senate were continued into the first state Senate. The switch from a national legislature to a state legislature did, however, occasion the demise of several committees for obvious reasons; there was no longer any need for committees devoted to foreign relations, naval affairs, or the post office.

Rules carried over, with the new state House quickly adopting those that had been used in the final Republic House (*Northern Standard* 1846). The legacy of the Republic Congress carried over to statehood in personnel as well. At least 24 members of the first state legislature had previously served in the Congress. Another 26 former Congress members eventually became state legislators. Indeed, as late as 1882 a former member of the Republic Congress served in the Texas state legislature.[13] Thus, in many ways, the national assembly lived on in the state legislature.

California and the Creation of a State Legislature with No Predecessor

As was the case with Texas, California had no territorial legislature. But unlike Texas, which immediately became a state once the United States took

TABLE 5.2. Standing Committees in the Senates of the Republic of Texas and the First Texas State Senate

Republic of Texas			State of Texas
First Session	Fourth Session	Sixth Session	First Session
Ways and Means	Finance	Finance	
Judiciary	Judiciary	Judiciary	Judiciary
Post Office and Post Roads	Post Office and Post Roads	Post Office and Post Roads	
State of the Republic			
Military Affairs	Military Affairs	Military Affairs	Military Affairs
Roads, Bridges, and Ferries		Roads, Bridges, and Ferries	
Claims and Accounts	Claims and Accounts		Claims and Accounts
Public Lands	Public Lands	Public Lands	
Indian Affairs	Indian Affairs	Indian Affairs	Indian Affairs
County Boundaries			County Boundaries
Naval Affairs	Naval Affairs	Naval Affairs	
	Foreign Relations	Foreign Relations	
	Contingent Expenses	Contingent Expenses	
	Enrolling and Engrossing	Engrossed Bills	Engrossed Bills
	Privileges and Elections		Enrolled Bills
			Privileges and Elections
	Printing		Printing and Contingent Expenses
	Education		Education
			Internal Improvements

Source: Smither 1931, 4; 1940, 5; Spaw 1990, 7, 178.

control of its territory, California operated under a military government for several years prior to statehood. As will be discussed later, during the military regime several local legislatures emerged, but these bodies had no impact on the state legislature when it was established. What model or models, then, did Californians use to design their new state legislature?

California's constitutional convention began in September 1849 and finished the following month. The delegates initially relied on Iowa's 1846 constitution as their model, but they later came to put equal emphasis on New York's 1846 constitution (Hunt 1895, 55–56). With one notable exception the provisions for the new state legislature were taken from Iowa. Only the initial clause, "The Legislative Power of this State shall be vested in a Senate and Assembly," was lifted from New York's constitution. (Iowa used the more common name "House of Representatives" for its lower chamber.)[14] Otherwise, the basic structure of the California legislature was much the same as Iowa's. One of the few notable differences was that California opted to use annual sessions, whereas Iowa, like many other state legislatures at the time, met biennially. The rationale given by delegates preferring annual sessions centered on California's lack of a territorial legislature. One argued that most recently admitted states "enjoyed from seven to thirty years experience under Territorial forms of government. There was comparatively but little change to make in their laws. That very fact would go to show the absolute necessity of annual Legislatures here." Another delegate agreed, observing, "We have no pre-existing laws that can form the basis of our legislation. With all this new material in the country—without previous territorial organization—we have to assemble together a Legislature to enact laws suitable to the condition of the country" (Browne 1850, 79–80).[15]

While there was considerable debate on the question of how often the legislature should meet, remarkably little was said about the body's basic structure. Bicameralism was assumed. Language largely taken from Iowa's constitution establishing the right of each chamber to determine its rules, the quorum standards to be used, the charge to keep and publish a journal, and the right to parliamentary privileges passed with almost no comment (Browne 1850, 86–87).

When the inaugural state legislature assembled—prior to California being formally admitted as a state—its experience was much like that of territorial bodies. A correspondent, who had witnessed the first meeting, later observed about the initial session in Montana Territory, "The Legislature reminds me very much of the first State Legislature of California.

. . . I notice a remarkable similarity in the methods used to accomplish the ends desired" (*MP* 1865a).

The legislature was scheduled to open in San Jose on December 15, 1849. The weather, however, was very wet, and muddy roads prevented a quorum from gathering until December 17 (Jones 1950, 5). When legislators finally arrived they found a small but rapidly expanding community. Some of the lawmakers lodged in the town's hotels, of which there were only a few. Others boarded with local families. One woman who opened her home recalled her boarders later.

> Everybody had to be hospitable. The legislature was in session, and the town was more than full. The first thing I knew I had thirteen boarders—senators, and representatives. . . . It was as good as a play to see them help me. Mr. Leek (he was the enrolling clerk in the legislature) was a wonderful hand to make batter-cakes. . . . [Assembly member] Mr. Bradford, from Indiana, could brown coffee to perfection. Mr. Orr and Mr. McMullen always brought the water; they were senators. I used to think they liked the job because there was a pretty girl in the house where they got the water. (Field 1887, 549)

Not every legislator enjoyed his accommodations. One Assembly member paid a considerable sum just to sleep on a dining table. In general, lawmakers found that their seemingly generous $16 per diem did not go far given gold rush–inflated prices (Ignoffo 1999, 51; Jones 1950, 8–9).

The facility appropriated for the legislature's use was a recently constructed two-story building that had been intended to be a hotel. The second floor was ready for the Assembly, but the first floor was unfinished. Consequently, the Senate spent its first week meeting nearby in the front room of Isaac Branham's adobe house (Bancroft 1888, 309; Ignoffo 1999, 53). When finished, the legislative chambers were not impressive. An English visitor described them this way.

> By a sort of solecism in the arrangement, the Senate, or Upper House, occupy the lower apartment, which is a large, ill-lit, badly ventilated room with a low ceiling, and a rough railing a little inside the door, beyond which none but the elect may pass. Each member had a rush-bottomed arm-chair, and a small desk with stationery, that was not in much requisition. At the further end, the Speaker was perched in a species of pulpit; the floor was covered with a number of little carpets, of various

shapes and patterns, looking as if every member contributed a patch to make up the robe, which had quite a mosaic appearance, the idea of antiquity being assisted by the threadbare state of the whole.

The room used by the Assembly came off only slightly better in the visitor's estimation: "The other apartment is precisely the same size, but has the advantage of greater loftiness, and exhibits at once the difference of grade betwixt the two bodies in the style of the furniture—plain common chairs, flat deal tables, and a strip of matting thrown where the feet are erroneously supposed to rest" (Kelly 1851, 308–9).

Given that very few of the lawmakers had any previous legislative experience, it is not surprising that parliamentary proprieties were largely absent. The English visitor proved to be even less impressed with the lawmakers than he was with their legislative chambers. After watching the legislature at work he reported, "The noise and jabbering was incessant as the twittering of a flock of swallows chatting over their intended migration."

Nothing can be more remote from the regularity, decency, or decorum of deliberative assemblies, than the proceedings of these bodies; there was no order of debate or system of discussion, but a turbulent dinning colloquy, made up of motions, interruptions, assertions, and contradictions; several members generally on their legs at the same time, and those with legs on the tables, adding to the tumult by the music of their heels. . . . They meet about ten o'clock, a.m., and are let loose for dinner at one o'clock, when they come out with a rush, like so many overgrown school boys. It is unnecessary to add, that smoking, chewing, and whittling, do not constitute an infraction of the rules of either house, privileges that are accorded also to a squad of slip-shod clerks or messengers who loll about the stores. (Kelly 1851, 309–10)

Whittling actually became such a problem that "Wood shavings littered the floor of the chambers," and small blocks of wood had to be provided to the legislators to keep them from shaving the furniture (Ignoffo 1999, 62).

As in territorial legislatures California's first lawmakers had to buy their own paper and ink (Barker 1945, 59). Among the first items lawmakers requested were locks for their desk drawers, suggesting some unease with their colleagues (Ignoffo 1999, 56). There may have been good reason for concern. According to Stephen J. Field, a member of the Assembly during its second session (and a future U.S. Supreme Court justice), most of his colleagues came to the floor armed with knives and guns. Accordingly, "It was a thing of every-day occurrence for a member, when he entered the House, before taking his seat, to take off his pistols and lay them in the drawer of his desk. He did it with as little concern and as much a matter of course, as he took off his hat and hung it up." Having weapons in close proximity to heated debates posed obvious problems. Field recalled that during one dispute, "When Mr. Moore rose to reply to me, he first ostentatiously opened his drawer, took out his revolvers, cocked them, and laid them in the open drawer before him. He then launched into a speech of the most opprobrious language, applying to me offensive epithets." Only a public apology on the Assembly floor averted a duel between the two lawmakers (Field 1893, 79–84).

Unlike most territorial legislatures, corruption did not appear to be a problem during California's initial session. One senator claimed, "At the first Legislature I think there was not much bribery: there was a different class of men in the first from what there was in the second: I think there was some jobbing in the second Legislature." He went on to offer a plausible explanation for the discrepancy, saying, "We had no revenue in the first Legislature, the state had not been admitted and there was no money to cover jobs; and after we were admitted the motive for jobbery was greater in the following Legislature" (Barker 1945, 60).

Alcohol did prove to be a problem. One senator was famous for keeping a supply of whiskey just outside the chamber and frequently exhorting his colleagues, "Well boys, let's go and take a thousand drinks." Another senator later recalled, "There were a few roystering fellows in the Legislature more in the Assembly because the Senate was a small body and composed mostly of very circumspect gentlemen. These fellows used to cut up there pranks and . . . those hangers on and lobbyists enjoyed themselves in that way" (Barker 1945, 59). Indeed, the legislature came to be known as the "Legislature of a Thousand Drinks" (*Daily Alta California* 1850, 1852).

The moniker may not have been altogether deserved. Much was accomplished by the first legislature, and both participants (Barker 1945, 59; Burnett 1880, 361) and later historians (Bancroft 1888, 311; Goodwin 1914, 307; Hittell 1898, 807) accorded it high marks, with one commenting, "But if they drank well, they worked well too" (Tuthill 1866, 285). Indeed, the man who encouraged his fellow lawmakers to "take a thousand drinks" was not a buffoon. Senator Thomas Jefferson Green (not to be confused with Thomas Jefferson White, the speaker of the first Assembly) had attended West Point and after returning to his native North Carolina was elected to the state House of Representatives. After marrying, he moved to Florida where he served in the territorial legislature. Following the death of his wife, Green relocated to Texas where he was a member of both houses of the Congress of the Republic. (He was the senator whose residency was questioned during the second session.) The gold rush drew him to California. In the Senate he chaired the Finance Committee, and while he usually focused his efforts on tax policies, he also authored the legislation creating the University of California (Ashe, Weeks, and Van Noppen 1905, 114–19; Green 2006, 17–18).

Only one other of California's first lawmakers had previous legislative service: Assembly member Thomas Jefferson Henley had served three terms in the U.S. House from Indiana. The legislature also had little in the way of staff: "In 1850, legislative staff consisted of a parliamentarian, a recorder of minutes, a chaplain, a sergeant of arms, and an occasional supernumerary" (Driscoll 1986, 125). Although both chambers lacked experienced personnel or much professional assistance, the lawmakers had the good sense to seize on rules and structures used by existing legislatures, which provided them the mechanisms they needed to overcome their limitations. On December 17, the Assembly temporarily adopted the rules of the U.S. House. On January 15, 1850, a committee to prepare rules for the Assembly was appointed. A slightly altered set of U.S. House rules was adopted by the House two days later (cf. *Jour. of the Proc. of the H. of Asm. of the St. of Calif.* 1850, 580, 661, 665–80; *Jour. of the H. of Reps. of the US* 1844, 1177–86). The Assembly's rules shuffled the order of the U.S. House rules slightly but made only small changes in a handful of rules. In the Assembly, a member could speak twice to a question without leave of the House (rule 24), while in the much larger U.S. House a member could speak only once (rule 37). The Assembly, with 104 rules, omitted or combined a number of the U.S. House's 146 rules. It also held that *Jefferson's Manual* would be used to fill any gaps.

A slightly different sequence unfolded in the upper house. On December 17, the Senate appointed a committee to draft its rules and then temporarily adopted *Jefferson's Manual*. After initially rejecting the committee's proposed rules on December 18, the Senate reconsidered its decision and passed them the next day (*Jour. of the Sen. of the St. of Calif.* 1850, 9, 12, 15). Unlike the Assembly, the Senate did not look to Washington for guidance. Instead, the rules they adopted appear to have been taken from those used by the New York Senate. Of the 37 rules adopted by the Senate, the vast majority of them were exactly the same as those used in New York, including the second rule, which presented the 12 orders of business in the same form and sequence. The assumption of New York's parentage is reinforced by the fact the chair of the committee drafting the rules, Nathaniel Bennett, was a native New Yorker who, although educated at Yale, had studied law in Buffalo and had been active in New York politics as recently as 1848 (Ignoffo 1999, 101–2). The rules used by the U.S. Senate in the late 1840s had been adopted in 1828 and were dissimilar to those used by the California and New York senates (cf. *Documents of the Sen. of the St. of N.Y.* 1835, 1–7; *Jour. of the Sen. of the St. of Calif.* 1850, 401–5; *Jour. of the Sen. of the USA* 1827, 160–66).

As was standard for legislatures of the time, both chambers also quickly established standing committee systems. On December 18, the Assembly initially created 10 committees, but within minutes decided to add 2 more. Ultimately, the body operated with 15 standing committees (*Jour. of the Proc. of the H. of Asm. of the St. of Calif.* 1850, 580–81, 680–81). On December 21, the Senate appointed the 10 committees previously created by their rules (*Jour. of the Sen. of the St. of Calif.* 1850, 28). Of these, 8 were either identical to or very similar to committees in the Assembly. But it was also the case that the first 4 committees established were exactly the same as the first 4 created in the New York Senate rules (cf. *Documents of the Sen. of the St. of N.Y.* 1835, 5).

California's first state legislature shared one more trait with territorial legislatures: a fixation on the issue of where the capital should be located. One of the first bills introduced in the Assembly was to "locate the Seat of Government of this State" (*Jour. of the Proc. of the H. of Asm. of the St. of Calif.* 1850, 586). The topic captured public attention. Taking note of the measure, a newspaper covering the legislature reported, "Nothing else transpired of interest with the exception of the reading of a bill submitted by Mr. Tingly of Sacramento, providing for the removal of the seat of Government to Monterey" (*Tri-Weekly Alta California* 1849). This proposal instigated a political battle that a member of the first Senate later lamented, saying, "I think it was a shameful thing to hawk the capital of the State around as was done afterwards" (Barker 1945, 60). But the pressure to move proved too great to resist. After spending a second session in San Jose, the legislature met briefly in Vallejo and Benicia before finally settling in Sacramento in 1854.

Tennessee and the General Assembly of the State of Franklin

As Americans pushed west over the Appalachians they found themselves living well beyond the reach of existing state governments. To fill this void the impulse of these isolated settlers was to create their own governments complete with representative legislatures. For instance, in 1775, a group of ambitious men in what is now Kentucky established the Colony of Transylvania, with an elected assembly that numbered Daniel Boone among its members. Because there were no facilities in Boonesborough able to house the assembly, during a three-day session its members met under a large elm tree (Ranck 1901, 28). But the "Journal of the Proceedings of the House of Delegates or Representatives of the Colony of Transylvania" (reprinted in Collins 1874, 501–8) reveals that the body elected a chair and a clerk, and, although it did not adopt a formal set of rules, it operated using accepted parliamentary procedures. The proprietor of the Transylvania Company, Richard Henderson, had previously served as a judge in North Carolina and is a likely source for the procedures used by the House. Thus, members were granted leave to introduce a bill, which was then assigned to an ad hoc committee. Each bill had to pass three readings to become law. A total of nine measures were passed; Boone was successful in authoring two laws, one for preserving game and the other to improve the breeding of horses. A measure put before the assembly proposed that once the polity achieved sufficient size legislative power would be split among a popularly elected House of Delegates, a Council of no more than 12 members drawn from men holding large estates, and the proprietors. The effort to transform Transylvania into the fourteenth state (following the declaration of American independence) was short-circuited when in late 1776 the Virginia state legislature annulled the settlers' land purchase and created the county of Kentucky (Brewster 1960, 246–55; Henderson 1920, 258–59; Hening 1821, 257–58; Toner 1896, 611–12). Not all frontier assemblies got as far as Transylvania's. A proposal to establish a legislature for Powell's Valley (now in east Tennessee) apparently went nowhere (Turner 1895, 79; Weeks 1894, 419).

A more concerted effort to establish the fourteenth state later occurred in the far western reaches of North Carolina. In 1784 the government of North Carolina ceded almost 30 million acres west of the Appalachian Mountains (called at the time the Alleghany Mountains) to the national government. Later that same year it rescinded the action and reclaimed the land. But to the inhabitants of western North Carolina, the initial act represented something of a final straw, and it prompted them to seek a political divorce (*Independent Journal* 1785a, 1785b). From their perspective the North Carolina government was too far away and too disinterested to govern them. The appeal for self-government resonated with residents of Washington County, just over the border in Virginia, who also felt isolated and ignored by their state government and, consequently, felt a tug to join the Franklin effort (Kastor 1997). The threat of independent government movements in the west was taken seriously in both Pennsylvania and Virginia, which passed laws disallowing any such efforts without the explicit consent of the state legislature (Turner 1896, 260).

Subsequently, residents of four counties in what is today northeastern Tennessee opted to create the State of Franklin. A convention produced a constitution for the breakaway government in December 1784. The new state, however, did not stray far from its roots. The constitution it adopted was based on North Carolina's 1776 constitution (Alden 1903, 274–75; Keedy 1953, 519–20; Williams 1933, 44, 341–47). The similarities between the legislative provisions of the two constitutions were particularly pronounced. Like North Carolina, Franklin created a bicameral General Assembly composed of a senate and a house of commons. Each chamber was authorized to elect its speaker and to judge the qualifications of its members. And as was the tradition, all bills were required to be read three times before they could become law.

Beyond the constitutional features of the Franklin legislature, little is known about its organization and procedures. It is likely that they too drew on the experience of the North Carolina legislature because the speaker of the Senate, Landon Carter, and the speaker of the House, William Cage, had each served in the North Carolina House (Williams 1933, 300, 313).[16] The supposition of similarity is further supported by the fact that the 15 laws passed by the Franklin legislature were largely adaptations of North Carolina laws (Ramsey 1853, 293–95). Finally, there is evidence that in 1787 the Franklin Senate used a "Committee of privileges and Elections" to resolve an election dispute ("An Old Document of the State of Franklin" 1896). The North Carolina Senate operated with a committee of the same name (*Jour. of the Senate* 1787, 1).

The first several Franklin assemblies met in Jonesboro (spelled Jonesborough in some sources). By 1787, Greeneville was established as Franklin's capital. Facilities there were rudimentary, as was to be expected on the frontier. The House met in the newly built courthouse, described as being "build of unhewn logs, and coverd with clapboards." The Senate used "the old court room in Carr's house, which, at this time, had become the village tavern." Because of a dearth of hard currency, legislative salaries were stated in shillings and pounds, but converted into the equivalent quantities of pelts and other commodities (Ramsey 1853, 297, 334–35). By the end of the Franklin experiment, assembly members were, depending on the source of the information, either being paid in beaver skins (Williams 1933, 220) or raccoon skins (*Independent Gazetter* 1789).

In 1785, there was a failed attempt to create a different governing structure for Franklin. A second convention convened and considered a draft constitution for the "Commonwealth of Frankland" that was intended to be submitted to the U.S. Congress as the basis for statehood (*Charleston Morning Post and Daily Advertiser* 1786; Ramsey 1853, 326–34; "The Provisional Constitution of Frankland" 1896, 48–63). The name *Frankland* was thought to represent the notion of freemen, but the name *Franklin* was ultimately kept to honor Benjamin Franklin (Ramsey 1853, 324). As in Vermont, the provisions of the legislature were largely lifted from the Pennsylvania constitution of 1776 because of its strong democratic character. Thus, a unicameral legislature was proposed. The "General Assembly of the Representatives of the Freemen of Frankland" was to be composed of "persons most noted for wisdom and virtue," the exact language used in the Pennsylvania (and Vermont) constitutions. The legislature was to be empowered to name its own officers, as well as the state treasurer, secretary of state, superior judges, and auditors. It was to be given the authority to "prepare bills, and to enact them into laws"; the governor was not to be granted a veto. All bills of "a public and general nature" were to be printed for review by the public prior to their final reading in the legislature. The doors of the legislative chamber were to be left open, all votes and proceedings were to be published weekly, and the people were to be allowed "to apply to the Legislature for redress of grievances." All of these provisions appeared in the Pennsylvania constitution using virtually the same words.

The proposed Frankland constitution did introduce a few differences with the Pennsylvania model. In Frankland, no military officers on active duty, ministers of the gospel, or lawyers would be allowed to serve as legislators, and men who were "guilty of such flagrant enormities as drunkenness, gaming, profane swearing, lewdness, sabbath breaking, and such like" also were prohibited from serving. In the end, however, the proposed Frankland constitution was rejected by the convention. Instead, the delegates opted to further revise the North Carolina constitution to suit their purposes.

By 1786 North Carolina reestablished a governmental presence in Franklin, and the two governments vied for political control. Within two years North Carolina had reasserted its dominance, and the government of the State of Franklin disintegrated. After a brief dalliance with the Spanish over possible unification with that country (Henderson 1920, 327–49), the inhabitants of Franklin were politically integrated back into North Carolina. Surprisingly, even leaders of the secession movement returned to politics. In 1789, both the former governor of Franklin and the first speaker of the Franklin Senate were allowed to take the seats in the North Carolina Senate to which they had been elected, although the debate over seating the former generated great passion and even physical altercations on the Senate floor (Brewster 1960, 215–16). One member of the Franklin General Assembly, Samuel Wear, went on to serve in the Tennessee territorial legislature (Williams 1933, 328). Some of the major figures in the Franklin movement even managed to maintain their political prominence well into Tennessee's statehood. The governor, John Sevier, not only went on to serve in the North Carolina Senate but was subsequently elected to the U.S. House from North Carolina in 1790. When Tennessee was admitted as a state Sevier served as its governor from 1796 to 1801 and again from 1803 to 1809.

The Oregon Provisional Legislatures

On February 15, 1841, Ewing Young, perhaps the wealthiest settler in Oregon, died unexpectedly. He left an impressive estate: vast property holdings, a large cattle herd, and a sawmill. Young, however, did not have any known heirs, and he did not leave a will designating how his property should be distributed. This created a problem because Oregon existed in a governing vacuum. Up to that point in time, Americans, French Canadians, and British citizens residing in the area under the auspices of the Hudson Bay Company had coexisted with little conflict. But Young's death highlighted the need for laws (at least estate laws) and some mechanism to enforce them (Carey 1922, 367–69; Hines 1850, 417–18; Holman 1912, 101–2).

A meeting of settlers to mull over the problems surrounding Young's estate was held following his funeral. This gathering selected a committee of twelve men to draft a code of laws for the land south of the Columbia

River. The next day the committee named one of its members to be the chair and two others to serve as secretaries. But the committee never produced a set of laws or a constitution (Grover 1853, 5–7). Pressure from an official of the Hudson Bay Company and from a U.S. military officer had apparently deflated the nascent effort to establish a governing authority (Carey 1922, 371–73; Hines 1850, 420–21).

The next attempt to organize a government occurred in 1843. A series of community meetings were held in February and March, ostensibly to devise a collective response to a problem with predatory wild animals— "bears, wolves, panthers, &c., &c."—killing livestock (Grover 1853, 9). These assemblies became known as the Wolf Meetings, and the Americans in attendance clearly angled to use them to push for the creation of a provisional government (Clark 1912, 146). Their French Canadian neighbors generally opposed the idea, although they supported the formation of a "senate or council" to "make the regulations suitable for the people" (Grover 1853, 12–13). During a subsequent mass meeting held on May 2 an American made a call for a vote on the question of creating a government, shouting either "All in favor of organization, come to the right" (Lyman 1900, 94) or "Who's for a divide? All in favor of the report and organization, follow me" (Holman 1912, 113). Regardless of the words used, the minutes of the meeting say that there was a call for a divide, with those in support going to the right and those opposed to the left (Grover 1853, 14). In dramatic fashion, the 50 Americans attending the meeting moved to the right, while the 52 French Canadians moved to the left. But one of the youngest Canadians reasoned that opposing the Americans meant supporting the British, something that, as survivor of the Canadian Rebellion of 1837, he refused to do. Consequently, he shifted to the American side, bringing along with him another Canadian (Holman 1912, 113; Lyman 1900, 94). The defections gave the movement to create a government a majority.[17] The meeting then named a committee of nine to draft a legal code (Grover 1843, 15). This committee was authorized to meet for no more than six days. Its members were to be paid a per diem of $1.25, the cost of which was to be covered not by taxes but by a voluntary subscription (Gray 1870, 336; Grover 1853, 15; Hines 1850, 424).

Meeting two weeks later, the nine-member group took the name Legislative Committee, as shown in table 5.3. Every member of the Committee subscribed the full amount to cover his own per diem. They met at Willamette in a room in the Methodist Mission granary, which also served as a church and a school. They were allowed to use the room for free (Gray

TABLE 5.3. Membership Continuity in Oregon Legislatures, 1843–49

	1843 Legislative Committee	1844 Legislative Committee	1845 Legislative Committee	1845 Special Session	1845 Provisional House	1846 Provisional House	1847 Provisional House	1848–49 Provisional House	1849 Territorial Legislature
Number of members[a]	9	8	13	13	13	17	19	27	Council: 10 House: 17
Number of members from previous session (percentage)	1 (11)	2 (25)	2 (15)	13 (100)	13 (100)	2 (12)	5 (26)	4 (15)	Council: 1 (10) House: 3 (18)
Number of members with previous service (percentage)	1 (11)	2 (25)	3 (23)	13 (100)	13 (100)	3 (18)	5 (18)	4 (15)	Council: 1 (10) House: 3 (18)
Did leader have previous legislative service	Yes	No	Yes	Yes	Yes	Yes	Yes	Yes	Council: Yes House: Yes

Source: Calculated by author from membership rosters at the Oregon State Archives, http://arcweb.sos.state.or.us/pages/records/legislative/recordguides/histleg/territorial/index.html.

[a]Total number who served in session.

TABLE 5.4. Standing Committees in Oregon Legislatures, 1843–49[a]

Legislative Committee, 1843	Legislative Committee, 1844	Legislative Committee, 1845 (June)	House of Representatives, 1845 (Aug.)	House of Representatives, 1845 (Dec.)	House of Representatives, 1846	House of Representatives, 1848–49	Territorial House of Representatives, 1849
Judiciary	Judiciary	Judiciary	Judiciary	Judiciary	Judiciary	Judiciary	Judiciary
Ways and Means	Ways and Means	Ways and Means	Ways and Means	Ways and Means	Ways and Means	Ways and Means	Ways and Means
Military Affairs	Military Affairs	Military Affairs	Military Affairs	Military Affairs	Militia	Military Affairs	Military Affairs
Private Land Claims	Land Claims	Private Land Claims	Private Land Claims	Private Land Claims		Land Claims	
Division of the Country	Roads	Roads and Highways	Roads, &c.	Roads and Highways		Roads and Highways	Roads
		Elections			Elections	Elections	Elections
		Claims	Claims	Claims	Claims	Claims	Claims
		Indian Affairs	Indian Affairs	Indian Affairs	Indian Affairs	Indian Affairs	Indian Affairs
			Revision				
			Districts	Districts			
			Education		Education	Education	Education
			Apportionment	Apportionment		Apportionment	
			Organic Law				
					Post Office and Post Roads		
					Seat of Government	Seat of Government	
					Commerce	Commerce	
					Foreign Affairs	Foreign Affairs	
					Currency	Currency	
						Enrolled Bills	Enrolled Bills
						Internal Improvements	
							Engrossed Bills

Source: Grover 1853, 16, 39, 72–73, 92, 124–45, 165–66, 276; *Jour. of the LA of the Terr. of Ore.* 1854, 8.

[a]No standing committees appear in the journals for the 1847 and first 1848 meetings.

1870, 336). The lawmakers' first action was to elect a chair—Robert Moore, who had served several terms in the Missouri legislature (Clark 1912, 148)—and a secretary. The Committee then named a committee of three members to prepare rules to govern the body's decision making (Grover 1853, 16). (It was referred to as a *committee;* technically it and others appointed should have been called *subcommittees.*) According to a Committee member's memoir, "This committee . . . at once, in a hasty manner, prepared eight rules" (Gray 1870, 338). Unfortunately, although they were quickly adopted, "article by article," neither the Committee journal nor the member's memoir lists them (Grover 1853, 16). Apparently, the secretary got so involved with the discussions that "he seemed to forget his work," and the minutes were abridged (Gray 1870, 339). The Committee's next action was to create five standing committees that, as table 5.4 reveals, were largely focused on the fundamental activities any government would need to perform, such as expenditures, military affairs, and a legal system. The standing committees were appointed by the chair, but the full membership forced a change in the composition of the Committee of Ways and Means. On the second day a motion to create a standing finance committee was defeated because it was argued that the government was to be funded by subscriptions and not through any taxes (Gray 1870, 339–40; Grover 1853, 16–17).

Their lack of legislative experience troubled some of the new lawmakers. One of the most contentious issues tackled by the Committee on its first day was whether to open its sessions to the public. Several members preferred to meet behind closed doors, because, according to one of their colleagues, "they did not want to expose their ignorance of making laws." The Committee ultimately opted to "sit with open doors," after a majority of members concluded they could benefit from any assistance observers might offer (Gray 1870, 338–39; Grover 1853, 16). Although the lawmakers may have lacked both confidence in their abilities and much time to do their work, they managed to produce a series of laws to govern the community. Some of the legislation the Committee produced was quite complex. The Judiciary Committee report contained 19 articles and incorporated 37 separate sections of the Iowa territorial statute laws of 1838–39 (Grover 1853, 28–32). That report and others generated by the Committee were approved by the people at a mass meeting in early July.

A new Legislative Committee was elected in 1844. One of its members argued that the Committee of 1843 deserved to be labeled a committee because its legislative proposals had to be ratified by the public. In contrast, he thought the 1844 Committee was a true legislature because all legislative power was vested in it (Burnett 1880, 199). As shown in table 5.3, very few members from the previous Committee continued in office. Most of the newcomers to the 1844 Committee were men who had only arrived in Oregon within the previous year. The change in personnel proved important because it altered the political atmospherics and allowed for the development of a less adversarial relationship between the provisional government and the Hudson Bay Company (Clark 1915, 319). Organizationally, however, the 1844 Committee picked up where its predecessor left off. Meeting again near Willamette, this time "at the house of Mr. Hathaway," the Committee established five standing committees during its initial afternoon session. The only change made from the previous session was to replace the Committee on Division of the Country with a Committee on Roads. The second day witnessed the adoption of "rules for the government of the house," which, again, were not specified. In form, however, the Committee operated like any well-developed legislature of the time. The journal entry for June 25, for example, reveals that the Committee referred several constituent petitions to select committees, received reports from four standing committees, suspended the rules in order to allow the introduction of a bill to prevent slavery, dissolved itself into a committee of the whole, and engrossed a bill prior to its third reading (Grover 1853, 38–40, 46–47).

The Committee of 1844 met for only a few days in June and a few more days in December. One member admitted "we had but little time to devote to public business. Our personal needs were too urgent, and our time too much occupied in making a support for our families" (Burnett 1880, 169–70). In spite of its time constraints, the Committee passed a considerable amount of legislation. W. H. Gray, who was a Committee member in 1843 but not in 1844, later dismissed the 1844 Committee's efforts, claiming, "The whole time of the session seems to have been taken up in the discussions of personal bills" (Gray 1870, 378). In response, Peter Burnett, a leading member of the 1844 Committee, wrote in his memoirs, "We passed forty-three bills, some of them of considerable length, and most of them of general importance. Among these forty-three acts there were not exceeding eight that could be properly termed personal" (Burnett 1880, 207). Part of the explanation for the difference in interpretations is that Gray and Burnett did not like one another. Gray characterized Burnett as "a very ambitious man—smooth, deceitful, and insinuating in his manners" (Gray 1870, 375). In response, Burnett headed a section of his memoirs,

"Misstatements of W. H. Gray" (Burnett 1880, 192). It may be worth noting that Gray was also quite catty in his comments about another member of the 1844 Committee, claiming, "He was favorable to all applications for divorces, and married a second wife, as near as we could learn, before he obtained a divorce (if he ever did) from his first wife" (Gray 1870, 375).

The "personal" bills authorized nontrivial activities such as the construction of canals and the development of ferries. Other acts passed by the Committee formed the basis for a tax system, created a mechanism to govern land claims, and established circuit courts and justices of the peace (Burnett 1880, 170, 200–204). Some of the legislation was actually quite clever. In a letter later published in an East Coast newspaper, a Committee member recounted, "We passed a tax bill, appointed an assessor, and permitted every man not to pay a tax, if he chose so to do, but if he did not pay, being able, we debarred him from suing in the courts as a plaintiff. At the same time we passed acts to protect all *bona fide* settlers in their claims to the extent of 640 acres." The member went on to boast, "The tax bill operated like a charm. Nearly all of the whole population paid without hesitation" (Burnet 1845).[18]

The final meeting of the Legislative Committee occurred in June 1845. In 1844 the Committee had voted to increase its size to 13 members in response to a surge in Oregon's population (Burnett 1880, 210–11). Meeting at the residence of J. E. Long in what was now known as Oregon City rather than Willamette, the slightly larger Committee began by administering a new oath of office to its members: "I do solemnly swear that I will support the Organic Laws of the Provisional Government of Oregon, so far as the said Organic Laws are consistent with my duties as a citizen of the United States, or a subject of Great Britain, and faithfully demean myself in office. So help me God" (Grover 1853, 71). The oath's inclusive language allowed British citizens and Hudson Bay Company officials to fully support the provisional government (Clark 1915, 325). Following the swearing in, the Committee adopted its governing rules, again failing to list them. But this time the proposed rules generated debate, and two rules were amended, providing a glimpse of their contents. The second rule established the standing committees—it was amended to insert the phrase "And such other standing committees as the house may, from time to time, adopt" after the words "Indian Affairs." The third rule appeared to delineate the role of the sergeant at arms (Grover 1853, 72–73).

The slightly larger Committee expanded its roster of standing committees, reflecting an increase in the scope of activities undertaken by the provisional government. The five committees used in 1844 were all used again, while three new ones on elections, claims, and Indian affairs were added. One noteworthy innovation was introduced during the session. The legislature's informational resources were greatly expanded when the "secretary of the Multnomah circulating library [tendered] the use of the Library to the Legislative committee." The Committee voted its gratitude for the offer (Grover 1853, 73).

In July 1844, Oregon voters adopted a revised Organic Law of Oregon prepared by the Legislative Committee. The law created a unicameral legislature called the House of Representatives. The House was to start with 13 members and be allowed to grow to 61 members, but it could increase by no more than 5 seats from one session to the next. The House was allowed to choose a speaker and other officers and to determine its rules of procedure. The quorum was set at two-thirds of the members (*Stat. of Ore.* 1855, 33–38).

Now calling themselves the House of Representatives, the same set of lawmakers who had met in June as the Legislative Committee assembled again in an August special session. After initially electing a new speaker, the previous speaker got the House to reverse the decision by successfully arguing that the current session was an extension of the previous one. The old speaker then proceeded to greatly expand the standing committee system, adding committees on revision, districts, education, apportionment, and organic law while dropping the committee on elections. Rules were again adopted but not listed (Grover 1853, 90–93). This session was notable for taking only an hour to introduce, pass, and have signed into law a measure banning dueling. This expeditious process was carried out under a suspension of the rules and was motivated by a desire to prevent an imminent encounter between two of Oregon's more prominent citizens. As it happened, one of the potential duelists had "implored" a representative to quickly introduce the measure (Brown 1892, 169).

The same House met once more in December 1845. They assembled again in J. E. Long's home before procuring "a room of T. McGruder, at $2.00 per day; fuel and light included." This time the speaker was replaced, although by a different member than the one who had been initially elected in August. The new speaker dropped the revision, education, and organic law committees but kept all of the others. More significantly, the House chose a different set of rules from those used by its predecessors. On the first day it met it passed a motion adopting "The rules of the house of representatives of the United States, contained in *Jefferson's Manual*" (Grover

1853, 124–25). A member later recalled, "Jefferson's Manual, which had for the first time strayed across the Rocky Mountains, was presented to the house, and used to govern its proceedings, so far as it was applicable. I think it must have come into the Multnomah Circulating Library" (Gray 1870, 439).

There was one curious episode during the session. A week after M. M. McCarver lost the speakership he failed to show for a session. After initially voting to ignore his absence, the House reversed itself and, "On motion, The serjeant-at-arms was authorized to require the attendance of Mr. Mc-Carver in the house." The sergeant at arms tracked down McCarver, who was brought before the House and permitted to offer an excuse, which was accepted. He was fined, however, and the body resolved, "That for members to absent themselves from the house, during the hours of session, without notice or leave, is a direct violation of the rules, and a contempt of the house." The following day, in a possibly passive-aggressive move, Mc-Carver again was absent for the first roll call. He managed to answer the second call (Grover 1853, 133–35).[19]

The 1846 House first met in the City Hotel in Oregon City before adjourning to a room they rented from Mr. Knighton for $2.00 a day (Grover 1853, 154–55). The House adopted the rules used in the previous session. The standing committee system was both shuffled and expanded. Several committees from the previous session were dropped, while a couple of others used in earlier sessions were revived. A few new committees were added, notably four committees with seemingly national jurisdictions: Post Office and Post Roads, Commerce, Foreign Affairs, and Currency.

After initially assembling in Dr. Prigg's office in Oregon City, the 1847 House rented a room from Stephen Meek for $1.25 a day. The next day, however, they rescinded the deal and decided instead to meet in the Methodist Church because, apparently, they could use it for free. Once again, the House voted to use the rules from the previous session (Geer 1912, 196–97; Grover 1853, 220–21, 223). Interestingly, there is no evidence in the journals that standing committees were appointed during the session.

The 1848 House confronted a problem that had not troubled its predecessors. Because gold had been discovered in California, when it came time for the legislature to assemble in December it was estimated that almost half of the lawmakers had headed south in pursuit of riches (Brown 1892, 449). The House did not have a quorum when it was scheduled to first meet on December 5, and it took until December 9 for enough members to arrive for one to be achieved. On the day it finally met the House took care of logistics. One select committee was appointed to procure stationery, another "to arrange the seats, stands, &c.," and third to locate a suitable room. The last of these quickly reported that G. W. Rice's house, "together with wood for the session, can be had at five dollars per day, in scrip," which was accepted (Grover 1853, 255–56). The next day the House opted to again use the previous session's rules. But confronted by a continuing shortage of members they spent the rest of the day fashioning a resolution calling on the sergeant at arms to bring 5 truant members to the session. It was not until February 7, 1849, with 17 members in attendance, that the speaker announced standing committee assignments. Of the standing committees created, eleven had been used in the 1846 session and three others had existed in earlier sessions. There were two completely new committees created, one on enrolled bills, the other on internal improvements (Grover 1853, 257–60, 276).

Within a few days of naming its committees, however, the provisional legislature was dissolved. The U.S. Congress had passed legislation in August 1848 creating the Oregon Territory. When the appointed governor arrived in March 1849 he initiated the establishment of a territorial government. As with other territories of its generation, Congress gave Oregon a bicameral legislature, with a council and a house of representatives. But the territorial legislature proved to be a continuation of the provisional legislature in significant ways. While there was only limited carryover in personnel, the leadership in both chambers was drawn from the ranks of provisional lawmakers. There was organizational continuity as well. Among its first acts, the territorial House adopted *Jefferson's Manual* for its rules (*Jour. of the LA of the Terr. of Ore.* 1854, 4), as its provisional predecessors had done in every session since 1845. The next day the territorial House created ten standing committees, nine of which had existed in the final provisional House. Only a committee on engrossed bills was new. Once organized, the legislature behaved like its territorial counterparts; the first legislation introduced was "A bill to locate the seat of government of Oregon Territory" (*Jour. of the LA of the Terr. of Ore.* 1854, 9).

Between 1841 and 1849 Oregon was governed by several different legislative bodies. Importantly for the analysis here, although these institutions were distinct, there were common threads running through them. Rules, committee structures, and personnel knitted them together. One notable issue spanned the provisional and territorial eras. It involved Ewing Young's estate, the problem that had prompted the initial move toward establishing a government. The matter dragged on for a number of years even after governmental institutions ostensibly created to settle it were established and even after a judge was specifically charged with resolving it. Finally, in 1852 a long-lost son that Young had fathered while living in New Mexico surfaced and established his legal claim. Three years later the territorial government of Oregon turned over the estate, worth $4,994.64—less $44.80 in court costs—to the rightful heir (Young 1920).

Utah and the General Assembly of Deseret

Like Oregon, Utah experienced a provisional government prior to becoming a territory. And like Tennessee, the provisional government promoted its prospects for statehood by organizing itself as a state, in this case the State of Deseret. A Mormon-dominated provisional government was assembled. It claimed a vast area of the West encompassing not only what is today Utah but also most of Nevada and Arizona, along with parts of Colorado, Idaho, New Mexico, Wyoming, and even a swath of California leading to the Pacific Ocean around San Diego.

A convention to write a constitution for the proposed state met in Great Salt Lake City in March 1849, and it quickly agreed on a document. The constitution adopted was based on Iowa's 1846 constitution (Crawley 1989, 15). It established a bicameral legislature with a House of Representatives whose members were given two-year terms and a Senate whose members enjoyed four-year terms. Each house was given the right to choose its officers and to judge the qualifications of its members (*Cons. of the St. of Deseret, with the Jour. of the Conv. which Formed it, and the Proc. of the Leg. Consequent Thereon* 1849, 5). While the structure of the Deseret General Assembly largely mimicked the structure of the Iowa General Assembly, there were a few notable differences. The Deseret legislature was to meet annually, while Iowa's had biennial sessions. Revenue bills in Iowa were required to start in the House, but no such procedure was set in Deseret. Finally, age qualifications differed, with Deseret adopting older standards exactly like those for the U.S. House and Senate (Crawley 1989, 15).

Although there is some confusion on this point, it appears that the first formal session of the Deseret General Assembly was in early December 1849. The *Constitution of the State of Deseret, with the Journal of the Convention which Formed it, and the Proceedings of the Legislature Consequent Thereon* (1849, 11–13) states that both the House and Senate met in early July 1849, and there are news reports confirming that a session of some sort was held

(*Barre Patriot* 1849), but there is convincing evidence for the December date from diaries kept by members of the legislature (Crawley 1989, 20; Morgan 1987, 44–45). Both the House and Senate met in Huber C. Kimball's schoolroom. The 14 rules and regulations adopted jointly by the two chambers in December 1850 appear to have been locally generated, although they were entirely consistent with established legislative practices. The rules focused almost entirely on matters of parliamentary etiquette rather than on legislative procedure. As with many of the colonial assemblies and early state legislatures there were rules imposing fines on members who failed to respond when the roll was called or who were more than 30 minutes late to a session. But Deseret's Rule 6 was unusual in where it directed the financial penalties to go: "The fine so imposed, shall be paid to the clerk of the house, to be applied in purchasing wood, lights, &c., and towards defraying the incidental expenses of the same" (Morgan 1987, 44, 194–95).

Organizationally, both houses were configured like other legislatures of the era. The House elected a speaker, a clerk, an assistant clerk, and a sergeant at arms and the Senate chose a president pro tem, a clerk, and a sergeant at arms (*Cons. of the St. of Deseret, with the Jour. of the Conv. which Formed it, and the Proc. of the Leg. Consequent Thereon* 1849, 11, 13). It also appears that the General Assembly employed standing committees. A list for the Senate identifies eleven standing committees, each of which had five or six members (Morgan 1987, 195). Again, the committees were standard issue for the time—Judiciary; Counties; Ways and Means; Civil Law; Claims; Criminal Codes; Elections; Military; Ordinances; Petitions; and Roads, Bridges, and Public Works. Given the use of joint rules it is likely that the House employed the same, or very similar, standing committees.

Legislatively, the General Assembly was an active body. It passed almost 50 ordinances over the year and a half that it held meetings (Morgan 1987, 129–93). Among other matters, it made laws regulating elections, creating a militia, and establishing a judiciary. A criminal code with novel features was fashioned (Keedy 1953, 527–28). Many of the ordinances were complex; the law incorporating Great Salt Lake City contained 48 sections. The General Assembly legislated up to its very last moments with the final ordinance making it a misdemeanor to gamble on "horse-racing, cock-fighting, dog-fighting, card-playing, or any other means by which the game may be tested and property won" (Morgan 1987, 193).

The General Assembly's demise came when Congress passed legislation establishing the Utah Territory. Gaining territorial status was a positive development in the push for statehood, and the General Assembly adopted a resolution saying it "cheerfully and cordially" accepted its termination in favor of a territorial legislature (*DN* 1851). But the General Assembly's legacy lived on in several ways. First, at least nine members of the first Utah territorial legislature had previously served in the Deseret legislature. Second, the new territorial legislature quickly reenacted all of the laws adopted by its provisional predecessor (Crawley 1989, 20). Third, the standing committees used by both the territorial House and Council were, at least partly, rooted in those used by the General Assembly. Of the 13 standing committees established by the Council, 7 had a direct analogue in the Deseret Senate. Of the 8 standing committees in the House, 6 had a counterpart in the Deseret Senate. It does not appear, however, that the General Assembly rules transferred to the territorial legislature. The territorial House adopted a set of 20 rules much more focused on parliamentary procedures than the rules used by the Deseret General Assembly. Again, the rules appear to have been locally generated, but in this case they bear sufficient resemblance to the rules used by the Iowa House to suggest that, again, Iowa was an important model for Utah.[20]

Finally, and most unusually, Brigham Young later revived a legislature of Deseret that held annual sessions between 1862 and 1870. In this incarnation the shadow Deseret legislature reenacted the laws adopted by that year's territorial legislature (*DN* 1868; Morgan 1987, 96–112; *NYT* 1868). Outside of Utah, this second version of the legislature of Deseret was treated as a curiosity. In 1864, for example, a *New York Times* correspondent remarked, "What business there is for these solons to transact is rather a puzzler. Failure having followed all attempts of Utah to become a State, the continuance of the shadow without the substance is illustrative of Mormon tenacity, and of the peculiar ways of doing things in this Territory" (*NYT* 1864). Eventually, Utahans determined that the existence of the ghost legislature was inhibiting advancement to statehood, and it ceased to be called into session.

The Legislatures of Hawaii

Like Oregon, Hawaii experienced a number of different legislative bodies prior to becoming a territory, as shown in table 5.5. Unlike Oregon, Hawaii's early legislatures were established by monarchs. The islands' first lawmaking body of any sort was created by Kamehameha III in 1829 and was a council composed of ten chiefs, the regent, and the king. In 1840,

Kamehameha III granted his subjects a constitution that established the first fully recognizable legislature, the Legislative Council.[21] This body was bicameral, with a House of Nobles and a House of Representatives. The king selected the nobles who were appointed for life, and the initial 16 chosen were specifically named in the constitution (Lydecker 1918, 3, 12). Some of the nobles held hereditary rank, others did not. Indeed, it was speculated that one member was appointed because he was "a drinking companion of the King's" (Simpson 1843, 37). Members of the House were elected annually by the voters. The range of seats in the House was set by law, and over the 12 years the constitution was in effect the body's membership size varied from a low of 5 seats to high of 24 seats. Although the first session of the Legislative Council met in 1841, it was not until 1845 that any members of the House appear to have participated (Lydecker 1918, 16–18).

Under the 1840 constitution both houses had to pass legislation for it to be sent to the king for assent. It also specified that the two houses were to sit separately, but it allowed them to sit together at their discretion. It appears from the records that the houses opted to meet as a single body through 1850. But over time pressure built to give the representatives a greater voice, and a law passed in 1850 quadrupled the number of House seats to 24 from 6. Several other significant changes quickly followed, marking the 1851 legislative session as a watershed. For the first time the two houses met separately, they each began keeping a journal, and they each named a formal leader: a speaker in the House of Representatives and a president—the king—in the House of Nobles (Lydecker 1918, 5–6).

The Legislative Council was notable for one other feature: women served as Nobles. There were four women in the first session in 1841. The 1845 and 1847 sessions each saw six women serve. The last woman noble held office in 1855. Their presence was routinely commented on by foreign observers (e.g., Bingham 1855, 568; Simpson 1847, 26). Noting the five women serving at the time of his residency, the British consul wondered, "What would our political peeresses give for permission to vote in their own right as do these Hawaiian ladies?" (Simpson 1843, 37).

In 1852 a new constitution, developed in consultation with the Legislative Council, was granted by Kamehameha III. The document formalized many of the changes introduced during the 1851 legislative session. The lawmaking body's name was changed to the Legislature of the Hawaiian Islands. The two houses kept their individual names, but they were directed to sit separately. Nobles were still named by the king and served for life,

TABLE 5.5. Characteristics of Hawaiian Legislatures Prior to the Territorial Legislature

Legislative Characteristic	Legislature				
	Legislative Council	Legislature of the Hawaiian Islands	Legislature of the Hawaiian Kingdom	Legislature of the Hawaiian Kingdom	Legislature of the Republic of Hawaii
Created by Constitution of:	1840	1852	1864	1887	1894
Bicameral status	Houses sat together and separately	Houses sat separately	Houses sat together	Houses sat together	Houses sat separately
Sessions	Annual	Annual	Biennial	Biennial	Biennial
Upper House	Nobles	Nobles	Nobles	Nobles	Senate
Membership size	16	No more than 30	No more than 20	24	15
Selected by	King	King	King	Voters, by district	Voters, by district
Term of office	For life	For life	For life	Six-year term	Six-year term
Leadership	President (king) (1851)	President	President	President[a]	President, Vice president
Lower House	Representatives	Representatives	Representatives	Representatives	Representatives
Membership size	5–24	No more than 30	24–40	24	15
Selected by	Voters, annually	Voters, annually	Voters, biennially	Voters, by district	Voters, by district
Term of office				Two-year term	Two-year term
Leadership	Speaker (1851)	Speaker	Vice President	Vice President[a]	Speaker, Vice Speaker

Source: Compiled by author from Lydecker 1918.
[a]Both the president and vice president were members of the House of Nobles.

while representatives continued to be elected by the voters to one-year terms. Both houses were increased slightly in size. And like American legislatures, each chamber was now allowed to judge the qualifications of its members, to choose its officers, and to adopt its rules of procedure. The constitution also granted lawmakers parliamentary privilege.

A few noteworthy differences between the two houses were established. Different membership qualifications were set. Nobles had to be at least 21 years old and an island resident for five years. In an unusual move, a higher age standard was set for the lower house; representatives had to be at least 25 years old, but a resident for only one year prior to election. In addition, they were required to know how to read and write and understand accounts. Representatives were paid, with a maximum set at $3 a day. Nobles were not compensated, although the constitution allowed for the possibility in the future.

There was only slight tinkering with the legislative process. Again, each house had to pass legislation, and any measure had to have the king's signature before becoming law. Revenue and spending bills, however, were to originate with the representatives, although the nobles were allowed to amend them. In practice, however, the separation of powers was a bit fuzzy. During several sessions in the 1850s the speaker of the House of Representatives was concurrently an associate justice of the Supreme Court. Another member of the Supreme Court served simultaneously in the House of Nobles. This interlocking practice had occurred under the previous constitution as well (Lydecker 1918, 6).

A new constitution introduced in 1864 by Kamehameha V prevented judges from holding legislative seats. It also made several other significant changes. Although they continued to be separately composed, the two chambers were now required to sit together, a fact confirmed by the Anglican bishop of Hawaii, who, in describing the government, wrote of a single chamber composed of roughly 20 nobles and 40 representatives (Staley 1868). This situation was, apparently, satisfactory to a majority of lawmakers. An attempt to force them to meet separately was defeated in the legislature a decade later (*NYT* 1874b). Another significant change introduced was to have the legislature meet biennially, rather than annually, a switch taking place at the same time in the American states.

While most other constitutional provisions on the legislature carried over from the 1852 constitution, there were a few changes. The term of office for representatives was increased to two years, and their pay was set at $150 per session. Their qualifications were altered slightly: the minimum age was dropped to 21 years, while the residency requirement was raised to three years. The fact that representatives were paid while nobles were not may explain the former's better attendance records (Kuykendall 1967, 288)

In terms of procedure, the Hawaiian legislature looked much like American legislatures of the time. As will be documented below, it used a standing committee system, albeit with nobles and representatives serving together on committees (*Hawaiian Gazette* 1880; *Saturday Press* 1884). And the rules it adopted were clearly derived from those given in *Jefferson's Manual*. But some were refashioned to meet local needs. The 1876 rules were printed in two columns, the left listing the rules in English and the right in Hawaiian. Rule 82 gave a nod to the islands' multinational population, saying that "The Rules of Parliamentary practice in England and the United States shall govern the House in all cases to which they are applicable" (*Rules and Orders for Conducting Business in the H. of the LA of the Hawaiian Islands* 1876).

There were a few dissimilarities. In 1874 the Legislative Assembly moved into the newly built Aliiolani Hale. Originally intended to be a royal palace, the building was characterized as being "admirably adapted in structure and accommodation in accordance with the present requirements of the population and resources of the country." When the legislature was out of session the Hale's Hall of Assembly was used by the Court of Equity and Common Pleas (Nicholson 1881, 66–67). The opening of each Legislative Assembly was accompanied by pomp and ceremony, including a military band and an address by the king in full uniform and a "rich yellow feather cloak" (*Hawaiian Hansard* 1886, 1–2). The institution, however, was not always revered. Following the Assembly's 1874 vote to name David Kālakaua as king, supporters of his opponent, Queen Dowager Emma, rioted. The protesters broke into the courthouse where the meeting had been held, destroyed furniture, and beat lawmakers with clubs and broken chair legs. A number of representatives were injured, and one later died. The disturbance was only put down with assistance from forces aboard two U.S. Navy ships and a British Royal Navy vessel (Cummings 1874, 37–38).

In 1887, King Kālakaua was forced to accept a new constitution developed by the Hawaiian League, a civic group dominated by wealthy Americans and Europeans with business interests in the islands. The League was backed by a volunteer militia. The specter of violence behind the push for a new governing structure prompted the king's acquiescence and gave the new document its popular moniker, "The Bayonet Constitution."

Superficially, the legislature remained unchanged under the new constitution. It continued to be a bicameral body with a House of Nobles and a House of Representatives sitting together. It continued to meet every other year. Language giving each house control of its procedures and leaders, and its members parliamentary privileges, carried over from earlier constitutions. But under the surface, the role of the legislature was greatly strengthened, and the monarchy was stripped of much of its authority. One reporter commented, "The humorous description of this document [is] one that deprives the monarch of all powers but those of drawing his salary and granting pardons" (*NYT* 1887a). While the king retained a veto, the legislature could now override it with a two-thirds majority in each house. In addition, the king could no longer appoint the nobles to life terms. Instead, the nobles were to be elected to six-year terms by a very tightly defined electorate that excluded a large percentage of native Hawaiians.

Under the Bayonet Constitution the nobles and representatives were equal in number but held to different qualification standards. Nobles had to be at least 25 years old, a resident for three years, and have property equity of at least $3,000 and an annual income of $600. Representatives had to be at least 21 years old, a resident for three years, have property equity of at least $500, an annual income of $250, plus the ability to read and write English, Hawaiian, or a European language and understand accounts. Representatives were to be paid $250 for each biennial term, while nobles received no compensation.

Some opposition to this legislative structure developed. By 1890, the moderate National Reform Party proposed splitting the nobles and representatives, arguing that the system of sitting together was "an anomaly not to be found in any office in any other constitutionally governed country." They also supported modifying the voting laws to allow "natives, small land owners and mechanics" the right to vote for the nobles (*National Herald* 1890).

The 1887 constitution was in place for only a few years. In 1894, after a serious political miscalculation, Queen Liliuokalani, King Kālakaua's sister and successor, was forced to abdicate by many of the same people who had pushed the Bayonet Constitution on Hawaii. The new regime's preference was to be annexed by the United States, but when that outcome appeared to be unlikely for the foreseeable future, they assembled a constitutional convention. The document they wrote creating the Republic of Hawaii was adopted without any popular vote.

Legislative powers in the new republic were similar to those granted

Congress by the U.S. Constitution. The legislature was bicameral, with a Senate and a House of Representatives sitting separately. Senators had to be at least 30 years old and were given 6-year terms while representatives had to be at least 25 years old and were given 2-year terms. Higher qualifications were imposed on members of the upper house than on members of the lower house: senators had to have property equity of $3,000 and an annual income of $1,200, while representatives had to have property equity of $1,000 and an annual income of $600. But members of both chambers were now required speak, read, and write either English or Hawaiian. And members of both chambers were to be paid $400 a session.

Provisions allowing each house to determine its own leaders and procedural rules carried over from earlier constitutions. The writers of the constitution opted not to create a vice president, figuring that the Senate could elect its own presiding officer and save the Republic the cost of a salary (Judd 1894, 56). A few changes in legislative procedure were introduced. The legislature was limited to a session of 90 legislative days. The requirement that a bill be read three times before becoming law was made a constitutional mandate rather than a rule adopted by the legislature as it had been (*Rules and Orders for Conducting Business in the H. of the LA of the Hawaiian Islands* 1876, 14). A procedure requiring a bill to be engrossed was added. More unusual was a requirement that no bill in either house could be introduced without first gaining the written endorsement of three members. According to an analysis of the constitution, "This provision was borrowed from one of the German States, and it is believed will prevent the introduction, expense of printing and waste of time upon bills that have no merit, and which might be introduced and kept alive for the purpose of extorting blackmail from individuals or corporations supposed to be injuriously affected by such legislation." The need for such a rule was seen in the "Proceedings in Legislatures of several of the States of the United States [which] furnish Hawaii with object lessons on this topic" (Judd 1894, 58).

The Republic of Hawaii legislature did not exist for long. In 1898 Hawaii was annexed by the United States and made a territory. In 1900 Congress passed an organic act establishing a territorial legislature. That legislature met for the first time in early 1901. The question of interest here is the extent to which this new body was grounded in its Hawaiian predecessors. There were a number of links. The territorial legislature met in the Iolani Palace, as earlier legislatures had since moving from the Aliiolani Hale in 1893. According to one account, the House met in the old throne room, "where some thirty desks are conveniently arranged"

(*Evening Bulletin* 1901). Another observer called it "a splendid room" with a "lofty ceiling," large windows, and "polished koa wood" (*Public* 1901, 827). The Senate did not fare as well. One report was charitable, noting that "The arrangement of the Senate was as in previous Legislatures. There were two rows of new desks running *mauka* and *makai*" (*Evening Bulletin* 1901).[22] Another observer commented that compared with the House chamber, the Senate chamber was "less commodious and well fitted." This reporter went on to add, "It is, in fact, nothing but the upper hall of the old palace, shut off from the stairway that leads from the main floor to it by movable screens" (*Public* 1901, 827). There was some carryover in personnel. In the territorial House three members, including the speaker, had previously served in earlier bodies, one going back as far as 1876. In the Senate five members had previous service in either the Republic Legislature or the latter Legislature of the Hawaiian Kingdom.[23]

There were procedural continuities as well. On the first day that the territorial House met it passed a motion, "that Rules of proceedings of the last Legislature of the Republic of Hawaii be adopted as temporary rules for the House" (*Jour. of the H. of Reps.* 1901, 3). Later in the session they adopted a sophisticated set of 89 rules. Rather than relying on *Jefferson's Manual* to supply answers to questions not addressed in the chamber's rules, Hawaii opted to use "The Rules of Parliamentary practice as laid down by Cushing, and as interpreted and practiced in the House of Representatives of the United States" (*Jour. of the H. of Reps.* 1901, 78). Hawaii's use of *Cushing's* was a nod to evolving legislative standards in the American states, as will be demonstrated in chapter 6.

Perhaps even more notably, there was remarkable continuity between the standing committees created by the territorial House and those used by its predecessors, as shown in table 5.6. All but one standing committee created by the first territorial House—Public Expenditures—had existed in some form in the Legislature of the Hawaiian Kingdom in 1876 and 1892 and in the Republic of Hawaii House of Representatives in 1898. Indeed, there were surprisingly few changes between 1876 and 1901, even though the legislatures existed under three different regimes. The committees on Finance, Judiciary, Public Lands and Internal Improvements, Military, and Accounts carried over directly. The Committee on Commerce, Agriculture and Manufactures dropped commerce from its name, the Sanitary Committee and the Committee on Education were combined to become the Committee on Public Health and Education, and the Committee on Enrollment and Revision was merged with the Committee on Printing, to

TABLE 5.6. Standing Committees in Hawaiian Legislatures: 1876, 1892, 1898, and 1901

Legislature of the Hawaiian Kingdom, 1876	Legislature of the Hawaiian Kingdom, 1892	Legislature of the Republic of Hawaii, House of Representatives, 1898	Legislature of the Territory of Hawaii, House of Representatives, 1901
Foreign Relations	Foreign Relations	Foreign Relations	
Judiciary	Judiciary	Judiciary	Judiciary
Finance	Finance	Finance	Finance
Military	Military	Military	Military
Public Lands and Internal Improvements	Public Lands and Internal Improvements	Public Lands and Internal Improvements	Public Lands and Internal Improvements
Commerce, Agriculture and Manufactures	Commerce, Agriculture and Manufactures	Commerce, Agriculture and Manufactures	Agriculture and Manufactures
Sanitary	Sanitary	Public Health and Education	Public Health and Education
Education	Education		
Accounts	Accounts	Accounts and Revenue	Accounts
	Rules		Rules
	Enrollment and Revision	Enrollment, Revision, and Printing	Enrollment, Revision, and Printing
	Printing		Miscellany
	Miscellaneous Petitions		Public Expenditures

Source: Committees in 1876 are taken from *Rules and Orders for Conducting Business in the H. of the LA of the Hawaiian Islands* (1876). The standing committees for 1892 and 1898 were graciously supplied by archivists at the Hawaii State Archives. Committees in the territorial House were taken from *Jour. of the H. of Reps.* 1901, 62.

become the Committee on Enrollment, Revision, and Printing. Standing committees on printing and enrollment, and revision had appeared by 1880 (*Hawaiian Gazette* 1880). A committee on Miscellaneous Petitions, which had been first created in 1886 as a catchall for matters that did not fit the existing committee structure (*Hawaiian Hansard* 1886, 8), resurfaced in the territorial legislature as a Committee on Miscellany. The only standing committee not carried over to the territorial era, for obvious reasons, was the Committee on Foreign Relations.

The Free State Legislature of Kansas

Legislative evolution in Kansas followed a different path than that taken by any other state that had a territorial legislature. This is because of events during the "Bleeding Kansas" period. When the first Kansas territorial legislature was elected, hordes of Missouri "border ruffians" illegally swelled the ranks of voters, producing a body dominated by proslavery members (Shoemaker 1954, 326–28). Consequently, Kansas residents who wanted to see the territory admitted to the union as a free state came to refer to it as the "Bogus Legislature" (Brewerton 1856, 288–92; Gladstone 1857, 90–91; Phillips 1856, 98–113). A sense of their revulsion can be gleaned from a resignation letter written by an antislavery member of the newly elected Council: "Their Legislature is substantially a Provincial Council, instituted and ordained by a daring and unscrupulous league in the State of Missouri and other parts of the South, to govern a people whose liberties they have ruthlessly stricken down." He went on to state, "Simply as a citizen and a man, I shall therefore yield no submission to the alien Legislature" (*NYDT* 1855b).

Unhappiness with the Bogus Legislature spawned an organized opposition, labeled the Topeka movement. In 1855 supporters of the Topeka movement drafted a constitution to submit to Congress to have Kansas admitted as a free state. The proposed constitution created an alternative territorial legislature, commonly called the Free State Legislature. In form, the Free State Legislature looked much like its territorial counterpart. It was a bicameral body with a House of Representatives, but like a state it called its upper house the Senate instead of the Council. The proposed constitution gave each house the right to choose its officers and to adopt its own rules and procedures, as in the federal and most state constitutions. The document did have one distinguishing provision: "Any member of either house shall have the right to protest against any act or resolution thereof; and such protest and reason therefor shall, without alteration, commitment or delay, be entered on the journal." This specific language was lifted from the New York constitution of 1846 and the Ohio constitution of 1851, and goes back to the Pennsylvania constitution of 1776 (Luce 1922, 363).

The initial meeting of the Free State Legislature was held in Topeka on March 4, 1856. The first action taken by the House was to elect its officers, starting with the speaker and chief clerk and then a host of assistant clerks and other functionaries. This process was, of course, a replay of the actions taken by the territorial House during its first day. But when it came to establishing rules and standing committees, the two Kansas legislatures relied on divergent models. The rules adopted by the first Kansas territorial House were taken from the rules then in use by the Missouri House, even to the extent that they employed the exact same ten article headings in the exact same order.[24] The standing committee structure created also mimicked that used in the Missouri House. Of the 14 committees established in the territorial House, 13 were found in the Missouri House; only the Committee on Bounds of Counties and Districts did not have a Missouri counterpart, probably because the latter was a well-established polity that no longer routinely confronted such issues (*Jour. of the H. of Reps. of the Terr. of Kan.* 1855, Appendix 29–34; *Jour. of the H. of Reps. of the St. of Mo.* 1855, 374–84). There were a few other small differences. Where Missouri had separate committees on Judiciary and Criminal Jurisprudence, Kansas combined them into a single committee. Missouri had a Committee on Ways and Means, while Kansas called its version the Committee on Finance. Finally, Missouri had several committees that Kansas did not replicate, among them a Committee on Lunatic Asylum, a Committee on Swamp Lands, and a Committee on Public Salines.

Given prevailing political passions, it comes as no surprise that the Free State Legislature opted not to model itself on Missouri. Instead, the rules the Free State Legislature adopted were based on those employed by the U.S. House, likely a version included in a recent volume of *Jefferson's Manual* (cf. Jefferson 1854, 135–62; "Journal of the House of Representatives of the State of Kansas, March 4, 1856" 1915, 173–76). In addition, the Free State Legislature created a somewhat more elaborate standing committee system than that created by its territorial counterpart, establishing 18 standing committees rather than 14. There were a number of other differences. Where the territorial House had a Committee on Agriculture, the Free State House had a Committee on Agriculture and Manufactures. The

Free State House had a Committee on Banking and Corporations that had no counterpart in the territorial House. Another committee found in the Free State House but not in the territorial House was a Committee on Vice and Immorality. Such a committee was not unique to Kansas; one with the same name had long been a feature of the Pennsylvania House (Sutherland 1827, 81). It appears that the Kansas committee was created to respond to a vocal constituency. During the second week of its first session the Free State Legislature received a petition from "56 Ladies of Topeka" saying, "the wives and daughters of your constituents beg leave . . . that suitable laws be immediately passed to prevent the manufacture and importation for sale or use as a beverage within the State of Kansas of any distilled or malted liquors" ("Journal of the House of Representatives of the State of Kansas, March 4, 1856" 1915, 209–10). The petition was referred to the Committee on Vice and Immorality, which failed to recommend it.

The convening of the Free State Legislature was seen by many in the territory and around the rest of the country as a provocative act. The enmity between the two territorial factions was palpable. A Free State supporter published an inflammatory comparison of the two sets of lawmakers.

> I saw the Border Ruffian "Barons" of Kansas when at Pawnee city, and I assure you that the contrast between the Free-State and Pro-Slavery Legislatures of Kansas is very gratifying to my sympathies and complementary to our creed. The Ruffians were drunkards, blasphemers and gamblers; they were personally as ignorant and unpolished as their "acts" demonstrated they were unprincipled and violent. These Free-State men, on the contrary, are intelligent, sober, decided yet liberal in creed. I wish I could get the daguerreotypes of both Assemblies and publish them in The Tribune. They would convert thousands of dough-faces to our party. (*Organization of the Free State Government in Kansas with The Inaugural Speech and Message of Governor Robinson* 1856, 4)[25]

Consequently, it was to be expected that, as a reporter warned following the March meeting of the Free State Legislature, "Violence is apprehended" (*NYT* 1856c). In turn, territorial and federal government officials sought to prevent the Free State government from taking root. In January 1856, President Franklin Pierce issued a proclamation that threatened to use the U.S. Army in support of the territorial government. A few days later Secretary of War Jefferson Davis sent orders to military commanders in Kansas authorizing the use of force if requested by the territorial governor. As a result, when Governor Wilson Shannon asked for assistance in advance of a planned July 4 session of the Free State Legislature, Colonel E. V. Sumner took five companies of his U.S. Army regiment to just outside of Topeka. Given his interpretation of his orders—he characterized the legislature as being "insurrectionary"—the colonel intended to prevent it from meeting (Mullis 2004; U.S. House 1856, 56–59).

On July 4, shortly before the legislature was scheduled to assemble at noon, Sumner galloped into Topeka with 200 dragoons. He had two cannons positioned on a rise above Constitutional Hall, the legislature's meeting place (*NYT* 1856d). The colonel then entered the House chamber, as recounted in the House journal.

> Col. E. V. Sumner U. S. Army having now taken a position upon the platform interrupted the proceedings of the House and said
>
> Gentlemen "I am called upon this day to perform the most painful duty of my whole life. Under the authority of the President's proclamation I am here to disperse this Legislature and therefore inform you that you cannot meet. I therefore in accordance with my order command you to disperse. . . .
>
> P. C. Schuyler a spectator asked
>
> "Col. Sumner are we to understand that the Legislature is dispersed at the point of the bayonet?
>
> Col. Sumner replyed "I shall use the whole force under my command to carry out my orders."
>
> The House thereupon dispersed. ("Journal of the House of Representatives of the State of Kansas, March 4, 1856," 235)

At that point, "Col. Sumner, who did not appear to be particularly enlightened on legislative matters, had got on his horse to go, when he learned that the Senate was still to be disperse" (Phillips 1856, 404). The colonel dismounted, proceeded upstairs to the Senate chamber, and forced it to cease its session.

Following its dispersal, the Free State Legislature managed to reassemble several times the following year ("Journal of the House of Representatives of the State of Kansas, March 4, 1856," 235–49). But once Free State supporters won control of the territorial legislature in the October 1857 elections there was no longer a need for the alternative body, and it disappeared from the political scene. In several important ways, however, the Free State Legislature lived on. Although there was almost no overlap in membership between the two bodies—only two members appear to have served in both ("Biographies of the Members of the Free-State Legislature of 1857-'58" 1908, 204–16)—the territorial legislature that organized following the election took its rules from those used in the Free State Legislature and not from its territorial predecessor. Similarly, the standing committees it established looked far more like those used in the Free State Legislature—including committees on Agriculture and Manufactures, Banking and Commerce, and Vice and Immorality—than the ones used by the previous territorial assembly ("Journal of the House of Representatives of the State of Kansas, March 4, 1856," 173–76; *Rules for the Gov. of the LA of the Terr. of Kan.* 1858, 3–19). Thus, in important ways, the evolution of the Kansas state legislature is rooted in the Free State Legislature and not the original territorial legislature.

The Legislative Assembly of San Francisco

California never had a territorial legislature, as noted above. When the United States took control of the territory it instituted a military government, which largely relied on carryover institutions from the Mexican era, notably *alcaldes* or municipal magistrates, to govern. In 1847, the military governor allowed San Francisco to establish a six-member town council. When the council's term expired at the end of 1848, electoral difficulties led to a brief period where the old council and two newly elected councils all claimed the right to govern (Burnett 1880, 307). Unhappy with the confusion, a convention of San Franciscans met in February 1849 to straighten out the political mess. The delegates chose to create a Legislative Assembly for the District of San Francisco, to consist of 15 members elected to one-year terms (Bancroft 1888, 210, 271; Buffum 1850, 151–52; Dwinelle 1867, 89).[26] The legislature was charged with keeping a journal of its proceedings and authorized to determine its own rules (Dwinelle 1867, 105).

Around this time district legislatures also formed in Sacramento and Sonoma (Browne 1850, xvii; Burnett 1880, 294–95; Royce 1886, 257). It appears that these other bodies were not very active. In May 1849, a Sacramento newspaper asked, "Where is the Legislative Assembly, elected a few weeks since, whose commendable zeal in the discharge of its high obligations promised so well? . . . We know many of the members to be absent" (*Placer Times* 1849). In contrast, San Francisco's assembly was busy. Its first meeting was held at the Public Institute on March 5. Using tellers, the assembly elected a speaker and a clerk. It also appointed a committee of three to "draw up rules of proceeding" (Dwinelle 1867, 106). The following week a set of 37 rules was adopted unanimously. The rules were surprisingly sophisticated, dealing with both protocol and procedure. They established standing committees and a voting process to appoint them and imposed a requirement that all bills be referred to committee. The final rule held that *Jefferson's Manual* would used to fill any gaps in parliamentary procedures (*Min. of the Proc. of the LA of the District of S.F.* 1860, 5, 8–10). The model for these rules was not specified, and there are no obvious candidates, but the first 20 rules are remarkably similar to those used around the same time by the Florida House (cf. *Jour. of the Proc. of the H. of Reps. of the First GA of the St. of Fla.* 1845, 15–16).

The second day the assembly met it created five standing committees: Ways and Means, Judiciary, Expenditures, Health and Police, and Public Buildings and Improvements. Each committee had three members. Membership sizes were later increased to five (*Min. of the Proc. of the LA of the District of S.F.* 1860, 11, 36).

Attendance was a chronic problem for the Assembly, even though sessions were conveniently scheduled for seven o'clock in the evening. The body's membership size was expanded in May in an effort to make attaining a quorum easier (Buffum 1850, 152–53). Among the new members elected was Peter Burnett, who had served on the 1844 Oregon Legislative Committee (Burnett 1880, 319). Like territorial legislatures of the time, the Assembly struggled to be supplied with the necessary stationery, candles, and fuel to carry out its tasks. Still, even with many impediments, it managed to pass a fair amount of legislation. The assembly created a harbor master and passed a revenue measure and an elections bill. Some of the issues it tackled, however, were typically associated with city councils, such as a bill prohibiting making fires in the streets (*Min. of the Proc. of the LA of the District of S.F.* 1860, 12, 22, 24–25, 28).

The military authorities were unhappy with the assembly's existence, seeing it as a challenge to their authority. On June 4, 1849, the military governor issued a proclamation denouncing the legislature.

> Whereas, proof has been laid before me that a body of men styling themselves "the Legislative Assembly of the District of San Francisco," have usurped powers which are vested only in the Congress of the United States, by making laws, creating and filling offices, imposing and collecting taxes, without the authority of law, and in violation of the

Constitution of the United States, . . . Now, therefore, all persons are warned not to countenance said illegal and unauthorized body, either by paying taxes or by supporting or abetting their officers. (Dwinelle 1867, 107)

The proclamation was delivered in Monterey and was not distributed in San Francisco for several days (Burnett 1880, 325). During that time the assembly, which enjoyed broad popular support (Buffum 1850, 154), published its own broadside against the federal government.

For the first time in the history of the "model Republic," and perhaps in that of any civilized government in the world, the Congress of the United States, representing a great nation of more than twenty millions of freemen, have assumed the right, not only to *tax us without representation*, but to *tax us without giving us any government at all*—thus making us feel, endure, and bear all of the BURTHENS of government, without giving us even a distant glimpse of its BENEFITS. (Burnett 1880, 320, italics in original)

The harsh rhetoric might have led to a political rupture, but tensions quickly abated when the military governor pressed the issue of statehood by scheduling a constitutional convention for September. That action siphoned off support for the Assembly. In early July, the Assembly's speaker resigned his seat. In a subsequent public vote on whether to continue the Assembly, the voters who showed up overwhelmingly wanted to do so. But turnout in the election was very light, which was widely interpreted as a signal that most San Franciscans had turned their attention to the upcoming convention and statehood. By mid-July, the Legislative Assembly ceased to exist (Burnett 1880, 338–39).

It did not leave much of a legacy. Scholars make no mention of the assembly in studies of the first state legislature (Ignoffo 1999; Jones 1950). None of its members went on to serve in the constitutional convention or the first state legislature. As noted above, the state legislature turned elsewhere for its rules and structures. One assembly member did go on to bigger things: Peter Burnett was elected California's first governor. Like several other legislatures examined here, however, the Legislative Assembly of San Francisco demonstrates a strong desire among nineteenth-century Americans to create legislative bodies to fill governing voids.

The General Assembly of the Indian Stream Republic

The final legislative oddity is perhaps the least known and most curious American legislature: the General Assembly of the Indian Stream Republic. The Indian Stream Republic was established in 1832 in a tiny land mass squeezed in between the northernmost corner of New Hampshire and British Canada. The area was contested by both Great Britain and the United States, but it was so small and isolated that neither government had much of a presence in it. Consequently, the community of several hundred households determined, as an 1834 letter from their representatives to Congress stated, that "imperative necessity required, that they should adopt some form of government which would secure the rights, happiness, and prosperity, of the people of this place" (U.S. House 1839, 7).

The constitution adopted by the 60 Indian Stream men who assembled to write it created an unusual legislative body. It was bicameral, with a General Assembly composed of every man over the age of 21 who would pledge a loyalty oath and a five-member Council elected by and from the larger assembly. The General Assembly was to meet annually, while the Council could meet as often as it wished. The legislative process concocted differed from that found in other American legislatures. Only the Council was authorized to propose legislation, and the General Assembly could only amend measures passed by the Council. If the Council did not agree to an amended bill, the General Assembly could override the veto with a two-thirds majority (Brown 1955, 59–61; Doan 1997, 163–71; Showerman 1915, 61–63; U.S. House 1839, 7). In selecting the upper house from among the membership of the lower house this system mimicked New England colonial assemblies and early state legislatures. But a closer analogue to the overall scheme would be the region's open town meetings (Bryan 2004, 6–8; Zimmerman 1999, 59–64).

Councilors were given one-year terms, and they exercised executive and judicial powers as well as legislative powers. When necessary they could call a special meeting of the General Assembly, but to do so they were required to post public notices at least 6 days in advance, "at or near the dwelling house of Ebenezer Fletcher, at the assembly rooms, and at the house of Peter Barnes" (Showerman 1915, 63). Legislative proposals developed by the Council had to be posted at the same three venues at least 14 days before the annual General Assembly session.

The General Assembly's first session took place in July 1832. Of the 52 men eligible to participate in the assembly, 44 agreed to do so. During the initial meeting, the assembly elected a speaker and a clerk, and "Voted that the former rules and regulations for the government of the house be adopted until others are made." They also charged the Council with developing a permanent set of rules (Showerman 1915, 68–69). It does not appear that a copy of either set of rules has survived.

The legislature enjoyed considerable continuity. The same individual served as speaker during its first four sessions, and he was elected to the Council during the first two sessions. In 1833, four of the six men elected to the Council had served on it the previous year. Only one councilor returned in 1834, but in 1835 three of the four members elected did (Doan 1997, 181). (Why only four councilors were elected that year is a mystery.) Legislatively, the assembly was active. During the first year eight laws were passed, among them measures establishing courts of justice and organizing a militia. Legislation passed in later years focused on taxes and the criminal justice system. It is not clear how members behaved, but a law passed the first year titled "An Act to Prevent Selling Spirituous Liquors in or Near the Assembly Rooms &c." suggests that there might have been some problems (Showerman 1915, 72, 79–92).

Indian Stream residents were divided on whether they would prefer to be annexed by Great Britain or the United States. By 1835 tensions between the two camps spilled over into confrontation and occasional violence. One of the prime movers behind the creation of the republic and an initial Council member, Luther Parker, agitated for joining with New Hampshire and got arrested by British officials for allegedly providing a neighbor with weapons to use to resist their authority (*New-Hampshire Patriot* 1835; *Portsmouth Journal of Literature and Politics* 1835). Eventually, Parker was released, and his desire for the republic to be united with the United States was fulfilled. After New Hampshire's militia occupied Indian Stream in late 1835, the republic's government ceased to exist, and the area became integrated in New Hampshire. Still, its legislature left a legacy. Following the turmoil, Parker moved his family to Wisconsin Territory. In 1846 he served in the territorial House, chairing the Committee on Agriculture and Manufactures and successfully shepherding the creation of Waukesha County (Showerman 1915, 118–24).

Conclusions

The evolutionary patterns laid out in chapters 3 and 4 were relatively straightforward. The colonial assemblies morphed into state legislatures with very few changes. Similarly, territorial legislatures were almost directly transformed into state legislatures. The question posed at the beginning of this chapter was whether the odd cases of predecessor legislatures enjoyed the same close relationship with their successor bodies. There are, of course, many reasons to anticipate that their structures and procedures might not transfer over, most obviously because the legal standing of many of these predecessor bodies was suspect. Yet the overall picture that develops from a close examination of these unusual legislatures is that they too influenced the legislative bodies that followed them, just as the colonial assemblies and territorial legislatures did.

In a few cases the influence of the predecessor on the successor is clear and unequivocal. The most obvious is the Maine legislature, which in terms of its constitutional features, procedural rules, and standing committee system was, as we might expect, the spitting image of the Massachusetts legislature. It is the contrast of Maine's process with how the West Virginia state legislature was created, however, that generates an important caveat on legislative evolution. West Virginia looked to Virginia, its parent, only for bits and pieces of its constitutional provisions and not at all for its rules and committees. This demonstrates that legislative DNA is chosen rather than inherited. West Virginia opted not to be like Virginia, perhaps because of the sharp political differences between the two polities. The same argument can be made with the exceptional case of the Kansas Free State Legislature. Rather than looking to its territorial rival, a body based on the legislature in detested Missouri, the Free-Staters chose to use different models on which to fashion their legislature. Arguably, the same was even true in Vermont, which did not look to either New Hampshire or New York—the states bickering over it—to guide the constitutional design of its general assembly. Thus, it appears that when the obvious legislative model is deemed politically unpalatable a substitute template is chosen. Clearly, politics can override familial ties in institutional design.

In most cases where the legislative lineage is obvious the influence of the predecessor legislature on the successor legislature is unquestionable. Remarkably, this is true even when the design of the successor legislature is in the hands of a different regime. The territorial legislatures in Hawaii, Oregon, Tennessee, and Utah were, as every territorial legislature was, created by the U.S. Congress and not by those in the territory. Yet, their predecessor legislatures influenced their successor bodies in a number of ways. In Hawaii and Oregon, parliamentary rules and committee structures largely carried over. To a lesser degree, that was also true in Utah.

And it is worth noting that the Deseret General Assembly devised the laws the new territorial legislature adopted. In Tennessee, as best we can tell from the limited information available, the State of Franklin's legacy surfaced through common governmental personnel.

In important ways the story lines of each of the 12 legislative oddities examined in this chapter reinforces the conclusions derived from the study of the development of the colonial assemblies, the original state legislatures, and the territorial legislatures. Each of these oddities adopted rules and structures used in existing legislatures, usually a parent, but in later cases often the U.S. House through the spread of *Jefferson's Manual.* The odd cases used existing rules and structures, and then, when they were replaced, many of these features were transferred to the new institutions. This transmission occurred through constitutional provisions, parliamentary rules, and committee systems. But it also happened through shared personnel. In almost every case the new institution had at least a few members who had served in the predecessor legislature. This represents an important aspect of continuity.

Finally, even the two instances of no legacies provide insights on the importance of legislatures in American history. Although neither the Legislative Assembly of San Francisco nor the General Assembly of the Indian Stream Republic influenced the state legislatures that absorbed their polities, they both evidence the pervasiveness of legislative institutions in American societies. Indeed, they demonstrate that the strong democratic impulse in nineteenth-century America manifested itself through the creation of legislatures. Keep in mind that at this time the established states were moving to constrain the power of legislatures. Yet, despite the temptation to appoint a governor or executive council to govern, in both of these odd cases an irrepressible desire for representative government surfaced. In an important sense, efficacy trumped efficiency. In these divergent situations small populations banded together, and by relying on familiar forms, they established legislatures and adopted sophisticated legislative rules and structures to govern themselves. Moreover, these legislatures successfully used those rules and structures to produce legislation that looked like laws developed by well-established legislative bodies operating in much less trying circumstances. The Legislative Assembly of San Francisco and the General Assembly of the Indian Stream Republic, along with legislatures in the State of Franklin, Oregon, the State of Deseret, and several other places, demonstrate the power of rules and structures to allow frontier lawmakers working in primitive conditions to successfully govern and to do so in a manner that was viewed as legitimate by the governed.

6 • The Institutionalizing of State Legislatures in the Nineteenth Century

Over the course of the nineteenth century, state legislatures institutionalized. In this context, I use *institutionalize* to mean that over time increasingly advanced structures and procedures become enmeshed in the organizational fabric. Although this perspective is consistent with Polsby's (1968) notion of institutionalization, it is, perhaps, even more directly aligned with Huntington's view. He proposed that "the level of institutionalization of any particular organization or procedure can be measured by its adaptability, complexity, autonomy and coherence" (Huntington 1965, 394). As will be documented in this chapter, newly established state legislatures adopted rules and structures then in use by existing legislatures, thereby starting their organizational lives as reasonably sophisticated organizations rather than as more primitive start-ups. This observation is, of course, entirely consistent with the story lines of the colonial assemblies, original state legislatures, territorial legislatures, and even the odd legislative cases presented in chapters 2 to 5. What is perhaps even more important to recognize about state legislatures during the nineteenth century is that they continued evolving, becoming increasingly complex bodies with more elaborate procedural rules and standing committee systems. In addition, they devised novel pay schemes and meeting schedules and added more staff and improved facilities. None of these changes, however, occurred uniformly across the states. Although the legislatures were all evolving in the same direction, each charted a somewhat different course. The colonial assemblies experienced similar patterns of change over their histories. The difference with state legislatures in the nineteenth century is that they started much farther along in terms of organizational evolution.

From Territorial Assemblies to State Legislatures: Continuities

It would be a mistake to assume that once territorial legislatures graduated to become state legislatures they crossed a magical threshold that made them distinctively different organizations. Actually, the shift in status was murky at times. One of the curiosities of the statehood process is the fact that a number of newly established state legislatures, among them Alabama, Indiana, Iowa, Michigan, Minnesota, Nebraska, Oregon, and Washington, met prior to their states being formally admitted to the union, raising questions about the legality of their decisions during the transition.[1] More important for the evolutionary story, however, were the tight connections between the state legislatures and their territorial predecessors. Most obviously, all of the new state legislatures were created as bicameral bodies as had been the case with their predecessor territorial bodies except in Michigan. Occasionally, the subject was debated. Tennessee's first constitutional convention initially voted in favor of a unicameral legislature but the draft was later amended to create a bicameral body, in part because Andrew Jackson argued that the new state ought to mirror the federal government's structure. The vote in favor of a bicameral system was razor thin, 28 to 27 (Buell 1904, 108; *Jour. of the Proc. of a Conv. Begun and Held at Knoxville* [1796] 1852, 9–10). The North Dakota constitutional convention discussed a proposal to create a unicameral legislature, and the idea garnered a fair amount of support (*Off. Report of the Proc. and Deb. of the First Constitutional Conv. of N.D.* 1889, 103–28; Kingsbury 1915, 1927–28). Interestingly, the South Dakota constitutional convention, held over the same days as the one in North Dakota, gave no consideration to unicameralism (*S.D. Constitutional Conv.* 1907).

Continuity prevailed in other ways. Lower houses mostly retained the name *House of Representatives*, but all of the upper houses that had been called *councils* took the name *Senate*. Sometimes, the institutional name used during the territorial era was kept. In Oregon, a delegate at the 1857 constitutional convention successfully argued to keep the title *Legislative Assembly* because it had been used in the territorial organic act and "We had got used to it." But there was debate. Another delegate argued for *general assembly* over *legislature* for a practical reason everyone who talks about legislatures can appreciate: "In making speeches legislator was sometimes confounded with legislature" (Carey 1926, 231). North Dakota also kept the territorial name, *Legislative Assembly*, for its state legislature, but it did so without any recorded discussion (*Off. Report of the Proc. and Deb. of the*

First Constitutional Conv. of N.D. 1889, 102–3). South Dakota, however, opted to call its state legislative body the Legislature.

More significantly, patterns of territorial legislative organization and behavior, both good and bad, carried over into statehood. This should not be a surprise because in important ways many new states were still on the frontier. A member of the first Kansas House recalled that for his journey to the state capital, "I . . . dumped into my saddle-bags a pair of blue woolen shirts, saddled the cayuse, and hiked to Topeka, across the boundless prairie, dressed in my only suit of clothes, which served me for weekdays and Sundays alike" (Ballard 1908, 233). Tobacco use in the legislative chamber continued to be an issue. A number of efforts were made to limit smoking in the Ohio General Assembly during the nineteenth century, all of which ended in failure (Gold 2009, 145). A rule prohibiting smoking was adopted by the first North Dakota House; the Dakota territorial House had had no such rule, and the first South Dakota House did not implement one (*Jour. of the H. of the Seventeenth Sess. of the LA, 1887* 1886; *Jour. of the H. of Reps. of the First Sess. of the S.D. Leg.* 1890, 18–25; *Legislative Man. Containing the Cons. of N.D. and the Rules of the First LA*, 1890, 15). Smoking in the Colorado House was only prohibited in 1895 when the "sustained pertinacity" of the chamber's first female members forced the issue. Reportedly, "The men members felt greatly annoyed because they could not solace their brains with tobacco, but they soon found out that they were closely watched by the women members, who, whenever they saw smoke curling up in the air over any desk, sprang to their feet and protested to the chair" (*Aspen Daily Times* 1895).

Rowdiness and violence failed to disappear from legislative life once a territory became a state. In the Wyoming House, parliamentary rules were manipulated to allow a controversial bill to pass on the final day of its first session.

> It was denounced with oaths, hands went to hip pockets, exposing revolvers, and disreputable trading was denounced in scathing terms. . . . A quiet member mounted the table, shook his fist in the face of the presiding officer, and swore roundly at the fraud. The sergeant at arms was called. He was threatened with violence and did not appear. A member who had a few hours before, in presenting a gavel, spoken in honeyed terms of the speaker's fairness, shouted that it was a miracle the words had not choked him. (*Kansas City Times* 1891)

Such behavior was not confined to Wyoming. During an early session of the Idaho House, a member called the speaker a liar, and, according to a newspaper account, "Each approached the other bent on fighting. There were cries of 'Form a ring,' but more peaceably-disposed members separated the combatants" (*NYT* 1893a). During the first Missouri Senate one member threw a pewter inkstand at a colleague, starting a fistfight that the governor had to break up (Stevens 1921, 115). Not every such incident ended peacefully. During the initial session of the Arkansas House, a debate over a bill to have the state pay a premium for the killing of wolves included a passing verbal jab questioning a local bank's integrity. The Speaker, and president of the bank in question, took umbrage, and the dispute escalated to the point that the Speaker and the representative who had made the cutting remark drew hunting knives on each other. The Speaker ended up stabbing the representative to death during a scuffle on the chamber floor (*Connecticut Courant* 1837; *Niles' Weekly Register* 1838, 258; Worley 1950, 409–10).[2]

Working conditions did not automatically improve once a territorial legislature became a state legislature. Lawmakers continued to be paid a pittance. Wisconsin legislators even took a cut in pay, with their $3.00 territorial per diem reduced to $2.50 a day in the new state constitution. That outcome was actually better than it might have been. The failed 1846 constitutional convention had settled on a per diem of $2.00, the wage the territorial legislature had foolishly proposed for convention delegates (Quaife 1919, 357–58). The 1847 constitutional convention (which produced the 1848 constitution) initially contemplated a per diem of $3.00. One delegate argued that $3.00 could only be afforded if the legislature were small and that members of a larger legislature should only be paid $1.50 a day, an amount at which he claimed "Grant County could send . . . able men." Another delegate reasoned that the convention should set a minimum per diem of $2.00 and a maximum of $3.00 and allow future lawmakers to choose the appropriate sum. The dispute was resolved when a third delegate offered a compromise setting the per diem at $2.50 (*Jour. of the Conv. to Form a Cons. for the St. of Wis.* 1848, 217, 226).

In response to such difficulties, lawmakers occasionally devised dubious schemes to supplement their meager wages. Minnesota's initial state legislators connived to draw $75 each from the state treasury to cover "stationery" costs incurred while on a long recess during which they were ineligible for their regular per diem. Filing for the reimbursement was voluntary, but all but two lawmakers took advantage of it (Hall 1904, 45–47).

Legislative facilities were usually not impressive in the new states, just as they had not been in most territories. The first Louisiana House held its initial meetings in the home of Mr. Tremoulet but quickly opted to join the Senate in the government house. A House committee charged with finding the new meeting place reported that the Senate had already taken the better space, leaving them "the north east room [which] although considerably out of repair, and otherwise inconvenient, on account of the very great descent of the floor, is sufficiently large and airy, and may at a small expense be filled up in such manner as to be sufficiently convenient at this time" (*Jour. of the H. of Reps. of the st. of La.* 1812, 17). Other new state legislatures also dealt with inadequate accommodations. A member of the inaugural Kansas House complained that during the session, "the spring rains began, and the old shack we were in let the water through like a sieve, and we had to move to the Congregational church" (Ballard 1908, 235). During the first session of the South Dakota legislature, the House met in the courthouse while the Senate assembled in the Presbyterian Church. To be fair, in this case it should be noted that officials in Pierre had been given only two weeks notice that the city was to serve as the state capital, and they had to scramble to find a place to house the legislature (Smith 1915, 1917). The first Utah legislature used rooms in the City and County building in Salt Lake City (Drumm 1896, 38). Perhaps the most unusual facilities situation occurred in Montana. A heated dispute over the vote count in Silver Bow County divided the first House, and each party convened its own version of the assembly in Helena: the Democrats in the county courthouse (the building used by recent territorial legislatures) and the Republicans in the "Iron building on lower Main street" (*Anaconda Standard* 1889; Bancroft 1890, 802; U.S. Senate 1913, 747; Lynch 1977, 8).[3] According to one account, GOP representatives were "creeping across back yards and under overhanging clothes lines" to get to their meeting place (*Anaconda Standard* 1889).

Fortunately, there was usually some membership overlap between the territorial and state legislatures, supplying connective tissue between the two institutions. The first speaker of the Tennessee Senate had been an influential member of the Southwest Council (Harrell 1958, 312–13). The first Indiana House speaker had served as the clerk for the territorial legislature (Lanman 1876, 35). The oldest member of the first Washington Senate had been the youngest member of the first territorial House 36 years earlier (*NYT* 1889a). In the initial Kansas legislature, 7 of the 26 members of the Senate had served in the territorial legislature. A lower proportion of House members, 12 out of 75, also had territorial legislative experience, and they were supplemented by one colleague who had served as the territorial House clerk and another who had been a Mississippi House member (Ballard 1908, 238–54). In the Minnesota Senate 6 of the 37 members had held seats in the territorial legislature (Hubbard and Holcombe 1908, 60–62). North Dakota, South Dakota, and Utah state legislators formally recognized the continuity between the new institutions and their predecessors in an interesting manner: their rules granted floor privileges to ex-territorial legislators, a right typically reserved for former members of a legislature (Drumm 1896, 46, 51; *Jour. of the H. of Reps. of the First Sess. of the S.D. Leg.* 1890, 24; *Legislative Man. Containing the Cons. of N.D. and the Rules of the First LA,* 1890, 13).

But, as had been the case in the territorial legislatures, while a few state legislators had previous legislative experience, most of them did not. This reality impacted the performance of the new legislatures. After extolling the performance of its fledgling state lawmakers, a Colorado newspaper made this observation.

> The only real delay to a rapid advancement of work has been the inexperience of a large number in legislative work. . . . The members themselves for the most part are getting tired of the work, especially those who are unaccustomed to the business. Being cramped behind desks and listening to the routine of prayer, roll calls, and the reading of bills, is to them a bore, and they will be glad when the adjournment occurs, so that they can go back to the chasing of steers over the plains and the killing of wild grasshoppers. (*Denver Daily Times,* 1877)

The adoption of rules developed in territorial legislatures was critical in allowing newly created state legislatures to overcome their lack of experienced members. As documented in chapter 4, new territorial legislatures had taken their rules and procedures from existing legislatures and, over time, molded them to meet their specific needs. For the most part, these territorial legislative rules became the basis of the rules used in the newly established state legislatures. In the first Louisiana House the transfer was explicit: "Resolved, that the house shall adopt the rules of the territorial legislature . . ." (*Jour. of the H. of Reps. of the st. of La.,* 1812, 2). Similarly, during the third day of the first meeting of the Iowa House, the Committee on Rules of Order recommended adoption of the territorial House rules, with the simple change of striking out the word *territorial* where it appeared and replacing it with the word *state*. The Committee's recommendations were adopted the following day. A similar sequence of events unfolded in the new Senate with the territorial rules of procedure being adopted with few modifications (*Jour. of the H. of Reps. of the GA of the St. of Iowa*, 1847; *Jour. of the Sen. of the First GA of the St. of Iowa* 1846). Both houses of the first Wisconsin state legislature turned to the rules used by their territorial predecessor as did the first Nebraska Senate, both chambers of the first Kansas legislature, the first Alabama House, and the first Washington House (*Freedom's Champion* 1861; *H. Jour. of the First Leg. of the St. of Wash.* 1890, 8; *Jour. of the Asm. of the First Leg. of the St. of Wis.* 1848, 11; *Jour. of the H. of Reps. of the GA of the St. of Ala.* 1820, 4–5; *Jour. of the Sen. of the First Leg. of the St. of Wis.* 1848, 7; *Sen. Jour. of the St. Leg. of Neb.* 1867, 5).[4]

In other state legislatures only a few changes were made to the territorial rules. Of the 55 rules adopted by the Northwest territorial House, 52 were taken virtually verbatim by the first Ohio House (*Jour. of the H. of Reps. of the Terr. of the US, North-west of the River Ohio*, 1799, 12–16; *Jour. of the H. of Reps. of the Terr. of the US, North-west of the Ohio* 1801, 6–11; *Jour. of the H. of Reps. of the St. of Ohio* 1803, 18–23). The three rules dropped were a requirement that the clerk take an oath, a standing order for the House to dissolve itself into a committee of the whole, and a holding that all proceedings involving appropriations first be moved and discussed in a committee of the whole. Almost all of the 63 rules adopted by the first North Dakota House were taken from the 55 rules used by the final Dakota House. The North Dakota House changed the rules in three areas: they altered the three-reading requirements to make them more flexible, they added rules explicitly allowing the speaker to control disturbances and legislative documents, and, as noted above, they prohibited smoking on the floor. The first South Dakota House hewed even more closely to the Dakota House rules (*Jour. of the H. of Reps. of the First Sess. of the S.D. Leg.* 1890, 18–25; *Jour. of the H. of the Seventeenth Sess. of the LA, January, 1887* 1886, 45–53; *Legislative Man. Containing the Cons. of N.D. and the Rules of the First LA*, 1890, 7–16).

An example of the transmission of legislative rules between a territorial legislature and its state successor is mapped in table 6.1. It shows that the rules adopted by the first Tennessee House were largely lifted from those used by its predecessor Southwest Territory House (*Jour. of the H. of Reps.*

of the St. of Tenn. [1796] 1852, 4–5; *Jour. of the Proc. of the H. of Reps. of the Terr. of the USA, South of the River Ohio* [1794] 1852, 3–4). In this case there were a few notable changes in the procedures adopted by the state House. Experience gained during the only territorial legislature likely played a role in the adoption of a new rule that gave the speaker the power to control lobbyist behavior. More important, the other new rules required a daily reading of the journal and provided for moving the previous question and making strategic use of adjournments. These rules were taken from those used by the U.S. House in 1795.

Standing committee systems also carried over to the new state legislatures from their territorial predecessors. As shown in table 6.2, the standing committee system in the first Iowa House was a continuation of the one established in the territorial House (Briggs 1916, 36–37; Horack 1916). The same was true in Florida. The standing committees that appeared in the territorial House in 1843 were replicated in the new state House in 1845, save for two that were no longer needed: a Committee on the State of the Territory and a Committee on Currency (*Jour. of the Proc. of the LC of the Terr. of Fla., 1843* 1843, 27–28; *Jour. of the Proc. of the H. of Reps. of the First GA of the St. of Fla. 1845* 1845, 21).

Toward the end of the nineteenth century this dynamic changed, but only slightly. The first Washington House largely carried over the 20 standing committees used by the final territorial House but supplemented them with another 18 committees (*H. Jour. of the First Leg. of the St. of Wash.* 1890, 24–25; *Jour. of the H. of Reps. of the Terr. of Wash.* 1888). Among those added were committees dealing with state lands; school lands; tidal lands; water; water rights; immigration; and state, county, and municipal indebtedness. The rise in the number of standing committees reflected the substantial increase in the number of seats. The new state House had 70 members compared to only 24 members in the last territorial House. More members, of course, meant more demands for committee assignments, prompting the creation of additional committees. From an organizational perspective, more members and committees allowed the House to further divide its workload.

A similar outcome occurred in the Dakotas. The new North Dakota House had 14 more members than the final territorial House, and it increased its number of standing committees to 36 from the 29 used earlier, and it added 6 joint committees. Again, almost all of the committees used in the territorial House were reestablished in the state House. The Committee on Territorial Affairs became the Committee on State Affairs. Sev-

TABLE 6.1. A Comparison of the Rules of Decorum in the 1794 Southwest Territorial House of Representatives and the Rules in the 1796 Tennessee House of Representatives

Southwest Territorial House of Representatives		Tennessee House of Representatives	
Rule Number	Rule	Rule Number	Rule
1st	When the Speaker is in the chair, every member may sit in his place with his head covered.	1	When the speaker is in the chair every member may sit in his place with his head covered.
2nd	That every member shall come into the house uncovered and shall continue so at all times, but when he sits in his place.	2	Every member shall come into the house with his head uncovered and shall continue so at all times but when he sits in his place.
3rd	No member, in coming into the house, or removing from his place, shall pass between the Speaker and a member speaking, nor shall any member go across the house, or from one part thereof to the other whilst another was speaking.		
4th	When any member stands to speak, he shall stand in his place uncovered, and address himself to the Speaker, but shall not proceed to speak until permitted so to do by the Speaker, which permission is granted by naming the member.	5	Every member when he speaks, shall, standing in his place, address himself to the speaker (or chairman) as the case may be, who shall give his attention by naming the member.
5th	When any member is speaking, no other shall stand or interrupt him; but when he is done speaking, and taken his seat, any other may rise, observing the rules.	4	While the journal or public papers are reading, or when any member is speaking, there shall be no interruption, nor shall any member read any printed paper, but the attention of the members is expected.
6th	When the Speaker desires to address himself to the house he shall rise, and be heard without interruption; and the member then speaking shall take his seat.		
7th	If more than one member attempt to speak at any time, the Speaker shall determine who was up first.	6	If two or more members rise to speak, at the same time, the speaker shall determine who shall speak first.
8th	When any motion shall be before the house and not perfectly understood, the Speaker may explain, but shall not attempt to sway the house by argument or debate.	7	When any motion shall be before the house, and not properly understood, the speaker may explain, but shall not attempt, in any such explanation, to sway the house by argument or debate.
9th	He that digresseth from the subject, to fall on the person of any member, shall be suppressed by the Speaker.	9	A member digressing from the subject, or using personal observation or reflection, may be called to order by the speaker or chairman, or any member of the house.

10th	Exceptions, taken to offensive words, to be taken the same day they shall be spoken, and before the member who spoke them shall go out of the house.	
11th	Whatever is spoken in the house, may be subject to the censure of the house.	
12th	Whenever any matter is in debate before the house, it shall be determined or postponed before any new business shall be introduced.	12 — No member to speak more than twice, without the leave of the house, to the same question, unless in a committee of the whole.
13th	No member shall speak more than twice without leave, in the same question, unless it be in a committee of the whole house.	11 — No question to be put upon motion, unless seconded.
14th	No question shall be put on any motion, unless seconded.	10 — All motions to be committed to writing and seconded, and handed to the speaker, before the same can be considered in the possession of the house, except a motion of course.
15th	Every member making any motion, which is not of course, shall before making such motion, reduce the same to writing.	
16th	If there shall be an equality of votes for and against any question, the Speaker shall declare whether he be a yea or nay; but shall in no other case give his vote.	14 — No member to depart the service of the house without leave.
17th	No member shall depart the service of the house without leave.	3 — The speaker having taken the chair, and a majority of the members being present, the clerk shall read the journal of the preceding day, in order that any mistake may be corrected that may have been made in the entries.[a]
18th	Upon adjournment, no member shall presume to move until the Speaker arises and goes before.	13 — When a question is before the house, no motion shall be received unless for amendment, for the previous question, or to commit to adjourn.[a]
		15 — It shall be the duty of the speaker (or chairman) to call gentlemen spectators, appearing among the members when in session, by name, to desire them to withdraw to the seats assigned them.

Source: Jour. of the Proc. of the H. of Reps. of the Terr. of the USA, South of the River Ohio [1794] 1852, 3–4; *Jour. of the H. of Reps. of the St. of Tenn.* [1796] 1852, 4–5.
[a]These rules appear in the rules adopted by the U.S. House of Representatives in 1795.

eral new committees were added, among them a Committee on Coal Lands and Mining that supplemented the carried-over Committee on Mines and Mining, a Committee on Apportionment, a Committee on Irrigation, a Committee on Public Debt, and a Committee on Taxes and Tax Laws. Interestingly, the South Dakota House, which had 76 more members than the Dakota House, created only 33 standing committees and no joint committees. Again, most were carried over, among them a Committee on Indian Affairs that the North Dakota House did not reestablish. Like the North Dakota House, the South Dakota House created a new Committee on Irrigation and Drainage and converted Territorial Affairs to State Affairs. One altogether new committee was established: Medicine, Surgery, and Pharmacy. Thus, although the North Dakota and South Dakota houses can be thought of as twins, they were clearly fraternal and not identical (*Jour. of the H. of Reps. of the First Sess. of the S.D. Leg.* 1890,

TABLE 6.2. Standing Committees in the First Iowa Territorial House of Representatives and the First Iowa State House of Representatives

First Territorial House of Representatives, 1838–39 (13 committees)	First State House of Representatives, 1846–47 (15 committees)
Judiciary	Judiciary
Common Schools	Schools
Internal Improvements[a]	
Military Affairs	Militia
Claims	Claims
Enrollments	Enrolled Bills
Expenditures	Expenditures
Territorial Affairs	
Roads and Highways	Roads and Highways
Elections	Elections
Township and County Boundaries	Township and County Organization
Corporations	Incorporations
Vetoes	
	Engrossed Bills[b]
	Public Buildings[c]
	Agriculture[d]
	Ways and Means[e]
	New Counties[f]

Source: Horack 1916, 574–85; *Jour. of the H. of Reps. of the GA of the State of Iowa* 1847.
[a]Committee appeared in the State House in 1850.
[b]Committee appeared in the Territorial House in 1839.
[c]Committee appeared in the Territorial House in 1840.
[d]Committee appeared in the Territorial House in 1841.
[e]Committee appeared in the Territorial House in 1845.
[f]Committee appeared in the Territorial House in 1845.

22–23; *Jour. of the H. of the Seventeenth Sess. of the LA* 1886, 50; *Legislative Man. Containing the Cons. of N.D. and the Rules of the First LA*, 1890, 11–12).

A Brief Digression on State Legislatures in the Confederacy

The rise of the Confederacy represented an opportunity for the secessionists to redesign their governmental institutions. For a brief time secession conventions competed with governors and legislatures to set policies in many of the Confederate states. Relatively quickly, however, the fundamental structures of Confederate state governments reverted to looking as they did prior to secession. During the war Confederate state legislatures came to carry much of the governing burden; to handle the increased workload six states switched to annual sessions from biennial sessions, while the others called numerous special sessions (Ringold 1966, 2, 4–5, 9). Most were handicapped by inexperienced leadership. Of 28 state house speakers, only 4 had previously served in the post before the war, and 15 had no previous legislative service (Wakelyn 2002, 38–39). As happened during the Revolutionary War, several Confederate state legislatures had to flee in the face of military attacks, with the Virginia General Assembly earning plaudits for its members' brave behavior, while their counterparts in Georgia and Tennessee were ridiculed for running (Ringold 1966, 8).

Organizationally, the existence of the Confederacy poses an interesting test for the theory of legislative evolution offered here. Did the (attempted) regime change affect organizational development in the 11 states that seceded? Perhaps surprisingly, the answer is almost not at all. Secession made virtually no difference to the way Confederate state legislatures operated. Take, for example, the Florida House. The body that convened in November 1861, after secession, labeled itself the legislature's eleventh session and adopted the same 56 rules that the tenth session had adopted in November 1860, before secession. The 1861 House continued to rely on *Jefferson's Manual* to resolve any problems not addressed by the chamber's rules, just as the 1860 House had. All 14 standing committees established by the House in 1860 were reestablished by the House in 1861—and the three seemingly new committees created had all existed during the House's 1859 meeting. The only substantive difference in the committee roster between 1860 and 1861 was that the Committee on Federal Relations in the former was refashioned as the Committee on Confederate Relations in the latter (cf. *Jour. of the Proc. of the H. of Reps. of the GA of the St. of Fla.* 1861, 20–26, 36–38; *Jour. of the Proc. of the H. of Reps. of the GA of the St. of Fla.* 1860,

18–19, 45–52; *Jour. of the Proc. of the H. of Reps. of the GA of the St. of Fla.*
1859, 58–59). Florida's behavior was typical. In December 1861 the Virginia House voted "that the rules of the last house of delegates be adopted for the government of this." Those rules also established the same standing committees (*Jour. of the H. of Dels. of the St. of Va.* 1861, 4, 7).

What about at the other end of the war? Again, it appears that the shift in regimes made almost no difference to the operations of the 11 state legislatures. In December 1865 the fourteenth Florida House adopted the same 56 rules used by the thirteenth House in 1864. Indeed, it was the same set of rules, complete with the use of *Jefferson's Manual*, which the House had employed before the war. And the 18 standing committees used by the 1865 House were almost the exactly the same set of 18 committees that had been established by the 1864 House. The only changes were that the Committee on Public Accounts was replaced by a Committee on Public Lands, and the Committee on Confederate Relations reverted to being a Committee on Federal Relations (*Jour. of the Proc. of the H. of Reps. of the GA of the St. of Fla.* 1865, 8, 12–13; *Jour. of the Proc. of the H. of Reps. of the GA of the St. of Fla.* 1864, 32–34, 37–43).

Developments in the other former Confederate state legislatures were similar. When the South Carolina Senate adopted rules for the extra session that met in October 1865, the committee that composed them reported, "They are in the main the Rules heretofore adopted by the Senate" (*Jour. of the Sen. of the St. of S.C.* 1865, 17). During the same session the House took a slightly different tack, opting to use "the Rules adopted by the House of Representatives in the year A. D. 1860" (*Jour. of the H. of Reps. of the St. of S.C.* 1865, 7). Both decisions document the continuity of organizational features. Thus, with a regime change more fundamental than that from territory to state, there was once again remarkable stability in legislative organization.[5]

The Institutionalizing of State Legislatures

State legislatures did not institutionalize quickly or easily during the nineteenth century, but they did develop into stable organizations. During this process they still endured occasional abuses of parliamentary procedures. Quorum rules, for example, continued to be exploited, sometimes in seemingly silly ways: As a young Whig member of the Illinois House, Abraham Lincoln jumped out of a window in Springfield's Second Presbyterian

Church, which was being used because the new capitol had yet to be finished, in a futile effort to deny the majority Democrats a quorum (Simon 1971, 228). Lincoln's successor in the White House, Andrew Johnson, acted to break a quorum for four straight days when he was a member of the Tennessee Senate (Phelan 1888, 408).

And at times lawmakers still responded to political frustrations in nonparliamentary ways. An Illinois House member wrote to his wife during a political struggle over whether a state judge should be removed from office.

> One of the Judge's persecutors, ([state Senator] Butterfield) and General Ewing, speaker of the House, came very near fighting a duel last Friday. Butterfield insulted Ewing without any cause. Ewing drew a chair on him and B. escaped the blow aimed at him. He then challenged Ewing, it was accepted, and the distance of ten feet was chosen, the distance to shoot with pistols. Butterfield by this time concluded to beg the privilege of apology, and back out, this ended the matter, the best for both parties, no doubt. (Pond 1949, 415)

Some duels did take place. After their heated debate escalated into a scuffle on the Kentucky House floor, representatives Henry Clay and Humphrey Marshall were separated by a large German immigrant colleague, who seized one of them in each hand and said, "come poys, no fighting here, I vips you both." Clay, however, took umbrage at several of Marshall's comments and challenged him to a duel. After several shots, Clay was wounded in the leg and the participants' seconds ended the showdown (Quisenberry 1892, 100–103).

Violence was not confined to frontier legislatures; even well-established bodies suffered. Following an animated exchange in the Ohio House in 1846, the two adversaries ran into each other on the street. Each representative pulled a knife, but bystanders kept the fracas from escalating into bloodshed (Gold 2009, 145). During his first term in the New York Assembly in 1882—when the institution was over 100 years old—Theodore Roosevelt secreted a broken chair leg near his desk to protect himself against some of his tougher colleagues (Roosevelt 1913, 82–83). A dispute over a gubernatorial veto in the final hour of the 1895 Indiana House session led to a riot on the floor: "Revolvers were flourished and blows struck with such articles of furniture as the combatants could lay hands on conveniently" (*NYT* 1895a). Even the U.S. Congress and British House of Commons experienced violent episodes (*NYT* 1893c; Polsby 1968, 167–68).

Alcohol abuse still bedeviled state legislatures. A Frankfort, Kentucky, paper castigated "two Senators, now in the legislative halls, [who] were beastly and disgracefully drunk in their seats during the sessions of the first two days" (*Weekly Roundabout* 1880). When a Georgia Senate committee went on an excursion to investigate conditions at a mine it was alleged by one lawmaker that "one end of the [railroad] coach [was] filled with whisky and champagne and the other end with cigars, and one member of the committee got maudlin drunk and fell out of his bunk" (*NYT* 1887b). Even more egregiously, it was reported in New York that "On the last night of the session there were so many members drunk that the Speaker had to declare the Assembly adjourned through his inability to transact business" (*Sun* 1894). And drink led to tragedy: An Arkansas lawmaker jumped into a Little Rock river and drowned while drunk (*Fort Worth Daily Gazette* 1883).

Capital cities often needed time to mature, and they were frequently found wanting in newer states. In 1840, an Illinois lawmaker wrote to his wife, confiding about his accommodations in Vandalia.

> I board with old Mr. Dickey (the Baker.) My room mates are [Rep.] Bainbridge of a county in the south of the name of Williamson; [Rep.] Allen of Franklin, and [Rep.] Holmes of Cass and Parish, also of Franklin, a member of the Senate. We fare well at $6.00 a week. I could do no better. Iles' great tavern, called the "American House," is crowded with its hundreds at $2.00 per day it is said. I was offered a place at Grimsley's, but I was to sleep by myself, this would not suit me, and no fire in the bed room. I concluded to lodge for these reasons with Dickey. Bainbridge is my bed fellow. (Pond 1949, 409)

Sharing beds was common. An eccentric member of the first Missouri legislature—his surname was Palmer but he went by Ringtail Painter—insisted on sharing one with the governor so he could return home and brag to his friends that he had slept with the state's chief executive (Stevens 1921, 115). Unappealing accommodations and difficult colleagues lessened the attractiveness of legislative service. This was of importance because a potential impediment to institutional development during the nineteenth century was high levels of membership turnover.

Membership Turnover

Over the nineteenth century state legislative memberships were shockingly unstable. As noted in chapter 3, turnover had been relatively low toward the end of the eighteenth century. But then things changed dramatically. In Connecticut, Georgia, and New York turnover increased spectacularly over the first half of the nineteenth century, reaching levels of between 70 percent and almost 100 percent (DeBats 1990, 430; Deming 1889; Gunn 1988, 75; Luce 1924, 355–56). And these states were not exceptions. High levels of turnover were commonplace across all state legislatures during the antebellum era (Bowers 1983, 443, 458; Davis 1988, 99; Levine 1977, 76–79; Wooster 1969, 41–42). When Abraham Lincoln first joined the Illinois House in 1834, he was one of 36 members in their first term. They were joined by 17 members in their second terms, one member in his third term and another member in his fourth term (Baringer 1949, 48–49). In Arkansas, 93 percent of lower-house members between 1836 and 1861 served only a single term (Wooster 1975, 43).

Turnover rates declined only slightly after the Civil War. In Pennsylvania in 1877, just 27 percent of members had served the previous term, and only 22 percent returned in 1879 (Harrison 1979, 338). Between 1886 and 1895, first-term members composed 68 percent of the Illinois House, 62 percent of the Iowa House, and 75 percent of the Wisconsin House (Campbell 1980, 228). In 1881, 81 percent of Indiana House members were in their first term (VanderMeer 1985, 165). Turnover rates in the Ohio legislature in the 1880s and 1890s often reached close to 100 percent (Gold 2009, 53–54). Such figures were the norm (Burns et al. 2008, 232–35).

It was recognized that high turnover levels made state legislatures less efficient organizations than they would be with more experienced members (Lowell 1897). In 1863, George Caleb Bingham, the Missouri state treasurer and a former state legislator (but better known today as a preeminent nineteenth-century artist), confided in a letter to a friend, "It is enough to say that two or three weeks have been wasted in a frui[t]less effort to elect U.S. Senators, and that no Legislation of general importance has yet been accomplished." The reason he cited for this failure was that "The Legislature is composed almost entirely of new members very few of whom seem to have much legislative ability or experience" (Rollins 1938, 59). A Massachusetts House reform committee lamented that new members "lack that experience in conducting the affairs of a deliberative body . . . which are essential to the rapid and accurate despatch of business" (*Deb. and Proc. in the Mass. Leg., 1857,* 1857, 287). Even leaders were often inexperienced, with repercussions for the institutions in which they served. On the first day of one Connecticut speaker's term, it was reported that as a result of his parliamentary rulings, "Mr. Paige was soon out of his depth and floundering in a sea of decisions . . . so contradictory that his advisors were astounded at his audacity" (*NYT* 1891a).

Legislative Salaries

Another plausible reason few members opted to serve for long may have been low salaries. By the end of the eighteenth century all state legislators were paid for their service, but the question of whether they should be was not yet fully settled. As late as 1799 a proposal to do away with the lawmakers' per diem was put before the Maryland legislature. After the motion was defeated, a resolution explaining the legislature's rationale was passed. It offered a strong defense of legislative salaries.

> Resolved, That in the opinion of this house, to repeal the per diem law would tend to exclude all persons, not possessed of affluent fortunes, from a seat in this house; that it would make the poorer classes of people subservient to the rich . . . and would subject the house of delegates to the control of the senate; inasmuch as no persons but those who possess enormous and extravagant fortunes, could afford to live here in a respectable manner, or as representatives of a free and virtuous people. (*Commercial Advertiser* 1799)

Even when the notion of legislative pay was no longer challenged, the question of how much to pay lawmakers continued to generate controversy. A central issue was whether they should be paid at a level that would help them make up for lost income or be compensated only for their expenses. In arguing that the Pennsylvania Assembly's per diem was too high, one newspaper asserted, "The idea in giving wages to that body, was to preserve their independence; not to enable them to make profit of their places: But in giving them each two dollars *per diem,* the latter idea seems to have prevailed" (*Pennsylvania Evening Herald* 1785).

When, a few years later, it was again proposed to cut legislative pay, Pennsylvania lawmakers revisited the question. One Assembly member held that a reduction in pay would promote the establishment of a governing "aristocracy" because anyone "connected with poverty would be excluded from the legislative body." He argued that "it was not enough that the state should provide for the bare maintenance of a member while on duty; but should also afford a sufficiency to compensate the loss his family must suffer by his absence." A colleague sought a middle-ground position, saying, "No man should suffer in his private interest . . . by devoting his time to the public service." But he added, "the salary should not be so considerable as to make the office desirable on account of pecuniary emolument" (*General Advertiser* 1791).

Maryland and Pennsylvania were not alone in grappling with this issue. A Connecticut newspaper reasoned that lawmakers deserved to be paid, but not at a premium. They believed, "a day's work at *hoeing*, will pay for a day's work at *legislation*—This not only *seems*, but is *really* equitable, for *hoers* are as necessary as *legislators*, and because the former are more plenty than the latter, it is no reason that the latter should have the highest wages" (*Weekly Advertiser* 1793, italics in original). A debate over the level at which to set legislative salaries during the 1834 Tennessee constitutional convention generated a similar analysis: "the compensation to the Members . . . of the Legislature, is vastly greater, than is allowed to other members of the community, for *services equally meritorious.*" Unfavorable comparisons were drawn between the privations suffered by the "citizen soldier" and those of "a Member of the Legislature who sits in a comfortable apartment, and spends six, or seven hours each day, in talking about matters and things in general, while at the same time he is enjoying all the comforts and luxuries of life" (*Jour. of the Conv. of the St. of Tenn.* 1834, 356–57, italics in original).

Given all this it is not surprising that legislative salaries cropped up as a campaign issue. A Maryland candidate wrote a letter to a local paper exclaiming, "Three Dollars and a half per day is more Money than a Member of the General Assembly ought to be allowed—Two Dollars: at *most*, two and an half Dollars is as much as should be allowed. If elected, I will endeavour to reduce the *per diem* to *two Dollars*" (*Maryland Herald* 1803a, italics in original). The following week the same paper carried another letter, this one signed by "A REPUBLICAN," supporting the pledge to cut the per diem.

The highest board which any member pays per day, is *eleven shillings and three pence;* but many of the members board for one dollar per day *only— what reason* can exist, to *justify a man,* who before he is elected a member of the General Assembly, is in the habit of making loud declarations, of his disinterestedness, & warmth of attachment to the substantial interests of the people; in drawing from the public treasury *three dollars and an half per day*, when *two dollars* will *most assuredly cover all his necessary expences?* . . . Sir, I would not wish, to reduce the allowance to a Sum, which will not enable a Member to defray his necessary expences—but I do wish, to see the daily pay of an Assemblyman, settled at *such* a rate, as would put it out of the power of *nine* men in *ten*—nay of *any* man, to convert a *legislative trust* into an *office* of *profit*. (*Maryland Herald* 1803b, italics in original)

In the face of such populist appeals, nineteenth-century state legislators zealously guarded their salaries, and they did not take kindly to those who challenged them on the subject. When, in 1841, an Illinois representative proposed taxing legislative per diems, his colleague, Abraham Lincoln, took to the floor in opposition, joking that ethical norms prevented lawmakers "from voting in cases in which they were interested and it appeared to him they were interested in this case." Lincoln and his laughing colleagues voted down the measure (Simon 1971, 270). Other legislators who tried to tinker with pay were made more than just the butt of jokes. In 1825, James B. Gardiner was elected to the Ohio House by pledging to reduce the per diem by a dollar and promising that if he failed to do so, he would donate his excess wages to his county treasury. When he appeared to take his seat his colleagues voted to expel him, claiming that his campaign promise constituted a bribe to gain votes. Gardiner's constituents disagreed and returned him to office in the special election to fill the vacant seat, but the House refused to seat him, citing a constitutional provision that kept those convicted of bribery from holding office for two years. In 1827 Gardiner was elected to the Ohio Senate, where his new colleagues declined to let him introduce a measure to reduce the per diem (*American Annual Register* 1827, 358–59; Gold 2009, 120).

Given this sort of behavior most observers came to expect state lawmakers to protect their salaries above all else. When Texas faced a tight state budget a newspaper noted, "The retrenchment fever has broken out with renewed violence in the legislature. Nothing save the salary of the governor and the per diem and mileage of the legislators are safe from the pruning knife" (*Daily Herald* 1895). Similar cynicism surfaced in a Nebraska paper, which at the beginning of one session predicted that "The relief bill and the appropriations bill for legislative salaries will be rushed through, but most other measures will take their natural order." This was not the only shot the paper took at legislative pay that session. When a lawmaker proposed cutting legal printing rates, a move that would hurt the paper's bottom line, an editorial countered, "This distinguished gentleman draws a salary of $5 a day from the state. He would be overpaid at $1 a day. Has anyone heard him suggest a reduction of legislative salary?" (*Omaha Daily Bee* 1891a, 1891b). Accordingly, legislators were sensitive to the political atmospherics surrounding their pay. When a bill proposing an annual salary was introduced in Minnesota, the local paper reported that it "was listened to with interest by the members present, but was sent to the committee on legislative expenses without comment" (*St. Paul Daily Globe* 1893).

Mileage reimbursements also generated resentment among the public who thought such payments were prone to abuse. Thus, when it was suggested during Iowa's 1857 constitutional convention that legislators be required to "receive mileage by the nearest mail route" the author of that stipulation admitted, "I inserted this provision with the view of preventing members from going by way of Illinois" (*Deb. of the Constitutional Conv. of the St. of Iowa* 1857, 528–29). Even small sums troubled people. Under a subtitle of "Look at These Figures, Taxpayers and then Weep," a Minnesota paper listed the travel reimbursements given to the state's lawmakers. Chastising their local solons, the paper scolded, "St. Paul's representatives are supposed to walk, but our more aristocratic senators have been allowed 30 cents each for coupes during the session" (*St. Paul Daily Globe* 1895).

Given the public furor surrounding the issue, how did legislative pay change over the nineteenth century? In 1832, every state paid its lawmakers a per diem, as shown in table 6.3. None of the per diems was particularly generous. The sums paid ranged from a low of $1.50 in the New England legislatures of Rhode Island, Vermont, and in the Connecticut House (Connecticut senators got a per diem of $2.00), to a high of $4.00 in Alabama, Georgia, Louisiana, Maryland, South Carolina, Tennessee, and Virginia (*American Almanac* 1832, 274). Following Kentucky's lead, many states began setting their per diems in their state constitutions. This practice became dominant by the 1850s, making it much more difficult to increase pay by taking the matter largely out of legislators' hands (Hough 1867, 60–62; Luce 1924, 528).

A few innovations in the way state legislators were paid were introduced between 1832 and 1861. In 1844 New Jersey began limiting the number of days its per diem would be given: $3 for the first 40 days and $1.50 for each additional day. This system gave lawmakers an incentive to conclude their business within the specified time period and limited their ability to pad their pay by extending the session (Luce 1924, 529). New York quickly seized on the idea. During that state's 1846 constitutional convention the chair of the committee examining the legislative branch proposed a more stringent version of New Jersey's scheme, arguing that "there was a necessity for adopting some measure by which the annual sessions of the legislature shall be limited to a certain term." During the debate alternatives were advanced. One delegate suggested paying an annual salary of $300, which would be the equivalent of paying a per diem of $3 for a 100-day session. But that proposal was shot down because it was reasoned that "if a salary were fixed without reference to the time of service, [lawmakers] might adjourn in twenty days without transacting the public business." The delegates settled on paying legislators a $3 per diem for 100 days (*Deb. and Proc. in the N.Y. St. Conv. for the Rev. of the Cons.* 1846, 337–38). But unlike its neighbor, New York cut off pay entirely after the limit was reached. By 1861 California, Illinois, and Iowa also followed the New Jersey two-tiered per diem model, although each set pay and day limits differently. California paid a per diem of $10.00 for 90 days and $5.00 for every day thereafter. Illinois paid $2.00 for 40 days and $1.00 every day thereafter. Iowa paid $2.00 for 50 days and $1.00 for every day thereafter. None emulated New York's strict cutoff.

Perhaps the most notable change in salary structure was introduced in Massachusetts in 1858 when that state took the step New York had been unwilling to take and paid its lawmakers an annual wage of $300 rather than a $3.00 per diem. While this might seem a striking innovation, it was

TABLE 6.3.   Annual Pay versus Per Diems in State Legislatures over the Nineteenth Century

	1832	1861	1889	1900
States with annual or biennial salary	0	2	11	11
States with per diem or weekly salary	24	31	27	34
Total number of states	24	33	38	45

Source: 1832, American Almanac 1832, 274; 1861, Acts of the Leg. of the St. of Mich. 1858, 45; Conn. Register 1860, 21, 28; Gold 2009, 154; Laws of the St. of Ind. 1865, 64–65; Public Acts of the St. of Tenn. 1861, 57–59; Acts and Resolutions Adopted by the GA of Fla. 1861, 61; American Almanac 1856, 333; American Almanac 1860, 287; American Almanac 1861, 248–370; Revised Code of the Statute Laws of the St. of Miss. 1857, 100; Revised Stat. of the St. of R.I. 1857, 24; Revised Stat. of the St. of Wis. 1858, 120; 1889, American Almanac 1889, 107; 1900, Off. Man. for the use of the Courts, St., and County Officials and GA of the St. of Ky. 1900, 147.

sold to voters in familiar terms. One paper reported that the $300 salary was to be "paid at the rate of $2 per diem, on the first of each month, during the session until the whole amount is paid" (*Pittsfield Sun* 1858). Thus, in many ways, the change was more apparent than real. Moreover, because the reform was adopted at the same time the number of seats was cut substantially, the state actually reduced its legislative payroll costs (*Deb. and Proc. in the Mass. Leg.*, *1857*, 1857, 285–86). But the idea of an annual salary began to take hold; by 1860 Pennsylvania was paying its lawmakers $700 a year (Ziegler 1860, 243).

Over the century, relatively few voices were heard in favor of raising legislative pay, and those that were, seized on well-worn arguments. In 1846, a New York lawmaker made an appeal on the basis of insufficiency, stating that "He doubted whether many members of the legislature made both ends meet at the end of a session." In his own case he claimed, "He had himself paid in postage alone, his entire per diem, as a member" (*Deb. and Proc. in the N.Y. St. Conv. for the Rev. of the Cons.* 1846, 336). That same year, an Iowa paper advanced the idea that higher salaries would produce a more diverse legislature, calculating that "A poor man cannot go to the legislature, because $2.00 per day will not justify him in leaving his domestic affairs, and spending his time at the capital" (Shambaugh 1900, 217). A third tack was offered by a New York paper, which made a comparative argument, noting, "At the present rate of pay even a subpoena-server gets more than a State Senator or Assemblyman. And yet there seems to be no universal outcry for the raising of Legislative salaries" (*NY Trib.* 1881).

Regardless of how they were pitched, such appeals typically fell on deaf ears, and legislative salaries grew only at a snail's pace over the nineteenth century, a trend that largely reflected wage growth in the larger economy (Hanes and James 2003). But by 1889 11 states offered an annual salary, as documented in table 6.3. That year New Hampshire voters set their lawmakers' salary at $100 annually (a figure unchanged since), motivated by a desire to cut the length of their legislative sessions, which they thought members extended to collect additional per diem payments (*NYT* 1889b). New York established the high-water mark. A constitutional commission in 1872–73 had proposed an annual salary of $1,000, but lawmakers raised the amount to $1,500, which the voters approved in 1874 (Luce 1924, 529). Within a few years it was claimed that "since the legislative salary has been fixed at $1,500 there has been a gradual improvement in the average character of the House." This was thought to be the case because there were now "a larger number of decent and respectable citizens of small means in it who can afford to accept the honor of a legislative term on the present compensation" (*NYT* 1878a).

When they did increase, legislative salaries did not always go up monotonically, and even payment methods occasionally reverted to an earlier mode. In Massachusetts, in 1864 lawmakers overrode a gubernatorial veto and raised their pay to $400 a year. The next year pay returned to $300 annually. In 1870, lawmakers reinstituted a per diem, setting the figure at $5. The following year they resumed an annual salary, this time set at $750. In 1872 legislators voted to pay themselves $100 a month. This lasted only until 1876 when the legislature decided to cut their annual wage to $650. Three years later that figure was reduced to $500 a year, and then six years later it was raised back to $650. In 1886 the legislature adopted an annual salary of $750, a level that was maintained until 1911 (Luce 1924, 530; Roe 1895, 24). These salary gyrations were likely driven by the economy because their rise and fall lags national economic fluctuations by only a year or two (Hanes and James 2003, 1417).

An important pattern in legislative salaries emerged by 1889. In addition to New York and Massachusetts, the other states with high salaries were also large and industrial: Pennsylvania paid $750 a year, Ohio $600, and New Jersey $500. In contrast, the states with the lowest wages were almost all small and agricultural: Rhode Island with a per diem of $1, and Delaware, Kansas, Michigan, Nebraska, Oregon, and Vermont with per diems of $3. In 1832 there had been no difference in legislative salaries between large, wealthy states and small, poorer states. By the end of the nineteenth century the contrast was obvious.

Overall, during the nineteenth century state lawmakers made relatively little money for their service. An Ohio lawyer recalled somewhat facetiously, "in the summer of 1875, I foolishly accepted a nomination to the legislature, was elected, and there ended my prosperity" (Dalzell 1888, 39). But he exaggerated his financial plight only slightly, and low pay did dissuade qualified people from running. When friends tried to persuade George Norris, a Nebraska lawyer who later served for many years in Congress, to run for the legislature, he demurred, recalling, "I could not afford to serve. . . . The pay of a Nebraskan legislator was very small, $300 a term—insufficient even to meet living expenses on a modest scale" (Norris 1961, 337). A Houston lawyer declined to run for the legislature because he could not afford "if elected to neglect important private business." In response, a local paper complained, "It is extremely difficult at the present time to get a first-class man to become a candidate for the legislature" (*Brenham Weekly Banner* 1886).

Low salaries likely contributed to the high turnover levels experienced by state legislatures in the nineteenth century. After analyzing legislative pay across the states, the Williamsport (Pa.) *Gazette & Bulletin* concluded, "these salaries do not seem to be so high as to warrant men without other visible means of support making 'going to the Legislature' a profession" (quoted in *NYT* 1872). Obviously, turnover could also result from incumbents losing reelection bids. Elections were competitive at many points during this time period. But most incumbents chose not to seek reelection. In some cases this may have been because rotation was practiced, with state lawmakers exiting after a term or two in order to allow another person the opportunity to serve (Deming 1889, 427; Harrison 1979, 338; Levine 1977, 79; VanderMeer 1985, 154, 193; Wooster 1969, 42; 1975, 42–44). In other cases it appears that continuing legislative service was simply not sufficiently attractive. Between 1870 and 1900 New York paid its legislators far more than other states paid their lawmakers, but only about 50 percent of incumbents sought reelection (Stonecash 1993, 306). Roughly 30 percent of Iowa House members sought reelection during the years from 1884 to 1894, even though that body paid better than many (Campbell 1977, 115). Figures from other states were similar (Ray 1976). Thus most legislators decided to leave on their own, with legislatures suffering losses in organizational continuity and memory.

It is likely that states suffered for paying poor salaries in another regard. Because wages were low, the temptation to supplement them raised ethical concerns about lawmaker behavior even as legislatures institutionalized. Corruption was not, of course, new to state legislatures. In the Yazoo land scandal in 1795, every member of the Georgia legislature who voted for the fraudulent sale save for one was a shareholder in one of the companies involved (Haskins 1891, 26). In 1806, a New York state senator was forced to resign over a corruption charge, and in response the legislature passed antibribery legislation (Hammond 1846, 233–34). But such problems became, if anything, more pronounced over the nineteenth century.

Some ethical breaches were seemingly trivial. For instance, as the railroads emerged as economic powerhouses they provided state legislators with free passes. The *New York Times* characterized these passes as "a small kind of bribery," meaningful, however, because they were a gateway to "the insidious progress of corruption among legislators." The paper remarked, "The sending of these passes by railroad companies is not an act of charity or philanthropy. Unquestionably they are intended to secure the favor of legislators, and there is no doubt that to a considerable extent they serve the purpose intended" (*NYT* 1886b). A Texas paper offered a similar analysis, noting that when a lawmaker "is caught with a free pass in his vest pocket . . . His constituents suspect him at once, because they consider that this pass increases his obligations to the corporations against which they expect him to exert himself" (*Fort Worth Daily Gazette* 1890). Even more distressing was evidence from places such as Virginia and Wisconsin that suggested it was legislators who pressed the railroads for the passes and not just for their own personal use, but also for the benefit of their relatives and friends (*NYT* 1888a, 1888b). Voters looked askance at the passes; the Illinois Farmers' State convention passed a resolution condemning them following a debate characterized as "not complimentary to the legislators" (*NYT* 1873c). Public skepticism of lawmaker motives was captured by Mr. Peck, a well-known humorist of the time.

> I beg to direct your attention to a series of diabolical outrages that have for years been perpetrated upon unsuspecting and innocent State . . . legislators . . . by those gigantic and uncontrollable monsters, the railroads. I am informed that for years it has been the custom of these corporations to thrust upon poor, unprotected members of the Legislature, free passes upon their roads, by which they were compelled to travel without paying fare. . . . I am told that in many instances, where members have refused to accept passes, the minions of these railroad monopolies have seized the unfortunate victim, and bound him hand and foot, and while in this helpless condition, thrust passes into his pocket, and ordered their conductors to shoot the poor member if he did not show his pass when on the car, instead of offering money. (Richardson 1880, 229–30)[6]

Lawmakers justified taking the passes on the grounds that their pay was low (Aldrich 1884, 91). They denied being influenced by them, pointing to instances when legislation unfriendly to the railroads' interests was passed (Hubbard 1884, 97–98; *NYT* 1885b). Some legislators even touted the passes as being a good thing because they allowed them to return home regularly to consult with their constituents (*NYT* 1886b). But at least a few of them felt guilty. One lawmaker confessed, "While I was down home the other day, I rode on the cars with one of my old farmer neighbors, as good a man as I am, and as worthy of any sort of favor; and I tell you what it is, I felt ashamed of myself when I presented my pass to the conductor, and he a ticket for which he had paid!" (Aldrich 1884, 94). In Massachusetts, the chairs of the joint committee overseeing railways refused to answer a witness before them who asked if they held free passes, saying it was "a private matter" (Felt 1875, 12–13). The following year, 12 lawmakers returned their passes, and it was reported that "the papers are working at the consciences of the remainder to make them do likewise" (*Providence Evening Press* 1876). Clearly, legislators were sensitive to charges of corruption on this score. When a Connecticut representative alleged that many of his colleagues were being bought by passes, his remarks were ruled out of order, and he was held in contempt and not allowed to vote again until he apologized. There was even talk of expelling him (*Meriden Daily Republican* 1885; *NYT* 1885a).

Some lawmakers acknowledged the conflict of interest posed by the passes, with a Utah senator claiming a railroad agent had admitted that the companies purchased influence through the passes (*Salt Lake Herald* 1897). Railroad officials denied such charges. During a New York state legislative hearing U.S. Senator Chauncey Depew, the former president of the New York Central Railroad, was asked by committee counsel (and future Chief Justice of the United States) Charles Evans Hughes, "It has been suggested . . . that one method of influencing legislation in Albany was through the granting of railroad passes at the request of members of the Legislature for their friends. . . . Is there any truth in it?" Depew responded, "No, I do not think there is any truth in it" (*Testimony Taken Before the Joint Committee of the Sen. and Asm. of the St. of N.Y.* 1905, 3187).

Many were unconvinced by such assertions, and a number of states took steps to stop railroads from giving legislators free passes. A few did it by statute ("Constitutional Law—Police Power—Railroad Passes" 1916, 834). Many enacted constitutional prohibitions against the practice. During the convention leading to the adoption of the 1874 Pennsylvania constitution, the delegate who proposed the ban on rail passes argued, "The amendment will be very acceptable to the people, and they will accept it as a proclamation against the exercise of a species of illegitimate influence of railroad companies." But the delegate also noted that because of the pressure by lawmakers to provide the passes, "I believe that every well regulated railroad company in the State will rejoice in accepting . . . an amendment of this kind" (*Deb. of the Conv. to Amend the Cons. of Pa.* 1873, 703). By 1900, eleven states had constitutional provisions prohibiting free rail passes.[7] But, as is often the case, at least one state rode off in the opposite direction from the others: New Jersey opted to deal with the problem by making mandatory the granting of railway passes to all legislators (*Acts of the Ninety-Sixth Leg. of the St. of N.J.* 1872, 1026).

Larger ethical problems than free passes, however, emerged in the second half of the nineteenth century. The Pennsylvania legislature in the 1870s was considered a cesspool of corruption (Harrison 1979).[8] Assessing the sway the country's largest oil company enjoyed over that state's lawmakers, an early muckraker cracked that "The Standard had done everything with the Pennsylvania legislature, except refine it" (Lloyd 1881, 322). Other state legislatures were similarly suspect. The Ohio General Assembly endured a number of ethics investigations in the 1870s and 1880s (Gold 2009, 173–75). When Theodore Roosevelt was a member of the New York Assembly in the early 1880s, he estimated a third of his colleagues were "thoroughly corrupt men," most because they introduced "blackmail" bills, measures designed to extort money from businesses opposed to policies in the proposed legislation. He was bipartisan in his scorn, finding "on one side there were corrupt and unscrupulous demagogues, and on the other side corrupt and unscrupulous reactionaries" (Roosevelt 1913, 77, 100). According to a news report, in the mid-1890s the New Jersey legislature "was owned body and soul by the corporations, and the third house controlled the situation." On the chamber floor a Garden State senator contended that "the lobbyists were rank and that their offenses in this Legislature smelled to heaven" (*NYT* 1895b). Colorado's governor vetoed a bill regulating the production and sale of oleomargarine because the measure "was passed by means of the most open and bare-faced bribery in both House and Senate" (*NYT* 1897). In 1899, 35 Montana legislators allegedly split a total of $431,000 in bribes for their votes for a U.S. Senate seat (Connolly 1906, 27). Around the same time the Missouri lieutenant governor assembled a list of state senators, categorizing them as either sheep ("pure, honest men, who can't be touched") or goats ("[men who are] out for all there is in it"). He labeled over half the Senate as goats (Wetmore 1904, 153). A global indictment of state legislatures was rendered by the U.S. House select committee investigating the Credit Mobilier scandal. In its report the select committee railed against the growth of corporate political influence, noting, "It is notorious in many State legislatures that these influences are often controlling, so that in effect they become the ruling power of the State" (U.S. H. 1873, *x*).

Not surprisingly, the public considered state legislatures corrupt. A joke about thieves was indicative of the contempt in which legislatures were held. One thief complained that he worked "as hard as anybody at thievin' an' I scarcely make a living." The punch line was "An' yet my brother Bill he's saved about $50,000 on a legislative salary of $1,500 a year an' they call him a statesman" (*Omaha Daily Bee* 1887). The *New York Times* cracked that if state politics were not cleaned up, "the State Capitol ought to be removed to Auburn or Sing Sing. Our legislators and convicts should change places" (*NYT* 1874a). In the same vein, Mark Twain quipped in an 1872 speech, "I think I can say, and say with pride, that we have some legislatures that bring higher prices than any in the world" (Twain 1910, 414). For the most part, these prices were paid by those with interests before the legislature rather than by the state on behalf of its citizens. But, as always, there were exceptions. Few accusations of corruption were leveled against legislatures in Illinois, Iowa, and Wisconsin (Campbell 1980, 200–202). And a news article actually lauded the Delaware legislature for being "Small but Incorruptible" (*NYT* 1891b).

Legislative Sessions

At the beginning of the nineteenth century, state legislatures met in annual sessions. They did so because when the original state constitutions were written frequent legislative meetings were seen as both a critical check on gubernatorial power and a significant boost to representation (Squire and Hamm 2005, 68). As documented in table 6.4, however, a shift to biennial sessions occurred slowly but inexorably. In 1832, 3 out of the 24 states limited their legislature to meeting only every other year: Illinois, Missouri, and Tennessee, all of which were newer states that had established biennial sessions in their first constitutions. Influenced by the republicanism of the Tennessee constitution and by a concern that annual sessions led to excessive legislation, Delaware became the first of the original states to switch when it adopted biennial sessions in 1833 (Still 1936, 196). Roughly 30 years later, the now 33 states tilted slightly in favor of meeting only every other year. By 1889 biennial sessions were being characterized as "a reform which has become one of the tests of enlightened thinking in politics nowadays" (*Boston Evening Transcript* 1879). Only 6 of the 38 states retained annual meetings. All of the holdouts were from among the first 13 states, sticking fast to their original values: Connecticut, Massachusetts, New Jersey, New York, Rhode Island, and South Carolina. In assessing a proposed switch to biennial sessions, the *Newark Advertiser* commented that annual sessions were "the heritage of a wise colonial government" and that "A system which would apply successfully to newer communities might be at variance with the fundamental principles of New Jersey government" (quoted in *Patterson Daily Press* 1880). But in 1889, Connecticut gave way and switched to biennial sessions, doing so over the objections that they "were departing from the custom of the last 200 years" (*Hartford Weekly Times* 1884; *Public Acts Passed by the GA of the St. of Conn.* 1887, 657). While the direction of the trend was clear, some states vacillated: Virginia adopted biennial sessions in 1850, returned to annual sessions in 1870, and then went back to meeting every other year in 1876. Georgia adopted biennial sessions in 1877 but reverted to annual sessions in 1892 (Oberholtzer 1900, 80).

What drove the shift? By the beginning of the nineteenth century serious reservations were being expressed about the tremendous power invested in state legislatures. Constitutions in the original states had promoted legislative supremacy (Squire and Hamm 2005, 39–40). As these states replaced their initial constitutions, the newer documents were written with provisions that greatly constrained lawmakers (Burgess 1886, 27–30; Still 1936). These limitations accumulated over the nineteenth century. In Virginia, the 1829 constitution generally maintained legislative supremacy, but the 1850 constitution "started in earnest the practice of circumscribing the powers of the general assembly," and the trend reached its zenith with the 1901 constitution (Pate 1930, 111, 114). As new states were admitted, their constitutions limited legislative power from the beginning. Prominent among these restraints were provisions allowing legislatures to meet only once every other year. In a number of states concerns about legislative abuse of power were so great that reformers even toyed with the idea of triennial sessions (*Deb. and Proc. of the Md. Reform Conv. to Revise the State Cons.* 1851, 276; *Jour. of the Conv. of the State of Tenn.* 1834, 358–59; *Report of the Deb. and Proc. of the Conv. for the Rev. of the Cons. of the State of Ind.* 1850, 43, 94; *Report of the Deb. and Proc. of the Conv. for the Rev. of the Cons. of the State of Ohio*

TABLE 6.4. Frequency of State Legislative Sessions across the Nineteenth Century

Frequency of Sessions	1832	1861	1889
Annual	21	15	6
Biennial	3	18	32
Total number of states	24	33	38

Source: 1832, *American Almanac* 1832, 275; 1861, *American Almanac* 1861, 238; 1889, *American Almanac* 1889, 107.

1851, 253; *Report of the Proc. and Deb. in the Conv. to Revise the Cons. of the State of Mich.* 1850, 115). And, as will be discussed in chapter 7, by the end of the century quadrennial sessions were being contemplated. These changes (along with others such as extended gubernatorial terms) increased the executive's power at the expense of the legislature.

Those who argued in favor of biennial sessions focused on two major points. The first was voiced by proponents in New York: "The complaint is universal of over-legislation and constant tinkering of laws to the infinite annoyance of those who must live under them" (*NY Trib.* 1898). Georgia's governor voiced a similar concern: "Annual sessions are prolific of much needless legislation, and too much legislation has a disturbing effect on business and commercial affairs" (*Macon Telegraph* 1898). A delegate to the 1834 Tennessee constitutional convention contended that a national legislature needed to meet annually, "But no such necessity exists for . . . a State Legislature, which has nothing to do with any thing except to make new laws or repeal old ones; and the less of that they do so much the better" (*Jour. of the Conv. of the State of Tenn.* 1834, 358–59). Some lawmakers concurred. During a floor debate New York Assembly member Theodore Roosevelt asserted that 90 percent of legislation passed in annual sessions "could be dispensed with and the State yet be a gainer" (*NYT* 1883).

The second line of argument taken by biennial session supporters was financial, and again it was pushed by those touting the reform in New York: "The expense of the annual session grows year by year more appalling" (*NY Trib.* 1898). A Michigan paper itemized legislative expenditures and calculated that a shift to biennial sessions would produce "a savings to the State of $52,624.51" (*Genesee Whig* 1850). Biennial session backers in Minnesota went so far as to forecast "the saving of expense alone being so considerable that a decrease of taxation will probably be practicable, at least in alternate years" (*Daily Globe* 1881a). Iowa's governor succinctly encapsulated all these claims: "less legislation, less expense, less work to do over remedying bad legislation, fewer errors, more satisfaction, and less complaints from the people" (*NYT* 1879). A delegate to the 1844 Louisiana constitutional convention similarly tied all the arguments together. Calling annual sessions "one of the greatest curses ever inflicted on our country," he maintained biennial meeting would remove an "excess of legislation; the enacting of laws one year to be repealed the next; to say nothing of this, the great saving to the public treasury" (*Proc. and Deb. of the Conv. of La.* 1845, 945).

Biennial session supporters saw avarice and venality lurking behind opposition to their proposed reform. Obviously, lawmakers were thought to have selfish motives for preferring annual sessions. The *Philadelphia Times* conjectured, "The newly discovered demand for annual sessions of the Legislature probably owes its origin to those who would like the salary of $1,500 a session every year, instead of every two years, as at present" (quoted by the *NYT* 1896). But others were also thought to be motivated by self-interest in preferring annual meetings. In New York, it was alleged, "The first opposition came, as was expected, from Albany. Every hotel and saloon keeper, hack driver, grocer or other person whose income is increased by the Legislature and its followers is, of course, bitterly opposed to having such harvest occur only once in two years." And Albanyites were not the only suspects: "All the hangers-on of the Legislature who come down like so many vultures on January 1 to secure as much pay for alleged services during four months as any business man would give them for their services during the whole year, would turn heaven and earth to defeat this bill" (*NY Trib.* 1898). Similar reasons were ascribed for the preference for annual sessions among residents of Connecticut's capital: "The proposed biennial sessions amendment . . . excites more interest in Hartford than anywhere else in the State, for the reason that its people want to have the Legislature in session here as long and frequently as possible on account of the money it brings" (*NYT* 1884).

Supporters of annual sessions countered that yearly meetings were needed to deal with the increasing number of problems states faced (Bridgman 1893). The *Duluth Herald* maintained, "In a young and rapidly growing state like Minnesota, where changes are so rapid and need of legislation is made apparent every day, biennial sessions result in great inconvenience, not to say serious embarrassment" (quoted in *St. Paul Daily Globe* 1886). Proponents of annual sessions in established states pushed a similar theme, as in New York: "This is a large State, with vast and complex interests and a great deal of public business. Emergencies frequently arise which demand prompt legislation" (*NYT* 1899). The *Richmond Dispatch* actually turned this line of argument into a taunt, observing, "It must be a poor, unprosperous, unenterprising State that does not need some sort of legislation every year" (quoted in *Georgia Weekly Telegraph* 1875).

What actually happened following the shift from annual to biennial sessions? First, it must be noted that the change was often accompanied by considerable cynicism. For instance, it was speculated by a Georgia newspaper that even if biennial sessions were to be adopted in that state, "Some excuse for the assembling of the Legislature every year will always be found" (*Macon Georgia Telegraph* 1847). Such skepticism proved warranted, if not in Georgia then in Ohio. After briefly observing an 1851 constitutional provision requiring biennial sessions, Ohio lawmakers concocted a method to get around the limitation by taking a recess at the end of the first year of a session and then holding "the adjourned session" the following year. It was believed that the lawmakers did this because "Two sessions meant more perquisites than one, and so there have been two regularly" (*NYT* 1893b; *Perrysburg Journal* 1894).

Some states claimed that the shift to biennial sessions saved money. After the first biennial session in Minnesota it was declared that allowing the legislature to only meet every other year reduced state expenses by about 25 percent and caused taxes to be reduced (*NYT* 1879). But opponents of biennial sessions in Georgia took issue with the assertion that they were less expensive than annual sessions. In that state it was calculated that during biennial sessions the legislature met for more days than it did during two annual sessions combined, a concern in a state that paid a per diem (*NYT* 1891c). Similar outcomes occurred elsewhere. For the first decade following the change to biennial sessions in Minnesota the legislature stuck to the 60-calendar-day limit it had followed under annual sessions. But after that point biennial sessions began consuming 106 calendar days, pushing the total number of days in a session over the two-year period close to what it had been before the reform.[9] The financial impact of the change was muted in another state for a different reason. In Pennsylvania the shift was accompanied by a dramatic increase in members—to 201 members from 100 members in the House and to 50 members from 33 members in the Senate—negating any salary savings from moving to biennial sessions (*NYT* 1879).

Occasionally, experience with biennial sessions produced more sophisticated arguments in favor of annual meetings. One was offered by the *Montpelier Watchman*, which editorialized, "We have always looked upon the annual session of the Legislature as the political normal school of the State, educating the best and the most noted men in every town, successively in legislative and administrative forms, knowledge and duties." The editorial went on to add, "We think we can see the growing disadvantages of the new [biennial] system, in the larger influence of inexperienced men, and in decreasing knowledge of the best elements and principles of political administration" (quoted in *NYT* 1874c). A few years later a Vermont lawmaker agreed, observing that the lack of experience caused by biennial sessions had "left [legislators] in a condition of less memory of, and acquaintance with, previous legislation, &c., than they had under the annual system" (*NYT* 1881). There were also claims that candidate recruitment had suffered. In Connecticut, it was thought that "The sessions since the adoption of the amendment have been greatly protracted, and the most capable and competent men cannot be persuaded to become members of either house in consequence" (*NYT* 1889c).

Such arguments were generally lost on the public, and it appears that biennial sessions were their clear choice. When Georgia voters were given the opportunity to express a preference between biennial sessions and annual sessions, 86 percent of them chose the former.[10] According to one paper, "We presume the people have become disgusted with our current cumbrous and expensive system of Legislation. . . . they are determined to resort to less frequent meetings of that body" (*Enquirer* 1840). Such views were common. As the century drew to a close, a scholar reported, "In those few States in which the legislatures still convene annually . . . there is no concealment of the public distrust for these bodies, while the conviction seems to grow that it would be a very much better arrangement should they meet less frequently" (Oberholtzer 1900, 80).

Staff and Facilities

At the beginning of the nineteenth century state legislatures had little in the way of staff other than a clerk or two and a few other functionaries, such as a doorkeeper and a sergeant at arms. Only very slowly did the number of support staff grow. New York was in the vanguard of the movement to add assistance. Among the workers employed by the Assembly by 1858 were a clerk, four deputy clerks (a journals clerk, an engrossing clerk, and two clerks performing miscellaneous work), a librarian, an assistant librarian, a postmaster, and an assistant postmaster (*Clerk's Man. of Rules, Forms, and Laws for the Regulation of Business in the Asm. of the St. of N.Y.* 1858, 18–19). While useful, these positions "performed routine clerical and housekeeping chores and had no discernable impact on public policy" (Gunn 1980, 284). By 1890, the number of staff had swelled considerably. Between them, the speaker and the Assembly clerk now filled 73 staff positions. Some supplemented long-existing offices. Thus, the clerk gained an assistant clerk and 9 deputy clerks, and the journals clerk added an assistant clerk. There continued to be a librarian and an assistant librarian. But a number of new positions were created, among them a superintendent and assistant superintendent of documents and 12 committee clerks. Each of the four busiest standing committees (Ways and Means, Judiciary, Affairs of Cities, and Railroads) was assigned a clerk, while the others worked for the remaining committees as needed (*Jour. of the Asm. of the St. of N.Y.* 1890, 51–52).

By the last quarter of the century more employees, including staff for at least some standing committees, were common in most state legislatures. In 1870, the Texas House employed 22 clerks, of whom 13 were assigned to committees (*H. Jour. of the Twelfth Leg., St. of Texas* 1870, 410). The Missouri Senate in 1879 had 3 enrolling clerks, 6 engrossing clerks, 1 revision clerk, 1 clerk to oversee printing, and 23 committee clerks (*Jour. of the Sen. of the St. of Mo.* 1879, 579). Similarly, "In the early nineties Illinois representatives hired 101 people, 22 of whom clerked for committees at three dollars a day" (Campbell 1980, 45).

There was resistance to the growth in legislative staff, particularly committee clerks. In 1870, a select committee charged with investigating the number of Texas House employees reported, "The committees on the Judiciary and Internal Improvements hold daily meetings, and should have the regular services of their clerks. It does not seem that the same necessity exists with the other standing committees of the House" (*H. Jour. of the Twelfth Leg., St. of Texas* 1870, 410). Two decades later the Texas speaker was authorized to "appoint as many committee clerks as necessary, not exceeding eight" (*Fort Worth Daily Gazette* 1889). That same year the Michigan Senate endured a running battle over the appropriate number of committee clerks after a member introduced a resolution stating, "We still believe that the appointment of any additional clerks would be ill advised and an unnecessary expense to the State" (*Jour. of the Sen. of the St. of Mich.* 1889, 161, 174, 241, 257, 324). Such efforts were common. In 1867, the Nevada Senate narrowly defeated a resolution to discharge all committee clerks (*Jour. of the Sen. During the Third Sess. of the Leg. of the St. of Nev.* 1867, 68). But over the final decades of the nineteenth century efforts to reverse the trend toward more committee staff were usually rebuffed. An effort in the Nebraska House to limit the hiring of more "useless clerks" was rejected when the Committee on Privileges and Elections maintained that it "could not possibly proceed to business without a clerk" (*Omaha Daily Bee* 1889). A crucial justification for increasing staff was identified during the Missouri Senate's examination of the issue: "the duties of clerks may be performed by a clerk and the Senators relieved" (*Jour. of the Sen. of Mo.* 1885, 109).

It would be a mistake to interpret the increase in the number of clerks over the course of the nineteenth century, even those for committees, as evidence that state legislatures were growing their capacity to generate and digest information. During this time most clerks were employed on a session-only basis, and in some legislatures committee clerks were hired and fired as needed. Moreover, in many states, if not most, staff positions, particularly committee clerks, were treated as political sinecures (e.g., *Mansfield Herald* 1869; *Milwaukee Journal* 1891; Morris 1982, 128). The Virginia Senate rules in 1880 even required that of the five committee clerks, "not more than one . . . shall be appointed from the same congressional district" (*Members, Officers, and Standing Committees and Rules of the Sen. of Va.* 1880, 16).

Perhaps because of this, staff positions were prone to exploitation by their occupants. In 1875 the South Carolina Senate clerk expressed two concerns in his diary: One was whether he could maintain sufficient support among the senators to keep his position; the other was whether he could get the state to pay its bill to the state printer, a company he owned (Woody 1936a, 1936b). He had another reason to want to hold on to his position. The governor had recently complained that the House and Senate clerks were paid five times more than lawmakers and received the highest salaries of "any officer in the State, except the Chief Justice" (*Jour. of the H. of Reps. of the St. of S.C.* 1872, 20). Questionable financial dealings involving clerks were common. The New York Assembly clerk gained notoriety for openly distributing railroad passes (*NYT* 1886b). In Ohio in the late 1860s, both the Senate clerk and the House clerk were concurrently employed by newspapers. Over one two-year session they collected their $5 per diem for 845 days and 1,106 days respectively, even while working two jobs (*Mansfield Herald* 1869).

The behavior of committee clerks was no better. Allegedly most of them in the Iowa House were "relatives of members" (*Dubuque Herald* 1897). Nepotism was also suspected in Texas, where it was said that committee clerks "had nothing to do except wear white winged collars, chew spruce gum, entertain the lady visitors and draw $5 per day from the state" (*Daily Herald* 1893). Unearned pay troubled a California paper which decried that committee clerks were provided "Sixty days at the public crib at a per diem of $5, and few of them [have] anything to do" (*Sacramento Daily Record-Union* 1887). An even more brutal assessment was offered a few years later by another California newspaper. Under a headline of "Bloodsuckers of the State Yet Hold On—Retrenchment at the Capital Regarded as a Joke—An Army of Useless Attaches Whose Salaries are Unwarranted—Raid on the Treasury—Hordes of Political Hangers-On Fed at the California Lawmakers' Crib," it found that while "Every committee in the Senate has its clerk. . . . Some committees meet [only] once or twice during the session of the Legislature." Turning its attention to the other side of the capitol, the paper reported similar dubious practices in the Assembly: "The Committee on Rules met once before a clerk was appointed. Since then it has had a clerk at $5 a day and has not met." The paper concluded that "Many [committees] need no clerk" (*Morning Call* 1895a, 1895b). There were allegations that phantom committee clerks were put on the South Carolina Senate's payroll (*Report of the Joint Investigating Committee on Public Frauds* 1878, 416). In Texas it was alleged that "Certificates for salary for services as committee clerks . . . were presented by men who had no sort of connection with either branch of the legislature" (*Fort Worth Daily Gazette* 1888). The same charge was leveled in Georgia (*Daily Atlanta Intelligencer* 1870). Even in Oregon, where resolutions gave preference to former Union soldiers to be hired as committee clerks, it was suspected that "In many cases there was no work whatever to do, and in other cases the job was created for clear gain" (*Capitol Journal* 1895; *Jour. of the H. of the LA of the St. of Ore.* 1887, 51; *Jour. of the Sen. of the LA of the St. of Ore.* 1889, 90). Given this, it may be no surprise that following the close of one legislative session, Oregon committee clerks were "to be seen wending their way toward their respective boarding houses . . . laden with inkstands, waste-paper baskets and such other articles of office furniture as their fancy suggested and their hands could reach" (*Daily Eugene Guard* 1898).

This sort of behavior infected the legislative process. Committee clerks were thought to have "misplaced" or reworded legislation without authorization (Harrison 1979, 345). But, as an investigation of the role of committee clerks in the unauthorized revisions of legislative proposals concluded, "It is hard to distinguish between the mistakes of haste and carelessness and the errors of intention" (*Sun* 1893). Indeed, it was thought that gaffes in the Ohio House occurred because the clerk's office was woefully understaffed (Gold 2009, 163). Still, as Missouri's governor observed of his legislature's staff, "The clerks are, as a rule, young men of great promise, but have little knowledge of the business with which they are entrusted; hence we find so many badly drawn, ambiguous, and often meaningless acts passed" (*Saint Joseph Daily Gazette* 1874).

Although the increase in the number of legislative staff during the course of the nineteenth century appears to have been driven more by clerical needs and patronage desires than by informational demands, the seeds of change were planted toward the end of the century. Notably, in 1890 the New York State Library established a legislative reference unit, the first of its kind in the nation. It was the brainchild of Melvil Dewey, who had recently taken over the state library. (As a younger man Dewey had developed the decimal classification system that bears his name.) In 1892, the Massachusetts State Library took steps in a similar direction (Rothstein 1990, 405; Weber 1919, 360–61). As will be discussed in chapter 7, these efforts blossomed into more robust forms of institutional assistance early in the twentieth century.

Finally, during the course of the nineteenth century state legislatures acquired permanent facilities dedicated to their use. Indeed, four capitols built toward the end of the eighteenth century and 16 capitols constructed during the nineteenth century are still in use by state legislatures in the twenty-first century.[11] Kentucky occupied its first permanent capitol in 1794, a three-story stone building described as "plain, but roomy and commodious" (Cuming [1810] 1904, 192). It was destroyed by fire in 1813. After meeting in a rented building, the legislature moved into its second permanent capitol, a two-story brick building, in 1816. It was largely destroyed by fire in 1824, forcing the Senate to relocate to a nearby seminary and the House to a large meetinghouse. The meetinghouse burned a year later, and the House had to move to a Methodist church. The legislature occupied its third permanent capitol, "a large and very handsome structure built of polished Kentucky marble" in 1829, and that building served (despite one notable fire) for the rest of the century (Hitchcock and Seale 1976, 317; *Off. Man. for the use of the Courts, St., and County Officials and GA of the St. of Ky.* 1900, v–vii).

Kentucky's legislature was far from the only one to be orphaned at some point by fire. During the nineteenth century capitols in Alabama (1849), California (1854), Illinois (1823), Louisiana (1862, while the building was being used as a barracks by Union troops), Minnesota (1881), Missouri (1837, although its replacement was already under construction), New Jersey (partly 1885), North Carolina (1831), Ohio (1852, although its replacement was already under construction), Oregon (1855, before completion), Pennsylvania (1897), South Carolina (1865, during Sherman's march), Texas (1881), and Vermont (1857) also burned (*Daily Alta California* 1854; Davidson and Stuvé 1877, 916; Gold 2009, 91; Hitchcock and Seale 1976, 143–44, 312–33; Viles 1919, 234–35). And these were not the only capitols lost: As noted in chapter 4, Wisconsin Territory's capitol in

Burlington (now Iowa) burned in 1837 as did New Mexico's in 1892. Moreover, fire was not the only calamity to strike statehouses during the nineteenth century. In 1870, an inadequately constructed courtroom the floor above the Virginia House chamber collapsed when too many people crowded in to hear a controversial case. Although the House chamber was empty at the time more than 60 people died in the tragedy (*Harper's Weekly* 1870). Severe flooding caused the 1862 California legislature to flee Sacramento "with all the furniture and appointments appertaining to it" for San Francisco, where it held its sessions in the Merchants' Exchange building. Despite discussions about a permanent relocation, the legislature returned to Sacramento the next year (*Jour. of the Asm, during the Thirteenth Sess. of the Leg. of the St. of Calif.* 1862, 127–28; *Sacramento Daily Union* 1862).

But it was fires that were prevalent and harrowing. Both the Minnesota and Pennsylvania legislatures were in session when the blazes broke out. In Minnesota flames threatened the Senate, and many senators had to escape through a small window in the cloakroom. A representative leapt to safety, "landing, happily, in the deep snow and sustaining no injury." Miraculously, no lives were lost. St. Paul residents, who were anxious to keep the legislature in their city, immediately rallied to reconfigure the Market Hall to serve as a temporary capitol, and it was ready the day after the fire. Senators were reasonably content with their makeshift chamber, which was the hall's dining room, although they had to use "chairs and tables of a variety of patterns,—extension tables, long tables, short tables, square tables, and round tables." Representatives were less enthused about their accommodations, which were "chilly in the extreme." Because of this, "Everybody kept their overcoats and wraps on, and by special permission those who chose to do so were allowed to wear their hats." During the session, members "kept themselves warm by vigorous exercise and by puffing their cigars" (*Daily Globe* 1881b; 1881c). The legislature used the Market Hall for two years until the capitol was rebuilt.

Pennsylvania's lawmakers and staff also had to flee, and with their capitol destroyed they faced the same relocation problems. The governor wanted to keep the legislature in session, thus the day after the fire the Senate met in the state Supreme Court chamber and the House assembled in the U.S. district courtroom, which fortuitously held 120 desks from the recent administration of a civil service test. Representatives got desks on a first-come, first-served basis; those who arrived too late had to stand. Eventually the legislature took up residence in the Grace Methodist

Church; the House occupied the first floor auditorium, the Senate the rear Sunday-school room, and committees and staff the lecture rooms (*Daily Free Press* 1897; "Destruction of the Capitol Building at Harrisburg" 1897).

All the destroyed capitols were eventually replaced by larger buildings that provided more space for legislators, staff, and other government offices. Other statehouses were expanded to meet growing needs. The Arkansas capitol was remodeled in 1885, increasing the size of one of the legislative chambers (Kennan 1950, 38).[12] And statehouses were upgraded with modern conveniences. In Minnesota's capitol gaslights replaced candles in 1866 and in 1871 a running water system was hooked up and steam heat replaced wood-burning stoves, providing lawmakers "some of the comforts of civilized life" (Dean 1908, 18).

By the end of the nineteenth century the few peripatetic state legislatures settled on a capital city. The Vermont legislature, which, as noted in chapter 5, had bounced around the state, became fixed in Montpelier in 1808. For many years the Connecticut Assembly met in Hartford in odd-numbered years and in New Haven in even ones. In 1875 Hartford became the sole capital. Rhode Island was the most nomadic. In the 1830s the General Assembly met in Newport in May, the start of the legislative year. It alternated its October meetings between Providence and South Kingston, and rotated its January meetings among East Greenwich, Bristol, and Providence (*American Almanac* 1832, 187). In 1854 it was decided to alternate sessions only between Newport and Providence. Providence became the sole capital in 1900, and the legislature moved into the current capitol when it was finished a few years later.

The Role of Rules and Standing Committees in Overcoming Organizational Instability

State legislatures in the nineteenth century were institutions that endured high levels of membership turnover, as discussed earlier in this chapter. It also is the case that the public turned on their legislatures. Constitutional provisions were adopted that constrained legislative powers, notably by limiting their ability to meet. And while facilities improved over time, staff resources did not advance much and were in many cases subject to the abuses of the spoils system. For instance, long after the removal of wood-burning stoves from the Minnesota capitol, an ex-lawmaker noted, "Each legislature . . . still continues to elect its firemen, who wander through the chambers and halls . . . in a vain search for the ancient stoves, while the per diem is still gathered in by their willing hands" (Dean 1908, 18).

All of this would suggest that state legislatures were organizationally inert during the nineteenth century. Yet, in important ways they institutionalized in that they became progressively more complicated institutions. This outcome can be documented by examining the growth in rules and standing committees over the course of the century. These institutional developments support the notion that the press of external demands made on the legislative system and the system's need to respond to those demands largely account for its development.

State legislative rules became more sophisticated over the course of the nineteenth century. In the Ohio House bill introduction procedures evolved significantly. During the early decades of the nineteenth century bills were introduced either by an individual by motion for leave (with a day's notice) or by order of the House on a report of a committee. At this point, most legislation was introduced by committees. By the 1860s lawmakers were allowed to introduce legislation without leave of the House, and bills were about as likely to be introduced by an individual as by a committee (Gold 2002, 637, 642, 651; 2009, 119–20). Similar transitions occurred in many other state legislatures, and they parallel almost perfectly the changes involving bill introductions in the U.S. House over the same time period (Cooper and Young 1989; Dodds 1918, 28). But, again there were exceptions. The older form of bill introduction survived in Massachusetts until 1893 (Dodds 1918, 27).

More generally, by the 1880s lower houses had greatly increased the total number of rules under which they operated. In most chambers the count of numbered rules had at least doubled from that found in 1818–19, as documented in table 6.5. Toward the end of the century most chambers used elaborate and sophisticated rules focused largely on managing the legislative process. The only state still using a limited set of rules was Delaware, and it was something of a special case. As noted in chapters 2 and 3, Delaware had long relied on far fewer rules than other legislatures. An analysis of its state legislature at the end of the nineteenth century noted that because the lower house had only 21 members and the Senate but 9 members, "The manner of conducting business is plain and simple. . . . Parliamentary tactics are seldom resorted to, and the previous question is a stranger to entire sessions" (*NYT* 1891b). Other lower houses were too large to conduct themselves in such relaxed fashion, and they had to rely on rules rather than personal relations to allow them to process legislation. But, importantly, rules differed in particulars across states and chambers. One scholar who in the mid-1850s visited most of the states to investigate their parliamentary procedures reported that "the rules of State Legislatures differed from each other, and from those of Congress . . . each [has] its separate and distinct forms for conducting public business" (Burleigh 1856, 2).

TABLE 6.5. The Growth of Standing Rules in the Nineteenth Century, Selected States

State	1817–19, Number of		1883–90, Number of		Supplemental Manual Used in 1880s (if specified)
	Seats	Standing Rules	Seats	Standing Rules	
Alabama	51	43	100	51	
Connecticut	201	22	249	43	
Delaware	21	16	21	26	Cushing's
Georgia	85	28			
Illinois	28	44	153	60	Cushing's
Kentucky	84	52	100	59	
Maryland	80	41	91	52	
Massachusetts	408	58	240	102	
New Hampshire	194	22	313	52	
New Jersey			60	58	Cushing's
New York	126	49	128	77	
North Carolina	118	36	120	53	
Ohio	58	43	110	100	Cushing's
Pennsylvania	97	33	201	66	
Rhode Island			72	47	
Tennessee	40	22	99	64	Robert's
Vermont	185	31	244	40	
Virginia	202	48	100	88	Jefferson's
Arkansas	—	—	95	19	U.S. House
California	—	—	80	85	Cushing's
Colorado	—	—	49	30	Jefferson's
Florida	—	—	76	59	Jefferson's
Iowa	—	—	100	68	Cushing's
Kansas	—	—	125	67	Cushing's
Maine	—	—	151	58	Cushing's
Michigan	—	—	100	70	Cushing's
Minnesota	—	—	103	63	Jefferson's
Missouri	—	—	140	91	Smith's
Nebraska	—	—	100	61	Jefferson's
Nevada	—	—	40	85	Robert's
West Virginia	—	—	65	100	Jefferson's
Wisconsin	—	—	100	96	Jefferson's

Source: Size of legislature is generally taken from Dubin 2007, although the size for several legislatures between 1817 and 1819 had to be gathered from the legislative journals. The size of the Virginia House of Delegates for 1817 was taken from http://fisher.lib.virginia.edu/collections/stats/valeg/php/main.php. Rules for

State legislatures in the 1880s differed from those in the 1810s in one obvious way that might have implications for rules: membership size. Most lower houses grew over the decades. It would seem reasonable to hypothesize that larger legislative bodies require more rules to make them work than would smaller bodies. As discussed above, the Delaware House, which held at 21 members from its first constitution in 1776 until 1898, operated with far fewer rules than did its larger counterparts in the other states. But even its rules grew to 26 in 1885 from 16 in 1819. Lower houses in New York and North Carolina, which barely grew at all in membership size, saw impressive increases in their number of rules.

The most dramatic evidence that the number of rules was largely unrelated to membership size is supplied by the Massachusetts House. Until 1857, its number of seats was a function of the number of towns in the state and how many of those towns in a particular year opted to cover the cost of sending their representatives to the legislature. Thus the size of the House fluctuated from session to session, reaching a high of 749 members in 1812 and a low of 160 members in 1822 (Dubin 2007, 91–92). By 1857, during a session in which 355 members were seated, the House Committee on Re-

---

Table 6.5—continued

1817–19: Clark 1816, 60–64; *Jour. of the Asm. of the St. of N.Y.* 1816, 14; *Jour. of the Asm. of the St. of N.Y.* 1818, 46; *Jour. of the Asm. of the St. of N.Y.* 1819, 47; *Jour. of the H. of Commons* 1819, 1–2, 4–6; *Jour. of the H. of Dels. of the Com. of Va.*, 1817, 4–6; *Jour. of the H. of Reps. of the Com. of Ky.* 1817, 6; *Jour. of the H. of Reps. of the Com. of Ky.* 1816, 8–13; *Jour. of the H. of Reps. of the Com. of Ky.* 1818, 3–4, 7; *Jour. of the H. of Reps. of the GA of the St. of Ala.* 1820, 18–23; *Jour. of the H. of Reps. at the First Sess. of the Thirteenth GA of the St. of Tenn.* 1819, 3–4, 18–20; *Jour. of the H. of Reps. of the First Sess. of the First GA of the St. of Ill.* 1818, 15–19; *Jour. of the H. of Reps. of the St. of Del.* 1819, 12–13; *Jour. of the H. of Reps. of the St. of Ga.* 1818, 3–4, 107–8; *Jour. of the H. of Reps. of the St. of N.H.* 1819, 96–100; *Jour. of the H. of Reps. of the St. of Ohio* 1819, 3–4, 70–75; *Jour. of the Twenty Ninth H. of Reps. of the Com. of Pa.* 1818, 66–69; *Jours. of the GA of the St. of Vt.* 1819, 3–4, 24–27; *Rules and Orders to be Observed in the House of Reps. of the Com. of Mass.* 1819, 3–14; *Rules of the H. of Reps. in the GA of Conn.* 1818; *Votes and Proc. of the House of Dels. of the St. of Md.* 1819, 6–7. Rules for 1883–90: *Blue Book of the St. of Wis.* 1889, 93–101; *H. Jour. of the GA of the St. of Colo.* 1889, 15–38; *Jour. of the Asm. During the Twenty-Eighth Sess. of the Leg. of the St. of Calif.* 1889, 17–25; *Jour. of the Asm. of the Fourteenth Sess. of the Leg. of the St. of Nev.* 1889, 194–206; *Jour. of the H. of Dels. of the St. of Va.* 1887, 8–16; *Jour. of the H. of Reps. of the GA of the St. of N.C.* 1889, 1057–65; *Jour. of the H. of Reps. of the St. of Ala.* 1887, 77–84; *Jour. of the H. of Reps. of the St. of Del.* 1885, 40–43; *Jour. of the H. of Reps. of the St. of Ohio* 1888, 236–44; *Jour. of the H. of Reps. of the St. of Vt.* 1889, 19–26; *Jour. of the H. of Reps. of the Thirty-Sixth GA of the St. of Ill.* 1889, 49–57, 70–78; *Jour. of the H. of Reps. of the Thirty-Third GA of the St. of Mo.* 1885, 101–21; *Jour. of the H. of Reps. of the Twenty-Second GA of the St. of Iowa* 1888, 83–89; *Jour. of the H. of Reps., St. of Ark.* 1889, 69–77; *Jour. of the Proc. of the Asm. of the St. of Fla.* 1885, 11–18; *Jour. of the Reg. Sess. of the H. of Reps. of the Com. of Ky.* 1887, 49–60; *Legislative Man. of the St. of Minn.* 1889, 561–73; *Maine Register or St. Year-Book and Legislative Man.* 1889, 157–70; *Man. for the Use of the GC* 1889, 347–68; *Man. for the Use of the Leg. of the St. of N.Y.* 1889, 387–412; *Man. of the Leg. and of the Executive and Judicial Departments* 1890, 13–29; *Man. of the Leg. of N.J.* 1888, 65–73; *Man. of the Leg. of the St. of Neb.* 1883, 112–24; *Man. with the Rules and Orders for the Use of the GA of the St. of R.I.* 1889, 291–97; *N.H. Man.* 1889, 436–47; *Off. Directory and Legislative Man. of the St. of Mich.* 1889, 118–27; *Off. and Political Man. of the St. of Tenn.* 1890, 149–55; *Proc. of the H. of Reps. of the St. of Kan.* 1889, 66–75; *Register and Man. of the St. of Conn.* 1889, 128–32; *Rules and Orders for the Regulation and Gov. of the H. of Dels. of Md.* 1888; *Smull's Legislative Hand Book* 1887, 559–72.

Note: — = not applicable.

trenchment and Reform concluded that the membership was "altogether too large to secure accuracy and despatch in the prosecution of business" (*Deb. and Proc. in the Mass. Leg., 1857* 1857, 286). At that point the voters agreed to cap the number of seats at 240, a membership size that was kept in place until 1978. As shown in table 6.5, the 408 members of the Massachusetts House in 1819 were governed by 58 rules, while the 240 members of the 1889 House were governed by 102 rules. A similar pattern is found in Virginia, which also substantially reduced its number of delegates while increasing the number of rules.

It is essential to point out that although by the second half of the nineteenth century almost every state gave each chamber of its legislature the right to establish its own rules and procedures, a contradictory impulse to constrain the power of the institution manifested itself in a substantial number of procedural rules being incorporated directly into the constitution.[13] As one scholar at the time noted, "the legislatures established by nearly all of these constitutions have been deprived of the control of the fundamental rules of their own procedure, and the constitutions themselves stuffed with . . . details of parliamentary law" (Burgess 1886, 27). Among the procedural limitations imposed by state constitutions in the early 1870s were restrictions on when bills could be introduced (3 states), requirements that bills be confined to a single subject (19 states), that bills defeated not be introduced again during the same session (3 states), that laws could not be reenacted only by reference to title or section (19 states), that all votes on final passage be taken by yeas and nays (20 states), and that no bills be passed on the final day of the session (Minnesota). Three-reading requirements were elevated to constitutional standing in 25 states.[14] Such a provision was added to the 1850 Virginia constitution to address a perceived problem with hasty legislation caused by existing rules requiring three readings being routinely ignored (Pate 1930, 113). Lawmakers, however, understood that the relaxation of three-reading rules was a response to a dramatic increase in the number of bills and a need to keep the legislative process efficient. Consequently, even constitutional provisions requiring three readings were largely sidestepped, sometimes with the complicity of the state courts (Gold 2002, 635, 647).

State constitutions also placed unambiguous limits on special laws the legislature might wish to pass. Special laws are measures that are designed for a narrow purpose and reference a particular place or person. Article IV, section 27 of the 1865 Missouri constitution provides an extreme example with a long list of such restrictions, among them prohibitions against "establishing, locating, altering the course, or affecting the construction of roads, or the building or repairing of bridges; or establishing, altering, or vacating any street, avenue, or alley in any city or town" and "extending the time for the assessment or collection of taxes, or otherwise relieving any assessor or collector of taxes from the due performance of his official duties." Limitations on special laws of one sort or another appeared in most nineteenth-century state constitutions (Burgess 1886, 28–30; Hough 1867, 78; 1872, 645).

Overall, rules systems, even those with externally imposed limitations, were important because they allowed state legislatures to overcome the challenges created by high membership turnover and limited legislative sessions. Newly established legislatures were advantaged in that they had the opportunity to adopt rules developed by existing legislatures. Over time, their own experiences would lead chambers to revise their rules to meet their changing organizational needs. The widespread distribution of legislative manuals focused on parliamentary procedures greatly aided this process. Originally published in 1801, *Jefferson's Manual* was the first to gain extensive use. Written by Thomas Jefferson while he was president of the U.S. Senate, it drew heavily on British precedents and on Jefferson's earlier work, *Parliamentary Pocket Book* (Peterson 1983). By the 1830s a few state-specific manuals appeared. Pennsylvania's was written by a former state legislator who noted, "The excellent Manual of Thomas Jefferson contains the landmarks of order, and must always be a useful guide; but it is well known to all conversant with the business of public bodies, that it does not supply all that is wanting to State Legislatures." The author added that his manual would help "to explain the detail that is necessary to a new member" (Sutherland 1827, vii–viii). A few years later a manual for New Jersey was published, embodying "the Legislative practice of New Jersey as settled by sixty successive Legislatures" (Sitgreaves 1836, v–vi). By the 1840s, new general manuals were in circulation. Burleigh's *Legislative Guide* was written explicitly to expand on Jefferson's rules. The author came to the topic from a different route than his competitors, deciding to study parliamentary procedures after encountering problems "presiding at the faculty meetings of a University" (Burleigh 1856).

Ultimately, it was *Cushing's Manual* that came to replace *Jefferson's* in many state legislatures. Luther Cushing was a clerk for the Massachusetts House, and his manual, first published in 1845, was designed to be useful for the nation's burgeoning voluntary associations as well as legislatures. A similar motive later prompted Henry Martyn Robert, a U.S. Army officer, to publish his manual in 1876 (Doyle 1980; Levmore 1989). During the latter part of the nineteenth century, *Cushing's Manual* became the leading parliamentary supplement in American legislatures. Some chambers, however, opted to retain *Jefferson's Manual*, or use *Robert's* or *Smith's*. But, as documented in table 6.5, by the late 1880s *Cushing's* was the plurality choice. Indeed, even territorial chambers and legislatures in Canada and Hawaii turned to it (Bourinot 1884, 189–90, 192, 216, 238, 393, 414, 649; *Hawaiian Hansard* 1886, 211; *Jour. of the First Sess. of the LA of Okla. Terr.* 1890, 56; *Jours. of the Fourteenth LA of the Terr. of Ariz.* 1887, 648; *Journaux de l'Assemblée Législative de la Province de Quebec* 1884, 108, 201, 275, 288). The popularity of *Cushing's* indicates that by the latter part of the nineteenth century many state legislatures found it useful to have a parliamentary supplement that was targeted to their needs rather than one focused on the congressional process as was the case with *Jefferson's*. Interestingly, all of the newer state legislatures named a supplementary manual, while many of the oldest bodies chose not do so.

Finally, it is instructive to point out that the development of procedural rules during the first half of the nineteenth century in state legislatures does not appear to have been driven primarily by the needs of political parties. Political parties developed in the states well before the Civil War. But in the early histories of many chambers these parties did not structure voting behavior or the allocation of leadership and committee posts (Bowers 1983, 451; Broussard 1977; Davis 1970; 1988, 103–4; Ershkowitz and Shade 1971; but see Levine 1975). Even during the second half of the nineteenth century, when partisan organizations were clearly established in new states, seemingly dominant majority parties often fractured in practice, reducing their effectiveness, as happened in Idaho and elsewhere (Lowell 1902, 337–39, 349–50; Morrissey 1976; Schiller and Stewart, 2008). Thus, it seems that the evolution of rules governing parliamentary procedure in state legislatures gained considerable momentum before parties took full control. This is important because it suggests that rule development was often motivated by the need to manage increasingly heavier workloads rather than a desire to allow a partisan majority to work its will.

In the first decades of the nineteenth century standing committee systems were still in the early stages of development in most state legislatures. As documented in chapter 3, they had evolved to become a feature of state legislative systems by the end of the eighteenth century. As can be seen in table 6.6, by 1818 and 1819 most state legislatures had some standing committees; a few had a good number of them. Whether or not to rely on joint standing committees was still being sorted out in many legislatures. In New Hampshire, the House decided it was "inexpedient for the House and Senate to conduct their ordinary business of legislation by joint committees as usual" (*Jour. of the H. of Reps. of the St. of N.H.* 1819, 65). But a few states relied heavily on them.

Over the next decades standing committee systems became fully established. The power to report bills that had been referred to committee developed relatively early in many states. In the Pennsylvania House, initially a committee was empowered to report a bill only when it was allowed to do so by a specific resolution. By 1825 the House granted such authorization to all committees through a single resolution. In 1830, the power to report a bill was incorporated directly into the chamber's rules (Dodds 1918, 37).

By the second half of the nineteenth century standing committees typically were potent entities in state legislative decision making (Gold 2009, 129–30; Harrison 1979, 342). A Massachusetts House reform committee asserted "that thoroughness and despatch in legislation depend vastly more upon the manner in which business is matured in committees, than upon any amount of care or diligence bestowed upon it by the whole body in regular session" (*Deb. and Proc. in the Mass. Leg.* 1857, 286). As can be seen in table 6.6, the sheer number of standing committees grew dramatically between the 1810s and the 1880s, growth that paralleled that in the U.S. House and Senate over the same time period (Deering and Smith 1997, 27). There were, of course, similarities in committee systems across the state legislatures, with a raft of standing committees given jurisdictions over core governmental responsibilities. But each legislature tailored some standing committees to meet its state's particular circumstances. Thus in the 1880s the Minnesota House had both a Committee on Logs and Lumber and a Committee on Forestry, the Virginia House had a Committee on the Chesapeake and its Tributaries, and the California Assembly had committees on Chinese Immigration and Emigration, Silk Culture, Viniculture and Viticulture, and Yosemite Valley and Mariposa Grove of Big Trees and Forestry (*Jour. of the Asm. during the Twenty-Eighth Sess. of the Leg. of the St. of Calif.* 1889, 19; *Jour. of the H. of Dels. of the St. of Va.* 1887, 10; *Legislative Man. of the St. of Minn.* 1889, 567). Both the first North Dakota House and first South Dakota House named a standing committee on Warehouses, Grain Grading and Dealing, continuing a body that had existed during the territorial era (*Jour. of the H. of Reps. of the First Sess. of the S.D. Leg.* 1890, 23; *Jour. of the H. of the Seventeenth Sess. of the LA* 1886, 50; *Legislative Man. Containing the Cons. of N.D. and the Rules of the First LA* 1890,

TABLE 6.6. The Growth of Standing Committees in the Nineteenth Century, Selected States

	1817–19, Number of			1885–90, Number of		
State	Seats	House Standing Committees	Joint Standing Committees	Seats	House Standing Committees	Joint Standing Committees
Alabama	51	7	1	100	25	
Connecticut	201	2		249	4	22
Delaware	21	3		21	14	
Georgia	85	1	3	130	32	
Illinois	28	2	3	153	46	
Indiana	28	3		100	37	
Kentucky	84	5		100	33	
Louisiana	40	5		98	30	
Maryland	80	5		91	28	
Massachusetts	408	6	11	240	9	34
Mississippi				130	30	5
New Hampshire	194	6		313	30	3
New Jersey	43	3		60	20	14
New York	126	8		128	41	
North Carolina	118	3		120	23	5
Ohio	58	2	5	110	42	
Pennsylvania	97	11		201	34	
Rhode Island				72	14	7
South Carolina				124	27	
Tennessee	40		5	99	25	
Vermont	185	12		244	22	6
Virginia	202	13	1	100	22	
Arkansas	—	—	—	95	34	2
California	—	—	—	80	45	
Colorado	—	—	—	49	29	
Florida	—	—	—	76	24	
Iowa	—	—	—	100	53	
Kansas	—	—	—	125	48	
Maine	—	—	—	151	8	30
Michigan	—	—	—	100	53	
Minnesota	—	—	—	103	40	2
Missouri	—	—	—	140	39	1
Nebraska	—	—	—	100	43	
Nevada	—	—	—	40	21	
Oregon	—	—	—	60	23	
Texas	—			106	37	
West Virginia	—	—	—	65	21	3
Wisconsin	—	—	—	100	25	3

Source: Size of legislature is generally taken from Dubin 2007, although the size for several legislatures between 1817 and 1819 had to be gathered from the legislative journals. The size of the Virginia House of Delegates for 1817 was taken from http://fisher.lib.virginia.edu/collections/stats/valeg/php/main.php. Standing Committees for 1817–19: *Jour. of the Asm. of the St. of N.Y.* 1819, 49–50, 55; *Jour. of the H. of Commons* 1819, 3; *Jour. of the H. of Dels. of the Com. of Va.* 1817, 8–9; *Jour. of the H. of Reps. at the First Sess. of the Thirteenth GA of the St. of Tenn.* 1819, 21; *Jour. of the H. of Reps. During the First Sess. of the Fourth Leg. of the St. of La.* 1819, 3–5, 7, 9–10, 14, 22; *Jour. of the*

21). There was another distinctive evolution of consequence: Joint standing committees became dominant in the Connecticut, Maine, and Massachusetts legislatures but largely lost influence elsewhere. Overall, although standing committees expanded universally, each chamber configured its system in a somewhat different fashion.

Again, it might seem reasonable to conjecture that larger membership sizes drove the increase in the number of standing committees. After all, there were more members to be put to work. The evidence, however, does not support such a simple relationship. In Delaware, which did not change in size, the House used only 3 standing committees in 1819, but had 14 in 1885. Massachusetts, which dramatically cut its number of representatives, grew from 17 standing committees in 1819 to 43 standing committees in 1889. Overall, it appears that increased workloads (and perhaps legislative fad) caused the jump in the number of standing committees rather than the burgeoning size of the legislature. But it is important to note that as in New York, "While the list of committees is a long one, those which exert

---

Table 6.6—continued

H. of Reps. of the Com. of Ky. 1818, 5–7; Jour. of the H. of Reps. of the First Sess. of the First GA of the St. of Ill. 1818, 20–21; Jour. of the H. of Reps. of the GA of the St. of Ala. 1820, 6–7, 17; Jour. of the H. of Reps. of the St. of Del. 1819, 5, 8, 91; Jour. of the H. of Reps. of the St. of Ga. 1818, 4, 9; Jour. of the H. of Reps. of the St. of Ind. 1819, 3–4, 9; Jour. of the H. of Reps. of the St. of N.H. 1819, 63–64; Jour. of the H. of Reps. of the St. of Ohio 1819, 5, 6, 9, 69, 84, 95, 234; Jour. of the Twenty Ninth H. of Reps. of the Com. of Pa. 1818, 11; Jours. of the GA of the St. of Vt. 1819, 9; Rules and Orders to be Observed in the H. of Reps. of the Com. of Mass. 1819, 37–41; Rules of the H. of Reps. in the GA of Conn. 1818; Votes and Proc. of the Forty-Third GA, of the St. of N.J. 1819, 6; Votes and Proc. of the H. of Dels. of the St. of Md. 1819, 4–5. Standing Committees for 1885–90: Blue Book of the St. of Wis. 1889, 479–80; Columbus Enquirer-Sun 1888, H. Jour. of the GA of the St. of Colo. 1889, 29; Jour. of the Asm. During the Twenty-Eighth Sess. of the Leg. of the St. of Calif. 1889, 19; Jour. of the Asm. of the Fourteenth Sess. of the Leg. of the St. of Nev. 1889, 12–14; Jour. of the H. of Dels. of the St. of Va. 1887, 9–10; Jour. of the H. of Reps., Being the Regular Sess., Twenty-First Leg., Begun and Held at the City of Austin 1889, 9, 49, 52, 77–78; Jour. of the H. of Reps. of the Com. of Mass. 1887, 16–21; Jour. of the H. of Reps. of the GA of the St. of N.C. 1889, 1062–63, 1068; Jour. of the H. of Reps. of the GA of the St. of S.C. 1889, 25–32; Jour. of the H. of the LA of the St. of Ore. 1885, 42–43; Jour. of the H. of Reps. of the St. of Ala. 1887, 63; Jour. of the H. of Reps. of the St. of Del. 1885, 44; Jour. of the H. of Reps. of the St. of Ind. 1887, 57–60; Jour. of the H. of Reps. of the St. of Miss. 1888, 52–54, 73; Jour. of the H. of Reps. of the St. of N.H. 1887, 52–59; Jour. of the H. of Reps. of the St. of Ohio 1888, 22, 27, 30, 36, 40, 240; Jour. of the H. of Reps. of the St. of Vt. 1889, 37–43; Jour. of the H. of Reps. of the Thirty-Sixth GA of the St. of Ill. 1889, 84–87; Jour. of the H. of Reps. of the Thirty-Third GA of the St. of Mo. 1885, 151–55; Jour. of the H. of Reps. of the Twenty-Second GA of the St. of Iowa 1888, 111–14; Jour. of the H. of Reps., Sess. of Ark. 1889, 72–73; Jour. of the Proc. of the Asm. of the St. of Fla. 1885, 49–53; Jour. of the Reg. Sess. of the H. of Reps. of the Com. of Ky. 1887, 62–65; Legislative Man. of the St. of Minn. 1889, 583–84; Maine Register or St. Year-Book and Legislative Man. 1889, 139–44; Man. for the Use of the Leg. of the St. of N.Y. 1889, 381–86; Man. of the Leg. and of the Executive and Judicial Departments 1890, 39–41; Man. with the Rules and Orders for the Use of the GA of the St. of R.I. 1889, 299–307; Min. of Votes and Proc. of the One Hundred and Ninth GA of the St. of N.J. 1885, 11–12; Neb. Blue Book and Legislative Man. 1889, 165–66; Off. and Political Man. of the St. of Tenn. 1890, 154; Off. Directory and Legislative Man. of the St. of Mich. 1889, 601–2; Jour. of the H. of Reps. of the St. of Kan. 1889, 106–9; Off. Jour. of the Proc. of the H. of Reps. of the St. of La. 1888, 67–68, 91, 96, 109, 141–43; Register and Man. of the St. of Conn. 1889, 114–20; Rules and Orders for the Regulation and Gov. of the H. of Dels. of Md. 1888, 12; Smull's Legislative Hand Book 1887, 672–78.

Note: — = not applicable.

an important influence upon legislation are comparatively few" (*NYT* 1886a). Workloads increased and committee systems grew in response, but a number of the new committees were of limited significance.

Conclusions

Did state legislatures institutionalize between 1800 and 1900? The evidence presented here suggests that they did. By the end of the nineteenth century state legislatures were far more complex organizations than they had been a hundred years before. Organizationally, their procedural rules became more numerous and more complex. Standing committee systems not only became established but expanded dramatically. By these important measures state legislatures clearly had evolved. And the evolutionary process during the century transpired as it had with the original state legislatures, with newly established legislatures lifting rules and structures from established legislatures, thereby starting well along in terms of organizational development.

Institutionalization was, of course, uneven across the states. Some legislatures, mostly those in states that were larger and more industrial, developed to become reasonably complex organizations, looking and operating much like the U.S. House did at the time. A few others, however, appeared only a bit different from what they had been in the past. But overall, organizational change was noticeable in most bodies. In some ways the fact that significant change occurred is surprising because state legislatures had to overcome many impediments to development. First, because they generally paid poorly, making legislative service financially unattractive, membership turnover was very high, even in the more developed legislatures. This was important because individual lawmakers typically did not serve long enough to have much incentive to alter organizational mechanics. Second, legislative development was not left exclusively in the lawmakers' hands. Instead, exogenous forces manifested considerable control over legislative structures and even procedural rules through state constitutional provisions. State legislatures were forced to meet biennially instead of annually, and they were prohibited from passing legislation on certain subjects. Finally, the institutions themselves created obstacles to their own development. Corruption gnawed at their organizational fabric. Patronage trumped informational needs in the use of legislative staff.

Yet, state legislatures managed to survive these problems. It is likely that they were able to overcome their limitations through the adoption of increasingly complex procedural rules and organizational structures. Indeed, by the end of the century many of the things needed to improve the legislatures' prospects for further development were already in place. There was some movement to pay state lawmakers an annual wage, something that might make service more attractive and potentially increase membership stability. And, although staff might not have employed effectively, the fact that assistance had become an accepted part of the legislative system laid the foundation for its future expansion and increased effectiveness. Thus two major components for greater institutional capacity were in place.

Finally, the development of more complex rules and structures in state legislatures over the nineteenth century is significant for two additional reasons. First, they are strong evidence in support of the notion that legislatures can have high membership turnover yet still experience increased institutionalization (Hibbing 1999, 157–58). Organizations can become more structured and individual behaviors routinized in such a way as to minimize the costs associated with a regular change in personnel. The second reason is that this outcome likely happened because state legislatures were forced to respond to increasing demands from the political environment. The evolution of rules and committees had a functional element to them in that they each advanced a legislature's capacity to make decisions on increasingly more complex issues. But if state legislatures institutionalized in the sense presented here, the question then becomes how they would continue to evolve in the twentieth century.

7 ◆ The Professionalizing of State Legislatures since 1900

State legislatures institutionalized during the nineteenth century. As chapter 6 documented, complex procedural rules and well-developed standing committee systems became permanent organizational fixtures. Once institutionalized, however, a legislature does not necessarily continue to become progressively more elaborate or complex, at least in the simple ways examined in chapter 6. At a certain point a legislature no longer expands its number of rules or standing committees. Indeed, lawmakers may choose to streamline an institutionalized body by pruning superfluous rules and committees. But being institutionalized does not mean that a legislature ceases to evolve. Since the beginning of the twentieth century the dominant form of institutional evolution in state legislatures has been the process of their professionalization.

Legislative professionalization is a related but distinct concept from institutionalization (Squire 1992a). As used here, institutionalization focuses on two types of institutional attributes. The first is the development of organizational boundaries, something that, as discussed in chapter 2, was accomplished during the colonial era. The second, as noted above, is the development and perpetuation of complex procedures and structures, something that was fully achieved during the nineteenth century. In contrast to institutionalization, professionalization focuses on a different set of organizational attributes: member pay, session length, and staff resources and facilities (Squire 1992b, 2000, 2007). The relationships posited by legislative professionalization are straightforward. As pay increases, members are given incentive to serve for more terms. Longer-serving members translate into more experienced lawmakers. Longer legislative sessions provide legislators more time to both generate and digest policy proposals. Increased staff and improved facilities expand the informational resources available to legislators. Where institutionalization influences the *processes* by which legislators and legislatures make decisions, professionalization affects the *substance* of the decisions they make through increasing their organizational capacity.

Aggregate Changes in State Legislatures since 1900

The changes undergone by state legislatures since 1900 will be examined in two ways. First, aggregate changes across the states in membership size, number of chambers, pay structures, frequency of legislative sessions, membership turnover, facilities, and rules and committees will be traced. This analysis will provide a broad overview of the transformation of the state legislatures over the last century from the point of view of institutionalization. Second, a state-level analysis will probe the changes in legislative professionalization, looking at how each state legislature changed over time compared to Congress with respect to member pay, session length, and staff resources.

Change in Membership Size

Perhaps the most visible change in state legislatures since 1900 has been their membership sizes. Not counting Nebraska for reasons explained below, of the 44 state legislatures in existence in 1900, only 12 have not changed the number of seats in their lower house in the time since then.[1] Another two lower houses—Iowa and New York—changed their membership sizes but ultimately reverted to the same number they had in 1900. The other 30 states have changed their lower-house size. Some have altered the number often—New Hampshire has changed the size 27 times since 1900, while Ohio has changed 22 times. Others, among them Massachusetts and Michigan, have made only a single change. Comparing those lower houses that have altered their size, 21 are now larger than they were in 1900; the other 9 are smaller. Many of the increases are substantial: Florida has added 52 seats and Georgia 50 seats. Utah has almost doubled the size of its lower house, to 75 seats from 45 seats. A few of the decreases have been trivial: Pennsylvania and Wisconsin each have only one fewer member than in 1900. Several lower houses, however, have undergone substantial cuts with New England chambers shedding the most seats: Connecticut 104 seats, Vermont 96 seats, and Massachusetts 80 seats.

The U.S. Supreme Court decision in *Reynolds v. Sims* (1964) prompted many states to shuffle the size of their legislative bodies to accommodate the judicial shift in apportionment rules (Squire and Hamm 2005, 46–47). The Court held that state legislative chambers could not be malapportioned along the lines of the U.S. Senate, forcing many states to change the way they drew legislative districts. Lower houses in New England, for example, had to apportion on the basis of one-person, one-vote, dropping traditional schemes that represented towns with little differentiation on population size. This apportionment revolution was, coincidentally, coterminous with the professionalization revolution examined in depth later in this chapter.

Change in the Number of Chambers

The most substantial change in state legislative organization during the twentieth century occurred in Nebraska in 1934, when after three previous failed efforts voters approved a constitutional amendment to create a unicameral legislature. Attempts to create unicameral bodies in Oregon (1912 and 1914), Oklahoma (1914), and Arizona (1916) had been rejected by the voters of those states, and proposals in nine other states never made it to the ballot. In 1917, an Arkansas constitutional convention voted to establish a unicameral legislature but later reversed the decision (Buck 1936, 26–28; *Constitutional Conv. Bulletin* 1920, 43; Thomas 1919, 87). Efforts in a number of states since 1934 have all been unsuccessful (Buck 1936, 32–36; Harrison 1992, 42–45; Omdahl 1974; Perkins 1946, 513; Squire and Moncrief 2010, 13–14). Thus, Nebraska's creation of a unicameral legislature remains the country's great exception. Only the confluence of two extraordinary forces was able to overcome the strong American proclivity for bicameralism. One was the economic depression that led Nebraskans to actively seek a less expensive legislative form. The other was U.S. Senator George Norris's (R-Neb.) passionate campaign for unicameralism, motivated by his hatred of what he saw as the lack of accountability and potentially corrupt behavior of conference committees in bicameral legislatures (Norris 1961, 344–45). The decisive role played by the senator was readily acknowledged in his home state. Indeed, the first act of the new unicameral legislature following the swearing-in of its members was to invite Norris to make an address, saying, "We are honored today by the presence of the one who has been more responsible than any other person for this occasion. We are assembled as the members of the first Nebraska Unicameral Legislature because of his leadership" (*Legislative Jour. of the St. of Neb.* 1937, 5). Only after hearing the senator's comments did the legislature move on to electing its leaders.

The transformation of a bicameral legislature into a unicameral body raises an interesting evolutionary question: To which parent does the new institution look for its rules and structures? In the case of Nebraska, the legislative genes were not evenly split. Of the 43 members of the first Unicameral, 18 had served previously in the 100-seat House, while 13 had served in the 33-seat Senate, and 1 had served in both chambers.[2] The 5-member committee assembled to write the standing rules for the new body was even more skewed toward former House members: 4 members had served in the lower house while the other member had been in the upper house.[3] Perhaps it is no surprise then that the rules the committee produced drew far more heavily from those used in the old House than from those used in the old Senate. At least 22 rules adopted by the first Unicameral were taken from the rules used by the old House, while only 5 rules appear to have been lifted from the old Senate's rules.[4] As a supplement, the committee chose to continue to rely on *Gregg's Parliamentary Law*, a volume written by a psychology professor at the Nebraska State Normal School that had been used by the bicameral legislature. As might be anticipated given the large percentage of the new Unicameral's members who had legislative experience, the committee's proposal was reworked on the floor. A total of 23 amendments were offered, 18 of which were adopted. Most of the amendments were proposed by veteran lawmakers (*Legislative Jour. of the St. of Neb.* 1937, 115–21).

In contrast to the committee that wrote the rules, the elected 11-member Committee on Committees was evenly split, with 4 members having had experience in the House, 4 having served in the Senate, and 1 having been in both chambers. Charged with establishing the standing committee system, the Committee on Committees took the opportunity to greatly streamline it, creating only 16 standing committees. In recent sessions each chamber in the bicameral legislature had used over 25 standing committees. Almost all of the committees created by the first Unicameral had direct analogues in both chambers of the old bicameral legislature.

The first Unicameral also had a facilities problem to solve. It met in the recently opened state capitol, Nebraska's third since statehood. Constructed between 1922 and 1932, the building was designed for a bicameral legislature and had two chambers. The Unicameral opted to meet in the larger west chamber that had been used by the old House. The east chamber that housed the old Senate was shuttered. During the first session lawmakers made do in the larger chamber by removing many of the excess desks and roping off unneeded space. Toward the end of the session they voted to appoint a Committee on Seating Arrangement in Legislative Chamber and accepted its proposal to install the desks from the Senate chamber and have additional desks built as needed (*Legislative Jour. of the St. of Neb.* 1937, 172, 1622–24). Thus, the Unicameral ended up housed in the House chamber but sitting at the Senate's desks.

Changes in Session Frequency

As documented in chapter 6, during the nineteenth century state legislatures shifted from holding annual sessions to biennial sessions. During the twentieth century they largely reversed course, as shown in table 7.1. Most of these switches occurred after 1960.[5]

The shift to biennial sessions had been driven by public revulsion at what they saw as legislative abuses of power. Voters reasoned that a legislature that met less often would write fewer laws, thereby engendering greater social and economic stability. Efforts along these lines reached their zenith toward the end of the nineteenth century when several states contemplated adopting quadrennial sessions. Among those that considered but rejected such a change were California and Kentucky (*Off. Report of the Proc. and Deb. in the Conv. Assembled at Frankfort* 1890, 4249–63; Willis and Stockton 1881, 742–45). During its constitutional convention of 1901–2, Virginia initially adopted quadrennial sessions but later reversed the decision by a single vote, staying instead with biennial sessions (Holt 1968,

TABLE 7.1. Frequency of State Legislative Sessions, 1906–2009

Frequency of Sessions	1906	1931	1960	1999	2009
Annual	6	6	19	43	45[a]
Biennial	38	41	31	7	5
Quadrennial	1	1			
Total number of states	45	48	50	50	50

Source: 1906, *Off. Man. of the St. of Mo.* 1907, 488; Reinsch 1907, 131–32; 1931, Schumacker 1931, 10; 1960, *Book of the States 1960–61*, 40–41; 1999, *Book of the States 1998–99*, 64–65; 2009, *Book of the States 2009*, 83–86.

[a]In 2010 Oregon voters approved a shift to annual sessions, making that state the 46th state to meet every year.

87–89). In 1918 Arkansas voters rejected a new constitution that would have established quadrennial sessions (Thomas 1919, 88). All of these states ultimately shied away from taking such a dramatic step because they worried that needed legislation would be delayed too long. A leading Virginia lawyer rejoiced at his state's failure to adopt quadrennial sessions, reasoning, "two years of rapid, whizzing modern life is as full of change, and of the necessity for legislation, as a decade of ante-bellum days" (Daniel 1902, 275).

There were two states that chose to undertake the experiment. In 1890 Mississippi established what they called quadrennial legislative sessions, but they scheduled regular limited special sessions at the two-year mid-point. This gave them quasi-biennial sessions. In its 1901 constitution, Alabama went its neighbor one better and created a quadrennial session system with no scheduled special meetings in the interim. The committee that proposed the radical change argued, "it will prevent hasty and ill-advised attempts to repeal general laws before they have been given long enough in force to admit of a fair test of their merits. . . . The tendency to permanency of the legislative enactments will be greatly increased, and much expense saved to the State" (*Jour. of the Proc. of the Constitutional Conv. of the St. of Ala.* 1901, 467). Mississippi voters rejected a return to full biennial sessions in 1902, and Alabama voters did likewise in 1908, leading one political scientist to forecast that "The movement for less frequent legislative sessions will hardly turn backward" (Dodd 1908, 160).

Mississippi, however, returned to a regular biennial system in 1910, at the behest of the legislature, which again put the proposal before the voters who approved it. Alabama held on to its quadrennial system for several decades, although the legislature regularly put measures on the ballot to return to biennial sessions, which the voters routinely rejected (Commission to Compile Information and Data for the use of the Constitutional Conv. 1918, 375). But elite opposition developed early on. When the governor addressed the legislature during its second extra session in 1909, he commented that "it is clear that quadrennial sessions are not well for the best interest of the people" (*Jour. of the Sen. of the St. of Ala.* 1909, 28). A few years later the state bar association concluded that "instead of preventing hasty, ill digested or ill advised legislation, the quadrennial system has only increased the evils sought to be abated" (*Proc. of the Fortieth Annual Meeting of the Alabama St. Bar Association* 1917, 201). A similar claim was made by a former governor, who commented that the quadrennial system "has proven to be the most prolific course yet devised for hasty and ill-prepared legislation." But a contrary position was taken by another ex-governor, who argued that all legislative session systems were susceptible to "ill-digested legislation" (Commission to Compile Information and Data for the use of the Constitutional Conv. 1918, 376).

It was not until 1939 that biennial sessions were reenacted as part of a larger administrative reorganization plan (Martin 1940a, 445–46). They recommenced in 1943. The decision was prompted by two major problems experienced with quadrennial sessions. The first was that in many areas the legislature was unable to successfully set policy to cover a four-year period, particularly in regard to budgets. This failure led to the second problem: A chronic need for special sessions. During the 1930s, the legislature should have met only in 1931, 1935, and 1939. But those regular sessions proved inadequate, and the legislature had to hold special sessions in 1932, 1933, 1936, 1936–37, and 1939. Those special sessions met for a total of 122 legislative days, evidencing a need for more frequent regular sessions (Martin 1940b).

Alabama's quadrennial sessions may have been unique, but its need to call special sessions was not. States with biennial systems frequently found themselves similarly pressured (Buck 1936, 18; Toll 1938, 3–4). Between 1927 and 1940, state legislatures held a total of 281 special sessions, with Illinois and Texas leading the way, each having to call 19 of them ("State Legislative Overtime: 1927–1940" 1940). In 1946, 17 states held special sessions, with California, Illinois, Michigan, and New Jersey each needing two special sessions, Arizona three special sessions, and Ohio four special sessions (Caldwell 1947, 283). A Washington state lawmaker from that era later admitted, "We virtually had annual sessions. We got to the point where we were having special sessions every year" (Kilgannon 2005, 366). Similarly, an Idaho newspaper commented that its state's "present system . . . has amounted in recent years to the ordained biennial sessions plus 'regular' special sessions" (*Lewiston Morning Tribune* 1949).

Legislative scholars had long been aware of these problems, and they began articulating arguments in favor of returning to annual meetings. As early as 1914 one reported, "Holding sessions as a rule only biennially, these bodies are under great pressure for legislation because of the infrequency of meetings" (Jones 1914, 196). A few years later another concluded that biennial sessions had "proved absolutely ineffective," adding, "An annual session not only permits the more timely consideration of legislation that is actually urgent, but makes it easier to defer partially considered measures until the following session" (Barrows 1917, 139). Later, the growth in public demands for governmental services was explicitly linked to this line of argument. A report by a Texas legislative agency observed, "Another reason put forward in favor of annual sessions is that state governments have developed in size and complexity sufficient to justify, if not require, annual supervision" (Texas Legislative Coun. 1956, 19). An analysis by the Council of State Governments' Committee on Legislative Processes and Procedures also pursued this line of argument: "Legislatures cannot properly fulfill their important functions without adequate time to dispose of questions before them. . . . The volume and complexity of legislative business has constantly increased, and constitutional or statutory measures which prevent the legislature from fulfilling its proper function cannot be held to be in the public interest" (Council of State Governments 1948, 4). Additional arguments against biennial sessions surfaced. Perhaps the most novel was advanced by the Legislative Council of Connecticut, which reported, "The worst aspect of the biennial session is that it encourages the expansion of executive power" (Perkins 1946, 514). There is evidence that a desire to reduce gubernatorial clout prompted some lawmakers to seek annual sessions (Kilgannon 2005, 367; *News and Courier* 1941; Seeberger 1997, 11). By the second half of the twentieth century these various rationales proved persuasive, and most state legislatures shifted to meeting annually.

As with many state legislative trends, however, the return to annual sessions was neither universal nor irreversible. In 1958, 59 percent of Nevada voters approved a constitutional amendment to switch to annual sessions. The regularly scheduled session in 1959 proved productive, but the 1960 session—the first annual meeting—produced little in the way of legislation. News reports highlighting this failure tipped public opinion against annual meetings, and later that year 58 percent of voters approved an amendment to revert to biennial sessions (Driggs and Goodall 1996, 79–80). Similarly, within two years after Montana's 1972 constitution established annual legislative sessions, the voters passed a referendum returning to biennial sessions, a decision they reaffirmed in 1982 and 1988 (Rosenthal 1996, 192).

Changes in Pay Mechanisms

Legislative pay was low during the nineteenth century, and by early in the twentieth century it was seen as a serious problem in many states. The arguments given for needing higher salaries, however, were basically the same ones that had been advanced ever since the issue was first raised in the 1630s (see chapter 2). A 1904 *Atlantic Monthly* article complained, "We do not pay our legislators a living wage, certainly not a wage that can attract ability" (Orth 1904, 738). A few years later a constitutional scholar agreed with that sentiment, noting, "The per diem amount paid is often barely sufficient for expenses at a cheap hotel and must be eked out from other sources of income" (Dealey 1907, 46). Those themes were picked up by political scientists who protested that legislators were "paid such a [stingy] salary that many able men who would otherwise be willing to serve cannot afford to do so" and that many "find it impossible to remain in public office because of the financial losses involved" (Shumate 1938, 196; Toll 1938, 1).

Some observers tied low pay to corruption. One claimed, "Small salaries mean that competent men must make sacrifices in order to serve their states, while dishonest men are subjected to the constant temptation to supplement their salaries by accepting money for serving special interests" (Shuler 1922, 106). The *New York Times* concurred, arguing, "Competence demands a competency. You cannot expect much from a man who gets $5 a day except subservience to the interests making it possible for him to serve the State at so [meager] a stipend" (*NYT* 1931). In Texas, the $5 per diem was thought to make lawmakers easy prey for lobbyists: "Because of this pittance, many members eagerly accepted standard-of-living gifts . . . in the form of free hotel lodging, meals and liquor, prostitutes, parties at the night spots on Congress Avenue, and railroad passes" (Steinberg 1975, 17). Austin lobbyists came to refer to an important measure as a "three B bill," meaning they had to ply low-paid legislators with "beefsteak, bourbon, and blondes" to get it passed (Vclic 1953b, 39).

In response to these sorts of problems reform advocates campaigned for both higher wages and replacing per diems with annual salaries (Buck 1936, 39). Calling for "fair living salaries," one newspaper asserted, "Arkansas needs the highest type of men" in its legislature and that "it is universally recognized that annual salaries are preferable . . . to per diem allowances" (*Journal-Advance* 1918). Such sentiments met some resistance, much of it rooted in the same concerns echoed over the centuries. Some critics cited the cost to state budgets. This was a potent appeal during the Depression, and legislatures occasionally responded with salary cuts (e.g., *NYT* 1933; Sullivan 1933). In vetoing a legislative pay raise a Minnesota governor even harkened back to colonial-era rationales. After acknowledging that lawmakers were underpaid for their services, he argued that they entered into legislative service out of a sense of public duty or honor, therefore it was "better not to put the matter on a purely money basis" (*NYT* 1929).

By midcentury, organized efforts to raise legislative pay emerged. In 1948, the Council of State Governments' Committee on Legislative Processes and Procedures asserted, "From the viewpoint of good public service the compensation of state legislators is now too low. Annual salaries sufficient to permit competent persons to [serve] in legislatures without financial sacrifice should be provided by statute" (Council of State Governments 1948, 5). The same concerns were registered a few years later by the American Political Science Association's Committee on American Legislatures, which reported, "salaries have been inadequate in most cases, and few men have been able to afford the sacrifice for many sessions" (Zeller 1954, 76). The Texas Legislative Council made a detailed analysis to substantiate these sorts of claims. They estimated that the cost of housing, meals, and travel consumed $1,785 of a Texas lawmaker's $3,000 salary. The average lost income from a member's regular occupation was calculated to be another $1,050. Once expenses associated with official activities during the period between sessions were added, serving in the legislature actually cost legislators money (Texas Legislative Coun. 1956, 42). These were not sterile calculations. A Washington lawmaker during this era who was also an educator recalled, "I lost money when I was a legislator because I took 180th out for every teaching day I was gone" (Boswell 1999, 56).

Over time these sorts of complaints accumulated, and many states responded by altering their legislative pay structures. As shown in table 7.2, during the midpart of the twentieth century many states shifted away from relying on per diem payments in favor of offering a set salary. This change was associated with an increase in the amount of money paid legislators for their service in many states. In South Dakota legislative pay had been left unchanged at $5.00 a day from 1889 to 1946. At that point, the state's voters passed a constitutional amendment to allow the legislature to set its own

TABLE 7.2. Annual Pay versus Per Diems in State Legislatures over the Twentieth Century

	1907	1918	1931	1960	1999	2009
Annual or biennial salary	12	21	22	31	42	42
Per diem or weekly	33	27	26	19	8	8
Total number of states	45	48	48	50	50	50

Source: 1907, *Off. Man. of the St. of Mo.* (1907, 489); 1918, *Off. Man. of the St. of Mo.* (1917, 580); 1931, Schumacker 1931, 10; 1960, *Book of the States 1960–61*, 38–39; 1999, *Book of the States 1998–99*, 80–81; 2009, *Book of the States 2009*, 99–101.

salary. They were encouraged to support the measure by a newspaper ad that said, "Suppose there was a law by which a South Dakota farmer had to pay his help at the same scale of wages his father or grandfather paid in 1889. Such a law would, of course, be absurd. Yet that is the way the state of South Dakota has had to do business." The following year lawmakers took advantage of the opportunity to set their wages and more than doubled their pay (South Dakota Legislative Research Coun. 1998, 2–4). At the time the South Dakota legislature was limited to meeting every other year for a maximum of 100 days. This gave them a salary of $500 for a biennium. In 1947 they set their salary at $1,050 for two years. The salary grab was not as egregious as it might appear; lawmakers simultaneously abolished their $200 expense account.

Changes in Membership Stability

Typically, it was hoped that higher pay would encourage state lawmakers to serve for more terms (e.g., Worsnop 1976). Perhaps it was to be expected then that as pay improved over the course of the twentieth century, state legislative memberships became more stable with turnover rates falling substantially from the 1930s through the 1980s. They then leveled off or rose slightly in the 1990s and the first decade of the twenty-first century (Burns et al. 2008, 232–35; Moncrief, Niemi, and Powell 2004; Ray 1974; Shin and Jackson 1979; Squire and Moncrief 2010, 63–64). The data presented in figure 7.1, which shows the percent new members in the Virginia House from 1900 to 2004, is illustrative of the general trend found across most of the states.[6] Declines in turnover rates had important consequences for legislative organization. For example, standing committee membership retention rates increased as chamber turnover rates decreased, as did tenure in top legislative leadership posts (Squire 1992c; Squire et al. 2005; Squire and Moncrief 2010, 132–34).

Modern state legislatures suffer two unusual sources of turnover. Some legislatures are considered springboard bodies because members have exceptional opportunities to use their current position to move to higher elective office (Squire 1988a, 1988b, 1992a; Squire and Moncrief 2010, 149–53). Turnover in these chambers is higher than might be expected because members regularly seize the opportunity to move up. Being a springboard has consequences for legislative organization, with seniority mattering less and committee memberships being more fluid (Squire 1988a, 1988b).

The other distinctive source of turnover is a more obvious one: term

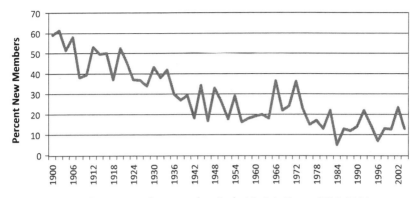

Fig. 7.1. Percentage of new members in the Virginia House, 1900–2004

limits. Term limits were a reaction against a trend toward greater member-ship stability or careerism. The uptick in turnover rates in the 1990s and the first decade of the twenty-first century is the result of term limits in a few states forcing out members who would otherwise continue to serve. Term limits have not changed the sort of person who gets elected to state legislatures, but they have reordered policy priorities and have increased the influence of the executive branch relative to legislative leaders in policy making (Carey, Niemi and Powell 1998; Kurtz, Cain, and Niemi 2007). Term limits have turned several legislatures into springboard bodies, orga-nized to meet the needs of ambitious politicians en route to other offices (Powell 2000; Squire and Moncrief 2010, 149–53). And they have tended to deflate organizational and behavioral aspects of legislative professional-ization (Kousser 2005).

Changes in Facilities

During the nineteenth century, state legislatures acquired buildings dedi-cated to their use. After 1900, some of those facilities were replaced, while others were renovated and expanded. Some states had to build new capitols because fires continued to consume them. Wisconsin's first capitol largely burned to the ground in 1904 (*NYT* 1904). In 1911, a lightning strike dur-ing a freak winter thunderstorm ignited Missouri's second permanent state-house. Lawmakers joined firefighters in the unsuccessful effort to save the building (*NYT* 1911a). North Dakota's original capitol succumbed to flames in 1930 (*NYT* 1930). Oregon's went up in smoke in 1935 (*NYT* 1935). West Virginia suffered twice. In 1921, only the brick shell of its existing statehouse remained following a massive fire (*NYT* 1921). A few years later, the temporary capitol being used while a new permanent facility was under construction also burned to the ground (*NYT* 1927).[7] All of these states constructed new capitols that provided lawmakers with more space.

In states where fire did not force the issue, decisions had to be made as to whether existing capitols could be remodeled to meet needs or if new facilities were required. Virginia opted for the former, adding two wings housing new legislative chambers in 1906. Upon completion of the project, the governor told lawmakers, "The improvement and enlargement of the Capitol will give you facilities for work never enjoyed by your predecessors" (*Jour. of the H. of Dels. of the St. of Va.* 1906, 22–23). A number of other states followed a similar path by expanding existing capitols (Goodsell 2001, 60–61). Repurposing of space sufficed to meet new demands in some capitols. Occasionally this happened after a considerable time lag: A women's restroom was only built off the Rhode Island House chamber in 2007–84 years after the first female representative was elected (Gudrais, Gregg, and Peoples 2007). But not all remodeling efforts were sufficient to meet the legislature's growing space requirements. Florida's 1840s capitol was renovated and expanded several times during the first half of the twentieth century, but in the 1970s the state replaced it with a much larger modern facility (Warner 1983).

Several other states also chose to build new capitols. In a few cases, decrepit conditions compelled the decision. While Arkansas lawmakers debated whether to push ahead with a new statehouse in 1899, a rain-soaked plaster ceiling in the senate chamber collapsed, injuring several solons and settling the issue (Treon 1972, 100–101). Idaho built a new capitol during the first decade of the twentieth century in part because legislators were inconvenienced by the old capitol's lack of indoor plumbing (Idaho Capitol Commission n.d.). Some states built new facilities because the old ones were too cramped and outmoded. In 1891 a Minnesota senator described the second permanent capitol then in use.

> The offices were all crowded . . . Every nook and cranny in the building was converted into a closet for storage of documents or a place for another desk. The ventilation, if there was any, was most imperfect. During the session seats were constantly vacant in each chamber, because of the illness of members suffering from the noxious air. The secretary of

the State Board of Health was called in to test the quality of the air in the senate chamber, and he pronounced it utterly unfit for human beings to breathe. For legislation to be well considered and carefully discussed under such conditions was wellnigh impossible. (Dean 1908, 22–23)

Lawmakers eventually agreed to build a larger capitol. Novel motives for new statehouses emerged elsewhere. In Louisiana, Governor Huey Long successfully pushed for a grand new capitol to improve the state's image. His cause was helped when one of his opponents complained that the roof of the existing statehouse leaked on his House desk (Jolly and Calhoun 1980, 15; Williams 1981, 427–28). There were allegations that Long had had a hole drilled in the ceiling to cause the problem (Goodsell 2001, 71–72).

In general, the new state capitols were impressive in their size and opulence (e.g., *NYT* 1932; Steffensen 2002). They provided more space for lawmakers to conduct their business, with more committee meeting rooms and, in some cases, member offices. Legislatures in Nevada and North Carolina even got their own buildings, separate from the capitol. But there were deviations from the pattern. Alaska's capitol in Juneau is a converted federal office building. And when Alabama's capitol was renovated during the 1980s the legislature was permanently exiled to a renovated state highway administration building.

Changes in Parliamentary Rules

By the beginning of the twentieth century parliamentary rules in most chambers were reasonably complex and sophisticated. They also tended to be stable; as one scholar noted, "In the great majority of states, the legislative rules adopted by each house persist through many years without much revision" (Buck 1936, 9). They were not as sophisticated or complex as those used in Congress: "Curiously enough though, our States are the units in which the greatest willingness has been shown to try experiments in the field of legislation proper, they have recast legislative procedure to a much less degree than has congress" (Jones 1914, 191). Thus rule development in the states was incremental; legislators usually only fixed parliamentary problems as they cropped up. Revisions that were made were geared toward increasing legislative efficiency. A leading state legislative parliamentarian wrote, "During recent years a number of changes have occurred in parliamentary law. . . . Most of these changes are of a type which expedite business or curtail debate" (Mason 1938, 152).

Overall, state legislative rule development since 1900 has been motivated as much by a need to manage workloads as by a desire to advance the goals of the majority party. In 1909, for example, the South Carolina House implemented a consent calendar to expedite the handling of noncontroversial legislation, the same year the innovation was adopted by the U.S. House. Many state legislative chambers followed suit, particularly after the reform movement of the 1960s touted the calendar's benefits. Eventually, 65 of the 99 state legislative chambers employed a consent calendar, with those operating under tighter time constraints being more likely to adopt one than those with unlimited sessions (Tucker 2005).

Workload issues drove the Virginia General Assembly to allow bill prefiling prior to a session and to impose bill introduction limits. Because the legislature operates under fairly strict time constraints, prefiling was instituted to allow lawmakers to begin processing legislative proposals at a session's commencement. The advent of prefiling did not reduce the number of bills introduced, but it did expedite their consideration. Reductions in the number of bills were produced through a series of progressively stricter limitations on introductions (Austin 2010). The vast majority of state legislative chambers now allow for prefiling. About a quarter limit the number of bills a member may introduce.[8] Efficiency concerns have driven these reforms.

Clearly, the interests of political parties also influence rule development. The shift in the South to two-party chambers from one-party chambers has been accompanied by changes in leadership structures, committee assignment procedures, and rules (Hamm and Harmel 1993; Harmel 1986). Procedural rights granted to the minority parties have generally expanded as the size of the majority party increased, because the majority enjoyed the freedom to be more generous (Martorano 2004). Discharge petition rules have changed for partisan reasons. In 2004, the Mississippi House voted along party lines to alter the required vote for discharging a bill to two-thirds of those present and voting from a majority of those present and voting. The change was prompted by the majority Democrats' concern that under the old rules the minority Republicans would successfully force two controversial bills out of committee (Kanengiser 2004). And following the GOP takeover of the Georgia House in 2005 the party pushed through a rule allowing the majority party leadership to directly shape committee decisions by giving the speaker the right to appoint an unspecified number of "hawks"; majority party lawmakers empowered to participate as full voting members on any standing committee at any point in the legislative process (Tharpe, Badertscher, and Jacobs 2005). So in a number of instances state legislative rules have been changed to enhance the majority party's ability to produce its preferred outcomes.

Of course, unlike the situation in Congress, state legislative rules are not set by state legislators alone. Voters can play a direct role through the initiative process in the states that allow for one. Thus among the measures adopted by Colorado voters in 1918 was an amendment that reduced the time period during which bills could be introduced from the first 30 to the first 15 days of the session (Kettleborough 1919, 431–32). In 1988, Colorado voters again interceded in parliamentary matters by passing the GAVEL (Give a Vote to Every Legislator) amendment. GAVEL requires that every bill referred to a committee be brought up for a committee vote and that all bills reported by committee go to the floor, and it prohibited party caucuses from taking binding votes (Strayer 2000, 88, 109, 231). Voter interventions in the state legislative process are not unusual.

State constitutions also establish legislative procedures to a far greater degree than does the U.S. Constitution for Congress. An analysis of the current Mississippi constitution identifies 27 sections specifying rules of procedures. Among the procedural details set in the constitution are section 67, "No new bill shall be introduced into either house of the Legislature during the last three (3) days of the session," and section 74, "No bill shall become a law until it shall have been referred to a committee of each house and returned therefrom with a recommendation in writing" (Mississippi Leg., n.d.). Such specificity is not unusual. Missouri's constitution (Article III, section 22) directs that a bill can be discharged from a committee on the vote of one-third of the members of either house. These sorts of procedural details are established at a level well beyond the machinations of legislative parties.

Superficially, in the aggregate, state legislative rule development over the last hundred years or so has been limited. The 84 rules used by the California Assembly in 1889 only grew to 121 rules by 2009. Over that same time period, the number of rules in Missouri's House grew to 119 from 91, in the Ohio House to 124 from 100, in the West Virginia House to 143 from 100, and in the Wisconsin Assembly to 99 from 96. These raw numbers, however, mask considerable evolution and refinement. Modern rules are far more detailed and complicated than were the rules a hundred years ago. And, of course, rules have changed to reflect new concerns that have emerged over time. By 2009, for example, the California Assembly incorporated rules prohibiting cell phone and text messaging use on the floor and requiring every employee to take courses on ethics and sexual harassment prevention.

There are two major points to keep in mind regarding the development of state legislative procedural rules since the end of the institutionalization era. First, as mentioned above, they usually changed only slowly and incrementally. Evidence of this is supplied by Hamm, Hedlund, and Martorano's (2006) detailed study of rules governing state legislative standing committees over the twentieth century. They examined the rules governing committee independence, openness, capacity to gather information, ability to protect its position on the floor, right to initiate legislation, and gatekeeping powers. On each of these six dimensions they scored the rules for each chamber in 33 states over four time periods, 1909–29, 1939–59, 1969–79, and 1989–99. In 27 percent of these four time period comparisons, the coding of the rules did not change at all, and in another 12 percent only one of the four scores changed. Thus, in 39 percent of the comparisons of rules governing state legislative standing committees over the period from 1909 to 1999, nothing, or very little, changed. This indicates considerable stability.

Second, although rules have universally become more detailed and complex over time, differences in the specific rules adopted have evolved. Limitations on debate have varied across the states. By 1950, state lawmakers could speak twice on an issue without leave in most chambers, but they could speak only once in several houses and three times in the Maine senate. Interestingly, these limitations did not always develop as one might predict: Members of the Indiana and Missouri senates were limited to speaking once without leave, while colleagues in their states' much larger lower houses could speak twice without leave. How long members were allowed to speak also varied by chamber. Senators in Colorado could speak for two hours, while senators in Wyoming were kept to five minutes. Rules on cutting off debate differed. Moving the previous question was authorized in 46 of the 48 lower houses, while the rules were silent on the issue in the other two. In 36 senates the previous question could be moved, but the rules were silent on the matter in 10 chambers, and the previous question was explicitly prohibited in 2 chambers. At the same time an explicit cloture rule existed in 12 upper houses and 10 lower houses (Zeller 1954, 112–13). The details of other rules, of course, also came to differ across the states. Although most legislatures imposed some variant of a single subject rule, the way the rule was interpreted varied widely (Gilbert 2006). Similarly, the rules governing the discharge of legislation from committees evolved very differently across the states (Dodds 1918, 52–56; Squire and Hamm 2005, 124–26; Zeller 1954, 103–4, 198).

With all of these differences in details, there have been a few areas of convergence. The most notable is the parliamentary manual used to supplement legislative rules. By 2009 the vast majority of state lower houses used *Mason's Manual of Legislative Procedure*, a volume first compiled in 1931 for the California Senate and designed specifically for state legislatures. But some differences still remained, with several chambers opting to rely instead on *Jefferson's Manual*, a few others on the U.S. House rules, and one each *Reed's Rules* or *Robert's Rules*.

There is one final observation to make. Although state legislatures came to operate using well-codified rules and procedures, they did not necessarily evolve into staid and decorous bodies. For instance, quorum requirements, among the oldest of all parliamentary rules, continued to be exploited for partisan purposes, occasionally in notorious fashion. A sufficient number of Tennessee House members fled to Alabama in 1911 and again in 1920 to prevent a quorum (Luce 1922, 35–36). In 1924, a dispute in the Rhode Island Senate between the minority Democrats and the majority Republicans led to an all-night session. Tensions were so high that the Democratic lieutenant governor feared to vacate his seat as the presiding officer because it might give the Republicans a chance to take control of the floor. Consequently, as the battle trudged on into the morning hours he summoned a barber to the podium to give him a shave so he would not have to leave his chair. GOP senators were desperate to end the session, but they could not get recognized by the lieutenant governor. The meeting was finally brought to an abrupt conclusion when gas fumes generated by a lit saturated newspaper—characterized in the press as a "gas bomb"—filled the chamber. Save for one member the Republicans, who alleged that the Democrats had packed the public gallery with "well-known thugs" to intimidate them, fled to Massachusetts where they were beyond the lieutenant governor's legal reach. They stayed there for the rest of the legislative session. Democrats were prevented from pursuing their policy agenda because the remaining GOP senator was available to raise a parliamentary point that a quorum was not present (Hubbard 1924; *NYT* 1924). These incidents presaged more recent episodes in Texas in 2003, when first House Democrats fled to Oklahoma and then Senate Democrats removed to New Mexico in an ultimately futile attempt to prevent Republicans from passing a partisan redistricting plan, and Wisconsin and Indiana in 2011 where Democratic senators in the former and Democratic representatives in the latter left for Illinois.

Boorish behavior also did not disappear. During a contentious 1981 debate in the Illinois Senate, a member addressed the presiding officer as "You son of a bitch" and then "threw aside his red leather chair, ripped the microphone from his desk and stormed toward [him] with all deliberate speed. A colleague, however, stepped in [the senator's] path and slugged him. The pair tussled for several moments before they were pulled apart." The story's kicker was, "It was the first time that violence had marred the orderly processes of the Illinois legislature since . . . ten days earlier, when armed officers were called in to break up a brawl on the floor of the house" (Kelly 1981, 12). In 2007, an Alabama senator called a colleague a "son of a bitch" on the chamber floor and in return got punched in the head. The scuffle was recorded by public television, and clips of the assault were immortalized on YouTube. As one senator noted, "It's certainly a black eye on the Legislature and the Senate in particular" (*Huntsville Times* 2007).

Even the use of tobacco on the chamber floor continued to be sorted out. By the early twenty-first century, at least one house in 42 states prohibited smoking (O'Donnell 2006). But these rules could be manipulated to serve different purposes. The Nevada Assembly prohibited smoking as early as 1873. The rule was, however, frequently waived. When the first women were elected to the body between 1919 and 1929, they often offered the waiver, not because they were comfortable with smoking but rather as a way to gain acceptance from their male colleagues (Bennett 2010, 93, 116).

Changes in Standing Committee Systems

Like complex parliamentary rules, standing committee systems became entrenched during the nineteenth century. And like rules, since then committee systems have been refined and reformed. As discussed in chapter 6, by the end of the 1800s standing committee systems in most states were bloated. Early in the twentieth century, a leading politics text commented, "In most state legislative bodies there are too many committees, and the committees are too large" (Dodd 1922, 197). There were some extreme examples: In 1915 the 32-member Michigan Senate had 65 standing committees, 14 of which dealt primarily with education issues (*Jour. of the Sen. of the St. of Mich.* 1915, 10–11). Lawmakers could be greatly burdened by committee service; in 1919 one Illinois senator had 28 standing committee assignments. The number of standing committees in a chamber was usually driven more by internal politics than by workload demands. In the Illinois Senate, the majority-party Republicans created as many standing committees as members in their caucus so that each GOP senator could be a committee chair. As their caucus grew, so did the number of standing committees (Dodd 1922, 198). This partisan dynamic was not confined to Illinois or to Republicans. Explaining the large number of standing committees in the Washington legislature at midcentury, a lawmaker recalled, "And you see how we got into this situation was the Democrats always took care of their members. Somebody would say, 'Boy! I don't have a committee chairmanship,' so they'd establish a new committee and make him the chairman" (Kilgannon 2005, 401). Occasionally the rules themselves caused the growth in the number of standing committees. From 1845 to 1925 the Florida House operated under a mandate that no more than nine members could serve on a particular committee. As new counties were created and the number of House seats expanded, the body was forced to create more committees to accommodate the growing number of lawmakers (Morris 1982, 128).

The problem got to the point that "in most state legislatures . . . many committees are useless and unnecessary" (Dodd 1922, 198). In 1931 the 95-member Florida House had 76 standing committees. Of those standing committees, 21 never had any bills referred to them, and another 7 had only one bill referred (Morris 1982, 128–29). This reality eventually forced most chambers to reduce their number of committees in the name of efficiency. Such reform was initially pursued in Wisconsin early in the twentieth century, and most other state legislative chambers followed suit over the next several decades (Council of State Governments 1948, 9–10; Dodds 1918, 41; Morris 1982, 128–30; Perkins 1946, 518–19; Zeller 1954, 98–99). The rationale for the reduction was practical: "to facilitate their functioning and thereby expedite the whole legislative process" (Perkins 1946, 518–19).

Thus, over the last century the number of standing committees has dropped in many chambers while increasing only slightly in a few others. The California Assembly, which had 45 standing committees in 1889, used 30 standing committees in 2009. In Ohio the number of committees dropped to 27 in 2009 from 42 in 1889. But in Missouri, the number of standing committees in the House grew to 42 in 2009 from 39 in 1889, and in West Virginia the number increased to 27 in 2009 from 21 in 1889.

From an evolutionary perspective there are two important aspects of standing committee system development to note. First, stark differences in the details of standing committee systems arose across the states. Most obviously, some chambers came to have many standing committees—in 2009 the Illinois House had 57—while other chambers evolved to have very few—in 2009 the Alaska, Maryland, and Rhode Island houses each had 9.[9] Other evolutionary deviations occurred across the states, perhaps most notably the powerful joint committee systems in Connecticut, Maine, and Massachusetts (Dodds 1918, 49–50; Zeller 1954, 256–61). And the procedures used to place lawmakers on committees have evolved differently across the states: many give appointment powers to the speaker, president, or other party leader, some allow a committee to make assignments, a few use chamber elections, party or district caucuses, or some form of a seniority rule (Squire and Moncrief 2010, 144–47).

Second, the powers granted standing committees evolved to vary substantially across legislative chambers. An extensive survey in the 1980s found that committees were central decision makers in 15 state legislative chambers, shared power with party leaders or caucuses in 66 chambers, and were weak in 18 chambers (Francis 1985). Similarly, the level of autonomy enjoyed by standing committees developed differently across state legislative chambers (Martorano 2006). And, of course, the power granted to a particular committee could change over time. In the New York Assembly a powerful Rules Committee emerged late in the nineteenth century. Originally intended to control the flow of legislation to the floor over only the final few days of a session, it slowly accrued power so that by 1911 the committee controlled legislation from April to October (Dodds 1918, 59–61; Jones 1914, 195). Decades later it was still considered by far the most powerful committee in the Assembly (Hevesi 1975, 20–22; Zimmerman 1981, 133).

Professionalization and the Evolution of State Legislatures since 1900

During the nineteenth century, the evolution of American legislatures was marked by an increase in the internal organizational complexity of the bodies, notably in the development of procedural rules and standing committees. While both rules and standing committee systems continued to change over the course of the twentieth century, the most prominent evolutionary development in state legislatures was their professionalization. In most states member pay increased, sessions became longer, and staff resources improved. These are the three characteristics commonly associated with legislative professionalization (Citizens Conference on State Legislatures 1971; Grumm 1971; King 2000; Moncrief 1988, 54–55; Squire 1988a, 1988b, 1992a, 1992b, 2000, 2007; Squire and Hamm 2005). They are pursued to increase the organizations' capacity to generate and digest information and are intended to make them more capable policymakers along the lines of the modern U.S. Congress.

The Coming of Legislative Professionalization

Congress began professionalizing roughly during the first decade of the twentieth century. Congressional pay was set at $5,000 from 1873 until 1907, at which time it was raised to $7,500. From that point on, salary adjustments (almost always increases) occurred with much greater frequency (Dwyer 2004). Congress verged on becoming a year-round institution by 1910 (Galloway 1961, 122). The 61st Congress (1909–11) was in session for 435 days, or an average of 217 days a year, a substantial figure although less than the 280 days or more spent in session in more recent decades (Congressional Quarterly 1993, 483–87; Ornstein, Mann, and Malbin 2000, 154–57). And by the beginning of the twentieth century all congressional committees had full-time staff and members had personal staff—albeit few in numbers (Fox and Hammond 1977, 15; Malbin 1980, 11; Rogers 1941, 3). Thus by 1910 the U.S. Congress was a professionalized legislature (Price 1975).

The Status of State Legislative Professionalization in 1910

If Congress was professionalized by the first decade of the twentieth century, what was the status of state legislatures in comparison? As institutions, state legislatures were held in low regard. An *Atlantic Monthly* article proclaimed, "The utterances of the press, the opinions of publicists and scholars, and the sentiments of the street and the market-place are quite at one in the denunciation of the legislature" (Orth 1904, 728). Indeed, in 1911 the California Assembly's chaplain began the year's session by beseeching the assembled members to "give us a square deal, for Christ's sake" (Mowry 1963, 139).

Perhaps it is no surprise, then, that state legislators began to look to Congress as a model to emulate. According to a leading text at the time, the state legislatures "have naturally, as the Federal Legislature has become more and more important, been profoundly influenced by the methods of procedure there evolved" (Reinsch 1907, 162). Around the same time, a newspaper wondered whether New York lawmakers would "fall in line with the Congressmen who voted themselves $7,500 a year last session" (*NYT* 1907). No state commanded the financial resources necessary to develop a legislature matching Congress in salary or staff. State legislatures could, however, aspire to become more like Congress and in doing so create greater capacity to meet the demands being made on them.

Table 7.3 offers a comparative measure of legislative professionalization in 1910, combining member pay, legislative days in session, and legislative staff in an index with Congress as the baseline. At this point in time, annual state legislative salaries lagged far behind the $7,500 paid to members of Congress (Squire and Hamm 2005, 72). The highest state legislative salary was $1,500 in New York; the lowest was $50 in Alabama with its quadrennial sessions. The mean annual salary across the states was just under $250, representing slightly more than 3 percent of congressional pay.

Almost no state legislature met for very long compared to Congress.[10] The U.S. Constitution requires Congress meet every year, and it places no limits on session length. The situation at the state level in 1910 was very different. As noted above, during the first decade of the twentieth century few states had annual sessions. In addition, most states imposed strict limits on the number of days their sessions could last. Given these constraints the mean number of annual days in session for state legislatures was only 28, compared to over 200 days for Congress.

In terms of staff resources, no state legislature in 1910 provided staff for individual lawmakers, and only limited staff was provided for committees, leaving them well behind Congress on both dimensions (Squire and Hamm 2005, 76). But some states had developed institutional staff resources, something that Congress did not enjoy. As noted in chapter 6, the New York State Library in 1890 was the first organization to routinely provide lawmakers reference assistance. In 1901 the Wisconsin Free Library Commission established a legislative reference collection, consisting of books that remained in the capitol after the commission moved to a new building. Charles McCarthy, a recent University of Wisconsin Ph.D. in history, was hired as a document cataloger to run the small library. As an undergraduate at Brown, McCarthy had been a star football player. A few years later he replaced Glenn "Pop" Warner as the University of Georgia's head coach and led the team to two winning seasons. Once McCarthy took over the reference library on his own initiative he began providing research

TABLE 7.3. State Legislative Professionalization, 1910

State[a]	Existence of a Legislative Reference Bureau	Existence of Legislative Reference in State Library or State Historical Department	Member Pay, Days in Session, and Reference Staff Compared to Congress
Wisconsin	X		0.43
Michigan	X		0.40
Pennsylvania	X		0.40
Iowa	X		0.40
Indiana	X		0.38
South Dakota	X		0.38
Montana	X		0.37
Kansas	X		0.37
Alabama	X		0.35
Connecticut		X	0.25
California		X	0.23
Virginia		X	0.21
Washington		X	0.21
Oregon		X	0.19
Illinois			0.09
Missouri			0.08
Ohio			0.07
Misssissippi			0.07
Tennessee			0.06
Minnesota			0.06
Colorado			0.06
Vermont			0.06
New Hampshire			0.06
Maine			0.05
Oklahoma			0.05
North Carolina			0.05
Delaware			0.05
Florida			0.04
Nevada			0.04
Idaho			0.04
Georgia			0.04
Utah			0.04
South Carolina			0.03
West Virginia			0.03
Wyoming			0.03
Mean			0.16
Median			0.07

Source: Member pay calculated from *Off. Man. of Ky.* 1910, 141; legislative reference services from Cleland 1910, 219; days in session from data collected by Keith Hamm and Ronald Hedlund; congressional days in session calculated from *Congressional Quarterly* 1993; and congressional pay from Dwyer 2004.

[a]Data on days in session are not available for 13 states.

assistance to legislators. In 1903 appreciative lawmakers appropriated funds to support his efforts. McCarthy's unit quickly evolved into the Legislative Reference Bureau (Fitzpatrick 1944, 40–47; Healey 2007, 38–39; McCarthy 1911; Rothstein 1990, 406–8; Weber 1919, 350). It became a national model, and by 1910, 19 states had created legislative reference services of some sort (Cleland 1910; Weber 1919). Even Congress followed Wisconsin's lead by establishing the Legislative Reference Service (now called the Congressional Research Service) in 1914. The provision of reference services was promoted as an efficient way to compensate for the inexperience of most legislators (Ray 1917, 574–76).

Columns one and two of table 7.3 identify the states that either had a clearly identifiable legislative reference unit or provided such services as part of a state library or state historical department. As a crude estimate of staff resources, states with legislative reference bureaus were coded 1, meaning the equivalent of institutional staff in Congress, and states providing other reference services .5, or half of what Congress offered. States with no staff resources were coded 0. The final column of table 7.3 gives a rudimentary professionalization measure comparing state legislatures to Congress on pay, time demands, and staff in 1910, with 1 being perfect resemblance and 0 being no resemblance.[11] Staffing resources clearly discriminate in this measure with the most professionalized states being those that had legislative reference bureaus. Overall, a few states posted respectable scores, but most lagged well behind Congress, as suggested by the median score of .07. Conspicuously, almost all the states that topped the rankings were large-population states, with small-population states bringing up the rear.

Wisconsin led the way in regard to another legislative innovation during this time period. In 1917 the Assembly became the first chamber in the country to employ an electronic voting device to capture roll call votes. Developed by a Milwaukee engineer, the machine was intended to make the Assembly a more efficient body. The expectation was that it would soon be deployed in the U.S. House, where it was estimated that two months of time each session was consumed by roll calls ("Congress May Vote with New Time-Saving Machine" 1916; Holmes 1915; "Voting Device for Use in Congress" 1916). A study by the New York legislature found that enough time would be saved to cover the cost of such a system (Buck 1936, 17). The second legislature to adopt the innovation, however, was Iowa in 1921 (Luce 1922, 378). By the late 1940s at least one chamber in 18 states voted electronically (Council of State Governments 1948, 28). The U.S. House did not install an electronic voting system until 1973 (Smith 1989, 27–28), and the U.S. Senate still does not have one.

State Legislative Professionalization from 1935 to 1960

By 1935 state legislatures were coming under increasing public pressure to improve their institutional performance. A 1933 *American Mercury* article was titled "The Clown as Lawmaker," and it castigated state legislatures for not being serious policy-making institutions, saying, "Scientifically re-garded, they have become simply so many auxiliary grand lodges of the tin-pot fraternal orders" (Seagle 1933, 330). A *Literary Digest* article, "Roman Holiday: Do Legislators Play Leap-Frog? Gracious, No! Well Hardly Ever," pushed a similar theme (*Literary Digest* 1937). But concerns about the ability of state legislators to do their jobs were not limited to muckrak-ing journalists. A legislative scholar concurred with their assessments, not-ing, "Almost any layman and some competent political observers and com-mentators, will tell you that our legislatures are filled with 'ward heelers,' 'petty politicians,' and 'yokels' or even worse" (Shumate 1938, 189). Evi-dence for the "even worse" was supplied by an article entitled "Crooks in the Legislatures," written by an anonymous lawmaker under the unimagi-native nom de plume State Senator (1937).

Contrary to the image conveyed by these articles, some institutional improvements had been made over the previous quarter century. By 1935, the mean annual state legislative salary had increased to $495, a substantial rise over 1910: $250 in 1913 dollars was worth $346 in 1935 dollars. Al-though it was an improvement the figure represented just 6 percent of con-gressional pay.[12] A few legislatures were beginning to approximate the time demands of Congress, notably Massachusetts, which had annual sessions that stretched over much of the year. But most were still restricted to meet-ing infrequently and for limited numbers of days.

By the mid-1930s, 42 states had some sort of legislative reference ser-vice (Witte 1938, 139). There are no direct data on the size of state legisla-tive staffs. The best estimate is that that fewer than 500 full-time staff worked for state legislatures in 1935 (Kurtz 2010, 88). There are, however, two indirect measures. The first is the overall cost of the legislature. This captures expenditures related to staff resources, but it confounds them by including legislator pay and whatever other costs a state swept into its legislative budget. The second is a more targeted measure calculating the appropriations to a state's legislative reference bureau or equivalent unit (McDermott 1934).

As can be seen in table 7.4, the professionalization measures for 1935 incorporating the two different measures of staff produce very similar results. (Many states share the same scores because they had the same session limits and paid the same per diems.) Again the states that more closely approximated Congress were among the largest population states, with Massachusetts and New York clearly ahead of the rest. Most state legislatures continued to trail well behind Congress.

From 1935 to 1945 state legislatures lost ground compared to Congress, as shown in the third column of table 7.4. By 1945 the mean annual state legislative salary increased to $605, but that figure again represented just 6 percent of the congressional salary. And although a few legislatures met for a substantial number of days, congressional sessions were far longer than those for most of them. Finally, the overall cost of state legislatures paled in comparison to the cost of Congress, indicating a substantial gap in staff resources. Indeed, there is an anecdotal evidence of backsliding on state legislative staff support: In 1943, the Colorado director of legislative reference had the effort he was to devote to the task cut from "his entire time" to a period of 60 days prior to the session to 30 days after its conclusion (Perkins 1946, 516).

Louder calls for reforms were heard by the 1950s (Teaford 2002, 163–69; Zeller 1954). *Reader's Digest*, for example, ran a series of articles criticizing state legislatures and calling for reforms (Velie 1953a, 1953b, 1953c, 1953d, 1953e). These stories garnered considerable attention. In an extended floor soliloquy, an Iowa representative challenged their claims on corruption. But he allowed that "we need to move in the direction of giving legislators better pay and more time to accomplish the tremendous job that they have before them" (*Jour. of the H. of the Fifty-Fifth GA* 1953, 1536).

States began to respond to such concerns. At roughly the same time Congress was attempting to make itself more efficient, leading a political scientist to counsel, "In some ways, the Congressional Reorganization Act points the way for strengthening and improvement of state legislatures." He specifically cited a need for higher salaries, more frequent sessions, better staff resources, and fewer standing committees (Harris 1947, 143–44, 146). But another scholar noted, "While much attention has been given to the efforts of Congress to improve itself, the activities of the state legislatures which have sought improvements as diligently . . . have gone virtually unnoticed." By his count, during the mid-1940s 28 states engaged in serious studies of the ways they might modernize their legislative structures and procedures (Perkins 1946, 510).

Perhaps not surprisingly, then, between 1945 and 1960 state legislatures made some progress relative to Congress, although the score for 1954 suggests slippage along the way. Overall, member pay and the number of session days both increased in many states between 1946 and 1960 (Fiorina 1994, 313–14). By 1960, the median annual state legislative salary was $1,939, or 9 percent of what members of Congress were paid. State legislatures still met for far fewer days each year than did Congress, but that gap too was narrowing a bit as 19 states held annual sessions. Indeed, a few states actually met for more days (at least on paper) than did Congress.

State spending on legislatures was still a small fraction of what the nation spent on Congress, indicating that staff resources continued to fall far short of the congressional standard. But here too efforts were being made to encourage improvements. In 1948, the Council of State Governments' Committee on Legislative Processes and Procedures recommended that legislative employees be hired on the basis of merit rather than patronage (Council of State Governments 1948, 8). A few years later the American Political Science Association's Committee on American Legislatures went further, issuing a report saying that "a good research and clerical staff is an indispensable aid to the legislature." By this point, clerical staff was provided to most committees in almost every state; only two states provided no such support. Research support was given to committees in most states, about a quarter directly through staff assigned to committees, the rest indirectly through access to legislative or executive agencies or outside contractors. Staff for individual members, however, was sparse; only Florida, Iowa, Missouri, Oregon, Pennsylvania, and Texas provided almost all of their lawmakers with clerical help. Many other states provided members access to a secretarial pool. Office facilities also were greatly limited. No state gave all of its legislators a capitol office, and only Maryland, Missouri, and Texas gave senators their own offices. In another eight states senators shared offices as did lower-house members in five states.[13] The Committee on American Legislatures concluded that the lack of offices for members was "partly . . . a question of cost, partly . . . a space problem" (Zeller 1954, 156–59).

The conditions of service in the Washington legislature in 1953 were typical. According to one lawmaker's recollection, "Your desk was your

TABLE 7.4. State Legislative Professionalization (using cost of legislature), 1935, 1945, 1954, and 1960

State	1935 Rank	1935 Score	1935ᵃ Rank	1935ᵃ Score	1945 Rank	1945 Score	1954 Rank	1954 Score	1960 Rank	1960 Score
Alabama	48	0.052	31	0.116	31	0.065	47	0.030	47	0.038
Arizona	36	0.108	22	0.162	38	0.062	20	0.078	19	0.153
Arkansas	21	0.141	25	0.150	24	0.071	35	0.042	41	0.071
California	14	0.192	8	0.329	12	0.101	5	0.177	8	0.242
Colorado	17	0.169	18	0.188	26	0.069	9	0.120	18	0.154
Connecticut	12	0.192	9	0.278	16	0.087	29	0.054	29	0.109
Delaware	31	0.112	32	0.112	33	0.065	12	0.110	5	0.280
Florida	37	0.108	40	0.104	39	0.061	42	0.035	37	0.075
Georgia	35	0.109	39	0.105	23	0.072	33	0.043	35	0.078
Idaho	41	0.104	41	0.103	42	0.059	41	0.035	36	0.076
Illinois	5	0.294	5	0.387	3	0.201	4	0.182	9	0.221
Indiana	29	0.115	23	0.153	18	0.077	26	0.060	34	0.082
Iowa	22	0.141	13	0.215	20	0.074	23	0.062	20	0.151
Kansas	45	0.087	38	0.107	46	0.049	37	0.040	31	0.104
Kentucky	30	0.112	34	0.109	32	0.065	25	0.060	32	0.089
Louisiana	33	0.112	36	0.109	30	0.066	28	0.057	28	0.115
Maine	27	0.116	33	0.112	19	0.075	30	0.052	27	0.115
Maryland	19	0.159	11	0.242	11	0.116	14	0.103	12	0.177
Massachusetts	1	0.554	1	0.696	1	0.294	1	0.295	1	0.498
Michigan	7	0.243	12	0.234	13	0.093	3	0.189	4	0.281
Minnesota	16	0.172	21	0.165	10	0.117	16	0.090	23	0.135
Mississippi	20	0.150	26	0.146	21	0.074	22	0.075	25	0.117
Missouri	23	0.141	27	0.136	4	0.178	13	0.107	17	0.154
Montana	32	0.112	35	0.109	34	0.065	45	0.034	43	0.061
Nebraska	18	0.165	14	0.197	29	0.067	15	0.094	14	0.158
Nevada	34	0.110	37	0.109	27	0.069	31	0.052	38	0.075
New Hampshire	11	0.196	17	0.192	15	0.091	32	0.047	24	0.127
New Jersey	2	0.428	3	0.555	9	0.130	11	0.111	7	0.256
New Mexico	43	0.104	41	0.103	36	0.064	44	0.034	44	0.061
New York	3	0.353	2	0.694	2	0.203	2	0.231	3	0.282
North Carolina	15	0.179	16	0.192	45	0.050	21	0.078	16	0.154

North Dakota	40	0.105	41	0.103	41	0.060	46	0.031	46	0.057
Ohio	13	0.192	19	0.172	6	0.164	6	0.154	10	0.203
Oklahoma	24	0.138	28	0.134	37	0.063	17	0.086	21	0.148
Oregon	47	0.069	48	0.067	44	0.052	24	0.062	26	0.115
Pennsylvania	8	0.220	6	0.345	8	0.135	8	0.136	6	0.265
Rhode Island	9	0.208	10	0.265	17	0.078	18	0.082	13	0.177
South Carolina	4	0.316	7	0.330	7	0.140	10	0.113	11	0.196
South Dakota	39	0.105	41	0.103	43	0.059	38	0.040	42	0.069
Tennessee	25	0.131	29	0.129	48	0.029	43	0.034	39	0.074
Texas	10	0.197	15	0.194	14	0.092	19	0.082	22	0.143
Utah	44	0.103	46	0.102	35	0.064	39	0.040	45	0.059
Vermont	42	0.104	20	0.167	40	0.061	40	0.038	15	0.157
Virginia	28	0.115	24	0.151	28	0.068	34	0.042	33	0.083
Washington	38	0.106	41	0.103	25	0.070	27	0.060	40	0.071
West Virginia	26	0.124	30	0.117	22	0.072	36	0.041	30	0.104
Wisconsin	6	0.283	4	0.435	5	0.166	7	0.139	2	0.295
Wyoming	46	0.074	47	0.073	47	0.044	48	0.024	48	0.038
Mean		0.165		0.200		0.091		0.083		0.145
Median		0.135		0.151		0.071		0.061		0.122

Source: 1935, Member pay, days in session, and cost of legislature calculated from Book of the States 1935, cost of legislative reference services, McDermott 1934; congressional days in session calculated from Congressional Quarterly (1993), congressional pay from Dwyer (2004), cost of Congress from Statistical Abstract of the United States 1935, and cost of the legislative reference service from Message of the President of the United States Transmitting the Budget for the Service of the Budget Year Ending June 30, 1934; 1945, State legislative pay and days in session calculated from data in Book of the States 1945–1946, cost of legislature is averaged from State Finances 1945 and State Finances 1946, congressional days in session calculated from data in Congressional Quarterly (1993), congressional pay from Dwyer 2004, and congressional cost from Statistical Abstract of the United States 1946; 1954, State legislative pay and days in session calculated from data in Book of the States 1954–55 (1954, 100–101, 106–7), cost of legislature is averaged from State Government Finances in 1953 and State Government Finances in 1954, congressional days in session calculated from data in Congressional Quarterly 1993, congressional pay from Dwyer 2004, and congressional cost from Statistical Abstract of the United States 1956; 1960, State legislative pay and days in session calculated from data in Book of the States 1960–61, cost of legislature is averaged from Compendium of State Government Finances in 1959 and State Government Finances in 1960, congressional days in session calculated from data in Congressional Quarterly 1993, congressional pay from Dwyer 2004, and congressional cost from Statistical Abstract of the United States 1960.

aProfessionalization measured using cost of legislative reference service rather than total cost of legislature.

office. There was a bookshelf behind the desk . . . and so you put most of your stuff in there and other than that it was right on top of your desk" (Kilgannon 2005, 80). Another legislator noted that because most members lacked their own space, "You'd try to find an empty room someplace, the committee rooms."[14] Lawmakers "had a steno pool and if you wanted to do any letters or news bulletins, you'd send a Page to the steno pool and they'd send a stenographer." Committee chairs were a bit better situated; "The committee chairmen had one of those big roll-top desks in their committee room, and with a secretary who would do the committee work" (Kilgannon 2005, 80). Along the same lines a Pennsylvania representative recalled that when he was first serving in 1955, "We had no offices, we had no telephones, we had no file cabinets, we had no desks except that which was assigned to us on the floor of the House Chambers, . . . and no regular secretarial service" (Fineman 2003, 88). A Florida lawmaker complained, "We get no professional help even on [complex policies] like insurance and utility regulation" (Velie 1953b, 37).

The same state of affairs prevailed a decade later. In Massachusetts, it was reported, "The secretarial pool for the 240-man Assembly consists of five stenographers. Their message center is a honeycomb of little alphabetical pigeonholes reminiscent of a fraternity house mailbox" (Miller 1965a, 178). Reflecting on his limited work space, a West Virginia lawmaker said, "I think the biggest shock I got was finding out you just about had to keep your legislative career in a pasteboard box under your desk." He added, "Every senator did get a single file cabinet drawer for the first time last session, so it wasn't quite that bad" ("There's Ferment in the Statehouse" 1967, 80).

Overall, with only slight improvements in their circumstances state legislatures were still roughly where they had been relative to Congress 25 years earlier. The most professionalized state legislature continued to be Massachusetts, a state where the legislature met annually for long sessions and that paid its members reasonably well. And once again, the more professionalized legislatures were found among the largest-population states, while the least professionalized bodies were from the smaller states. Indeed, few states changed their relative positions from 1935 to 1960: the professionalization scores using legislative costs for 1935 and 1960 correlate with each other at an impressive .84 ($p < .01$). But it is important to recognize that some momentum for state legislative reform developed during the 1940s and 1950s (Smith and Lyons 1977). Moreover, some legislatures, notably California's, were grasping for ways to cope with the increased policy demands being made by the public (Cloner and Gable 1959, 715–21). Thus, they were primed for a concerted effort to professionalize.

Jesse Unruh, California, and the Professionalization Movement

State legislatures changed in significant ways during the professionalization movement of the 1960s and 1970s (King 2000; Pound 1992; Rosenthal 1996, 1998; Squire 1992a, 1997, 2007; Squire and Hamm 2005). In part, these changes were driven by the reforms promoted in the California legislature in the 1960s by Assembly Speaker Jesse Unruh. The speaker's influence on the national scene was acknowledged by his contemporaries. One scholar declared, "Mr. Unruh is perhaps the most prominent state legislator in the United States. His California legislature has perhaps done more to improve its capacity to meet the extraordinary problems it faces than has any other" (Heard 1966, 158). Others observed that under his direction, California was "in the forefront of the movement to give professional assistance to individual legislators and legislative committees" (Crane and Watts 1968, 67). A journalist labeled Unruh "the captain of this new reform movement" (Beetle 1966, 475).

The Assembly that Unruh had first entered in 1955 enjoyed few of the characteristics associated with a professional body. The legislature had just emerged from a long period where it had been dominated by the legendary lobbyist Artie Samish, known as the "Secret Boss of California." Samish had influenced legislative behavior by providing lawmakers both campaigns funds and spending money to help meet their Sacramento living expenses (Samish and Thomas 1971, 122; Buchanan 1963, 59–60). His demise began with a national magazine article that had a picture of him seated with a ventriloquist's dummy on his knee. The caption had Samish asking the dummy, "And how are you today, Mr. Legislature?" (Velie 1949, 11). But even after a subsequent conviction for income tax evasion removed Samish from the political scene, corruption still festered in the legislature. When Unruh arrived in Sacramento two former speakers were under indictment for bribery (Buchanan 1963, 55–56).

The annual legislative salary had been raised the year Unruh started in the Assembly, but only to $6,000. It was supplemented by a per diem and additional compensation for interim service, bringing the average yearly stipend to an estimated $7,200 to $8,000 (Buchanan 1963, 60). This sum allowed for a modest standard of living while the legislature was in session, but most members still needed another job. As a new legislator with a young family, Unruh added to his income by counting boxcars for a railroad (Cannon 1969, 93). But even working two jobs he found it difficult to make ends meet. Unruh recalled that by the late 1950s as he was lobbying his colleagues in an attempt to move up the leadership ranks, "I was running around the state soliciting votes . . . in a borrowed car because my used car at the point was simply not in good enough condition to drive from Los Angeles to San Francisco and other far reaches of the state." A friend had to buy Unruh some new suits to wear (Boyarsky 2008, 163–64).

The formal time demands that Assembly service placed on members were restricted. In 1946, California voters had approved an amendment to revert to annual sessions. But those sessions were limited: Odd-year meetings could be no longer than 120 days, and even-year meetings were held to 30 days and could only consider budget bills. Working conditions were adequate. A 1951 addition to the state capitol provided each member a private office, and during the legislative session members were given the use of a full-time secretary (Buchanan 1963, 49; Wyner 1973). Although no other personal staff was provided, some assistance was available through the offices of the Legislative Counsel and the Legislative Analyst (Beek 1980).

On the whole, by 1960 the conditions of legislative service in California were tolerable, but not impressive. In comparison, the situation was actually better than in most other states. Still, the legislature's capacity to perform its assigned tasks was limited, and the body was in no way comparable to Congress. Not surprisingly, most legislators did not serve for long. Although turnover had decreased from approximately 70 percent at the turn of the century, it was still quite significant, with the majority of legislators serving three or fewer terms (Burns et al. 2008, 232–35; Fisher, Price, and Bell 1973, 12).

Unruh recognized and in some ways exploited the legislature's weaknesses to become speaker in 1961, and after he took power he dominated the institution. A 1963 *Life* magazine profile referred to him by his capitol nickname, "Big Daddy"—a reference to the character in *Cat on a Hot Tin Roof* (Mills 1987, 11)—and claimed that "He has the legislature virtually in the pocket of his vast trousers" ("Big Daddy Unruh" 1963). A *Harper's Magazine* article that same year ratcheted up the hyperbole, asserting that Unruh was "the most powerful . . . of America's political bosses" (Fuller 1963, 64). Like the *Harper's* article, most of the stories on Unruh at this point focused on his role as a party leader rather than as an institutional reformer (Cray 1963; Harris 1962, 1963), suggesting the latter was not of much public interest. Under Unruh's direction the California legislature—at the Assembly's behest (Cannon 1969, 119; Wyner 1973, 53)—instituted a series of reforms designed to strengthen it. Unruh was motivated by a desire to make the legislature a more equal policy-making competitor to the governor (Unruh 1967). In his own words, the Speaker wanted the legislature "to raise its decision-making ability, to scrutinize, to originate, and yes to innovate, . . . to ask the right questions and grope with more insight for better settlements" (Boyarsky 2008, 166). In other words, he wanted to build a "professional" legislature along the lines of Congress.

Politically, Unruh saw professionalizing the legislature as a two-track process: one to increase staff resources, the other to raise member pay and make the legislature full-time. The first track was relatively easy to achieve because the speaker could accomplish most of it on his own initiative, although there was some surprising resistance from senior legislators along the way (Putnam 2005, 65). But Unruh overcame the opposition by persuading his colleagues that giving them staff would provide them with an independent source of information and make the legislature more powerful in relation to the executive branch (Unruh 1964a, 1964b, 1965). Starting in 1961 Unruh provided each Assembly member funds for a full-time administrative assistant, a secretary, and a district office. He also increased standing committee staff, with all of them getting at least one professional consultant. Additional institutional resources were created by establishing the Legislative Reference Bureau in 1962. Finally, aides were provided to leadership positions and party caucuses (Bell and Price 1984, 187–89; Bolton 1971, 59; Cannon 1969, 113–16; Unruh 1964b, 56–57; 1965; Wyner 1973, 59–66). Allocating staff to both parties was, of course, a politically astute move intended to garner broad support for the professionalization effort. But Unruh also believed spreading informational resources benefited the institution, arguing that "the quality of the legislative product is immeasurably improved if the minority has independent staffing" (Herzberg and Unruh 1970, 23).

The speaker understood that staff would help make lawmakers less dependent on interest groups for information (Unruh 1964b, 54). But Unruh's main goal was to place the legislature on an equal footing with the governor. He thought, "If legislators are not equipped with staff to scrutinize material provided by the executive, it is extremely unlikely that they can determine what is fact and what is fancy if the material involves anything but the simplest and most obvious kind of issue" (Herzberg and Unruh 1970, 23). The challenge these staffing reforms posed to the executive did not go unnoticed in the governor's mansion. According to one of Unruh's legislative lieutenants, after the speaker instituted his staffing enhancements, "[Governor] Pat [Brown] made noises like a screech owl about the whole program. He knew that the development of analytical capabilities on the part of Assembly committees would reduce the power of the administration to influence the lawmaking process" (Mills 1987, 71). But the governor was persuaded to go along because he wanted Unruh's endorsement for his reelection bid, and his own executive office was also promised more personnel.

After achieving these staffing improvements Unruh considered the California legislature the strongest in the country. But he acknowledged, "we still have a long way to go," because accomplishing his second reform track, increasing member pay and making the legislature full-time, was far more challenging (*Los Angeles Times* 1963). As noted above, annual sessions were allowed under the state constitution but limits were set on how long the legislature could meet. The constitution also held that no pay increase could be instituted without voter approval. This requirement was a serious impediment because raises were not politically popular; voters had rejected them four times between 1958 and 1962. Consequently, Unruh seized on a circuitous scheme to overcome the electorate's resistance to raising legislative pay. In 1959, the legislature had charged the Citizens' Legislative Advisory Commission with investigating procedures that could be used to revise the constitution. Building on the Commission's findings, the next year the Assembly Interim Committee on Constitutional Amendments reported that the constitution was in need of fundamental revision and that the legislature was empowered to propose amendments to the voters. In 1961 legislators voted to put a proposal on the 1962 general election ballot asking the voters to grant the legislature the power to act as a constitutional convention and to propose revisions to the state constitution. The voters subsequently approved the request. In 1963, at Unruh's urging the legislature passed a concurrent resolution creating a Constitutional Revision Commission (Cannon 1969, 199). The commission was appointed by the Joint Committee on Legislative Organization and had six legislators among its members.[15] In early 1966, the commission submitted its report which proposed a series of constitutional changes to the executive, judicial, and legislative branches. This collection of reforms was placed on the November 1966 general election ballot as Proposition 1A. The decision to push ahead with the complicated proposition was driven by Unruh and the Assembly over opposition from the governor and Senate (Unruh 1967, 10–11).

Embedded in the complex proposal were two provisions central to the speaker's plan to professionalize the legislature. The first gave the legislature the ability to set its own salary subject to only a few constraints: Annual increases could not exceed 5 percent and any raise could not go into effect until the following legislative session. (Prior to the general election vote on Proposition 1A the legislature passed a measure to increase their pay from $6,000 to $16,000, contingent on the proposition's passage. They justified the large percentage increase by retroactively raising pay 5 percent for each year since the last adjustment.) The second provision removed restrictions on the number of days the legislature could meet. The Constitutional Revision Commission had recommended limiting annual sessions to 166 days, which they calculated would continue the existing 120-day limit used in odd-year sessions but also count Saturdays and Sundays. The legislature altered the proposal to allow for unlimited sessions (Hyink 1969, 643). Taken together, the two proposed changes allowed proponents to make an argument that full-time legislators deserved full-time pay. Backed by the speaker, supporters from both parties—among them Ronald Reagan, the Republican candidate for governor (Cannon 1969, 200)—and most of the state's major newspapers, Proposition 1A passed easily. With its passage the California Legislature was professionalized, establishing a model for the rest of the states to emulate.

Legislative Professionalization after Unruh: 1979 to 2009

The 1960s and 1970s were momentous decades for state legislatures with the professionalization movement pushing many of them to become more like the U.S. Congress (Jewell and Patterson 1986, 159; Rosenthal 1971a, 9–10). Unruh was evangelical in his zeal to promote reform nationally. In 1965 he said, "After watching a number of other legislatures try to function around this country without adequate tools . . . I don't believe it's possible for them to service the needs of their people" (Blanchard 1965). So he took his reform campaign on the road. A Wisconsin newspaper editorial noted the speaker had been "in the state in furtherance of his mission to make state legislatures more effective arms of government." They admitted that the Wisconsin legislature "could use plenty of the Unruh prodding" (*Milwaukee Journal* 1965). When Unruh addressed the Florida Senate on professionalization, the member who invited him, Lawton Chiles, wanted the speaker to "give us some idea what they (California) have been doing, in a bipartisan way" to improve the legislature. Chiles opined that under Unruh's direction California "has done more in legislative reform" than any other state (*St. Petersburg Times* 1967).

The professionalization movement, however, was more than just Jesse Unruh. In 1961, the National Legislative Conference—an organization established in 1948 by a group of legislative service agency directors (Kurtz 1999)—issued a report making a number of recommendations promoting modernization, among them longer legislative sessions, higher compensation, and more staff.[16] Several years later the organization followed up with another report, this time focusing exclusively on promoting the development of improved staff resources (National Legislative Conference 1961, 1963). The reports gained considerable attention around the country (Herzberg and Unruh 1970, 104), and efforts to address institutional weaknesses soon followed. In 1965, the Colorado Governor's Committee on Legislators' Compensation (1965) recommended improvements in legislative pay and pensions. The following year, the West Virginia legislature created a Citizens Advisory Committee to investigate questions about the appropriate level of salaries, session lengths, and staffing ("West Virginia Citizens to Study Legislature" 1966). In 1968 the Pennsylvania General Assembly created a Commission on Legislative Modernization—better known as the "Michener Commission" after one of its cochairs, author James Michener—to reform the body in such a way as to elevate it to being a coequal with the executive (Fineman 2003, 100). The following year the Commission published a report titled *Toward Tomorrow's Legislature* (Commission for Legislative Modernization 1969).

Interest in improving state legislatures built over the several years. Some efforts managed to seep into popular venues. In 1965, a *National Civic Review* article touting legislative reform was condensed and republished the following month as the lead piece in *Reader's Digest* (Miller 1965a, 1965b). Around the same time the Citizens Conference on State Legislatures (CCSL) was established with an organizational mission to improve state legislative capabilities. The CCSL developed out of a meeting in Chicago in May 1964. The organization was created as a nonprofit headquartered in Kansas City, and it held its first formal meeting in January 1965.[17] A journalist asserted that the CCSL emerged out of the "Ford lobby," and the organization did benefit greatly from financial support provided by the Ford Foundation (Beetle 1966, 476). Between 1969 and 1971 the CCSL conducted the Legislative Evaluation Study, which assessed the 50 state legislatures on a number of dimensions. The somewhat incestuous nature of the reform movement was indicated by the fact that the study was led by Larry Margolis, who had previously served as Jesse Unruh's chief of staff. The CCSL's analysis was made public in an accessible book and a more technical volume (Burns 1971; Citizens Conference on State Legislatures 1971), each of which garnered national attention (Morse 1971; *NYT* 1971; "The States: Appraising the Legislatures" 1971). The CCSL's rankings were seized on by members of lower-rated legislatures and used as a cudgel to promote greater public investment in their institutions (Fineman 2003, 97; Lemon 1973; *Lewiston Daily Sun* 1971; *Meriden Journal* 1971; *Rome News-Tribune* 1971; *Tuscaloosa News* 1971).

The CCSL's comparative work was complemented by a series of single-state studies on legislative reform conducted by Rutgers University's Eagleton Institute of Politics (Chartock and Berking 1970; Craft 1972; Ogle 1970, 1971; Rosenthal 1968; Smith 1970; Tantillo 1968), by other academic units (Institute of Gov. 1970), and by the organization's own analyses (CCSL 1974a, 1974b, 1974c, 1974d, 1974e, 1974f, 1974g). Around the same time the American Political Science Association instituted the State Legislative Service Fellows program, and at least three volumes on state legislatures emerged from that effort (Fisher, Bell, and Price 1973; Palmer 1973; Wise 1971). All of these reports generally hit the same reform themes: the need to increase legislative pay and session lengths and to improve staff and facilities. Over time these basic ideas percolated down and became standard talking points in public discussions of state legislative reform (Cohn 1971; Meikle 1968). And they received broad-based support; the magazine for the U.S. Chamber of Commerce published a favorable article, and an organization of national business leaders issued a study calling for similar improvements (Committee for Economic Development 1967; "There's Ferment in the Statehouse" 1967).

The public initially responded positively to the professionalization movement. As table 7.5 reveals, popular support for state legislative reforms peaked in the late 1960s and early 1970s.[18] Between 1967 and 1970, voters passed measures to increase lawmaker pay in Arizona, Idaho, Iowa, Nebraska (twice), North Carolina, Oklahoma, and Utah. Proposals allowing for annual sessions were adopted in Connecticut, Idaho, Indiana, Iowa, Maine, Mississippi, Missouri, Nebraska, Utah, West Virginia, and Wisconsin. Backing for these sorts of changes, however, was never universal. During the same time period voters rejected legislative pay increases in Idaho, Nevada, New Hampshire, Rhode Island, and Texas (twice), and annual sessions were turned down in Kentucky, Montana, Nevada, New Hampshire (although a majority supported the proposal), and Oregon. But

41 percent of all the legislative pay raise measures passed by voters between 1955 and 1990 were adopted during the eight years from 1965 to 1972, as were 53 percent of all the measures increasing legislative sessions.

Improvements in staff resources usually did not require public approval. A 1967 survey of lower-house speakers listed increased staff as their most pressing need ("There's Ferment in the Statehouse" 1967, 80). Con-

TABLE 7.5. Voter Support for Legislative Professionalization Ballot Measures, 1955–90

	Voters Supported			Voters Rejected		
Election Cycle	Pay or Benefits Increase	Annual Sessions or Increase in Session Length	Staff Increase	Pay or Benefits Increase	Annual Sessions or Increase in Session Length	Staff Increase
1955–56	AZ		CA	MO, ND, OR		
1957–58	AZ, AR, CT	CA, NV		CA, MO, NE, OR, TX, UT	TX	
1959–60	NE, TX	PA		CA, OK, OR	NM, NV[a]	
1961–62	KS, OR	SD, MN	LA	CA(2), MA, MD, OK, RI,[b] WV	OK	
1963–64		MD, NM	CO	MA, NH,[b] OK(2)	IL[b]	
1965–66	CA, TN	CA, KS, NH,[c] OK		MD, NE, UT, TX, WV	KY, UT, WV	UT
1967–68	AZ, IA, NE(2), NC, OK, UT	IA, ID, MS, UT, WI		ID, NH, TX	MT	
1969–70	ID	CT, IN, MO, ME, NE, WV		NV, RI, TX	KY, NH,[b] NV, OR	
1971–72	NM	CA, MN, WY		AL, AZ, ID, NE(3), TX	AL, LA, NH[b]	
1973–74		OH		AZ, NE, OH, RI, TX	KY, MT,[a] TX	
1975–76	AR, DE, GA	AL, ME, ND		AK, ND, NE	NH[b]	
1977–78				AZ, NE, NM	NH[b]	
1979–80	AZ, KY	WA		ND, NM, NV, UT		

TABLE 7.5.—Continued

Election Cycle	Voters Supported			Voters Rejected		
	Pay or Benefits Increase	Annual Sessions or Increase in Session Length	Staff Increase	Pay or Benefits Increase	Annual Sessions or Increase in Session Length	Staff Increase
1981–82	ND, NM	CO		AZ, NE	MT	
1983–84		NH, UT		TX	AK[a]	
1985–86				AZ, CA, RI		MI
1987–88	NE			AZ, MA[a]	CO,[a] MT	
1989–90		FL		AZ, CA,[a] NM, TX(2)	OK,[a] OR	CA[a]
Total	27	34	3	69	27	2

Source: Data collected by author from http://www.ncsl.org/default.aspx?tabid=16580; http://www.cslib .org/constitutionalAmends/index.htm; http://www.sosweb.state.ar.us/elections/elections_pdfs/initiatives _amendments_1938-2006.pdf; http://holmes.uchastings.edu/cgi-bin/starfinder/16996/calprop.txt; http:// election.dos.state.fl.us/initiatives/initiativelist.asp; http://www.sos.idaho.gov/elect/inits/initinfo.htm; http://contentdm.legis.state.ia.us/cdm4/document.php?CISOROOT=/redbooks&CISOPTR =18773&REC=19; http://www.maine.gov/legis/lawlib/const.htm; http://www.sec.state.ma.us/ELE/ele balm/balmpdf/balm1988.pdf; http://www.legislature.mi.gov/documents/publications/MichiganManual% 5C2009-2010MichiganManual/09-10-MM_II_pp_68-74_Proposed.pdf; http://www.house.leg.state.mn .us/hrd/pubs/ss/ssregses.htm; http://www.legis.nd.gov/information/library/docs/pdf/measuresbeforethe voters.pdf; http://nebraskalegislature.gov/pdf/bluebook/243-272.pdf; http://www.sos.state.oh.us/sos/up load/elections/historical/issuehist.pdf; http://www.scvotes.org/2008/11/21/election_reports; http://sd-sos.gov/content/html/elections/electvoterpdfs/BallotQuestions1890-2010.pdf; http://www.legis.wiscon-sin.us/lrb/bb/09bb/pdf/191-242.pdf; Andersen 1971, 23–27; 1972, 20; 1973a, 22, 26, 31; 1973b, 614; 1974, 87; 1976, 26; 1977, 84, 87; Blair 1988, 164; Boyd 1968, 416; 1969a, 23; 1969b, 69; H. Research Or-ganization (Texas) 1989; H. Study Group (Texas) 1984; Jewell and Miller 1988, 4; "Many Amendments Get Voter Approval" 1967, 19, 21–22; Md. Man. 1968, 518; Olmsted 1958, 566; 1961, 94; 1962a, 379; 1962b, 615–18; 1963, 24; 1964, 593; Rausch 1994, 6-7; Seeberger 1997, 9; St. of N.H. Man. for the GC 1965, 702; 1967, 523; 1969, 801–3; 1973, 956; 1977, 687; 1979, 297; 1985, 443; Sturm 1981, 32–33, 36; 1983, 42, 47–48; 1985, 41; Texas Legislative Coun. 1968, 1972; Valentine 2008; Zeigler and Smith 1971, 336.

[a]Measure passed by the voters that reduced legislative pay, sessions, or staff.

[b]Measure to increase legislative pay or session length that gained majority support, but vote percentage was insufficient to pass state constitutional amendment threshold.

[c]Measure was passed by the voters but later overturned by the state court of last resort.

sequently, although they were nearly invisible to the public, staffing en-hancements were made in many legislatures between the mid-1960s and the mid-1970s (Rosenthal 1981, 205). These improvements had a pro-found impact on the institutions. In 1967, the Illinois General Assembly had no full-time professional committee staff. Ten years later professional staff was assigned to every policy-making committee (Van Der Slik and Redfield 1986, 99). In 1965, Wisconsin initiated a pilot program to provide party caucuses full-time policy staff and then quickly expanded it (Rosen-thal 1971b, 77–78). Professional staff was provided to all committees in the Pennsylvania House in 1969 with the speaker making clear that these positions were not to be treated as political patronage (Fineman 2003, 89). The Washington state legislature gained full-time staff in 1973, and the additions produced the sort of outcomes professionalization reformers had envisioned. As one lawmaker recalled, "If someone from the governor's office walked into a committee hearing, he no longer knew more about the subject at hand than anyone else in the room" (Chasan 1990, 153). A similar observation was made by a Florida representative following staffing increases in that body: "Today, when a lobbyist testifies, I can look at him and say, 'That's very interesting, but it's not what my staff tells me'" (Miller 1971a, 370). When asked two decades later, longtime legislative veterans cited increased staff resources as one of the most important reforms they had witnessed, with a Kansas representative saying it was "both fortunate and necessary because the issues dealt with [now] are so much more complex" (Moncrief, Thompson, and Kurtz 1996, 60–61).

By the early 1970s legislative observers were touting the success of the reform movement. Florida, in an explicit attempt to level the playing field with the governor, had raised lawmaker pay and shifted to annual sessions (*St. Petersburg Times* 1969). An early evaluation of the changes extolled, "In less than six years the state has revolutionized its legislature, hauling it bodily out of the 19th century and converting it into an efficient mechanism for the handling of 20th-century problems" (Miller 1971a, 366; 1971b). Systematic evidence that the professionalization efforts largely succeeded is presented in table 7.6, which shows how state legislatures compared to Congress on member pay, time demands, and staff in 1979, 1986, 1996, 2003, and 2009. Most important, the mean and median professionalization scores in 1979 were substantially above what they had been in 1960 and earlier.[19] These findings are consistent with anecdotal accounts of how state legislatures changed during the 1960s and 1970s.

It is vital to note that even many of the less professional bodies underwent significant changes. In a study of the reforms in the Kentucky legislature from the mid-1960s to the mid-1980s, Jewell and Miller observed, "over the last twenty years or so, the Kentucky legislature has changed as much or more than those in other states." In particular, they highlighted an increase in the legislature's capacity to process information: "As a consequence of these developments, the legislature—through its committees—gained sufficient time to study issues and achieved sufficient expertise to make informed judgments about them" (Jewell and Miller 1988, 14, 283). Similarly, under the leadership of E. L. "Bubba" Henry, the "Young

Turks," a group of Louisiana House members in the late 1960s and early 1970s, pushed to reform that institution. Their efforts led to, among other changes, a streamlined standing committee system, increased member staff, and the creation of a Legislative Fiscal Office. All of this was done with an eye toward increasing legislative independence from the governor (Parent and Henderson 2002).

By the early 1980s, most of the significant professionalization reforms had been put in place, and, as signaled by the election of Ronald Reagan as president (and substantiated by the data in table 7.5), public support for continued investment in improved governmental institutions was eroding. State legislatures generally maintained their overall gains through the mid-1980s. The scores for 1986 show that while a few legislatures continued to advance compared to Congress, most simply held their own. The mean and median scores (in this case, directly comparable with 1979) show only slight movement from a few years before. The effects of changing political winds reveal themselves most clearly in the scores for 1996, 2003, and 2009. The mean and median scores for all 3 years are lower than they were a decade or two decades before. The progress made between 1960 and 1980 stopped over the next 30 years, and state legislative professionalization, on average, regressed slightly compared with Congress.[20] As the data in table 7.5 reveal, on the relatively few occasions when the voters were given the opportunity to enhance legislative professionalization, they usually declined to do so.

The Status of State Legislatures in 2009

Although the professionalization movement had long since waned, state legislatures in 2009 were far different organizations from what they had been at the start of the twentieth century. That is not to say that everything changed. Certainly, corruption did not disappear, with state legislatures suffering a series of embarrassing scandals in recent decades (Squire and Moncrief 2010, 108–9). In response to these failures, state lawmakers adopted progressively tighter ethics laws, and they came to operate under much more stringent regulations than their predecessors (Rosenson 2005; Rosenthal 2009, 420–21). Indeed, by 2006 legislators in 47 states faced more rigorous ethics rules than did members of Congress (Rush and Jimenez 2006).

Setting aside ethics, there was a notable change in the behavior of state

TABLE 7.6. State Legislative Professionalization (using staff per legislator), 1979, 1986, 1996, 2003, and 2009

State	1979 Rank	1979 Score	1986 Rank	1986 Score	1996 Rank	1996 Score	2003 Rank	2003 Score	2009 Rank	2009 Score
Alabama	45	0.085	30	0.158	46	0.067	32	0.131	45	0.078
Alaska	8	0.320	7	0.311	12	0.232	11	0.227	12	0.217
Arizona	11	0.269	16	0.250	18	0.185	10	0.232	8	0.271
Arkansas	41	0.115	43	0.105	39	0.104	42	0.106	42	0.110
California	1	0.526	3	0.625	1	0.570	1	0.626	2	0.581
Colorado	9	0.284	9	0.300	21	0.172	14	0.202	16	0.199
Connecticut	23	0.200	17	0.233	20	0.178	19	0.190	17	0.196
Delaware	28	0.179	25	0.192	26	0.151	26	0.148	30	0.159
Florida	19	0.224	14	0.255	10	0.249	13	0.223	15	0.210
Georgia	37	0.142	38	0.133	38	0.107	38	0.116	38	0.116
Hawaii	17	0.246	11	0.276	9	0.252	12	0.225	9	0.262
Idaho	29	0.179	40	0.125	36	0.110	29	0.138	36	0.120
Illinois	7	0.344	8	0.302	11	0.236	8	0.261	6	0.281
Indiana	36	0.143	36	0.139	39	0.106	43	0.102	22	0.174
Iowa	12	0.266	19	0.225	23	0.164	22	0.170	24	0.167
Kansas	31	0.169	31	0.152	37	0.067	35	0.125	31	0.140
Kentucky	47	0.078	44	0.101	43	0.087	27	0.148	33	0.137
Louisiana	35	0.150	27	0.185	29	0.144	34	0.129	26	0.163
Maine	27	0.180	33	0.147	41	0.098	44	0.089	43	0.088
Maryland	14	0.252	22	0.204	16	0.189	18	0.194	19	0.189
Massachusetts	4	0.386	4	0.614	5	0.332	4	0.385	7	0.280
Michigan	2	0.463	2	0.653	2	0.516	5	0.342	4	0.461
Minnesota	22	0.211	24	0.199	19	0.179	23	0.169	27	0.162
Mississippi	26	0.185	29	0.160	31	0.127	41	0.107	39	0.115
Missouri	13	0.266	10	0.287	15	0.198	21	0.174	18	0.194
Montana	42	0.114	42	0.110	44	0.073	45	0.076	44	0.079
Nebraska	20	0.216	26	0.186	22	0.172	24	0.162	25	0.166
Nevada	40	0.130	34	0.146	24	0.161	30	0.138	29	0.159

State										
New Hampshire	50	0.062	50	0.042	50	0.034	50	0.027	50	0.031
New Jersey	30	0.175	13	0.255	6	0.320	9	0.244	11	0.221
New Mexico	44	0.092	45	0.098	40	0.093	40	0.109	40	0.110
New York	3	0.407	1	0.659	3	0.515	2	0.480	1	0.606
North Carolina	25	0.190	23	0.203	28	0.149	16	0.198	21	0.180
North Dakota	48	0.077	48	0.075	48	0.058	49	0.051	49	0.049
Ohio	5	0.355	6	0.329	7	0.315	7	0.304	5	0.380
Oklahoma	15	0.249	15	0.250	17	0.188	20	0.187	20	0.181
Oregon	18	0.233	28	0.183	25	0.153	25	0.159	23	0.172
Pennsylvania	6	0.345	5	0.336	8	0.283	6	0.339	3	0.479
Rhode Island	38	0.142	32	0.148	35	0.113	31	0.133	34	0.134
South Carolina	10	0.281	20	0.212	30	0.135	37	0.124	28	0.161
South Dakota	43	0.104	46	0.083	47	0.065	47	0.064	47	0.068
Tennessee	34	0.149	37	0.135	32	0.117	39	0.116	37	0.118
Texas	24	0.191	21	0.210	13	0.215	15	0.199	14	0.210
Utah	46	0.082	47	0.082	45	0.067	46	0.065	46	0.072
Vermont	39	0.130	35	0.145	33	0.117	28	0.144	41	0.110
Virginia	32	0.164	39	0.133	27	0.150	33	0.131	32	0.138
Washington	21	0.212	18	0.230	14	0.198	17	0.197	13	0.212
West Virginia	33	0.150	41	0.125	34	0.116	36	0.125	35	0.121
Wisconsin	16	0.249	12	0.270	4	0.459	3	0.439	10	0.242
Wyoming	49	0.075	49	0.056	49	0.057	48	0.054	48	0.061
Mean		0.209		0.221		0.182		0.185		0.191
Median		0.188		0.189		0.152		0.154		0.165

Source: The measure for 1986 (with corrections for Alabama, Idaho, Maine, Missouri, South Carolina, and Virginia) is from Squire 1992b. The measure for 1996 (with corrections for Nevada and New Mexico) is from Squire 2000. The measures for 1979 and 2003 are from Squire 2007. The measure for 2009 was calculated by the author.

lawmakers. Following the Unruh reforms, close observers of the California legislature claimed that there were fewer alcoholics, and that members were more serious about their duties than before (Salzman 1976, 79–81). Around the same time Arkansas banned both lobbyists and liquor from the legislative floor (Blair 1988, 162). More recently, a veteran of 30 years in the Georgia legislature noted the change in the behavior of his colleagues, saying, "It's a different world now. You've got different people in the General Assembly. I don't know of any of them that's hanky-pankying around" (Smith 2004). Overall, many noted improvement in state legislative performance over the latter part of the twentieth century (Greenawalt and Madonna 1992; Hansen 1994; Pound 1992; Rosenthal 2009; Thompson and Moncrief 1992).

As documented earlier in this chapter there have not been major changes in rules and committee systems. These had institutionalized during the nineteenth century, and, although they continued to evolve at the margins in response to changing organizational environments, they were still fundamentally the same at the beginning of the twenty-first century. The major institutional differences over time manifested themselves in the characteristics associated with professionalization. In 2009 most states paid lawmakers a set wage, with the mean salary being $28,230 and the median being $20,806.[21] Because many states also supplement legislative salaries with per diems (which receive favorable federal tax treatment) and other sums, the actual income received by state lawmakers was higher than these figures (Squire and Moncrief 2010, 79–88). Even the lower figures, however, represent a considerable increase over time; the $250 mean state legislative salary paid in 1910 would have been worth roughly $5,500 in 2009 dollars. Time demands made on state legislators also increased over the last century. The median days in session figure for 1909 was 28; in 2009 it was 60. Staff resources expanded greatly. In 2009 all standing committees in 39 states had professional staff, and only 3 states failed to supply at least some standing committees with professional assistance. Only 4 states failed to provide clerical support to standing committees; again the vast majority of state legislatures provided clerical staff to all standing committees. But it is in the provision of personal staff that the greatest change is found. No personal staff was provided at the beginning of the twentieth century. In 2009, lawmakers in 25 upper houses and 22 lower houses had year-round personal staff, and in another 6 upper houses and 3 lower houses they received session-only personal staff. And in almost all of the other state legislatures members shared some personal staff.[22]

What Difference Does Professionalization Make?

Professionalization matters because it influences lawmaker behavior, the way a legislature operates, and the policy decisions it makes. In terms of member behavior, the most obvious impact is on membership turnover, which declines as professionalization levels increase (Berry, Berkman, and Schneiderman 2000; Moncrief, Niemi, and Powell 2004). But there are other important differences as well. Lawmakers in more professional legislatures have more contact with their constituents, are more attentive to their concerns, and are more representative of their views than are their counterparts in less professional legislatures (Lax and Phillips 2009; Maestas 2003; Squire 1993; Wright 2007). Voting behavior is affected, with legislators in more professionalized legislatures asserting greater independence from their party (Jenkins 2010). Among institutional effects, legislative efficiency—the percentage of bills passed and the number of bills enacted per legislative day—goes up with professionalization (Squire 1998). Lawmakers invest their leaders with less power as professionalization increases (Richman 2010). And, as reformers hoped, more professionalized legislatures are better able to counter gubernatorial influence in the budget process, to better resist a governor's policy agenda, and to more effectively constrain the bureaucracy (Huber, Shipan, and Pfahler 2001; Kousser and Phillips 2009, 2010).

Perhaps the greatest impact of professionalization is on the sorts of policy decisions legislatures make. The inclination to reform government personnel and procurement practices increases with legislative professionalization, as does the willingness to adopt increasingly complex regulatory policies and income tax systems (Coggburn 2003; Ka and Teske 2002; Kellough and Selden 2003; Slemrod 2005). Increased professionalization is associated with the adoption of more innovative e-government architectures and stronger environmental programs (Thomson and Arroyo 2011; Tolbert, Mossberger, and McNeal 2008; Woods 2008). The stringency of lobbying regulations and the vigor with which they are enforced increases with professionalization, as does the propensity to adopt stricter campaign finance laws (Opheim 1991; Witko 2007). It also produces greater investments in higher education and better-funded state pension systems (Coggburn and Kearney 2009; McLendon, Hearn, and Mokher 2009). As professionalization levels increase legislatures are more likely to increase the number of economic enterprise zones and to respond to local government pressures to adopt antismoking ordinances (Shipan and Volden 2006;

Turner and Cassell 2007). More professionalized legislatures also are better able to mediate policy disputes, thereby reducing the motivation for interest groups to turn to citizen initiatives in the states that allow them (Boehmke 2005). More generally, professionalized legislatures are better able to learn from the policy successes of other states and to generate more innovative policies of all sorts of their own (Kousser 2005, 197–98; Shipan and Volden n.d). Thus, the increased analytical capacity produced by professionalization translates into a different set of policy choices.

Explanations for Differences in Levels of Professionalization over Time

The preceding discussion documents the trend toward the professionalization of state legislatures from 1909 to 2009. During this period most state legislatures became a little more like Congress, a handful made impressive strides, and a few floundered. But which legislatures tended to close the gap with Congress, and which continued to lag?

Studies of state legislative professionalization trends from the 1960s to the 1990s reached similar conclusions on this question. The one variable consistently associated with legislative professionalization is state population: professionalization increases with state population (King 2000; Mooney 1995). In a twist on that theoretical relationship other studies found that the level of total state income rather than population accounts for the level of legislative professionalization. The idea was that states that enjoy greater total wealth provide their legislature with more support. It is important to note that, from an economic perspective, membership sizes of American state legislatures do not vary much (Stigler 1976). Thus, theoretically, the important relationship is between the total number of lawmakers and the size of the population that finances them. It is easy to envision how 38 million Californians can more generously support their 120 state legislators than 1.3 million New Hampshirites can support their 424 state legislators. Large populations generate more income that can be used to finance the legislature and can spread those costs across more people. The critical variable, however, is not population but the wealth it generates. A small population in a poor state will not be able to support its legislature at the same level as a similarly small population in a wealthier state. But total wealth matters, not per capita wealth. A large-population state of moderate per capita wealth will still be able to generate more revenue with which to support its legislature than will a small-population state, even if it is one of substantial per capita wealth (Squire 2006b; Squire and Hamm 2005).

In addition to capacity to finance legislative professionalization, total state income likely taps another dimension as well. Generally speaking, where state income is greater populations are larger, and, as a result, states are more socially and economically diverse. This diversity generates more conflict and, in turn, greater demands on government. It seems reasonable to expect that increased demands should produce greater support for legislative professionalization to facilitate adequate governmental response. Consequently, total state income probably captures the level of demands on the state legislature as well as the state's capacity to pay for professionalization. Analyses of legislative professionalization over time confirm that it is overwhelmingly driven by state wealth (Squire 2006b; Squire and Hamm 2005). Partisanship and region play only a small role. A separate line of analysis by Malhotra is consistent with this explanation, finding that state legislatures professionalize in response to increases in state spending. Indeed, he argues that professionalization is pursued to give the institution the capacity it needs to handle increased demands on it (Malhotra 2006, 2008). Thus, the dynamic driving the differentiation based on state wealth (and population) among state legislatures on the various dimensions of professionalization that first surfaced in the second half of the nineteenth century (see chapter 6) only became stronger through the twentieth century and into the twenty-first century.[23]

There is an alternative explanation for professionalization during the twentieth century that focuses on changes in lawmaker occupations. As the American economy changed, so too did the occupational composition of state legislatures. In the nineteenth century farmers dominated membership rosters, although toward the end of the period the percentage of lawyers grew substantially. In the early twentieth century lawyers replaced farmers as the leading occupation of state lawmakers. Over the course of the twentieth century the percentage of state legislators who were farmers declined dramatically, but the percentage of lawyers also dropped, although not by as much. By 1999 the plurality of state lawmakers was not from agriculture or the law but from business (Squire and Hamm 2005, 133–34).

Fiorina (1994) speculated that beginning in the mid-twentieth century Democratic state legislators were drawn from different occupational groups than were Republican state legislators. This mattered because Democrats supposedly came from livelihoods that made legislative service seem attractive while Republicans held jobs that made continued service in the legislature less appealing. Thus Fiorina argued that professionalization was driven less by the external demands made on the legislature than by the financial needs of Democratic lawmakers planning on legislative careers. A similar argument was offered by Ehrenhalt (1991).

An examination of the occupations of the more than 3,200 members of the Iowa legislature who served between 1880 and 1980 offers a test of this hypothesis.[24] Iowa presents an interesting case to examine. The state was heavily Republican during much of this time period, but starting in the 1960s it became highly competitive (Patterson, Hedlund, and Boynton 1975, 23–24; Squire 1992d). Over the century the economy diversified with the agricultural sector becoming less prominent. Finally, the legislature drifted from being one of the better-paid bodies in the country to falling somewhere in the middle of the pack. All of this suggests that if the parties began to draw from different occupational groups starting around the 1940s, some evidence of this change should surface among Iowa lawmakers.

Data on legislator occupation were aggregated by party and decade of first election and are presented graphically in figures 7.2 and 7.3. As can be seen, they do not support Fiorina's conjecture. The percentage of farmers in the General Assembly peaks in the 1920s and declines from that point as we might expect, but the percentage in each party's caucus tracks almost perfectly. Similarly, the percentage of lawyers in the two party member-ships is almost alike and largely moves in tandem. In data not presented here few differences appear between the parties in the percentages of real estate agents, insurance agents, and funeral directors serving, or in the per-centage of housewives, students, or retired members. Thus, while the oc-cupational mix of Iowa legislators changed significantly over the twentieth century, there is no evidence in these data that the change had any partisan component, and it likely had no institutional consequences. Overall, pro-fessionalization appears to be more a response to the external demands made on state legislatures than a movement prompted by the career needs of Democratic lawmakers.

The Public and Professionalization

The public opinion trends developed in table 7.5 suggest that legislative professionalization has not enjoyed much support in recent decades. Sur-vey analyses confirm a relationship: the more professional the legislature, the less people approve of it (Kelleher and Wolak 2007; Squire 1993; Squire and Moncrief 2010, 237–40). In part, these results are driven by the public's limited understanding about legislatures and the legislative process

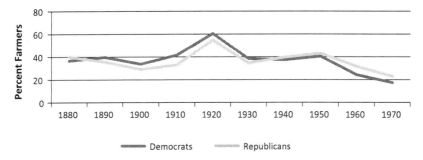

Fig. 7.2. Farmers in the Iowa legislature by party and decade, 1880–1980

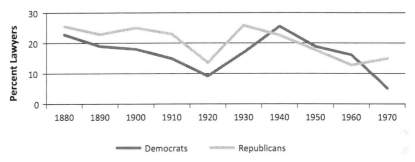

Fig. 7.3. Lawyers in the Iowa legislature by party and decade, 1880–1980

and the fact that the legislature is always an easy target for political cynicism (Rosenthal 2009, 18–27; Squire and Moncrief 2010, 240–41). But it also appears that lower opinions of professional legislatures are held mostly by political conservatives who see them as the drivers of big government; liberals express more positive feelings (Richardson, Konisky, and Milyo 2010). Regardless, there appears to be a disconnect between the demands the public makes on state legislatures and what they think the institutions need to meet those demands.

These conflicts are on display in the current debate over whether state legislatures should be full-time or part-time bodies. In several of the less professional state legislatures there are pressures to become more professionalized. The motivation, in the words of one state senator, is to "see the Legislature get more proactive in getting involved in the nitty-gritty of running the state" (Coleman 2006; Gregg, Mayerowitz, and Gudrais 2006; Wilson 2006). The other side is taken by a Rhode Island representative who echoes claims made as long ago as the early nineteenth century: "I think we do enough damage being in here part-time. The last thing people need is to have us here full-time" (Gregg, Mayerowitz, and Gudrais 2006). At the same time, many of the most professionalized legislatures are hearing calls to return to part-time status (Bell, Christoff, and Gray 2007; Marelius 2010; Marley 2006; Swift 2010). Clearly, the public is, at best, ambivalent about legislative professionalization.

Conclusions

Over the last century, most state legislatures became more like the U.S. Congress, albeit many of them only marginally so. In 1910, most state legislatures were similar to each other. Over the next 99 years, substantial differences across the states emerged. A few states became well-paid, full-time bodies much like Congress. A large number of other legislatures improved their lot relative to Congress, at least a little bit. But a handful failed to make up any ground at all.

The findings reported here also highlight the important effect that the professionalization revolution had on state legislatures between 1960 and 1979. Although many professionalization trends were already apparent by the time Jesse Unruh and the Citizens Conference rallied state legislatures to become more like Congress, their efforts did make a difference. But the data also reveal how the professionalization fervor dissipated by the 1980s. Indeed, many state legislatures lagged as far behind Congress in 2009 as they had in 1960. Thus, at the beginning of the twenty-first century only a few state legislatures had professionalized to the extent that they were in any way akin to the U.S. Congress.

Finally, it appears that efforts to professionalize state legislatures were driven primarily by external pressures. Clearly, some lawmakers, notably Jesse Unruh, had their own motives for pressing legislative reform. But starting early in the twentieth century demands were made of state legislatures to improve their policy-making capacity. By midcentury public demands, combined with the efforts of several national organizations, successfully pushed state legislatures to increase member pay and session lengths, and increase staff resources. This movement changed state legislatures. But the question then becomes whether these reforms are permanent or if, as some observers suggest, state legislatures have begun regressing.

8 • Where Does Legislative Evolution Go from Here?

In November 1990, California voters passed Proposition 140. Its three provisions directly affected the state legislature in ways that were relevant to its evolution. The first provision enacted term limits. The second provision abolished legislative pensions. The final provision imposed a 38 percent reduction in spending on the legislature, thus cutting staff.

As noted in chapter 7, public support for enhancing state legislatures waned by the mid-1980s. But 1990 arguably marked a watershed in state legislative evolution because at that point decisions directly or indirectly brought to a halt many aspects of legislative professionalization. Most important, in addition to California, both Oklahoma and Colorado passed term limits on their state legislatures in 1990. Within a few years term limits would be adopted by 21 states.[1] This is significant because limitations on legislative service reflect public unhappiness with career legislators, and career legislators are a by-product of professionalization and, perhaps, institutionalization as well (Polsby 1968; Squire 2007). Other scattered events since 1990 raise additional questions about the evolutionary process. In 1993, Louisiana voters cut even-numbered-year legislative sessions to 30 days from 60 days and limited them to only considering fiscal matters. In 2009, the California Citizens Compensation Commission—a body created by the state's voters in June 1990 to take away from legislators the power to set their own wages—reduced lawmaker salaries to $95,291 from $116,208. In 2010, Missouri abolished its legislative budget office (an informational resource it had created only two years before), an effort to qualify a ballot measure to reduce the California state legislature to part-time status was launched but failed, and a Pennsylvania grand jury produced a recommendation calling for the legislature to be deprofessional-ized.[2] At the same time the recession forced many states to cut legislative expenditures, reducing staff and in some bodies cutting member pay (Greenblatt 2010).

Such events raise an important question about the direction of legisla-tive evolution. Polsby's (1968) study of changes in the U.S. House sug-gested that the body became progressively more institutionalized over time.[3] Similarly, the expectation from the literature is that over time legis-latures become more professionalized, not less. But the possibility that leg-islatures can travel both directions on evolutionary dimensions has been suggested by Hibbing (1999, 156), and some analyses of state legislatures since 1990 argue that they are deprofessionalizing or deinstitutionalizing (Brace and Ward 1999; Parent and Henderson 2002; Rosenthal 1996, 1998). To assess where state legislative evolution goes from here, we need to determine whether state legislatures have, in fact, deinstitutionalized or deprofessionalized in recent years.

Are State Legislatures Deinstitutionalizing?

As developed in this study, institutionalization has two characteristics: boundedness and complexity. In chapter 2, the rise of representative as-semblies and bicameral legislatures are cited as evidence of institutional boundedness. No developments since 1990 suggest that on these two char-acteristics legislatures today are less bounded than they once were. A ques-tion might be raised, however, about the impact of various forms of direct democracy on the boundedness of state legislatures. Over the last two decades voters have imposed a number of constraints on state legislative actions, not only through term limits but also through various forms of tax and expenditure limitations (TELs). In a number of states, voters have put in place TELs that establish supermajority vote requirements for taxes to be raised, greatly restricting the legislatures' ability to respond to changing revenue environments (Martell and Teske 2007). Certainly, in the states that allow initiatives, the voters can substitute their own policy judgments for those of their lawmakers, and in that way they can breach the legisla-ture's boundedness. But clever legislators often blunt the impact of voter initiatives (Gerber et al. 2001; Kousser, McCubbins, and Moule 2008), thereby reestablishing boundaries.

Given the line of argument offered in earlier chapters, it also is important to ask whether there is any evidence that state legislatures are deinstitutionalizing in terms of internal complexity. In this study internal complexity has largely been measured by parliamentary rules and standing committee systems. As discussed in chapter 7, parliamentary procedures usually change only very slowly and incrementally. To be sure, there are occasional bursts of rules reforms, but they are typically associated with the rare instances of a change in party control following a long period of dominance by the other party, as in Florida in 1999 and Georgia in 2005 (Jewett and Handberg 1999, 27; Squire and Moncrief 2010, 143). Similarly, standing committee systems usually change only at the margins from session to session (Hamm, Hedlund, and Martorano 2001, 2006). Moreover, the changes we do see have not resulted in legislatures becoming less complicated. Thus, in terms of internal complexity, it does not appear that state legislatures have begun to deinstitutionalize in recent decades. This is what we should expect because once an organization is highly institutionalized, organizational inertia or "stickiness" will exert a strong enough pull that institutional features do not decay, at least very quickly, even in the face of other significant changes (Pierson and Skocpol 2002, 700).

Are State Legislatures Deprofessionalizing?

Perhaps the more compelling question to investigate is whether state legislatures have begun deprofessionalizing since 1990. As discussed in chapter 7, there are three components to legislative professionalization: member pay, session length, and staff resources. The overall measure of state legislative professionalization compared to Congress, presented in table 7.6, suggests a slight decay in the average legislature since the mid-1980s. But how have state legislatures fared in regard to each component over the last two decades?

The question of whether state lawmakers in 2009 were getting paid more or less money than they had been at the peak of the professionalization movement in 1979 is answered in table 8.1. Here, legislative pay is calculated in 2009 dollars for each legislature in 1979 and 2009. As can be seen, the picture is muddled. In 2009 lawmakers were making more money than their counterparts had been four decades earlier in 23 states and less money in 27 states. The bottom half of table 8.1 presents a slightly different look at these data, examining whether state lawmaker pay had increased by more or less than $1,950 in 2009 dollars ($1,950 representing

10 percent of the median legislative pay). Again, by this measure 21 states had increased their pay substantially, 23 states had decreased their pay substantially, and 6 states paid roughly what they had in 1979.[4]

Interestingly, no particular pattern emerges as to which states raised salaries substantially and which let them lag. The states that increased legislative salaries by $10,000 or more in 2009 dollars included California, Delaware, Hawaii, Kentucky, Louisiana, New Jersey, Rhode Island, and Washington. Some of these states have generally been found near the top of the professionalization rankings, while others, notably Kentucky and Rhode Island, have been found toward the bottom. But as discussed in chapter 7, from the mid-1960s to the mid-1980s Kentucky made a concerted effort to improve its legislature, and in the mid-1990s voters in Rhode Island amended their constitution to improve legislative pay (Squire and Moncrief 2010, 89). Similarly, the states that allowed legislative wages to fall by $10,000 or more included Alaska, Iowa, Minnesota, Mississippi, South Carolina, and Texas, all of which have usually been found in the midranks on professionalization.

Thus, the data in table 8.1 do not present a clear picture on deprofessionalization. Slightly more states saw legislative salaries fall between 1979 and 2009 than saw them increase. In the vast majority of states this does not suggest that they were deprofessionalizing, but at the same time it is clear that efforts to continue to raise legislative salaries have foundered.

What of session lengths? As noted in chapter 7, most state legislatures returned to annual sessions during the twentieth century. Although many

TABLE 8.1. Deprofessionalization? Change in State Legislative Pay, 1979–2009

Pay Condition	Number of States
Pay increased in constant dollars between 1979 and 2009	23
Pay decreased in constant dollars between 1979 and 2009	27
Pay increased more than $1,950 in constant dollars between 1979 and 2009	21
Pay decreased more than $1,950 in constant dollars between 1979 and 2009	23
Pay changed less than $1,950 in constant dollars between 1979 and 2009	6

Source: Calculated by author from data in *Book of the States 1980–81* (1980, 90–91), and *Book of the States 2009 Edition* (2009, 99–101).

state legislatures still operate with some limitations on session lengths (Squire and Hamm 2005, 69), there has been a general increase in the number of days state legislatures meet. Has that trend been arrested over the last two decades?

As can be seen in table 8.2, a majority of states met for roughly the same number of days in 2007–8 as they did in 1977–78. Only 8 states saw the number of days they met drop by 10 days or more, while 13 states saw an increase of 10 days or more. Once again, however, no clear pattern emerges. Among the states that increased the number of days that they met were those with highly professionalized legislatures, such as California, New York, Ohio, and Pennsylvania, but also states with much less professional bodies such as Kentucky and Vermont. Likewise, among the states meeting for fewer days were Maine and Massachusetts, states on the opposite ends of the professionalization spectrum. Consequently, it is hard to argue from these data that state legislatures are either professionalizing or deprofessionalizing.

The third component of professionalization is staff. As revealed in the bottom of table 8.3, the total number of legislative staff during the session did not fluctuate much between 1979 and 2009. In the four time periods examined for change, a majority of states increased their number of legislative staff during three of them, and the states were evenly split between those that gained and those that lost during the other period. The discrepancy between these two observations—more states adding staff than losing them while the overall number of staff did not change much—can be reconciled by examining which states added staff and which states lost staff. Overall, most legislatures did not experience dramatic changes one way or the other. Interestingly, only two states saw declines with each measurement from 1988 to 2009: California and New York. California had 2,978 staff members in 1988, but only 2,106 in 2009. Similarly New York wit-

TABLE 8.2. Deprofessionalization? Change in Mean Number of Days in Session, 1977–78 and 2007–8

Number of Days in Session	Number of States
Increased 10 days or more from 1977–78 to 2007–8	13
Decreased 10 days or more from 1977–78 to 2007–8	8
Change from 1977–78 and 2007–8 was within 10 days	28

Source: Calculated by author from data in *Book of the States 1980–81* (1980, 104–5); *Book of the States 2008 Edition* (2008, 130–31); and *Book of the States 2009 Edition* (2009, 132–33).

nessed a decline from 4,157 staff members in 1988 to 2,751 in 2009. Thus the most professionalized legislatures experienced dramatic losses in staff support. In contrast, only five states increased staff with each measurement from 1979 to 2009: Arkansas, Kentucky, Nevada, New Hampshire, and New Mexico. To be sure, in several of these cases the increases were small. Session staff in New Hampshire, for example, grew to 179 in 2009 from 140 in 1979. But these results suggest an intriguing pattern. It may be that deprofessionalization on the staff component is occurring with the most professionalized state legislatures. But among the least professionalizing bodies, there is evidence of a continuing effort to improve their meager informational resources.

Legislative Evolution to This Point and into the Future

American legislatures were first established early in the seventeenth century. As discussed in chapter 2, they developed into recognizable legislative institutions by the eighteenth century. The assemblies became bounded institutions in that they rapidly evolved into representative houses in bicameral legislatures. They also started the process of becoming more complex organizations by adopting increasingly sophisticated rules and establishing the beginnings of standing committee systems. Even hints of professional-

TABLE 8.3. Deprofessionalization? Change in Total Staff during Legislative Session, 1979–2009

	Change from 1979 to 1988	Change from 1988 to 1996	Change from 1996 to 2003	Change from 2003 to 2009
Number of state legislatures with staffing numbers that increased or stayed the same	39	28	25	32
Number of state legislatures with staffing numbers that decreased	11	22	25	18
	1988	1996	2003	2009
Total number of staff during legislative sessions	33,330	35,884	34,903	34,110

Source: Tabulated by the author from National Conference of State Legislatures data: http://www.ncsl.org/default.aspx?tabid=14843.

ization began to appear with the provision of member salaries, the lengthening of legislative sessions, and the hiring of minimal staff.

The evolution of the colonial assemblies was driven by their objective to become powerful political actors. Eventually, they emerged as the leading forces promoting independence. The resulting break with Britain created an evolutionary challenge, as detailed in chapter 3. Those charged with designing new governing systems might have regarded the break as an opportunity to rethink their legislative institutions. Although a competing model in the form of the provisional congresses and the Continental Congress was available, the new state legislatures were created in the image of their colonial predecessors. Importantly, their most important features carried over despite the regime change. As the new state legislatures aged, they continued to become increasingly complex organizations.

Remarkably, organizational continuities were maintained even with territorial legislatures, which, as discussed in chapter 4, were institutions established in challenging environments. These legislatures were modeled on existing legislatures, and those that existed for decades became increasingly more complex organizations. Perhaps, even more strikingly, the odd evolutionary cases examined in chapter 5 reinforce this line of argument, even when the transition was from an independent republic to a state legislature (Texas), an independent kingdom to an independent republic to a territorial legislature (Hawaii), or various provisional legislatures to a territorial legislature to a state legislature (Oregon).

How existing legislatures changed over time was examined in chapter 6, which showed that state legislatures became institutionalized during the nineteenth century, and in chapter 7, which documented the professionalization trend since 1900. This brings us to the present, with institutionalized legislatures of various professionalization stripes. All of them are rooted in (mostly) the same set of predecessors, but none looks exactly like any other legislature. Over the last two decades, none has deinstitutionalized, and, perhaps, a few have deprofessionalized, if only at the margins.

Where does legislative evolution go from here? Given the long continuity in American legislatures, stretching out almost four centuries, there is little reason to think that state legislatures four or five decades from now, or even a century from now, will look particularly different from what they look like today. After all, their rules and procedures and their organizational structures are institutionalized, and institutions do not change easily or often. If American legislatures are apt to change, it is likely the change will occur in the components of professionalization. Given the pattern of the last two decades, a scenario can be spun where the most professional state legislatures lose some ground. Thus, given current trends, California and New York will probably never become the organizational equivalents of Congress; indeed they may fall further behind. But, at the same time, it may also be the case that many of the legislatures that lag in terms of professionalization will push to improve their status. Thus, the New Hampshires of the American legislative world may professionalize, at least a little bit. But they likely will never completely close the gap with their most professional counterparts.

The reason for this general pattern is that the expectations placed on state legislatures to make increasingly important public policy decisions will likely push them to continue to evolve. Such external pressures have done so for four centuries. Colonial assemblies became more complex organizations as an increasing number of issues were placed on their agendas. During the nineteenth century state legislatures were buffeted by demands to both do less and do more. Again, over time, they responded by increasing their internal complexity. In the twentieth century state legislatures dramatically increased the informational resources available to them, sometimes with public support, sometimes without it. They did so to better inform themselves as they were confronted by more complex problems to solve. As the public continues to make greater demands on them, state legislatures will continue to evolve in response, although the exact path each takes will likely differ.

Notes

1. Jillson and Wilson (1994) is an exception in linking colonial assemblies to the Continental and Confederal Congress. My early efforts on evolution can be found in Squire (2005, 2006a) and Squire and Hamm (2005).

2. For a provocative attempt to fit a biological model to the study of legislative evolution, see Hedlund, Patzelt, and Olson (2008).

3. Polsby's (1968) third indicator, universalistic criteria and automatic methods, is the least translatable to legislatures beyond the U.S. Congress (Squire 1992a). It is given scant attention here.

4. Military governments operated for a period in New Mexico and California and arguably in Florida and Orleans as well (Grivas 1963; Thomas 1904). There were 31 state legislatures from 30 territorial legislatures because Dakota Territory was split into North Dakota and South Dakota.

CHAPTER 2

1. The exception to the early emergence of representative assemblies is New York, where it took some 60 years to establish one (Bonomi 1971, 28–29; Lincoln 1909, 1–5).

2. A *feme sole trader* was a married woman authorized by law to engage in trade or business as if she were unmarried (Robey 1922, 30).

3. The Crown or corporation appointed the governor and councilors in Massachusetts and later in New Hampshire. They were elected in Connecticut, New Haven, Plymouth, and Rhode Island. In Massachusetts, the council would eventually be elected by the lower house.

4. The use of the word *Comittes* here means individuals to whom certain responsibilities were committed, not an organized body as in current usage (Kukla 1989, 56; McConachie 1898, 4–6). Here and elsewhere I use language as given in the original source, with a few exceptions. I replaced the long *s* with

an *s* and symbols that are not reproducible with the letters they represent. I have left the letters *u* and *v* as given in the originals.

5. Moran (1895, 50) says bicameralism developed in 1694, but it seems clear from the 1692 House journal (Salley 1907) that the chambers were already separate at that point.

6. West Florida reverted to Spanish control following the American Revolution. Thus its assembly did not transition into a state legislature. Rather, as discussed in chapter 4, once the United States took control of Florida several decades later it established it as a territory and created a territorial legislature following a brief period of military rule.

7. These means were calculated by the author using data in Bonomi (1971, 295–311).

8. The decision to pay the speaker and not other Assembly members reinforces the idea that the position was seen as serving more of an administrative or support role. Although Pory was called the speaker and played the leading role in the General Assembly, he was not speaker in the sense the title would suggest in later years (Billings 2004, 8–9; Kukla 1981, 8–9; 1989, 51–52).

9. Olson (1992, 562) puts the move in the 1730s, while Hitchcock and Seale (1976) say the Assembly first met in the new facility in 1746, and Etting (1891, 5) gives 1747 as the date.

10. Additional evidence can be found in Cook (1931, 266); Corey (1929, 123); Frakes (1970); Greene (1959); Harlow (1917, 1–23); Jameson (1894, 261–67); Leake (1917); Leonard (1948a, 237–38); Pargellis (1927a, 84–86; 1927b, 143–45); and Ryerson (1986, 114). There is disagreement over the number of standing committees used in the South Carolina Commons House. In 1757, there were five standing committees: Courts of Justices; Grievances; Priveledges and Elections; Religion; and Trade (Lipscomb 1996, 10). Smith (1903, 103) reports the existence of the same five standing committees but without specifying a date. Harlow (1917, 18) argues that there were only two standing committees: (1) Grievances and (2) Privileges and Elections. Frakes (1970, 22) says there were six standing committees, again without giving a date. The data I report were collected from microfilm of the unpublished, handwritten journals for 1769, available at the South Carolina Department of Archives and History.

11. The number of ad hoc committees was taken from the index compiled by the clerk and found at the end of the unpublished, handwritten journal, available on microfilm at the South Carolina Department of Archives and History.

12. A committee for Private Causes also was established in several years during the mid-1650s, but it focused on judicial rather than legislative matters (Billings 2004, 38; Hening 1809, 422, 512; McIlwaine 1915, 93, 103).

13. Such committees were also created in Jamaica (1677), the Bahamas (1734), and Bermuda (1747).

14. Volume 1 of the journal can be found at http://www.british-history .ac.uk/source.aspx?pubid=14.

15. Calling the presiding officer *the moderator* still continues today in New England town meetings. The Rhode Island General Assembly began referring to its presiding officer as *the speaker* in 1664 (Bartlett 1857, 22, 25, 71).

16. For examples of cloture and moving the previous question being invoked, see the journal of Samuel Foulke (1884, 411).

17. The Bahamas Assembly drew on the experiences of the Bermuda Assembly (Kammen 1969, 50). In turn, Bermuda's rules were drawn from Parliament's (Lefroy 1882, 197–99).

CHAPTER 3

1. The provincial congress was preceded by a 60-member Committee of Inspection, which was later transformed into a 100-member Provisional War Committee. It was this latter body that issued the call for the election of a provisional congress (Lincoln 1906, 472, 476).

2. All three committee members had also served in the assembly; Follsom (whose name usually appears as Folsom) and Bartlett were serving concurrently in the final assembly (Walker 1905, 47–48, 52–53, 55–56). Given their service in both bodies, the fact that the rules adopted by the provincial congress are more like those adopted in Massachusetts rather than their own assembly is consistent with the supposition advanced here.

3. These data are taken from The Virginia Elections and State Elected Officials Database Project, 1776–2007, http://fisher.lib.virginia.edu/collec tions/stats/valeg/php/statistics.php?type=Turnover&office=VAH&end=1789 &begin=1776.

4. Following John Hale's (n.d., 16) short volume on Boone published sometime in the 1880s most scholars have given the date of the order to take him into custody as December 7, 1781. According the House journal, the order was issued on December 28, 1781.

CHAPTER 4

1. The figure for Arizona was calculated by the author from data in Wagoner (1970, 43).

2. Clay had served in the U.S. Senate prior to the required age of 30 but the reference should have been to John Randolph, who was alleged to have given the response when asked by either the speaker or the clerk if he was the required age to be sworn in as a member of the U.S. House (Bruce 1922, 154–55; Colton 1904, 268).

3. These data were calculated by the author from "Catalogue of the Members and Officers of Both Houses of the First Legislative Assembly of

Kansas Territory, Convened on the 2nd Day of July, 1855"; found at http://www.territorialkansasonline.org/cgiwrap/imlskto/index.php?SCREEN=view_image&<le_name=k301920&scale=1.5625&document_id=100108&FROM_PAGE=.

4. These data were calculated by the author from Brazier (2000, 29–31).

5. As another example of the dominance of Spanish in New Mexico, in 1865 the territorial House proposed printing 500 copies of the governor's annual address in English and 2,000 copies in Spanish (*Jour. of the H. of Reps. of the Terr. of N.M.* 1866, 46). Printing a governor's address in multiple languages was common. The Wisconsin territorial House voted to print 1,000 copies of their governor's message in English, 500 copies in German, and 250 copies in Norwegian (*Jour. of the H. of Reps, First Annual Sess. of the Fifth LA of the Terr. of Wis.* 1847, 19). The Michigan Council voted to have 1,000 copies of their governor's address printed in English and 150 copies in French (*Jour. of the Proc. of the Sixth LC of the Terr. of Mich.* 1834, 7). The Nebraska Legislative Assembly voted to have 1,000 copies of the governor's address printed in German (*Coun. Jour. of the LA of the Terr. of Nebraska* 1860, 43, 56).

6. Green I. Currin (sometimes the initial is given as J.) served in 1890, and David J. Wallace in 1893. See http://digital.library.okstate.edu/encyclopedia/entries/C/CU005.html; and http://digital.library.okstate.edu/encyclopedia/entries/W/WA010.html.

7. These data were calculated by the author from membership rosters in Gilkey (1901, 131–43) and Brantley (1947, 228–29).

8. These data were calculated by the author from membership rosters in *Iowa Off. Register* (1907, 107–8), *Neb. Blue Book* (1922, 36–42), *Legislative Man. of the St. of Wis.* (1872, 185–96).

9. Technically, the speaker was not a neophyte; almost a decade earlier he had served for a year in the Legislature of the Hawaiian Kingdom (Lydecker 1918, 182).

10. A *cayuse* is a native range horse.

11. Henry S. Baird. "Letters from the Territorial Convention in Belmont." Wisconsin Historical Society Archives (Wis Mss V, Box 1 Folder 4). Online facsimile at http://www.wisconsinhistory.org/turningpoints/search.asp?id=43.

12. This information can be found in "Alaska gets a Legislature," on the Alaska History and Cultural Studies webpage, http://www.akhistorycourse.org/articles/article.php?artID=135.

13. Another lawmaker, Ephraim Cutler (1890, 55), recounts a similar episode, although some of the details vary, notably that his assaulted colleague drew a dirk and not a pistol. It is likely, but not certain, that this was the same incident that Burnet described.

14. Henry S. Baird, "Letters from the Territorial Convention in Belmont," Wisconsin Historical Society Archives (Wis Mss V, Box 1 Folder 4). Online facsimile at http://www.wisconsinhistory.org/turningpoints/search.asp?id=43.

15. *Bug juice* was poor quality whiskey.

16. A *slung-shot* is a personal weapon consisting of a heavy weight attached to a cord.

17. The assailant was James R. Vineyard. Amazingly, the incident only ended one legislative career. Acquitted of manslaughter charges, Vineyard was elected to the Wisconsin state Assembly in 1849. He moved to California during the gold rush and was elected to the state assembly in 1855 and the state senate in 1861.

18. *Buncombe* means nonsense. In colloquial English today, *buncombe* (or *bunkum*) is usually shortened to *bunk*.

19. *Pipe-laying* and *wire-working* were nineteenth-century terms for political and financial corruption respectively (Grimsted 1998, 195; Hammond 1948, 13).

20. See "Alaska gets a Legislature," on the Alaska History and Cultural Studies webpage, http://www.akhistorycourse.org/articles/article.php?artID=135.

21. This quote can be found in "Alaska gets a Legislature," on the Alaska History and Cultural Studies webpage, http://www.akhistorycourse.org/articles/article.php?artID=135.

22. As will be discussed in chapter 5, the rules adopted by the Kentucky House were largely taken from the rules adopted by the U.S. House in 1789 (*Jour. of the H. of Reps. of the US* 1789, 9–12). There were a few notable changes in the U.S. House rules between 1789 and 1795.

23. The initial Missouri House in 1812 met for only a few days and focused on selecting names to submit for the Council. The 1813 House was the first to deal with policy issues and thus had a need for a standing committee or committees.

CHAPTER 5

1. The nine cities in the order in which they first hosted the legislature were Windsor, Bennington, Manchester, Westminster, Charlestown (New Hampshire), Rutland, Norwich, Newbury, and Castleton. The legislature met in Charlestown on the east side of the Connecticut River at a time when it and a number of other towns in that region were contemplating being annexed by Vermont. Several of these communities gained seats in the Vermont Assembly (Hall 1868, 339–40, 357).

2. In its 1790 constitution, South Carolina had included a maximum legislative per diem of seven shillings.

3. The few substantive differences in rules between the Kentucky House and the U.S. House were largely driven by the contrasts in membership sizes and by Kentucky's use of a standing committee system. By comparison, in 1792 the Pennsylvania House used a much smaller set of 20 rules (*Jour. of the First Session of the Third H. of Reps. of the Com. of Pa.* 1792, 20–21). There may have been a tie between Kentucky's rules and those used by Pennsylvania because the latter influenced U.S. House rules (McConachie 1898, 10, 13).

4. One minor difference appears in the rule governing committee appointments. In Kentucky, the speaker appointed all committees with the House being allowed to add members. In the U.S. House the speaker appointed committees of three or fewer members; larger committees were filled by a ballot of the House. Another difference was that failure to respond to a call of the Kentucky House would result in a specified fine; no fines were imposed in the U.S. House. A Kentucky rule not found in the U.S. House rules specified that the all fines be turned over to the sergeant at arms.

5. The printer in Maine got the Roman numeral wrong for Chapter VI, mistakenly printing Chapter IV (*Rules and Orders to be Observed in the H. of Reps. of the St. of Maine* 1820, 11).

6. See Mr. Lamb's comments in the debates of January 8, 1862, at http://www.wvculture.org/HISTORY/statehood/cc010862.html.

7. See Mr. Van Winkle's comments in the debates of January 7, 1862, at http://www.wvculture.org/HISTORY/statehood/cc010762.html.

8. See Mr. Lamb's comments in the debates of January 7, 1862, at http://www.wvculture.org/history/statehood/cc010762.html.

9. Wheeling, where the first West Virginia legislature met, is 120 miles from Columbus, Ohio, 200 miles from Harrisburg, Pennsylvania, and almost 250 miles from Richmond, Virginia. Maryland and Kentucky also border West Virginia. Annapolis is over 300 miles from Wheeling, and the rules and standing committees used at that time by the House of Delegates bear almost no resemblance those adopted by West Virginia (cf. *Rules and Orders for the Regulation and Gov. of the H. of Dels.* 1861).

10. The provisions are 1836, Article I, section 13; 1845, Article III, section 12; 1861, Article III, section 12; 1866, Article III, section 11; 1869, Article III, section XV; and 1876, Article III, section 10. See http://tarlton.law.utexas .edu/constitutions/text/q.html.

11. These data were tabulated by the author from membership rosters in Lindley (1942).

12. Of the members with previous American service, three had served in Alabama, two each in Florida and North Carolina, and one each in Kentucky, Maine, Mississippi, Missouri, and Tennessee. One Texas Congress member had served in both North Carolina and Florida. One senator had been a member of the Mexican legislature at Saltillo, a representative had served in the Coahuila legislature, and another representative had served in both the Coahuila legislature and the Mexican Congress (Lindley 1942).

13. These data were tabulated by the author from membership rosters in Lindley (1942).

14. Wisconsin's lower house also came to be called the Assembly because that state's constitutional convention used New York's constitution as its model (Paxson 1915, 9). Nevada took much of its first constitution from California's (Driggs and Goodall 1996, 66), accounting for its use of the name.

15. In its initial constitution, Nevada devised a creative solution to this

dilemma, specifying that the legislature would meet annually for its first two sessions and then meet biennially (*Off. Rep. of the Deb. and Proc. in the Constitutional Conv. of the St. of Nev., 1864* 1866, 138–39).

16. The names of most of the other members of the Franklin General Assembly have been lost.

17. The first defector, F. X. Matthieu, was later elected to the Oregon House in 1874 and 1878.

18. The letter was published over the name of Peter H. Burnet, which was likely a typographical error and should have been Peter H. Burnett.

19. McCarver left for California during the gold rush. He was elected a delegate to the California constitutional convention and was an active participant in the discussions on legislative provisions (Browne 1850, 79–91). One of McCarver's convention colleagues recalled that he continually mixed up references to California and Oregon (Barker 1945, 39–40).

20. The membership of the General Assembly of Deseret was taken from the *Constitution of the State of Deseret, with the Journal of the Convention which Formed it, and the Proceedings of the Legislature Consequent Thereon* (1849, 11, 13) and supplemented with committee lists reported by Morgan (1987, 51, 195) and information from Evans (1875, 86). The membership list of the first Utah Territorial Legislature can be found at http://www.archives.state.ut.us/re search/guides/legislative-assembly.htm. The list of the standing committees in the first territorial legislature and the rules for the first territorial House were supplied by the reference staff at the Utah State Archives. They were located in the Utah Territorial Legislative Assembly, Journals, First Session, 1851–1852, Series 3145, Reel 1 (pages 10–12).

21. My discussion of the various Hawaiian constitutions is grounded in Lydecker (1918), which contains copies of each of the documents.

22. *Mauka* and *makai* mean "toward the mountains" and "toward the ocean."

23. By 1918 another seven territorial lawmakers had first served in the Republic or Kingdom legislatures. These data were tabulated by the author from rosters in Lydecker (1918, 286–301).

24. The House initially adopted the rules used by the U.S. House and then subsequently adopted its own set of rules (*Jour. of the H. of Reps. of the Terr. of Kan.* 1855, 9, 29).

25. A *doughface* was a Northerner who sympathized with Southern slave interests.

26. Dwinelle mistakenly dates the convention in March.

CHAPTER 6

1. Although it did not have a territorial predecessor, California's state legislature also met prior to statehood, with accompanying concerns about the legality of its decisions.

2. As with the Wisconsin Council murder discussed in chapter 4, the Arkansas assailant, John Wilson, was expelled from the House but found not guilty at trial. Within a few years Wilson moved to a new county and was again elected to the House, where he got involved in another floor altercation over a banking bill and once more brandished a knife (Rolfe 1904, 304). Soon thereafter, he moved to Texas, where he failed in efforts to get elected to the legislature (http://www.encyclopediaofarkansas.net/encyclopedia/entry-detail.aspx?entryID=5664).

3. Each source gives a slightly different name for the building used by House Republicans. The *Anaconda Standard* (1889) gave the name quoted. A U.S. Senate report on contested elections (a category in which both of Montana's initial Senate elections fell) gave the name as "Iron Hall," while Bancroft referred to it as "Iron block" and Lynch as the "Old iron front building." The Montana Senate met in the courthouse, although Democrats boycotted the first several weeks to prevent a quorum. As a result of the election dispute, the first state legislature accomplished almost nothing.

4. In Washington, the rules were those used in the 1887–88 Washington territorial House, which, in turn, were originally adopted in 1883 (*Jour. of the H. of Reps. of the Terr. of Wash.* 1888, 7).

5. Legislation passed by Confederate state legislatures was, with the exception of bills directly supporting the rebellion, effectively deemed legitimate by the U.S. Supreme Court in 1869 (*Texas v. White* 74 U.S. 700).

6. George W. Peck was a newspaper publisher who became well known as the author of "Peck's Bad Boy." He later was elected mayor of Milwaukee and governor of Wisconsin.

7. In addition to Pennsylvania (1874), state constitutions with a similar provision were Alabama (1875), Arkansas (1874), California (1879), Florida (1885), Kentucky (1890), Louisiana (1898), Mississippi (1890), Missouri (1875), New York (1894), and Washington (1889).

8. Corruption became a serious problem in the Pennsylvania legislature by the 1840s (Bowers 1983, 459).

9. Calculated by the author from data found at http://www.leg.state.mn.us/lrl/histleg/sessions.asp.

10. The vote totals were 9,340 in favor of biennial sessions and 1,503 in favor of annual sessions. But more than 75,000 votes were cast during the election, and the vast majority of voters opted not to express an opinion. In 1879, Connecticut voters defeated a proposal to move to biennial sessions (with over 89 percent of the votes in Hartford against the reform). But in 1884 the state's voters changed their minds and passed such a measure (*NYT* 1889b).

11. The capitols still in use and the year the initial construction was completed (but not necessarily the year the legislature first occupied the building) are New Jersey (1792), Maryland (1797), Massachusetts (1798), Virginia (1798), New Hampshire (1819), Maine (1832), Ohio (1857), Tennessee (1859). Vermont (1859), South Carolina (1868), California (1869), Michigan (1878), Connecticut (1879), Iowa (1886), Illinois (1888), Texas (1888), Indiana (1888),

Wyoming (1888), Georgia (1889), New York (1899). See Gold (2009, 92); Goodsell (2001, 60–61); Hitchcock and Seale (1976, 312–33).

12. In addition to Arkansas, capitols expanded in the nineteenth century included Alabama, Delaware, Georgia, Maine, Massachusetts, Minnesota, New Hampshire, New Jersey, North Dakota, and Pennsylvania (Hitchcock and Seale 1976, 312–33).

13. At the time, 34 states had provisions allowing each chamber to determine the rules of its proceedings. No such provision appeared in the Georgia, Maine, and North Carolina constitutions (Hough 1872, 630).

14. All of these data were tabulated by the author from information in Hough (1872, 638–43).

CHAPTER 7

1. The 12 states that have kept the same number of lower-house seats since 1900 are Arkansas, California, Colorado, Indiana, Kansas, Kentucky, Maine, North Carolina, Oregon, South Carolina, Tennessee, and Virginia. These data were gathered by the author from Dubin (2007).

2. These data were gathered from *Sen. and H. Jours. of the Leg. of the St. of Neb.* (1935, 6–7, 276–80); and *2008–9 Neb. Blue Book*, http://nebraskalegisla ture.gov/about/blue-book.php, pages 327–88.

3. The Committee on Committees recommended the composition of the Rules Committee, which was approved by the full chamber (*Legislative Jour. of the St. of Neb.* 1937, 23).

4. Comparisons were made among the standing rules used in the 1931 Senate of Nebraska (http://www.usgennet.org/usa/ne/topic/resources/OLLi brary/Legislature/1933/pages/nelj0032.htm), the 1931 House of Representatives of Nebraska (http://www.usgennet.org/usa/ne/topic/resources/OLLi brary/Legislature/1933/pages/nelj0050.htm), the 1935 House of Representatives (*H. Jour. of the Leg. of the St. of Neb.* (1935, IX–XXIII), and the first unicameral legislature in 1937 (*Legislative Jour. of the St. of Neb.* 1937, xv–xxxii).

5. In addition to the states that had formally adopted annual sessions given in table 7.1, several other states had moved to meeting every year using informal mechanisms, usually by taking recesses and not adjourning *sine die* (Owsley 1969, 401; Wiltsee 1966, 42).

6. These data were gathered by the author from http://fisher.lib.virginia .edu/collections/stats/valeg/php/stats_main.php.

7. The west wing and reference library in the New York capitol were destroyed by fire in 1911 (*NYT* 1911b), but the building was repaired.

8. See the electronic version of National Conference of State Legislatures, Inside the Legislative Process, http://www.ncsl.org/documents/legis mgt/ILP/02Tab3Pt6.pdf.; http://www.ncsl.org/documents/legismgt/ILP/96 Tab3Pt1.pdf.

9. These data are from the *Book of the States 2009*, page 140.

10. Data on days in session in 1909 were generously provided by Keith Hamm and Ronald Hedlund who gathered them as part of their project on state legislative committees.

11. This professionalization measure and the others presented here are calculated in the same manner as Squire (1992b, 2000, 2007).

12. Legislative pay was calculated from data in the *Book of the States 1935*. For Congress I used the salary at the beginning of 1934 ($8,500) to make it comparable to the data available for the states. In early 1934 Congress raised its pay back to $9,000, the figure it had been in 1932, and then increased it again to $9,500 toward the end of that year. In 1935 they raised it again to $10,000, where it stayed for 12 years (Dwyer 2004). Using the higher congressional salaries would deflate the state professionalization scores.

13. The eight states where senators enjoyed shared office space were Florida, New York, Oklahoma, Pennsylvania, Vermont, Washington, West Virginia, and Wisconsin. The five states where at least most members could share office space were Maryland, Missouri, Oklahoma, Washington, and West Virginia.

14. This quote is taken from page 23 of an oral history provided by William A. Gissberg as part of the Washington State Oral History Program, http://apps.leg.wa.gov/oralhistory/gissberg.pdf.

15. See pages 2 and 3 of the summary of the Commission's archives, http://www.oac.cdlib.org/data/13030/zp/tf096n96zp/files/tf096n96zp.pdf; and Hyink (1969, 641).

16. In 1975 the National Legislative Conference merged with two other organizations to form the National Conference of State Legislatures (Kurtz 1999).

17. See the discussion based on the organization's archives housed at the Auraria Library in Denver, Colorado.

18. This table includes all professionalization-related measures put before the voters across the states. On salaries, measures to directly increase legislative pay or to allow the legislature to set its own wages were included in this tally. Measures to create salary commissions were not included. On legislative sessions, measures to allow for annual sessions or to increase session lengths were included. Measures to allow the legislature to call itself into special session or to hold organizational sessions were not included.

19. The scores in table 7.6 are not directly comparable to those in table 7.4 because the staff components of the scores for 1979 and later are comparisons between the state legislatures and Congress on the number of staff members per legislator, rather than on funding measures. Measures using legislative expenditures or legislative operating budgets for the final component of professionalization produce consistent state rankings with measures using staffing numbers (Berkman 1991, 675; Maestas 2003, 448; Mooney 1994).

20. As noted in Squire (2007), in an absolute sense professionalization in state legislatures can increase over time, but at a slower rate than in Congress,

making it look as if state legislatures are becoming less professional. There is some evidence suggesting that this has happened.

21. These figures were calculated with California's salary set at $116,208. In December 2009, the state's compensation commission cut that salary by 10 percent. Using the reduced salary the mean state legislative salary in 2009 was $27,812.

22. These data were gathered from the *Book of the States 2009*, pages 136–39.

23. State or provincial wealth also has been found to be the most powerful variable in explaining differences in legislative salaries in a comparative analysis of national assemblies and subnational legislatures in federal systems (Squire 2008).

24. These data were gathered from Iowa GA (1980). Information on member occupation was provided for members earlier than 1880, but the reporting of party membership was irregular. The necessary data are complete for the period between 1880 and 1980.

CHAPTER 8

1. State courts of last resort tossed out term limits in Massachusetts, Oregon, Washington, and Wyoming. State legislatures repealed them in Idaho and Utah. Thus they went into full effect in 15 states.

2. The failure of the effort to make California a part-time legislature can be found at http://blogs.kqed.org/capitalnotes/2010/03/29/part-time-legisla ture-not-this-year/. The Pennsylvania grand jury report can be found at http://www.post-gazette.com/downloads/20100525GrandJuryReport.pdf.

3. Polsby's (2004) final book, *How Congress Evolves*, can be seen as a story about the deinstitutionalization of the U.S. House.

4. A Council of State Governments analysis of legislative pay from 1975 to 2005 reports a similar finding. The report can be found at http://trendsi namerica.org/knowledgecenter/docs/sn0702LegislativePayDaze.pdf.

Abbreviations

In the references and citations, commonly cited sources and words that appear repeatedly have been abbreviated according to the following list.

Legislative and Other Public Documents

Ala.	Alabama
Ariz.	Arizona
Ark.	Arkansas
Asm.	Assembly
Calif.	California
Col.	Colony
Colo.	Colorado
Com.	Commonwealth
Cong.	Congress
Conn.	Connecticut
Cons.	Constitution
Conv.	Convention
Convs.	Conventions
Coun.	Council
Deb.	Debates
Del.	Delaware
Dels.	Delegates
Ext.	Extract
Exts.	Extracts
Fla.	Florida
Ga.	Georgia

GA	General Assembly
GC	General Court
Gov.	Government
H.	House
Ill.	Illlinois
Ind.	Indiana
Jour.	Journal
Jours.	Journals
Kan.	Kansas
Ky.	Kentucky
La.	Louisiana
LA	Legislative Assembly
LC	Legislative Council
Leg.	Legislature
Man.	Manual
Mass.	Massachusetts
Md.	Maryland
Mich.	Michigan
Min.	Minutes
Minn.	Minnesota
Miss.	Mississippi
Mo.	Missouri
Mont.	Montana
N.C.	North Carolina
N.D.	North Dakota
Neb.	Nebraska
Nev.	Nevada
N.H.	New Hampshire
N.J.	New Jersey
N.M.	New Mexico
N.Y.	New York
Off.	Official
Okla.	Oklahoma
Ore.	Oregon
Pa.	Pennsylvania
Proc.	Proceedings
Prov.	Province
Reg.	Regular
Reps.	Representatives

Rev.	Revision
R.I.	Rhode Island
S.C.	South Carolina
S.D.	South Dakota
Sen.	Senate
Sess.	Session
S.F.	San Francisco
St.	State
Stat.	Statutes
Tenn.	Tennessee
Terr.	Territory
US	United States
USA	United States of America
Va.	Virginia
Vt.	Vermont
Wash.	Washington (state)
Wis.	Wisconsin
W.Va.	West Virginia
Wyo.	Wyoming

Newspapers

DN	*Deseret News*
MP	*Montana Post*
NYDT	*New York Daily Times*
NYT	*New York Times*
NY Trib.	*New-York Tribune*

Other Sources

AHQ	*Arkansas Historical Quarterly*
AHR	*American Historical Review*
Annals	*Annals of the American Academy of Political and Social Science*
APSR	*American Political Science Review*
JAH	*Journal of American History*
JOP	*Journal of Politics*
JSH	*Journal of Southern History*
LSQ	*Legislative Studies Quarterly*
MVHR	*Mississippi Valley Historical Review*

NCR   *National Civic Review*
PMHB   *Pennsylvania Magazine of History and Biography*
PSQ   *Political Science Quarterly*
QOHS   *Quarterly of the Oregon Historical Society*
SPPQ   *State Politics and Policy Quarterly*
VMHB   *Virginia Magazine of History and Biography*
WMQ   *William and Mary Quarterly*
WPQ   *Western Political Quarterly*

References

LEGISLATIVE JOURNALS AND OTHER PUBLIC DOCUMENTS

Acts and Laws of the St. of Conn., in America. 1784. New-London, Conn.: Timothy Green.

Acts and Resolutions Adopted by the GA of Fla., at its Tenth Sess., Begun and Held at the Capitol, in the City of Tallahassee, on Monday, November 26, 1860. 1861. Tallahassee, Fla.: Floridian and Journal.

Acts of the LA of the Terr. of N.M., Twenty-First Sess., Convened at the Capital, at the City of Santa Fe, on Monday the First Day of December, 1873, and Adjourned on Friday the Ninth Day of January, 1874. 1874. Santa Fe, N.M.: Manderfield and Tucker.

Acts of the Leg. of the St. of Mich., Passed at the Extra Sess. of 1858, with an Appendix, Containing Certified Statements of Boards of Supervisors relative to the Erection of New Townships; also State Treasurers' Annual Report for Year 1857. 1858. Lansing, Mich.: Hosmer and Kerr.

Acts of the Ninety-Sixth Leg. of the St. of N.J. and Twenty-Eighth under the New Cons. 1872. Trenton, N.J.: Naar, Day & Naar.

Acts Passed at the First Sess. of the First Leg. of the Terr. of Orleans, Begun and Held in the City of New-Orleans, on the 25th Day of January, in the Year of Our Lord One Thousand Eight Hundred and Six, and of the Independence of the USA the Thirtieth. 1807. New Orleans: Bradford & Anderson.

Acts Passed at the First Sess. of the Leg. Coun. of the Terr. of Orleans, Begun and Held at the Principal, in the City of New-Orleans, on Monday the Third Day of December, in the Year of Our Lord, One Thousand Eight Hundred and Four, and of the Independence of the US the Twenty-Ninth. 1805. New Orleans: James. M. Bradford.

Acts Passed at the First Sess. of the Second Leg. of the Terr. of Orleans, Begun and Held in the City of New-Orleans, on Monday, the Eighteenth Day of January, in the Year of Our Lord, One Thousand Eight Hundred and Eight, and of the Independence of the USA, the Thirty-Second. 1808. New Orleans: Bradford & Anderson.

Acts Passed at the First Sess. of the Third Leg. of the Terr. of Orleans, Begun and Held in the City of New-Orleans, on Tuesday, the Ninth Day of January, in the Year of Our Lord One Thousand Eight Hundred and Ten, and of the Independence of the USA, the Thirty-Fourth. 1810. New Orleans: Thierry & Dacqueny.

Acts Passed at the Second Sess. of the First GA of the Ala. Terr. in the Forty Third Year of American Independence. 1818. St. Stephens, Ala.: Thomas Eastin.

Acts Passed at the Second Sess. of the First Leg. of the Terr. of Orleans, Begun and Held in the City of New-Orleans, on the 12th Day of January, in the Year of Our Lord One Thousand Eight Hundred and Seven, and of the Independence of the USA the Thirty-First. 1807. New Orleans: Bradford & Anderson.

Acts Passed at the Second Sess. of the Second Leg. of the Terr. of Orleans, Begun and Held in the City of New Orleans, on Friday, the Thirteenth Day of January, in the Year of Our Lord One Thousand Eight Hundred and Nine, and of the Independence of the USA, the Thirty-Third. 1809. New Orleans: Louisiana Courier.

Acts Passed at the Second Sess. of the Third Leg. of the Terr. of Orleans, Begun and Held in the City of New-Orleans, on Monday, the Twenty-Third Day of January, in the Year of Our Lord One Thousand Eight Hundred and Eleven, and of the Independence of the USA, the Thirty-Fifth. 1811. New Orleans: Thierry.

Acts, Resolutions, and Memorials, Passed by the First Annual, and Special Sessions, of the LA, of the Terr. of Utah, Begun and Held at Great Salt Lake City, on the 22nd Day of September, A. D. 1851. 1852. Great Salt Lake City, Utah: Brigham H. Young.

Bartlett, John Russell, ed. 1856. *Records of the Col. of R.I. and Providence Plantations, in New England,* vol. I. Providence, R.I.: A. Crawford Greene and Brother.

Bartlett, John Russell, ed. 1857. *Records of the Col. of R.I. and Providence Plantations, in New England,* vol. II. Providence, R.I.: A. Crawford Greene and Brother.

Bartlett, John Russell, ed. 1858. *Records of the Col. of R.I. and Providence Plantations, in New England,* vol. III. Providence, R.I.: Knowles, Anthony & Co.

Bartlett, John Russell, ed. 1862. *Records of the Col. of R.I. and Providence Plantations in New England,* vol. VII. Providence, R.I.: A. Crawford Greene.

Bartlett, John Russell, ed. 1863. *Records of the St. of R.I. and Providence Plantations in New England,* vol. VIII. Providence, R.I.: Cooke, Jackson.

Barton, C. M. 1891. *Barton's Legislative Hand-Book and Man., Containing Historical, Political, Commercial, Agricultural, and Other Data; Together with Interesting Statistics, from the Organization of the Terr. to the Close of the Second Leg. of the St.* Olympia, Wash.: State Printing and Publishing Co.

Batchellor, Albert Stillman, ed. 1891. *Early St. Papers of N.H. Including the Cons. of 1784, Jours. of the Sen. and H. of Reps., and Records of the President and Coun., from June 1784 to June 1787, with an Appendix Containing an Abstract of the Official Records Relative to the Formation, Promulgation, Consideration, and Adoption of the Federal Cons., and Illustrative Notes.* Manchester, N.H.: John B. Clarke.

Batchellor, Albert Stillman, ed. 1892. *Early St. Papers of N.H. Including the Jours. of the Sen. and H. of Reps. and Records of the President and Coun., from June 1787 to June 1790, with an Appendix Containing Biographical Sketches of Men Who Sustained Important Relations to the State Gov. During that Period, Taken from the Manuscript Biographies of Governor William Plumer; Also Correspondence and Acts of the Leg. Pertaining to the Federal Cons. and the Relations of N.H. to the Federal Gov.* Concord, N.H.: Ira C. Evans.

Batchellor, Albert Stillman, ed. 1904. *Laws of N.H. Including Public and Private Acts and Resolves and the Royal Commissions and Instructions, with Historical and Descriptive Notes, and an Appendix,* vol. one. Manchester, N.H.: John B. Clarke Co.

Blue Book of the St. of Wis. 1889. Madison, Wis.: State Printing Board.

Bouton, Nathaniel, ed. 1868. *Documents and Records Relating to the Prov. of N.H., from 1686 to 1722: Being Part I of Papers Relating to that Period.* Manchester, N.H.: John B. Clarke.

Bouton, Nathaniel, ed. 1869. *Documents and Records Relating to the Prov. of N.H., from 1692 to 1722: Being Part II of Papers Relating to that Period.* Manchester, N.H.: John B. Clarke.

Bouton, Nathaniel, ed. 1870. *Documents and Records Relating to the Prov. of N.H., from 1722 to 1737: Containing Important Records and Papers, Pertaining to the Settlement of the Boundary Lines between N.H. and Mass.* Manchester, N.H.: John B. Clarke.

Bouton, Nathaniel, ed. 1871. *Documents and Records Relating to the Prov. of N.H., from 1738 to 1749: Containing Very Valuable and Interesting Records and Papers Relating to the Expedition against Louisbourg, 1745.* Nashua, N.H.: Orren C. Moore.

Bouton, Nathaniel, ed. 1873. *Documents and Records Relating to the Prov. of N.H., from 1764 to 1776; Including the Whole Administration of Gov. John Wentworth; the Events Immediately Preceding the Revolutionary War; the Losses at the Battle of Bunker Hill, and the Record of all Proc. Till the End of Our Provincial History.* Nashua, N.H.: Orren C. Moore.

Bouton, Nathaniel, ed. 1874. *Documents and Records, During the Period of the American Revolution, From 1776 to 1783; Including the Cons. of N.H., 1776; N.H. Declaration for Independence; the "Association Test," with Names of Signers, &c.; Declaration of American Independence, July 4, 1776; the Articles of Confederation, 1778.* Concord, N.H.: Edward A. Jenks.

Browne, J. Ross. 1850. *Report of the Deb. in the Conv. of Calif., on the Formation of the State Cons., in September and October, 1849.* Washington, D.C.: John T. Towers.

Browne, William Hand, ed. 1883. *Proc. and Acts of the GA of Md., January 1637/8–September 1664.* Baltimore: Maryland Historical Society.

Browne, William Hand, ed. 1884. *Proc. and Acts of the GA of Md., April 1666–June 1676.* Baltimore: Maryland Historical Society.

Bushman, Claudia L., Harold B. Hancock, and Elizabeth Moyne Homsey, eds. 1986. *Proc. of the Asm. of the Lower Counties on the Del., 1770–1776, the Constitutional Conv. of 1776, and of the H. of Asm. of the Del. St., 1776–1781.* Newark: University of Delaware Press.

Candler, Allen D., ed. 1907a. *The Colonial Records of the St. of Ga.*, vol. XIII. Atlanta: Franklin-Turner.

Candler, Allen D., ed. 1907b. *The Colonial Records of the St. of Ga.*, vol. XV. Atlanta: Franklin-Turner.

Candler, Allen D., ed. 1907c. *The Colonial Records of the St. of Ga.*, vol. XIV. Atlanta: Franklin-Turner.

Candler, Allen D., ed. 1908a. *The Revolutionary Records of the St. of Ga.*, vol. I. Atlanta: Franklin-Turner.

Candler, Allen D., ed. 1908b. *The Revolutionary Records of the St. of Ga.*, vol. III. Atlanta: Franklin-Turner.

Carey, Charles Henry. 1926. *The Ore. Cons. and Proc. and Deb. of the Constitutional Conv. of 1857.* Salem, Ore.: State Printing Department.

Carter, Clarence Edwin, ed. 1936. *The Territorial Papers of the United States*, vol. IV. Washington, D.C.: U.S. Government Printing Office.

Carter, Clarence Edwin, ed. 1937. *The Territorial Papers of the United States*, vol. V. Washington, D.C.: U.S. Government Printing Office.

Carter, Clarence Edwin, ed. 1938. *The Territorial Papers of the United States*, vol. VI. Washington, D.C.: U.S. Government Printing Office.

Carter, Clarence Edwin, ed. 1949. *The Territorial Papers of the United States*, vol. XIV. Washington, D.C.: U.S. Government Printing Office.

Carter, Clarence Edwin, ed. 1950. *The Territorial Papers of the United States*, vol. XVII. Washington, D.C.: U.S. Government Printing Office.

Carter, Clarence Edwin, ed. 1952. *The Territorial Papers of the United States*, vol. XVIII. Washington, D.C.: U.S. Government Printing Office.

Carter, Clarence Edwin, ed. 1956. *The Territorial Papers of the United States*, vol. XXII. Washington, D.C.: U.S. Government Printing Office.

Carter, Clarence Edwin, ed. 1958. *The Territorial Papers of the United States*, vol. XXIII. Washington, D.C.: U.S. Government Printing Office.

Clark, Aaron. 1816. *Man. Compiled and Prepared for the Use of the Asm.: Exemplifying Particularly the Mode of Proceeding, Conformably to the National and State Constitutions, and the Rules and Orders of the H. of Asm. of the State of N.Y.* Albany, N.Y.: J. Buel.

Clerk's Man. of Rules, Forms, and Laws for the Regulation of Business in the Asm. of the St. of N.Y. 1858. Albany, N.Y.: Weed, Parsons & Company.

Compendium of State Government Finances in 1959. 1960. Washington, D.C.: U.S. Government Printing Office.

Conn. Register: Being a State Calendar of Public Officers and Institutions in Conn. for 1860. 1860. Hartford, Conn.: Brown & Gross.

Connor, R. D. W., ed. 1913. *A Man. of N.C. Issued by the N.C. Historical Commission for the Use of the Members of the GA.* Raleigh, N.C.: E. M Uzzell & Co.

Cons. of the St. of Deseret, with the Jour. of the Conv. which Formed it, and the Proc. of the Leg. Consequent Thereon. 1849. Kanesville, Iowa: Orson Hyde.

Constitutional Conv. Bulletin. 1920. Springfield, Ill.: Legislative Reference Bureau.

Coun. Jour. of the LA of the Terr. of Neb., Sixth Sess. 1860. Nebraska City, Neb.: Thomas Morton.

Coun. Jour. of the Tenth LA of the Terr. of Wyo., Convened at Cheyenne on the Tenth Day of January, 1888. 1888. Cheyenne, Wyo.: Bristol and Knabe Printing Co.

Crockett, Walter H., ed. 1924. *St. Papers of Vt.,* vol. 3, *Jours. and Proc. of the GA of the St. of Vt.,* vol. I. Bellow Falls, Vt.: P. H. Gobie Press.

Crockett, Walter H., ed. 1925. *St. Papers of Vt.,* vol. 3, *Jours. and Proc. of the GA of the St. of Vt.,* vol. II. Bellow Falls, Vt.: P. H. Gobie Press.

Crockett, Walter H., ed. 1928. *St. Papers of Vt.,* vol. 3., *Jours. and Proc. of the St. of Vt.,* vol. III. Bellow Falls, Vt.: Wyndham Press.

Crockett, Walter H., ed. 1929. *St. Papers of Vt.,* vol. 3, *Jours. and Proc. of the St. of Vt.,* vol. IV. Bellow Falls, Vt.: Wyndham Press.

Deb. and Proc. in the Mass. Leg., at the Reg. Sess., Which was Begun at the St. H. in Boston, on Wednesday, the Seventh Day of January, and Ended on Saturday, the Thirtieth Day of May; and Also at the Special Sess., Which was Begun on Tuesday, the Fourteenth Day of July, and Ended on Friday, the Thirty-First Day of the Same Month, 1857. 1857. Boston: Charles Hale.

Deb. and Proc. in the N.Y. State Conv. for the Rev. of the Cons. 1846. Albany, N.Y.: Albany Argus.

Deb. and Proc. of the Md. Reform Conv. to Revise the St. Cons., vol. I. 1851. Annapolis, Md.: William M'Neir.

Deb. of the Constitutional Conv.; of the St. of Iowa, Assembled at Iowa City, Monday, January 19, 1857, vol. I. 1857. Davenport, Iowa: Luse, Lane & Co.

Deb. of the Conv. to Amend the Cons. of Pa.: Convened at Harrisburg, November 12, 1872; Adjourned November 27, to Meet at Philadelphia, January 7, 1873, vol. VI. 1873. Harrisburg, Pa.: Benjamin Singerly.

Documents of the Sen. of the St. of N.Y., Fifty-Eighth Sess., 1835. 1835. Albany, N.Y.: E. Croswell.

Dwyer, Paul E. 2004. "Salaries of Members of Congress: A List of Payable Rates and Effective Dates, 1789–2004." CRS Report for Congress 97-1011 GOV.

Easterby, J. H., ed. 1958. *Jour. of the Commons H. of Asm., September 10, 1746–June 3, 1747.* Columbia, S.C.: South Carolina Archives Department.

Ewbank, Louis B., and Dorothy L. Riker. 1934. *The Laws of Ind. Terr. 1809–1816.* Indianapolis: Indiana Historical Bureau.

Exts. from the Jour. of Proc. of the Provincial Cong. of N.J., Held at Trenton in the Months of May, June and August, 1775. 1775. Burlington, N.J.: Isaac Collins.

Exts. from the Jours. of the Provincial Cong. of S.C. 1775. Charles-Town, S.C.: Peter Timothy.

Exts. from the Jours. of the Provincial Cong. of S.C. 1776. Charles-Town, S.C.: Peter Timothy.

Gammel, H. P. H., comp. 1898. *The Laws of Texas, 1822–1897*, vol. 1. Austin, Tex.: Gammel Book Company.

Governor's Committee on Legislators' Compensation. 1966. "Legislators' Compensation and Retirement in Colo." Colo. Legislative Coun., Research Publication No. 108, December.

Grover, La Fayette. 1853. *The Ore. Archives: Including the Jours., Governor's Messages and Pubic Papers of Ore., from the Earliest Attempt on the Part of the People to Form a Gov., Down to, and Inclusive of the Sess. of the Territorial Leg. Held in the Year 1849, Collected and Published Pursuant to an Act of the LA Passed Jan. 26. 1853.* Salem, Ore.: Asahel Bush.

Hawaiian Hansard. 1886. Honolulu, Hawaii: Daily Bulletin Steam Printing Office.

Hening, William Waller, ed. 1809. *The Stat. at Large; Being a Collection of all the Laws of Va., from the First Sess. of the Leg., in the Year 1619*, vol. I. Richmond, Va.: Samuel Pleasants, Junior.

Hening, William Waller, ed. 1821. *The Stat. at Large; Being a Collection of all the Laws of Va., from the First Sess. of the Leg., in the Year 1619*, vol. IX. Richmond, Va.: J. & G. Cochran.

Hening, William Waller, ed. 1823. *The Stat. at Large; Being a Collection of all the Laws of Va., from the First Sess. of the Legis., in the Year 1619*, vol. II. New York: R. & W. & G. Bartow.

Hoadly, Charles J., ed. 1857. *Records of the Col. and Plantation of New Haven, from 1638 to 1649.* Hartford. Conn.: Case, Tiffany and Company.

Hoadly, Charles J., ed. 1868. *The Public Records of the Col. of Conn., from August, 1689, to May, 1706.* Hartford, Conn.: Case, Lockwood and Brainard.

Hoadly, Charles J., ed. 1870. *The Public Records of the Col. of Conn., from October, 1706, to October, 1716.* Hartford, Conn.: Case, Lockwood and Brainard.

Hoadly, Charles J., ed. 1894. *The Public Records of the St. of Conn., from October, 1776 to February, 1778, Inclusive, with the Journ. of the Coun. of Safety, from October 11, 1776, to May 6, 1778, Inclusive, with an Appendix.* Hartford, Conn.: Case, Lockwood & Brainard Co.

House of Commons Information Office (United Kingdom). 2009. "Members' Pay, Pensions, and Allowances." Factsheet M5, Members Series, Revised May.

H. Jour. 1899. Santa Fe, N.M.: New Mexican Printing Co.

H. Jour. of the First Leg. of the St. of Wash. 1890. Olympia, Wash.: O. C. White.

H. Jour. of the GA of the St. of Colo. 1889. Denver: Collier & Cleaveland Lith. Co.

H. Jour. of the LA of the Terr. of Colo. 1864. Denver: Byers & Dailey.

H. Jour. of the Leg. of the St. of Neb. Fiftieth Sess. 1935. Lincoln, Neb.: House of Representatives.

H. Jour. of the Twelfth Leg., State of Texas. 1870. Austin, Tex.: Tracy, Siemering & Co.

H. Research Organization (Texas). 1989. "1989 Constitutional Amendments." Special Legislative Report No. 151, August 29.

H. Study Group (Texas). 1984. "1984 Constitutional Amendments." Special Legislative Report No. 105, August 8.

Idaho Capitol Commission. N.d. "About the History of Idaho's Capitol."

In Asm. Jour. of Proc. of the Thirty-Sixth Sess. of the Wis. Leg. 1883. Madison, Wis.: Democrat Printing Co.

In Congress at Exeter, January 5ᵗʰ, 1776. 1776. Portsmouth, N.H.: Daniel Fowle.

Iowa GA. 1980. *The Iowa GA: Our Legislative Heritage, 1846–1980.* Des Moines, Iowa: Senate Rules and Administration Committee.

Iowa Off. Register for the Years 1907–1908. 1907. Des Moines, Iowa: Emory H. English.

James, Edmund J. ed. 1901. *The Territorial Records of Ill., Number III. Jour. of the H. of Reps., 1812.* Springfield, Ill.: Phillips Bros.

Jour. and Votes of the H. of Reps. of the Prov. of Nova Cesarea, or N.J., in the First Sessions of Asm., Began at Perth Amboy, the 10ᵗʰ Day of November, 1703. 1872. Jersey City, N.J.: John H. Lyon.

Jour. of the Asm, during the Thirteenth Sess. of the Leg. of the St. of Calif: 1862. 1862. Sacramento: Benj. P. Avery.

Jour. of the Asm. during the Twenty-Eighth Sess. of the Leg. of the St. of Calif., 1889. 1889. Sacramento: State Office.

Jour. of the Asm. of the First Leg. of the St. of Wis., Held at Madison June 5, A. D. 1848. 1848. Madison, Wis.: Rhenodyne A. Bird.

Jour. of the Asm. of the Fourteenth Sess. of the Leg. of the St. of Nev., 1889. 1889. Carson City, Nev.: State Printing Office.

Jour. of the Asm. of the St. of N.Y., at the First Meeting of the Thirteenth Sess., Begun and Holden at the City of Albany, the Sixth Day of July 1789. 1789. New York: Samuel and John Loudon.

Jour. of the Asm. of the St. of N.Y.: at Their Fortieth Sess., Begun and Held at the Capitol, in the City of Albany, the Fifth Day of November, 1816. 1816. Albany, N.Y.: J. Buel.

Jour. of the Asm. of the St. of N.Y.: at Their Forty-First Sess., Begun and Held at the Capitol, in the City of Albany, the Twenty-Seventh Day of January, 1818. 1818. Albany, N.Y.: J. Buel.

Jour. of the Asm. of the St. of N.Y.: at Their Forty-Second Sess., Begun and Held at the Capitol, in the City of Albany, the Fifth Day of January, 1819. 1819. Albany, N.Y.: J. Buel.

Jour. of the Asm. of the State of N.Y., at Their One Hundred and Thirteenth Sess., Begun and Held at the Capitol, in the City of Albany, on the Seventh Day of January 1890. 1890. Albany, N.Y.: James B. Lyon.

Jour. of the Conv. of the St. of Tenn., Convened for the Purpose of Revising and Amending the Cons. Thereof. 1834. Nashville, Tenn.: Banner & Whig Office.

Jour. of the Conv. to Form a Cons. for the St. of Wis., with a Sketch of the Deb., Begun and Held at Madison, on the Fifteenth Day of December, Eighteen Hundred and Forty-Seven. 1848. Madison, Wis.: Tenney, Smith & Holt.

Jour. of the Coun., First Annual Sess. of the Fifth LA of The Terr. of Wis.; Held at Madison, on the First Monday of January, One Thousand Eight Hundred and Forty-Seven. 1847. Madison, Wis.: H. A. Tenney.

Jour. of the Coun. of the First LA of Wis., Begun and Held at Belmont, on the Twenty-Fifth Day of October, One Thousand Eight Hundred and Thirty-Six. 1836. Belmont, Wis.: James Clarke.

Jour. of the Coun., First Sess. of the Second LA of Wis., Begun and Held at Madison, on Monday the Twenty-Sixth Day of November, in the Year of Our Lord One Thousand Eight Hundred and Thirty-Eight. 1838. Madison, Wis.: Josiah A. Noonan.

Jour. of the Coun. of the LA of Wis.; Begun and Held at Madison, The Seat of Gov., on Monday, The Seventh Day of December, In the Year of Our Lord One Thousand Eight Hundred and Forty. 1841. Madison, Wis.: William W. Wyman.

Jour. of the Coun. of the LA of Wis.; Begun and Held at Madison, The Seat of Gov., on Monday, The Sixth Day of December, In the Year of Our Lord One Thousand Eight Hundred and Forty-One. 1842. Platteville, Wis.: Alonzo Platt.

Jour. of the Coun. of the Third Annual Sess. of the Fourth LA of the Terr. of Wis.; Held at Madison, on the First Monday of January, One Thousand Eight Hundred and Forty-Five. 1845. Madison, Wis.: Simeon Mills.

Jour. of the Coun. of the Terr. of Kan. At Their First Sess. 1855. Shawnee, Kan.: John T. Brady.

Jour. of the First Sess. of the LA of Okla. Terr. 1890. Guthrie, Okla.: Oklahoma News Publishing Co.

Jour. of the First Sess. of the Third H. of Reps. of the Com. of Pa., Which Commenced at Philadelphia, on Tuesday, the Fourth Day of December, in the Year of Our Lord One Thousand Seven Hundred and Ninety-Two. 1792. Philadelphia: Francis Bailey and Thomas Lang.

Jour. of the Honorable H. of Reps. of His Majesty's Prov. of the Mass.-Bay in New-England, Begun and Held at Boston, in the County of Suffolk, on Wednesday the Thirtieth Day of May, Annoque Domini, 1750. 1750. Boston: Samuel Kneeland.

Jour. of the Honorable H. of Reps. of His Majesty's Prov. of the Mass.-Bay in New-England, Begun and Held at Boston, in the County of Suffolk, on Wednesday the Eighth Day of July, Annoque Domini, 1750. 1750. Boston: Samuel Kneeland.

Jour. of the Honorable H. of Reps. of His Majesty's Prov. of the Mass.-Bay in New-England, Begun and Held at Boston, in the County of Suffolk, on Wednesday the Twenty-Sixth Day of May, Annoque Domini, 1756. 1756. Boston: Samuel Kneeland.

Jour. of the Honorable H. of Reps. of His Majesty's Prov. of the Mass.-Bay in New England, Begun and Held at Harvard-College in Cambridge, in the County of Middlesex, on Wednesday the Thirtieth Day of May, Annoque Domini, 1770. 1770. Boston: Edes and Gill.

Jour. of the H. of Asm. 1771. New Bern, N.C.: James Davis.

Jour. of the H. of Commons. 1778. New Bern, N.C.: James Davis.

Jour. of the H. of Commons. 1789. Edenton, N.C.: Hodge & Wills.

Jour. of the H. of Commons. 1790. Edenton, N.C.: Hodge & Wills.

Jour. of the H. of Commons, St. of N.C., At a GA, Begun and Held at Fayetteville, on the Second Day of November, in the Year of Our Lord One Thousand Seven Hundred and Eighty-Nine, and in the Fourteenth Year of the Independence of the USA the Seventeenth : Being the First Sess. of This Asm. 1790. Edenton, N.C.: Hodge & Wills.

Jour. of the H. of Commons at a GA Begun and Held in the City of Raleigh, on Monday the 16th Day of November, in the Year of Our Lord 1818 and in the Forty Second Year of the Independence of the USA: It Being the First Sess. of this Asm. 1819. Raleigh, N.C.: Henderson.

Jour. of the H. of Dels. of the Com. of Va., Begun and Held at the Capitol, in the City of Richmond, on Monday the First Day of December, One Thousand Eight Hundred and Seventeen. 1817. Richmond, Va.: Thomas Ritchie.

Jour. of the H. of Dels. of the Com. of Va., Begun and Held at the Capitol in the City of Richmond, on Monday, the Nineteenth of October, in the Year of Our Lord, One Thousand, Seven Hundred and Eighty-Nine, and of the Com. the Fourteenth. 1789. Richmond, Va.: John Dixon.

Jour. of the H. of Dels. of the Com. of Va., Begun and Held at the Capitol in the City of Richmond, on Monday, the Seventeenth of October, in the Year of Our Lord, One Thousand, Seven Hundred and Ninety-One. 1791. Richmond, Va.: Augustine Davis.

Jour. of the H. of Dels. of the Com. of Va.; Begun and Held in the Town of Richmond, in the County of Henrico, on Monday, the Seventh Day of May, in the Year of Our Lord One Thousand Seven Hundred and Eighty-One. 1828. Richmond, Va.: Thomas W. White.

Jour. of the H. of Dels. of the St. of Va., for the Sess. of 1861–62. 1861. Richmond, Va.: William Ritchie.

Jour. of the H. of Dels. of the St. of Va., for the Sess. of 1887–'88. 1887. Richmond, Va.: Superintendent of Public Printing.

Jour. of the H. of Dels. of the State of Va. for the Sess. of 1906. 1906. Richmond, Va.: Superintendent of Public Printing.

Jour. of the H. of Dels. of the St. of W.Va. 1863. Wheeling, W.Va.: John. F. M'Dermot.

Jour. of the H. of Reps. 1901. Honolulu, Hawaii: Bulletin Publishing Company.

Jour. of the H. of Reps. at the First Sess. of the GA for the Com. of Ky., Begun and Held at the Town of Lexington, on Monday, the Fourth of June in the Year of Our Lord, One Thousand Seven Hundred and Ninety-Two. 1792. Lexington, Ky.: John Bradford.

Jour. of the H. of Reps. at the First Sess. of the Thirteenth GA of the St. of Tenn., Begun and Held at Murfreesborough on Monday the Twentieth Day of September, One Thousand Eight Hundred and Nineteen. 1819. Murfreesborough, Tenn.: G. A. & A. C. Sublette.

Jour. of the H. of Reps., Being the Reg. Sess., Twenty-First Leg., Begun and Held at the City of Austin January 8, 1889. 1889. Austin, Tex.: Smith, Hicks & Jones.

Jour. of the H. of Reps. during the First Sess. of the Fourth Leg. of the St. of La. 1819. New Orleans: J. C. de St. Romes.

Jour. of the H. of Reps., First Annual Sess. of the Fifth LA of the Terr. of Wis. Held at Madison on the First Monday of January, One Thousand Eight Hundred and Forty-Seven. 1847. Madison, Wis.: H. A. Tenney.

Jour. of the H. of Reps. for his Majestie's Prov. of N.Y. in America. [1695] 1903. New York: Dodd, Mead, & Co.

Jour. of the H. of Reps., of the Ala. Terr. at the First Sess. of the First GA in the Forty-Second Year of American Independence. 1818. St. Stephens, Ala.: Thomas Eastin.

Jour. of the H. of Reps., of the Ala. Terr. at the Second Sess. of the First GA in the Forty-Third Year of American Independence. 1818. St. Stephens, Ala.: Thomas Eastin.

Jour. of the H. of Reps. of the Com. of Ky., Begun and Held in the Town of Frankfort, on Monday the First Day of December 1817, and of the Com. the Twenty-Sixth. 1817. Frankfort, Ky.: Kendall and Russells.

Jour. of the H. of Reps. of the Com. of Ky., Begun and Held in the Town of Frankfort, on Monday the Second Day of December, 1816, and of the Com. the Twenty-Fifth. 1816. Frankfort, Ky.: Gerard & Kendall.

Jour. of the H. of Reps. of the Com. of Ky., Begun and Held in the Town of Frankfort, on Monday the Seventh Day of December 1818, and of the Com. the Twenty-Seventh. 1818. Frankfort, Ky.: Kendall and Russells.

Jour. of the H. of Reps. of the Com. of Mass. 1887. Boston: Wright & Potter Printing Co.

Jour. of the H. of Reps. of the First Sess. of the First GA of the St. of Ill., Begun and Held in the Town of Kaskaskia, on Monday the Fifth Day of October, A. D. 1818. 1818. Kaskaskia, Ill.: Blackwell & Berry.

Jour. of the H. of Reps. of the First Sess. of the S.D. Leg. 1890. Pierre, S.D.: Free Press Co.

Jour. of the H. of Reps. of the First Territorial Asm. of Wis., Begun and Held at Belmont, on the Twenty-Fifth Day of October, One Thousand Eight Hundred and Thirty-Six. 1836. Belmont, Wis.: James Clarke.

Jour. of the H. of Reps. of the Fourteenth LA of the Terr. of Idaho. 1887. Boise City, Idaho: Henry Gibson.

Jour. of the H. of Reps. of the GA of the St. of Ala. Begun and Held in the Town of Huntsville, on the Fourth Monday in October, in the Year of Our Lord One Thousand Eight Hundred and Nineteen and of American Independence the Forty Fourth. 1820. Cahawba, Ala.: Press Office.

Jour. of the H. of Reps. of the GA of the State of Iowa, First Sess. 1847. Burlington, Iowa: Hawkeye-Office.

Jour. of the H. of Reps. of the GA of the St. of N.C. at its Sess. of 1889. 1889. Raleigh, N.C.: Josephus Daniels.

Jour. of the H. of Reps. of the GA of the St. Of S.C., Being the Reg. Sess. Commencing November 26, 1889. 1889. Columbia, S.C.: James H. Woodrow.

Jour. of the H. of Reps. of the LA of Wis.; Being the Second Sess. 1837. Green Bay, Wis.: Charles C. Sholes.

Jour. of the H. of Reps., of the Miss. Terr. at the Second Sess. of the Eight GA in the Thirty-Ninth Year of the American Independence. 1814. Natchez, Miss.: P. Isler & J. M'Curdy.

Jour. of the H. of Reps. of the St. of Ala., Sess. of 1886–87, Held in the City of Montgomery, Commencing November 9ᵗʰ, 1886. 1887. Montgomery, Ala.: W. D. Brown & Co.

Jour. of the H. of Reps. of the St. of Del., at a Sess. of the GA, Commenced and Held at Dover, Agreeably to the Directions of an Act of the GA, on Tuesday the Fifth Day of January, in the Year of Our Lord, One Thousand Eight Hundred and Nineteen, and in the Forty-Third Year of Independence of the US. 1819. Dover, Del.: J. Robertson.

Jour. of the H. of Reps. of the St. of Del., at the Sess. of the GA, Convened and Held at Dover on Tuesday, the Sixth Day of January, A.D. One Thousand Eight Hundred and Eighty-Five, and the One Hundred and Ninth Year of the Independence of the US. 1885. Dover, Del.: James Kirk & Son.

Jour. of the H. of Reps. of the St. of Ga., at an Annual Sess. of the GA, Begun and Held at Milledgeville, the Seat of Government, in November and December, 1818. 1818. Milledgeville, Ga.: S. & F. Grantland.

Jour. of the H. of Reps. of the St. of Idaho. 1891. Boise City, Idaho: Statesman Printing Co.

Jour. of the H. of Reps. of the St. of Ind., Being the Fourth Sess. of the GA. 1819. Corydon, Ind.: Brandon & McCullough.

Jour. of the H. of Reps. of the St. of Ind., During the Fifty-Fifth Sess. of the GA, Commencing Thursday, January 6, 1887. 1887. Indianapolis: Wm. B. Burford.

"Journal of the House of Representatives of the State of Kansas, March 4, 1856." 1915. *Collections of the Kan. St. Historical Society, 1913–1914,* vol. XIII. Topeka: Kansas State Printing Plant.

Jour. of the H. of Reps. of the St. of La., first session, first legislature. 1812. New Orleans: n.p.

Jour. of the H. of Reps. of the St. of Miss., at a Reg. Sess. Thereof, Convened in the City of Jackson, January 8, 1888. 1888. Jackson, Miss.: R. H. Henry.

Jour. of the H. of Reps. of the St. of Mo., at the First Sess. of the Eighteenth GA, Begun and Held at the City of Jefferson, on Monday, the Twenty-Fifth Day of December, in the Year of Our Lord, One Thousand Eight Hundred and Fifty-Four. 1855. Jefferson City, Mo.: James Lusk.

Jour. of the H. of Reps. of the St. of N.H., at Their Sess., Begun and Holden at Concord, on the First Wednesday of June, Anno Domini, 1819. 1819. Concord, N.H.: Hill and Moore.

Jour. of the H. of Reps. of the St. of N.H., June Sess., 1887. 1887. Manchester, N.H.: John B. Clarke.

Jour. of the H. of Reps. of the St. of Ohio, Being the First Sess. of the Eighteenth GA, Begun and Held in the Town of Columbus, in the County of Franklin, Monday, December Sixth, 1819: and in the Eighteenth Year of Said State. 1819. Columbus, Ohio: P. H. Olmsted.

Jour. of the H. of Reps. of the St. of Ohio: Being the Second Sess. of the Fifty-Second GA, Commencing on Monday, January 5, 1857 [Being the Fourth Sess. under the New Cons.]. 1857. Columbus, Ohio: Richard Nevins.

Jour. of the H. of Reps. of the St. of Ohio, First Sess. of the Leg., Held under the Cons. of the St., A.D. 1803, and of the Independence of the US the Twenty-Seventh. 1803. Chillicothe, Ohio: N. Willis.

Jour. of the H. of Reps. of the St. of Ohio, for the Reg. Sess. of the Sixty-Eighth GA, Commencing Monday, January 2d, 1888. 1888. Columbus, Ohio: Columbus Printing Co.

Jour. of the H. of Reps. of the St. of S.C. 1865. Columbia, S.C.: Julian A. Selby.

Jour. of the H. of Reps. of the St. of S.C., Being the Regular Session of 1871–'72. 1872. Columbia, S.C.: Republican Printing Co.

Jour. of the H. of Reps. of the St. of Tenn. Begun and Held at Knoxville on Monday, the Twenty-Eight of March, One Thousand Seven Hundred and Ninety Six. [1796] 1852. Nashville, Tenn.: McKennie & Brown, True Whig Office.

Jour. of the H. of Reps. of the St. of Vt., Biennial Sess., 1888. 1889. Montpelier, Vt.: Argus and Patriot Job Printing House.

Jour. of the H. of Reps. of the Terr. of Kan. at the First Sess. of the First Terr. LA Begun and Held at the Town of Pawnee, on Monday the 2d Day of July, in the Year of Our Lord One Thousand Eight Hundred and Fifty-Five. 1855. Shawnee, Kan.: John T. Brady.

Jour. of the H. of Reps. of the Terr. of N.M. Of the Sess. Begun and Held in the City of Santa Fe, Terr. of New Mexico, on Monday the Fourth Day of December, A.D. One Thousand Eight Hundred and Sixty-Five It Being the Fifteenth LA for the Said Terr. 1866. Santa Fe, N.M.: Manderfield & Tucker.

Jour. of the H. of Reps. of the Terr. of the US, North-west of the Ohio, at the First Sess. of the Second GA, A.D. 1801 and of the Independence of the USA the Twenty-Sixth. 1801. Chillicothe, Ohio: N. Willis.

Jour. of the H. of Reps. of the Terr. of the US, North-west of the River Ohio at the First sess. of the GA, A.D. 1799, And of the Independence of the US the Twenty-Fourth. 1799. Cincinnati: Carpenter and Findlay.

Jour. of the H. of Reps. of the Terr. of Wash., Together with the Memorials and Joint Resolutions of the First Sess. of the LA Begun and Held at Olympia, February 27ᵗʰ, 1854, and of the Independence of America, the Seventy-Ninth. 1855. Olympia, Wash.: Geo. B. Goudy.

Jour. of the H. of Reps. of the Terr. of Wash. 1888. Olympia, Wash.: Tmos. H. Cavanaugh.

Jour. of the H. of Reps. of the Thirty-Sixth GA of the St. of Ill., Convened at Springfield, January 9, 1889, and Adjourned Sine Die May 28, 1889. 1889. Springfield, Ill.: Springfield Printing Co.

Jour. of the H. of Reps. of the Thirty-Third GA of the St. of Mo. 1885. Jefferson City, Mo.: Tribune Printing Co.

Jour. of the H. of Reps. of the Twenty-Second GA of the St. of Iowa. 1888. Des Moines, Iowa: Geo. E. Roberts.

Jour. of the H. of Reps. of the US. 1789. New York: Francis Childs and John Swaine.

Jour. of the H. of Reps. of the US, at the First Sess. of the Fourth Cong. 1795. Philadephia: Francis Childs.

Jour. of the H. of Reps., St. of Ark. 1889. Little Rock, Ark.: Press Register.

Jour. of the H. of the Fifty-Fifth GA. 1953. Des Moines: State of Iowa.

Jour. of the H. of the LA of the St. of Ore. for the Fourteenth Reg. Sess. with Appendix. 1887. Salem, Ore.: Frank C. Baker.

Jour. of the H. of the LA of the St. of Ore., for the Thirteenth Reg. Sess., 1885. 1885. Salem, Ore.: W. H. Byars.

Jour. of the H. of the Seventeenth Sess. of the LA, January, 1887. 1886. Bismarck, N.D.: Tribune.

Jour. of the LA of the Terr. of Ore.: During the First Reg. Sess. Thereof Begun and Held at Oregon City, July 16, 1849. 1854. Salem, Ore.: Asahel Bush.

Jour. of the LC, at the First Sess. of the Fourth GA of the Miss. Terr., Began and Held at the Town of Washington, on Monday the First Day of December, in the Year of Our Lord One Thousand Eight Hundred and Six, and of the Independence of the USA the Thirty-First. 1807. Natchez, Miss.: Samuel Terrell.

Jour. of the LC of the Ala. Terr. at the First Sess. of the First GA, in the Forty Third Year of American Independence. 1818. St. Stephens, Ala.: Thomas Eastin.

Jour. of the LC of the Terr. of Mich., Being the First Sess. of the Third Coun. Begun and Held at the City of Detroit, May 5, 1828. 1828. Detroit: John P. Sheldon.

Jour. of the Proc. of a Conv. Begun and Held at Knoxville, January 11, 1796. [1796] 1852. Nashville, Tenn.: McKennie & Brown, True Whig Office.

Jour. of the Proc. of the Asm. of the St. of Fla., at the Thirteenth Sess. of the Leg., Begun and Held at the Capitol, in the City of Tallahassee, on Tuesday, January 6, 1885. 1885. Tallahassee, Fla.: Charles E. Dyke.

Jour. of the Proc. of the Constitutional Conv. of the St. of Ala., Held in the City of Montgomery, Commencing May 21st, 1901. 1901. Montgomery, Ala.: Brown Printing Co.

Jour. of the Proc. of the GA of the St. of Vt. at their Sess. at Windsor, October 13th, 1791. 1791. Windsor, Vt.: Alden Spooner.

Jour. of the Proc. of the H. of Asm. of the St. of Calif.; at its First Sess. Begun and Held at Puebla de San José, on the Fifteenth Day of December, 1849. 1850. San José, Calif.: J. Winchester.

Jour. of the Proc. of the H. of Reps. of the First GA of the St. of Fla. at its First Sess. Begun and Held in the City of Tallahassee on Monday, June 23, 1845. 1845. Tallahassee, Fla.: Floridian Office.

Jour. of the Proc. of the H. of Reps. of the GA of the St. of Fla., at an Adjourned Sess., Begun and Held at the Capitol, in the City of Tallahassee, on Monday, November 28, 1859, A. 1859. Tallahassee, Fla.: Floridian and Journal.

Jour. of the Proc. of the H. of Reps. of the GA of the St. of Fla., at its Eleventh Sess., Begun and Held at the Capitol, in the City of Tallahassee, on Monday, November 26, 1861, A. 1861. Tallahassee, Fla.: Floridian and Journal.

Jour. of the Proc. of the H. of Reps. of the GA of the St. of Fla., at its Fourteenth Sess., Begun and Held at the Capitol, in the City of Tallahassee, on Monday, December18, 1865, A. 1865. Tallahassee, Fla.: Floridian.

Jour. of the Proc. of the H. of Reps. of the GA of the St. of Fla., at its Tenth Sess., Begun and Held at the Capitol, in the City of Tallahassee, on Monday, November 18, 1860, A. 1860. Tallahassee, Fla.: Floridian and Journal.

Jour. of the Proc. of the H. of Reps. of the GA of the St. of Fla., at its Thirteenth Sess., Begun and Held at the Capitol, in the City of Tallahassee, on Monday, November 21st, 1864, A. 1864. Tallahassee, Fla.: Floridian and Journal.

Jour. of the Proc. of the H. of Reps. of the Terr. of the USA, South of the River Ohio. [1794] 1852. Nashville, Tenn.: McKennie & Brown, True Whig Office.

Jour. of the Proc. of the LC of the Terr. of Fla. at its Fourth Sess. Begun and Held in the City of Tallahassee on Monday, January 2nd, 1843. 1843. Tallahassee, Fla.: J. Knowles, Printer.

Jour. of the Proc. of the Provincial Cong., of N.C. 1775. New Bern, N.C.: James Davis.

Jour. of the Proc. of the Provincial Cong. of N.C., Held at Halifax on the 4th Day of April, 1776. 1776. New Bern, N.C.: James Davis.

Jour. of the Proc. of the Sixth LC of the Terr. of Mich.: Begun and Held in the Capitol, at the City of Detroit, on Tuesday, January 7, 1834. 1834. Detroit: S. M'Knight.

Jour. of the Provincial Cong. of S.C., 1776. 1776. London: J. Almon.

Jour. of the Reg. Sess. of the H. of Reps. of the Com. of Ky., Begun and Held in the City of Frankfort, on Friday, the Thirtieth Day of December, in the Year of Our Lord 1887, and of the Com. the Ninety-Sixth. 1887. Frankfort, Ky.: Capitol Office.

Jour. of the Sen. 1776. Williamsburg, Va.: Alexander Purdie.

Jour. of the Sen. 1787. New Bern, N.C.: Hodge & Blanchard.

Jour. of the Sen. during the Second Sess. of the First Leg. of the St. of La. 1813. New Orleans: Peter K. Wagner.

Jour. of the Sen. During the Third Sess. of the Leg. of the St. of Nev., 1867, Begun on Monday, the Seventh Day of January, and Ended on Thursday, the Seventh Day of March; and Special Sess., Begun on Friday, the Fifteenth Day of March, and Ended on Wednesday, the Third Day of April. 1867. Carson City, Nev.: Joseph E. Eckley.

Jour. of the Sen. of Mo. of the Thirty-Third GA. 1885. Jefferson City, Mo.: Tribune Publishing Co.

Jour. of the Sen. of the First GA of the St. of Iowa. 1846. Iowa City, Iowa: A. H. Palmer.

Jour. of the Sen. of the First Leg. of the St. of Wis., Held at Madison June 5, A. D. 1848. 1848. Madison, Wis.: Rhenodyne A. Bird.

Jour. of the Sen. of the LA of the St. of Ore. for the Fifteenth Reg. Sess. 1889. 1889. Salem, Ore.: Frank C. Baker.

Jour. of the Sen. of the St. of Ala., Extra Sess. of 1909. 1909. Montgomery, Ala.: Brown Printing Co.

Jour. of the Sen. of the St. of Calif.; at its First Sess. Begun and Held at Puebla de San José, on the Fifteenth Day of December, 1849. 1850. San José, Calif.: J. Winchester.

Jour. of the Sen. of the St. of Mich. 1889. Lansing, Mich.: Darius D. Thorp.

Jour. of the Sen. of the St. of Mich., vol. 1. 1915. Lansing, Mich.: Wynkoop, Hallenbeck Crawford Co.

Jour. of the Sen. of the St. of Mo. 1879. Jefferson City, Mo.: Carter & Regan.

Jour. of the Sen. of the St. of S.C. Being the Extra Sess. of 1865. 1865. Columbia, S.C.: Julian A. Selby.

Jour. of the Sen. of the USA: Being the First Sess. of the Twentieth Cong.; Begun and Held at the City of Washington, December 3, 1827, and in the Fifty-Second Year of the Independence of the Said US. 1827. Washington, D.C.: Duff Green.

Jour. of the Sen., St. of N.C., At a GA, Begun and Held at Newbern, on the Fifteenth Day of November, in the Year of Our Lord One Thousand Seven Hundred and Ninety-Two, and of the Independence of the USA the Seventeenth : It Being the First Sess. of This Asm. 1793. Edenton, N.C.: Hadge & Wills.

Jour. of the Twenty Ninth H. of Reps. of the Com. of Pa., Commenced at Harrisburg, Tuesday the First of December, in the Year of Our Lord One Thousand Eight Hundred and Eighteen, and of the Com. the Forty Third. 1818. Harrisburg, Pa.: James Peacock.

Jour. of the Votes and Proc. of the Conv. of N.J. 1776. Burlington, N.J.: Isaac Collins.

Jour. of the Votes and Proc. of the GA of His Majesty's Col. of N.Y., in America, A. 1738. New York: John Peter Zenger.

Jour. of the Votes and Proc. of the GA of the Col. of N.Y. 1771. New York: H. Gaine.

Jour. of the Votes and Proc. of the GA of the Col. of N.Y.; Began the 10th of January, 1775, And adjourned the 3d April, to the 3d of May following. 1775. New York: Hugh Gaine.

Jour. of the Votes and Proc. of the Lower H. of Asm. of the Prov. of Md., at the Sess. begun and held September 21, 1742, A. 1742. Annapolis, Md.: Jonas Green.

Jour. of the Votes and Proc. of the Lower H. of Asm. of the Prov. of Md., June Sess., 1773. 1773. Annapolis, Md.: Anne Catharine Green.

Jour. of the Votes and Proc. of the Reps. of the Prov. of Pa. 1725. Philadelphia: Samuel Keimer.

Jour. of the Votes of the H. of Reps. of His Majestys Prov. of N.J. 1716. New York: William Bradford.

Jours. of the Fourteenth LA of the Terr. of Ariz. 1887. Prescott, Ariz.: Courier Book and Job Printing.

Jours. of the GA of the St. of Vt., at their Sess. Begun and Held at Montpelier, in the

County of Washington, on Thursday, the fourteenth of October, A.D. 1819. 1819. Bennington, Vt.: William Haswell.

Jours. of the H. of Reps. of the Com. of Pa., vol. the First, 1782. Philadelphia: John Dunlap.

Jours. of the Provisional Cong. of Mass. in 1774 and 1775, and the Committee of Safety, with an Appendix, Containing the Proc. of the County Conventions—Narratives of the Events of the Nineteenth of April, 1775—Papers Relating to Ticonderoga and Crown Point, and Other Documents, Illustrative of the Early History of the American Revolution. 1838. Boston: Dutton and Wentworth.

Jours. of the Thirteenth LA of the Terr. of Ariz. 1885. San Francisco: H. S. Crocker & Co.

Journaux de l'Assemblée Législative de la Province de Quebec, Depuis le 27 Mars Jusqu'au 10 Juin 1884. 1884. Quebec: Léger Brousseau.

Kennedy, John Pendleton, ed. 1906. *Jours. of the H. of Burgesses of Va. 1766–1769.* Richmond, Va.: Virginia State Library.

Laws of the Prov. of Pa., Passed by the Governour and General Assemblies of Said Prov., held at Philadelphia in the Years 1715, 1717 and 1718 being the second and fourth Year of his present Majesty King George over Great Britain, France and Ireland, &c. 1718. Philadelphia: Andrew Bradford.

Laws of the Republic of Texas, in Two Volumes, vol. I. 1838. Houston, Tex.: Office of the Telegraph.

Laws of the St. of Ind., Passed at the Forty-Third Reg. Sess. of the GA, Begun on the Fifth Day of January, A. D 1865. 1865. Indianapolis: W. R. Holloway.

Leaming, Aaron, and Jacob Spicer, ed. 1758. *The Grants, Concessions, and Original Constitutions of the Prov. of N.J. The Acts Pased during the Proprietary Governments, and other Material Transactions before the Surrender there of to Queen ANNE.* Philadelphia: W. Bradford.

Legislative Jour. of the St. of Neb. 1937. Lincoln, Neb.: Commercial Printing.

Legislative Man. Containing the Cons. of N.D. and the Rules of the First LA, Also the Declaration of Independence, the Cons. of the US, the Enabling Act of Cong. and Political and Off. Statistics. 1890. Bismarck, N.D.: Daily Tribune.

Legislative Man. Containing the Cons. of N.D., The Cons. of the US, also Rules and Standing Committees of the Eighth LA and Historical, Statistical, and Political Information. 1903. Bismarck, N.D.: Tribune.

Legislative Man. of the St. of Minn. 1889. St. Paul: Minnesota Legislature.

Legislative Man. of the St. of Wis.; Comprising Jefferson's Man., Rules, Forms and Laws for the Regulation of Business; Also Lists and Tables for Reference, etc. 1872. Madison, Wis.: Atwood & Culver.

"Letter from His Excellency William Franklin, Esquire; to the Honorable Gentlemen of His Majesty's Council, and the Gentlemen of the House of Representatives of His Majesty's Province of New-Jersey." 1776. Burlington, N.J.: Isaac Collins.

Lincoln, Charles Z., ed. 1909. *Messages from the Governors Comprising Executive Communications to the Leg. and Other Papers Relating to Legislation from the*

Organization of the First Colonial Asm. in 1683 to Including the Year 1906. Albany, N.Y.: J. B. Lyons.

Lincoln, Charles Z., William H. Johnson, and A. Judd Northrup, eds. 1894. *The Colonial Laws of N.Y. from the Year 1664 to the Revolution : Including the Charters to the Duke of York, the Commissions and Instructions to Colonial Governors, the Duke's Laws, the Laws of the Dongan and Leisler Assemblies, the Charters of Albany and N.Y. and the Acts of the Colonial Legislatures from 1691 to 1775 Inclusive.* Albany, N.Y.: James B. Lyon.

Lipscomb, Terry W., ed. 1996. *Jour. of the Commons H. of Asm. October 6, 1757–January 24, 1761.* Columbia, S.C.: South Carolina Department of Archives and History.

Maine Register or St. Year-Book and Legislative Man. from April 1, 1889, to April 1, 1890. 1889. Portland, Maine: G. M. Donham.

Man. for the Use of the GC. 1889. Boston: Wright & Potter.

Man. for the Use of the Leg. of the St. of N.Y. 1889. Albany, N.Y.: Weed, Parsons and Co.

Man. of the Leg. and of the Executive and Judicial Departments for the Year 1889. 1890. Charleston, W.Va.: Moses W. Donnally.

Man. of the Leg. of N.J. 1888. Trenton, N.J.: T. F. Fitzgerald.

Man. of the Leg. of the St. of Neb. for the Year 1883. 1883. Lincoln, Neb.: Journal Company.

Man. of Rules for the Gov. of Both Branches of the Leg. of Pa., Preceded by the Constitutions of the US and of Pa.: With a List of the Members and Officers of the Sen. and H. of Reps., with Their Places of Residence While in Harrisburg, and their Post Office Address When at Home. 1863. Harrisburg, Pa.: Singerly & Myers.

Man. with the Rules and Orders for the Use of the GA of the St. of R.I. 1889. Providence, R.I.: E. L. Freeman & Sons.

Md. Man. 1967–1968. 1968. Annapolis, Md.: Hall of Records Commission.

McCain, William D., ed. 1940. *Jours. of the GA of the Miss. Terr. Jour. of the H. of Reps. Second GA, Second Sess. October 3–November 19, 1803.* Hattiesburg, Miss.: Book Farm.

McIlwaine, H. R., ed. 1910. *Jours. of the H. of Burgesses of Va. 1727–1734 1736–1740.* Richmond, Va.: The Colonial Press.

McIlwaine, H. R., ed. 1912. *Jours. of the H. of Burgesses of Va. 1712–1714, 1715, 1718 1720–1722, 1723–1726.* Richmond, Va.: The Colonial Press.

McIlwaine, H. R., ed. 1914. *Jours. of the H. of Burgesses of Va. 1659/60–1693.* Richmond, Va.: The Colonial Press.

McIlwaine, H. R., ed. 1915. *Jours. of the H. of Burgesses of Va. 1619–1658/59.* Richmond, Va.: The Colonial Press.

Members, Officers, and Standing Committees and Rules of the Sen. of Va., also the Cons. of Va., &c., &c. 1880. Richmond, Va.: R. F. Walker.

Message of the President of the United States Transmitting the Budget for the Service of the Budget Year Ending June 30, 1934. 1932. Washington, D.C.: U.S. Government Printing Office.

Min. of the Coun. of the Del. St., from 1776–1792. 1887. Wilmington, Del.: Historical Society of Delaware.

Min. of the First Sess., of the Eighth GA of the Com. of Pa.; Which Commenced at Philadelphia, on Monday the Twenty-Seventh Day of October, in the Year of our Lord One Thousand Seven Hundred and Eighty-Three. 1783: Philadelphia: Hall and Sellers.

Min. of the First Sess. of the Fourth GA of the Com. of Pa. 1780. Philadelphia: John Dunlap.

Min. of the First Sess. of the Fourteenth GA of the Com. of Pa., Which Commenced at Philadelphia, on Monday, the Twenty-sixth Day of October, in the Year of our Lord One Thousand Seven Hundred and Eighty-nine. 1789. Philadelphia: Hall and Sellers.

Min. of the First Sess., of the Ninth GA of the Com. of Pa.; Which Commenced at Philadelphia, on Monday the Twenty-Fifth Day of October, in the Year of our Lord One Thousand Seven Hundred and Eighty-Four. 1784. Philadelphia: Francis Bailey.

Min. of the First Sess., of the Seventh GA of the Com. of Pa.; Which Commenced at Philadelphia, on Monday the Twenty-Eighth Day of October, in the Year of our Lord One Thousand Seven Hundred and Eighty-Two. 1782. Philadelphia: John Dunlap.

Min. of the Proc. of the Convention of the St. of Pa., Held at Philadelphia, the Fifteenth Day of July, 1776. 1776. Philadelphia: Henry Miller.

Min. of the Proc. of the LA of the District of San Francisco, from March 12th, 1849, to June 4th, 1849, and a Record of the Proc. of the Ayuntamiento or Town Coun. of San Francisco, from August 6th, 1849 until May 3d, 1850. 1860. San Francisco: Towne and Bacon.

Min. of the Provincial Cong. and the Coun. of Safety of the St. of N.J. 1879. Trenton, N.J.: Naar, Day & Naar.

Min. of Votes and Proc. of the One Hundred and Ninth GA of the St. of N.J. 1885. Camden, N.J.: Courier Publishing Association.

Miss. Leg. N.d. "Constitutional Provisions Affecting the Legislature and Legislation." http://billstatus.ls.state.ms.us/htms/cp_rules.pdf.

Neb. Blue Book and Legislative Man. for the Year 1889. 1889. Lincoln, Neb.: State Journal Co.

Neb. Blue Book 1922. 1922. Lincoln, Neb.: Nebraska Legislative Reference Bureau.

N.H. Man. of Useful Information. 1889. Manchester, N.H.: John. B. Clarke.

O'Callaghan, E. B., ed. 1853. *Documents Relative to the Colonial History of the St. of N.Y.; Procured in Holland, England and France,* vol. III. Albany, N.Y.: Weed, Parsons and Company.

O'Callaghan, E. B., ed. 1854. *Documents Relative to the Colonial History of the St.*

of N.Y.; Procured in Holland, England and France, vol. IV. Albany, N.Y.: Weed, Parsons and Company.

O'Callaghan, E. B., ed. 1855. *Documents Relative to the Colonial History of the St. of N.Y.; Procured in Holland, England and France*, vol. V. Albany, N.Y.: Weed, Parsons and Company.

Off. and Political Man. of the St. of Tenn. 1890. Nashville, Tenn.: Marshall & Bruce Stationers.

Off. Directory and Legislative Man. of the St. of Mich. for the Years 1887–8. 1887. Lansing, Mich.: Thorp & Godfrey.

Off. Directory and Legislative Man. of the St. of Mich. for the Years 1889–90. 1889. Lansing, Mich.: Darius D. Thorp.

Off. Jour. of the Proc. of the H. of Reps. of the St. of La. at the First Reg. Sess. of the Third GA Begun and held in the City of Baton Rouge, May 14, 1888. 1888. Baton Rouge, La.: Leon Jastremski.

Off. Man. for the use of the Courts, St., and County Officials and GA of the St. of Ky. 1900. Louisville, Ky.: Geo. G. Fetter Printing.

Off. Man. for the use of the Courts, St., and County Officials and GA of the St. of Ky. 1910. Louisville, Ky.: Geo. G. Fetter Printing.

Off. Man. of the St. of Mo. for the Years 1907–1908. 1907. Jefferson City, Mo.: Hugh Stephens Printing Co.

Off. Man. of the St. of Mo. for the Years 1917–1918. 1917. Jefferson City, Mo.: Hugh Stephens Printing Co.

Off. Report of the Deb. and Proc. in the Constitutional Conv. of the St. of Nev., Assembled at Carson City, July 4th, 1864. 1866. San Francisco: Frank Eastman.

Off. Report of the Proc. and Deb. in the Conv. Assembled at Frankfort on the Eight Day of September, 1890, to Adopt, Amend, or Change the Cons. of the St. of Ky., vol. III. 1890. Frankfort, Ky.: E. Polk Johnson.

Off. Report of the Proc. and Deb. of the First Constitutional Conv. of N.D., Assembled in the City of Bismarck, July 4th to August 17th, 1889. 1889. Bismarck, N.D.: Tribune.

Pease, Theodore Calvin. 1925. *The Laws of the Northwest Terr., 1788–1800.* Springfield, Ill.: Illinois State Historical Library.

Perley, Jeremiah. 1820. *The Deb., Resolutions, and Other Proc., of the Conv. of Del., Assembled at Portland on the 11th, and Continued until the 29th Day of October, 1819, for the Purpose of Forming a Cons. for the St. of Maine.* Portland, Maine: A. Shirley.

Philbrick, Francis S. 1930. *The Laws of the Ind. Terr. 1801–1809.* Springfield: Illinois State Historical Library.

Philbrick, Francis S. 1950. *The Laws of the Ill. Terr. 1809–1818.* Springfield: Illinois State Historical Library.

Proc. and Deb. of the Conv. of La. 1845. New Orleans: Besancon, Ferguson & Co.

Proc. of the Conv. of Del. for the Counties and Corporations in the Col. of Va., Held at

Richmond town, in the county of Henrico, on Monday the 17ᵗʰ of July, 1775. 1775. Williamsburg, Va.: Alexander Purdie.

Proc. of the Conv. of Del. for the Counties and Corporations in the Col. of Va., Held at Richmond town, in the county of Henrico, on the 20ᵗʰ of March 1775. 1775. Williamsburg, Va.: Alexander Purdie.

Proc. of the Conv. of Del., Held at the Capitol, in the City of Williamsburg, in the Col. of Va., on Monday the 6ᵗʰ of May 1776. 1776. Williamsburg, Va.: Alexander Purdie.

Proc. of the Conv. of the Del. St., Held at New-Castle on Tuesday the Twenty-Seventh of August, 1776. 1776. Wilmington, Del.: James Adams.

Proc. of the Convs. of the Prov. of Md., Held at the City of Annapolis, in 1774, 1775, & 1776. 1836. Baltimore: James Lucas & E. K. Deaver.

Proc. of the H. of Reps. of the St. of Kan. 1889. Topeka: Kansas Publishing House.

"A Proclamation." 1774. Boston: M. Draper.

Public Acts of the St. of Tenn., Passed at the Extra Sess. of the Thirty-Third GA, April 1861. 1861. Nashville, Tenn.: J. O. Griffith & Co.

Public Acts Passed by the GA of the St. of Conn., in the Year 1887. 1887. Hartford, Conn.: Case, Lockwood & Brainard Company.

Pulsifer, David. 1861. *Records of the Col. of New Plymouth in New England.* Boston: William White.

Register and Man. of the St. of Conn. 1889. Hartford, Conn.: Case, Lockwood & Brainard Co.

Report of the Deb. and Proc. of the Conv. for the Rev. of the Cons. of the St. of Ind. 1850. Indianapolis: A. H. Brown.

Report of the Deb. and Proc. of the Conv. for the Rev. of the Cons. of the St. of Ohio, 1850–51. 1851. Columbus, Ohio: S. Medary.

Report of the Joint Investigating Committee on Public Frauds and Election of Hon. J. J. Patterson to the US Sen., Made to the GA of S.C. at the Reg. Sess. 1877–78. 1878. Columbia, S.C.: Calvo & Patton.

Report of the Proc. and Deb. in the Conv. to Revise the Cons. of the St. of Mich. 1850. Lansing, Mich.: R. W. Ingals.

Report of the Secretary of the Terr., 1909–1910 and Legislative Man., 1911. 1911. Santa Fe, N.M.: New Mexican Printing Co.

Revised Code of the Statute Laws of the St. of Miss. 1857. Jackson, Miss.: E. Barksdale.

Revised Stat. of the St. of R.I. and Providence Plantations: to which are Prefixed, the Constitutions of the US and of the St. 1857. Providence, R.I.: Sayles, Miller, and Simons.

Revised Stat. of the St. of Wis.: Passed at the Annual Sess. of the Leg. Commencing Jan. 13, 1858, and Approved May 17, 1858. 1858. Chicago: W. B. Keen.

Roll Call of State Officers and Members of GA of Conn., from 1776 to 1881. 1881. Hartford, Conn.: Case, Lockwood & Brainard Co.

Rules and Orders for Conducting Business in the H. of the LA of the Hawaiian Islands. 1876. Honolulu, Hawaii: n.p.

Rules and Orders for the Regulation and Gov. of the H. of Dels. 1861. Annapolis, Md.: Elihu S. Riley.

Rules and Orders for the Regulation and Gov. of the H. of Dels. of Md., January Sess. 1888. 1888. Annapolis, Md.: James Young.

Rules and Orders to be Observed in the H. of Reps. of the Com. of Mass. for the Year 1818. 1818. Boston: Russell, Cutler & Co.

Rules and Orders to be Observed in the H. of Reps. of the Com. of Mass. for the Year 1819. 1819. Boston: Russell and Gardner.

Rules and Orders to be Observed in the H. of Reps. of the St. of Maine, during the Continuance of the First Leg. 1820. Portland, Maine: Francis Douglas.

Rules for the Gov. of the LA of the Terr. of Kan. 1858. Lawrence, Kan.: W. W. Ross.

Rules of the H. of Reps. in the GA of Conn. 1818. Hartford, Conn.: n.p.

Salley, A. S., Jr., ed. 1907. *Jour. of the Commons H. of Asm. of S.C. for the Sess. Beginning September 20, 1692, and Ending October 15, 1692.* Columbia, S.C.: Historical Commission of South Carolina.

Salley, A. S., Jr., ed. 1908. *Jour. of the Commons H. of Asm. of S.C. for the Sess. Beginning January 30, 1696, and Ending March 17, 1696.* Columbia, S.C.: Historical Commission of South Carolina.

Salley, A. S., Jr., ed. 1914. *Jour. of the Commons H. of Asm. of S.C. for the Two Sessions of 1698.* Columbia, S.C.: Historical Commission of South Carolina.

Saunders, William L., ed. 1886a. *The Colonial Records of N.C.*, vol. III. Raleigh, N.C.: P. M. Hale.

Saunders, William L., ed. 1886b. *The Colonial Records of N.C.*, vol. IV. Raleigh, N.C.: P. M. Hale.

Sen. and H. Jours. of the Leg. of the St. of Neb. Fifty-First Sess. (Extraordinary). 1935. Lincoln, Neb.: Nebraska Legislature.

Sen. Jour. of the St. Leg. of Neb. 1867. Omaha, Neb.: St. A. D. Balcombe.

Shurtleff, Nathaniel B., ed. 1853a. *Records of the Governor and Company of the Mass. Bay in New England*, vol. I. Boston: William White.

Shurtleff, Nathaniel B., ed. 1853b. *Records of the Governor and Company of the Mass. Bay in New England*, vol. II. Boston: William White.

Shurtleff, Nathaniel B., ed. 1854. *Records of the Governor and Company of the Mass. Bay in New England*, vol. III. Boston: William White.

Smither, Harriet ed. 1931. *Jours. of the Fourth Cong. of the Republic of Texas 1839–1840 to which are Added the Relief Laws.* Austin, Tex.: Von Boeckmann-Jones Co.

Smither, Harriet ed. 1940. *Jours. of the Sixth Cong. of the Republic of Texas 1841–1842 to which are Added the Special Laws.* Austin, Tex.: Von Boeckmann-Jones Co.

Smull's Legislative Hand Book. 1887. Harrisburg, Pa.: E. K. Meyers.

S.D. Constitutional Conv., vol. 2. 1907. Huron, S.D.: Huronite.

S.D. Legislative Research Coun. 1998. "State Legislator Compensation." Issue Memorandum 98-02 Update, May 1.

State Finances 1945. 1947. Washington, D.C.: U.S. Government Printing Office.

State Finances 1946. 1947. Washington, D.C.: U.S. Government Printing Office.

State Government Finances in 1953. 1954. Washington, D.C.: U.S. Government Printing Office.

State Government Finances in 1954. 1955. Washington, D.C.: U.S. Government Printing Office.

State Government Finances in 1959. 1960. Washington, D.C.: U.S. Government Printing Office.

St. of N.H. Man. for the GC 1965. 1965. Concord, N.H.: Department of State.

St. of N.H. Man. for the GC 1967. 1967. Concord, N.H.: Department of State.

St. of N.H. Man. for the GC 1969. 1969. Concord, N.H.: Department of State.

St. of N.H. Man. for the GC 1973. 1973. Concord, N.H.: Department of State.

St. of N.H. Man. for the GC 1977. 1977. Concord, N.H.: Department of State.

St. of N.H. Man. for the GC 1979. 1979. Concord, N.H.: Department of State.

St. of N.H. Man. for the GC 1985. 1985. Concord, N.H.: Department of State.

Statistical Abstract of the United States 1935. 1935. Washington, D.C.: U.S. Government Printing Office.

Statistical Abstract of the United States 1946. 1946. Washington, D.C.: U.S. Government Printing Office.

Statistical Abstract of the United States 1956. 1956. Washington, D.C.: U.S. Government Printing Office.

Statistical Abstract of the United States 1960. 1960. Washington, D.C.: U.S. Government Printing Office.

Stat. of Ore. 1855. Salem, Ore.: Asahel Bush.

Testimony Taken Before the Joint Committee of the Sen. and Asm. of the St. of N.Y. to Investigate and Examine into the Business and Affairs of Life Insurance Companies Doing Business in the St. of New York, vol. IV. 1905. Albany, N.Y.: Brandow Printing Company.

Texas Legislative Coun. 1956. *Compensation of Legislators and Frequency of Legislative Sessions.* Austin: Texas Legislative Council.

Texas Legislative Coun. 1968. "Proposed Constitutional Amendments Analyzed."

Texas Legislative Coun. 1972. "Proposed Constitutional Amendments Analyzed."

Thornbrough, Gayle, and Dorothy Riker, eds. 1950. *Jours. of the GA of Ind. Terr. 1805–1815.* Indianapolis: Indiana Historical Bureau.

Trumbull, J. Hammond, ed. 1850. *The Public Records of the Col. of Conn., Prior to the Union with the New Haven Colony, May 1665; Transcribed and Published, (in Accordance with a Resolution of the GA,) with Occasional Notes, and an Appendix.* Hartford, Conn.: Brown & Parsons.

Trumbull, J. Hammond, ed. 1852. *The Public Records of the Col. of Conn., from 1665 to 1678; with the Jour. of the Council of War, 1675 to 1678; Transcribed* and Edited, in Accordance with a Resolution of the GA, with Notes and an Appendix. Hartford, Conn.: F. A. Brown.

U.S. H. 1839. *Rep. No. 176. Claim of N.H. [To accompany bill H.R. No. 1088].* January 16.

U.S. H. 1856. *Message from the President of the US to the Two Houses of Cong., at the Commencement of the Third Sess. of the Thirty-Fourth Cong.,* vol. II. Washington, D.C.: Cornelius Wendell.

U.S. H. 1873. *Report of the Select Committee to Investigate the Alleged Credit Mobilier Bribery, Made to the H. of Reps., February 18, 1873.* Washington, D.C.: Government Printing Office.

U.S. Sen. 1900. *Organic Acts for the Territories of the US with Notes Thereon Compiled from Stat. at Large of the US; Also, Appendixes Comprising other Matters Relating to the Gov. of the Territories.* Washington, D.C.: Government Printing Office.

U.S. Sen. 1913. *Compilation of Sen. Election Cases from 1789 to 1913.* Washington, D.C.: Government Printing Office.

Van Schreeven, William J., and George H. Reese, eds. 1969. *Proc. of the GA of Va. July 30–August 4, 1619 Written & Sent from Va. to England by Mr. John Pory Speaker of the First Representative Asm. in the New World.* Jamestown, Va.: Jamestown Foundation of the Commonwealth of Virginia.

Votes and Proc. of the Asm. of the St. of N.Y., At their first Sess., begun and holden in the Asm. Chamber at Kingston, in Ulster County, on Wednesday, the tenth Day of September, 1777. 1777. Kingston, N.Y.: John Holt.

Votes and Proc. of the Asm. of the St. of N.Y., At their second Sess., begun and holden in the Asm. Chamber at Poughkeepsie, in Dutchess County, on Thursday, the first Day of October, 1778. 1779. Poughkeepsie, N.Y.: John Holt.

Votes and Proc. of the Forty-Third GA, of the St. of N.J. 1819. Trenton, N.J.: James J. Wilson.

Votes and Proc. of the Fourteenth GA of the St. of N.J. 1789. New-Brunswick, N.J.: Abraham Blauvelt.

Votes and Proc. of the GA of the Col. of N.J. 1772. Burlington, N.J.: Isaac Collins.

Votes and Proc. of the GA of the Prov. of N.J. 1769. Woodbridge, N.J.: James Parker.

Votes and Proc. of the GA of the St. of N.J. 1777. Burlington, N.J.: Isaac Collins.

Votes and Proc. of the H. of Asm. of the Del. St., At a Sess. Commenced at Dover, on Wednesday, the Twentieth Day of October, in the Year of Our Lord, One Thousand Seven Hundred and Eighty-Six. 1786. Wilmington, Del.: Jacob A. Killen & Co.

Votes and Proc. of the H. of Asm. of the Del. St., At a Sess. Commenced at Dover, on Monday, the Twenty-Seventh Day of August, in the Year of Our Lord, One Thousand Seven Hundred and Eighty-Seven. 1787. Wilmington, Del.: Frederick Craig and Co.

Votes and Proc. of the H. of Asm. of the Del. St., At a Sess. Commenced at Dover, on Monday, the Twentieth Day of October, in the Year of Our Lord, One Thousand

Seven Hundred and Eighty-Eight. 1788. Wilmington, Del.: James Adams & Sons.

Votes and Proc. of the H. of Asm. of the Del. St., At a Sess. Commenced at Dover, on Tuesday, the Twentieth Day of October, in the Year of Our Lord, One Thousand Seven Hundred and Eighty-Nine. 1789. Wilmington, Del.: Frederick Craig and Co.

Votes and Proc. of the H. of Asm. of the Del. St., Commenced at Dover, on Wednesday, the Twentieth Day of October, in the Year of Our Lord, One Thousand Seven Hundred and Eighty-Four. 1785. Wilmington, Del.: Jacob A. Killen & Co.

Votes and Proc. of the H. of Asm. of the Del. St., Commenced at Dover, on Wednesday, the Twentieth Day of October, in the Year of Our Lord, One Thousand Seven Hundred and Eighty-Five. 1786. Wilmington, Del.: Jacob A. Killen & Co.

Votes and Proc. of the H. of Asm. of the Del. St., At a Sess. Commenced at Dover, on Tuesday the Twentieth Day of October, in the Year of Our Lord One Thousand Seven Hundred and Eighty-nine. 1789. Wilmington, Del.: Frederick Craig.

Votes and Proc. of the H. of Dels. of the St. of Md. 1819. Annapolis, Md.: Jonas Green.

Votes and Proc. of the H. of Dels. of the St. of Md. February Sess. 1777. 1777. Annapolis, Md.: Frederick Green.

Votes and Proc. of the H. of Dels. of the St. of Md. October Sess. 1778. 1778. Annapolis, Md.: Frederick Green.

Votes and Proc. of the H. of Dels. of the St. of Md. October Sess. 1780. 1781. Annapolis, Md.: Frederick Green.

Votes and Proc. of the H. of Dels. of the St. of Md. November Sess. 1785. 1786. Annapolis, Md.: Frederick Green.

Votes and Proc. of the H. of Dels. of the St. of Md. November Sess. 1789. 1790. Annapolis, Md.: Frederick Green.

Votes and Proc. of the H. of Reps. of the Gov. of the Counties of New-Castle, Kent, and Sussex, *upon* Del., *as a Sess. of Asm. held at* New-Castle *the Twenty-First Day of* October *(the Twentieth being* Sunday*) 1765.* 1770. Wilmington, Del.: James Adams.

Votes and Proc. of the H. of Reps. of the Prov. of Pa. Beginning the Fourth Day of December, 1682, vol. the first. In two parts. 1752. Philadelphia: B. Franklin and D. Hall.

Votes and Proc. of the H. of Reps. of the Prov. of Pa. Beginning the Fourth Day of December, 1682, vol. the first. Part the second. 1752. Philadelphia: B. Franklin and D. Hall.

Votes and Proc. of the H. of Reps. of the Prov. of Pa., *Met at Philadelphia, on the Fifteenth of* October, Anno Domini *1770, and continued by Adjournments.* 1771. Philadelphia: Henry Miller.

Votes and Proc. of the H. of Reps. of the Prov. of Pa., Met at PHILADELPHIA, *on the Fourteenth of* October, Anno Domini *1763, and continued by Adjournments.* 1764. Philadelphia: B. Franklin and D. Hall.

Votes and Proc. of the H. of Reps. of the Prov. of Pa., vol. the sixth. 1776. Philadelphia: Henry Miller.

Votes and Proc. of the Lower H. of Asm. of the Prov. of Md. 1771. Annapolis, Md.: Anne Catharine Green.

Votes of the H. of Reps. 1734. Philadelphia: Benjamin Franklin.

Whitmore, William H., ed. 1889. *The Colonial Laws of Mass.* Boston: Rockwell and Churchill.

Willis, E. B., and P. K. Stockton. 1881. *Deb. and Proc. of the Constitutional Conv. of the St. of Calif., Convened at the City of Sacramento, Saturday, September 28, 1878,* vol. II. Sacramento: State Office.

Winkler, Ernest William, ed. 1911. *Secret Jours. of the Sen., Republic of Texas, 1836–1845.* Austin, Tex.: Austin Printing Co.

Ziegler, J., ed. 1860. *A Man. for the Gov. of the Sen. and the H. of Reps. of the Com. of Penn.* Harrisburg, Pa.: George Burgner & Co.

NEWSPAPERS

Anaconda Standard (Mont.). 1889. "The Road to Order." November 24.

Arizona Champion. 1885a. "The Legislature." March 28.

Arizona Champion. 1885b. "The Solons of the Thirteenth Legislature." April 4.

Arizona Champion. 1885c. "That the last Legislature . . ." May 30.

Arizona Daily Citizen. 1901. "Saturday; Gazette; Various; Mr. Morgan." March 12.

Arizona Silver Belt. 1885a. "The Legislature." January 31.

Arizona Silver Belt. 1885b. "Capitol Capers." March 7.

Arizona Silver Belt. 1885c. "Arizona Disgraced." March 21.

Aspen Daily Times (Colo.). 1895. "Those Women." June 6.

Barre Patriot (Mass.). 1849. "State of Deseret." October 19.

Boston Evening Transcript (Mass.). 1879. "Evening Transcript." September 27.

Boston Post Boy (Mass.). 1774. "At a meeting of the Delegates." September 12.

Brenham Weekly Banner (Texas). 1886. "State News." July 8.

Capitol Journal (Ore). 1895. "The Clerkship Evil." May 1.

Charleston Morning Post and Daily Advertiser (S.C.). 1786. "New State of Franklin, August Session, 1785." February 17.

Columbian (Wash.). 1853. "The Legislative Assembly of Oregon." January 15.

Columbus Enquirer-Sun (Ga.). 1888. "Georgia Legislature." November 20.

Commercial Advertiser (N.Y.). 1799. "By Mail. Baltimore, Nov. 20." November 23.

Connecticut Courant. 1837. "Extract of a Letter from a Gentleman at Little Rock, Arkansas, to His Friend in Louisville, Kentucky Dated December 10, 1837." December 30.

Daily Alta California. 1850. "Liberality." July 2.

Daily Alta California. 1852. "Legislative Intelligence." April 2.

Daily Alta California. 1854. "Letter from Sacramento." July 17.

Daily Atlanta Intelligencer (Ga.). 1870. "Georgia Legislature." August 2.

Daily Colorado Republican and Rocky Mountain Herald. 1861a. "Council Chambers." September 14, 1861.

Daily Colorado Republican and Rocky Mountain Herald. 1861b. "House of Representatives." September 14, 1861.

Daily Colorado Republican and Rocky Mountain Herald. 1861c. "House of Representatives." September 17, 1861.

Daily Eugene Guard (Ore.). 1898. "They Took Everything." October 18.

Daily Free Press (Pa.). 1897. "The Capitol Fire." February 4.

Daily Globe (Minn.). 1881a. "Biennial Sessions—Special Legislation." January 7.

Daily Globe (Minn.). 1881b. "Incendiary Torch." March 2.

Daily Globe (Minn.). 1881c. "A Big Blaze." March 3.

Daily Herald (Texas). 1893. "Things that Resemble Nepotism." January 21.

Daily Herald (Texas). 1895. "The Retrenchment Fever." March 19.

Daily Picayune (La.). 1838. "Committee; Territorial Legislature; Wisconsin; Alexander M'Gregor." February 8.

Daily Tombstone Epitaph (Ariz.). 1886. "An Awful Example." February 3.

Denver Daily Times (Colo.). 1877. "Legislative Work." March 7.

Denver Daily Tribune (Colo.). 1878. "New Mexico." January 8.

DN (Utah). 1851. "Deseret News." April 8.

DN (Utah). 1856a. "Affairs at the Capital." January 2.

DN (Utah). 1856b. "Fillmore City." January 2.

DN (Utah). 1856c. "Legislative Assembly." December 17.

DN (Utah). 1856d. "Resolutions." December 24.

DN (Utah). 1856e. "The Legislative Assembly." December 24.

DN (Utah). 1857. "Names of Members and Officers of the Legislative Assembly of the Territory of Utah." January 2.

DN (Utah). 1858a. "The Legislative Assembly." January 27.

DN (Utah). 1858b. "Legislative Assembly." December 22.

DN (Utah). 1859. "Meeting of the Legislature." December 7.

DN (Utah). 1860a. "Adjournment of the Legislature." January 25.

DN (Utah). 1860b. "Tenth Annual Session of the Legislative Assembly." December 5.

DN (Utah). 1860c. "Legislative Proceedings." December 19.

DN (Utah). 1861a. "From Nevada Territory." December 18.

DN (Utah). 1861b. "Eleventh Annual Session of the Legislative Assembly." December 18.

DN (Utah). 1862a. "Legislative Proceedings." December 17.

DN (Utah). 1862b. "Legislative Proceedings." December 24.

DN (Utah). 1863a. "The Last Evening of the Session." January 21.

DN (Utah). 1863b. "Legislative Proceedings." January 21.

DN (Utah). 1868. "Home Items." February 26.

DN (Utah). 1869. "Legislative Assembly." January 13.

Dubuque Herald (Iowa). 1897. "State Finances." January 26.

East Florida Herald. 1826. "Communication for the Herald to the Electors of the Eastern District of Florida." August 22.

Enquirer (Ga.). 1840. "Biennial Sessions." November 4.

Evening Bulletin (Hawaii). 1901. "Law Makers Begin Their Arduous Work." February 20.

Fort Worth Daily Gazette (Texas). 1883. "A Drunk Legislator." March 2.

Fort Worth Daily Gazette (Texas). 1888. "The Past Invoked." December 3.

Fort Worth Daily Gazette (Texas). 1889. "Legislative." January 10.

Fort Worth Daily Gazette (Texas). 1890. "The Pass to Public Officials Must Go." June 13.

Freedom's Champion (Kan.). 1859. "The Territorial Legislature." January 22.

Freedom's Champion (Kan.). 1861. "Kansas Legislature." April 6.

Freedom's Champion (Kan.). 1867. "Another Minneola Swindle." June 20.

General Advertiser and Political, Commercial, Agricultural and Literary Journal (Pa.). 1791. "Legislature of Pennsylvania, House of Representatives February 16." February 17.

Genesee Whig (Mich.). 1850. "Legislative Expenses—Contrast of Cost Between Annual and Biennial Sessions." June 29.

Georgia Weekly Telegraph and Journal & Messenger. 1875. "Biennial Sessions." December 14.

Hartford Weekly Times (Conn.). 1884. "The State Legislature." April 3.

Hawaiian Gazette. 1880. "The Legislature." May 5.

Huntsville Times (Ala.). 2007. "Alabama Senator Throws Punch in Scuffle in Senate Chamber." July 7.

Idaho Tri-Weekly Statesman. 1866. "Territorial Legislature." December 1.

Independent (Hawaii). 1901a. "Our Legislature." February 18.

Independent (Hawaii). 1901b. "Topics of the Day." February 27.

Independent (Hawaii). 1901c. "The Legislature." April 16.

Independent Gazetter (Pa.). 1789. "Extract of a Letter from a Gentleman in Fayetteville (N.C.) to His Friend in Frederick-Town, Dated Jan. 1, 1789." February 26.

Independent Journal (N.Y.). 1785a. "Philadelphia." June 1.

Independent Journal (N.Y.). 1785b. "New-York, September 24."

Journal-Advance and Gentry Index (Ark.). 1918. "Proposed New Constitution." November 29.

Kansas City Times (Mo.). 1891. "Ended with Ill Feeling." January 13.

Lewiston Daily Sun (Maine). 1971. "Maine Flunked the Test." February 9.

Lewiston Morning Tribune (Idaho). 1949. "Overworked Legislatures." March 29.

Los Angeles Times (Calif.). 1963. "State Has Best Legislators, Unruh Asserts." October 2.

Macon Georgia Telegraph. 1847. "The Georgia Legislature." November 7.

Macon Telegraph (Ga.). 1898. "Atkinson's Message." October 28.

Mansfield Herald (Ohio). 1869. "Facts for All Tax-Payers." August 26.

Maryland Herald and Elizabeth-Town Weekly Advertiser. 1803a. "Mr. Grieves." September 14.

Maryland Herald and Elizabeth-Town Weekly Advertiser. 1803b. "Voters of Washington County." September 21.

Mercantile Advertiser (N.Y.). 1818. "Usury." October 2.

Meriden Daily Republican (Conn.). 1885. "Connecticut Egislature." February 5.

Meriden Journal (Conn.). 1971. "General Assembly Middles Along." February 5.

Milwaukee Journal (Wis.). 1891. "Expense of Legislatures." June 30.

Milwaukee Journal (Wis.). 1965. "Better Legislatures." December 11.

Milwaukee Sentinel (Wis.). 1842. "Territorial Legislature." December 14.

Milwaukee Sentinel (Wis.). 1844. "Territorial Legislature." November 9.

Milwaukee Sentinel (Wis.). 1848. "Territorial Legislature." February 21.

Missouri Gazette. 1808. "St. Louis." December 8.

Missouri Gazette. 1812. "Journal of the House of Representatives, of the Missouri Territory: begun and held at the Town of St. Louis, in the County of St. Louis and Territory of Missouri on Monday the seventh day of December, one thousand and eight hundred and twelve being the day appointed by a law of the United States, entitled 'an act providing for the Government of the Territory of Missouri' passed June 4[th,] 1812." December 19.

Missouri Gazette. 1814. "Missouri Territory. Journal of the House of Representatives, begun and held at the Town of St. Louis, and Territory of Missouri, on Monday the sixth day of December, one thousand and eight hundred and thirteen, being the second session of the first legislature held under a law of the Congress of the United States, entitled 'an act providing for the Government of the Territory of Missouri' passed June 4[th,] 1812." January 1.

Mohave County Miner (Ariz.). 1887. "The Arizona Legislature." March 19.

Morning Call (Calif.). 1895a. "Bloodsuckers of the State Yet Hold On—Retrenchment at the Capital Regarded as a Joke—An Army of Useless Attaches Whose Salaries are Unwarranted—Raid on the Treasury—Hordes of Political Hangers-On Fed at the California Lawmakers' Crib." February 20.

Morning Call (Calif.). 1895b. "On a Kite-Shaped Track—Fast Race of Senate and Assembly in Extravagance." February 20.

MP. 1864. "Bannack Correspondence." December 17.

MP. 1865a. "Bannack Correspondence." January 21.

MP. 1865b. "Bannack Correspondence." February 4.

MP. 1866a. "Legislative Proceedings." March 24.

MP. 1866b. "Weekly Post." November 3.

MP. 1866c. "Weekly Post." December 8.

MP. 1868a. "Death of Gen. J. P. Slough." January 18.

MP. 1868b. "Our Virginia Letter." December 18.

National Herald (Hawaii). 1890. "National Reform Party." January 25.

National Republican (Washington, D.C.). 1867. "From St. Louis—Murder of Col. Slough."

Newburyport Herald (Mass.). 1798. "New State House." January 19.

New-Hampshire Patriot and State Gazette. 1835. "House." June 22.

News and Courier (S.C.). 1941. "Assembly Harm to Trade Denied." February 6.

Niles' Weekly Register. 1838. "Murder in Arkansas." June 23.

Northern Standard (Texas). 1846. "Texas Legislature." March 11.

NYDT. 1853. "News of the Morning." March 8.

NYDT. 1855a. "Interesting from Kansas." September 4.

NYDT. 1855b. "Resignation of M. F. Conway, One of the Kansas Territorial Legislature." July 21.

NYDT. 1856a. "Affairs in Nebraska." January 18.

NYDT. 1856b. "Nebraska." February 1.

NYDT. 1856c. "News from Kansas." March 13.

NYDT. 1856d. "Kansas." July 18.

NYDT. 1857. "From Nebraska." January 27.

NYT. 1858a. "Kansas Affairs." February 16.

NYT. 1858b. "A Legislative Rumpus in Nebraska—The Split." January 22.

NYT. 1859. "From Utah." February 19.

NYT. 1863. "Close of the Session of the Legislature." February 8.

NYT. 1864. "Affairs in Utah; The Legislature Miscellaneous." February 14.

NYT. 1867. "Murder of Chief-Justice Slough in New-Mexico, by a Member of the Senate." December 28.

NYT. 1868. "Affairs in Utah." March 10.

NYT. 1872. "Legislative Pay." February 11.

NYT. 1873a. "New-Mexico: Affairs of the Territory." December 6.

NYT. 1873b. "Wyoming." December 5.

NYT. 1873c. "Railroad Extortion." April 3.

NYT. 1874a. "Corruption at Albany." March 30.

NYT. 1874b. "The Sandwich Islands. Meeting of the Hawaiian Legislature." May 22.

NYT. 1874c. "The Vermont Legislature." October 5.

NYT. 1878a. "Debate in the Assembly." March 13.

NYT. 1878b. "The Wyoming Affair." March 19.

NYT. 1879. "Biennial Legislative Sessions." October 20.

NYT. 1881. "Mr. Edmunds on Biennial Sessions." February 6.

NYT. 1883. "Work of the Legislators." February 27.

NYT. 1884. "Biennial Sessions in Connecticut." October 6.

NYT. 1885a. "All About Free Passes." February 6.

NYT. 1885b. "Use of Railroad Passes." March 20.

NYT. 1886a. "Committees of the Legislature." January 14.

NYT. 1886b. "Free Passes." January 24.

NYT. 1887a. "Hawaii's New Constitution." August 9.

NYT. 1887b. "Georgia's Legislature." October 7.

NYT. 1888a. "Lent His Railroad Pass." February 17.

NYT. 1888b. "No More Railroad Passes." December 4.

NYT. 1889a. "A Washington Legislator." December 16.

NYT. 1889b. "Changing a Constitution." March 11.

NYT. 1889c. "The Biennial Session Plan." June 2.

NYT. 1890a. "Excitement in Guthrie." October 3.

NYT. 1890b. "The Two Browns Meet: A Disgraceful Scuffle in the Oklahoma Legislature." December 11.

NYT. 1891a. "A Democratic Surprise." January 8.

NYT. 1891b. "Small But Incorruptible—The Little Legislature Which Rules Delaware." January 16.

NYT. 1891c. "Biennial Sessions Costly." October 10.

NYT. 1893a. "Idaho's Lively Legislature." March 11.

NYT. 1893b. "Biennial Sessions in Ohio—How Legislatures for Years Have Evaded the Constitution." May 26.

NYT. 1893c. "Riot in the British House." July 28.

NYT. 1895a. "King May Die of His Injuries." March 13.

NYT. 1895b. "The Third House Rules—Disgraceful Record of the New-Jersey Legislature." March 25.

NYT. 1896. "One Session in Two Years Satisfies." March 15.

NYT. 1897. "Oleomargarine Bill Vetoed." April 22.

NYT. 1899. "Biennial Sessions." January 23.

NYT. 1901. "The Hawaiian Legislature." March 8.

NYT. 1904. "Wisconsin's Capitol Destroyed by Fire; The Loss Is Estimated at Approximately $1,000,000." February 28.

NYT. 1907. "Insists on Higher Legislative Pay." April 10.

NYT. 1911a. "Flames Destroy Missouri Capitol." February 6.

NYT. 1911b. "$5,000,000 LOSS IN CAPITOL FIRE; West Wing Wrecked and State Library, with Historic Records, Almost Destroyed." March 30.

NYT. 1921. "Fire Ruins Capitol of West Virginia." January 4.

NYT. 1924. "Gassed Solons Flee in Rhode Island." June 21.

NYT. 1927. "State Offices Burn in Charleston, W. Va.; Occupants of Temporary Capitol Have Narrow Escapes—Valuable Records Lost." March 3.

NYT. 1929. "Most Legislators Get Low Salaries." May 5.

NYT. 1930. "Fire Razes Capitol of North Dakota; Documents of Incalculable Value Are Lost in Flames of Undetermined Origin." December 29.

NYT. 1931. "Legislative Salaries." February 25.

NYT. 1932. "Louisiana to Open New Capitol Tomorrow." May 15.

NYT. 1933. "Legislators Take $155 Salary Cut." February 8.

NYT. 1935. "OREGON'S CAPITOL SWEPT BY FLAMES; Dome Collapses as Fire Engulfs 60-Year-Old Building—Loss Put at $1,500,000." April 26.

NYT. 1971. "Ranking of Legislatures." February 4.

NY Trib. 1881. "Our Wretched Police Courts." February 15.

NY Trib. 1898. "Biennial Sessions." February 19.

Omaha Daily Bee (Neb.). 1887. "Mingling with the Wits." May 1.

Omaha Daily Bee (Neb.). 1889. "Lively Wrangle in the House." January 11.

Omaha Daily Bee (Neb.). 1891a. "The Power of Two Senators." January 28.

Omaha Daily Bee (Neb.). 1891b. "A Blow at Country Papers." February 1.

Patterson Daily Press (N.J.). 1880. "Biennial Legislative Sessions." April 5.

Pennsylvania Evening Herald and the American Monitor. 1785. "Postscript. Philadelphia, October 29." October 29.

Perrysburg Journal (Ohio). 1894. "Governor's Message." January 6.

Pioneer and Democrat (Wash.). 1854a. "Washington Legislature—First Session." March 4.

Pioneer and Democrat (Wash.). 1854b. "The Legislature." April 1.

Pioneer and Democrat (Wash.). 1856. "Remarks of Mr. Smith." December 19.

Pittsfield Sun (Mass.). 1858. "Massachusetts Legislature." January 21.

Placer Times (Calif.). 1849. "The Placer." May 26.

Portsmouth Journal of Literature and Politics (N.H.). 1835. "Madawasca Troubles." July 25.

Providence Evening Press (R.I.). 1876. "Hon. Charles Jackson." January 24.

Public (Ill.). 1901. "The First Territorial Legislature of Hawaii." 157:827–28.

Puget Sound Argus (Wash.). 1881. "Now That Our Legislative Representative has Returned." December 16.

Rocky Mountain News (Colo.). 1874. "The Tenth Legislative Assembly." Feb. 15.

Rome News-Tribune (Ga.). 1971. "Legislature Ranks Low." February 3.

Sacramento Daily Record-Union (Calif.). 1887. "Legislative Notes." March 4.

Sacramento Daily Union (Calif.). 1862. "News of the Morning." January 24.

Saint Joseph Daily Gazette (Mo.). 1874. "Governor's Message." January 9.

Salt Lake Herald (Utah). 1888. "A State House." January 12.

Salt Lake Herald (Utah). 1897. "Legislators and Passes." March 13.

Saturday Press (Hawaii). 1884. "The Legislature." May 3.

Seattle Gazette (Wash.). 1864. "Olla Podrida." January 9.

Sheboygan Press (Wis.). 1936. "Centennial of First Wisconsin Legislature is Observed Sunday." October 26.

St. Paul Daily Globe (Minn.). 1886. "Favoring Annual Sessions." December 17.

St. Paul Daily Globe (Minn.). 1889. "The Speaker of the Idaho Legislature." February 18.

St. Paul Daily Globe (Minn.). 1893. "Downed for a Day." February 10.

St. Paul Daily Globe (Minn.). 1895. "How the Money Goes." January 20.

St. Petersburg Times (Fla.). 1967. "Senate Okays Bid to Noted Lawmaker." August 17.

St. Petersburg Times (Fla.). 1969. "Legislative Firsts Cited." June 13.

Sun (N.Y.). 1893. "Legislation at Albany." May 21.

Sun (N.Y.). 1894. "Legislators on a Drunk." May 5.

Telegraph and Texas Register. 1836. "First Congress—First Session." October 11.

Tri-Weekly Alta California. 1849. "Doings of the Legislature." December 24.

Tuscaloosa News (Ala.). 1971. "Legislative Reform Issue Revived." Feb. 4.

Weekly Advertiser (Conn.). 1793. "The Voter, No. V." April 2.

Weekly Roundabout (Ky.). 1880. "Weekly Roundabout." January 3.

Wisconsin Enquirer (Wis.). 1841 "Territorial Legislature." March 20.

Wiscousin Territorial Gazett, and Burlington Advertiser (Iowa). 1837a. "The Capitol." October 12.

Wiscousin Territorial Gazett, and Burlington Advertiser (Iowa). 1837b. "Legislature, Monday." November 2.

Wiscousin Territorial Gazett, and Burlington Advertiser (Iowa). 1837c. "House of Representatives." December 16.

Wiscousin Territorial Gazett, and Burlington Advertiser (Iowa). 1838. "The Council and the Secretary." December 8.

OTHER SOURCES

"The Address of Liberty, to the Buckskins of Pennsylvania, on hearing of the intended Provincial Congress." 1775. Philadelphia: n.p.

Alden, George Henry. 1903. "The State of Franklin." *AHR* 8:271–89.

Aldrich, Charles. 1884. "Bribery by Railway Passes." *North American Review* 138:89–94.

Altshuler, Constance Wynn. 1989. "The Scandalous Divorce: Governor Safford Severs the Tie that Binds." *Journal of Arizona History* 30:181–92.

American Almanac and Repository of Useful Knowledge, for the Year 1832. 1832. Boston: Gray and Bowen.

American Almanac and Repository of Useful Knowledge, for the Year 1857. 1856. Boston: Crosby, Nichols and Company.

American Almanac and Repository of Useful Knowledge, for the Year 1860. 1860. Boston: Crosby, Nichols, Lee and Company.

American Almanac and Repository of Useful Knowledge, for the Year 1861. 1861. Boston: Crosby, Nichols, Lee and Company.

American Almanac and Treasury of Facts, Statistical, Financial, and Political, for the Year 1889. 1889. New York: American News Company.

American Annual Register; for the Year 1825–6, or the Fiftieth Year of American Independence. 1827. New York: G. and C. Carvill.

Andersen, W. G., Jr. 1971. "42 States Vote on Amendments." *NCR* 60:22–33.

Andersen, W. G., Jr. 1972. "14 States Vote on Amendments." *NCR* 61:19–28.

Andersen, W. G., Jr. 1973a. "45 States Vote on Amendments." *NCR* 62:21–31.

Andersen, W. G., Jr. 1973b. "Courts Resolve Election Issues." *NCR* 62:608–15.

Andersen, W. G., Jr. 1974. "1973 Developments on Constitutions." *NCR* 63:83–90.

Andersen, W. G., Jr. 1976. "State Constitutional Developments during 1975." *NCR* 65:25–34.

Andersen, W. G., Jr. 1977. "State Constitutional Developments during 1976." *NCR* 66:8–90.

Andrésen, Karen E. 1976. "A Return to Legitimacy: New Hampshire's Constitution of 1776." *Historical New Hampshire* 31:155–62.

Andrews, Charles M. 1926. "The American Revolution: An Interpretation." *AHR* 31:219–32.

Andrews, Charles McLean. 1944. "On the Writing of Colonial History." *WMQ* 1:27–48.

Ashe, Samuel A., Stephen B. Weeks, and Charles L. Van Noppen. 1905. *Biographical History of North Carolina from Colonial Times to the Present*, vol. II. Greensboro, N.C.: Charles L. Van Noppen.

Austin, Robert J. 2010. "Too Much Work, Not Enough Time: A Virginia Case Study in Improving the Legislative Process." *Journal of the American Society of Legislative Clerks and Secretaries* 16:25–40.

Bailey, Raymond C. 1979. *Popular Influence upon Public Policy: Petitioning in Eighteenth-Century Virginia*. Westport, Conn.: Greenwood.

Ballard, David E. 1908. "The First State Legislature." *Transactions of the Kansas State Historical Society, 1907–1908* X:232–54.

Bancroft, Hubert Howe. 1888. *History of California*. Vol. VI., 1848–1859. San Francisco: The History Company.

Bancroft, Hubert Howe. 1890. *History of Washington, Idaho, and Montana*. San Francisco: The History Company.

Banks, Ronald F. 1970. *Maine Becomes a State*. Middletown, Conn.: Wesleyan University Press.

Baringer, William E. 1949. *Lincoln's Vandalia*. New Brunswick: Rutgers University Press.

Barker, Charles Albro. 1940. *The Background of the Revolution in Maryland*. New Haven: Yale University Press.

Barker, Charles Albro, ed. 1945. *Memoirs of Elisha Oscar Crosby*. San Marino, Calif.: Huntington Library.

Barnhart, John D. 1941. "Frontiersmen and Planters in the Formation of Kentucky." *JSH* 7:19–36.

Barns, C. R., ed. 1877. *The Commonwealth of Missouri; a Centennial Record*. St. Louis: Bryan, Brand & Co.

Barrows, David P. 1917. "Legislative Failure and Reform." *California Law Review* 5:129–41.

Bassett, John Spencer. 1894. *The Constitutional Beginnings of North Carolina (1663–1729)*. Baltimore: Johns Hopkins University Press.

Batinski, Michael C. 1987. *The New Jersey Assembly, 1738–1775*. Lanham, Md.: University Press of America.

Beck, J. Murray. 1957. *The Government of Nova Scotia*. Toronto: University of Toronto Press.

Bedini, Silvio A. 1997. "The Mace and the Gavel: Symbols of Government in America." *Transactions of the American Philosophical Society* 87 Part 4:1–21.

Beek, Joseph Alan. 1980. *The California Legislature*. Rev. ed. Sacramento: California Office of State Printing.

Beeman, Richard R. 1972. *The Old Dominion and the New Nation, 1788–1801*. Lexington: University Press of Kentucky.

Beeman, Richard R. 1985. "The Political Response to Social Conflict in the Southern Backcountry: A Comparative View of Virginia and the Carolinas during the Revolution." In *An Uncivil War: The Southern Backcountry during the American Revolution*, ed. Ronald Hoffman, Thad W. Tate, and Peter J. Albert. Charlottesville: University Press of Virginia.

Beeman, Richard R. 1992. "Deference, Republicanism, and the Emergence of Popular Politics in Eighteenth-Century America." *WMQ* 49:401–30.

Beetle, David H. 1966. "Legislatures: The 100-Year Lag." *Nation* 196:475–78.

"The Beginnings of Burlington." 1921. *Palimpsest* 11:351–65.

Belknap, Jeremy. 1784. *The History of New-Hampshire*, vol. I. Philadelphia: Robert Aitken.

Belknap, Jeremy. 1791. *History of New Hampshire*, vol. II. Boston: Isaiah Thomas and Ebenezer T. Andrews.

Bell, Charles G., and Charles M. Price. 1984. *California Government Today: The Politics of Reform*. 2nd ed. Homewood, Ill.: Dorsey.

Bell, Dawson, Chris Christoff, and Kathleen Gray. 2007. "Idea of a Part-Time Legislature Gains Favor." *Detroit Free Press*, May 24.

Bennet, H. P. 1898. "The First Territorial Legislature of Nebraska." *Proceedings and Collections of the Nebraska State Historical Society*, 2nd series, vol. II: 88–92.

Bennett, Dana R. 2010. "Smokin' in the Boys Room: A Case Study of Women State Legislators in Nevada, 1919–1931." *Frontiers: A Journal of Women Studies* 31:89–122.

Bensel, Richard. 2000. "Of Rules and Speakers: Toward a Theory of Institutional Change for the U.S. House of Representatives." *Social Science History* 24:349–66.

Berkhofer, Robert F., Jr. 1972. "Jefferson, the Ordinance of 1784, and the Origins of the American Territorial System." *WMQ* 29:231–62.

Berkman, Michael B. 2001. "Legislative Professionalism and the Demand for Groups: The Institutional Context of Interest Population Density." *LSQ* 26:661–79.

Beverley, Robert. [1722] 1855. *The History of Virginia, in Four Parts*. Richmond, Va.: J. W. Randolph.

Bicknell, Thomas Williams. 1920. *The History of the State of Rhode Island and Providence Plantations*, vol. II. New York: American Historical Society.

"Big Daddy Unruh." 1963. *Life* 55 (September 27): 47–52.

Billings, Warren M. 1974. "The Growth of Political Institutions in Virginia, 1634–1676." *WMQ* 31:225–42.

Billings, Warren M. 2004. *A Little Parliament: The Virginia General Assembly in the Seventeenth Century.* Richmond: Library of Virginia, Jamestown 2007/Jamestown-Yorktown Foundation.

Billon, Frederick L. 1888. *Annals of St. Louis in Its Territorial Days from 1804 to 1821.* St. Louis: Frederick L. Billon.

Binder, Sarah A. 1995. "Partisanship and Procedural Choice: Institutional Change in the Early Congress, 1789–1823." *JOP* 57:1093–1118.

Binder, Sarah A. 1996. "The Partisan Basis of Procedural Choice: Allocating Parliamentary Rights in the House, 1789–1990." *APSR* 90:8–20.

Bingham, Hiram. 1855. *A Residence of Twenty-One Years in the Sandwich Islands; or the Civil, Religious, and Political History of Those Islands: Comprising a Particular View of the Missionary Operations Connected with the Introduction and Progress of Christianity and Civilization among the Hawaiian People.* Canandaigua, N.Y.: H. D. Goodwin.

"Biographies of the Members of the Free-State Legislature of 1857–'58." 1908. *Transactions of the Kansas State Historical Society, 1907–1908,* vol. X:204–16.

Bird, Annie Laurie. 1958. "William Henson Wallace, Pioneer Politician." *Pacific Northwest Quarterly* 49:61–76.

Blackmar, Frank Wilson. 1904. "State of Kansas." In *The Province and the States,* vol. IV, ed. Weston Arthur Goodspeed. Madison, Wis.: Western Historical Society.

Blair, Diane D. 1988. *Arkansas Government and Politics.* Lincoln: University of Nebraska Press.

Blanchard, Robert M. 1965. "Legislature: Change Coming—but What?" *Los Angeles Times,* April 22.

Boehmke, Frederick J. 2005. "Sources of Variation in the Frequency of Statewide Initiatives: The Role of Interest Group Populations." *Political Research Quarterly* 58:565–75.

Bolton, Arthur. 1971. "Expanding the Power of State Legislatures." In *Strengthening the States: Essays on Legislative Reform,* ed. Donald G. Herzberg and Alan Rosenthal. Garden City, N.Y.: Doubleday.

Bonomi, Patricia U. 1971. *A Factious People: Politics and Society in Colonial New York.* New York: Columbia University Press.

Book of the States 1935. 1935. Chicago: Council of State Governments and American Legislators' Association.

Book of the States 1945–1946. 1945. Chicago: Council of State Governments.

Book of the States 1954–55. 1954. Chicago: Council of State Governments.

Book of the States 1960–61. 1960. Chicago: Council of State Governments.

Book of the States 1980–81. 1980. Lexington, Ky.: Council of State Governments.

Book of the States 1998–99 Edition. 1998. Lexington, Ky.: Council of State Governments.

Book of the States 2008 Edition. 2008. Lexington, Ky.: Council of State Governments.

Book of the States 2009 Edition. 2009. Lexington, Ky.: Council of State Governments.

Bosher, Kate Langley. 1907. "The First House of Burgesses." *North American Review* 184:733–39.

Boswell, Sharon. 1999. *Frank B. Brouillet: An Oral History.* Olympia, Wash.: Washington State Oral History Program.

Bourinot, John George. 1884. *Parliamentary Procedure and Practice with an Introductory Account of the Origin and Growth of Parliamentary Institutions in Dominion of Canada.* Montreal: Dawson Brothers.

Bowers, Douglas E. 1983. "From Logrolling to Corruption: The Development of Lobbying in Pennsylvania, 1815–1861." *Journal of the Early Republic* 3:439–74.

Boyarsky, Bill. 2008. *Big Daddy: Jesse Unruh and the Art of Power Politics.* Berkeley: University of California Press.

Boyd, William J. D. 1968. "Bay State Has District Woes." *NCR* 57:411–18.

Boyd, William J. D. 1969a. "Many Amendments on State Ballots." *NCR* 58:20–27.

Boyd, William J. D. 1969b. "Local Government Progress on Remap." *NCR* 58:67–72.

Brace, Paul, and Daniel S. Ward. 1999. "The Institutionalized Legislature and the Rise of the Antipolitics Era." In *American State and Local Politics*, ed. Ronald E. Weber and Paul Brace. New York: Chatham House.

Bradley, Jared William, ed. 2002. *Interim Appointment: W. C. C. Claiborne Letter Book, 1804–1805.* Baton Rouge: Louisiana State University Press.

Brantley, William H. 1947. *Three Capitals: A Book about the First Three Capitals of Alabama, St. Stephens, Huntsville, & Cahawba.* Privately Printed.

Brazier, Don. 2000. *History of the Washington Legislature, 1854–1963.* Olympia, Wash.: Washington State Senate.

Brenaman, J. N. 1902. *A History of Virginia Conventions.* Richmond, Va.: J. L. Hill.

Brewerton, G. Douglas. 1856. *The War in Kansas.* New York: Derby & Jackson.

Brewster, William. 1960. *The Fourteenth Commonwealths: Vermont and the States that Failed.* Philadelphia: George S. MacManus Co.

Bridgman, Raymond L. 1893. "Biennial Elections and Legislative Sessions." *New England Magazine* 8:206–21.

Briggs, John E. 1916. "History and Organization of the Legislature in Iowa." In *Statute Law-making in Iowa*, ed. Benjamin F. Shambaugh. Iowa City: State Historical Society of Iowa.

Brodhead, John Romeyn. 1871. *History of the State of New York*, second volume. New York: Harper & Brothers.

Broussard, James H. 1977. "Party and Partisanship in American Legislatures: The South Atlantic States, 1800–1812." *JSH* 43:39–58.

Brown, J. Henry. 1892. *Brown's Political History of Oregon*, vol. I. Portland, Ore.: Wiley B. Allen.

Brown, Roger Hamilton. 1955. *The Struggle for the Indian Stream Territory.* Cleveland, Ohio: Western Reserve University Press.

Bruce, Philip Alexander. 1910. *Institutional History of Virginia in the Seventeenth Century,* vol. II. New York: G. P. Putnam's Sons.

Bruce, William Cabell. 1922. *John Randolph of Roanoke 1773–1833,* vol. I. New York: G. P. Putnam's Sons.

Brunkow, Robert de V. 1980. "Officeholding in Province, Rhode Island, 1646, 1686: A Quantitative Analysis." *WMQ* 37:242–60.

Bryan, Frank M. 2004. *Real Democracy: The New England Town Meeting and How It Works.* Chicago: University of Chicago Press.

Buchanan, William. 1963. *Legislative Partisanship.* Berkeley: University of California Press.

Buck, A. E. 1936. *Modernizing Our State Legislatures.* Philadelphia: American Academy of Political and Social Science.

Buell, Augustus C. 1904. *History of Andrew Jackson,* vol. I. New York: Charles Scribner's Sons.

Buffum, E. Gould. 1850. *Six Months in the Gold Mines: From a Journal of Three Years Residence in Upper and Lower California, in 1847–8–9.* London: Richard Bentley.

Burgess, John W. 1886. "The American Commonwealth: Changes in its Relation to the Nation." *PSQ* 1:9–35.

Burleigh, Joseph Bartlett. 1856. *The Legislative Guide, Containing All the Rules for Conducting Business in Congress; Jefferson's Manual; and the Citizens' Manual, Including a Concise System of Rules of Order Founded on Congressional Proceedings; with Copious Notes and Marginal References, Explaining the Rules and the Authority Therefor; Designed to Economize Time and Secure Uniformity in the Proceedings of all Deliberative Assemblies; and also to Meet the Wants of Every Private Citizen Who Desires to Understand the Right Way to Transact Public Business.* 4th ed., rev. ed. Philadelphia: J. B. Lippincott & Co.

Burnet, Jacob. 1847. *Notes on the Early Settlement of the North-Western Territory.* New York: D. Appleton & Co.

Burnet, Peter H. 1845. "Falatine Plains, Oregon, Nov. 4, 1844." *Pittsfield Sun,* September 4.

Burnett, Peter H. 1880. *Recollections and Opinions of an Old Pioneer.* New York: D. Appleton and Company.

Burns, John. 1971. *The Sometime Governments: A Critical Study of the 50 American Legislatures.* New York: Bantam Books.

Burns, Nancy, Laura Evans, Gerald Gamm, and Corrine McConnaughy. 2008. "Pockets of Expertise: Institutional Capacity in Twentieth-Century State Legislatures." *Studies in American Political Development* 22:229–48.

Caldwell, Lynton K. 1947. "Strengthening State Legislatures." *APSR* 41:281–89.

Callahan, Maud Fulcher. 1909. *Evolution of the Constitution of West Virginia.* Morgantown: Department of History and Political Science, West Virginia University.

Campbell, Ballard C. 1977. "Did Democracy Work? Prohibition in Late Nineteenth-Century Iowa: A Test Case." *Journal of Interdisciplinary History* 8:87–116.

Campbell, Ballard C. 1980. *Representative Democracy*. Cambridge: Harvard University Press.

Cannon, Lou. 1969. *Ronnie and Jesse*. Garden City, N.Y.: Doubleday.

Carey, Charles Henry. 1922. *A History of Oregon*. Chicago: Pioneer Historical Publishing.

Carey, John M., Richard G. Niemi, and Lynda W. Powell. 1998. "The Effects of Term Limits on State Legislatures." *LSQ* 23:271–300.

Cash, Marie. 1942. "Arkansas in Territorial Days." *AHQ* 1:223–34.

Cashin, Edward J. 1985. "But Brothers, It Is Our Land We Are Talking About: Winners and Losers in the Georgia Backcountry." In *An Uncivil War: The Southern Backcountry during the American Revolution*, ed. Ronald Hoffman, Thad W. Tate, and Peter J. Albert. Charlottesville: University Press of Virginia.

Chacón, Rafael. 1986. *Legacy of Honor: The Life of Rafael Chacón, a Nineteenth-Century New Mexican*. Albuquerque: University of New Mexico Press.

Chartock, Alan S., and Max Berking. 1970. *Strengthening the Wisconsin Legislature*. New Brunswick: Rutgers University Press.

Chase, Philander D., ed. 1987. *The Papers of George Washington*, Revolutionary War Series 2 September–December 1775. Charlottesville: University Press of Virginia.

Chasen, Daniel Jack. 1990. *Speaker of the House: The Political Career and Times of John L. O'Brien*. Seattle: University of Washington Press.

Chesnutt, David R., ed. 1985. *The Papers of Henry Laurens*, vol. Ten: Dec. 12, 1774–Jan. 4, 1776. Columbia: University of South Carolina Press.

Chesnutt, David R., ed. 1988. *The Papers of Henry Laurens*, vol. Eleven: Jan. 5, 1776–Nov. 1, 1777. Columbia: University of South Carolina Press.

Childs, Ebenezer. 1859. "Recollections of Wisconsin Since 1820." *Wisconsin Historical Collections* 4:153–95.

Chipman, Daniel. 1849. *A Memoir of Thomas Chittenden, the First Governor of Vermont; with a History of the Constitution during His Administration*. Middlebury, Vt.: Daniel Chipman.

Citizens Conference on State Legislatures. 1971. *State Legislatures: An Evaluation of Their Effectiveness*. New York: Praeger.

Citizens Conference on State Legislatures. 1974a. *How Citizens Can Improve the Arizona Legislature*. Kansas City, Mo.: Citizens Conference on State Legislatures.

Citizens Conference on State Legislatures. 1974b. *How Citizens Can Improve the Colorado General Assembly*. Kansas City, Mo.: Citizens Conference on State Legislatures.

Citizens Conference on State Legislatures. 1974c. *How Citizens Can Improve the Louisiana Legislature*. Kansas City, Mo.: Citizens Conference on State Legislatures.

Citizens Conference on State Legislatures. 1974d. *How Citizens Can Improve the Massachusetts General Court*. Kansas City, Mo.: Citizens Conference on State Legislatures.

Citizens Conference on State Legislatures. 1974e. *How Citizens Can Improve the Minnesota Legislature*. Kansas City, Mo.: Citizens Conference on State Legislatures.

Citizens Conference on State Legislatures. 1974f. *How Citizens Can Improve the New Hampshire General Court*. Kansas City, Mo.: Citizens Conference on State Legislatures.

Citizens Conference on State Legislatures. 1974g. *How Citizens Can Improve the Ohio General Assembly*. Kansas City, Mo.: Citizens Conference on State Legislatures.

Clark, Robert Carlton. 1912. "How British and American Subjects Unite in a Common Government For Oregon Territory in 1844." *QOHS* 13:140–59.

Clark, Robert Carlton. 1915. "The Last Step in the Formation of a Provisional Government for Oregon in 1845." *QOHS* 16:313–29.

Clarke, Mary Patterson. 1943. *Parliamentary Privilege in the American Colonies*. New Haven: Yale University Press.

Cleland, Ethel. 1910. "Legislative Reference." *APSR* 4:218–20.

Cloner, Alexander, and Richard W. Gable. 1959. "The California Legislator and the Problem of Compensation." *WPQ* 12:712–26.

Coggburn, Jerrell D. 2003. "Exploring Differences in the American States' Procurement Practices." *Journal of Public Procurement* 3:3–28.

Coggburn, Jerrell D., and Richard C. Kearney. 2009. "Trouble Keeping Promises? An Analysis of Underfunding in State Retiree Benefits." *Public Administration Review* 70:97–108.

Cohn, Mary W. 1971. "State Legislatures Regain Vitality, Esteem." *St. Petersburg Times*, December 29.

Coleman, Tobin A. 2006. "Reps Consider Full-Time Legislature." *Greenwich Time* (Conn.), January 3.

Collier, G. Loyd. 2000. "The Cultural Geography of Folk Building Forms in Texas." In *Built in Texas*, 2nd ed., ed. Francis Edward Abernathy. Denton: University of North Texas Press.

Collins, Richard H. 1874. *Collins' Historical Sketches of Kentucky. History of Kentucky*, vol. II. Covington, Ky.: Collins & Co.

Colton, Calvin. 1904. *The Works of Henry Clay Comprising His Life, Correspondence, and Speeches*, vol. 3. New York: G. P. Putnam's Sons.

Colvin, David Leigh. 1913. "The Bicameral Principle in the New York Legislature." Ph.D. diss. Columbia University.

Commission for Legislative Modernization. 1969. *Toward Tomorrow's Legislature*. Harrisburg, Pa.: Commission for Legislative Modernization.

Commission to Compile Information and Data for the use of the Constitutional Convention. 1918. *Bulletins for the Constitutional Convention 1917–1918*, vol. I. Boston: Wright & Potter Printing Co.

Committee for Economic Development. 1967. *Modernizing State Government.* New York: Committee for Economic Development.

"Congress May Vote with New Time-Saving Machine." 1916. *Popular Mechanics* 26:88–89.

Congressional Quarterly. 1993. *Congress A to Z.* Washington, D.C.: Congressional Quarterly Inc.

Connolly, C. P. 1906. "The Story of Montana IV: The Sale of the Montana Legislature, and Clark's Election." *McClure's Magazine* 28:27–43.

Conrad, Henry C. 1908. *History of the State of Delaware*, vol. I. Wilmington, Del.: Henry C. Conrad.

The Constitution of the State of Vermont. 1891. Brattleboro, Vt.: C. H. Davenport & Co.

"Constitutional Law—Police Power—Railroad Passes." 1916. *University of Pennsylvania Law Review and American Law Register* 64:834–36.

Cook, Florence. 1931. "Procedure in the North Carolina Colonial Assembly, 1731–1770." *North Carolina Historical Review* 8:258–83.

Cooper, Joseph. 1977. "Congress in Organizational Perspective." In *Congress Reconsidered*, ed. Lawrence C. Dodd and Bruce I. Oppenheimer. New York: Praeger.

Cooper, Joseph, and David W. Brady. 1981. "Toward a Diachronic Analysis of Congress." *APSR* 75:988–1006.

Cooper, Joseph, and Cheryl D. Young. 1989. "Bill Introduction in the Nineteenth Century: A Study of Institutional Change." *LSQ* 14:67–105.

Corey, John Pitts. 1929. "Procedure in the Commons House of Assembly in Georgia." *Georgia Historical Quarterly* 13:110–27.

Coulter, E. Merton. 1924. "Early Frontier Democracy in the First Kentucky Constitution." *PSQ* 39:665–77.

Council of State Governments. 1948. *Our State Legislatures. Report of the Committee on Legislative Processes and Procedures.* Rev. ed. Chicago: Council of State Governments.

Coward, Joan Wells. 1979. *Kentucky in the New Republic.* Lexington: University Press of Kentucky.

Cox, Elizabeth M. 1996. *Women, State and Territorial Legislatures, 1895–1995: A State-by-State Analysis, with Rosters of 6,000 Women.* Jefferson, N.C.: McFarland.

Cox, Gary W. 2000. "On the Effects of Legislative Rules." *LSQ* 25:169–92.

Craft, Ralph. 1972. *Strengthening the Arkansas Legislature.* New Brunswick: Rutgers University Press.

Crane, Wilder, Jr., and Meredith W. Watts Jr. 1968. *State Legislative Systems.* Englewood Cliffs, N.J.: Prentice-Hall.

Craton, Michael. 1962. *A History of the Bahamas.* London: Collins.

Crawley, Peter. 1989. "The Constitution of the State of Deseret." *BYU Studies* 29:1–29.

Cray, Ed. 1963. "Big Daddy of California." *Nation* 196:199–207.

Cuming, F. [1810] 1904. *Sketches of a Tour to the Western Country, Through the States of Ohio and Kentucky; A Voyage Down the Ohio and Mississippi Rivers, and a Trip Through the Mississippi Territory, and Part of Western Florida.* Pittsburgh: Cramer, Spear & Eichbaum. Reprinted in Reuben Gold Thwaites, *Early Western Travels 1748–1846*, vol. IV. Cleveland, Ohio: Arthur H. Clark Co., 1904.

Cummings, Henry. 1874. *A Synopsis of the Cruise of the U. S. S. 'Tuscarora' from the Date of Her Commission to Her Arrival in San Francisco, Cal., Sept. 2d, 1874.* San Francisco: Cosmopolitan Steam Printing Company.

Cushing, Harry A. 1896. "History of the Transition from Provincial to Commonwealth Government in Massachusetts." Ph.D. diss. Columbia University.

Cutler, Julia Perkins. 1890. *Life and Times of Ephraim Cutler Prepared from his Journals and Correspondence.* Cincinnati: Robert Clarke & Co.

Dabney, Virginius. 1961. "Jack Jouett's Ride." *American Heritage* 13 (December): 56–59.

Dalzell, James McCormick. 1888. *Private Dalzell, His Autobiography, Poems, Comic War Papers, Sketch of John Gray, Washington's Last Soldier, Etc.* Cincinnati: Robert Clarke & Co.

Daniel, Jean Houston, and Price Daniel. 1969. *Executive Mansions and Capitols of America.* Waukesha, Wis.: Country Beautiful.

Daniel, John W. 1902. "The Work of the Constitutional Convention." In *Report of the Fourteenth Annual Meeting of the Virginia State Bar Association*, ed. Eugene C. Massie. Richmond, Va.: Everett Waddey Co.

Daniels, Bruce C. 1986. "Diversity and Democracy: Officeholding Patterns among Selectmen in Eighteenth-Century Connecticut." In *Power and Status*, ed. Bruce C. Daniels. Middletown, Conn.: Wesleyan University Press.

Darcy, R. 2005. "The Oklahoma Territorial Legislature, 1890–1905." *Chronicles of Oklahoma* 83:144–77.

Davidson, Alexander, and Bernard Stuvé. 1877. *A Complete History of Illinois from 1673 to 1873; Embracing the Physical Features of the Country; Its Early Explorations; Aboriginal Inhabitants; French and British Occupation; Conquest by Virginia; Territorial Condition, and the Subsequent Civil, Military, and Political Events of the State.* Springfield, Ill.: D. L. Phillips.

Davidson, Roger H., and Walter J. Oleszek. 1976. "Adaptation and Consolidation: Structural Innovation in the U.S. House of Representatives." *LSQ* 1:37–65.

Davis, Rodney O. 1970. "Partisanship in Jacksonian State Politics: Party Divisions in the Illinois Legislature, 1834–1841." In *Quantification in American History*, ed. Robert Swierenga. New York: Atheneum.

Davis, Rodney O. 1988. "'The People in Miniature,' The Illinois General Assembly, 1818–1848." *Illinois Historical Journal* 81:95–108.

Davis, Sam P. 1912. *The History of Nevada.* Las Vegas: Nevada Publications.

Davis, W. W. H. 1857. *El Gringo; or, New Mexico and Her People.* New York: Harper & Brothers.

Dealey, James Quayle. 1907. *Our State Constitutions.* Philadelphia: American Academy of Political and Social Science.

Dean, David. 1996. *Law-Making and Society in Late Elizabethan England: The Parliament of England, 1584–1601.* Cambridge: Cambridge University Press.

Dean, William B. 1908. "A History of the Capitol Buildings of Minnesota. With Some Account of the Struggles for their Location." *Collections of the Minnesota Historical Society* 12:8–42.

DeBats, Donald A. 1990. "An Uncertain Arena: The Georgia House of Representatives, 1808–1861." *JSH* 56:423–56.

Deering, Christopher J., and Steven S. Smith. 1997. *Committees in Congress.* 3rd ed. Washington, D.C.: CQ Press.

Deming, Clarence. 1889. "Town Rule in Connecticut." *PSQ* 4:408–32.

"Destruction of the Capitol Building at Harrisburg." 1897. *The School Journal: Organ of the Department of Public Instruction and the State Teachers' Association* 45:395–401.

Detweiler, Robert. 1972. "Political Factionalism and the Geographic Distribution of Standing Committee Assignments in the Virginia House of Burgesses, 1730–1766." *VMHB* 80:267–85.

Dickens, Charles. 1898. *American Notes: and Pictures from Italy.* New York: Charles Scribner's Sons.

Dill, Alonzo Thomas. 1955. *Governor Tryon and His Palace.* Chapel Hill: University of North Carolina Press.

Doan, Daniel. 1997. *Indian Stream Republic.* Hanover, N.H.: University Press of New England.

Dodd, W. F. 1908. "Some Recent Tendencies in State Constitutional Development, 1901–1908." *Proceedings of the American Political Science Association* 5:149–64.

Dodd, Walter F. 1922. *State Government.* New York: The Century Co.

Dodds, H. W. 1918. "Procedure in State Legislatures." *Annals* 17: May supplement.

Doyle, Don H. 1980. "Henry Martyn Robert and the Popularization of American Parliamentary Law." *American Quarterly* 32:3–18.

Draper, Lyman C. 1872. "Naming of Madison and Dane County, and the Location of the Capital." *Wisconsin Historical Collections* 6:388–96.

Drayton, John. 1821a. *Memoirs of the American Revolution, from its Commencement to the Year 1776, Inclusive; as Relating to the State of South-Carolina: and Occasionally Refering to the States of North-Carolina and Georgia,* vol. I. Charleston, S.C.: A. E. Miller.

Drayton, John. 1821b. *Memoirs of the American Revolution, from its Commencement to the Year 1776, Inclusive; as Relating to the State of South-Carolina: and*

Occasionally Refering to the States of North-Carolina and Georgia, vol. II. Charleston, S.C.: A. E. Miller.

Driggs, Don W., and Leonard E. Goodall. 1996. *Nevada Government and Politics*. Lincoln: University of Nebraska Press.

Driscoll, James D. 1986. *California's Legislature*. Sacramento: Center for California Studies.

Drumm, Mark. 1896. *Drumm's Manual of Utah and Souvenir of the First State Legislature, 1896*. Salt Lake City, Utah: Drumm.

Dubin, Michael J. 2007. *Party Affiliations in the State Legislatures: A Year By Year Summary, 1796–2006*. Jefferson, N.C.: McFarland & Co.

Dunbar, Willis F., and George S. May. 1980. *Michigan: A History of the Wolverine State*. Grand Rapids, Mich.: William B. Eerdmans.

Dwinelle, John W. 1867. *The Colonial History City of San Francisco: Being a Narrative Argument in the Circuit Court of the United States for the State of California, For Four Square Leagues of Land, Claimed by the City under the Laws of Spain, and Confirmed to it by That Court, and by the Supreme Court of the United States*. 4th ed. San Francisco: Towne & Bacon.

Eblen, Jack Ericson. 1968. *The First and Second United States Empires*. Pittsburgh: University of Pittsburgh Press.

Ehrenhalt, Alan. 1991. *The United States of Ambition: Politicians, Power, and the Pursuit of Office*. New York: Times Books.

Ehrlich, Karen Lynn. 1981. "Arizona's Territorial Capital Moves to Phoenix." *Arizona & the West* 23:231–42.

Elkins, Zachary, and Beth Simmons. 2005. "On Waves, Clusters, and Diffusion: A Conceptual Framework." *Annals* 598:33–51.

Elton, G. R. 1986. *The Parliament of England, 1559–1581*. Cambridge: Cambridge University Press.

Emery, Robert A. 2006. "What Happened to Colonial Statutes? New York As an Example." *Legal References Services Quarterly* 25:129–39.

Ershkowitz, Herbert, and William G. Shade. 1971. "Consensus or Conflict? Political Behavior in the State Legislatures during the Jacksonian Era." *JAH* 58:591–621.

Etting, Frank M. 1891. *An Historical Account of the Old State House of Pennsylvania Now Known as The Hall of Independence*. Philadelphia: Porter and Coates.

Eustis, William Henry. 1904. "State of Minnesota." In *The Province and the States*, vol. VI, ed. Weston Arthur Goodspeed. Madison, Wis.: Western Historical Society.

Evans, David W. 1875. *Journal of Discourses by President Brigham Young, His Counselors, and the Twelve Apostles*, vol. XVII. Liverpool: Albert Carrington.

Fairlie, John A. 1917. "The Veto Power of the State Governor." *APSR* 11:473–93.

Falb, Susan Rosenfeld. 1986. *Advice and Ascent: The Development of the Maryland Assembly, 1635–1689*. New York: Garland.

Faragher, John Mack. 1992. *Daniel Boone: The Life and Legend of an American Pioneer*. New York: Henry Holt and Co.

Farish, Thomas Edwin. 1916. *History of Arizona*, vol. III. San Francisco: Filmer Brothers Electrotype Co.

Felt, Charles W. 1875. *Political Dead-Heads*. New York: English-American Office.

Field, M. H. 1887. "Grandma Bascom's Story of San Jose in '49." *Overland Monthly and Out West Magazine* 9:543–51.

Field, Stephen J. 1893. *Personal Reminiscences of Early Days in California, with Other Sketches*. Washington, D.C.: n.p.

Fineman, Herbert. 2003. "Looking Back on the Legislative Modernization Movement in Pennsylvania: Remarks of Herbert Fineman, Former Speaker of the Pennsylvania House of Representatives, Given at the Annual Meeting of the Pennsylvania Political Science Association, April 4, 2003 at Villanova University (with an Introduction and Commentary by Michael Cassidy)." *Commonwealth: A Journal of Political Science* 12:87–110.

Fiorina, Morris. 1994. "Divided Government in the American States: A Byproduct of Legislative Professionalism?" *APSR* 88:304–16.

Fisher, David Hackett. 1989. *Albion's Seed: Four British Folkways in America*. New York: Oxford University Press.

Fisher, Joel M., Charles M. Price, and Charles G. Bell. 1973. *The Legislative Process in California*. Washington, D.C.: American Political Science Association.

Fisher, Lucius G. 1918. "Pioneer Recollections of Beloit and Southern Wisconsin." *Wisconsin Magazine of History* 1:266–86.

Fisher, Sydney George. 1897. *The Evolution of the Constitution of the United States*. Philadelphia: J. B. Lippincott.

Fitzpatrick, Edward A. 1944. *McCarthy of Wisconsin*. New York: Columbia University Press.

Flandrau, Charles E. 1900. *The History of Minnesota and Tales of the Frontier*. St. Paul: E. W. Porter.

Ford, Paul Leicester, ed. 1893. *The Writings of Thomas Jefferson*, vol. II. New York: G. P. Putnam's Sons.

Fortier, Alcée. 1904. *A History of Louisiana*, vol. III, part I. New York: Manzi, Joyant & Co.

Foulke, Samuel. 1881. "Fragments of a Journal Kept by Samuel Foulke, of Bucks County, while a Member of the Colonial Assembly of Pennsylvania, 1762-3-4." *PMHB* 5:60–73.

Foulke, Samuel. 1884. "The Pennsylvania Assembly in 1761-2." *PMHB* 8:407–13.

Fowell, William Watts. 1956. *A History of Minnesota*, vol. 1. St. Paul: Minnesota Historical Society.

Fox, Harrison W., Jr., and Susan Webb Hammond. 1977. *Congressional Staffs*. New York: Free Press.

Frakes, George Edward. 1970. *Laboratory for Liberty: The South Carolina Legislative Committee System, 1719-1776*. Lexington: University Press of Kentucky.

Francis, Wayne L. 1985. "Leadership, Party Caucuses, and Committees in U.S. State Legislatures." *LSQ* 10:243–57.

Franklin, Benjamin. 1921. *Autobiography of Benjamin Franklin.* New York: Macmillan.

Frothingham, Richard. 1886. *The Rise of the Republic of the United States.* Boston: Little, Brown.

Fuller, Helen. 1963. "The Man to See in California." *Harper's Magazine* 226:64–72.

Galbreath, C. B. 1921. "Legislature of the Northwest Territory, 1795." *Ohio Archaeological and Historical Quarterly* 30:13–53.

Gallay, Alan. 1988. "Jonathan Bryan's Plantation Empire: Land, Politics, and the Formation of a Ruling Class in Colonial Georgia." *WMQ* 45:253–79.

Galloway, George B. 1961. *History of the House of Representatives.* New York: Thomas Y. Crowell.

Gamm, Gerald, and Kenneth Shepsle. 1989. "Emergence of Legislative Institutions: Standing Committees in the House and Senate, 1810–1825." *LSQ* 14:39–66.

Gammel, H. P. H., comp. 1898. *The Laws of Texas, 1822–1897,* vol. 1. Austin, Tex.: Gammel Book Company.

Gaston, Joseph. 1912. *The Centennial History of Oregon 1811–1912.* Chicago: S. J. Clarke.

Geer, T. T. 1912. *Fifty Years in Oregon.* New York: Neale Publishing.

Gerber, Elisabeth R., Arthur Lupia, Mathew D. McCubbins, and D. Roderick Kiewiet. 2001. *Stealing the Initiative: How State Government Responds to Direct Democracy.* Upper Saddle River, N.J.: Prentice-Hall.

Gibson, James E. 1934. "The Pennsylvania Provincial Conference of 1776." *PMHB* 58:312–41.

Gilbert, Michael D. 2006. "Single Subject Rules and the Legislative Process." *University of Pittsburgh Law Review* 67:803–70.

Gilkey, Elliot Howard. 1901. *The Ohio Hundred Year Book.* Columbus, Ohio: Fred J. Heer.

Gilmore, James R. 1887. *John Sevier as a Commonwealth-Builder.* New York: D. Appleton and Company.

Gladstone, T. H. 1857. *The Englishman in Kansas: or Squatter Life and Border Warfare.* New York: Miller & Company.

Gold, David M. 2002. "Rites of Passage: The Evolution of the Legislative Process in Ohio, 1799–1937." *Capital University Law Review* 30:630–55.

Gold, David M. 2009. *Democracy in Session: A History of the Ohio General Assembly.* Athens: Ohio University Press.

Goodsell, Charles T. 2001. *The American Statehouse: Interpreting Democracy's Temples.* Lawrence: University Press of Kansas.

Goodwin, Cardinal. 1914. *The Establishment of State Government in California 1846–1850.* New York: Macmillan.

Gosnell, Cullen B., and C. David Anderson. 1956. *The Government and Administration of Georgia.* New York: Thomas Y. Crowell.

Graham, A. A. 1888. "Legislation in the Northwest Territory." *Ohio Archaeological and Historical Quarterly* 1:303–18.

Gray, W. H. 1870. *A History of Oregon, 1792–1849, Drawn from Personal Observation and Authentic Information.* Portland, Ore.: Harris & Holman.

Green, Stephen. 2006. "'T. J. Green and 'The Legislature of a Thousand Drinks.'" *California State Library Foundation Bulletin* 85:17–18.

Greenawalt, Charles E., II, and G. Terry Madonna. 1992. "The Pennsylvania General Assembly—The House of Ill Repute Revisited." In *The Reform of State Legislatures,* ed. Eugene W. Hickok Jr. Lanham, Md.: Commonwealth Foundation.

Greenblatt, Alan. 2010. "Going Lean." *State Legislatures* 36 (April): 24–27.

Greene, Jack P. 1959. "Foundations of Political Power in the Virginia House of Burgesses, 1720–1776." *WMQ* 16:485–506.

Greene, Jack P. 1961. "The Role of the Lower Houses of Assembly in Eighteenth-Century Politics." *JSH* 27:451–74.

Greene, Jack P. 1963. *The Quest for Power: The Lower Houses of Assembly in the Southern Royal Colonies, 1689–1776.* Chapel Hill: University of North Carolina Press.

Greene, Jack P., ed. 1965. *The Diary of Colonel Landon Carter of Sabine Hall, 1752–1778,* vol. I. Charlottesville: University Press of Virginia.

Greene, Jack P. 1969. "Political Mimesis: A Consideration of the Historical and Cultural Roots of Legislative Behavior in the British Colonies in the Eighteenth Century." *AHR* 75:337–60.

Greene, Jack P. 1975. "The Growth of Political Stability: An Interpretation of Political Development in the Anglo-American Colonies, 1660–1760." In *The American Revolution: A Heritage of Change,* ed. John Parker and Carol Urness. Minneapolis: Associates of the James Ford Bell Library.

Greene, Jack P. 1979. "Character, Persona, and Authority: A Study of Alternative Styles of Political Leadership in Revolutionary Virginia." In *The Revolutionary War in the South,* ed. W. Robert Higgins. Durham: Duke University Press.

Greene, Jack P. 1981. "Legislative Turnover in British America, 1696 to 1775: A Quantitative Analysis." *WMQ* 38:442–63.

Greene, Jack P. 1994. "Colonial Assemblies." In *The Encyclopedia of the American Legislative Process,* vol. I, ed. Joel H. Silbey. New York: Scribners.

Gregg, Katharine, Scott Mayerowitz, and Elizabeth Gudrais. 2006. "A Full-Time Legislature for R.I.?" *Providence Journal,* January 5.

Grey, Anchitell. 1769. *Debates of the House of Commons, From the Year 1667 to the Year 1694.* London: T. Becket and P. A. De Hondt.

Griffith, Lucille. 1970. *The Virginia House of Burgesses, 1750–1774.* Rev. ed. University: University of Alabama Press.

Grimsted, David. 1998. *American Mobbing, 1828–1861: Toward Civil War.* New York: Oxford University Press.

Grivas, Theodore. 1963. *Military Governments in California, 1846–1850.* Glendale, Calif.: Arthur H. Clark.

Grumm, John G. 1971. "The Effects of Legislative Structure on Legislative Performance." In *State and Urban Politics,* ed. Richard I. Hofferbert and Ira Sharkansky. Boston: Little, Brown.

Gudrais, Elizabeth, Katherine Gregg, and Steve Peoples. 2007. "Political Scene: After 84 Years, Female Legislators of the House Get Their Own Restroom." *Providence Journal.* April 30.

Gunn, L. Ray. 1980. "The New York State Legislature: A Developmental Perspective: 1777–1846." *Social Science History* 4:267–94.

Gunn, L. Ray. 1988. *The Decline of Authority: Public Economic Policy and Political Development in New York, 1800–1860.* Ithaca: Cornell University Press.

Haight, Elizabeth S. 1984. "The Northampton Protest of 1652: A Petition to the General Assembly from the Inhabitants of Virginia's Eastern Shore." *American Journal of Legal History* 28:364–75.

Hailey, John. 1910. *The History of Idaho.* Boise, Idaho: Syms-York Company.

Hale, John P. n.d. *Daniel Boone.* Wheeling, W.Va.: Lewis Baker & Co.

Hall, Frank. 1904. "State of Colorado." In *The Province and the States,* vol. IV, ed. Weston Arthur Goodspeed. Madison, Wis.: Western Historical Society.

Hall, H. P. 1904. *H. P. Hall's Observations, Being More or Less a History of Political Contests in Minnesota from 1849 to 1904.* 3rd ed. St. Paul: H. P. Hall.

Hall, Hiland. 1868. *The History of Vermont, from its Discovery to its Admission into the Union in 1791.* Albany, N.Y.: Joel Munsell.

Hall, Van Beck. 1972. *Politics Without Parties: Massachusetts, 1780–1791.* Pittsburgh: University of Pittsburgh Press.

Hamm, Keith E., and Robert Harmel. 1993. "Legislative Party Development and the Speaker System: The Case of the Texas House." *JOP* 55:1140–51.

Hamm, Keith E., Ronald D. Hedlund, and Nancy Martorano. 2001. "Structuring Committee Decision-Making: Rules and Procedures in US State Legislatures." *Journal of Legislative Studies* 7:13–34.

Hamm, Keith E., Ronald D. Hedlund, and Nancy Martorano. 2006. "Measuring State Legislative Committee Power: Change and Chamber Differences in the 20th Century." *SPPQ* 6:88–111.

Hammond, Bray. 1948. "Banking in the Early West: Monopoly, Prohibition, and Laissez Faire." *Journal of Economic History* 8:1–25.

Hammond, Jabez D. 1846. *The History of Political Parties in the State of New-York, from the Ratification of the Federal Constitution to December 1840,* vol. I. Cooperstown, N.Y.: H. & E. Phinney.

Hanes, Christopher, and John A. James. 2003. "Wage Adjustment under Low Inflation: Evidence from U.S. History." *American Economic Review* 93:1414–24.

Hanson, Karen. 1994. "Our Beleaguered Institution." *State Legislatures* 20 (1): 12–17.

Hardaway, Roger D. 1991. "William Jefferson Hardin: Wyoming's Nineteenth Century Black Legislator." *Annals of Wyoming* 63:2–13.

Harlow, Ralph Volney. 1917. *The History of Legislative Methods in the Period before 1825*. New Haven: Yale University Press.

Harmel, Robert. 1986. "Minority Partisanship in One-Party Predominant Legislatures: A Five-State Study." *JOP* 48:729–40.

Harper's Weekly Journal of Civilization. 1870. "The Richmond Calamity." May 14.

Harrell, David Edwin. 1958. "James Winchester: Patriot." *Tennessee Historical Quarterly* 17:301–17.

Harris, Joseph P. 1947. "Modernizing the Legislature." *National Municipal Review* 36:142–46.

Harris, T. George. 1962. "Big Daddy's Big Drive." *Look* 26 (September 25): 78–82.

Harris, T. George. 1963. "Big Daddy Goes to Yale." *Look* 27 (February 12): 28–30.

Harrison, Gordon S. 1992. "Streamlining the Legislature: Pursuit of Unicameral Reform in Alaska." *Alaska History* 7:33–51.

Harrison, Robert. 1979. "The Hornet's Nest at Harrisburg: A Study of the Pennsylvania Legislature in the Late 1870s." *PMHB* 103:334–55.

Haskins, Charles Homer. 1891. *The Yazoo Land Companies*. New York: Knickerbocker Press.

Hasse, A. R. 1903. "The First Published Proceedings of an American Legislature." *The Bibliographer* 2:240–42.

Hatfield, Joseph T. 1976. *William Claiborne: Jeffersonian Centurion in the American Southwest*. Lafayette: University of Southwestern Louisiana.

Haynes, George H. 1894. *Representation and Suffrage in Massachusetts, 1620 1691*. Baltimore: Johns Hopkins University Press.

Healey, Paul D. 2007. "Go and Tell the World: Charles R. McCarthy and the Evolution of the Legislative Reference Movement, 1901–1917." *Law Library Journal* 99:33–53.

Heard, Alexander. 1966. "Reform: Limits and Opportunities." In *State Legislatures in American Politics*, ed. Alexander Heard. Englewood Cliffs, N.J.: Prentice-Hall.

Hedlund, Ronald D., Werner J. Patzelt, and David M. Olson. 2008. "Capacity Building in Parliaments and Legislatures: Institutionalization, Professionalization and Evolutionary Institutionalism." Presented at the International Political Science Association Conference, "International Political Science: New Theoretical and Regional Perspectives," Montreal, Canada.

Henderson, Archibald. 1920. *The Conquest of the Old Southwest*. New York: The Century Co.

Hening, H. B., ed. 1958. *George Curry, 1861–1947: An Autobiography*. Albuquerque: University of New Mexico Press.

Herndon, Dallas T., ed. 1922. *Centennial History of Arkansas*, vol. I. Chicago: S. J. Clarke.

Herzberg, Donald G., and Alan Rosenthal. 1971. *Strengthening the States: Essays on Legislative Reform*. Garden City, N.Y.: Doubleday.

Herzberg, Donald G., and Jess Unruh. 1970. *Essays on the State Legislative Process*. New York: Holt, Rinehart and Winston.

Hevesi, Alan G. 1975. *Legislative Politics in New York State*. New York: Praeger.

Hibbing, John R. 1988. "Legislative Institutionalization with Illustrations from the British House of Commons." *American Journal of Political Science* 32:681–712.

Hibbing, John R. 1999. "Legislative Careers: Why and How We Should Study Them." *LSQ* 24:149–71.

Hibbing, John R., and Samuel C. Patterson. 2006. "The U.S. Congress's Modest Influence on the Legislatures of Central and Eastern Europe." In *Exporting Congress? The Influence of the U.S. Congress on World Legislatures*, ed. Timothy J. Power and Nicol C. Rae. Pittsburgh: University of Pittsburgh Press.

Higginson, Stephen A. 1986. "A Short History of the Right to Petition Government for the Redress of Grievances." *Yale Law Journal* 96:142–66.

Higham, C. S. S. 1926. "The General Assembly of the Leeward Islands." *English Historical Review* 41:190–209.

Hill, Alice Polk. 1915. *Colorado Pioneers in Picture and Story*. Denver: Brock-Haffner Press.

Hines, Gustavus. 1850. *A Voyage Round the World: With a History of the Oregon Mission: and Notes of Several Years Residence on the Plains, Bordering the Pacific Ocean: Comprising an Account of Interesting Adventures among the Indians West of the Rocky Mountains*. Buffalo, N.Y.: George H. Derby and Co.

History of Tennessee. 1887. Nashville: Goodspeed Publishing.

Hitchcock, Henry-Russell, and William Seale. 1976. *Temples of Democracy*. New York: Harcourt Brace Jovanovich.

Hittell, Theodore H. 1898. *History of California*, vol. II. San Francisco: N. J. Stone & Company.

Hoffer, Peter C., and N. E. H. Hull. 1978. "The First American Impeachments." *WMQ* 35:653–67.

Hoffer, Peter C., and N. E. H. Hull. 1979. "Power and Precedent in the Creation of an American Impeachment Tradition: The Eighteenth-Century Colonial Record." *WMQ* 36:51–77.

Holman, Frederick V. 1912. "A Brief History of the Oregon Provisional Government and What Caused its Formation." *QOHS* 13:89–139.

Holmes, Fred L. 1915. "Voting by Electricity." *Illustrated World* 24:528.

Holt, Wythe W., Jr. 1968. "The Virginia Constitutional Convention of

1901–1902: A Reform Movement Which Lacked Substance." *VMHB* 76:67–102.

Horack, Frank E. 1916. "The Committee System." In *Statute Law-making in Iowa*, ed. Benjamin F. Shambaugh. Iowa City: State Historical Society of Iowa.

Hosmer, James Kendall, ed. 1908. *Winthrop's Journal, "History of New England," 1630–1649*. New York: Charles Scribner's Sons.

Hough, Franklin B. 1867. *Constitution of the State of New York, Adopted in 1846. With a Comparative Arrangement of the Constitutional Provisions of Other States, Classified by Their Subjects*. Albany, N.Y.: Weed, Parsons & Company.

Hough, Franklin B. 1872. *American Constitutions: Comprising the Constitution of Each State in the Union, and of the United States, with the Declaration of Independence and Articles of Confederation; Each Accompanied by a Historical Introduction and Notes, Together with a Classified Analysis of the Constitutions, According to Their Subjects, Showing, by Comparative Arrangement Every Constitutional Provision Now in Force in the Several States; with References to Judicial Decisions, and an Analytical Index*, vol. II. Albany, N.Y.: Weed, Parsons & Co.

Housman, Robert L. 1935. "The First Territorial Legislature in Montana." *Pacific Historical Review* 4:376–85.

Howard, Clinton N. 1947. *The British Development of West Florida, 1763–1769*. Berkeley: University of California Press.

Hubbard, C. C. 1924. "Legislative 'War' in Rhode Island." *National Municipal Review* 13:477–80.

Hubbard, Lucius F., and Return I. Holcombe. 1908. *Minnesota in Three Centuries*. Mankato, Minn.: Publishing Society of Minnesota.

Hubbard, N. M. 1884. "Bribery by Railway Passes." *North American Review* 138:95–99.

Huber, John D., Charles R. Shipan, and Madelaine Pfahler. 2001. "Legislatures and Statutory Control of Bureaucracy." *American Journal of Political Science* 45:330–45.

Hudson, Thomas J. 1904. "State of Iowa." In *The Province and the States*, vol. V, ed. Weston Arthur Goodspeed. Madison, Wis.: Western Historical Society.

Hunt, Rockwell Dennis. 1895. *The Genesis of California's First Constitution (1846–49)*. Baltimore: Johns Hopkins Press.

Huntington, Samuel P. 1965. "Political Development and Political Decay." *World Politics* 17:386–430.

Huntington, Samuel P. 1968. *Political Order in Changing Societies*. New Haven: Yale University Press.

Hutchinson, Thomas. 1765. *The History of the Colony of Massachuset's Bay, from the Settlement Thereof in 1628, until Its Incorporation with the Colony of Plimouth, Province of Main, &c. by the Charter of King William and Queen Mary in 1691*. London: M. Richardson.

Hutchinson, Thomas. 1768. *The History of the Province of Massachusets-Bay*, *from the Charter of King William and Queen Mary, in 1691, Until the Year 1750.* London: J. Smith.

Hyink, Bernard L. 1969. "California Revises Its Constitution." *WPQ* 22:637–54.

Hyman, Harold Melvin. 1954. *Era of the Oath.* Philadelphia: University of Pennsylvania Press.

Ignoffo, Mary Jo. 1999. *Gold Rush Politics: California's First Legislature.* Sacramento: California State Senate.

"Illinois' First State House." 1938. *Journal of the Illinois State Historical Society* 31:100.

Institute of Government. 1970. *Strengthening the Georgia General Assembly: Research Papers.* Athens: Institute of Government, University of Georgia.

Jackson, Harvey H. 1985. "The Rise of Western Members: Revolutionary Politics and the Georgia Backcountry." In *An Uncivil War: The Southern Backcountry during the American Revolution,* ed. Ronald Hoffman, Thad W. Tate, and Peter J. Albert. Charlottesville: University Press of Virginia.

Jackson, W. Turrentine. 1943. "Montana Politics during the Meagher Regime, 1865–67." *Pacific Historical Review* 12:139–56.

Jackson, W. Turrentine. 1945. "Indian Affairs and Politics in Idaho Territory, 1863–1870." *Pacific Historical Review* 14:311–25.

Jameson, J. Franklin. 1894. "The Origin of the Standing-Committee System in American Legislative Bodies." *PSQ* 9:246–67.

Jefferson, Thomas. 1854. *A Manual of Parliamentary Practice: Composed originally for the use of The Senate of the United States.* New York: Clark, Austin & Smith.

Jenkins, Jeffrey A. 1998. "Property Rights and the Emergence of Standing Committee Dominance in the Nineteenth-Century House." *LSQ* 23: 493–519.

Jenkins, Shannon. 2010. "Examining the Influences over Roll Call Voting in Multiple Issue Areas: A Comparative US State Analysis." *Journal of Legislative Studies* 16:14–31.

Jenks, William T. 1918. "Territorial Legislation by Governor and Judges." *MVHR* 5:36–50.

Jewell, Malcolm E., and Penny M. Miller. 1988. *The Kentucky Legislature: Two Decades of Change.* Lexington: University Press of Kentucky.

Jewell, Malcolm E., and Samuel C. Patterson. 1986. *The Legislative Process in the United States.* 4th ed. New York: Random House.

Jewett, Aubrey, and Roger Handberg. 1999. "GOP Rules Changes in the Florida House." *Comparative State Politics* 20 (August): 27–48.

Jillson, Calvin, and Rick K. Wilson. 1994. *Congressional Dynamics: Structure, Coordination, and Choice in the First American Congress, 1774–1789.* Stanford: Stanford University Press.

Johannsen, Robert W. 1951. "National Issues and Local Politics in Washington Territory, 1857–1861." *Pacific Northwest Quarterly* 42:3–31.

Johnson, Alvin W. 1938. *The Unicameral Legislature*. Minneapolis: University of Minnesota Press.

Johnson, Richard R. 1987. "'Parliamentary Egotisms': The Clash of Legislatures in the Making of the American Revolution." *JAH* 74:338–62.

Jolly, Ellen Roy, and James Calhoun. 1980. *The Pelican Guide to the Louisiana Capitol*. Gretna, La.: Pelican Publishing Co.

Jones, Charles C., Jr. 1883. *The History of Georgia*, vol. I. New York: Houghton, Mifflin.

Jones, Chester Lloyd. 1914. "The Improvement of Legislative Methods and Procedure." In *Proceedings of the American Political Science Association at its Tenth Annual Meeting held at Washington, D.C., December 30, 1913–January 1, 1914*. Baltimore: Waverly Press.

Jones, Herbert C. 1950. *The First State Legislature of California*. Sacramento: Senate of the State of California.

Jones, Matt Bushnell. 1939. *Vermont in the Making, 1750–1777*. Cambridge: Harvard University Press.

Jordan, David W. 1987. *Foundations of Representative Government in Maryland, 1632–1715*. New York: Cambridge University Press.

Jordan, John W. 1899. "A Description of the State-House, Philadelphia, in 1774." *PMHB* 23:417–19.

Judd, A. F. 1894. "The Constitution of the Republic of Hawaii." *Yale Law Journal* 4:53–60.

Ka, Sangjoon, and Paul Teske. 2002. "Ideology and Professionalism—Electricity Regulation and Deregulation Over Time in the American States." *American Politics Research* 30:323–43.

Kammen, Michael. 1969. *Deputyes and Libertyes: The Origins of Representative Government in Colonial America*. New York: Knopf.

Kanengiser, Andy. 2004. "Tort, Voter ID Bills Appear Dead." *Clarion-Ledger* (Miss.), March 4.

Kastor, Peter J. 1997. "'Equitable Rights and Privileges': The Divided Loyalties in Washington County, Virginia, during the Franklin Separatist Crisis." *VMHB* 105:193–226.

Katz, Jonathon N., and Brian R. Sala. 1996. "Careerism, Committee Assignments, and the Electoral Connection." *APSR* 90:21–33.

Keedy, Edwin R. 1953. "The Constitutions of the State of Franklin, the Indian Stream Republic and the State of Deseret." *University of Pennsylvania Law Review* 101:516–28.

Kelleher, Christine A., and Jennifer Wolak. 2007. "Explaining Public Confidence in the Branches of State Government." *Political Research Quarterly* 60:707–21.

Kellough, J. E., and S. C. Selden. 2003. "The Reinvention of Public Personnel Administration: An Analysis of the Diffusion of Personnel Management Reforms in the States." *Public Administration Review* 63:165–76.

Kelly, James. 1981. "One Man, One Vote, One Mess." *Time* (July 13): 12–15.

Kelly, William. 1851. *An Excursion to California over the Prairie, Rocky Mountains, and Great Sierra Nevada*, vol. II. London: Chapman and Hall.

Kennan, Clara B. 1950. "Arkansas's Old State House." *AHQ* 9:33–42.

Kettleborough, Charles. 1919. "Amendments to State Constitutions." *APSR* 13:429–47.

Kilgannon, Anne, ed. 2005. *Don Eldridge: An Oral History*. Olympia, Wash.: Washington State Oral History Program.

King, James D. 2000. "Changes in Professionalism in U.S. State Legislatures." *LSQ* 25:327–43.

Kingsbury, George W. 1915. *History of Dakota Territory*, vol. II. Chicago: S. J. Clarke Publishing.

Klain, Maurice. 1955. "A New Look at the Constituencies: The Need for a Recount and a Reappraisal." *APSR* 49:1105–19.

Kolp, John G. 1992. "The Dynamics of Electoral Competition in Pre-Revolutionary Virginia." *WMQ* 49:652–74.

Kousser, Thad. 2005. *Term Limits and the Dismantling of State Legislative Professionalism*. New York: Cambridge University Press.

Kousser, Thad, Mathew D. McCubbins, and Ellen Moule. 2008. "For Whom the TEL Tolls: Can State Tax and Expenditure Limits Effectively Reduce Spending?" *SPPQ* 8:331–61.

Kousser, Thad, and Justin H. Phillips. 2009. "Who Blinks First? Legislative Patience and Bargaining with Governors." *LSQ* 34:55–86.

Kousser, Thad, and Justin H. Phillips. 2010. "The Roots of Executive Power." Paper presented at the 2010 State Politics and Policy Conference, Springfield, Ill..

Krehbiel, Keith. 1991. *Information and Legislative Organization*. Ann Arbor: University of Michigan Press.

Kruman, Marc W. 1997. *Between Authority and Liberty: State Constitution Making in Revolutionary American*. Chapel Hill: University of North Carolina Press.

Kukla, Jon. 1981. *Speakers and Clerks of the Virginia House of Burgesses, 1643–1776*. Richmond: Virginia State Library.

Kukla, Jon. 1985. "Order and Chaos in Early America: Political and Social Stability in Pre-Restoration Virginia." *AHR* 90:275–98.

Kukla, Jon. 1989. *Political Institutions in Virginia, 1619–1660*. New York: Garland.

Kurtz, Karl T. 1999. "The History of Us." *State Legislatures* 25 (7): 16–21.

Kurtz, Karl T. 2010. "75 Years of Institutional Change in State Legislatures." In *Book of the States 2010 Edition*. Lexington, Ky.: Council of State Governments.

Kurtz, Karl T., Bruce Cain, and Richard G. Niemi, eds. 2007. *Institutional Change in American Politics: The Case of Term Limits*. Ann Arbor: University of Michigan Press.

Kurtz, Karl T., Gary F. Moncrief, Richard G. Niemi, and Lynda W. Powell.

2006. "Full-Time, Part-Time and Real Time: State Legislators' Perceptions of Time on the Job." *SPPQ* 6:322–38.

Kuykendall, Ralph S. 1967. *The Hawaiian Kingdom*, vol. 3. Honolulu: University of Hawaii Press.

Labaree, Leonard Woods. 1930. *Royal Government in America*. New Haven: Yale University Press.

Labaree, Leonard W., ed. 1967. *The Papers of Benjamin Franklin*, vol. 11. New Haven: Yale University Press.

Lamar, Howard Roberts. 1956. *Dakota Territory, 1861–1889: A Study of Frontier Politics*. New Haven: Yale University Press.

Langdon, George D., Jr. 1966. *Pilgrim Colony: A History of New Plymouth, 1620–1691*. New Haven: Yale University Press.

Lanman, Charles. 1876. *Biographical Annals of the Civil Government of the United States during its First Century*. Washington, D.C.: James Anglim.

Larson, Robert W. 1968. *New Mexico's Quest for Statehood, 1846–1912*. Albuquerque; University of New Mexico Press.

Larson, T. A. 1978. *History of Wyoming*. 2nd ed. Lincoln: University of Nebraska Press.

Lathrop, H. W. 1888. "The Capitals and Capitols of Iowa." *Iowa Historical Record* 4:97–124.

Lawson, Gary, and Guy Seidman. 2004. *The Constitution of Empire: Territorial Expansion and American Legal History*. New Haven: Yale University Press.

Lax, Jeffrey R., and Justin H. Phillips. 2009. "Gay Rights in the States: Public Opinion and Public Responsiveness." *APSR* 103:367–86.

Leake, James Miller. 1917. *The Virginia Committee System and the American Revolution*. Baltimore: Johns Hopkins Press.

Leder, Lawrence H. 1963. "The New York Elections of 1769: An Assault on Privilege." *MVHR* 49:675–82.

Lefroy, J. Henry. 1882. *The Historye of the Bermudaes or Summer Islands*. London: Hakluyt Society.

"Legislative Divorces." 1844. *Western Law Journal* 1:6.

Lemon, John J. 1973. "Study of 50 States is Showing Influence." *Spokane Daily Chronicle*, December 7.

Leonard, Sister Joan de Lourdes. 1948a. "The Organization and Procedure of the Pennsylvania Assembly 1682–1776 I." *PMHB* 72:215–39.

Leonard, Sister Joan de Lourdes. 1948b. "The Organization and Procedure of the Pennsylvania Assembly 1682–1776 II." *PMHB* 72:376–412.

Levine, Peter D. 1975. "State Legislative Parties in the Jacksonian Era: New Jersey, 1829–1844." *JAH* 62:591–608.

Levine, Peter D. 1977. *The Behavior of State Legislative Parties in the Jacksonian Era: New Jersey, 1829–1844*. Rutherford, N.J.: Fairleigh Dickinson University Press.

Levmore, Saul. 1989. "Parliamentary Law, Majority Decisionmaking, and the Voting Paradox." *Virginia Law Review* 75:971–1044.

Lincoln, Charles Z. 1906. *The Constitutional History of New York from the Beginning of the Colonial Period to the Year 1905, Showing the Origin, Development, and Judicial Construction of the Constitution*, vol. I. Rochester, N.Y.: The Lawyers Co-operative.

Lindley, E. R., comp. 1942. *Biographical Directory of the Texan Conventions and Congresses, 1832–1845*. Huntsville, Tex.: n.p.

Littler, Robert M. C. 1929. *Governance of Hawaii*. Stanford: Stanford University Press.

Lloyd, H. D. 1881. "Story of a Great Monopoly." *Atlantic Monthly* 47:317–22.

Loewenberg, Gerhard. 2011. *On Legislatures*. Boulder: Paradigm.

Lokken, Roy N. 1959a. "The Concept of Democracy in Colonial Political Thought." *William and Mary Quarterly* 16:568–80.

Lokken, Roy N. 1959b. *David Lloyd: Colonial Lawmaker*. Seattle: University of Washington Press.

Longmore, Paul K. 1995. "From Supplicants to Constituents: Petitioning by Virginia Parishioners, 1701–1775." *VMHB* 103:407–42.

Longmore, Paul K. 1996. "'All Matters and Things Relating to Religion and Morality': The Virginia House of Burgesses' Committee for Religion, 1769 to 1775." *Journal of Church and State* 38:775–97.

Loomis, Burdett A. 1994. *Time, Politics, and Policies*. Lawrence: University Press of Kansas.

Lounsbury, Carl R. 2001. *From Statehouse to Courthouse: An Architectural History of South Carolina' Colonial Capitol and Charleston County Courthouse*. Columbia: University of South Carolina Press.

Lowell, A. Lawrence. 1902. *The Influence of Party upon Legislation in England and America*. Washington, D.C.: Government Printing Office.

Lowell, Francis C. 1897. "Legislative Shortcomings." *Atlantic Monthly* 79:366–77.

Lubbock, Francis Richard. 1900. *Six Decades in Texas or Memoirs of Francis Richard Lubbock*. Austin, Tex.: Ben C. Jones & Co.

Luce, Robert. 1922. *Legislative Procedure*. Boston: Houghton Mifflin.

Luce, Robert. 1924. *Legislative Assemblies*. Boston: Houghton Mifflin.

Lutz, Donald S. 1999. "The Colonial and Early State Legislative Process." In *Inventing Congress: Origins and Establishment of the First Federal Congress*, ed. Kenneth R. Bowling and Donald R. Kennon. Athens: Ohio University Press.

Lydecker, Robert C. 1918. *Roster Legislatures of Hawaii 1841–1918*. Honolulu: Hawaiian Gazette Co.

Lyman, H. S. 1900. "Reminiscences of F. X. Matthieu." *QOHS* 1:73–104.

Lynch, Neil J. 1977. *Montana's Legislature through the Years*. Butte, Mont.: self-published.

Lyon, William H. 1984. "Arizona Territory and the Harrison Act of 1886." *Arizona & the West* 26:209–24.

MacKinnon, Frank. 1951. *The Government of Prince Edward Island*. Toronto: University of Toronto Press.

Maestas, Cherie. 2003. "The Incentive to Listen: Progressive Ambition, Resources, and Opinion Monitoring among State Legislators." *JOP* 65:439–56.

Magruder, Drake W., ed. 1981. "A Discourse on Divorce: Orleans Territorial Legislature, 1806." *Louisiana History* 22:434–37.

Maier, Pauline. 1976. "Reason and Revolution: The Radicalism of Dr. Thomas Young." *America Quarterly* 28:229–49.

Main, Jackson Turner. 1966. "Government by the People: The American Revolution and the Democratization of the Legislatures." *WMQ* 23:391–407.

Main, Jackson Turner. 1967. *The Upper House in Revolutionary America, 1763–1788*. Madison: University of Wisconsin Press.

Main, Jackson Turner. 1973a. *Political Parties before the Constitution*. Chapel Hill: University of North Carolina Press.

Main, Jackson Turner. 1973b. *The Sovereign States, 1775–1783*. New York: New Viewpoints.

Malbin, Michael J. 1980. *Unelected Representatives*. New York: Basic Books.

Malhotra, Neil. 2006. "Government Growth and Professionalism in U.S. State Legislatures." *LSQ* 31:563–84.

Malhotra, Neil. 2008. "Disentangling the Relationship between Legislative Professionalism and Government Spending." *LSQ* 33:387–414.

"Many Amendments Get Voter Approval." 1967. *NCR* 56:18–24.

Marelius, John. 2010. "Critics Seek a Part-Time California Legislature." San Diego *Union-Tribune*, March 1.

Marley, Patrick. 2006. "Walker Proposes State Term Limits." Milwaukee *Journal Sentinel*, February 21.

Martell, Christine R., and Paul Teske. 2007. "Fiscal Management Implications of the TABOR Bind." *Public Administration Review* 67:673–87.

Martin, Roscoe C. 1940a. "Alabama's Administrative Reorganization of 1939." *JOP* 2:436–47.

Martin, Roscoe C. 1940b. "Alabama Falls in Line." *State Government* 13:43–53.

Martin, Sidney Walter. 1944. *Florida during the Territorial Days*. Athens: University of Georgia Press.

Martorano, Nancy. 2004. "Cohesion or Reciprocity? Majority Party Strength and Minority Party Procedural Rights in the Legislative Process." *SPPQ* 4:55–73.

Martorano, Nancy. 2006. "Balancing Power: Committee System Autonomy and Legislative Organization." *LSQ* 31:205–34.

Mason, Paul. 1938. "Methods of Improving Legislative Procedure." *Annals* 195:151–58.

Massicotte, Louis. 2006. "So Close, Yet So Far: Congressional Influences on Canadian Legislatures." In *Exporting Congress? The Influence of the U.S. Congress on World Legislatures*, ed. Timothy J. Power and Nicol C. Rae. Pittsburgh: University of Pittsburgh Press.

McCarthy, Charles. 1911. "Legislative Reference Department." In *Readings on American State Government*, ed. Paul S. Reinsch. Boston: Ginn.

McClure, A. K. 1869. *Three Thousand Miles through the Rocky Mountains.* Philadelphia: J. B. Lippincott & Co.

McConachie, Lauros G. 1898. *Congressional Committees.* New York. Thomas Y. Crowell.

McConnell, W. J. 1913. *Early History of Idaho.* Caldwell, Idaho: Caxton Printers.

McCormick, Richard P. 1997. "Ambiguous Authority: The Ordinances of the Confederation Congress, 1781–1789." *American Journal of Legal History* 41:411–39.

McCrady, Edward. 1902. *The History of South Carolina in the Revolution, 1780–1783.* New York: Macmillan.

McDermott, Malcolm. 1934. "Paying the Piper." *State Government* 7:270–71.

McLendon, Michael K., James C. Hearn, and Christine G. Mokher. 2009. "Partisans, Professionals, and Power: The Role of Political Factors in State Higher Education Funding. *Journal of Higher Education* 80:686–713.

Meany, Edmond S. 1909. *History of the State of Washington.* New York: Macmillan.

Meikle, Don. 1968. "Overhaul of State Legislature is Urged." *The Day* (Conn.), December 14.

Miller, Elmer I. 1907. *The Legislature of the Province of Virginia; Its Internal Development.* New York: Columbia University Press.

Miller, James Knox Polk. 1960. *The Road to Virginia City: The Diary of James Knox Polk Miller.* Norman: University of Oklahoma Press.

Miller, James Nathan. 1965a. "Hamstrung Legislatures." *NCR* 54:178–87.

Miller, James Nathan. 1965b. "Our Horse-and-Buggy State Legislatures." *Reader's Digest* (May): 49–64.

Miller, James Nathan. 1971a. "How Florida Threw Out the Pork Chop Gang." *NCR* 60:366–80.

Miller, James Nathan. 1971b. "Florida Fires the Pork Chop Gang." *Reader's Digest* (August): 109–13.

Mills, James R. 1987. *A Disorderly House: The Brown-Unruh Years in Sacramento.* Berkeley, Calif.: Heyday Books.

Moncrief, Gary F. 1988. "Dimensions of the Concept of Professionalism in State Legislatures: A Research Note." *State and Local Government Review* 20:128–32.

Moncrief, Gary, and Malcolm E. Jewell. 1980. "Legislators' Perceptions of Reform in Three States." *American Politics Quarterly* 8:106–27.

Moncrief, Gary, Richard G. Niemi, and Lynda W. Powell. 2004. "Time, Term Limits, and Turnover: Membership Stability in U.S. State Legislatures." *LSQ* 29:357–81.

Moncrief, Gary F., Joel A. Thompson, and Karl T. Kurtz. 1996. "The Old Statehouse, It Ain't What It Used to Be." *LSQ* 21:57–72.

Mooney, Christopher Z. 1994. "Measuring U.S. State Legislative Profession-alism: An Evaluation of Five Indices." *State and Local Government Review* 26:70–78.

Mooney, Christopher Z. 1995. "Citizens, Structures, and Sister States: Influences on State Legislative Professionalism." *LSQ* 20:47–67.

Moran, Thomas Francis. 1895. *The Rise and Development of the Bicameral System in America.* Baltimore: Johns Hopkins University Press.

Morey, William C. 1893–94. "The First State Constitutions." *Annals* 4:201–32.

Morgan, Dale L. 1987. *The State of Deseret.* Logan: Utah State University Press.

Morgan, Robert. 2007. *Boone: A Biography.* Chapel Hill, N.C.: Algonquin.

Morris, Allen. 1982. "Florida Legislative Committees: Their Growth since 1822." *Florida Historical Quarterly* 61:125–47.

Morris, Allen, and Amelia Rea Maguire. 1978. "Beginnings of Popular Gov-ernment in Florida." *Florida Historical Quarterly* 57:19–39.

Morris, Allen, and Amelia Rea Maguire. 1980. "The Unicameral Legislature in Florida." *Florida Historical Quarterly* 58:303–15.

Morrissey, David. 1976. "Idaho's First State Legislature." *Rendezvous* 11:26–31.

Morse, Charles F. J. 1971. "Assembly—Tsk, Tsk—Rates 24th in Nation." *Hartford Courant,* February 7.

Mowry, George E. 1963. *The California Progressives.* Chicago: Quadrangle Books.

Mullis, Tony R. 2004. "The Dispersal of the Topeka Legislature." *Kansas History: A Journal of the Central Plains* 27:62–75.

Munroe, John A. 1979. *History of Delaware.* Newark: University of Delaware Press.

Murray, William P. 1908. "Recollections of Early Territorial Days and Legis-lation." *Collections of the Minnesota Historical Society* 12:103–30.

National Legislative Conference. 1961. *American State Legislatures in Mid-Twentieth Century.* Chicago: Council of State Governments.

National Legislative Conference. 1963. *Mr. President . . . Mr. Speaker . . .* Chicago: Council of State Governments.

Neale, J. E. 1949. *The Elizabethan House of Commons.* London: Jonathan Cape.

Nevins, Allan. 1924. *The American States During and After the Revolution, 1775–1789.* New York: Macmillan.

Nicholson, H. Whalley. 1881. *From Sword to Share; a Fortune in Five Years at Hawaii.* London: W. H. Allen & Co.

Niemi, Richard G., and Laura R. Winsky. 1987. "Membership Turnover in U.S. State Legislatures: Trends and Effects of Districting." *LSQ* 12:115–23.

Norris, George W. 1961. *Fighting Liberal: The Autobiography of George W. Nor-ris.* New York: Collier.

Norton, Philip. 1989. "The Glorious Revolution of 1688/9: Its Continuing Relevance." *Parliamentary Affairs* 42:135–47.

Noyes, Richard. 1976. "Time Frame as a Variable in the Fifth Provincial Congress." *Historical New Hampshire* 31:192–216.

Oberholtzer, Ellis Paxson. 1900. *The Referendum in America Together with Some Chapters on the History of the Initiative and Other Phases of Popular Government in the United States.* New York: Charles Scribner's Sons.

O'Donnell, Natalie. 2006. "The Importance of Decorum." *National Conference of State Legislatures LegisBrief* 14 (40).

Ogle, David B. 1970. *Strengthening the Connecticut Legislature.* New Brunswick: Rutgers University Press.

Ogle, David B. 1971. *Strengthening the Mississippi Legislature.* New Brunswick: Rutgers University Press.

"An Old Document of the State of Franklin." 1896. *American Historical Magazine* 1:298–300.

Olmsted, H. M. 1958. "Voters Pass on Many Proposals." *NCR* 47:562–67.

Olmsted, H. M. 1961. "Organizing by Public Employees." *NCR* 50:86–95.

Olmsted, H. M. 1962a. "New Michigan Constitution Ready." *NCR* 51:373–83.

Olmsted, H. M. 1962b. "Voters Amend Constitutions." *NCR* 51:613–22.

Olmsted, H. M. 1963. "Urges Revision for Anti-Strike Law." *NCR* 52:21–29.

Olmsted, H. M. 1964. "Congress Is Urged to Adopt Reforms." *NCR* 53: 591–99.

Olson, Alison G. 1992. "Eighteenth-Century Colonial Legislatures and Their Constituents." *JAH* 79:543–67.

Omdahl, Lloyd B. 1974. "Drive for Unicameralism Needs National Support." *NCR* 63:526–30.

Onuf, Peter S. 1981. "State-Making in Revolutionary America: Independent Vermont as a Case Study." *JAH* 67:797–815.

Opheim, Cynthia. 1991. "Explaining the Differences in State Lobby Regulation." *WPQ* 44:405–21.

Organization of the Free State Government in Kansas with The Inaugural Speech and Message of Governor Robinson. 1856. Washington, D.C.: Buell & Blanchard.

Ornstein, Norman J., Thomas E. Mann, and Michael J. Malbin. 2000. *Vital Statistics on Congress, 1999–2000.* Washington, D.C.: AEI.

Orth, Samuel P. 1904. "Our State Legislatures." *Atlantic Monthly* 94:728–39.

Owsley, Roy H. 1969. "For Annual Sessions." *NCR* 58:401–40.

Palmer, Kenneth T. *The Legislative Process in Maine.* 1973. Washington, D.C.: American Political Science Association.

Parent, Wayne, and Michael B. Henderson. 2002. "The Party's Over: The Rise and Stall of Louisiana Legislative Independence." *Loyola Law Review* 48:527–49.

Pargellis, S. M. 1927a. "The Procedure of the Virginia House of Burgesses I." *William and College Quarterly Historical Magazine* 7:73–86.

Pargellis, S. M. 1927b. "The Procedure of the Virginia House of Burgesses II." *William and College Quarterly Historical Magazine* 7:143–57.

Parvin, Theodore S. 1865. "Iowa Territorial Legislature." *Annals of Iowa* 3:506–11.

Parvin, Theo. S. 1900. "Territorial Legislature of 1838." In *Pioneer Lawmakers' Association of Iowa*. Des Moines: F. R. Conaway.

Pate, James E. 1930. "Constitutional Revision in Virginia Affecting the General Assembly." *William and Mary College Quarterly Historical Magazine* 10:105–22.

Patterson, Samuel C., Ronald D. Hedlund, and G. Robert Boynton. 1975. *Representatives and Represented*. New York: John Wiley & Sons.

Patterson, Stephen E. 1973. *Political Parties in Revolutionary Massachusetts*. Madison: University of Wisconsin Press.

Paxson, Frederic L. 1915. "A Constitution of Democracy—Wisconsin, 1847." *MVHR* 2:3–24.

Pedersen, Gilbert J. 1966. "The Founding First." *Journal of Arizona History* 7:45–58.

Peery, Dan W. 1929a. "The First Two Years." *Chronicles of Oklahoma* 7:281–322.

Peery, Dan W. 1929b. "The First Two Years (continued from last issue)." *Chronicles of Oklahoma* 7:419–57.

Pepys, Samuel. 1905. *The Diary of Samuel Pepys*. London: Macmillan.

Perkins, John A. 1946. "State Legislative Reorganization." *APSR* 40:510–21.

Peterson, Merrill D. 1965. "Louisiana!" In *The Louisiana Purchase Bicentennial Series in Louisiana History*, vol. III, ed. Dolores Egger Labbe. Lafayette: Center for Louisiana Studies, University of Southwestern Louisiana.

Peterson, Sanford W. 1983. "The Genesis and Development of Parliamentary Procedure in Colonial America, 1609–1801." Ph.D. diss. Indiana University.

Petrik, Paula. 1985. "Strange Bedfellows: Prostitution, Politicians, and Moral Reform in Helena, 1885–1887." *Montana: The Magazine of Western History* 35:2–13.

Phelan, James. 1888. *History of Tennessee*. Boston: Houghton, Mifflin.

Phelps, John B. 2004. "Notes on the Early History of the Office of Legislative Clerk." *Journal of the American Society of Legislative Clerks and Secretaries* 10:5–11.

Phillips, William. 1856. *The Conquest of Kansas by Missouri and Her Allies*. Boston: Phillips, Sampson and Company.

Pierson, Paul, and Theda Skocpol. 2002. "Historical Institutionalism in Contemporary Political Science." In *Political Science: The State of The Discipline*, ed. Ira Katznelson and Helen V. Milner. New York: Norton.

Pioneer Law-Makers' Association of Iowa. 1894. *Reunion of 1894*. Des Moines: G. H. Ragsdale.

Plaisted, Thais M. 1976. "The Source of Colonial Parliamentary Rules." *Parliamentary Journal* 17:7–12.

Pole, J. R. 1969. *The Seventeenth Century; The Sources of Legislative Power*. Charlottesville: University Press of Virginia.

Polishook, Irwin H. 1969. *Rhode Island and the Union, 1774–1795*. Evanston: Northwestern University Press.

Polsby, Nelson W. 1968. "The Institutionalization of the U.S. House of Representatives." *APSR* 62:144–68.

Polsby, Nelson W. 2004. *How Congress Evolves: Social Bases of Institutional Change*. New York: Oxford University Press.

Pomfret, John E. 1956. *The Province of West New Jersey, 1609–1702*. Princeton: Princeton University Press.

Pond, Fern Nance, ed. 1949. "Letters of an Illinois Legislator: 1839–40." *Abraham Lincoln Quarterly* 5:405–21.

Potts, James B. 1988. "The Nebraska Capital Controversy, 1854–59." *Great Plains Quarterly* 8:172–82.

Pound, William. 1992. "State Legislative Careers: Twenty-Five Years of Reform." In *Changing Patterns in State Legislative Careers*, ed. Gary F. Moncrief and Joel A. Thompson. Ann Arbor: University of Michigan Press.

Powell, William S. 1977. *John Pory, 1572–1636: The Life and Letters of a Man of Many Parts*. Chapel Hill: University of North Carolina Press.

Power, Timothy J., and Nicol C. Rae. 2006. "Barriers and Carriers: Legislative Diffusion and the Selective Imitation of Congress." In *Exporting Congress? The Influence of the U.S. Congress on World Legislatures*, ed. Timothy J. Power and Nicol C. Rae. Pittsburgh: University of Pittsburgh Press.

Price, H. Douglas. 1975. "Congress and the Evolution of Legislative 'Professionalism.'" In *Congress in Change: Evolution and Reform*, ed. Norman J. Ornstein. New York: Praeger.

Proceedings of the Fortieth Annual Meeting of the Alabama St. Bar Association held at Birmingham, ALA. 1917. July 12, 13, and 14.

"The Provisional Constitution of Frankland." 1896. *American Historical Magazine* 1:48–63.

Purcell, Richard J. 1918. *Connecticut in Transition, 1775–1818*. Washington, D.C.: American Historical Association.

Purvis, Thomas L. 1986. *Proprietors, Patronage, and Paper Money: Legislative Politics in New Jersey, 1703–1776*. New Brunswick: Rutgers University Press.

Putnam, Jackson K. 2005. *Jess: The Political Career of Jesse Marvin Unruh*. Lanham, Md.: University Press of America.

Quaife, M. M. 1922. "Wisconsin's Saddest Tragedy." *Wisconsin Magazine of History* 5:264–83.

Quaife, Milo M. 1919. *The Convention of 1846*. Madison: State Historical Society of Wisconsin.

Quincy, Josiah, Jr. 1915–16. "Journal of Josiah Quincy, Junior, 1773." *Massachusetts Historical Society Proceedings* 49:424–81.

Quisenberry, A. C. 1892. *The Life and Times of Hon. Humphrey Marshall*. Winchester, Ky.: Sun Publishing.

Quitt, Martin Herbert. 1970. "Virginia House of Burgesses 1660–1706: The

Social, Educational & Economic Bases of Political Power." Ph.D. diss. Washington University.

Rainbolt, John C. 1970. "The Alteration in the Relationship between Leadership and Constituents in Virginia, 1660 to 1720." *WMQ* 27:411–34.

Ramsay, David. 1858. *Ramsay's History of South Carolina, from Its First Settlement in 1670 to the Year 1808.* Newberry, S.C.: W. J. Duffie.

Ramsey, J. G. M. 1853. *The Annals of Tennessee to the End of the Eighteenth Century: Comprising its Settlement, as the Watauga Association, From 1769 to 1777; A Part of North-Carolina, from 1777 to 1784; The State of Franklin, From 1784 to 1788; A Part of North-Carolina, From 1788 to 1790; The Territory of the U. States, South of the Ohio, From 1790 to 1796; The State of Tennessee, From 1796 to 1800.* Charleston, S.C.: John Russell.

Ranck, George W. 1901. *Boonesborough: Its Founding, Pioneer Struggles, Indian Experiences, Transylvania Days, and Revolutionary Annals.* Louisville, Ky.: John P. Morton & Company.

Rausch, John David, Jr. 1994. "Anti-Representative Direct Democracy: The Politics of Legislative Constraint." *Comparative State Politics* 15 (2): 1–16.

Ray, David. 1974. "Membership Stability in Three State Legislatures: 1893–1969." *APSR* 68:106–12.

Ray, David. 1976. "Voluntary Retirement and Electoral Defeat in Eight State Legislatures." *JOP* 38:426–33.

Ray, P. Orman. 1917. *An Introduction to Political Parties and Practical Politics.* New York: Charles Scribner's Sons.

Redlich, Josef. 1908. *The Procedure of the House of Commons: A Study of its History and Present Form,* vol. 2. London: Archibald Constable & Co.

Reinsch, Paul S. 1907. *American Legislatures and Legislative Methods.* New York: The Century Co.

Remy, Jules, and Julius Brenchley. 1861. *A Journey to Great-Salt-Lake City.* London: W. Jeffs.

Reynolds, John. 1855. *My Own Times, Embracing Also, The History of My Life.* Chicago: B. H. Perryman and H. L. Davison.

Rice, M. M. 1928. "The Thirteenth Arizona Territorial Legislature." *Arizona Historical Review* 1:80–96.

Richardson, Lilliard E., Jr., David M. Konisky, and Jeffrey Milyo. 2010. "Public Approval of State Legislatures." Presented at the 2010 State Politics and Policy Conference, Springfield, Ill..

Richardson, Rupert N. 1928. "Framing the Constitution of the Republic of Texas." *Southwestern Historical Quarterly* 31:191–220.

Richardson, V. W. 1880. *Peck's Fun: Being Extracts from the "La Crosse Sun," and "Peck's Sun," Milwaukee Carefully Selected with the Object of Affording the Public in One Volume The Cream of Mr. Peck's Writings of the Past Ten Years.* Chicago: Belford, Clarke & Co.

Richman, Jesse. 2010. "The Logic of Legislative Leadership: Preferences, Challenges, and the Speaker's Powers." *LSQ* 35:211–33.

Ridgely, David, ed. 1841. *Annals of Annapolis, Comprising Sundry Notices of that Old City.* Baltimore: Cushing & Brother.

Riley, Elihu S. 1887. *"The Ancient City." A History of Annapolis, in Maryland.* Annapolis, Md.: Record Printing Office.

Riley, Elihu S. 1905. *A History of the General Assembly of Maryland 1635–1904.* Baltimore: Nunn & Co.

Ringold, May Spencer. 1966. *The Role of the State Legislatures in the Confederacy.* Athens: University of Georgia Press.

Risjord, Norman K., and Gordon DenBoer. 1974. "The Evolution of Political Parties in Virginia, 1782–1800. *JAH* 60:961–84.

Robey, Louis W. 1922. *Real Estate and Conveyancing in Pennsylvania.* Philadelphia: George T. Bisel Co.

Rodolf, Theodore. 1900. "Pioneering in the Wisconsin Lead Region." *Collections of the State Historical Society of Wisconsin* 15:338–89.

Roe, Alfred Seelye. 1895. *The Old Representatives' Hall, 1798–1895.* Boston: Wright and Potter Printing Co.

Rogers, George C., Jr. 1974. *The Papers of Henry Laurens.* Vol. Four: Sept. 1, 1763–Aug. 31, 1765. Columbia: University of South Carolina Press.

Rogers, Lindsay. 1941. "The Staffing of Congress." *PSQ* 56:1–22.

Rolfe, Maro O. 1904. "State of Arkansas." In *The Province and the States,* vol. III, ed. Weston Arthur Goodspeed. Madison, Wis.: Western Historical Society.

Rollins, C. B. 1938. "Letters of George Caleb Bingham to James S. Rollins. Part V." *Missouri Historical Review* 33:45–78.

"Roman Holiday: Do Legislators Play Leap-Frog? Gracious, No! Well Hardly Ever." 1937. *Literary Digest* 123 (May 15):13–14.

Roosevelt, Theodore. 1913. *Theodore Roosevelt. An Autobiography.* New York: Macmillan.

Rosenson, Beth A. 2005. *The Shadowlands of Conduct.* Washington, D.C.: Georgetown University Press.

Rosenthal, Alan. 1968. *Strengthening the Maryland Legislature.* New Brunswick: Rutgers University Press.

Rosenthal, Alan. 1971a. "The Scope of Legislative Reform: An Introduction." In *Strengthening the States: Essays on Legislative Reform,* ed. Donald G. Herzberg and Alan Rosenthal. Garden City, N.Y.: Doubleday.

Rosenthal, Alan. 1971b. "The Consequences of Legislative Staffing." In *Strengthening the States: Essays on Legislative Reform,* ed. Donald G. Herzberg and Alan Rosenthal. Garden City, N.Y.: Doubleday.

Rosenthal, Alan. 1974. "Turnover in State Legislatures." *American Journal of Political Science* 18:609–16.

Rosenthal, Alan. 1981. *Legislative Life.* New York: Harper & Row.

Rosenthal, Alan. 1993. "The Legislative Institution: In Transition and at Risk." In *The State of the States*, 2nd ed., ed. Carl E. Van Horn. Washington, D.C.: CQ Press.

Rosenthal, Alan. 1996. "State Legislative Development: Observations from Three Perspectives." *LSQ* 21:169–98.

Rosenthal, Alan. 1998. *The Decline of Representative Democracy: Process, Participation, and Power in State Legislatures.* Washington, D.C.: CQ Press.

Rosenthal, Alan. 2009. *Engines of Democracy: Politics and Policymaking in State Legislatures.* Washington, D.C.: CQ Press.

Ross, Margaret. 1971. "The Hinderliter House: Its Place in Arkansas History." *AHQ* 30:181–92.

Rossiter, Clinton. 1953. "Richard Bland: The Whig in America." *WMQ* 10:33–79.

Rothstein, Samuel. 1990. "The Origins of Legislative Reference Services in the United States." *LSQ* 15:401–11.

Rowland, Dunbar. 1905. *The Mississippi Territorial Archives, 1798–1803*, vol. I. Nashville: Press of Brandon Printing Co.

Rowland, Dunbar. 1925. *History of Mississippi*, vol. 1. Chicago: S. J. Clarke.

Rowland, Kate Mason. 1892. *The Life of George Mason 1725–1792*, vol. I. New York: G. P. Putnam's Sons.

Royce, Josiah. 1886. *California: From the Conquest in 1846 to the Second Vigilance Committee in San Francisco.* Boston: Houghton, Mifflin, and Co.

Rush, Leah, and David Jimenez. 2006. "States Outpace Congress in Upgrading Lobbying Laws." The Center for Public Integrity, March 1, http://projects.publicintegrity.org/hiredguns/report.aspx?aid=781.

Ryerson, Richard Alan. 1986. "Portrait of a Colonial Oligarchy: The Quaker Elite in the Pennsylvania Assembly, 1729–1776." In *Power and Status*, ed. Bruce C. Daniels. Middletown, Conn.: Wesleyan University Press.

Salzman, Ed. 1976. "The Deceptive Image of the State Legislature." *California Journal* 7:79–81.

Samish, Arthur H., and Bob Thomas. 1971. *The Secret Boss of California.* New York: Crown.

Sanders, Wilber Edgerton. 1910. "Montana: Organization, Name and Naming." *Contributions to the Historical Society of Montana* 7:15–60.

Scharf, J. Thomas. 1883. *History of Saint Louis City and County, from the Earliest Periods to the Present Day: Including Biographical Sketches of Representative Men*, vol. I. Philadelphia: Louis H. Everts & Co.

Schickler, Eric. 2001. *Disjointed Pluralism: Institutional Innovation and the Development of the U.S. Congress.* Princeton: Princeton University Press.

Schiller, Wendy, and Charles Stewart III. 2008. "Party Loyalty and the Election of U.S. Senators, 1871–1913." Presented at the Annual Meeting of the Midwest Political Science Association, Chicago.

Schoepf, Johann David. 1911. *Travels in the Confederation [1783–1784].* Philadelphia: William J. Campbell.

Schumacker, Waldo. 1931. "What Price Law-Makers?" *State Government* 4 (6): 10.

Seagle, William. 1933. "The Clown as Lawmaker." *American Mercury* 28: 330–37.

Sceberger, Edward D. 1997. *Sine Die: A Guide to the Washington State Legislative Process.* Seattle: University of Washington Press.

Selsam, J. Paul. 1936. *The Pennsylvania Constitution of 1776.* Philadelphia: University of Pennsylvania Press.

Shambaugh, Benjamin F. 1900. *Fragments of the Debates of the Iowa Constitutional Conventions of 1844 and 1846.* Iowa City: State Historical Society of Iowa.

Sherer, Timothy. 1979. "The Resistance to Representative Government in Early Michigan Territory." *Old Northwest* 5:167–79.

Sherfy, Marcella. 1999. "Bannack State Park: A Gate in Time." *Montana: The Magazine of Western History* 49:92–93.

Sherwood, Diana. 1947. "The Code Duello in Arkansas." *AHQ* 6:186–97.

Shin, Kwang S., and John S. Jackson III. 1979. "Membership Turnover in U.S. State Legislatures: 1931–1976." *LSQ* 4:95–114.

Shipan, Charles R., and Craig Volden. 2006. "Bottom-Up Federalism: The Diffusion of Antismoking Policies from U.S. Cities to States." *American Journal of Political Science* 50:825–43.

Shipan, Charles R., and Craig Volden. N.d. "When the Smoke Clears: Expertise, Learning, and Policy Diffusion." Typescript, University of Michigan.

Shoemaker, Floyd C. 1914. "A Sketch of Missouri Constitutional History During the Territorial Period." *Missouri Historical Review* 9:1–32.

Shoemaker, Floyd C. 1954. "Missouri's Proslavery Fight for Kansas, 1854–1855. Part II." *Missouri Historical Review* 48:325–40.

Showerman, Grant. 1915. *The Indian Stream Republic and Luther Parker.* Concord, N.H.: New Hampshire Historical Society.

Shuler, Marjorie. 1922. *The State Legislature and Its Work under the Party System.* Brooklyn, N.Y.: Stebbins & Company.

Shumate, Roger V. 1938. "A Reappraisal of State Legislatures." *Annals* 195:189–97.

Siegel, Stanley. 1956. *A Political History of the Texas Republic.* Austin: University of Texas Press.

Silbey, Joel H. 1983. "'Delegates Fresh from the People': American Congressional and Legislative Behavior." *Journal of Interdisciplinary History* 13:603–27.

Silver, John Archer. 1895. *The Provisional Government of Maryland (1774–1777).* Baltimore: Johns Hopkins University Press.

Simon, Paul. 1971. *Lincoln's Preparation for Greatness: The Illinois Legislative Years.* Urbana: University of Illinois Press.

Simpson, Alexander. 1843. *The Sandwich Islands: Progress of Events since Their Discovery by Captain Cook.* London: Smith, Elder and Co.

Simpson, George. 1847. *An Overland Journey Round the World, During the Years 1841 and 1842.* Philadelphia: Lea and Blanchard.

Sirmans, M. Eugene. 1961. "The South Carolina Royal Council, 1720–1763." *WMQ* 18:373–92.

Sirmans, M. Eugene. 1966. *Colonial South Carolina*. Chapel Hill: University of North Carolina Press.

Sitgreaves, Charles. 1836. *Manual of Legislative Practice and Order of Business in the Legislature of the State of New Jersey*. Trenton, N.J.: B. Davenport.

Slemrod, Joel. 2005. "The Etiology of Tax Complexity: Evidence from U.S. State Income Tax Systems." *Public Finance Review* 33:279–99.

Smith, Ben. 2004. "General Assembly Cleans Up Act, Say Legislators." *Atlanta Journal-Constitution*, April 3.

Smith, George Martin, ed. 1915. *South Dakota: Its History and Its People*, vol. 2. Chicago: S. J. Clarke.

Smith, Lynwood C., Jr. 1970. *Strengthening the Florida Legislature*. New Brunswick: Rutgers University Press.

Smith, Russell L., and William Lyons. 1977. "Legislative Reform in the American States: Some Preliminary Observations." *State and Local Government Review* 9:35–39.

Smith, Steven S. 1989. *Call to Order: Floor Politics in the House and Senate*. Washington, D.C.: Brookings.

Smith, Sir Thomas. [1583] 1906. *De Republica Anglorum*. Cambridge: Cambridge University Press.

Smith, W. Roy. 1903. *South Carolina as a Royal Province, 1719–1776*. New York: Macmillan.

Smith, William R. 1854. *The History of Wisconsin*, Part I—Historical, vol. I. Madison, Wis.: Beriah Brown.

Snow, Vernon F. 1977. *Parliament in Elizabethan England*. New Haven: Yale University Press.

Sparks, Jared. 1832. *The Life of George Mason, with Selections from His Correspondence and Miscellaneous Papers; Detailing Events in the American Revolution, the French Revolution, and in the Political History of the United States*. Boston: Gray & Bowen.

Sparks, Jared. 1844. *The Works of Benjamin Franklin; Containing Several Historical Tracts Not Included in Any Former Edition, and Many Letters Official and Private Not Hitherto Published; with Notes and a Life of the Author*, vol. I. Boston: Charles Tappan.

Sparks, Jared. 1847. *The Writings of George Washington; Being His Correspondence, Addresses, Messages, and Other Papers, Official and Private, Selected and Published from the Original Manuscripts, with a Life of the Author, Notes and Illustrations*. New York: Harper & Brothers.

Spaw, Patsy McDonald, ed. 1990. *The Texas Senate*, vol. 1. College Station: Texas A&M University Press.

Spence, Clark C. 1975. *Territorial Politics and Government in Montana, 1864–89*. Urbana: University of Illinois Press.

Spicer, George Washington. 1927. *The Constitutional Status and Government of Alaska*. Baltimore: Johns Hopkins University Press.

Squire, Peverill. 1988a. "Member Career Opportunities and the Internal Organization of Legislatures." *JOP* 50:726–44.

Squire, Peverill. 1988b. "Career Opportunities and Membership Stability in Legislatures." *LSQ* 13:65–82.

Squire, Peverill. 1992a. "The Theory of Legislative Institutionalization and the California Assembly." *JOP* 54:1026–54.

Squire, Peverill. 1992b. "Legislative Professionalization and Membership Diversity in State Legislatures." *LSQ* 17:69–79.

Squire, Peverill. 1992c. "Changing State Legislative Leadership Careers." In *Changing Patterns in State Legislative Careers*, ed. Gary F. Moncrief and Joel A. Thompson. Ann Arbor: University of Michigan Press.

Squire, Peverill. 1992d. "Iowa and the Drift to the Democrats." In *Party Realignment and State Politics*, ed. Maureen Moakley. Columbus: Ohio State University Press.

Squire, Peverill. 1993. "Professionalism and Public Opinion of State Legislatures." *JOP* 55:479–91.

Squire, Peverill. 1997. "Another Look at Legislative Professionalization and Divided Government in the States." *LSQ* 22:417–32.

Squire, Peverill. 1998. "Membership Turnover and the Efficient Processing of Legislation." *LSQ* 23:23–32.

Squire, Peverill. 2000. "Uncontested Seats in State Legislative Elections." *LSQ* 25:131–46.

Squire, Peverill. 2005. "The Evolution of American Colonial Assemblies as Legislative Organizations." *Congress & the Presidency* 32:109–31.

Squire, Peverill. 2006a. "Historical Evolution of Legislatures in the United States." *Annual Review of Political Science* 9:19–44.

Squire, Peverill. 2006b. "The Professionalization of State Legislatures in the United States over the Last Century." Presented at the 20th International Political Science Association World Congress, Fukuoka, Japan.

Squire, Peverill. 2007. "Measuring Legislative Professionalism: The Squire Index Revisited." *SPPQ* 7:211–27.

Squire, Peverill. 2008. "The State Wealth-Legislative Compensation Effect." *Canadian Journal of Political Science* 41:1–18.

Squire, Peverill, and Keith E. Hamm. 2005. *101 Chambers: Congress, State Legislatures, and the Future of Legislative Studies*. Columbus: Ohio State University Press.

Squire, Peverill, Keith E. Hamm, Ronald D. Hedlund, and Gary Moncrief. 2005. "Electoral Reforms, Membership Stability, and the Existence of Committee Property Rights in American State Legislatures." *British Journal of Political Science* 35:169–81.

Squire, Peverill, and Gary Moncrief. 2010. *State Legislatures Today: Politics Under the Domes*. Boston: Longman.

St. Stephens Historical Commission. 2001. "Functional Analysis & Records Disposition Authority." Montgomery, Ala.: State Records Commission.

Staley, Thomas Nettleship. 1868. *Five Years' Church Work in the Kingdom of Hawaii.* London: Rivingtons.

"State Legislative Overtime: 1927–1940." 1940. *State Government* 13:117–21.

State Senator. 1937. "Crooks in the Legislature." *American Mercury* 41:269–75.

"The States: Appraising the Legislatures." 1971. *Time* (February 15):16–17.

Steffensen, Ingrid. 2002. "Toward an Iconography of a State Capitol: The Art and Architecture of the Pennsylvania State Capitol in Harrisburg." *PMHB* 126:185–216.

Steinberg, Alfred. 1975. *Sam Rayburn: A Biography.* New York: Hawthorn.

Stevens, Michael E. 1989. "Legislative Privilege in Post-Revolutionary South Carolina." *WMQ* 46:71–92.

Stevens, Walter B. 1921. *Centennial History of Missouri,* vol. I. St. Louis: S. J. Clarke.

Stewart, Charles, III. 2001. *Analyzing Congress.* New York: Norton.

Stigler, George J. 1976. "The Sizes of Legislatures." *Journal of Legal Studies* 5:17–34.

Still, Bayrd. 1936. "An Interpretation of the Statehood Process." *MVHR* 23:189–204.

Stokes, Anthony. 1783. *A View of the Constitution of the British Colonies in North-America and the West Indies, at the Time the Civil War Broke Out on the Continent of America.* London: B. White.

Stonecash, Jeffrey M. 1993. "The Pursuit & Retention of Legislative Office in New York, 1870–1990: Reconsidering Source of Change." *Polity* 26:301–15.

Stourzh, Gerald. 1953. "Reason and Power in Benjamin Franklin's Political Thought." *APSR* 47:1092–1115.

Straayer, John A. 2000. *The Colorado General Assembly.* 2nd ed. Boulder: University Press of Colorado.

Strong, Moses M. 1870. *Territorial Legislation in Wisconsin: Annual Address before the State Historical Society of Wisconsin, Thursday Evening, February 4th 1870.* Madison, Wis.: Atwood & Culver.

Sturm, Albert L. 1981. "State Constitutional Developments during 1980." *NCR* 70:22–36.

Sturm, Albert L. 1983. "State Constitutional Developments during 1982." *NCR* 72:35–50.

Sturm, Albert L. 1985. "State Constitutional Developments during 1984." *NCR* 74:26–42.

Sullivan, James A. 1933. "Legislature Votes to Cut Pay in 1935." *Greensburg* (Pa.) *Daily Tribune,* April 19.

Surrency, Erwin C. 1965. "Revision of Colonial Laws." *American Journal of Legal History* 9:189–202.

Sutherland, Joel B. 1827. *A Manual of Legislative Practice and Order of Business in Deliberative Bodies.* Philadelphia: Jacob Frick & Co.

Swift, Robert. 2010. "Cost, Corruption in Pennsylvania Legislature Bring Calls for Reform." *Republican Herald* (Pa.), April 25.

Swift, Zephaniah. 1795. *A System of the Laws of the State of Connecticut*, vol. I. Windham, Conn.: John Byrne.

Tantillo, Charles. 1968. *Strengthening the Rhode Island Legislature*. New Brunswick: Rutgers University Press.

Taswell-Langmead, Thomas Pitt. 1946. *English Constitutional History*, 10th ed. Boston: Houghton Mifflin.

Taylor, Hawkins. 1890. "The First Territorial Legislature of Iowa." *Iowa Historical Record* 6:516–22.

Taylor, P. A. 1884. Personal Rights. *Speeches of P. A. Taylor, Esq., (Late M. P. for Leicester)*. London: Vigilance Association for the Defense of Personal Rights.

Taylor, William Harrison. 1900. *Legislative History and Souvenir of Rhode Island 1899 and 1900*. Providence, R.I.: E. L. Freeman and Sons.

Teaford, Jon C. 2002. *The Rise of the States: Evolution of American State Government*. Baltimore: Johns Hopkins University Press.

Tharpe, Jim, Nancy Badertscher, and Sonji Jacobs. 2005. "Legislature '05: Republicans Write Rules; New GOP Majority Locks in Power as Democratic Unity Noticeably Erodes." *Atlanta Journal-Constitution*, January 11.

"There's Ferment in the Statehouse." 1967. *Nation's Business* 55 (June):78–82.

Thomas, David Y. 1919. "Constitution Making in Arkansas." *APSR* 13:87–89.

Thomas, David Yancey. 1904. "A History of Military Government in the Newly Acquired Territory of the United States." Ph.D. diss. Columbia University.

Thompson, Francis M. 2004. *A Tenderfoot in Montana: Reminiscences of the Gold Rush, the Vigilantes, and the Birth of Montana Territory*. Helena: Montana Historical Society Press.

Thompson, Joel A., and Gary F. Moncrief. 1992. "The Evolution of the State Legislature: Institutional Change and Legislative Careers." In *Changing Patterns in State Legislative Careers*, ed. Gary F. Moncrief and Joel A. Thompson. Ann Arbor: University of Michigan Press.

Thompson, Neil B. 1973. "A Half Century of Capital Conflict: How St. Paul Kept the Seat of Government." *Minnesota History* 43:238–54.

Thomson, Vivian E., and Vicki Arroyo. 2011. "Upside-Down Cooperative Federalism: Climate Change Policymaking and the States." *Virginia Environmental Law Journal* 29:3–61.

Thorpe, Francis Newton. 1898. *A Constitutional History of the American People 1776–1850*, vol. one. New York: Harper & Brothers.

Thwaites, Reuben Gold, ed. 1906. *Travels in the Interior of North America By Maximilian, Prince of Wied*, part I. Cleveland, Ohio: Arthur H. Clark Co.

Timberland, Ebenezer. 1742. *The History and Proceedings of the House of Lords from the Restoration in 1660, to the Present Time*. London: Ebenezer Timberland.

Tolbert, Caroline J., Karen Mossberger, and Ramona McNeal. 2008. "Institutions, Policy Innovation, and E-Government in the American States." *Public Administration Review* 68:549–63.

Toll, Henry W. 1938. "Today's Legislature." *Annals* 195:1–10.

Toner, J. M. 1896. "Colonies of North American and the Genesis of the Commonwealths of the United States." In *Annual Report of the American Historical Association for the Year 1895*. Washington, D.C.: Government Printing Office.

Treon, John A. 1972. "Politics and Concrete: The Building of the Arkansas State Capitol, 1899–1917." *AHQ* 31:99–133.

Tripp, Bartlett, and John Henry Worst. 1904. "Territory of Dakota." In *The Province and the States*, vol. VI, ed. Weston Arthur Goodspeed. Madison, Wis.: Western Historical Society.

Tucker, Harvey J. 2005. "The Use of Consent Calendars in American State Legislatures." *Journal of the American Society of Legislative Clerks and Secretaries* 11:13–21.

Tully, Alan. 1977. *William Penn's Legacy: Politics and Social Structure in Provincial Pennsylvania, 1726–1755*. Baltimore: Johns Hopkins University Press.

Turner, Frederick Jackson. 1895. "Western State-Making in the Revolutionary Era." *AHR* 1:70–87.

Turner, Frederick Jackson. 1896. "Western State-Making in the Revolutionary Era II." *AHR* 1:251–69.

Turner, Robert C., and Mark K. Cassell. 2007. "When Do States Pursue Targeted Economic Development Policies? The Adoption and Expansion of State Enterprise Zone Programs." *Social Science Quarterly* 88:86–103.

Turner, Sylvie J. 1975. *Journal Kept by William Williams of the Proceedings of the Lower House of the Connecticut General Assembly, May 1757 Session*. Hartford: The Connecticut Historical Society.

Tuthill, Franklin. 1866. *The History of California*. San Francisco: H. H. Bancroft and Co.

Twain, Mark. [1872] 1996. *Roughing It*. New York: Oxford University Press.

Twain, Mark. 1910. *Mark Twain's Speeches*. New York: Harper & Brothers.

Twitchell, Ralph Emerson. 1912. *The Leading Facts of New Mexican History*. Cedar Rapids, Iowa: Torch.

Tyler, Lyon Gardiner. 1900. *The Cradle of the Republic: Jamestown and James River*. Richmond, Va.: Whittet & Shepperson.

Unruh, Jesse. 1964a. "The Integrity of the Legislature." *California Social Science Review* 3:3–6.

Unruh, Jesse M. 1964b. "Scientific Inputs into Legislative Decision Making." *WPQ* 17:53–60.

Unruh, Jesse M. 1965. "Science in Law-Making." *NCR* 54:466–72.

Unruh, Jesse. 1967. "A Reformed Legislature." *Journal of Public Law* 16:9–15.

Valentine, David C. 2008. "Constitutional Amendments, Statutory Revision and Referenda Submitted to the Voters by the General Assembly or by Initiative Petition, 1910–2008." Missouri Legislative Academy, Institution of Public Policy, Harry S Truman School of Public Affairs, Report 25–2008.

Van Der Slik, Jack R., and Kent D. Redfield. 1986. *Lawmaking in Illinois*. Springfield, Ill.: Office of Public Affairs Communication.

Van Koughnet, Donald E. 1933. "The Creation of the Territory." *Minnesota History* 14:127–34.

VanderMeer, Philip R. 1985. *The Hoosier Politician*. Urbana: University of Illinois Press.

Velie, Lester. 1949. "The Secret Boss of California." *Collier's* (August 13): 11–13, 71–73.

Velie, Lester. 1953a. "The Great Unwatched." *Reader's Digest* (January): 7–11.

Velie, Lester. 1953b. "Do You Know Your State's Secret Boss?" *Reader's Digest* (February): 35–40.

Velie, Lester. 1953c. "Do the Mobs Dictate Your Crime Laws?" *Reader's Digest* (March): 139–43.

Velie, Lester. 1953d. "Shakedown in the State House." *Reader's Digest* (April): 93–96.

Velie, Lester. 1953e. "Too Many Lawmakers Spoil the State." *Reader's Digest* (May): 35–40.

Viles, Jonas. 1919. "Missouri Capitals and Capitols, Second Article." *Missouri Historical Review* 13:232–50.

"Voting Device for Use in Congress." 1916. *National Magazine* 44:718–19.

Wagoner, Jay J. 1970. *Arizona Territory, 1863–1912: A Political History*. Tucson: University of Arizona Press.

Wakeley, Arthur C., ed. 1917. *Omaha: The Gate City and Douglas County Nebraska*. Chicago: S. J. Clarke.

Wakelyn, Jon L. 2002. *Confederates against the Confederacy: Essays on Leadership and Loyalty*. Westport, Conn.: Praeger.

Walker, Joseph B. 1905. *New Hampshire's Five Provincial Congresses*. Concord, N.H.: Rumford.

Walthoe, N. 1910. "The Council and the Burgesses." *William and Mary College Quarterly Historical Magazine* 19:1–10.

Walsh, Justin E. 1987. *The Centennial History of the Indiana General Assembly, 1816–1978*. Indianapolis: The Select Committee on the Centennial History of the Indiana General Assembly.

Warner, Lee H. 1983. "Florida's Capitols." *Florida Historical Quarterly* 61:245–59.

Warren, James R. 1988. "Seattle's First Lawyer: The Short Life of George N. McConaha." *Portage* 9:26–27.

Waterhouse, Richard. 1986. "Merchants, Planters, and Lawyers: Political Leadership in South Carolina, 1721–1775." In *Power and Status*, ed. Bruce C. Daniels. Middletown, Conn.: Wesleyan University Press.

Weber, Gustavus A. 1919. *Organized Efforts for the Improvement of Methods of Administration in the United States*. New York: D. Appleton and Company.

Weeks, Stephen B. 1894. "General Joseph Martin and the War of the Revolution in the West." In *Annual Report of the American Historical Association for the Year 1893*. Washington, D.C.: Government Printing Office.

Weir, Robert M. 1969. "'The Harmony We Were Famous For': An Interpretation of Pre-Revolutionary War South Carolina Politics." *WMQ* 26:473–501.

Wells, Merle, ed. 1976. "S. R. Howlett's War with the Idaho Legislature, 1866–67." *Idaho Yesterdays* 20:20–27.

Welsh, Miss Mary. 1888–89. "Reminiscences of Old Saint Stephens of More than Sixty-Five Years Ago." *Transactions of the Alabama Historical Society* 3:208–26.

Wenger, Mark R. 1993. "Thomas Jefferson and the Virginia State Capitol." *VMHB* 101:77–102.

Wendel, Thomas. 1973. "The Speaker of the House, Pennsylvania, 1701–1776." *PMHB* 97:3–21.

Wendel, Thomas. 1986. "At the Pinnacle of Elective Success: The Speaker of the House in Colonial America." In *Power and Status*, ed. Bruce C. Daniels. Middletown, Conn.: Wesleyan University Press.

"West Virginia Citizens to Study Legislature." 1966. *NCR* 56:547.

Wetmore, Claude. 1904. *The Battle Against Bribery*. St. Louis: Pan-American Press.

White, Lonnie J. 1964. *Politics on the Southwestern Frontier: Arkansas Territory, 1819–1836*. Memphis, Tenn.: Memphis State University Press.

Whitehead, William A., ed. 1880. *Documents Relating to the Colonial History of the State of New Jersey*, vol. I. Newark, N.J.: Daily Journal.

Whitney, Edson Leone. 1895. *Government of the Colony of South Carolina*. Baltimore: Johns Hopkins University Press.

Williams, Robert F. 1989. "The State Constitutions of the Founding Decade: Pennsylvania's Radical 1776 Constitution and Its Influences on American Constitutionalism." *Temple Law Review* 62:541–85.

Williams, Samuel Cole. 1933. *History of the Lost State of Franklin*. New York: The Press of Pioneers.

Williams, T. Harry. 1981. *Huey Long*. New York: Vintage.

Williamson, William D. 1832. *The History of the State of Maine from Its First Discovery, A.D. 1602, to the Separation, A.D. 1820, Inclusive*, vol. II. Hallowell, Maine: Glazier, Masters, & Co.

Wilson, Adam. 2006. "Swecker Calls for Full-Time Legislature." *The Olympian* (Wash.), January 27.

Wilson, Rick K. 1999. "Transitional Governance in the United States: Lessons from the First Federal Congress." *LSQ* 24:543–68.

Wiltsee, Herbert L. 1966. "Structures and Procedures." In *Book of the States, 1966–1967*. Chicago: Council of State Governments.

Winkler, Allan M. 1968. "Drinking on the American Frontier." *Quarterly Journal of Studies on Alcohol* 29:413–45.

Winslow, Walter C. 1908. "Contests over the Capital of Oregon." *Quarterly Journal of the Oregon Historical Society* 9:173–78.

Wise, Sidney. 1971. *The Legislative Process in Pennsylvania*. Washington, D.C.: American Political Science Association.

Witko, Christopher. 2007. "Explaining Increases in the Stringency of State Campaign Finance Regulation, 1993–2002." *SPPQ* 7:369–93.

Witte, Edwin E. 1938. "Technical Services for State Legislators." *Annals* 195:137–43.

Woods, Neal D. 2008. "The Policy Consequences of Political Corruption: Evidence from State Environmental Programs." *Social Science Quarterly* 89:258–71.

Woody, R. H. 1936a. "Behind the Scenes in the Reconstruction Legislature of South Carolina: Diary of Josephus Woodruff." *JSH* 2:78–102.

Woody, R. H. 1936b. "Behind the Scenes in the Reconstruction Legislature of South Carolina: Diary of Josephus Woodruff." *JSH* 2:233–59.

Woolworth, James Mills. 1904. "State of Nebraska." In *The Province and the States*, vol. V, ed. Weston Arthur Goodspeed. Madison, Wis.: Western Historical Society.

Wooster, Ralph A. 1969. *The People in Power: Courthouse and Statehouse in the Lower South 1850–1860*. Knoxville: University of Tennessee Press.

Wooster, Ralph A. 1975. *Politicians, Planters and Plain Folk: Courthouse and Statehouse in the Upper South, 1850–1860*. Knoxville: University of Tennessee Press.

Worley, Ted R. 1950. "The Control of the Real Estate Bank of the State of Arkansas, 1836–1855." *MVHR* 37:403–26.

Worsnop, Richard L. 1976. "Does Higher Pay Improve a Legislature?" *St. Petersburg Times*, February 3.

Wright, Gerald. 2007. "Do Term Limits Affect Legislative Roll Call Voting? Representation, Polarization, and Participation." *SPPQ* 7:256–80.

Wyllie, John Cook. 1960. "Daniel Boone's Adventures in Charlottesville in 1781: Some Incidents Connected with Tarleton's Raid." *Magazine of Albemarle County History* 19:5–18.

Wyner, Alan J. 1973. "Legislative Reform and Politics in California: What Happened, Why, and So What?" In *State Legislative Innovation*, ed. James A. Robinson. New York: Praeger.

Yonge, Samuel H. 1904a. "The Site of Old 'James Towne,' 1607–1698." *VMHB* 12:33–53.

Yonge, Samuel H. 1904b. "The Site of Old 'James Towne,' 1607–1698." *VMHB* 12:113–133.

Young, Chester Raymond. 1968. "The Evolution of the Pennsylvania Assembly, 1682–1748." *Pennsylvania History* 35:147–68.

Young, F. G. 1920. "Ewing Young and His Estate." *QOHS* 21:171–315.

Zagarii, Rosemarie. 1987. *The Politics of Size*. Ithaca: Cornell University Press.

Zeigler, L. Harmon, and Barbara Leigh Smith. 1971. "The 1970 Election in Oregon." *WPQ* 24:325–38.

Zeller, Belle, ed. 1954. *American State Legislatures.* New York: Crowell.

Zemsky, Robert M. 1969. "Power, Influence, and Status: Leadership Patterns in the Massachusetts Assembly, 1740–1755." *WMQ* 26:502–20.

Zemsky, Robert M. 1971. *Merchants, Farmers, and River Gods.* Boston: Gambit.

Zimmerman, Joseph F. 1981. *The Government and Politics of New York State.* New York: New York University Press.

Zimmerman, Joseph F. 1999. *The New England Town Meeting.* Westport, Conn.: Praeger.

Index